INTRODUCING PSYCHOLOGICAL RESEARCH

Third edition

Also by Philip Banyard

Psychology: Theory and Application (with Nicky Hayes)
Applying Psychology to Health
Controversies in Psychology
Psychology in Practice (Health)
Ethical Issues and Guidelines in Psychology (with Cara Flanagan)
OCR Psychology: The core studies (with Cara Flanagan)
Understanding and Using Statistics in Psychology: A Practical Introduction (with Jeremy Miles)

Also by Andrew Grayson

Psychological Development and Early Childhood (with John Oates and Clare Wood)
Cognitive and Language Development in Children (with John Oates)

INTRODUCING PSYCHOLOGICAL RESEARCH

250702 $46.00

PHILIP BANYARD
and
ANDREW GRAYSON

Third edition

palgrave
macmillan

First published 2008 by
PALGRAVE MACMILLAN
Houndmills, Basingstoke, Hampshire RG21 6XS and
175 Fifth Avenue, New York, N.Y. 10010
Companies and representatives throughout the world

PALGRAVE MACMILLAN is the global academic imprint of the Palgrave
Macmillan division of St. Martin's Press, LLC and of Palgrave Macmillan Ltd.
Macmillan® is a registered trademark in the United States, United Kingdom
and other countries. Palgrave is a registered trademark in the European
Union and other countries.

ISBN-13: 978–1–4039–0038–8
ISBN-10: 1–4039–0038–8

This book is printed on paper suitable for recycling and made from fully
managed and sustained forest sources. Logging, pulping and manufacturing
processes are expected to conform to the environmental regulations of the
country of origin.

A catalogue record for this book is available from the British Library.

A catalog record for this book is available from the Library of Congress.

10   9   8   7   6   5   4   3   2   1
17   16   15   14   13   12   11   10   09   08

Printed in China

CONTENTS

TABLES

FIGURES

PREFACE

Psychology is based on evidence from research studies. In this book we present the details of 84 research studies that we think reflect the discipline of psychology. Our aim is to provide clear and accurate summaries of these important pieces of work so that you can weigh up the evidence for yourself and come to your own conclusions about what it means.

The studies

Some of the studies might surprise you, and we hope that all of them will interest you. We include in our selection:

- a study that creates a mock prison to see how people behave when they are asked to take on the role of guard or prisoner;
- an account of the first successful attempt to teach a form of language to a chimpanzee;
- one of the first accounts of the phenomenon of multiple personality;
- an experimental study that explores the mental world of people with autism;
- a study that examines the effect on a person of having their brain surgically divided into two;
- an account of a serious attempt to train pigeons to be pilots of flying bombs;
- a comparison of the perceptual skills of people from different parts of the world who have different experiences;
- a summary of the collection of phenomena we call phantom limb pain, where people experience sensations in non-existent parts of their body;
- an account of the curious behaviour of the stickleback;
- a summary of one of Sigmund Freud's most famous case studies;

- an experimental study on a New York commuter railway that examines how people behave when they see a stranger in distress;
- an analysis of why children in the same family are different from one another;
- the use of scanning techniques to look at the differences between the brains of murderers and non-murderers;
- ... and many more.

These studies are summarized in enough detail to give you the flavour of what went on and what was discovered. We leave the implications and conclusions largely up to the reader, because we want to encourage critical reflection on the pieces of work.

The student

Students often do not have the opportunity to read original research articles. There are a number of reasons for this, including the major problem that many of the important articles are not readily available. Even if you have access to a good library, it takes a long time to search out the material you are looking for, and when you find the original research study it is often written in an impenetrable style. Even the technological advances of recent years have not provided free-to-air access to academic journals so you might be able to find a link to an article only to then discover that it is held on a subscription site.

We have tried to address these problems in this book. We are presenting the studies in a clear style (we hope), with enough detail for you to be able to get a good idea of the research, and all in one volume so you do not have to trail round the local university library. The summaries are written with a brief introduction to provide some background for the research. Then we describe how the work was carried out and what was found, and we add some comments at the end to suggest one or two possible critical evaluations or further developments. Questions are included after each summary (with suggested answers at the back of the book) to help consolidate and develop what you have learned.

Having read the summaries, you should find the original papers relatively easy to follow, and we would encourage you to track down any that you find particularly interesting. Our feeling is that reading journal articles is a skill that needs to be developed, rather than something we can all just (magically) do. Indeed, one intention of this book is to provide an intermediate stage between standard textbooks and the original articles upon which those textbooks (and the entire discipline of psychology) are based.

In the limited space of one book we can only present a small number of studies. We have been incredibly selective, especially when you consider that thousands of pieces of research are published every year. We have chosen our studies to illustrate how psychology has developed over the years, and we have tried to present a range of studies that illustrate the breadth of psychological research and psychological applications. We have also taken care to include studies that reflect the wide range of methods used by psychologists in their research, from hard-nosed experimentation to in-depth interviewing and literature searches.

Psychological evidence is still mainly presented in the form of research papers, and the studies we have chosen reflect the way that psychology is being conducted and reported. The summaries are presented in chapters that are based on the traditional research areas of the subject. It is worth noting, however, that the divisions between the different areas are sometimes quite arbitrary and most of the studies have relevance in more than one area.

We hope that this book encourages you to read further in the subject and to dig out some of the original papers if you can. We also hope that you enjoy reading the material and find it as provocative and interesting as we do. Most importantly, though, we hope that you develop your own opinions about psychology, drawing on the evidence presented in this text.

New in the third edition

In this third edition, in response to suggestions from users of the first two editions, we have rearranged the studies into six sections and added 14 new studies. The first five sections represent the core areas of psychology: social, biological and comparative, diversity, developmental and cognitive psychology. The sixth section is on methodology, and mops up some studies we didn't fit in elsewhere and looks at some of the research problems that provide a challenge to psychological research. In the last chapter on psychological methods we offer a summary of the key issues in psychological research and provide examples of these issues by cross-referencing to the studies that are summarized in the book. In fact, we only use examples from the studies in the book. We hope this chapter will help the reader to gain more from the individual studies and achieve a better understanding of how psychological research is conducted.

The new studies we have introduced in this edition offer ideas about the directions in which psychology is moving at the start of this century. In summary, the ideas about social behaviour that were established in US psychology nearly 50 years ago are under threat, and the work of Milgram and Zimbardo, for example, while still offering some insights into human behaviour can increasingly be seen to present a partial view of people. Elsewhere in psychology big ideas that are taking hold are in neuroscience with the mapping of cognition and behaviour to components of the brain, and also in evolutionary psychology where a greater understanding of genetics is leading towards more theories about the evolutionary origins of human behaviour.

Psychology is a controversial subject. This is inevitable because it is about people and how we think, feel and behave. At the moment we can be sure of very little about these things and that is one reason why it is controversial. You might argue that it is a good thing that we do not know all that much about why people do the things they do because if we did then someone would exploit that to make people do things they do not want to do. The final paper in the text by George Miller is a call to psychology that echoes from 40 years ago but still presents a fresh challenge to us. What is psychology for? And who should own it?

We have highlighted throughout the text particular words, concepts and terms where we feel a definition would be useful, and have put a definition alongside them. These usually appear at the point at which they are first used in each summary. All these words and phrases also appear in the full glossary at the back of the book. Use these to check your understanding of key concepts as you read through the text.

Acknowledgements

We would like to acknowledge the support of our colleagues in the Psychology Division at Nottingham Trent University who provide a remarkably positive and friendly working environment. We would also like to thank the many people who commented on the previous editions and so helped in the development of this new edition. We would particularly like to thank the following in no particular order for their helpful comments, Alex Haslam, Steve Reicher, Patrick Hylton, Mark Griffiths, Dan Simons, William Merrin, Glenn Williams, Mark Sergeant, Kathy Bach, Rachel Horsley, Susannah Lamb, Andrew Dunn and Richard Nordquist.

Phil Banyard would also like to acknowledge the inspiration given to him by his parents, The Gladstone in Carrington, Nottingham Forest and Ted 'The Count' Hankey. Andy would like to acknowledge the inspiration given to him by Chris and Nick.

Phil Banyard
Andy Grayson

The authors and publishers wish to thank the following for permission to use copyright material:

Academic Press, Inc. for material from A.M. Collins and M.R. Quillian, 'Retrieval time from semantic memory', *Journal of Verbal Learning and Verbal Behavior*, 8, 1969, pp. 240–7; E.F. Loftus and J.C. Palmer, 'Reconstruction of auto-mobile destruction', *Journal of Verbal Learning and Verbal Behavior*, 13, 1974, Tables 1 and 2. Alamy Limited for image of a PET Scan, Medical-on-Line/Alamy. Gerianne Alexander and Melissa Hines for material from Alexander and Hines, 'Sex differences in response to children's toys in nonhuman primates', in *Evolution and Human Behavior*, 23, 2002, pp. 467–79. American Association for the Advancement of Science for material from W.S. Condon and L.W. Sander, 'Neonate movement is synchronized with adult speech: interactional participation and language acquisition', *Science*, 183, 1974, Tables 1 and 2, adapted, pp. 99–100, figure 1, p. 100 © 1974 American Association for the Advancement of Science; D.L. Rosenhan, 'On being sane in insane places', *Science*, 179, 1973, Tables 1 and 2 © 1973 American Association for the Advancement of Science. American Psychological Association for material from A. Bandura, D. Ross and S. Ross, 'Transmission of aggression through imitation of aggressive models', *Journal of Abnormal and Social Psychology*, 63, 1961, pp. 575–82; L. Festinger and J. Carlsmith, 'Cognitive consequences of forced compliance', *Journal of Abnormal and Social Psychology*, 58, 1959, pp. 203–10; B. Forer, 'The fallacy of personal validation: a classroom demonstration of gullibility', *Journal of Abnormal and Social Psychology*, 44, 1949; P.J. Lang and A.D. Lazovik, 'Experimental desensitisation of a phobia', *Journal of Abnormal and Social Psychology*, 66, 1963, Tables 1, 2 and 3, pp. 522, 523; J. Hraba and G. Grant, 'Black is beautiful: a re-examination of racial preference and identification', *Journal of Personality and Social Psychology*, 16, 1970, Table 1, adapted, p. 399; an illustration from I Piliavin, J. Rodin and J. Piliavin, 'Good Samaritanism: an underground phenomenon?', *Journal of Personality and Social Psychology*, 13, 1969; Tables 2.1, 2.2 and 2.3 from R.E. Nisbett, C. Caputo, P. Legant and J. Maracek, 'Behaviour as seen by the actor as seen by the observer', *Journal of Personality and Social Psychology*, 27, 1973, Table 1, p. 157, adapted, Table 2, p. 159, adapted, and Table 5, p. 161 © 1961, 1959, 1949, 1963, 1976, 1970, 1969, 1973 by the American Psychological Association. J. Olds and P. Milner, 'Positive reinforcement produced by electrical stimulation of the septal area and other regions of the rat brain', *Journal of Comparative and Physiological Psychology*, 47, 1954, pp. 419–29; D.O Sears 'College sophomores in the laboratory: influences of a narrow data base on psychology's view of human nature', *Journal of Personality and Social Psychology*, 51, 1986, pp. 513-530, Tables 1 and 2. Association for Child and Adolescent Mental Health for material from J. Hodges and B. Tizard, 'Social and family relationships of ex-institutional adolescents', *Journal of Child Psychology and Psychiatry*, 30, 1989, Elsevier, Table 11, p. 88, Figure 2, p. 89; J. Samuel and P. Bryant, 'Asking only one question in the conservation experiment', *Journal of Child Psychology and Psychiatry*, 25, 1984, Elsevier, Table 2, p. 317; S. Baron-Cohen, T. Jolliffe, T., C. Mortimore and M. Robertson, 'Another advance test of theory of mind: evidence from very high functioning adults with autism or Asperger Syndrome', *Journal of Child Psychology and Psychiatry*, 38, 1997, Blackwell Publishing, 813–22. *Behavioural Science* for material from R. Rosenthal and K.L. Fode, 'The effect of experimenter bias on the performance of the albino rat', *Behavioural Science*, 8, 1963, Tables 1, 2, pp. 185, 186. Cambridge University Press for illustrations from F.C. Bartlett, *Remembering: A Study in Experimental and Social Psychology*, 1932, pp. 178–80. Chapman and Hall for an illustration from P. Banyard and N. Hayes, *Psychology: Theory and Application*, 1994, p. 17. Elsevier Science Ltd for material from T.H. Holmes and R.H. Rahe, 'The social re-adjustment rating scale', *Journal of Psychosomatic Research*, 11, 1967, Table 3, p. 216. Experimental Psychology Society for material from J.A. Gray and A.A.T. Wedderburn, 'Grouping strategies with simultaneous stimuli', *Quarterly Journal of Experimental Psychology*, 12, 1960, pp. 180–4. Gene Glass for material from M.L. Smith and G.V. Glass, 'Meta-analysis of psychotherapy outcome studies', *American Psychologist*, 32, 1977, 752–60, Figure 1, pp. 754 and Table 3, pp. 756. Getty Images for photographs including those by Spencer Platt, Al Fenn. Sharon Golub for material from E. Koff, 'Through the looking glass of menarche: what the adolescent girl sees', from *Menarche*, ed. S. Golub, 1983, Figures 5.1a–c, 5.2a–c, pp. 80–4. Ikuyo Tagawa Garber for illustrations by Bunji Tagawa from John B. Calhoun, 'Population density and social pathology', *Scientific American*, 206, February 1962, pp. 140–1. Edward Hubbard for the illustration of a mirror box from http://en.wikipedia.org/wiki/Image:MirrorBox.jpg. Alexandra Milgram for material from S. Milgram, 'Behavioural study of obedience', *Journal of Abnormal and Social Psychology*, 67, 1963, Table 1. Eric Mose Jr for illustrations by E. Mose, from N. Tinbergen, 'The curious behaviour of the stickleback', *Scientific American*, 187, December 1952, pp. 24, 25. *New Scientist* for graphic from R. Rawlins, 'Forty years of rhesus research', *New Scientist*, 82, 1979, p. 110. W.W. Norton and Company and Penguin Books for material from Stephen Jay Gould, 'The Mismeasure of Man', Figure 5.5, p. 211, © 1981 by Stephen Jay Gould. Popperfoto for the photograph on page 403. Psychonomic Society, Inc. for material from L.T. Kozlowski and J.E. Cutting. 'Recognising the sex of a walker from a dynamic point-height display', *Perception and Psychophysics*, 21(6), 1977, pp. 575–80. Sage Publications for material from Shawn O. Utsey, *Extended Self: Rethinking the So-Called Negro Self-Concept*, W.W. Nobles, *Journal of Black Psychology*, Vol. 2, 1976, Table 2, reprinted by permission of Sage Publications. *Scientific American*, Inc. for illustrations by Carol Woike Donner from J.B. Deregowski, 'Pictorial perception and culture', *Scientific American*, 227, November 1972, pp. 83, 86; M. Sherif, 'Experiments in group conflict', Scientific American, 195, 1956, pp. 54–8, Figure p. 57. The Royal Society, Edward Hubbard and V.S Ramachandran for material from 'Psychophysical investigations into the neural basis of synaesthesia', *Proceedings of the Royal Society of London*, 268, 2001. 979–83. Daniel Simons for images from D.J Simons and C.F Chabris, 'Gorillas in our midst: sustained inattentional blindness for dynamic events', *Perception*, 28, 1999, 1059–74. Niko Troje for the photo showing point light display, his description of which appeared in N.F. Troje, 'Decomposing biological motion: a framework for analysis and synthesis of human gait patterns', *Journal of Vision*, 2, 2002, pp. 371–87.

Every effort has been made to trace all the copyright holders, but if any have been inadvertently overlooked the publishers will be pleased to make the necessary arrangement at the first opportunity.

part i

SOCIAL PSYCHOLOGY

SOCIAL psychology, as the label suggests, is concerned with the social side of human life. Social psychologists look at the numerous complex issues which surround human interaction and human relationships. They look at how the individual behaves rather than how groups behave because this is psychology, not social anthropology or sociology. However, the individual is studied against the background of the social contexts which both frame and direct their actions and experiences.

When we study social psychology it is important to bear in mind that we are at one and the same time the producers of, and the products of, the relationships, groups, cultures and societies we belong to. Society moulds us, but we also mould society. Indeed, one of the ongoing tensions in social psychology is how much importance to give to the individual or to the society in our explanations of social behaviour. In other words, when we are trying to understand why someone has done or said something, do we look to that person or do we look to the society for the causes of that action? When someone does or says something, do their actions and words 'belong' to that person, or to the culture of which they are a part?

Intuitively we tend to say that it is the person that is really behind actions and words. We may acknowledge social constraints and influences, but in the end we believe that individuals are responsible for what gets done and what gets said. We see that their actions and words belong to them. Who or what else could they belong to?

However, this intuition may be a culturally specified thing. For a start, when we used the word 'we' in the previous paragraph we were probably talking about people in US and British cultures who place great emphasis on the individual; not all cultures have this same emphasis. This perspective (we would argue) is very strong and ingrained within us, such that answering the 'who or what else could they belong to?' question is actually a very difficult thing to do.

So, let us just think about this idea of who owns what gets done and said. Take for example the actions of a police officer or of a judge. Many of the things that these people do are specifically set down for them by society. When a police officer says, 'I arrest you. Anything you say may be taken down in evidence ...' (or whatever it is that they say; both authors claim no direct personal experience of

▶ role A social part that one plays in society.

this situation), they are not really doing or saying their own thing. The same goes for a judge who says, 'I sentence you to five years in prison ...'. These people are fulfilling the requirements of roles, and doing and saying things that in a sense belong to all of us. How many of the things that you say and do are in fact laid down for you by culture and society?

When you read the summaries of studies that are included in this part of the book we would like you to bear these issues in mind. The topics that are covered (social influence, social judgement and social interaction) represent three major concerns of traditional social psychology, and provide a good starting point for your own explorations of these sorts of questions.

chapter **1**

SOCIAL
INFLUENCE

SOCIAL influence is about how our actions can be affected by others. It is an important area of social psychology because the findings from many studies on social influence challenge some of our most deep-seated beliefs about our own autonomy. We like to think that we are true to ourselves in what we do and say, and that we only follow everyone else when we want to. But a number of social psychological investigations have suggested that we may be more susceptible to social influence than we think, and two of these are summarized in this section. Asch (1955), for example, observed a proportion of his subjects going along with a strong majority decision about something even though that decision was blatantly wrong. And Milgram (1963) showed the extent to which ordinary people are susceptible to following the demands of an authority figure, even when those demands require them to do something which is morally indefensible.

There are many things that you might note about the studies in this chapter, but two things are particularly important. First, the studies are all concerned with behaviour. That is, they are direct studies of what research participants (commonly referred to as subjects) actually did in

real situations. This is important because if you were to ask people how they would behave in situations like those set up by Milgram and Asch (Milgram actually did ask people this question), most people would give answers in line with their beliefs about their own autonomy; most people would predict that they would be unmoved by the social influences that were exerted. For example, many people will say that advertisements have no effect on them, but advertisers know that this is not the case because an advertising campaign can dramatically increase the sales of a product. By studying behaviour, rather than opinion, Milgram and Asch were able to show that most people's predictions about their own behaviour in this respect are wrong!

Second, we should note that although Milgram and Asch both studied actual behaviour in *real* situations, they were not studying actual behaviour in *realistic* situations. By this we mean that the 'real situations' that were set up were rather artificial, and somewhat removed from everyday experience. One thing which separates their situations from everyday life situations is that in everyday life we are usually with other people whom we know. We rarely find ourselves having to make decisions, for example, in the

▶ **behaviour (also spelt 'behavior')** Anything a person (or animal) does that can be observed and measured by a third party. Behaviour can be thought of as the public side of human life, in contrast to 'experience' (thoughts and feelings) which can be thought of as the private side.

disorienting context of having no one else around except complete strangers. Yet this is exactly what Asch's and Milgram's subjects had to do.

The other two studies in this chapter provide a methodological contrast to the two above, as well as illustrating some other issues in the study of social influence. The naturalistic experiment by Piliavin *et al.* (1969) examined the way in which people behaved in a real-life setting (on a subway train in New York). It constitutes part of the tradition of work on bystander intervention which is most closely associated with Latané and Darley (1970), and which set out to understand the role of social influences on the decision we make of whether or not to help someone in trouble. The work was stimulated by a news report of the murder of a young woman in New York which suggested that a number of people had witnessed the event but had not intervened. The report captured the public imagination and psychologists tried to explain the apparent non-intervention of the bystanders.

The final study in this chapter takes another look at the behaviour of bystanders by also looking at a real-life crime that captured the public imagination and still features in the news agenda. The murder of James Bulger by two 10-year-old boys shocked the general public. Levine (1999) used the testimony of the witnesses at the trial of the two murderers to examine why bystanders did not intervene in a situation they recognized to be worrying.

▶ **role** A social part that one plays in society.

ASCH, S.E. (1955)

Opinions and social pressure.

Scientific American, 193, 31–5.

Eight out of ten owners said their cats preferred it

Introduction

How conformist are you? Do you say, and do, and think what you like, or are you influenced by the behaviour of people around you? The obvious answer is that we are all influenced to some extent by the people around us. If we were not, then we would not be a member of any social group. To belong to a group means to adjust to other people and to conform to at least some of the social norms of the group. But how, and to what extent, we are influenced by others are important questions.

These questions about social conformity are important for many reasons, one of which is that some people try to manipulate our sociability for their own ends. These ends can be political or personal or commercial. Attempts are made to influence us to do and believe things because 'the electorate feels that ...', or because 'everyone else I know is doing this ...' or because 'eight out of ten owners said their cats preferred it'.

Asch was interested in the circumstances in which people would be most likely to conform. In his paper he refers to hypnosis as an extreme form of suggestibility, and suggests we should view everyday social behaviour as being susceptible to this suggestibility. Early studies conducted by, among others, Edward Thorndike, had demonstrated that the opinions of students could be changed by giving an account of the (fictitious) opinions of a majority of their peers. Asch chose to look at the process more systematically.

The study

In the basic design of the Asch study, a group of seven to nine male college students were assembled in a classroom for a 'psychological experiment in visual judgement'. The experimenter told them that they would be comparing the lengths of lines. He showed them two white cards. On one was a vertical dark line, the standard which was to be judged. On the other card were three vertical lines of various lengths. The subjects were asked to choose the one that was the same length as the standard. One of the three lines was actually the same length as the standard, and the other two were substantially different. The subjects were asked to give their judgements out loud and they did so in the order in which they were seated.

There was, in fact, only one subject in each group. The rest of the people giving judgements were confederates of the experimenter. The real subject would sit one from the end of the row, so all but one of the confederates gave their answers before them. On certain prearranged trials the confederates were instructed to give unanimous incorrect answers. The experimenters then looked to see the response of the one subject to this majority opinion. Each

▶ **behaviour (also spelt 'behavior')** Anything a person (or animal) does that can be observed and measured by a third party. Behaviour can be thought of as the public side of human life, in contrast to 'experience' (thoughts and feelings) which can be thought of as the private side.

▶ **conformity** The process of going along with other people – that is, acting in the same way that they do.

series of line judgements had 18 trials, and on 12 of these the majority gave unanimous incorrect answers.

Results

The trials that were of interest, of course, were the 12 on which incorrect answers had been set up. On these, around 75 per cent of the 123 subjects went along with the majority at least once. Under the pressure of the group, the subjects accepted the judgement of the majority on 37 per cent of the trials. Figure 1.1 shows the percentage of correct responses (that is, when the subject disagreed with the deliberately wrong judgment of the confederates) for each of the 12 test trials.

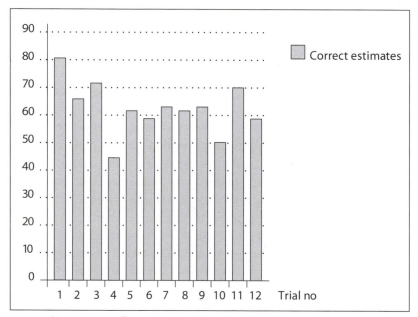

Figure 1.1   *The percentage of correct answers for each critical trial*

There were considerable individual differences, with about 25 per cent of the subjects never agreeing with the majority, while some other subjects agreed with the majority most of the time. The subjects were interviewed after the study and their reasons for their behaviour were recorded. Among the independent individuals (Asch's description of the non-conformers), many had staunch confidence in their own judgement and a capacity to recover from doubt. Also, some believed that the majority was correct but continued to dissent because it was their obligation to 'call it as they saw it'. Among the yielding individuals (Asch's description of the people who conformed), some took the line 'I am wrong, they are right', some suspected that the others were sheep following the first person to answer, but still yielded, and some saw it as a general sign of deficiency in themselves and tried to merge with the majority to cover up.

A number of variations of the study were carried out, including adjusting the size of the majority group. The results of these studies are shown in

Figure 1.2. It would appear that the conforming pressure peaks with three or four experimenter confederates. Another variation looked at the effect of a dissenting partner. In this case one of the confederates also disagreed with the majority, though halfway through the trials the support of this other dissenter was removed. In half of the cases the support was removed by the person leaving the room, after which the conformity rate rose a little. In the other half, the dissenter 'went over' to the other side and started to agree with the majority. This desertion induced high levels of conformity in the subjects.

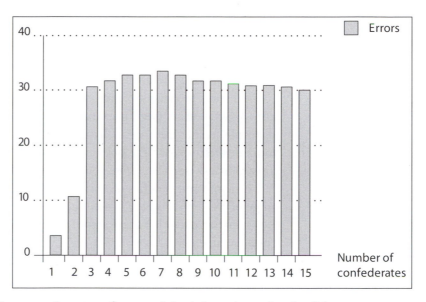

Figure 1.2 *Percentage of errors made in relation to the number of confederates*

Discussion

Some studies which give a further insight into Asch's work are the replications of the original study carried out by Perrin and Spencer. In the first replication (Perrin and Spencer, 1980), they used engineering undergraduates as the experimental confederates who had been instructed to give incorrect answers. The experimental subjects were also engineering undergraduates. This replication produced no conformity and the researchers initially concluded that the Asch study was 'a child of its time' (p. 405), a product of the pressures towards social conformity in the 1950s.

This finding, however, was challenged by Doms and Avermaet (1981), who pointed out that engineering students were particularly inclined to value accurate measurement, and so to use them as the subjects in a study of conformity based on judgements of line length was to introduce a bias against conformity which did not show in replications performed with other students.

Following this, Perrin and Spencer (1981) performed two further replications which did not involve students. In one, the experimental confederates were probation officers, and the subjects were young men on probation. The subjects had an average age of 19, and so were very different from the majority group on the basis of three factors: age, professional status and power. In this case, Perrin and Spencer achieved conformity levels which were similar to those achieved by Asch. In the third replication, the experimental confederates were unemployed young men from inner London of Afro-Caribbean back-grounds, again with an average age of 19. The experimental subjects were also Afro-Caribbean youths, and the experimenter was White. In this case, too, the researchers obtained conformity levels similar to those obtained by Asch.

In each of these cases, the level of conformity which was being displayed by the research subjects made extremely good social sense, given the situation and context. Perrin and Spencer argued that conformity is actually a socially adaptive strategy, rather than a social problem. They concluded that those social problems which are associated with conformity arise from people exploiting the social responsibility of their fellow citizens, not from a personal weakness in the general population.

Returning to Asch's comments about hypnosis, it is worth noting that some psychologists (see for example Orne, 1966) believe that the behaviour of people in the presence of hypnotists is more a sign of social conformity and a desire to please the hypnotist than an indication of an altered state of consciousness (see also Orne, 1962, Chapter 18 of this volume).

The conformity studies of Asch and his colleagues created a template for a range of research studies. These studies still challenge the reader to consider their own behaviour but there are important limitations of the research design. These include:

(a) The research concentrates on individuals rather than the situation they are in.
(b) The research invariably deals with very trivial tasks or judgements. For example, 'how long is a line?' Well, who cares?
(c) The research does not distinguish between independent action (doing what you think is right) and anti-conformity (awkward for the sake of it).
(d) There is an underlying assumption that conformity is 'bad' and independence is 'good'.
(e) The research is usually conducted on students.

Nevertheless, the studies still stimulate us to ask questions about why we do some of the things we do and about what factors affect our behaviour in our social worlds.

suggested
answers
→ p. 473

Questions

1. What features of the Asch study made the research participants more likely to conform?

2. What requests do you conform to and what requests do you resist? Make two lists and compare the differences.

3. List some positive aspects of conformity and some negative aspects of conformity.

4. What criticisms can you make of the method used by Asch to investigate conformity?

Be a good boy and do as you are told

MILGRAM, S (1963)

Behavioural study of obedience.

Journal of Abnormal and Social Psychology, 67, 371–8.

Introduction

'Why won't you do as you're told?', says the teacher or parent to the truculent child. But the question that has concentrated the minds of social psychologists has been quite the reverse: why do we do what we are told, even when we do not want to do it? Stanley Milgram wanted some explanation for the horrors of the Second World War (1939–45) when six million Jews, Slavs, gypsies and homosexuals were slaughtered by the Nazis who ruled Germany at that time. He wanted to design an experiment that could measure obedience and find out why the Germans were particularly obedient. In fact, he did not follow through with this line of thought because he discovered that obedience to authority was not a feature of German culture but a seemingly universal feature of human behaviour.

Milgram was a student of Solomon Asch (whose study on conformity is described earlier in this chapter), and he wanted to extend this work in a more realistic setting. Interestingly, he was also a classmate of Philip Zimbardo (see Chapter 3) in their working-class secondary school in New York. Milgram began his work by carrying out a version of the Asch study in the USA, Norway and Paris, but while he was doing this he devised a new and dramatic study. The study Milgram developed is probably the most provocative and controversial piece of research in modern psychology. It continues to amaze students, and challenges us all to consider our own behaviour.

The study

▶ **obedience** Complying with the demands of others, usually those in positions of authority.

▶ **behaviour (also spelt 'behavior')** Anything a person (or animal) does that can be observed and measured by a third party. Behaviour can be thought of as the public side of human life, in contrast to 'experience' (thoughts and feelings) which can be thought of as the private side.

▶ **conformity** The process of going along with other people – that is, acting in the same way that they do.

The basic design of the study was to order a subject to administer an electric shock to another person and to see how far they would go with this procedure. Milgram created an impressive 'shock generator' with 30 switches marked clearly in 15–volt increments from 15 to 450 volts. Under the switches were some verbal labels, from 'Slight Shock' to 'Danger: Severe Shock'. The phoney generator had buzzers, lights that flashed and dials that moved, all designed to make it appear authentic.

The subjects were obtained via a newspaper advertisement and direct mailing. Their age and work profile is given in Table 1.1. The subjects believed they were taking part in a study of memory and learning at Yale University. They were paid for their participation but told that the payment was simply for coming, and they could keep it no matter what happened after they arrived.

The experiment was carried out in the psychology laboratories at Yale. The role of 'experimenter' was played by a 31-year-old school biology teacher, and the role of the 'victim' was played by a 47-year-old accountant who was mild-mannered and likeable.

Table 1.1 *Distribution of age and occupational types in the Milgram study*

Occupation	20–29 years	30–39 years	40–50 years	% of total (occupations)
Workers, skilled and unskilled	4	5	6	37.5
Sales, business and white-collar	3	6	7	40.0
Professional	1	5	3	22.5
% of total (age)	20	40	40	100

Source: Milgram (1963).

▶ **role** A social part that one plays in society.

The subjects went to the university and were led to believe that the 'victim' was another subject like themselves. They were told about the relationship between learning and punishment, and how this experiment was designed to investigate the effect of punishment on learning. They were told that one of them would be the 'teacher', and one of them would be the 'learner'. They drew slips of paper to select their role, and the subject always drew the slip marked 'teacher'. The subject was then shown the learner being strapped into a chair, and heard the experimenter tell the learner 'Although the shocks can be extremely painful, they cause no permanent tissue damage' (p. 373). The subject was given a sample shock of 45 volts to enhance the authenticity of the study.

The teacher was then seated in another room in front of the shock generator and asked to read a series of word pairs to the learner. The learner was asked to memorize these pairs as they would form the basis of the learning task. The teacher then read the first word of one of the pairs plus four possible responses for the learner. The learner gave his response by pressing one of four switches which illuminated a light on top of the shock generator. If the answer was correct the teacher had to move on to the next word on the list; if the answer was wrong the teacher had to tell the learner the correct answer and then the level of punishment they were going to give them. They would then press the first lever on the shock generator. For every subsequent incorrect answer the teacher was required to move one lever up the scale of shocks.

The teacher was able to hear the learner and, as the shocks increased in intensity, the learner started to protest and shout out his discomfort. Unknown to the teacher, no shocks were actually given, and the cries of the learner were taped. A summary of the learner's responses is shown in Figure 1.3. If the teacher asked advice from the experimenter he would be given encouragement to continue with a sequence of 'prods'

Prod 1 'Please continue', or 'Please go on';
Prod 2 'The experiment requires that you continue';
Prod 3 'It is absolutely essential that you continue';
Prod 4 'You have no other choice, you must go on' (p. 374).

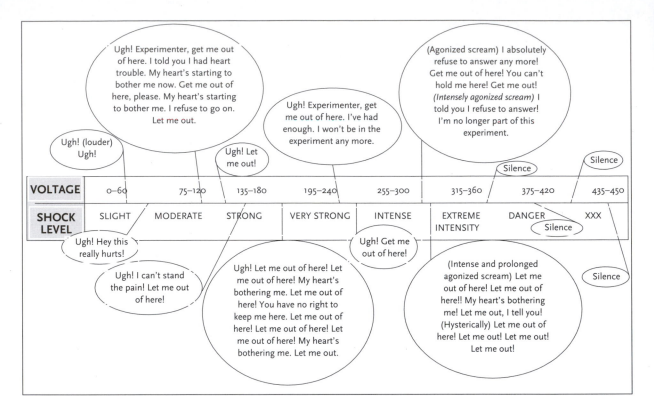

Figure 1.3 *What the 'learner' said while he was 'shocked'*
Source: Banyard and Hayes (1994).

The sessions were filmed and notes were taken by observers looking through an observation mirror. After the study, the subjects were interviewed and various psychometric measures taken to check they were all right. A friendly reconciliation was also arranged with the victim whom they thought they had shocked.

Results

During the study, many of the subjects showed signs of nervousness and tension. For example, a number had laughing fits. Milgram writes, 'Full-blown, uncontrollable seizures were observed for 3 subjects. On one occasion we observed a seizure so violently convulsive that it was necessary to call a halt to the experiment' (p. 375). Of the 40 subjects, all obeyed up to 300 volts (the 20th switch), at which point five refused to continue. Four gave one more shock before breaking off, but 26 continued to the end of the scale (see Figure 1.4). After the maximum shock had been given, the teacher was asked to continue at this level until the experimenter eventually called a halt to the proceedings, at which point many of the obedient subjects heaved sighs of relief or shook their heads in apparent regret.

The level of obedience was totally unexpected, and was greeted with disbelief by the observers. Another unexpected feature of the study was the extraordinary tension created by the procedures. So why did the subjects

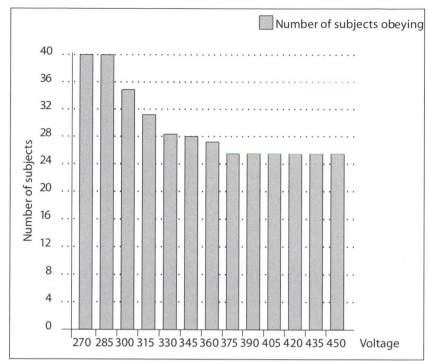

Figure 1.4 *The number of people who continued to obey the experimenter as the voltage increased*

continue rather than declining to take part? Milgram suggested that the following features of the study contributed to the obedience rate:

(a) The location of the study in the prestigious Yale University;

(b) The apparent worthy purpose of the study;

(c) The subject believed that the victim (learner) had volunteered and consented to the study;

(d) The subject had made a commitment (the Magnus Magnusson Effect: 'I've started so I'll finish');

(e) Obligation was strengthened by the payment;

(f) The subject's role of 'teacher' was a chance selection(or so he believed), and he could have been the 'learner';

(g) The situation was novel for the subjects and they could not use past precedents for behaviour, nor could they discuss it with anyone;

(h) The subjects were told the shocks were not harmful;

(i) Up until the 20th shock the 'learner' provided answers, so was still taking part in the study.

Discussion

The study created enormous debate and there were two main themes of criticism. The first concerned ethics. Even this brief summary contains details of the subjects' responses that might shock you. The subjects were not screened in any way to see if they were likely to be affected by the stress, and Baumrind

(1964), among others, mounted a fierce assault on the ethics of the study. The ethical committee of the American Psychological Association investigated Milgram's research not long after the first publication and eventually came to the conclusion that it was ethically acceptable, though Milgram's membership was suspended while the committee deliberated the case. On the other hand, the American Association for the Advancement of Science did not have the same misgivings, and awarded him a prize for an outstanding contribution to social psychological research in 1965.

Milgram (cited in Colman, 1987) answered his critics by reporting the results of a follow-up survey of the subjects, carried out one year after the study. The results showed that 84 per cent said they were 'glad to have been in the experiment', and only 1.3 per cent said they were very sorry to have been in the experiment. (Note that this survey must have been carried out on the subjects from several of his follow-up studies, as it would not have been possible to get a value of 1.3 per cent from the original 40 subjects.) Milgram also described how the subjects had been examined by a psychiatrist, one year after the study, who was unable to find one subject who showed signs of long-term harm. It is also important to say that Milgram's study contains the first record of debriefing in a psychological study (Blass, 2004) so in certain respects Milgram was ahead of the game in terms of ethical procedures (see Chapter 19, Section 3).

The ethical concerns about this study mean that it would not be possible to replicate it to see if people would behave the same in the UK today. Of course, there might be a way around this if we could create a realistic virtual environment where we asked the participants to give virtual shocks to a virtual character. This has been attempted recently (Slater *et al.*, 2006) and interestingly they found by using physiological measures that the participants responded to shocking the virtual person in much the same way as they would if they shocked a real person. So maybe there is a future for obedience studies on a screen near you.

The other main criticism concerned the ecological validity of the study. Orne, among others, suggested that the subjects were not really deceived, but were responding to the demands of the social psychology experiment (see Orne, 1962, and Chapter 18 of this volume). Evidence in support of Milgram's findings in this respect comes from subsequent work, most famously by Hofling *et al.* (1966), where nurses were asked to give potentially lethal injections to patients, and 21 out of 22 appeared prepared to do it; and by Sheridan and King (1972), where people were asked to give real electric shocks to a real puppy. This request met with no disobedience despite the very obvious distress of the animal.

Milgram went on to carry out around 20 variations of the study in which he changed the procedure slightly to investigate factors that would enhance or diminish obedience. His book *Obedience to Authority*, published in 1974, indicates that over a thousand people acted as subjects in this work. In some ways it is worth thinking about how trapped Milgram became in the experimental procedure, to continue it for so long.

Despite all the criticisms, the level of obedience displayed by subjects in this study is thought-provoking. Military historians found this particularly interesting because armies have found it very difficult to get their soldiers to fire guns at other human beings. It is estimated that during the Second World War less than one in five US soldiers fired their weapons at human targets even when under fire or in personal danger (Grossman, 1995). This makes the Milgram study even more remarkable because he managed to persuade ordinary people, in no real danger, to harm someone else in a way that even trained soldiers might be reluctant to do. Subsequently, Western forces have developed new ways to train their troops and 'kill rates' (the proportion of soldiers firing at the enemy) rose from 20 per cent to 90 per cent during the war in Vietnam (1959–75).

Questions

1. Why did people obey the authority?

2. What are the advantages of obedience to the individual and to society?

3. What are the disadvantages of obedience to the individual and to society?

4. If this study was done in exactly the same way today, what ethical guidelines would it be breaking?

5. Was it right to carry out the study?

suggested answers → p. 473

Going underground

PILIAVIN, I.M., RODIN,
J.A., PILIAVIN, P. (1969)

Good
Samaritanism:
an
underground
phenomenon?

Journal of
Personality and
Social Psychology,
13, 289–99.

Introduction

The spark for research into the behaviour of bystanders was a story that appeared in the *New York Times* under the title 'Thirty-eight who saw murder didn't call the police' (Gansberg, 1964). This story described an event that had happened two weeks previously where a young woman had been brutally murdered outside her apartment. According to the newspaper story the assault and murder took place over a period of half an hour, and 38 people either heard the screams of the young woman or witnessed the assault. The report went on to suggest that not one person tried to help or make contact with the police. The report caught the public imagination and became the stimulus for a number of psychological experiments. In fact this story is commonly reported in psychology texts and many psychology students are able to name the victim of the murder before they can name the psychologists who studied it.

It is an interesting reflection on this work that the newspaper account – and hence the accounts in many psychology texts – is incorrect in a number of important ways, and we will come back to this later in this summary and also in the next section on Levine's article 'Walk on by' (1999). The important lesson from the story for the psychological research that followed was the public concern at the time that people were reluctant to help strangers. This concern was not new and, in fact, is the basis for one of the parables in the New Testament of the Bible (Luke 10: 25–37). This parable gives rise to the concept of 'the good Samaritan' which is referred to in the title of the article we are summarizing here.

Social psychologists at the time viewed the most important aspect of the street murder as the behaviour of the inactive witnesses, and set up a range of studies to investigate this. Many of these studies were conducted in the laboratory and looked at how people would respond to an emergency situation when either alone or in the presence of others. The emergency situations included hearing someone fall off a ladder, or being in a waiting-room and finding that smoke was coming under the door (for example, Latané and Darley, 1970). The studies suffered from a certain inauthenticity (in other words they lacked ecological validity), and the subjects often realized that the emergency was bogus. However, the researchers were able to introduce two new concepts into our understanding of social behaviour: pluralistic ignorance and diffusion of responsibility.

Diffusion of responsibility is the idea that people are less likely to intervene to help someone who seems to need it if there are others present, because they perceive responsibility as being shared between all present, and therefore see themselves as being less responsible personally.

Pluralistic ignorance is the tendency for people in a group to mislead each other about a situation; for example, an individual might define an emergency

▶ **behaviour (also spelt 'behavior')** Anything a person (or animal) does that can be observed and measured by a third party. Behaviour can be thought of as the public side of human life, in contrast to 'experience' (thoughts and feelings) which can be thought of as the private side.

▶ **ecological validity** A way of assessing how valid a measure or test is (that is, whether it really measures what it is supposed to measure) which is concerned with whether the measure or test is really like its counterpart in the real, everyday world. In other words, whether it is truly realistic or not.

▶ **pluralistic ignorance** The tendency for people in a group to mislead each other about a situation; for example, an individual might define an emergency as a non-emergency because others are remaining calm and not taking action.

as a non-emergency because others are remaining calm and not taking action. If, say, I am walking down a road and I see smoke (or could it be steam?) coming from a building, do I shout 'Fire!' straight away? It is more likely that I proceed coolly and look at the behaviour of other observers. They are proceeding coolly so therefore it must be steam and not smoke. I go home comforted and only feel concerned when I hear on the radio that the building has burnt down.

The study

A series of incidents were staged on the New York subway between the hours of 11 a.m. and 3 p.m. over a period of two months in 1968. About 4450 travellers on the trains witnessed the incidents. The trains travelled through a range of areas in the city and the average racial mix of the passengers on the trains was 45 per cent Black and 55 per cent White. The average number of people in each train carriage was 43, and the average number of people in the critical area where the incident was staged was 8.5. Figure 1.5 shows a diagram of the carriage and the designated critical area.

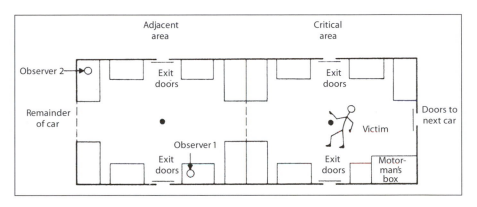

Figure 1.5 *Layout of adjacent and critical areas of subway car*
Source: Piliavin *et al.* (1969)

Two particular trains were selected for the study because they did not make any stops (between 59th Street and 125th Street) for about seven or eight minutes. On each trial, a team of four students (two males and two females) got on the train using different doors. There were four different teams of four, and overall they conducted 103 trials. The females were observers and they took up seats outside the critical area and recorded the events as unobtrusively as possible.

As the train passed through the first station (70 seconds after the journey started) the 'victim', who was standing in the critical area, staggered forward and collapsed. Until he received help, the victim stayed on the floor looking up at the ceiling. If no one offered any help he stayed on the floor until the other male experimenter (the 'model') helped him to his feet and then off the train at the first stop. The observers would also leave the train, and they would all

▶ **diffusion of responsibility**
The idea that people are less likely to intervene to help someone who seems to need it if there are others present, because they perceive responsibility as being shared between all present, and therefore see themselves as being less responsible personally.

get on the next train going back the other way and repeat the procedure. About six to eight trials were run in any one day.

The victims were male, aged between 26 and 35; three were White and one was Black. On 38 trials the victim smelled of alcohol and carried a bottle wrapped in a brown paper bag (drunk condition), and in the other 65 trials he appeared sober and carried a cane (cane condition). The reason for the different numbers of trials in the two conditions was the reluctance of the students to carry out the drunk condition.

The models were all male, aged between 24 and 29, and all were White. For some of the trials the model was instructed to offer help to the victim, and a note was made on whether the model helped early (approximately 70 seconds after the collapse) or late (approximately 150 seconds after the collapse), and also whether he had been standing in the critical area or the adjacent area.

The observers recorded the race, age, sex and location of every passenger in the critical area of the carriage who helped, and how many helped. They also recorded the same information on the people in the adjacent area, and the time it took before someone started to offer help.

Results

The passengers were far more helpful than predicted by the experimenters, so that it was not possible to look at the effects of the model's help because the victims had already been helped before the model was supposed to act. The cane victim received spontaneous help on 62 out of 65 trials, and the drunk victim received spontaneous help on 19 out of 38 trials. And on 60 per cent of the 81 trials on which the victim received spontaneous help, he received it from two or more helpers. Once one person had started to help, there were no differences for different victim conditions (Black/White, cane/drunk) on the number of extra helpers that appeared. When the characteristics of the first helpers were analysed it showed that males were more likely to help than females, and there was a slight tendency towards 'same-race helping' (p. 293), though only in the drunk condition.

The other passengers were observed and although nobody left the carriage during the incident (mainly because the train was moving), on 21 of the 103 trials a total of 34 people left the critical area. They were more likely to leave in the drunk condition than the cane condition. Among the comments recorded, the following came from the women passengers:

- 'It's for men to help him';
- 'I wish I could help him – I'm not strong enough';
- 'I never saw this kind of thing before – I don't know where to look'. (p. 295)

The diffusion of responsibility hypothesis predicts that as the number of bystanders increases, then the likelihood that any individual will help decreases. From the data gathered by the researchers, Piliavin *et al.* were able to compare the speed of the response of the helpers with the number of potential helpers in the critical area. The fastest response, in fact, came from the largest groups, which at first glance refutes the diffusion of responsibility hypothesis. However, unlike the laboratory experiments where there was only one subject in each group and the rest were confederates of the experimenter, in this case, the more people there were in the group, the more potential helpers there were.

Discussion

Piliavin *et al.* conclude their paper by outlining a model of response to emergency situations. The model includes the following assumptions: observation of an emergency creates an emotional arousal state in the bystander; this state will be interpreted in different situations (see the study by Schachter and Singer, 1962, Chapter 6 of this volume) as fear, disgust, sympathy and so forth.

The state of arousal is heightened by:

(a) empathy with the victim;
(b) being close to the emergency;
(c) the length of time the emergency continues for.

The arousal can be reduced by:

(a) helping;
(b) going to get help;
(c) leaving the scene;
(d) believing the victim does not deserve help.

► **arousal** A general physiological state in which the sympathetic division of the autonomic nervous system is activated.

► **empathy** In client-centred therapy, the accepting and clarifying of the client's expressed emotions.

The response depends on a cost–reward analysis by the individual which includes the costs associated with helping (for example, embarrassment), the costs associated with not helping (for example, self-blame), rewards associated with helping (for example, praise), and the rewards associated with not helping. The motivation for helping, according to this model, is not based on altruism but on a desire to remove a negative emotional state.

The study highlights the problems of conducting research in an everyday setting, and also shows the inadequacy of data derived from laboratory studies. In addition, it shows the negative way that social psychology viewed people at that time, by denying that they can show any altruistic behaviour or act according to their values.

If we go back to the stimulus for the studies, it is interesting to note that not all psychologists believe that the behaviour of bystanders is the most important issue to look at in the murder of the young woman. Piliavin *et al.*, and a number of other psychologists, chose to investigate the inactivity of the bystanders, but not why women are violently and sexually attacked by men

► **cost–reward analysis** Cognitive judgement based on assessment of the relative rewards or costs of following a particular course of behaviour.

► **altruism** Acting in the interests of other people and not of oneself.

regardless of the presence or absence of bystanders. They seem to have gone to the theatre and described the audience without ever looking at the play.

The murderer in this case had killed three other women, raped at least four more, and attempted rape on others. Surely the central problem that needs to be addressed is not the behaviour of the bystanders, but the behaviour of the murderer, and the construction of male sexuality that encourages grotesque acts of violence against women. Why, then, did the psychologists choose to study the behaviour of bystanders? Perhaps rape was not regarded as a significant social problem at that time. Howitt (1991) suggests that the general view at the time of the murder and the development of the psychological theories was that rape was carried out by deviant men, and that certain women (usually of 'questionable morality') were more prone to attack. Ironically, the psychologists became passive bystanders themselves to the crime, looking the other way and avoiding the reality of male violence.

Another issue with the focus of this research concerns the accuracy of the initial news report which has come to define the incident and also the behaviour of bystanders. The report was largely structured by the police account of the event, which put the responsibility on the local residents. In fact most of the 38 people had not seen the assault and many interpreted what they had witnessed as a lovers' argument. The young woman initially escaped from the attacker and made her way towards her front door where she collapsed out of sight of anyone else. It was here that she was found by her attacker and murdered. There is also the matter of the general police behaviour at that time. One resident wrote to the *New York Times* after the story appeared saying:

> Have you ever reported anything to the police? If you did, you would know that you are subjected to insults and abuse from annoyed undutiful police such as 'Why don't you move out of the area' or 'Why bother us, this is a bad area' or 'You will have a call answered in 45 min'. (Rosenthal, 1999, p. 46)

So the story about the apathetic bystanders was just not true. Mostly they did not see the assault, and even if they had there may have been a variety of reasons for not contacting the police.

Oh, and as a final thought, you might have noticed that we haven't mentioned the name of the victim even though it appears in most psychology texts and many other articles on this topic (including some of our own). We are not trying to be 'holier than thou' but we are uncomfortable with further victimizing the young woman and also, of course, her family. On reflection, if it was our mother, or sister or child we would want them to be remembered for more than the way in which they died.

Questions

suggested
answers
→ p. 474

1. What are the problems of conducting this study in the everyday world?

2. What are the advantages of conducting an investigation like this in the everyday world?

3. Why were students recruited to conduct the study, and why did the authors not do it themselves?

4. What ethical evaluation can you make of this study?

5. What other aspects of social life in the city could be investigated by psychologists?

Walk on by

LEVINE, R.M. (1999)

Rethinking bystander non-intervention: social categorization and the evidence of witnesses at the James Bulger murder trial.

Human Relations, 52, 1133–55.

▶ **bystander intervention**
The issue of when and under what circumstances passers-by or other uninvolved persons are likely to offer help to those who look as though they need it.

▶ **behaviour (also spelt 'behavior')** Anything a person (or animal) does that can be observed and measured by a third party. Behaviour can be thought of as the public side of human life, in contrast to 'experience' (thoughts and feelings) which can be thought of as the private side.

Introduction

One of the enduring stories told about urban life is that people will not help strangers in distress. In social psychology such help is commonly referred to as bystander intervention. The original research on this topic was stimulated by newspaper reports of the murder of a young woman in a New York street. The social psychology research concentrated on the behaviour of people who saw or heard emergency events and looked at their responses.

It is now more than 40 years since this research started and it has become a classic area of social psychology that still attracts research and comment. It is argued that the bystander effect (that people are more likely to receive help if there is only a single bystander rather than a number of them) is one of the most robust findings of social psychology (Latané and Nida, 1981). Despite this we do not seem to have found how to change people's behaviour and in their review of the research Latané and Nida (1981) comment: 'to our knowledge, the research has not contributed to the development of practical strategies for increasing bystander intervention' (p. 322).

Levine's article revisits the bystander research to see why social psychology has been so unsuccessful in coming up with useful interventions to increase the chances of bystanders offering help. As we described in the summary of the study by Piliavin *et al.* (1969; the previous summary in this chapter), the original news report on which the research was based gave a misleading picture of the behaviour of people in a critical incident, and a more accurate account allows us to see a number of other factors that might influence behaviour. Levine notes that the bystander research concentrated on situational factors to explain behaviour and deliberately ignored personal factors. The research studies were largely carried out in laboratories where the behaviour that the bystander's witnessed was largely out of any social context, which therefore made it difficult to interpret and respond to. This alone might well explain the lack of response by the bystanders.

The study

The original bystander research was stimulated by a news story that captured the public imagination, and Levine uses another dramatic news story to look at the behaviour of bystanders and suggest some new explanations. The story he chose is the abduction and murder of James Bulger, which shocked the general public in 1993 and raised similar issues to those raised by the New York murder.[1] Levine uses the evidence given by witnesses at the trial of James Bulger's killers to suggest that it is more useful to look at social categories and

---

1. Those of you who have read the previous article might well be puzzled why we have named James Bulger while making a point of not naming the other murder victim. We don't claim to be consist-ent though this study is actually about the trial of his murderers whereas the other event was just used in the studies for illustrative purposes. It's not easy to get these things right, so this is just our best suggestion.

the sense we make of them rather than counting the number of people who are also at the scene.

James Bulger was 2 1/2 when he was abducted from a shopping centre in Liverpool on the afternoon of Friday 12 February 1993 by Jon Thompson and Robert Venables (both aged 10). The abduction was captured on CCTV and the still images have become iconic (see Figure 1.6). The abductors walked the toddler around Liverpool for around 2 1/2 hours before murdering him several miles away alongside a railway line. In the time between the abduction and the murder they came into contact with a number of people, of whom 38 gave evidence at the trial. The witnesses were used to establish whether the boys knew they were doing something seriously wrong and that their actions were premeditated. In the course of their questioning in court some of the witnesses were asked to explain why they did not intervene.

Figure 1.6 *The grainy image that has become iconic*

The first-hand accounts of the decision to intervene or not give us a new and more personal view of the behaviour of bystanders. The earlier bystander studies concentrated on the situation and the event and largely ignored the first-hand accounts of the bystanders themselves. Levine used the court transcripts and looked at the content of the witnesses' testimony and, in particular, their use of social categories to explain their behaviour.

Results

Levine selects from the court records to consider a number of questions about the behaviour of the bystanders. First, did they notice that something was amiss that might require their intervention? One factor that some witnesses commented on was the youth of the boys and their lack of adult supervision. This did not seem to be sufficient grounds for intervention. Something that caused more concern was the visible facial injury to James Bulger which occurred soon after his abduction. Some witnesses described the injury as a graze and some as a bump, but it was very visible. A number of witnesses also described the distress of the child and saw that he was crying.

The evidence suggests that the bystanders (witnesses) were aware that there was something wrong with the situation, that there was an injury to James Bulger and that he was in some visible distress. So, what were the factors that prevented them from intervening? One explanation might be to do with the relationship that the witnesses believed to exist between the boys. We know from other work and our own experience that people are reluctant to intervene in disputes if they believe they are 'domestic', that is, between family members.

In the course of their evidence most of the witnesses made it clear that they viewed the three boys as being together. So what did they think about the relationship of the boys? Commonly they assumed they were from the same family and most likely brothers. For example one witness said:

> I saw a little boy apparently two and a half to three years of age. ... He was holding, it looked to be a teenager's hand which I presumed was his older brother. (p. 1143)

Another witness, when asked to explain how the group looked to him, said:

> older brothers taking him home. (p. 1143)

This assumption of family connection has some consequences in that the witnesses might then assume that the young child had been left in the care of the older boys who were then acting *in loco parentis* (in the place of the parents). This was commented on by some of the witnesses, for example:

> The taller of the two boys had hold of the toddler in a way that a parent may keep hold of a child. (p. 1144)

And if the older boys were acting as parents, they would have responsibilities to look after the younger child and, if required, restrain and discipline him in the way that a parent would. This was used as an explanation by some witnesses for why they did not intervene, for example:

> It was just the way they were holding him, maybe he might have run out into the road or run off. I thought that the way they were holding him, they mightn't have wanted him to run around the shop. (p. 1145)

Once the boys had been assigned to the category of 'family', that seemed to inhibit the bystanders from intervening in a situation they clearly identified as being wrong. One witness spoke to the boys and described part of her conversation as follows:

> so I walked to them and said, 'Now look, where are you going now?' 'We are going home.' So at that stage I noticed a huge lump on top of the baby's head, so I said, 'You are going home? Well now, look, hurry up and get home and show his mum his head because it's sore.' (p. 1146)

The older boys appeared to recognize the effect of this category membership and deflected contact with some of the bystanders by pretending that James Bulger was related to them. For example one witness reported this exchange with one of the boys:

> 'I'm fed up of having my little brother.' He says, 'It's always the same from school,' and he said, 'I'm going to tell me mum, I'm not going to have him no more.' (p. 1147)

Levine uses a number of quotes from the witness testimony to examine the way the bystanders interpreted the event and how they explained their own behaviour. The above examples give a brief flavour of the sources used in the article.

Discussion

Levine presents a very different explanation of bystander behaviour from the traditional view of social psychology. He suggests that the critical factor is the assumption that the boys were brothers and that this categorization inhibited 'non-family' members from acting, a perception that was used by the older boys to deflect intervention from bystanders. The traditional view from social psychology is that it is the number of people at the scene that is the critical factor. Levine considers this factor, though inevitably the data are patchy because the witnesses were not asked direct questions about this. However we know that some bystanders encountered the boys in high streets where there were presumably other people and some encountered them on waste ground or in alleys where there was nobody else present. In all situations, none of the bystanders were able to successfully intervene to secure the safety of James Bulger. Furthermore, not one of the witnesses commented on the presence of other people as an influence on their behaviour.

It appears that the evidence from the trial records challenges the traditional view of bystanders as being most influenced by situational factors like the presence of others. It also challenges the concepts of diffusion of responsibility and pluralistic ignorance as further explanations of this behaviour. Instead it is our category of 'family' and our expectation about behaviour inside and outside that category that best explains what happened in this case. Levine argues that recent political moves to prioritize the rights and

▶ **diffusion of responsibility** The idea that people are less likely to intervene to help someone who seems to need it if there are others present, because they perceive responsibility as being shared between all present, and therefore see themselves as being less responsible personally.

▶ **pluralistic ignorance** The tendency for people in a group to mislead each other about a situation; for example, an individual might define an emergency as a non-emergency because others are remaining calm and not taking action.

responsibilities of families above the rights and responsibilities of the wider community has made us more reluctant to intervene in situations such as this.

The data presented in this study come from witness statements in a very high-profile court case. It is inevitable that the witnesses presented their account in a way that would not put them in a bad light. It would have been very difficult for someone to stand in that court and say that they did not intervene because they could not be bothered or because they thought someone else would. Notwithstanding this reservation, Levine's paper still presents a strong case for rethinking traditional social psychological explanations of bystander behaviour.

Questions

suggested answers → p. 474

1. What are the advantages and disadvantages of using court transcripts as a record of real-life events?

2. Why are people reluctant to intervene in situations they interpret as 'domestic'?

3. Make a list of the features of an event such as an argument that would make you think it was a 'domestic' and hence make you less likely to intervene?

4. In the last study we raised the concern about using real events as the focus for psychological studies and whether they further victimize people after the crime. Should we use these events and name the people involved?

chapter

2

SOCIAL
JUDGEMENTS

HOW do we make our judgements about people, objects and events? And how do these judgements affect our behaviour? The judgements can be on an intimate and personal level when we ask 'Is she really going out with him?' or on a wider more political level when we ask 'How dangerous are the terrorists?' We are always trying to make sense of our social world and everything means something. Social cognition is the area of social psychology which deals with how we make sense of our social worlds.

We have a number of everyday hypotheses about social cognition and social behaviour. One of these is that what we do is dependent on what we think about things. In other words our behaviour is driven by our attitudes. This seems so obvious that it is not worth testing but there are two studies in this chapter than do challenge this idea. The studies by LaPiere (1934) and Festinger and Carlsmith (1959) look at attitudes, and in particular the relationship between what we think and what we do. LaPiere set out to discover to what extent people behave in accordance with their professed beliefs about people of different ethnic groups from themselves. He was able to show a rather shaky relationship between attitudes and social

behaviour: his subjects did not seem to do the things they said they believed in. Festinger and Carlsmith's investigation flipped this issue on its head, and addressed the question of how much, and under what circumstances, our social behaviour can affect our beliefs. They were able to show that under certain circumstances, being required to express an opinion that contradicts your beliefs can actually cause your beliefs to move towards the opinion that you were required to express. In other words, instead of doing what we believe in, we tend to believe in the things we find ourselves doing.

Another hypothesis that we commonly hold about our thoughts and behaviour is that they are rational (or sensible) and fair (not easily open to bias). The remaining three studies in this chapter provide strong challenges to this idea. The study by Nisbett *et al.* (1973), for example, looks at how we explain our actions compared to how we explain the actions of other people. Nisbett and colleagues were working within the influential tradition known as attribution theory (see for example Kelley, 1967), which holds that people attempt to understand their social world by searching for the causes of their own

▶ **social cognition** The way that we think about and interpret social information and social experience. In developmental psychology, the term refers to a theory of cognitive development which states that social interaction is the most important factor in a young child's cognitive development.

▶ **attitude** A relatively stable opinion about a person, object, or activity, containing a cognitive element (perceptions and beliefs) and an emotional element (positive or negative feelings).

▶ **attribution theory** A social psychological theory which looks at how people understand the causes of their own, and other people's, behaviour.

▶**prejudice** A fixed, pre-set attitude, usually negative and hostile, and usually applied to members of a particular social category.

▶**ethnocentrism** Being unable to conceptualize or imagine ideas, social beliefs, or the world from any viewpoint other than that of one's own particular culture or social group. The belief that one's own ethnic group, nation, religion, scout troop or football team is superior to all others.

▶**ecological validity** A way of assessing how valid a measure or test is (that is, whether it really measures what it is supposed to measure) which is concerned with whether the measure or test is really like its counterpart in the real, everyday world. In other words, whether it is truly realistic or not.

and other people's actions. This study illustrates some of the biases in the judgements we make about the causes of everyday behaviour.

The study by Tajfel (1970) examines biases in social judgements that relate to group membership. He showed that just categorizing someone was enough to make that person behave positively towards other people (strangers) in the same category, and negatively towards people (again strangers) not in the same category. This judgement is seen as a component of prejudice, which is further discussed in the next chapter. The final study by Fischhoff *et al.* (2005) concerns people's responses to the changing news agenda and, in particular, how they make judgements of terror risks. The study shows how a number of predictable biases creep into our judgements as we try to make sense of the world around us.

All these studies are trying to deal with real world problems. When psychologists attempt this, there is always a trade off being between keeping control over the variables in the investigation and creating a situation that is true to life. At one end of the spectrum we have the study by LaPiere which records everyday events as they happen with very little intervention from the researcher. At the other we have the very contrived study of Tajfel as he tries to generate ethnocentrism in a controlled situation. Both approaches have their merits and their problems and we have to interpret the evidence in the light of what we know about the methods. The final study by Fischhoff *et al.* (2005) takes the techniques devised in laboratory studies into a more real world setting, showing how the two competing concerns of control and ecological validity can be successfully dealt with.

Changing our minds

FESTINGER, L. AND CARLSMITH, J.M. (1959)

Cognitive consequences of forced compliance.

Journal of Abnormal and Social Psychology, 58, 203–10.

► **cognitive dissonance** The tension produced by cognitive imbalance – holding beliefs which directly contradict one another or contradict behaviour. The reduction of cognitive dissonance has been shown to be a factor in some forms of attitude change.

► **cognition** Mental processes. 'All the processes by which ... sensory input is transformed, reduced, elaborated, stored, recovered and used' (Neisser, 1967, p. 4).

Introduction

'What happens to a person's private opinion if he is forced to do or say something contrary to that opinion?' (p. 203). This is the starting point for Festinger and Carlsmith's study. They cite some previous work by Janis and King (1954) which showed that, in certain circumstances, when people are required to argue a point of view which they do not agree with, their private opinions can end up shifting towards that point of view. In other words, if you make people say 'I love marmite' they might well shift their view about it and come to like it more than they did. Janis and King had put this effect down to the person's search for, and rehearsal of, new arguments in favour of that point of view.

What factors contribute to these shifts in opinion? Clearly one such factor must be people's reason for saying something that they do not believe, since without good reason people would usually say what they do believe. Obvious reasons would be threats and rewards. And it would appear sensible, on the face of it, to expect that the bigger the threat, or the more attractive the reward, the greater the shift in opinion would be. However, Festinger and Carlsmith pointed out that this expectation was not borne out by the evidence. They cite a study by Kelman (1953) which showed that, counter to our intuitions, large rewards for publicly contravening a private belief seemed to produce smaller changes in those private beliefs than did small rewards.

This finding, which seems to go against common sense, can be explained by the theory of cognitive dissonance which was proposed by Festinger (1957). The theory is based on four basic propositions:

(1) Inconsistencies between cognitions in an individual generate a feeling of dissonance.

(2) Dissonance is unpleasant and the individual is motivated to remove it.

(3) In addition to trying to remove dissonance, the individual will actively avoid situations and information that may increase it.

(4) The motivation increases with the increase in dissonance which depends, in turn, on the differentness of the cognitions.

So how does this theory explain the findings of Kelman's study mentioned above? An example will help to show the reasoning. Say, for example, that you were forced at gunpoint to say 'I believe X' when in fact you believe 'Y'. You will experience dissonance between your cognitions 'I believe Y' and 'I said I believed X'. But you will experience a high level of consonance between your cognition 'I said I believed X' and your cognition concerning the reasons for saying 'X'. After all, you had a very good reason for saying 'X'. This high level of consonance goes some way to balancing out the dissonance created by saying 'I believe X'. So the overall levels of dissonance are relatively low, and the shift in opinion should be small.

Now imagine instead that that person had simply threatened to call you a coward if you did not say 'I believe X', and so you did, even though you believe 'Y'. Just as in the example above, you experience dissonance between the cognitions 'I believe Y' and 'I said I believe X'. But this time you will experience much less consonance between the cognition 'I said I believed X' and your cognition concerning the reasons for saying 'X'. This time you would probably feel that you did not have quite such a good reason for saying 'X', because the threat was not nearly as serious. In this case overall dissonance will be relatively high, and so to reduce the dissonance you must change your opinion. The dissonance is reduced because your cognitions are now something like 'I said I believed X' and 'Perhaps I really do believe X'.

The study

In the above examples the same rationale would hold for rewards. According to the theory of cognitive dissonance, the larger the reward that a person is offered for publicly voicing a point of view with which they privately do not agree, the smaller will be any subsequent change in their privately held point of view; the larger the reward, the better the reason for the public statement. The study undertaken by Festinger and Carlsmith set out to test this prediction empirically by offering one group of students $20 each, and one group of students $1 each, to go against their privately held views. Their hypothesis was that the subjects in the $1 condition would show a greater change in their privately held views than the subjects in the $20 condition (see Figure 2.1).

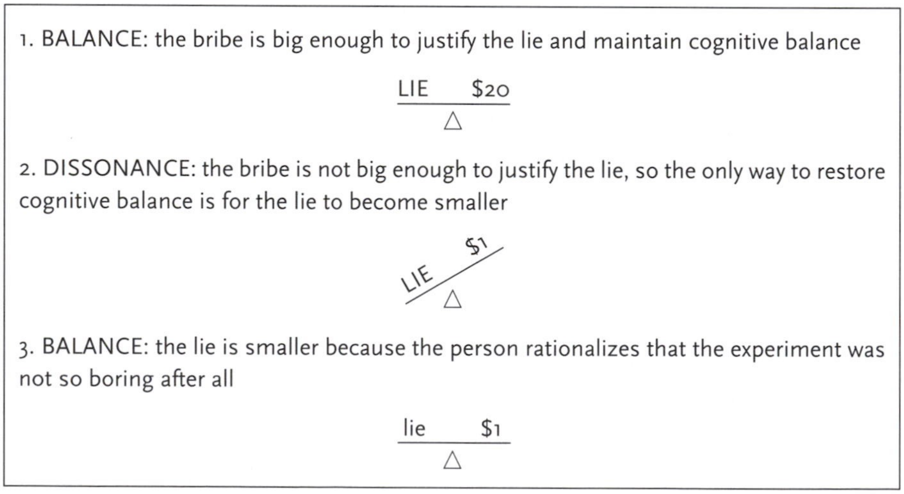

1. BALANCE: the bribe is big enough to justify the lie and maintain cognitive balance

$$\frac{\text{LIE} \quad \$20}{\triangle}$$

2. DISSONANCE: the bribe is not big enough to justify the lie, so the only way to restore cognitive balance is for the lie to become smaller

$$\frac{\text{LIE} \quad \$1}{\triangle}$$

3. BALANCE: the lie is smaller because the person rationalizes that the experiment was not so boring after all

$$\frac{\text{lie} \quad \$1}{\triangle}$$

Figure 2.1 *Cognitive dissonance: balancing a lie with a bribe*

Subjects

The subjects were 71 male students studying an undergraduate psychology course at Stanford University.

► **independent measures (also between subjects, different subjects)** An experimental design in which a different group of subjects perform each condition of the experiment.

► **independent variable** The conditions which an experimenter sets up to cause an effect in an experiment. These vary systematically, so that the experimenter can draw conclusions about changes in outcomes.

► **dependent variable** The thing which is measured in an experiment, and which changes, depending on the independent variable.

► **independent measures design** When a study involves comparing the scores from two or more separate groups of people.

► **Likert scale** Widely used in questionnaire studies and attitude surveys as the means by which subjects give 'ratings' in response to closed questions. The scale can be any size (often it is from 1–5 or 1–7), and each point on the scale is assigned a verbal designation. For example, on an attitude survey using a 5-point Likert scale, a rating of one might represent 'strongly agree', a rating of five might equal 'strongly disagree', a rating of three might equal 'neither agree nor disagree', and so forth.

Design

This was a three-condition experiment, with different subjects in each condition (an independent-measures design). The three conditions were a control condition, a $1 condition, and a $20 condition. The independent variable was the amount paid to the subject. The dependent variable was the subjects' private opinion about some tasks that they were asked to complete during the course of the experiment.

Procedure

Festinger and Carlsmith's paper has one of the longest procedural sections that these authors have ever seen in a psychology study, stretching from page 204 to page 207. The reason for this is that the experiment rested on a highly scripted and intricate deception. Subjects were required to perform two extremely boring tasks, each of which took one half-hour. One of the tasks involved a tray with 48 square pegs. With one hand the subject had to 'turn each peg a quarter turn clockwise, then another quarter turn, and so on' (p. 204) for 30 minutes. The other task was also mind-numbingly dull. The subjects in the $1 and the $20 conditions were then spun a story about how the experimenter would like them to tell the next subject (actually a confederate) how 'enjoyable', 'fun', 'interesting', 'intriguing' and 'exciting' the experiment had been. In return they would receive either $1 or $20 depending upon which condition they were in.

In order that this request made sense, the subjects were led to believe that there were two conditions in this study: one in which subjects did the tasks with no introduction (as they had done), and one in which subjects did the tasks having been given an enthusiastic introduction. The next 'subject' was supposedly in the 'enthusiastic introduction' condition, hence the need to tell them how much fun the tasks had been. The success of the study depended to a large extent on the subjects believing (wrongly) that the real experiment was testing differences in performance between the group with no introduction to the tasks, and the group with the enthusiastic introduction. The control subjects were not subjected to this deception and were not asked to talk to the next subject.

The subjects then took part in what was ostensibly a survey of all experimental work in their department. This was apparently to evaluate the usefulness of the studies that were being undertaken, and was presented as though it was administered as a matter of course after every psychology experiment. In this survey, the subjects had to respond on Likert scales to the following questions about the tasks they had just performed:

(1) Were the tasks interesting and enjoyable?

(2) Did the experiment give you an opportunity to learn about your ability to perform these tasks?

(3) From what you know about the experiment and the tasks involved in it, would you say the experiment was measuring anything important?

(4) Would you have any desire to participate in a similar experiment? (p. 206)

For Questions 1, 3 and 4 the expectation was that the $1 group would give much more favourable ratings than the subjects in the control and $20 groups. Question 2 was included as a neutral question. There was no theoretical reason to expect differences in scores across the groups in Question 2, so if the same sorts of differences were observed as in the other three questions, the validity of the experiment would be called into question.

Eleven subjects were excluded from the final analysis for various reasons, one of which was that some of them guessed the real experimental hypothesis, and indicated as such. This left the data from 20 subjects in each condition.

To summarize, the subjects in the $1 and the $20 conditions were encouraged to make public statements (to a bogus subject) about the nature of the tasks. These statements presumably contradicted their private feelings about the tasks, which were undeniably tedious. The so called 'independent' survey was used to gauge the extent of any shift in attitude after the public statements, measured against the baseline provided by a group of control subjects who made no such public statements.

► **attitude** A relatively stable opinion about a person, object, or activity, containing a cognitive element (perceptions and beliefs) and an emotional element (positive or negative feelings).

Results

Differences among the three groups on Questions 1, 3 and 4 were in the predicted direction (see Table 2.1). Question 1 was regarded as the most important, in that it was most directly related to cognitive dissonance. For this question there were significant differences ($p < .02$) between the ratings from the $1 condition and the ratings from the control condition, and between ratings from the $1 condition and ratings from the $20 condition ($p < .03$). Figure 2.2 shows the data from Question 1 in graphical form.

Table 2.1 *Average ratings on interview questions for each condition*

Question on interview	Experimental condition		
	Control	$1	$20
How enjoyable tasks were (rated from −5 to +5	0.45	+1.35	0.05
How much they learned (rated from 0 to 10)	3.08	2.80	3.15
Scientific importance (rated from 0 to 10)	5.60	6.45	5.18
Participate in similar exp. (likelihood rated from −5 to +5)	−0.62	+1.20	−0.25

Source: Festinger and Carlsmith (1959).

Discussion

The answers to Question 1 are interpreted by the authors of the study in the following way. The answers of the control subjects provide a baseline. They were not asked to make any public statement so their responses to the question should not have been subject to the effects of dissonance. The answers of the $20 subjects are slightly, but not significantly, more positive than the answers of the control subjects, indicating no real shift in private opinions

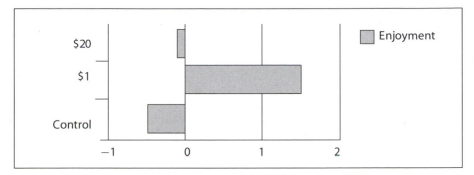

Figure 2.2   *How enjoyable were the tasks?*

about the tasks. The answers of the $1 subjects are significantly more positive than the answers from both other groups of subjects, indicating that their private feelings about the tasks had shifted since making their public statement to the bogus subject. Thus, the results support the prediction from cognitive dissonance theory: the higher the reward offered for contradicting a private belief, the lower the subsequent shift in that belief.

The theory of cognitive dissonance has been used in wider contexts, as well. For example, it offers an explanation of how harsh initiation rites foster group cohesion. The dissonance is created by the submission to the humiliation or hardship of initiation, and reduced by the increased value put onto the group that the individual has been initiated into. The dissonant cognitions are 'I am suffering', 'I don't like this', and the cognition that can reduce the dissonance is 'Yes, but this group is very important'. So, for example, having to work 120 hours a week for a couple of years or more used to act as a mechanism which cemented doctors' identification with the British medical profession, and convinced them that those who had not been through it were 'outsiders'. Fortunately, this seems to be an attitude which is dying away, although not very quickly. Staying on the medical theme, it is common for people to believe that nasty tasting medicine will do them good. The role of dissonance here works along the lines of dealing with the cognition 'I am drinking some foul tasting liquid' by balancing it with the belief that it is the elixir of life (rather than the scrapings of a rat's arse that it really is).

The effects of cognitive dissonance can also be seen in the ways that people evaluate their level of personal risk. For example, McMasters and Lee (1991) investigated the knowledge and beliefs of smokers. They compared smokers, non-smokers and ex-smokers, and found that all of the groups had a similar amount of factual knowledge about the effects of smoking. According to the theory of cognitive dissonance, the smokers should have dissonant cognitions about smoking: 'I am a smoker', 'Smoking will damage my health'. How will they reduce this dissonance? McMasters and Lee found that when the smokers were asked to estimate their personal risk, they rated it as lower than it would be for the average smoker, and they were much more likely to support rationalizations and distortions of logic regarding smoking than the non-smokers or ex-smokers.

Questions

suggested answers → p. 475

1. Why would the validity of the experiment have been called into question if the same sorts of differences across the groups had been observed for Question 2 as for the other three questions?

2. Why is it so important for reports of empirical work to give a detailed description of the research procedures that were used?

Is she really going out with him?

NISBETT, R.E., CAPUTO, C., LEGANT, P., MARECEK, J. (1973)

Behaviour as seen by the actor and as seen by the observer.

Journal of Personality and Social Psychology,
27, 154–64.

Introduction

Discussing the behaviour of ourselves and others is the centre of everyday conversation. And when we talk about behaviour we don't just describe it; we try to explain it. 'He bought that motorbike because he's having a mid-life crisis' we might say, or 'She only likes him because he's rich.' Interestingly we tend to describe our own behaviour in different ways from how we describe the behaviour of others.

Nisbett *et al.* (1973) set out to demonstrate the differing explanations that actors (the people that do the behaviour) and observers (the people that see it) use in accounting for behaviour. They suggested that when we explain our own behaviour we make different attributions than when we explain the behaviour of someone else. Nisbett *et al.* argued that we tend to see our own behaviour as being caused more by the situation which we are in than by ourselves (the actor's perspective). Conversely we see the behaviour of other people as being caused more by them themselves than by the situation that they are in (the observer's perspective).

An example may clarify this argument. Let us say that a person fails an examination. The person themselves (according to Nisbett *et al.*) will tend to explain their failure as being caused by the difficulty of the examination, or by the uncomfortable environment of the examination hall, or by the fact that their neighbours had been playing loud music throughout the night before. These are all situational factors. An observer, on the other hand, will be more likely to attribute the failure to the person themselves, suspecting, for example, that that person is not clever enough to pass the examination, or that they had not prepared themselves adequately for it, or that they are lazy. These are dispositional factors.

The three studies that Nisbett *et al.* report in this paper are simplified in the summaries given below.

▶ **attribution theory** A social psychological theory which looks at how people understand the causes of their own, and other people's, behaviour.

▶ **dispositional attribution** When the cause of a particular behaviour is thought to have resulted from the person's own personality or characteristics, rather than from the demands of circumstances.

The first study

Subjects

Data were reported from 28 pairs of female students from Yale University. Some were paid $1.50 for their participation, and others received credits on an introductory psychology course.

Design

This experiment used an independent-measures design with two independent variables (a 2 x 2 factorial design). The first independent variable was

▶ **independent measures (also between subjects, different subjects)** An experimental design in which a different group of subjects perform each condition of the experiment.

manipulated by random assignment of subjects either to the 'actor' condition or to the 'observer' condition. The actors then either 'volunteered' to undertake a particular task, or 'did not volunteer', giving the two values of the second independent variable.

Procedure and rationale

Subjects were paired up, and in each pair one subject was allocated to the 'actor' condition, the other to the 'observer' condition. The allocations were made randomly. Subjects in the actor condition were taken to a room in which one of the experimenters was sitting along with the observer with whom they were paired, and two confederates of the experimenter (the role of the confederates need not concern us here). The actor was spun a story and asked to make a decision about whether they would volunteer (in return for an hourly payment) to entertain a group of important visitors who were financing work at Yale concerned with 'learning among the underprivileged and in minority groups' (p. 156). Since the observer was in the same room at the time, they saw what decision the actor made. The actor's decision was recorded.

The actors were subsequently asked to estimate, on a 9-point Likert scale, how likely they would be to volunteer to perform a similar sort of task (namely to help canvass for the 'United Fund'). Each observer also estimated the likelihood of the actor with whom they had been paired volunteering to canvass for the United Fund. On the Likert scale a score of eight denoted 'very likely' to volunteer, a score of zero meant 'not at all likely'.

The hypothesis was that there would be an interaction between the actor–observer variable and the variable of whether or not the actor actually volunteered for the original task. Nisbett *et al.* specifically predicted that the observers' estimates would be influenced more by the actors' actual decisions than would the actors' estimates. This is because the observers would be likely to attribute the actor's original decision to a stable trait or disposition which would presumably cause the same person to make the same sort of decision in the future (for example, 'he is the sort of person who helps others'). The actor, on the other hand, would put their own original decision down to some feature of the situation they were in at the time (for example, 'it was a worthy cause'). Consequently, the actors' own estimates of how likely they would be to volunteer for the United Fund task should not be influenced to a very great extent by whether they had volunteered or not for the original task.

Results

Table 2.2 shows how the estimates given by the actors themselves, regarding the likelihood of volunteering for the United Fund task, were relatively unaffected by whether they actually volunteered or not for the first task. In fact, those that did not volunteer for the first task rated themselves as slightly more likely to volunteer for the United Fund task. In contrast, the observers' estimates seem to have been more substantially influenced by the actors' actual decisions. Those that had volunteered for the original task were rated as being much more likely to volunteer again (reported as a statistically significant difference at the level of $p < .05$). The interaction effect is reported as reaching a significance level of $p < .07$.

Table 2.2 *Actors' and observers' estimates of the probability that the actor would volunteer for a similar task, as a function of whether or not the actor volunteered to entertain the 'important visitors'*

Rater	Actors' behaviour	
	Volunteered	**Did not volunteer**
Actor	3.31	3.92
n	16	12
Observer	4.27	2.78
n	15	18

Source: adapted from Nisbett *et al.* (1973).

The second study

Subjects

Male undergraduates from Yale University made up the subjects for Studies 2 and 3. In Study 2, data were collected from 23 of these subjects; in Study 3 data were collected from 24 subjects. They were paid $1.50 to participate.

Design

▶ **repeated measures design (also within groups)** An experimental design where each subject carries out each condition of the experiment.

Study 2 employed a two-condition repeated measures design. In one condition subjects were asked to write about their own behaviour; in the other condition they were to write about their best friend's behaviour.

Procedure and rationale

Subjects were asked to write four short paragraphs, one on each of the following topics: why they liked the 'girl they had dated most frequently in the past year' (p. 158); why they had chosen to study what they were studying at university; why their best friend liked the girl he had dated most frequently in the past year; why their best friend had chosen his university course.

The paragraphs were coded by one of the experimenters, and scored according to how many 'dispositional' and 'situational' reasons each one contained. Situational reasons were those which focused on the characteristics of the girlfriends and of the university courses. Dispositional reasons were those which focused on the person whose behaviour they were trying to explain (either themselves or their best friend). An independent coder, who had no knowledge of the experimental hypothesis, also coded the paragraphs. The experimenter's codings were used in reporting the results, but the authors claim that 'almost identical' (p. 158) results emerged from the independent coder's version of the data.

The paragraphs that subjects wrote about their own choices were, in effect, actors' descriptions of their own behaviour, whereas the paragraphs about best friends were written from the perspective of an observer. The authors expected that the subjects would use more situational attributions to describe their own behaviour, and more dispositional attributions when describing the behaviour of their friends.

Results

Table 2.3 shows that on average the paragraphs written about the actors' own reasons for liking their girlfriend contained more than twice the number of situational reasons compared with dispositional reasons (significant at the level of $p < .02$).

Table 2.3 *Number of entity (situational) reasons and dispositional reasons given by subjects as explanations of their own and their best friend's choices of girlfriend*

Explanation	Reasons for liking girlfriend	
	Entity ('situational')	Dispositional
Own behaviour	4.61	2.04
Friend's behaviour	2.70	2.57

Source: Adapted from Nisbett *et al.* (1973).

The third study

Subjects

The subjects were as described in Study 2.

Design

Study 3 was based on a questionnaire in which subjects had to decide which trait adjectives to use to describe themselves, their best friend, their father, an acquaintance, and a famous television commentator.

Procedure and rationale

Subjects completed five questionnaires, one on each of five people: themselves, their best friend, their father, an acquaintance, and a famous television commentator of that time (Walter Cronkite). Each questionnaire consisted of the same 20 items. The items consisted of a trait term (for example, 'bold'), its opposite ('cautious'), or the phrase 'depends on the situation'. The subjects had to choose the most apt description of the 'stimulus person'. The order in which subjects completed the questionnaires was counterbalanced; in other words, the order in which the subjects thought about each stimulus person was systematically varied from subject to subject.

If Nisbett *et al.*'s claims about actor–observer differences are correct, then you would expect the questionnaires that the subjects completed about themselves to include, on average, more 'depends on the situation' responses than the other questionnaires. Their ideas imply that we have fewer trait terms available to describe ourselves than we have to describe others, since when we are explaining our own behaviour we tend to focus on characteristics of the situation that we are in, rather than on characteristics of ourselves.

Results

Table 2.4 shows how, on average, fewer trait descriptions were ascribed to the self than to all other stimulus persons. In other words, people selected 'depends on the situation' more frequently on the questionnaires about themselves than on the questionnaires about others. The differences between the average self-ratings and the ratings on the other four questionnaires were all significant at the level of at least $p < .05$.

Table 2.4 *Mean number of traits (out of a possible 20) that were ascribed to each stimulus person*

Item	Stimulus person				
	Self	**Best friend**	**Father**	**Acquaintance**	**Cronkite**
Actor	11.92[a]	14.21[bc]	13.42[b]	13.42[b]	15.08[c]

Note: Means not sharing a superscript differ from each other at the .05 level or more: N = 24.
Source: Nisbett *et al.* (1973).

Discussion

All three studies lend support to Nisbett *et al.*'s claims regarding the different perspectives of actor and observer when it comes to explaining behaviour. The observers in Study 1 seemed to attribute the actors' original decisions to some stable personal disposition, which would make them likely to make the same sorts of decision in the future. In Study 2, actors used more situational than dispositional reasons to account for their liking for their girlfriend; observers used more dispositional than situational reasons to account for their best friend's choice of university course. Study 3 suggested that people have fewer trait terms available to describe themselves than they have available to describe others.

To the extent that the studies suggest people have 'a tendency to hold a different implicit personality theory for the self than for others' (p. 162), the results are interesting. But the authors acknowledge other explanations for the patterns within the data. For example, in Study 1, the only information the observers had to go on in making their estimate of the actor's likelihood to volunteer for the United Fund task was the decision they had seen the actor make, since the actor–observer pairs were strangers to one another. No wonder the observers were more influenced by this one decision than the actors themselves, since the actors presumably knew themselves considerably better, and had much more information to go on in making their estimate. In other words, the results of Study 1 may be an artefact of the experimental procedures.

But the authors treat their data sensibly and put a lot of effort into arguing against alternative explanations. It is not possible in this short summary to explore in detail the authors' efforts to stand up for their hypothesis of actor–observer differences in explaining behaviour, but it is worth noting that in the end they do not claim too much for the studies they have carried out:

▶ **artefact** An artificial finding that has been produced by some aspect of the research procedures, and which therefore does not really tell us anything relevant to the actual research question. For example, research participants who know that they are being observed may behave very differently from normal. This effect is known as 'reactivity', and is one form of artefact.

The studies cannot be said to indicate that the hypothesis generally holds true. The studies should be regarded merely as demonstrations of some interest in their own right, which are consistent with a proposition that is too widely applicable to be either proved or disproved by anything short of a very large and extremely variegated research program. (p. 163)

This level of modesty may be one of the secrets of good research.

suggested answers ➤ p. 475

Questions

1. Why did the experimenters get an independent person to code the paragraphs of text in Study 2? And why was this person unaware of the experimental hypothesis?

2. Write down a list of things that you have done in the past year. Then write an explanation of each item in your list. Are the explanations situational or dispositional?

Introduction

Common sense would suggest that we have a set of values, beliefs and attitudes that shape our behaviour. Consequently, psychologists have expended considerable effort in attempts to measure and to change our attitudes in the belief that this would bring about changes in our behaviour. This connection between attitudes and behaviour was challenged as early as 1934 in this classic piece of work by LaPiere.

Although the study does not have the rigorous control of more modern work, it raises a number of issues about attitudes and research in social psychology that are relevant today. It also sets out to study behaviour as it happens in everyday life rather than as it happens in a psychology laboratory.

The study

LaPiere suggests that attitudes are acquired from social experience, and provide the individual with some degree of preparation to adjust in a well-defined way to certain social situations if they arise. However, these attitudes are usually measured by asking people to make a verbal response to a hypothetical situation. The use of questionnaires and interviews is controlled, cheap and creates massive databases, but questions remain about their effectiveness in measuring attitudes.

Questionnaires on controversial or embarrassing topics are particularly suspect. For example, on surveys of prejudice or racism it is difficult to find out what people's attitudes and behaviour really are because they have learned the appropriate social responses. So, in this study, LaPiere investigated the behavioural responses of people and then attempted to obtain a measure of their reported attitudes.

Starting in 1930, and continuing for two years, LaPiere travelled extensively in the United States with a young Chinese student and his wife. According to LaPiere, 'both were personable, and charming, and quick to win the admiration and respect of those they had the opportunity to become intimate with' (p. 231). They were born in China and they were easily identified as 'not-American'. At this time, there was considerable hostility towards Chinese people down the western coast of the USA.

LaPiere describes how he entered a hotel in a small and famously narrow-minded town with some concern about whether his Chinese companions would be accommodated. The concern was misplaced and they obtained rooms with ease. But when LaPiere telephoned the hotel two months later to ask whether they could accommodate 'an important Chinese gentleman' (p. 232), the response was a definite 'No'. This event stimulated the study.

▶ **attitude** A relatively stable opinion about a person, object, or activity, containing a cognitive element (perceptions and beliefs) and an emotional element (positive or negative feelings).

▶ **behaviour (also spelt 'behavior')** Anything a person (or animal) does that can be observed and measured by a third party. Behaviour can be thought of as the public side of human life, in contrast to 'experience' (thoughts and feelings) which can be thought of as the private side.

▶ **prejudice** A fixed, pre-set attitude, usually negative and hostile, and usually applied to members of a particular social category.

During their travels they investigated this contradiction between what people say and what people do. In their 10,000-mile motor journey, twice across the United States and up and down the western coast, they received the following responses: received at 66 hotels, auto-camps and 'tourist homes' and rejected only once; served in 184 restaurants and cafes, receiving very good service in 72 of them.

Wherever possible, the Chinese people made the reservations or the orders, but LaPiere had not told them about the study (to prevent them becoming self-conscious) and so he had to invent a number of ruses to be absent or distracted when they went into the various establishments. LaPiere came to believe that the main factors affecting behaviour towards the travellers were not race, but other features such as appearance, cleanliness, an air of self-confidence, and smiling. LaPiere also noted that when some tension did develop with the Chinese people, it would evaporate when they spoke in unaccented English.

From this survey it would appear reasonable to conclude that the attitudes of US citizens in 1930 were relatively positive towards Chinese people. However, negative attitudes towards Chinese people did exist and were commonly shown in attitude surveys.

Six months after the initial visit, LaPiere sent a questionnaire with an accompanying letter to every place they had visited. The questionnaires all asked the same question, 'Will you accept members of the Chinese race as guests in your establishment?' In half the questionnaires, this question was presented alone, and in the other half it was embedded in similar questions about Germans, Jews, Japanese, Italians and so forth. There was very little difference between the results from the two sets of questionnaires, so the data are combined in Table 2.5. Of the 251 establishments, 128 replied. The replies showed that 92 per cent of the visited establishments, and also 92 per cent of a further group of unvisited establishments answered 'No' to the question.

Table 2.5 *Replies to the question, 'Will you accept members of the Chinese race as guests in your establishment?'*

	Hotels etc. visited	Hotels etc. not visited	Restaurants etc. visited	Restaurants etc. not visited
No	43	30	75	88
Undecided: depends on circumstances	3	2	6	7
Yes	1	0	0	1
Total	47	32	81	96

Source: LaPiere (1934).

LaPiere notes the contradictory results of his two alternative methods of measuring attitudes towards Chinese people. The attitudes expressed by representatives of the visited hotels did not match up with the behaviour of the people at those hotels. He suggests that conventional attitude surveys have limited applications. For example, a political survey might be a good predictor of voter behaviour at an election, but it will not predict how particular voters will behave when they meet the candidate on the street. The questionnaire, says LaPiere, is limited because it asks for a verbal reaction to an entirely symbolic situation, and it will not indicate what a person will actually do in a real situation. He concludes by writing:

> The questionnaire is cheap, easy and mechanical. The study of human behaviour is time consuming, intellectually fatiguing, and depends for its success upon the ability of the investigator. The former method gives quantitative results, the latter mainly qualitative. Quantitative measurements are quantitatively accurate; qualitative measures are always subject to errors of human judgement. Yet it would seem far more worthwhile to make a shrewd guess regarding that which is essential than to accurately measure that which is likely to prove quite irrelevant (p. 237) .

▶**quantitative data** Data which focus on numbers and frequencies rather than on meaning or experience.

▶**qualitative data** Data which describe meaning and experience rather than providing numerical values for behaviour such as frequency counts.

Discussion

There are a number of factors in the study that influence the low relationship between the two measures. First, the request for service was made to the desk clerk or the waiter or waitress, but the questionnaire probably went to the proprietor or manager. Second, the request for service was a specific act that did not allow time for reflection before the person responded. The questionnaire, on the other hand, asked for a general statement that could be thought about at leisure.

The poor relationship between attitudes and behaviour has been demonstrated in other studies, and most recently in studies on health behaviour. Although many of us hold attitudes that value healthy living and healthy eating, at least one of the authors is inclined to relax with a beer and a bag of chips in front of the television. This lack of relationship between health attitudes and health behaviour undermines many attempts to promote health. In particular, the early health education literature on HIV and AIDS was remarkably unsuccessful in changing people's sexual behaviour, despite changing some of their attitudes towards sexual behaviour. It is clear that the relationship between attitudes and behaviour is a complex one, and is affected by a range of social, personal and environmental factors.

▶**Human Immunodeficiency Virus (HIV)** HIV is the virus that is believed to cause AIDS by attacking the immune system.

▶**Acquired Immune Deficiency Syndrome (AIDS)** AIDS is an infectious disease, most likely caused by a virus, that attacks the immune system making the host vulnerable to a variety of diseases that would be readily controlled by a healthy immune system.

Questions

1. What attitudes do you have that you do not act on? (If you're stuck, think of all the things you do that you know are unhealthy.)

2. Why do you not act in accordance with these attitudes?

3. What methodological problems are there with this study?

suggested answers → p. 475

The minimal group studies

TAJFEL, H. (1970)

Experiments in intergroup discrimination.

Scientific American, 223, 96–102.

Introduction

What does it take to make you believe you are a member of a group? The tradition of the British pantomime usually has one piece where the audience is asked to sing, divided into two groups, and encouraged to compete against each other to see who sings the loudest. The members of the audience invariably oblige by singing their hearts out. Each person believes they are a member of a team and acts to support that team. Ingroup favouritism can develop remarkably easily, so for example people are more likely to cooperate with someone if they believe they share a birthday with them (Miller *et al.*, 1998). Even more surprising is the observation that people are influenced in their choice of where they live by their names, so people named Louis are more likely to live in St Louis, people named Paul to live in St Paul, people named Helen to live in St Helen, and people named Raine are likely to live in Manchester (Pelham *et al.*, 2002).[1]

Not all groups are as harmless as pantomime audiences and our sense of group membership can lead us to behave in some hostile ways towards people who we believe are not in our group. This sense of group membership can be exploited by those who want to sell us things or who want to encourage us to wage war against other nations.

The studies by Sherif (summarized in Chapter 3) suggested that groups only develop strong intergroup feelings when there is conflict, and this conflict is the crucial precursor of ethnocentrism. However, although conflict is not present in all interactions between groups, ethnocentrism can still develop. Ethnocentrism can be described as the following syndrome of behaviours:

(1) The tendency to undervalue the products of the outgroup (any group that we do not belong to).
(2) Increased hostility to and rejection of outgroup members.
(3) The tendency to overvalue the products of the ingroup (any group that we do belong to).
(4) Increased liking for ingroup members, along with a pressure for conformity and group cohesion.

The first two features of ethnocentrism are what we commonly recognize as prejudice, where we have hostile thoughts and feelings, and maybe act in a

▶ **ethnocentrism** Being unable to conceptualize or imagine ideas, social beliefs, or the world from any viewpoint other than that of one's own particular culture or social group. The belief that one's own ethnic group, nation, religion, scout troop or football team is superior to all others.

▶ **behaviour (also spelt 'behavior')** Anything a person (or animal) does that can be observed and measured by a third party. Behaviour can be thought of as the public side of human life, in contrast to 'expe rience' (thoughts and feelings) which can be thought of as the private side.

▶ **outgroup** A group you define yourself as not belonging to.

▶ **ingroup** A group you define yourself as belonging to.

---

1. We made the last one up but it's probably true.

▶ **prejudice** A fixed, pre-set attitude, usually negative and hostile, and usually applied to members of a particular social category.

▶ **attitude** A relatively stable opinion about a person, object, or activity, containing a cognitive element (perceptions and beliefs) and an emotional element (positive or negative feelings).

discriminatory manner towards a certain group or individual. The concept of ethnocentrism sees this behaviour as having a companion set of attitudes and behaviours that enhance the social cohesion of the group you are in. It does not seem to take much to create ethnocentrism.

One curious observation from Sherif's summer-camp studies suggests that just being in a group is enough to create ethnocentrism, and that conflict is not necessary. In one of Sherif's studies, the boys were initially separated into two groups and did not know of each other's existence. However, when they became aware that another group was in the vicinity, they showed signs of competitiveness towards the other group before the intergroup competitions were announced by the experimenters. Just being in one group and becoming aware of a second group was enough to trigger feelings of rivalry. Henri Tajfel took this one step further and showed, in his minimal group studies, that merely being categorized is enough to create intergroup rivalry.

The study

▶ **minimal group paradigm** An approach to the study of social identification which involves creating artificial groups in the social psychology laboratory on the basic of spurious or minimal characteristics (for example, tossing a coin), and then studying the ingroup/ outgroup effects which result.

▶ **intergroup rivalry** Competition between different social groups, which can often lead to powerful hostility.

▶ **discrimination** The behavioural expression of prejudice.

Tajfel begins his article with a brief review of psychological approaches to prejudice. He observes that much of the research was concerned with attitudes rather than behaviour, with prejudice rather than discrimination. This approach has certain drawbacks because of the weak links between attitudes and behaviour (see LaPiere, earlier in this chapter). Tajfel suggests that the most important feature of our attempts to make sense of the social world we live in is our classification of groups as 'we' and 'they'. To put this in psychological terms, we talk about ingroups (which are groups we belong to) and outgroups (which are groups we do not belong to). Tajfel goes on to suggest that we experience so many ingroups and outgroups that we develop norms of behaviour towards them. We learn how to behave towards 'one of us' or 'one of them' regardless of how that distinction is defined.

Tajfel and his colleagues carried out two experiments to investigate the factors that will enhance discrimination in groups.

Experiment 1

The subjects were 64 boys aged between 14 and 15 years who all came from a state school in Bristol (UK). They went to the psychology laboratory in separate groups of eight, and all of the boys in each of the groups knew each other well before the experiment. The first part of the experiment was designed to create group categorization, and the second part of the experiment investigated the effects of this.

In the first part, the boys were told that the psychologists were interested in the study of visual judgements. Forty clusters of varying numbers of dots were flashed onto a screen. The boys were asked to estimate the number of dots in each cluster. The experimenters then pretended to assess the judgements of the boys, and told them what kind of judgements they had made. Some of the groups were categorized on the basis of accuracy, and some were categorized on the basis of over or underestimation. The boys were assigned to groups at random and were told they were either an 'overestimator' or 'underestimator' in one condition, or highly accurate or poorly accurate in the other condition.

The boys were then asked to give rewards of real money (though not very much) to the other boys in the experiment. They did not know the identity of the boys they were giving the money to, but they did know which group they were in (for example, whether or not they were an overestimator). Each boy was given an 18-page booklet with sets of numbers. They were asked to choose a pair of numbers that would allocate money to two other boys. The numbers were arranged in a style similar to that shown below:

Choice number	1	2	3	4	5
Boy number 1	9	11	12	14	16
Boy number 2	5	9	11	15	19

They were required to make three types of choice:

(a) *Ingroup choices*: where both top and bottom row referred to members of the same group as the boy.
(b) *Outgroup choices*: where both top and bottom row referred to members of the different group from the boy.
(c) *Intergroup choices*: where one row referred to the boys' own group and one row referred to the other group.

Results of Experiment 1

The important choice for Tajfel is the intergroup choice, and he found that a large majority of the boys gave more money to members of their own group than to members of the other group. Bear in mind that the boys came into the psychology laboratory as a group of eight, were arbitrarily divided into two subgroups of four by the psychologists, and were not aware of who else was in their subgroup. Tajfel investigated this phenomenon further in a second experiment.

Experiment 2

Three new groups of 16 boys were tested, and this time they were divided on the basis of their supposed artistic preferences. The boys were shown 12 paintings by the abstract expressionist painters Paul Klee and Wassily Kandinsky.[2] The boys were then randomly told that they had preferred either Klee or Kandinsky. Tajfel then asked the boys to fill out similar sets of reward booklets to the first experiment. However, in this experiment he was interested in which of three variables would have the greatest effect on the boys' choices. The three variables were:

2. Kandinsky is interesting to neuro-psychologists because it is believed he experienced synesthesia, which is a merging of the senses. People who experience this phenomena might well be able to answer the question 'What colour is Wednesday?' (see the paper by Ramachandran and Hubbard in Chapter 15). Kandinsky's art tries to show the experience of music in a visual way.

(a) *Maximum joint profit*: where the boys could give the largest reward to members of both groups.

(b) *Largest possible reward to ingroup*: where the boys could choose the largest reward for the member of their own group regardless of the reward to the boy from the other group.

(c) *Maximum difference*: where the boys could choose the largest possible difference in reward between members of the different groups (in favour of the ingroup).

If we look again at our example choices (shown below) then we can see how these three variables can be examined.

Choice number	1	2	3	4	5
Boy number 1 (ingroup)	9	11	12	14	16
Boy number 2 (outgroup)	5	9	11	15	19

Maximum joint profit and giving the largest reward to the ingroup would both be achieved by choosing the last pair in the row, giving 16 to a member of your own group, and 19 to a member of the other group. However, to maximize your own rewards while also maximizing the difference, you might well choose pair number 2 and give 11 to a member of your own group and only 9 to a member of the other group.

Results of Experiment 2

When Tajfel examined the boys' choices he found that maximum joint profit had very little effect at all, and the most important factor in their choices was maximizing the difference between the two groups. This is a relatively surprising result because it meant that the boys left the study with less money than if they had all given each other the most amount of money available.

Tajfel concludes that outgroup discrimination is extraordinarily easy to trigger. Once it has been triggered, then we have norms of behaviour for outgroups which include discriminating against them.

Discussion

There are a number of criticisms of Tajfel's studies, including his interpretation of the results. Brown (1988), for example, suggests that the behaviour of the boys can be seen in terms of fairness as much as discrimination. Although the boys showed bias towards their own group, this bias was not very extreme and seemed to be moderated by a sense of fairness (for example, choosing pair number 3 from the choices above, awarding 12 to the ingroup, and 11 to the outgroup). Another criticism concerns the artificial nature of the studies, and the suggestion that the design is so unlike a real-life situation that the results might well be just a product of the experiment itself. In other words, the boys just conformed to the demand characteristics of the experimental design (see the study by Orne, Chapter 18 of this volume), perhaps interpreting the task

▶ **demand characteristics**
Those aspects of a psychological study (or other artificial situation) which exert an implicit pressure on people to act in ways that are expected of them.

as a competitive game of the sort that boys play in Western societies. Related to this point is Brown's observation that the research evidence suggests that the effect demonstrated by Tajfel happens to a much lesser extent in other cultural settings.

The study is important because it contributed to the development of social identity theory. Social identity theory states that the social groups and categories to which we belong are an important part of our self-concept, and therefore a person will sometimes interact with other people, not as a single individual, but as a representative of a whole group or category of people. A simple example of this is the common experience of doing something to make your family proud of you, when you feel as if you are representing your family and do not want to let them down. Sometimes you act as an individual and sometimes as a group member and during one conversation you might change between these two identities. In business meetings people sometimes suggest that they are wearing 'a different hat' to convey the idea that they are adopting a social identity.

There are three basic psychological processes underlying social identification:

(a) *Categorization*: a basic tendency to classify things into groups. This is what Tajfel demonstrates in this study.

(b) *Social comparison*: the tendency to compare our groups to other groups. The comparison has inbuilt bias in favour of groups like ourselves because we know more about them.

(c) *Self-concept*: the way we see ourselves. According to Tajfel and Turner (1979) people want to belong to groups which will reflect positively on their self-esteem. If the group does not compare favourably with others, and membership of it brings about lowered self-esteem, people will try to leave the group, or to distance themselves from it. If leaving the group is impossible, then they may look for ways that group membership may provide a positive source of self-esteem. We also deal with social identity in this text in the summaries of the studies by Reicher and Haslam (2006) and Levine (1999).

▶ **social identity theory**
An approach which states that the social groups and categories to which we belong are an important part of our self-concept, and therefore a person will sometimes interact with other people, not as a single individual, but as a representative of a whole group or category of people. There are three basic psychological processes underlying social identification which are categorization, social comparison and self-concept.

Questions

1. The study was carried out on teenage boys. What effect do you think this had on the results?

2. What groups do you belong to? And what groups do you not belong to?

suggested answers → p. 476

part i

Shock and awe

FISCHHOFF, B., GONZALEZ, R., LERNER, J. AND SMALL, D. (2005) Evolving judgements of terror risks: foresight, hindsight and emotion. *Journal of Experimental Psychology: Applied,* 2, 124–39.

Introduction

Terrorism was not invented on 11 September 2001,[3] but the destruction of the World Trade Center in New York City on that date changed the way the West viewed the world. The attack on the twin towers was the first military attack by an outside force on the USA and suddenly US citizens did not feel safe.

After the attacks, President George W. Bush used the phrase 'War on Terror' to describe the USA's response to this act. Some would argue, however, that the war was already over and the USA had lost (Merrin, 2005). In one day the terrorists had destroyed the World Trade Center, created a global media explosion that still reverberates today and destroyed the sense of safety held by citizens of the USA (see Figure 2.3). Terror was created on a huge scale on one day and nothing that has happened since has reduced that. In modern history it is a hard to think of one event that has created such a sense of shock and awe. It was the One Day War.

Figure 2.3   *The destruction of the World Trade Center*

If we look at the attack on the World Trade Center or the London bombs of 2005 in a logical way, then the actual threat to our personal safety from terror attacks is quite low. Less than 3,000 people died in the World Trade Center;

---

3.   For example, there is 'the other 11 September' when in 1973 a US-backed military coup in Chile overthrew the democratic government of Salvador Allende. In the aftermath of the coup the loss of life was similar to that at the World Trade Center.

that is not to belittle each life lost but if you compare it to the number of people who die each year from other events it is not a great loss of life. Look at the following statistics and consider what you (logically) have more to be frightened of:

- The World Health Organization estimates that 1.7 million people die each year from tuberculosis (TB) (that's more than three people every minute), which is a preventable and curable disease (http://www.who.int/tb/en/). The recommended treatment, commonly referred to as DOTS, costs around £10 per person.
- Traffic accidents in 2005 were responsible for 43,443 deaths and 2,699,000 injuries in the USA (http://www.nhtsa.dot.gov/).
- Traffic accidents in 2002 in the UK were responsible for 3431 deaths and 302,600 injuries (Department of Transport, available at http://www.statistics.gov.uk/StatBase/ssdataset.asp?vlnk=4031andPos=1andColRank=1andRank=272).
- In 2003 in the USA 17,732 people were murdered (78 per cent male) of which 11,920 were killed by firearms (USA Department of Health and Human Services, available at http://www.cdc.gov/nchs/data/statab/Mortfinal2003_worktable210f.pdf).
- Oh, and it is estimated that between 67,265 and 73,611 civilians have been killed as a result of the military intervention in Iraq since the 2003 invasion (http://www.iraqbodycount.org/ accessed July 2007).

The study

One area of interest for psychologists is to look at how people judge risks in their everyday life. The recent political events and the West's War on Terror have provided an ideal source for these investigations. The paper by Fischhoff *et al.* starts by suggesting that the events of 11 September 2001 started a learning process in the general public of the USA to evaluate the level of risk and to balance protection from terrorism against other factors such as cost, civil liberties and protection from other risks.

Psychology has a history of studying how people make judgements relating to risk. Previous research had suggested the following factors might influence such judgements:

- *Availability*: People tend to judge the likelihood of an event happening by how easily they can think of an example (Kahneman and Tversky, 1973). However, the ease with which examples of an event come to mind can be misleading in framing judgments about their likelihood. In the UK there have been a few high-profile train crashes which have resulted in fatalities. Train crashes are extremely rare, but people will tend to overestimate their likelihood simply because they can remember key examples so readily (not remembering the thousands of people that die on the roads each year). A similar effect occurs with our judgements of disease risk, which are framed by inaccurate portrayals in television dramas which tend to concentrate on serious events like heart attacks and comas (see Casarett *et al.*, 2005).

- *Hindsight*: People tend to integrate new observations into their memories and not realize that they have done this. This gives them the 'gift of hindsight' where they exaggerate how much they knew at the time about a particular event. After the events of 11 September many people will say they were not surprised and they cannot understand why the US government did not prevent it. But check the news reports before the attack and you have to look a long way to find anyone suggesting that civilian aircraft might be used as weapons.

- *Emotion*: We can use our emotions to make judgements of risk. If we feel scared or uncomfortable we can use this to 'colour' the event we are judging. Our memories of events often have an emotional content, and this might influence our judgements of risk in the future. For example, in an experiment in which people were made to experience either anger or fear (Lerner *et al.*, 2003), the people in the 'fear' condition rated the consequences of terror as more negative than the people in the 'anger' condition. And this emotional manipulation also affected other judgements that were non-terror related such as the likelihood of getting flu.

However, many of the laboratory studies that have been used to illustrate these effects might not apply well to the situation of judging terror risks. Judgements of terror risks are different from other risk judgements because they involve very high stakes, they create intense public discussion and they raise some complex emotions.

Method

The authors report using 'a two-factor experimental design, embedded in the natural experiment created by 11 September and its aftermath' (p. 124). The study was a follow-up to previous work carried out in 2001 just after the World Trade Center attack (reported by Lerner *et al.*, 2003) which surveyed 973 adults from the USA on their judgements of terror risks. The participants had been recruited from a panel of people run by a commercial company that provides free WebTV and Internet access in return for completing three or four Internet surveys per month. The follow-up work, carried out a year later in 2002 when terror was still very much in the news but the war in Iraq had not yet started, used the same group of people. Of the original group, 869 were still on the panel, of which 582 (67 per cent) agreed to participate.

In the original study half the participants were primed to feel some anger and half were primed to feel some fear. In this follow-up study (labelled here the '2002 study') these same participants were either asked to relive the same emotion or view the events from a neutral perspective. The researchers looked at the following measures:

- *2001 predictions*: In 2001 the participants were asked to judge the probability that each of eight risks (five terror-related, and three routine) would occur during the next 12 months. They were asked to make the judgement between 0 (the event is impossible) and 100 (the event is certain to happen).

■ *Recall 2001*: In 2002 they were asked, 'Please remember what you predicted a year ago or, if you cannot remember, write what you would have said then.'

■ *Update 2001 (postdiction – like a pre-diction only it comes after the event rather than before)*: In 2002 they were asked, 'Please estimate what the probability was, knowing what you know now about the United States and its enemies.'

■ *Prediction 2002*: The participants were again asked to judge the probability of eight risks occurring during the next 12 months.

■ *Experience:* The participants were asked to say whether during the previous 12 months any of the risk events had occurred (a) to them, (b) to a close friend or relative, (c) someone else they knew.

■ *Emotion self-reports*: At the end of the study the participants were asked to rate the emotions they had felt during the emotion-provoking task at the start of the study.

Results

There are a lot of data in this study but we only present a brief summary here. Table 2.6 shows the responses to the first five measures.

Table 2.6   *Mean probability judegements of risk events (in order of task completion)*

Event	Prediction 2001	Recall 2001	Update 2001	Prediction 2002	% reporting personal experience
Terror risks					
Being hurt	20.3	16.9	14.6	19.2	0.3
Travelling less	33.6	20.7	23.4	26.9	30.0
Trouble sleeping	23.5	11.4	12.9	14.6	22.0
Screening mail	55.3	19.5	23.2	29.9	34.0
Anthrax antibiotic	22.4	10.7	9.6	14.5	0.7
Routine risks					
Getting flu	46.9	30.9	30.2	34.5	28.0
Violent crime	22.2	17.9	14.4	15.8	0.9
Dying	33.0	22.4	19.1	21.6	0.0

The data are presented in a graphical form in Figure 2.4. This shows the response to the four prediction questions for each risk. The interesting thing here is that for all the terror and routine risks people's *recall* of their risk assessment was lower than the assessment that they had actually made at the time. Furthermore their prediction of the future risk was again higher than their recalled 'prediction'. It is as if they were saying 'I didn't think it was so scary then but I think it will be scary in the future.' In Figure 2.5 we have added all the risk estimates together to get an overall risk score and you can see this effect more clearly. Overall risk assessment is down for the future compared with 2001 but it is higher than the recalled and updated risks.

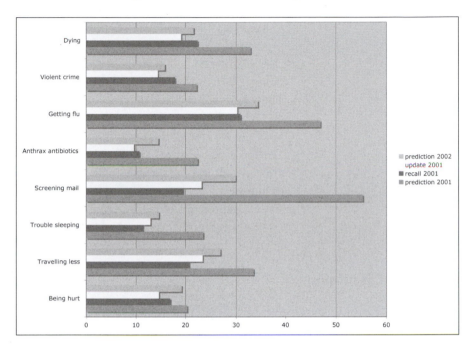

Figure 2.4 *Probability predictions for terror and routine risks*

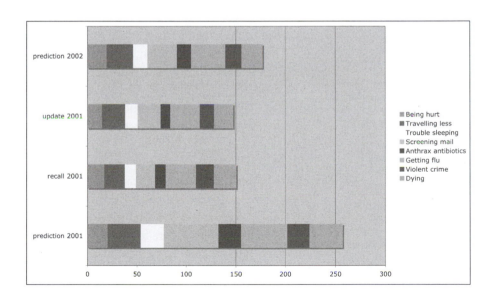

Figure 2.5 *Cumulative probability predictions for the eight risks*

In their extensive analysis of the data Fischhoff *et al.* make the following points:

- There was a correlation between the 2001 predictions and participants' reports of personal experiences suggesting that they had some insight into their relative degree of risk. So using these real world events it was possible to show that *availability* (as defined by self-reports of personal experience) predicts future judgements of risk. Interestingly, previous judgements of risk also correlated with subsequent events, meaning that more events happened to those that judged the risks to be higher.
- The world was not as dangerous in 2002 as the participants had predicted, and when they looked back to their previous view they showed considerable *hindsight bias* for all the risks.
- The emotions of anger and fear that were induced in the 2001 study had an effect on all the predictions, with anger producing lower estimates of risk than fear.
- Asking people to look back on the events in a neutral way rather than reliving the emotion they were asked to feel in 2001 had no effect on judgements of risk. In other words this particular 'debiasing' strategy was not effective.

Discussion

The research was able to show that some psychological concepts developed in laboratory studies can be used to explain real-life judgements of terror risk. It shows that availability and hindsight affect these judgements and that people who are primed to be fearful are likely to judge risks as being greater. This last point is not lost on those who try to move public opinion. Fear is the key. Don't be angry about it, just be fearful of those weapons of mass destruction that can be launched in 45 seconds (or was it minutes?).

The researchers note that carrying out a study of real-life events and collecting the data from people's homes rather than a laboratory leads to some loss of experimental control. On the other hand this method greatly enhances the ecological validity of the study and allows for more connections to be made to real-life events. They suggest that the following three points can be drawn from the study:

1. Citizens' judgements of risk are made in an orderly way and take account of their experiences and observations. It is therefore important to provide them with access to accurate and relevant information.
2. Hindsight bias occurs for a wide range of judgements. As a result, ensuring fair judgement of past actions and events requires special efforts beyond asking people simply to recall 'what it was like'.
3. 'People need protection from emotional manipulation, even (or especially) with fateful topics.' (page 137)

And we say Amen! to point 3.

▶ **experiment** A form of research in which variables are manipulated in order to discover cause and effect.

▶ **control group** A group which is used for comparison with an experimental group.

▶ **ecological validity** A way of assessing how valid a measure or test is (that is, whether it really measures what it is supposed to measure) which is concerned with whether the measure or test is really like its counterpart in the real, everyday world. In other words, whether it is truly realistic or not.

Questions

suggested
answers
→ p. 476

1. What are the factors that affect our judgements of risk?

2. What difficulties did the researchers have in carrying out a study on real-life events rather than a simple laboratory study?

chapter 3

SOCIAL
INTERACTION

THE studies that we have included on social interaction all say something about how our dealings with other people affect the way we think, feel and behave. We do not exist in isolation from other people and we are part of a number of formal and informal social groups. Our membership of these groups structures our view of the world and the way we act in it. The psychological research on social interaction is as vast and varied as the experiences we have during our lives, and the selection of studies in this chapter is inevitably limited. However, there are other studies in this text that tell us something about human interaction, especially in the sections on Diversity (for example Rosenhan's study of being sane in insane places) and Development (for example, Fernald's study on the response of newborn babies to motherese).

The first study in our selection, by Sherif (1956), looks at how interaction inside a group and interaction between groups can change the experience and judgements of the group members. The study is often used to illustrate how prejudice develops, and this issue rightly attracts a lot of attention in psychology. One approach in psychology sees prejudice and ethnocentrism as developing from interactions between groups and within groups. Sherif's work suggests that competition between groups is the key to understanding prejudice. This provides some clues to our hostile attitudes and behaviour to outsiders but cannot be the whole story. Elsewhere in this text we consider other factors that influence our judgements of others; see for example the paper by Tajfel and the study on terror risk by Fischhoff *et al*. (Chapter 2). And if you want to follow it up some more then look also at the papers by LaPiere on responses to Chinese Americans (also Chapter 2) and Hraba and Grant on Black identity (Chapter 7).

The Sherif paper goes beyond looking at the causes of prejudice and provides ideas about how we can resolve conflicts that are created between groups. This aspect of the work means that the paper is often used on studies of positive psychology or peace studies.

The next paper looks at what happens within a group which is charged with making decisions. This is an important topic because so many decisions that affect our lives are taken by groups (a.k.a. committees or cabinets or diagnostic teams). Bales devised a coding system to record the behaviour of individuals in groups to see if he could tease out the differences between successful and unsuccessful groups. Interestingly, this was also studied by Sherif in his studies, though it is not often reported in summaries of his work.

The next two studies should be seen as a pair. The Stanford Prison Experiment (SPE: Haney, Banks and Zimbardo, 1973) and the BBC prison study (Haslam and Reicher, 2006) were carried out 30 years apart and give us a fantastic insight into the changing agenda of social psychology and the changing view that we have of ourselves. They also give a surprising insight into academic life, and in particular to how scientists sometimes try to protect their own view despite a weight of evidence that challenges it. Zimbardo effectively waged an academic war on the UK psychologists who initially sought his advice and support for their work. Look at the following comment from Zimbardo on the Haslam and Reicher study, and then make your own mind up about whether it says more about Zimbardo or the work he is criticizing.

It was unfortunate that this 'Made for TV Experiment' was ever conducted. The SPE is now judged to be unethical, so BBC-TV had no right to try to replicate it.

I cannot go into all the ways that this alleged replication should never be considered as an 'experiment' or even as serious social science, which I have done at great length in my review

that recommended rejecting its publication.

It is sad for me to see these researchers not content to take their hired gun big salary for this job and go back to their labs and do some real serious research instead of using that mockery of research to challenge the value of my mock prison study. (Zimbardo, cited in Banyard and Flanagan, 2006)

The academic debate is very real between the two sets of researchers because they are aiming to explain why people seem to be capable of acts of great inhumanity. If we look, for example, at the prison of Abu Ghraib in Iraq, which after the Western invasion was run by troops from the USA, we see a number of examples of mistreatment of prisoners that were recorded and later broadcast. How did this come about and what can we do to stop future occurrences? Zimbardo provides a different answer from Haslam and Reicher.

The final paper by Dodds *et al.* looks at one of the new opportunities for social interaction provided by technology. In an age where email, blogs, text messaging, uploading, downloading, MySpace and YouTube are just some of the new ways to interact, could it be that we are creating new social conventions for our interactions or are we using old conventions in a new way? This study looks at email and asks whether it is making the world a smaller place.

The robber's cave

SHERIF, M. (1956)
Experiments in group conflict.
Scientific American, 195, 54–8.

▶ **prejudice** A fixed, pre-set attitude, usually negative and hostile, and usually applied to members of a particular social category.

▶ **racism** Using the pervasive power imbalance between races/peoples to oppress dominated peoples by devaluing their experience, behaviour and aspirations.

▶ **psychoanalysis** Freud's theory of personality which describes how human behaviour is affected by unconscious thought and feelings.

▶ **ethnocentrism** Being unable to conceptualize or imagine ideas, social beliefs, or the world from any viewpoint other than that of one's own particular culture or social group. The belief that one's own ethnic group, nation, religion, scout troop or football team is superior to all others.

Introduction

Why do groups of people end up in conflict with each other and, perhaps even more remarkably, how is it that we get on with each so well most of the time? Conflict and cooperation are good issues for psychologists to explore. The more pressing of the two in psychology is commonly the issue of conflict as we struggle to explain interpersonal conflict such as prejudice and racism and group conflict such as warfare. On reflection, though, it is just as difficult to explain the much more common behaviour of interpersonal cooperation and intergroup cooperation.

Muzafer Sherif had considerable personal experience of conflict and cooperation. He was born in Turkey in 1906 and was lucky to escape with his life during a conflict with Greece when soldiers invaded his local province (Trotter, 1985). He studied in Germany, France and Turkey before settling in the USA to follow his career studying intergroup behaviour. The study we are considering illustrates a number of key ideas including: how prejudice can develop, how group structure can affect the success of a group, and how conflict can be resolved. Because of this, the work can be found in discussions of racism, efficiency in work groups, and also peace studies.

Let's start by looking at prejudice. Psychology has offered two basic approaches to describe the phenomenon of prejudice. One line of argument sees it as an individual problem: a 'sick person' model of prejudice. The major influence here is psychoanalysis and the work of Freud, with the root of prejudice being seen to be in childhood experiences that create a damaged adult personality. For example, Adorno *et al.* (1950) presented the picture of the authoritarian personality who projects his or her unresolved childhood conflicts onto minority groups. The authoritarian personality is narrow minded, a stickler for rules, inhibited about sex, unquestioningly submissive to authority, intolerant of ambiguity and politically conservative. The basic flaw in this approach to prejudice is the insistence that prejudice is a sign of a sick personality, and by implication, that most people are not prejudiced.

The other major line of argument sees prejudice as a result of group membership and group interaction. An example of this approach is the work of Sherif and his associates, who proposed a conflict model of prejudice. Their model suggests that when groups interact they inevitably generate attitudes towards each other. If the groups are 'positively independent', and working towards common goals, then good intergroup relations develop and the intergroup attitudes are positive. On the other hand, if the groups are 'negatively independent', in competition for scarce resources perhaps, then group conflict develops and ethnocentric attitudes appear. Sherif and his associates tested this theory in a number of field studies. They also went on to test whether they could resolve conflict and reduce prejudice through the use of cooperative tasks.

The basic questions under investigation were: could they take a group of people without any hostile attitudes towards each other, divide them into groups, create conflict in the groups through introducing competition, and thereby create ethnocentric attitudes and behaviour? And when they have created conflict and ethnocentrism, can they remove it again?

The study

The field experiments were conducted in 1949, 1953 and 1954, and this article gives composite findings. Sherif wanted to study informal groups so that he could observe the natural and spontaneous development of group organization and attitudes. To do this the researchers created an isolated summer camp as an experimental setting.

The subjects were boys aged 11 to 12. According to Sherif they were picked by a 'long and thorough procedure' involving interviews with family, teachers and school officials, and also by the use of school and medical records, scores on personality tests, and observations of them in class and at play. The boys were unknown to each other and 'all were healthy, socially well adjusted, somewhat above average in intelligence and from stable, White, Protestant, middle-class homes' (p. 54). The sample was deliberately homogeneous to reduce the chances of bringing in established social conflicts (such as class or race prejudice) to the study.

The boys were unaware that they were part of an experiment on group relations. The investigators appeared as regular camp staff, and the boys met the staff and each other for the first time in the buses on the way to camp. To maintain ecological validity, the experiments were conducted within the framework of regular camp activities and games. The researchers made unobtrusive records of behaviour, and, on occasions, used cameras and microphones.

In the first phase of the study, Sherif and his associates observed the development of group structure. To start with the boys were housed in one large bunkhouse where they were able to choose their own 'buddies' (Sherif's term). After a few days they divided the boys into two groups and took care to separate 'best friends' into different groups.

The boys were given a range of challenging activities including hikes and campouts, and athletics and sports. In each group, the boys divided up the tasks and organized duties. Leaders and lieutenants emerged, and each group developed its own jargon, special jokes, secrets and special ways of performing tasks. They maintained social control through ridicule, threats and ostracism; for example, insulting any boy who did not pull his weight at a particular task. Each group selected a symbol and a name which was put on their baseball caps and T-shirts (fashion point: it is interesting to note that in 1954 the style for boys was very close to the style of the twenty-first century). The 1954 study was carried out near to a famous hideaway of Jesse James called the Robber's Cave (the study is often referred to as the Robber's Cave Experiment), and the groups called themselves 'The Eagles' and 'The Rattlers'.

To test the social evaluations of the boys, the researchers invented a game

▶ **ecological validity** A way of assessing how valid a measure or test is (that is, whether it really measures what it is supposed to measure) which is concerned with whether the measure or test is really like its counterpart in the real, everyday world. In other words, whether it is truly realistic or not.

of target practice. There were no marks on the target board, and a judgement of accuracy was made by the watching peers. However, the board was also secretly wired to give an objective measure of accuracy. The boys consistently overestimated efforts of highly regarded boys and underestimated efforts of the lowly regarded. The researchers also made diagrammatic records of group structure, one of which is shown in Figure 3.1. They asked each boy to name his friends in the group. The boy who was chosen most times was regarded as having the highest status, and the boy who was chosen the least was regarded as having the lowest status.

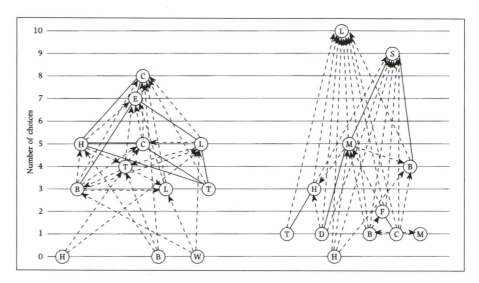

Figure 3.1 *Sociograms of group structure*

Sociograms represent patterns of friendship choices within the fully developed groups. One-way friendships are indicated by broken arrows; reciprocated friendships by solid lines. Leaders were among those highest in the popularity scale. The group on the left had a close-knit organisation with good group spirit. Low-ranking members participated less in the life of the group but were not rejected. The right-hand group lost the tournament of games between the two. They had less group unity and were sharply stratified.
Source: Sherif (1956).

The two groups shown in Figure 3.1 have very different structures; the group on the right is very hierarchical with one clear leader and lieutenant along with seven low-status boys. The group on the left has a clear leader but also a number of other boys of intermediate status. This latter group was reportedly better at a range of tasks.

Observations

Sherif's prediction had been that 'when two groups have conflicting aims, their members will become hostile to each other even though the groups are composed of normal well adjusted individuals' (p. 57). In the second phase of the study the researchers introduced conflict through games. The tournament started in good spirit but the boys soon started to call their rivals 'stinkers', 'sneaks' and 'cheaters' (fashion point 2: clothes style might not have changed but language certainly has). The boys refused contact with the opposing group, and turned against their previous buddies. When they were asked to give ratings to the other boys in the camp, they gave negative ratings to boys in the other group. During this period solidarity increased within each group. Name calling, scuffles and 'raids' (for example, stealing the other group's flag and setting fire to it) became the pattern of behaviour.

The hypothesis was supported alarmingly easily and this created a problem of how to reduce the conflict. The initial attempts involved bringing the groups together for an activity, but these occasions ended in fights and abuse. So a further hypothesis developed: 'working in a common endeavour should promote harmony' (p. 57).

In the third and final phase, the researchers had to establish superordinate goals for the two groups. They created a series of urgent and natural situations, for example by interrupting the water supply, and making the camp truck break down on an outing. This latter 'crisis' had to be resolved by the boys pulling the truck. The boys developed new friendships in the opposing groups as they worked through these crises and, according to Sherif, by the end of the camp the groups were 'actively seeking opportunities to mingle, to entertain and to "treat" each other'" (p. 57). The boys made far less negative ratings of the opposing group, and the hostility seemed to have disappeared.

▶ **hypothesis** Experiments are designed to test one or more hypotheses. An hypothesis is a prediction of what will happen in an experiment. It is worded in such a way that the results of a well-designed experiment will clearly show whether the prediction is right or wrong.

▶ **superordinate goal** A goal that over-rides existing goals.

Discussion

This is a remarkable piece of research on a number of counts. The methods are very inventive, with a number of measures of social behaviour being seamlessly introduced into everyday situations. It would not be possible to carry out a study like this with children today because we are more cautious about the effects of our research on the participants. Having said that, it is fair to point out that broadcasters don't share our concerns and people in reality shows are commonly subjected to social manipulations that are designed to create intergroup and interpersonal hostility.

The Sherif study has considerable ecological validity, which was a feature of social psychology conducted before 1960 (see Sears, 1986, Chapter 18 of this volume). The study lacks a certain amount of control, but the trade-off with relevance seems a good one. You cannot help but wonder whether the level of hostility alarmed the researchers, and whether they were able to reduce this hostility quite as successfully as they claim. Alternatively you might ask whether the researchers' expectations influenced what they saw and what they reported (see Rosenthal and Fode, 1963 in Chapter 18 on experimenter effects).

The study tells us one of the ways of creating intergroup hostility and, thereby, ethnocentric attitudes and behaviour. This suggests that we should see, for example, racial prejudice as a consequence of competition for resources between different ethnic groups. In this case, we would predict that prejudice would rise when economic hardship increased, and to a certain extent this is supported by observation. However, the model does not explain why some groups should be singled out for racism and not others. For example, in Nottingham, where the authors live, there are a number of large ethnic groups which include Irish, Ukrainian and Polish, as well as a number of Black and Asian groups. All these groups are in the same competition for a limited number of jobs, houses and welfare resources, but the Black and Asian groups are subject to more racism than the Europeans. Clearly the conflict model does not tell us the whole story.

The study also goes on to suggest a blueprint for resolving hostility and reducing prejudice by finding a superordinate goal for people to work towards. We might hope that concerns about the environment, global warming and the fate of the penguins might help governments and people around the world stop fighting each other and work together to avoid being drowned by melting ice caps. Don't hold your breath on that one though.

Questions

suggested answers → P. 476

1. What is the conflict model of prejudice?

2. What measures of social behaviour and social judgement did the researchers take?

3. List some of the (numerous) ethical concerns with this study.

4. What groups in everyday life are in conflict with each other?

5. What are the advantages of carrying this study out in 'the field'?

The mother (and father) of all groups

BALES, R.F. (1955)

How people interact in conferences.

Scientific American, 192, 31–5.

Introduction

Many of the most famous and influential studies in social psychology have focused on, or at least been set within the context of, 'people in groups'. For example, Sherif (1956) and Tajfel (1970) (in this and the previous chapter in this book) examined the issue of intergroup conflict; Asch (1955) (see Chapter 1) studied the effects that a group can have on the behaviour of its individual members; Moscovici *et al.* (1969) investigated the phenomenon of 'minority influence'; and Lewin *et al.* (1939) and Fiedler (1967) analysed group leadership. The emphasis within social psychology on groups is welcome, because being in groups is such a fundamental feature of our social lives.

Bales' concern with groups arose out of his early fieldwork on the effectiveness of Alcoholics Anonymous in helping hardened alcoholics to reform. He became particularly interested in the characteristics of communication within groups. Having become somewhat uncomfortable about observing real-life groups with real-life problems, he left the field and returned to the laboratory so that he could work under more controlled conditions. The studies which he describes in this paper were undertaken in his laboratory at Harvard University in 1947.

The study

▶ **fieldwork** Research which is conducted outside the laboratory.

Although Bales had given up fieldwork, he was still clearly interested in questions which bore directly on everyday life. In this paper he examines in detail the dynamics of communication which operate within decision-making groups. Since many important things are decided for us by people in decision-making groups (a government's decision to go to war, a board of directors decision to close a factory, and so forth) it is very important that we understand clearly how such groups operate. Perhaps such an understanding could lead to decision-making groups making better decisions.

Having said this, it is important to bear in mind that the first stage of 'understanding' in any scientific discipline involves careful description of the thing which we are trying to understand. In this paper, Bales is not concerned with improving the performance of decision-making groups; he simply sets out to examine and document some of the characteristics of such groups. The specific questions which guided his study were: What proportion of communications within a decision-making group are directly concerned with solving the problem at hand? What stages does a typical decision-making group go through in pursuit of its goal? And what roles do the different group members play?

▶ **role** A social part that one plays in society.

Subjects

Each group that Bales studied was composed of between two and seven people. No details are given in this paper about who the subjects were. Each group followed the procedure outlined below.

Design

This is a study based on techniques of structured observation. There is no manipulation of variables. The observations were carried out in a laboratory under controlled conditions in order that sensible comparisons could be made across different groups of subjects. Despite taking place in the laboratory, the task was designed to be as true to life as possible.

Procedure

Each group of subjects met four times for up to 40 minutes each time. Their task was to discuss 'a complex human relations problem of the sort typically faced by an administrator' (p. 32), and make recommendations about how the problem should be addressed. All subjects in each group had been briefed about the problem before the first meeting. They did not know one another and were unsure about whether they had received the same information about the problem as the other group members.

The subjects performed this series of joint decision-making tasks in a laboratory, where they were observed by a team of researchers sitting in an adjoining room behind a one-way mirror. Audiotape recordings of the discussions were made. The observers were watching for, and recording, the occurrence of communicative acts. Each observer used a type of event recorder which produced a continuously moving paper tape on which every communicative act was written. The codes that were used to identify acts, included a way of identifying who performed the act, and to whom the communication was directed.

The 12-category taxonomy which Bales developed in order to classify communicative acts is shown in the results section below. The 12 acts shown in the middle column of Table 3.1 are grouped into four types of acts, shown in the left-hand column.

The subjects were aware that they were being observed and that their communicative behaviour was being recorded. All subjects completed questionnaires after each session, which among other things asked for each person's opinion of who had the best ideas in the group, and which group member was the best liked.

Results

Table 3.1 shows that 56 per cent of the acts in the 'average' group session were classified as 'problem-solving attempts'. Bales suggests that these directly task-related acts were balanced by questions and reactions (positive and negative) which made up the remaining 44 per cent.

Table 3.1 *The average proportion of acts in each category of Bales' taxonomy, over 96 group sessions*

Area	Act	Percentage
Positive reactions	Shows solidarity Shows tension release Shows agreement	3.4 6.0 16.5
Problem-solving attempts	Gives suggestion Gives opinion Gives information	8.0 30.1 17.9
Questions	Asks for information Asks for opinion Asks for suggestion	3.5 2.4 1.1
Negative reactions	Shows disagreement Shows tension Shows antagonism	7.8 2.7 0.7

Source: Bales (1955).

The paper also shows that the rate of information giving within a group decreased across the first, middle and last stages of an average meeting, whilst the rates of suggestions, positive reactions and negative reactions increased. The giving of opinions seemed to occur most frequently in the middle phase of the meeting.

Bales identifies two particular types of role within the groups: the 'ideas' role, which was filled by the person who took a lead in terms of the problem-solving task at hand, and the 'most-liked' role, filled (of course) by the most popular group member. In some groups there was a high level of agreement in response to the questionnaire items about who had the best ideas, and who was best liked in the group. Bales also asserts that the subjects' subjective ratings usually matched up with the more objective measures taken by the observers. In other words, those who were identified by group members as having had the best ideas also tended to talk the most, and to give the most suggestions. Those identified by the group as being the most-liked person also tended to score more highly than average in the 'shows tension release' category (laughing and smiling are examples of this kind of act). By the end of four discussion sessions it was unlikely that the person with the best ideas was also seen as the most-liked person. Bales does not cite raw data in support of these assertions concerning the different roles of the group members.

Discussion

Perhaps the most interesting feature of this piece of work is the emphasis on how group interactions develop over the course of time. Bales likens the processes engaged in by his laboratory groups to the processes involved in 'a large-scale communication and control system such as an air-defence network' (p. 32), and outlines a complex seven-stage structure for problem-solving which is grounded in this analogy. The seven stages take the group from the starting point of 'making an observation' to the finishing point of proposing a 'specific action'. His data appear to support the stages he proposes. For example, information-giving ('making an observation') is most prevalent at the beginning of the process at the stage when the group is gathering together the knowledge of all its individual members. As time wears on, progressively more of the communications within the group are geared towards making suggestions (proposing 'specific actions').

The changes in task-oriented communications are counterbalanced by changes in the more social and emotional communications. At the outset, negative reactions are relatively infrequent, since information-giving is less controversial than the expression of opinions and the suggestion of strategies and ideas. Needless to say, as the number of suggestions increases, so too does the number of negative reactions from group members who do not agree with these suggestions. But note that positive reactions, which from the beginning occur at a much higher rate, increase in parallel with the negative reactions. It is as if groups need to maintain a surplus of positive acts in order to move forward in pursuit of their goal. The intricate interweaving of all these different acts, and the way that changes in the frequency of one act are related to changes in the frequency of other types of acts, indicate that the group operates as a kind of self-regulating system. Indeed, Bales' analysis of group dynamics is often referred to as a 'systemic' analysis.

It appears from Bales' findings that successful groups need two roles to be fulfilled. The role of task leader and the role of group-builder. Someone to boldly go where no one has gone before and someone to make sure we all feel OK about it. It is not unreasonable to suggest that there is a similarity here to the traditional family roles of mother and father. Maybe we learn some patterns of group behaviour as children and then recreate them when we form new groups as adults.

Bales went on to become an influential researcher and writer in the field of group dynamics, and his 12-category taxonomy for studying verbal communication within decision-making groups is still used today.

suggested answers → p. 477

Questions

1. What information is captured by recording acts on a moving paper tape which is harder to capture on a standard observation checklist?

2. Why are there several observers? Give at least two possible reasons.

3. Why is it important that we know that the group members knew they were being observed?

4. Bales' work was carried out on 'decision-making groups'. How do these groups differ from the everyday groups to which you belong or just find yourself in?

The prison simulation

HANEY, C., BANKS, W.C. AND ZIMBARDO, P.G. (1973)

A study of prisoners and guards in a simulated prison.

Naval Research Review, 30, 4–17.

► **role** A social part that one plays in society.

► **tyranny** 'An unequal social system involving the arbitrary or oppressive use of power by one group or its agents over another.' (Reicher and Haslam, 2006, p. 2)

Introduction

Some psychological studies produce very surprising results for the researchers and the participants. Sometimes the results are so striking that they challenge our explanations of human behaviour and human motivation. One example is the Milgram study described earlier. Another one is the work of Zimbardo and his associates.

The central question in this study concerns how much of our behaviour is structured by the social roles that we occupy. One of the famous soundbites from Shakespeare is: 'All the world's a stage, And all the men and women merely players' (*As You Like It*, II, vii, 139–43). The 'life is drama' metaphor is developed in role theory and the work of, among others, Erving Goffman. This approach to human behaviour and experience suggests that we are what we play, and a limited sense of selfhood and identity is shaped by the demands of the situation we are in.

The study has become fixed in psychology texts and the work is still commonly cited (often by Zimbardo) to explain recent events such as terrorist attacks and the behaviour of prisoners and guards at military prisons such as Abu Ghraib in Iraq. There was no major attempt to replicate or further develop the ideas in this study for 30 years, so Zimbardo's interpretation remained largely unchallenged. That is no longer the case following the BBC Prison Study (Reicher and Haslam, 2006) which we describe later in this chapter, and we suggest you read the next two studies together to get a sense of how this work has developed. At the heart of the work lies the important question of how tyranny develops and how it can be challenged. Needless to say, this is a question that affects us all.

The study

Twenty-four subjects were selected from an initial pool of 75 respondents to a newspaper advertisement which had asked for male volunteers to participate in a psychological study of prison life. The volunteers completed a questionnaire and interview designed to screen subjects, and the selected people were described as 'normal', healthy, male college students who were predominantly middle class and White.

The simulated prison was created in the basement of the Psychology Department at Stanford University. It was made up of three cells (each 6ft by 9ft) with three prisoners to a cell. A broom cupboard (2ft by 2ft by 7ft) was converted into a 'solitary confinement room'. Several rooms in an adjacent wing of the building were used as guards' rooms, interview rooms and a bedroom for the 'warden' (Zimbardo). There was also a small enclosed room used as a 'prison yard' in which there was an observation window behind which was video equipment, and room for several observers.

The subjects were randomly assigned their roles of either 'prisoner' or 'guard', and signed contracts on that basis. The contract offered $15 a day and guaranteed basic living needs, though it was made explicit to the prisoners that some basic civil rights (for example, privacy) would be suspended. The prisoners were given no information about what to expect and no instructions on how to behave. The guards were told to 'maintain the reasonable degree of order within the prison necessary for its effective functioning' (p. 6), though they were explicitly prohibited from using physical aggression.[1]

The prisoner subjects remained in the mock prison 24 hours a day for the duration of the study. Nine were arbitrarily assigned three to each cell, and the remaining three were on stand-by at home. The 'guard' subjects worked on three-man eight-hour shifts, and went home after their shifts.

Both sets of subjects were given uniforms to promote feelings of anonymity. The guards' uniform (plain khaki shirt and trousers, whistle, baton, and reflecting sunglasses) was intended to convey a military attitude and to give symbols of power. The prisoners' uniform (loose-fitting smock, number on front and back, no underwear, light chain and lock around ankle, rubber sandals and a cap made from nylon stocking) was intended to be uncomfortable, humiliating and to create symbols of subservience and dependence.

Zimbardo obtained the help of the local police department to unexpectedly 'arrest' the prisoner subjects. A police officer charged them with suspicion of burglary or armed robbery, advised them of their rights, handcuffed them, thoroughly searched them (often in full view of the neighbours!) and drove them to the police station. Here they had their fingerprints and picture taken and were put in a detention cell. They were then blindfolded and driven to the mock prison. During the induction period the arresting officers did not tell the subjects that this was part of the study. When they arrived at the mock prison, the prisoner-subjects were stripped, deloused, made to stand alone and naked in the 'yard' and then given their uniform and cell and told to remain silent.

The prisoners were then greeted by the warden (Zimbardo) who read them the rules which had to be memorized. After this they were referred to only by their number. The prisoners were to be given three meals a day, allowed three supervised toilet visits, two hours' privilege time for reading and letter writing, two visiting periods a week, exercise periods and film rights. They were also required to conduct work assignments and line up for a 'count' on each new guard shift. The initial purpose of the count was to check that all the prisoners were present, and to test their knowledge of the rules and their ID (identity) numbers. The first counts took around ten minutes, but, as conditions in the prison deteriorated, they increased in length until some lasted for several hours.

---

1. Zimbardo gave the guards further instructions but they are not described in this article. We deal with these in our discussion of the article by Reicher and Haslam (2006) which follows this study.

Results

The prison had a much more dramatic effect on all the players in the drama than had been anticipated. The mood of the prisoners and guards became increasingly negative. The prison was internalized by prisoners and guards (in other words, they started to believe in it) and they adopted very contrasting behaviours, which were appropriate for their respective roles. Five prisoners were released early due to extreme emotional depression, crying, rage and acute anxiety, and the simulation was brought to an end after six days rather than the projected 14 days.

One question that arises from simulations is 'were the behaviours shown by the subjects merely some very good acting or had the situation become real to them?' One answer to this comes from the private conversations of prisoners, which were monitored by the researchers. These conversations were 90 per cent on the prison, which shows that they actually reinforced the experience even when they could have escaped in their minds by discussing something else. The prisoners also adopted the guards' negative attitude towards them, and referred to each other in deprecating ways. When the prisoners were introduced to a priest, they referred to themselves by number, asked for a lawyer to help get them out, and asked for immediate bail and a parole board.

Guard aggression showed a steady increase throughout the study, even after resistance had ceased. They attempted to 'hide' one prisoner in the broom cupboard overnight because the experimenters were being 'too soft'.

The most dramatic demonstration of the reality of the prison came with the mock parole board. The five remaining prisoners were asked by Zimbardo in turn whether they would forfeit the money they had earned as a prisoner if they could be paroled (released from the study). Three of the five said 'yes', which meant they were effectively terminating their contract to take part in the study. Yet, when they were told to return to their cells while it was considered, they did so rather than just walk out.

If you want more details on this then just type 'Stanford prison simulation' into your browser and scan through the comments and descriptions and slideshows of the study.

Discussion

Zimbardo suggested that the reason for the deterioration in guard behaviour was power. The guards were able to exert control over the lives of other human beings and they did not have to justify their displays of power as they would have to in their daily lives. After day one, all prisoner rights became redefined as privileges, and all privileges were cancelled.

Zimbardo describes the social deterioration of the prisoners as the *pathological prisoner syndrome*. To start with, the prisoners rebelled against their conditions, but every attempt was undermined by the guards, and social cohesion collapsed among the prisoners. Half of the prisoners responded by becoming sick, and eventually had to be released before the study was finally brought to a conclusion. For those who remained, the model prisoner reaction that developed was passivity, dependence and flattened affect (emotions). Zimbardo suggested that there were a number of processes that contributed to the deterioration of the prisoners including:

(a) The loss of personal identity.

(b) The arbitrary control exerted by the guards. This made the prisoners' lives increasingly unpredictable and their treatment increasingly unfair. Their behaviour showed signs of learned helplessness (see the study by Seligman and Maier, 1967, Chapter 4 of this volume).

(c) Dependency and emasculation. The guards created a dependency in the prisoners which emasculated them to the extent that when the prisoners were debriefed they suggested that they had been assigned to be prisoners because they were smaller than the guards. In fact, there was no difference in average height between the prisoners and the guards, and the perceived difference was a response to the prisoners' perceptions of themselves and their lack of power.

▶ **learned helplessness** The way that the experience of being forced into the role of passive victim in one situation can generalize to other situations, such that the person or animal makes no effort to help themselves in unpleasant situations even if such effort would be effective.

▶ **emasculation** Removing a man's sense of his masculinity.

What does all this mean? Zimbardo describes it as a simulation of prison life, but that is not quite the case. None of the subjects had any experience of prison life before the study, and their roles were played from the social perceptions of how prison life should be. It is, in fact, a simulation of what we expect prison life to be, rather than what it is. However, the study still gives a powerful demonstration of the effect of social roles, and also the power of the social psychological experiment to make us behave in ways we did not think possible (see Orne, 1962, Chapter 18 of this volume).

One of the puzzles about this study concerns the differences between the design of the prison experience for the people who took part, and the real experience of going to prison. Watson (1980) noted the following differences:

- The prisoners had no record of criminal behaviour, and there was no attempt to simulate this;
- The removal of personal belongings and the removal of personal identifiers through the symbolic shaving of heads does not commonly take place in Western prisons;
- The guards were given khaki uniforms, which made them look more military;
- The prisoners were snatched arbitrarily from their homes rather than being transferred to prison in an orderly way after a court appearance.

These features are not part of going to prison in Western countries, but they are part of being taken prisoner of war. Watson (1980) noted that the research was funded by the US Navy and suggested that they were probably more concerned at the time of the study with the behaviour of military personnel in South East Asian prisoner-of-war camps (in the Korean and Vietnam wars) than they were in the behaviour of civilian prisoners. Watson argued that the study appears to be a basis for a course on how to train soldiers or sailors to cope with the stresses of captivity. More recently in the prisons of Abu Ghraib (Iraq) and Guantanamo Bay (Cuba), the US military have used just these techniques to contain and presumably de-stabilize their prisoners.

Not altogether surprisingly, there were numerous ethical objections to the study, though, like Milgram, Zimbardo made a robust defence (Zimbardo, 1973, and MacDermott, 1993). He argued that the studies provide a special insight into human behaviour and experience, and illuminate 'a dark side'. His personal criticism of the study concerns his own role as both researcher and warden. He became as trapped in his warden role as the other players in the simulation, and that prevented him responding appropriately as the lead researcher. There is video evidence from the study that challenges Zimbardo's description of the study and also underlines the ethical issue. He appears to have prevented the prisoners from withdrawing. In one of the few bits of video that is available it is evident that the prisoners want to leave at one point. In fact one of the prisoners can be heard screaming 'I want out! I want out!' In another harrowing segment where the prisoners are engaged in a physical struggle with the guards a prisoner can be heard screaming 'F*** the experiment and f*** Zimbardo!' while another voice screams 'It's a f****** simulation.' Zimbardo refused to let the prisoners out after this outburst and gave them the impression that they could not get out (Zimbardo, 1989).

In a strange twist on this, Zimbardo has used the ethical concerns about this study to argue against any replications and hence any challenge to his ideas (Zimbardo, cited in Banyard and Flanagan, 2006; see the introduction to this chapter) but in the next study we will see another interpretation of what is happening here.

Questions

suggested answers
→ p. 477

1. What were the main features of the prisoners' behaviour?

2. What ethical objections can be made to this study?

3. Was the study justified?

4. Why do you think the researchers chose the subjects they did? And what would be the differences in the outcome of the study if the subjects had not been predominantly young students?

5. Look at the last two paragraphs. How many asterisks (*) do you need to put in a book so that rude words don't look rude any more? Is 'f*ck' ruder that 'f***'? Is reporting that someone else used this word (in the course of doing science) less offensive than if the authors used the word themselves? Why?

Tyranny

REICHER, S. AND HASLAM, S.A. (2006) Rethinking the psychology of tyranny: the BBC prison study. *British Journal of Social Psychology,* 45, 1–40.

Background

In December 2001, Reicher and Haslam carried out perhaps the most substantial and bravest psychological field study since the Stanford Prison Experiment (SPE) 30 years before (see the previous summary in this chapter). The study was designed and run by the researchers and filmed by the BBC, which subsequently broadcast their edit under the title of *The Experiment.* In this summary we will try to capture the flavour of this major piece of work including the response from the psychological community.

The work of Milgram (1963) and Zimbardo (Haney *et al.*, 1973) formed part of social psychology's attempts to explain the horrors of genocide carried out in Europe during the middle of the last century (although this was by no means the only act of genocide of the twentieth century). One important outcome of this work was to change the question that is typically asked from 'how could *they* do these things?' to 'how could *we* do these things?'

These studies played an important part in shifting explanations from individuals to groups. In this view, tyranny is not created by one person and imposed on the general population but can grow from the tacit agreement of that population if the situation allows it. Reicher and Haslam define tyranny as 'an unequal social system involving the arbitrary or oppressive use of power by one group or its agents over another' (p. 2). So it is not just a few bad people who make these things happen but social structures that create the climate where terrible behaviours become easy and acceptable, or at least unchallenged.

Milgram's obedience experiments and Zimbardo's prison simulation still resonate through psychology texts and are commonly referred to when there are discussions about inhumanity. In response to the recent 'War on Terror' Zimbardo has written extensively (for example, 2004) on how situations create tyranny. He continues to support the conclusions he drew from the SPE where he argued that the guard aggression 'was emitted simply as a natural consequence of being in the uniform of a guard and asserting the power inherent in that role' (Haney *et al.*, 1973, p. 12). These views have not been challenged by any experimental work since the original study because no one has attempted a replication. But do they really describe what happened in the SPE and do they explain how tyranny develops?

Zimbardo has controlled access to data from the SPE but even those that are available cast doubt on his explanation of events. Did the participants in the study behave in the way they did because of their natural acceptance of their *role* or because of the *leadership* provided by the experimenters? Look at how Zimbardo briefed the guards and think about how this might have affected their behaviour:

> You can create in the prisoners feelings of boredom, a sense of fear to some degree, you can create a notion of arbitrariness that their life is

▶**tyranny** 'An unequal social system involving the arbitrary or oppressive use of power by one group or its agents over another.' (Reicher and Haslam, 2006, p. 2)

▶**obedience** Complying to the demands of others, usually those in positions of authority.

▶**War on Terror** The rhetorical centrepiece of US foreign policy in the early years of the twenty-first century; refers to unlimited military action against undefined people in undefined places with undefined ideas, loosely described as 'the bad guys'.

▶**role** A social part that one plays in society.

totally controlled by us, by the system, you, me and they'll have no privacy. They'll have no freedom of action, they can do nothing, say nothing that we don't permit. We're going to take away their individuality in various ways. In general what all this leads to is a sense of powerlessness. That is, in this situation we'll have all the power and they'll have none. (Zimbardo, 1989 cited in Haslam and Reicher, 2003)

The study

The work of Zimbardo and Milgram raised many ethical concerns at the time and this has meant that neither study can be replicated, and therefore cannot be challenged. Following these studies social psychology has been dominated by laboratory experiments in which participants respond to simple stimuli, rarely interact with other people and bring little or nothing of their personal histories into the work. The studies are often brilliantly controlled and scientifically rigorous but bear as much resemblance to social interaction as an Oxo cube does to a cow. Such studies can be described as 'impeccable trivia' (Haslam and McGarty, 2001): clever, precise, replicable but not about anything of any importance.

Reicher and Haslam's study reverses this trend and explores big questions (the nature of tyranny) through a grand study of human interaction (the BBC prison study). The study draws on a social identity theory approach (see Tajfel, 1970 and Levine, 1999, elsewhere in this text) and puts forward an alternative view of behaviour to Zimbardo's.

According to this approach people do not act automatically in the role given to them by, for example, their uniform. Instead, their behaviour depends on how much they internalize membership of the group they are assigned to and how the group matches up to their self-concept. In other words we are not empty husks waiting to be given a uniform and a script but we make sense of any situation through our membership of social groups and our view of ourselves.

Social identity theory offers some explanations for the behaviour of people in groups and for the ways they deal with group inequalities. It suggests that people who are in a positively valued or high-status group (such as guards) will tend to identify with the group and go along with it. On the other hand the willingness of people who are in negatively valued or low-status groups (such as prisoners) to act as group members will depend on features of social structure. Two factors are particularly important. First *permeability*, which is their belief about their opportunities to move from one group to another and hence get promotion to the valued group. The second factor is beliefs about the *security* of the intergroup relations, specifically their *legitimacy and stability*. If people believe that relations between the groups are insecure (i.e. illegitimate and unstable) then they may become aware of *cognitive alternatives* to the status quo and can speculate on ways the existing structure can be changed. Only where (a) there is no permeability in the system and (b) there are cognitive alternatives to the system does it make sense to commit to a devalued or low-status group as a means of improving one's lot. These are

▶ **impeccable trivia** Clever, precise, replicable but not about anything of any importance.

▶ **social identity theory** An approach which states that the social groups and categories to which we belong are an important part of our self-concept, and therefore a person will sometimes interact with other people, not as a single individual, but as a representative of a whole group or category of people. There are three basic psychological processes underlying social identification which are categorization, social comparison and self-concept.

▶ **self-concept** The idea or internal image that people have of what they themselves are like, including both evaluative and descriptive dimensions.

> **hypothesis** Experiments are designed to test one or more hypotheses. An hypothesis is a prediction of what will happen in an experiment. It is worded in such a way that the results of a well-designed experiment will clearly show whether the prediction is right or wrong.

a complex set of ideas, but the core point is that people do not automatically identify with groups. They only do so when this makes sense in terms of their understanding of the situation they are in and of how to make it better.

Reicher and Haslam set out to create a situation where they could test hypotheses derived from the social identity approach. They did not set out to simulate a prison but to create something that resembled a prison in order to investigate how people deal with inequalities between groups. Their study was not intended to be an exact replication of the SPE and they describe their work as 'an experimental case study of the behaviour of members in dominant or subordinate positions and of the developing relations between them' (p. 7).

Participants

Over 300 people applied to take part in the study and this was reduced to 27 possibles after extensive screening that included: (a) assessment by independent clinical psychologists, (b) medical references, and (c) police checks. The final sample of 15 was chosen to ensure a diverse group of people by class, age and ethnicity. They were randomly divided into two groups of five guards and ten prisoners.

Measures

The environment was designed so that the participants could be recorded wherever they were. The participants were tested every day on a range of measures including

- social variables (e.g. social identification);
- organizational variables (e.g. compliance with rules);
- clinical variables (e.g. self-efficacy, depression).

Ethics

The study had the following safeguards:

- Participants went through a three-phase clinical, medical and background screening.
- Participants signed a comprehensive consent form that explained the potential risks of the study.
- The study was monitored throughout by two independent clinical psychologists who had the right to see any participant or demand their removal;
- There was an on-site paramedic.
- There were also on-site security guards.
- An independent five-person ethics committee was led by a Member of Parliament and included the co-founder of the Beth Shalom Holocaust Memorial, a Council Member of the Howard League for Penal Reform and a close associate of Zimbardo.

After the study the ethics committee published an independent report (McDermott *et al.*, 2002) and described the conduct of the study as exemplary.

Set-up

Five participants were told they were to be guards and given instructions about their responsibility to ensure the institution ran as smoothly as possible. They were asked to draw up some prison rules and to draw up a series of punishments for rule violations.

Nine participants were taken the next day to the prison and given a full briefing by the experimenters (a tenth prisoner was introduced later as one of the experimental manipulations).

The guards had a number of ways of enforcing their authority, including access to keys, surveillance systems and resources such as snacks. They also had far better living conditions than the prisoners.

Interventions

The experimenters designed three interventions to explore their hypotheses about group behaviour;

- *Permeability*: The guards and prisoners were to be told that there was an opportunity for a prisoner to be promoted to the position of guard on Day 3. The guards would select who should be promoted and after that it would be announced that no more promotions were possible.
- *Legitimacy*: Three days after the promotion the participants were to be told that observations had shown there were no differences between the guards and prisoners but it was impractical to reassign them so the groups would be kept as they were.
- *Cognitive alternatives*: Within a day of the legitimacy intervention a new prisoner was to be introduced who was selected from the pool of ten prisoners because of his experience as a trade union official. It was anticipated that he would bring his experience of collective action to create cognitive alternatives.

Results

The study lasted eight days and produced a wealth of data that are reported by Reicher and Haslam (2006; see also Haslam and Reicher, 2005, 2006). In summary, in the first phase the guards failed to identify with each other as a group. This went against one of the predictions of the study, and also conflicted with findings from the SPE. On the other hand, after the promotion of one prisoner to the position of guard on Day 3 (in other words once boundaries were impermeable), the prisoners did increasingly identify as a group and act collectively to challenge the guards. At the same time, the guards' inability to work together as a group made them increasingly unable to resist this challenge and so the system appeared increasingly fragile. This supported the hypothesis that impermeability of group boundaries and the insecurity of intergroup relations makes those in a subordinate position more willing to identify with their group and to challenge the status quo.

As the study progressed, the prisoners' challenge led to a shift in power and to the collapse of the prisoner–guard system. The guards were overthrown and a new self-governing 'commune' was created. However, the commune was unable to deal with internal dissent and the inmates lost confidence in the commune system. At this point some of the participants (a mixture of former prisoners and former guards) moved to impose a new power structure that was much harsher than the original prisoner–guard regime. These 'new guards' now wanted to run the prison 'the way it should have been run from the start', with strict rules and punishments to ensure that everyone 'toed the line'.

The study was brought to a close by the experimenters when they judged that the study had become gridlocked. The commune was not working but the new social structure could not be imposed. The study was terminated for both (a) practical reasons, since imposing the new regime would have required force which was not allowed under prison rules, but also (b) for ethical reasons since, if the new regime was created, it would clearly have resembled that in the SPE. After the study was terminated the participants stayed for a day to take part in a series of debriefings which were designed 'to obtain and provide feedback on their experience, to explain the rationale for the study and to overcome any hostility deriving from events in the study' (p. 24).

Discussion

The soundbite conclusion of the study concerns the response to inequality. At the start of the BBC prison study almost all of the participants (guards and prisoners) rejected the unequal system that was imposed on them. However, by the end of the study they were close to bringing in their own tyrannical social system. Why?

Clearly this regime was not the product of conformity to role (as Haney *et al.* had argued from the SPE), because the 'new guards' were a mixture of prisoners and guards. Reicher and Haslam focus on two factors in the answer they offer: (a) social identification and (b) group history. In the first instance, they note that a tyrannical regime only emerged when those who would lead it identified with their group. They note too that this regime was also a response to a history of group failure, which made the promise of order more attractive.

Such an analysis offers quite a different explanation of events like the Holocaust from that offered by Zimbardo. It suggests that people are not passive victims of circumstance, but rather make active choices that take them, and their groups, in particular directions. The true horror here is not that people slip carelessly into evil, but that they do so because they *really believe* it is the right thing to do (Haslam and Reicher, 2007).

Reicher and Haslam consider four possible criticisms of the study:

- *The role of television:* Did the cameras affect the behaviour? Well they clearly had an effect, but it would be impossible to fake behaviour 24/7 so it is implausible that the events were all 'staged'. Furthermore it would be difficult to fake all the psychometric and physiological findings which, along with the observational data, converge in support of Reicher and Haslam's analysis. Note too that the SPE was also filmed and surveillance is, after all, an everyday occurrence in of contemporary life in the UK. Clearly this in itself does not make events 'unreal'.

- *The role of personality:* Do the results tell us more about the people or about the situation? On the basis of their behaviour, Zimbardo (2006) claims that the BBC and the researchers hand-picked the guards and prisoners, but this was not the case. Although individual differences must play a part in the story they do not explain the whole series of events.

- *The reality of inequality and power:* Did the prisoners and guards believe in the social system that was created for them? There is a weight of evidence to suggest they did, including interviews with the participants. For example one given to the *London Evening Standard*:

  > 'I knew it was an experiment but it honestly felt like a real jail ...' (Murfitt, 2002, p. 30)

- *The impact of interventions:* In the complex social world of the prison, did the interventions such as the promotion of the prisoner actually create the effect that the experimenters wanted? The researchers argue that their wide range of data support their view of events.

Conclusion

▶ **pro-social** Any behaviour intended to help or benefit another person, group or society.

The message of Zimbardo's Stanford Prison Experiment, as every psychology students knows, is 'that the toxic combination of groups and power leads to tyranny' (p. 33). The BBC Prison Study challenges this idea that group behaviour is inevitably uncontrolled, mindless and antisocial. The results suggest that 'the way in which members of strong groups behave depends on the norms and values associated with their specific social identity and may be either anti- or pro-social' (p. 33).

The authors suggest that rather than groups creating tyranny, it is the breakdown of groups and powerlessness that create the conditions under which tyranny can thrive.

Postscript

It is no surprise that a study such as this would generate a certain amount of controversy but it is the nature of the controversy that has been surprising. Zimbardo was initially asked to advise on the project but declined and has subsequently subjected the study to fierce criticism.

suggested answers
→ p. 477

Questions

1. What were the interventions that were used to affect the behaviour in the prison?

2. What ethical objections can be made to this study?

3. Why do you think Zimbardo objected to this study?

4. Are there any extra problems for psychologists if their research is filmed and then edited for television?

Small world and getting smaller

DODDS, P. MUHAMAD, R. AND WATTS, D. (2003)

An experimental study of search in global social networks.

Science, 301, 827–9.

Introduction

'It's a small world isn't it?' is a phrase we commonly hear when two apparent strangers make a connection in their social worlds. Although there are now over 7 billion human beings on the planet there is a belief that the world is getting smaller and people are more able to contact each other. Milgram (1967) devised a novel way to test this idea that everyone in the world can be connected through a very short chain of acquaintances which he referred to as the 'small-world problem'.

In Milgram's original study he asked some randomly selected people from the rural midwest of the USA to send a package to a stranger in Massachusetts on the east coast. They were told the stranger's name, occupation and general area where they lived but not, fairly obviously, their address. They were told to pass the package to someone they were on first name terms with who they thought would be most likely of all their acquaintances to know the target. That person was then asked to do the same and so on until the package reached the target.

Milgram was an excellent communicator and when he reported his results the idea caught the public imagination. He found that some of his packages made it to the target in only six hops, and this gave rise to the famous phrase 'six degrees of separation'. A closer inspection of the work reveals that it was not quite as successful as people commonly believe because in the original study, although the packages that made it through did so in six hops, only 5 per cent actually reached the target. His subsequent studies (for example, Travers and Milgram, 1969) had mixed results though it has been possible to achieve some higher success rates.

In the Western world, people's social lives and patterns of social contact are going through some dramatic changes. The use of mobile phones and text messaging allows people to make contact anywhere, anyplace anytime. On the Internet people join a range of online groups, make contact through sites such as MySpace, upload their home videos on sites such as YouTube and reach out to others in cyberspace with their blogs. It is estimated that there are in excess of 27 million weblogs and the blogosphere continues to double about every 5.5 months. There are about 75,000 new weblogs created everyday and 1.2 million posts per day on average, or 50,000 posts per hour (Sifry, 2006). By the time this text is published these data will already be very dated, such is the rate of change.

The question for social psychology is to describe and study these new relationships and see whether they represent new ways of relating to each

▶ **small-world problem** The idea that everyone in the world can be connected through a very short chain of acquaintances.

▶ **six degrees of separation** The theory that anyone on the planet can be connected to any other person on the planet through a chain of acquaintances that has no more than five intermediaries. The theory was first proposed in 1929 by the Hungarian writer Frigyes Karinthy in a short story called 'Chains'.

▶ **blogosphere** All weblogs or blogs; weblogs have many connections and bloggers read others' blogs, link to them, reference them in their own writing, and post comments on each others' blogs.

other or whether we are just using new technology to carry out old rituals. The use of email is widespread if not ubiquitous and it might be changing the number, type and style of social contacts that individuals have. Email is therefore an ideal medium to revisit Milgram's small world problem, because if the world is getting smaller then email is probably part of that process.

The study

Dodds *et al.* noted that although the belief in six degrees of separation is widely held there had been very little research work on it since the original studies by Milgram. Most of the subsequent studies have looked at non-social networks or task-based groups such as scientific collaboration. This paper describes 'a global, Internet-based social search experiment' (p. 827). Participants registered online and were randomly allocated to one of 18 target people from 13 countries. These targets included a journalist from Munich (Germany), a computer analyst from Managua (Nicaragua), a retired man from Welwyn Garden City (UK), an unemployed man from Bandung (Indonesia) and a life insurance agent from Omaha (USA). In the first instance, participants were recruited through requests to commercially obtained email lists. The response rate was very low (less than 0.5 per cent) but the work attracted wide media coverage around the world and more participants were able to join via the website.

Participants were informed that their task was to help relay a message to their allocated target by passing it to an acquaintance who they thought would be closer to the target than they were themselves. Just under 100,000 people registered on the site, of which about 25 per cent provided personal information about themselves and started a message chain. These messages effectively recruited more participants as they went towards their targets. To keep track of the chains, all the emails were forwarded through the experiment's website. Each sender was given two weeks to select and make contact with the next person in the chain and they were given a reminder at the end of the first week. If the next person in the chain did not respond the sender was re-contacted to come up with an alternative contact.

The project recorded data on over 60,000 people from 166 countries who initiated over 24,000 message chains. Participants came from all over the world, though around half of them were college-educated professional people from the USA. Participants were asked to say how they knew the next person in the chain and what was the nature and strength of that relationship. Most commonly, participants chose friends (67 per cent) who they had met at work (25 per cent) or school/college (22 per cent) and described their relationship as fairly close (33 per cent). Men were more likely to send a message to another man (57 per cent) and women to another woman (61 per cent). Participants were also asked why they chose the next person in the chain, with the most common responses referring the location or to similarity of occupation.

The average participation rate was 37 per cent, which is high for email surveys, but because this project required multiple participation in chains the completion rate was low, with only 384 out of the 24,163 message making it through. Perhaps not surprisingly the targets in the USA received the most completions, except for the life insurance agent from Omaha who received two (which was twice as many as the retired man from Welwyn Garden City, who in turn received one more than the unemployed man from Indonesia).

The authors argue that the most likely reason for the low completion rate was random failure due to individual apathy and not wanting to take part. Their evidence for this is first that the response rate was not affected by the length of the chain, and second that when they contacted people who were not responding they only rarely said (0.3 per cent) they could not think of anyone to send the message on to. They speculate whether incentive might be the key to completion, and if people see some value in completing the chain they will be more likely to move the message along. Of the successful chains, the most frequent length was four hops and very few chains made it beyond six hops.

Discussion

> **hypothesis** Experiments are designed to test one or more hypotheses. An hypothesis is a prediction of what will happen in an experiment. It is worded in such a way that the results of a well-designed experiment will clearly show whether the prediction is right or wrong.

The experimental approach used in this research has reinvigorated the small world work and shown how new technologies can be used to investigate social relationships and social interaction. It seems to offer some limited support to the six degrees of separation hypothesis, but we can only speculate on the proportion of chains that would have been completed if people were motivated to make the contacts.

The new technologies raise a number of questions for social psychologists about our social relationships. Are people forming more relationships using the new technologies and are they forming different types of relationships?

An example of development of social interaction in cyberspace can be seen in the growth of online multiplayer role-playing games. The Massive Multiplayer Role-playing Games (MMORPGs) as run by companies such as Blizzard (*World of Warcraft*), Sony (*EverQuest*) and Microsoft (*Asheron's Call*) have a large global audience. For example, *World of Warcraft* claims to have 7 million subscribers. The games create a multiplayer universe that allows a range of identities to be explored by playing a character created by the player. Character identity creation typically involves a number of dimensions such as gender, race and profession. Players are immersed in a detailed and complex social world governed by complex physical and social rules. To succeed it is necessary to be able to communicate within supportive groups and operate within the virtual world's commodities market (Underwood *et al.*, in press). In other words the players have to enter a social world that has some similar rules to those in face-to-face interactions, though there are some major differences as well.

Players develop long-term interactions (relationships?) with the cyberidentities of other people but are unaware of some of the dimensions that are commonly seen as most important in face-to-face interactions such as appearance, age, ethnicity and sex. Cyber-identities also have no past that can be

▶**cyber-identity** A social identity that people create on the internet. Some people prefer to use their real names but many users create pseudonyms and reveal varying amounts of personal information which might or might not be accurate.

verified and an unpredictable future. Interactions can be terminated at the flick of a switch and extreme actions such as killing another cyber-identity need have no consequences as the victim can just create another cyber-identity for themselves. Questions arise about how much a person's cyber-identity is like their real-life identity and how much interactions in cyberspace are similar to interactions in real life.

Postscript

At the time of writing this text a new version of the small world study is still in progress, and you can join in by going to the authors' website at Columbia University, USA http://smallworld.columbia.edu/

This article along with extra materials is available online at http://www.sciencemag.org/cgi/content/full/301/5634/827/DC1.

Questions

1. Do the original data support Milgram's idea about six stages of separation? Make a case for and against.

2. What groups of people do think will be hard to contact in a 'small world study' and what groups do you think will be easy to contact?

suggested answers ➤ p. 478

part **ii**

BIOLOGICAL AND COMPARATIVE PSYCHOLOGY

▶ **behaviour (also spelt 'behavior'** Anything a person (or animal) does that can be observed and measured by a third party. Behaviour can be thought of as the public side of human life, in contrast to 'experience' (thoughts and feelings) which can be thought of as the private side.

▶ **evolution** The development of bodily form and behaviour through the process of natural selection.

▶ **altruism** Acting in the interests of other people and not of oneself.

▶ **ethology** The study of behaviour in the natural environment.

▶ **behaviourism** A school of thought which holds that the observation and description of overt behaviour is all that is needed to comprehend the human being, and that manipulation of stimulus–response contingencies is all that is needed to change human behaviour.

SINCE Darwin held up a mirror to the human race and showed us the reflection of a monkey we have had a very different view about who and what we are. This new awareness leads us to explore our connectedness to other animals and also to look at the nuts and bolts of this biological machine that we call our body.

Comparative psychology explores human behaviour and experience by comparing people with other species. The basic argument is that it is not just our bodies that have evolved over the centuries, but also our behaviour. The evolution of behaviour can be seen, for example, in species of birds who are often far easier to spot by what they do (for example the way they build a nest) rather than by what they look like. Evolutionary studies have shown how the three factors of behaviour, biology and environment interact to develop a species. Animals adapt behaviourally (for example, feeding and mating patterns) and biologically (for example, size and digestive system) over a number of generations, to fit with their changing environment.

Animal psychologists have come up with some remarkable insights into animal behaviour and experience, but the question to be answered is how

much these insights can be applied to people. Are there some major differences between humans and the animals, or are we just another animal with a little more dress sense? Depending on your point of view you can concentrate on the similarities or the differences. The danger of the human-animal metaphor is that we see human behaviour as just being due to evolutionary forces. In this argument we view acts of kindness or altruism as being simple animal displays and, more worryingly, accept bad behaviour as 'natural'. For example, according to Rose *et al.* (1984), the famous Austrian animal psychologist Konrad Lorenz wrote a paper during the 1939–45 war giving an evolutionary argument in favour of the Final Solution (the Nazi policy of killing people they regarded as inferior: Jews, Slavs, homosexuals, gypsies, the mentally ill and so forth).

Comparative psychology has developed from two academic traditions: ethology and behaviourism. Ethology attempts to study animals behaving as naturally as possible in as natural an environment as possible. The behaviourist tradition, on the other hand, studied animals in very restricted environments while they carried out very limited tasks, such as running a T-maze.

part ii

The laboratory animals were commonly rats or pigeons, which were chosen not for their evolutionary significance, but because of their size and docility (well, would you fill your laboratory with polar bears?), and the psychologists bred special strains of the animals to the extent that it is unlikely that they could survive outside the laboratory.

One of the major interests of comparative psychologists is learning, and in Chapter 4 we summarize four papers on this topic. Some of the other concerns of comparative psychologists, both laboratory and ethological, are illustrated in the four studies included in Chapter 5.

Biological psychology explores human behaviour and experience by looking at people as if they are biological machines. This idea has some value because it is clear that our biology affects our behaviour and experience. On a simple level we know certain foodstuffs such as coffee or alcoholic drinks will affect the way we see the world and the way we behave. Also, it has been observed for a long time that damage to the brain and nervous system can have an effect on behaviour and experience. So the structure of the nervous system and the action of chemicals are two of the main themes of physiological psychology. However, the question that arises is very similar to the one we have to answer for comparative psychology, namely, to what extent are we determined by our biological make-up? In this selection we include five studies that show some of the concerns of physiological psychology, and highlight the interaction between biological and psychological variables. Some further issues of biological psychology are considered on the nature of pleasure (Olds and Milner, 1954, in Chapter 4), the influence of biological on our sense of gender (Diamond and Sigmundson, 1997, in Chapter 7), the relationship between drugs and the experience of psychosis (Griffith *et al.*, 1972, in Chapter 8) and the experience of synaesthesia (Ramachandran and Hubbard, 2001, in Chapter 15).

chapter **4**

LEARNING

▶ **learning** A change in behaviour, or the potential for behaviour, that occurs as a result of environmental experience, but is not the result of such factors as fatigue, drugs or injury.

▶ **behaviour (also spelt 'behavior'** Anything a person (or animal) does that can be observed and measured by a third party. Behaviour can be thought of as the public side of human life, in contrast to 'experience' (thoughts and feelings) which can be thought of as the private side.

▶ **behaviourism** A school of thought which holds that the observation and description of overt behaviour is all that is needed to comprehend the human being, and that manipulation of stimulus–response contingencies is all that is needed to change human behaviour.

LEARNING can be defined as 'a relatively permanent change in behavioural potential which accompanies experience but which is not the result of simple growth factors or of reversible influences such as fatigue or hunger' (Kimble, 1961, cited in Gross, 1992). This definition takes in the following points:

(a) *Relative permanence*: A change in behaviour is a sign of learning, but our behaviour often just fluctuates without learning, so psychologists include the phrase 'relatively permanent' to distinguish learning from the everyday fluctuations in performance.

(b) *Behavioural potential*: When we have learned something we do not always act on it; for example, the fact that I go to see the same football team lose every week does not mean that I haven't learned what the consequences will be (unhappiness, depression, irritability). It just means that I am too stupid to respond to what I've learned.

(c) *Growth factors*: Some behaviour and experience develops through maturation (a biological unfolding)

and this is usually distinguished from learning. However, this distinction is far from simple and there is an interaction between maturation and learning.

The psychological study of learning has been dominated by behaviourism – the movement founded by John B. Watson in the early part of this century, which concentrated on behaviour (what someone does) rather than experience (what someone thinks or feels). A paper by Watson is included in Part IV of this book, on Developmental Psychology. The behaviourists suggested that we learn by the simple process of associating one event with another. The work of Pavlov in developing the concept of classical conditioning is an important part of this perspective. Pavlov showed that dogs will learn to associate simple reflex behaviours, like salivating, with a previously neutral stimulus, such as a bell. In this way they can be taught to salivate at the sound of a bell. This type of learning can only explain a limited range of behaviour, but the work of Thorndike and Skinner provided an explanation for much more of our learning.

Thorndike made some ingenious

▶**classical conditioning** A form of learning which involves the pairing of a neutral stimulus with a reflex.

▶**reflex** An automatic reaction to a stimulus: often inborn but can also be learned or modified by experience.

▶**neutral stimulus** A stimulus that has no meaning for a person or animal before the onset of conditioning.

▶**Law of Effect** The learning principle that actions which have a pleasant effect on the organism are likely to be repeated.

▶**operant conditioning** The process of learning identified by B.F. Skinner, in which learning occurs as a result of positive or negative reinforcement of an animal or human being's action.

▶**reinforcement** Any consequence of any behaviour that increases the probability that that behaviour will recur in similar circumstances. The term is usually used of learned associations, acquired through operant conditioning, but it may also be applied to other forms of learning.

▶**punishment** According to behaviourist theory: anything that decreases the probability that a behaviour will recur in similar circumstances. More popularly: an aversive stimulus.

▶**Social Learning Theory** The approach to understanding social behaviour which emphasizes how people imitate action and model their behaviour on that of others.

▶**imitation** Copying someone else's behaviour and specific actions.

puzzle boxes from which cats had to learn to escape. He showed that they were able to learn how to escape without ever showing any sign of understanding how they managed to do it. He proposed the Law of Effect which says that the result of a successful behaviour is that it will be repeated in similar circumstances. Skinner elaborated on this work and developed the concept of operant conditioning which showed how animals (and people) can learn a whole range of behaviours through reinforcement and punishment. One of the strengths of this work is the experimental rigour which the behaviourists employed, but this is also one of the weaknesses. The controlled nature of the studies meant that the animals were observed in very restricted situations with a very limited range of behaviours to show, so the relevance of this work to learning in everyday life is seriously questioned.

The five papers chosen for this chapter all show how the basic concepts of behaviourism have been applied to wider concerns. The first paper is a delightful report by Skinner (1960) on his attempts to encourage the US military to let his pigeons pilot their missiles. Strangely, they declined the offer (the military that is, not the pigeons), but Skinner provided a powerful case for his suggestion. The paper by Olds and Milner (1954) considers the nature of reinforcement. The paper by Seligman and Maier (1967) starts with a simple learning experience in dogs and looks at how this might be applied to a range of human experience including depression. The paper by Bandura *et al.* (1961) takes a Social Learning Theory approach to understanding the role of imitation in learning. The final study by Gardner and Gardner (1969) looks at attempts to teach language to a chimpanzee, and enables us to ask questions about the differences between the way in which animals learn to communicate and the way children learn language.

The flight of the killer pigeons

Pigeons in a pelican.

SKINNER, B.F. (1960)

American Psychologist,
15, 28–37.

Introduction

Around the turn of the twentieth century, American psychologist Edward Lee Thorndike investigated how animals learn. In one series of observations he placed a cat in a 'puzzle box' and measured the time it took to escape. Over a number of trials the time taken to escape decreased, yet the animal showed no sign of insight into the problem. It got out but it did not understand how it did it. From his observations he developed the Law of Effect, which states that the consequence of a successful behaviour is that it is more likely to recur in similar circumstances. This provided a description of animal behaviour that did not require notions such as consciousness or thought.

This work was developed by the behaviourists, including B.F. Skinner. They argued that all behaviour in human or non-human animals is caused, shaped and maintained by its consequences. This can happen in a number of ways including:

- *Positive reinforcement*: When a pleasant stimulus follows a particular response it strengthens that response: for example, giving your pet a doggo-choc when it sits on command will make it more likely to sit next time you tell it to.
- *Negative reinforcement*: When an aversive stimulus is removed following a response it is also likely to strengthen that response. This is sometimes referred to as escape conditioning.
- *Punishment*: When an aversive stimulus follows a behavioural response it weakens that response and makes it less likely to recur.

The above procedures can be used to shape new behaviours into an animal by reinforcing successive approximations to the required response. For example, if you wanted your pet to learn to jump through a hoop of fire, you would not start by showing it a lighted hoop and saying 'Jump!' Instead, you would reward the animal for walking through an unlit hoop on the ground, and then gradually raise the hoop and reward the animal for every new height achieved. Finally, when the animal will jump through the hoop, you can try it with a lighted one. In this way, the animal learns the behaviour step by step until the whole complex action has been shaped by the careful use of rewards.

Skinner used these procedures to explain an array of complex behaviours in humans, believing that it was unnecessary to look for underlying causes beyond the reinforcement contingencies that could be used to change that behaviour. We recommend that you try and read some of Skinner's own writings (for example, Skinner, 1973 and 1974) because his work has been so influential in psychology.

▶**learning** A change in behaviour, or the potential for behaviour, that occurs as a result of environmental experience, but is not the result of such factors as fatigue, drugs or injury.

▶**Law of Effect** The learning principle that actions which have a pleasant effect on the organism are likely to be repeated.

▶**behaviour** Anything a person (or animal) does that can be observed and measured by a third party. Behaviour can be thought of as the public side of human life, in contrast to 'experience' (thoughts and feelings) which can be thought of as the private side.

The study

Skinner describes in this paper how, during the Second World War (1939–45), he developed a programme to train pigeons to guide missiles. With startling originality, but admirable directness, the programme was called 'Project Pigeon'. This was not the first time, nor the last, that the potential of animals has been exploited in warfare. Skinner reports that the British Navy used seagulls to detect submarines in the First World War (1914–18). The Navy would send its own submarines into the English Channel to release food. This would attract flocks of seagulls which would then learn to associate the sight of an underwater vessel with the appearance of food. They would then follow any submarine, whether it was British or German. Therefore, a flock of seagulls in the Channel would be the sign of an approaching German submarine. Dogs and dolphins are among the other animals that have been used for military purposes, and the consequence for these animals was often not a good meal, but an early death as the explosives which were attached to them were detonated.

The original studies by Skinner tested the ability of a pigeon to steer towards a target by using a moving hoist. The pigeon was held in a jacket and harnessed to a block, and was immobilized except for its neck. It could eat grain from a dish and move its head in appropriate directions. Movement of the head operated the motors of the hoist. The bird could make the apparatus move upwards by lifting its head, downwards by lowering it, and travel from side to side by moving its head to the side it wanted to travel to. The whole apparatus was mounted on wheels and pushed across a room towards a bulls-eye. The task of the pigeon was to adjust the position of the hoist while it was being pushed across the room so that it would end up at the bulls-eye where the bowl of grain could be found. The pigeons were remarkably successful and could direct the apparatus to the bulls-eye regardless of the starting position and also during rapid approaches.

The American military were initially unimpressed by the work and it took support from a private company to develop it further. This work found that a guiding system that was dependent on the movements of the pigeon would respond too late to accurately direct the missile to its target. Skinner and his associates then developed a screen that showed the target to the pigeon. The screen was arranged so that when the pigeon pecked the screen it activated the guidance system, and the position of the pecks would alter the orientation of the visual display. The visual display was constantly in motion and the target would go out of view unless the pigeon continued to control it with its pecks. Once again the perceptual skills of the pigeons were remarkable and they were able to direct the guidance system towards particular object shapes such as ships, to ignore other objects and concentrate on just one, and to guide the system towards a particular road junction on a city map. The researchers studied ways of enhancing the performance of the pigeons though changes in reinforcement schedules and the use of energizing drugs. They also investigated the effects of changes in temperature, pressure, sound, acceleration, oxygen levels and centrifugal force.

▶ **behaviourism** A school of thought which holds that the observation and description of overt behaviour is all that is needed to comprehend the human being, and that manipulation of stimulus–response contingencies is all that is needed to change human behaviour.

▶ **reinforcement** Any consequence of any behaviour that increases the probability that that behaviour will recur in similar circumstances. The term is usually used of learned associations, acquired through operant conditioning, but it may also be applied to other forms of learning.

▶ **positive reinforcement** In operant conditioning, strengthening learned behaviour by direct reward when it occurs.

▶ **negative reinforcement** Encouraging a certain kind of behaviour by the removal or avoidance of an unpleasant stimulus.

▶ **punishment** According to behaviourist theory: anything that decreases the probability that a behaviour will recur in similar circumstances. More popularly: an aversive stimulus.

▶ **successive approximations** From the vocabulary of behaviourism, this refers to behaviours that are increasingly similar to a target behaviour.

▶ perceptual acuity Visual resolution or clarity.

The argument for the pigeon-controlled missiles was strong. They had better perceptual acuity than humans, they were lighter, cost less and were regarded as expendable. At this stage of the project, in 1943, the military became interested and provided Skinner and his associates with details of the missile (the Pelican) which might be flown by the pigeons. They were able to use the specifications to design a pigeon-controlled version of the missile. The mechanism was relatively simple and, according to Skinner, foolproof. They also designed the apparatus to work with three pigeon pilots rather than one, so that the majority vote would help to avoid embarrassing mistakes.

Despite some excellent results from the laboratory, the team of scientists who examined the data and the project were unable to recommend its progress, probably because they were uneasy at the thought of large quantities of explosives being controlled by pigeons. The project was cancelled.

Discussion

Skinner refers to the idea behind 'Project Pigeon' as 'crackpot', yet he showed how the birds could be trained using simple operant techniques to carry out a seemingly very complex function. In the world of 1990s warfare, we are asked to marvel at cruise missiles, yet they are probably less accurate than the pigeons would have proved to be. Behaviourists see the success of 'Project Pigeon' (and its peacetime follow-up 'Project Orcon' – for ORganic CONtrol) as evidence that apparently complex tasks such as guidance can be brought under the control of very simple learning contingencies.

It is surprising just how discriminating pigeons can be in their perception. For example, they have been trained to discriminate between colour slides of paintings by Monet and Picasso (Watanabe *et al.*, 1995). After they had been trained they were able to discriminate between more paintings by the artists that they had not seen before. This is remarkable given the difficulty experienced by most humans in recognizing the artist of a painting. The pigeons were able to go one step further and respond to artists similar to Monet (expressionists such as Cezanne) and ones similar to Picasso (cubists such as Braque). This suggests that pigeons can categorize visual information and identify schools of art!

Many readers will be appalled at the callous disregard for the pigeons in the missile project. If the project had been brought into operation, Skinner would have trained pigeons who would then unwittingly be the agents of their own destruction as they guided themselves, and their missiles, towards detonation on an enemy ship. However, ethics must always be seen in the context of the times, and during the Second World War it appeared to many that it was right to go to war against Nazism, and that this war should be concluded as soon as possible to avoid defeat and further loss of life. In the paper Skinner writes: 'The ethical question of our right to convert a lower creature into an unwitting hero is a peace-time luxury' (p. 28). You might still not accept this as a justification for the use of animals in warfare, but it does highlight the idea that ethics is not a simple matter and that people sometimes choose to act by criteria that conflict with their normal ethical standards. As Spock suggested in *Star Trek II*, perhaps 'the needs of the many outweigh the needs of the few.'

suggested
answers
→ p. 479

Questions

1. Summarize how the pigeons were trained.

2. What are the advantages of using pigeons rather than people in spotter tasks?

3. Do you think the use of animals in warfare is ever justified? Try and give an example where it might be justified and where it would not be justified.

4. What other tasks would the perceptual skills of pigeons be useful for?

What's your pleasure?

OLDS, J. AND MILNER, P. (1954)

Positive reinforcement produced by electrical stimulation of the septal area and other regions of the rat brain.

Journal of Comparative and Physiological Psychology, 47, 419–27.

Introduction

What is pleasure? Some things make us feel happy, or warm, or relieved or exhilarated. We refer to this as the sensation of pleasure. People are prepared to go through a lot for the feeling of pleasure. They part with money (for example, to hear music), they risk their health (for example, by taking mind-altering drugs), they risk injury (for example, with extreme sports), and they risk their mental health (for example, by watching their favourite football team). All that for passing feelings of pleasure.

To put this question in a different way, we might ask 'what is reinforcement?' Behaviourists define reinforcement in terms of its effect on behaviour and say it is anything that increases the likelihood of a behaviour recurring in similar circumstances. If we take one step back and ask why a reinforcer increases the probability of a behaviour then we might choose to look at events inside the animal or person. The study by Olds and Milner (1954) looked at brain activity to investigate the nature of reinforcement.

The study

▶ **reinforcement** Any consequence of any behaviour that increases the probability that that behaviour will recur in similar circumstances. The term is usually used of learned associations, acquired through operant conditioning, but it may also be applied to other forms of learning.

▶ **behaviourism** A school of thought which holds that the observation and description of overt behaviour is all that is needed to comprehend the human being, and that manipulation of stimulus–response contingencies is all that is needed to change human behaviour.

▶ **behaviour (also spelt 'behavior'** Anything a person (or animal) does that can be observed and measured by a third party. Behaviour can be thought of as the public side of human life, in contrast to 'experience' (thoughts and feelings) which can be thought of as the private side.

The study was conducted on 15 male hooded rats. Each rat had an electrode inserted into its brain, and the electrode was connected to a loose wire which could be used to conduct an electric current. The rats were tested in a Skinner box, which is a piece of apparatus commonly used in behavioural studies. The Skinner box has a lever which the rat can press to receive some stimulation like a piece of food, or in this case an electrical current in the brain. You would imagine that an electrical current to the brain would be very unpleasant, in which case the rat would press the lever only once or twice before scuttling off to the other side of the cage as far away from the lever as possible. This was not, however, the outcome of the study.

Four days after the operation to insert the electrode, the rats were individually placed in a Skinner box and given an hour-long pre-testing session. This session was used to allow the rat to learn the effect of pressing the lever (brain stimulation) and to allow the experimenter to work out the minimum amount of electricity that would bring about a behavioural response. On the following days the rats were put in the box for 3.5 hours a day, of which 3 hours was acquisition time (the current was on) and 0.5 hours was extinction time (the current was off). The first rats were tested over four days, giving them a total of 12 hours of acquisition time, but there were few changes in the pattern of behaviour after the first two days so the later rats were only tested for two days (6 hours acquisition time).

Animals were scored on the percentage of time they spent pressing the bar regularly. If they pressed the bar regularly when the current was on (acquisition time) then it suggested that the current in that part of the brain was reinforcing. The time spent pressing the bar when the current was off (extinction time) was used as a control. 'After testing the animal was sacrificed' (p. 419), and its brain was examined to find the exact location of the electrode.

Results

The results of the study appear in two forms and we include examples of both forms in this summary. Table 4.1 shows the time spent bar pressing by some of the rats. You will notice a different pattern of behaviour for different regions of the brain.

Table 4.1 *The acquisition and extinction scores for some of the rats, showing the location of the electrode and the threshold voltage used*

Animal number	Location of electrode	Voltage used	% of time spent lever pressing during acquisition	% of time spent lever pressing during extinction
32	septal area	2.2–2.8	75	16
34	septal area	1.4	92	6
M-1	septal area	1.7–4.8	85	21
M-4	septal area	2.3–4.8	88	13
40	corpus callosum	0.7–1.1	6	3
41	caudate nucleus	0.9–1.2	4	4
6	medial geniculate bodies	0.5	0	31
11	medial geniculate bodies	0.5	0	21

The table shows the rats stimulated the septal area of their brain when given the opportunity. They spent, on average, 85 per cent of the time regularly pressing the lever to obtain the stimulation. Rat 34 stimulated itself with over 7500 lever presses in 12 hours at an average of 742 responses an hour, or more than once every 5 seconds (the response pattern of rat 34 is shown in Figure 4.1). We have to conclude that the lever pressing, and hence the stimulation, was very reinforcing.

If we examine the data from other areas of the brain then we come to different conclusions about the effects of electrical stimulation. If the electrode was adjacent to the septal area, in the caudate nucleus (rat 41) or the corpus callosum (rat 40), then the effect of stimulation appeared to be neutral. The time spent lever pressing was the same when the current was on (acquisition) as when it was off (extinction).

The pattern of behaviour of the rats with electrodes in the medial geniculate nucleus suggests that stimulation here was aversive. These rats required the least voltage to bring about behaviour, and once they had learned the effect of lever pressing they failed to press the lever at all when the current was on, but pressed it fairly enthusiastically when it was off.

Discussion

The study shows that there are some areas of the brain where electrical stimulation is reinforcing in the sense that an animal will stimulate itself in these

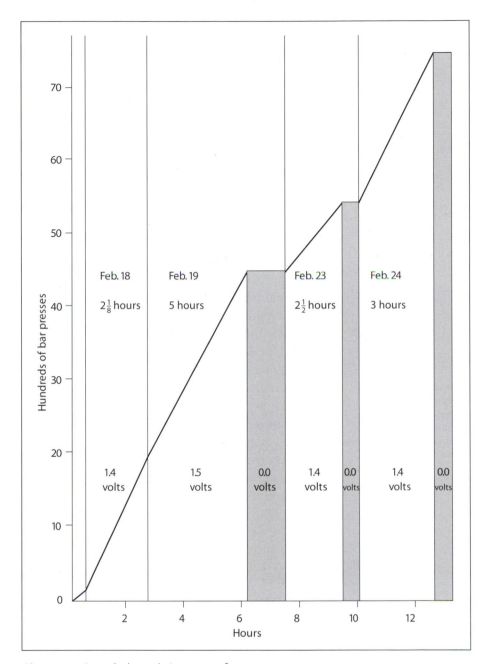

Figure 4.1 *Smoothed cumulative response for rat 34*

places frequently when given the opportunity. The area that produced the most consistent results was the septal area. One possible alternative explanation for the results is that the animals were in pain after their operation and the electrical stimulation provided pain relief. The authors discount this hypothesis by pointing out that the animals showed no other signs of discomfort and appeared to eat, drink and sleep normally. The study also shows that there are brain sites where stimulation will have the opposite effect and animals will try and avoid that stimulation.

This study by Olds and Milner is often described in terms of finding pleasure centres in the brain, though the authors never use these terms, preferring 'reinforcing structures' to describe the areas of the brain that affect behaviour in this way. Subsequent research has confirmed the presence of reinforcing structures in the brain, and stimulation of these areas has even been shown to interfere with normal behaviour. For example, mother rats have abandoned their young in order to press a lever for brain stimulation (see Kalat, 1992). A limited amount of work has also been conducted on humans, for example a 36-year-old woman with epilepsy received electrical stimulation to the right temporal lobe of her cortex. She described a pleasant tingling sensation on the left side of her body, said she enjoyed the sensation, giggled and began flirting with the psychologist (Delgardo, 1969).

It has been argued that the behaviour associated with self-stimulation of the brain is like the behaviour associated with addiction (Kalat, 1992). It might be that we develop repetitive behaviours (such as drug-taking or gambling) because they stimulate certain nervous pathways and certain reinforcing structures in the brain. The area of the brain that is commonly cited as the most reliable for bringing about self-stimulation is the medial forebrain bundle which is associated with pathways for the neurotransmitter dopamine. Dopamine levels can be increased by, among other things, the use of amphetamines or cocaine. There is, then, the potential for a partial explanation of reinforcement (and hence pleasure) in terms of brain structures and neurotransmitters (Concar, 1994). It is unlikely that this explanation will ever be complete, however, because how can you explain repetitive behaviours that have no obvious pleasurable (reinforcing) outcome, such as going to see your football team every week?

▶**dopamine** A neuro-transmitter. Neurotransmitters are chemicals that carry information from one nerve cell to another.

Questions

suggested answers ➤ p. 479

1. Make a list of the activities and experiences you find pleasurable (you know the sort of thing – raindrops on roses and whiskers on ... need we say more?).

2. What do your experiences of these things have in common?

3. Why do people need 'pleasure centres'?

4. Can you have too much pleasure?

5. How do you feel about what happened to the animals after testing?

Learning to be helpless

SELIGMAN, M.E.P. AND MAIER, S.F. (1967)

Failure to escape traumatic shock.

Journal of Experimental Psychology, 74, 1–9.

Introduction

We have all experienced feelings of helplessness at one time or other in our lives. The feelings are not pleasant. They are experienced when we are unable to control what happens to us, when whatever we do seems to have no effect on events. For most people this is a temporary state of affairs, associated perhaps with a mild bout of depression. But for some people feelings of helplessness persist, even when events are, in fact, potentially within their control.

Sometimes we clearly are unable to control events. In such cases our feelings of helplessness are grounded in some kind of reality. But at other times these feelings may be misguided. We may have the potential to exercise more control than we realize, but for one reason or another we fail to realize that potential.

One cause of this problem could be the phenomenon of learned helplessness. Consider the following scenario. You continually find yourself in situations where whatever you do seems to have no effect on what happens to you. Gradually your coping and problem-solving actions become extinguished, because if you learn that your actions have no important consequences for you, then you will stop bothering to act. So when you now encounter a situation in which you do have the potential to control events, you have long since lost the capability to exercise that control. You have learned to be helpless.

▶ **learned helplessness** The way that the experience of being forced into the role of passive victim in one situation can generalize to other situations, such that the person or animal makes no effort to help themselves in unpleasant situations even if such effort would be effective.

The study

That is the theory which Seligman and his colleague Maier set out to investigate in the simplified arena of the psychology laboratory. They wanted to see whether learned helplessness could be experimentally induced in laboratory dogs. The experiment had three conditions and involved two phases. In the first phase, some of the dogs (the 'escape' group and the 'yoked control' group) were placed, one at a time, in an apparatus which delivered electric shocks to them through their feet. Some of the animals (the escape group) were able to stop the shock by pressing a panel with their heads, but the others (the yoked control group) were unable to do anything to escape the shock. The dogs in the escape group successfully learned to terminate the shocks.

In Phase 2, all the dogs were placed in shuttle boxes. The shuttle boxes were divided into two by a barrier set at shoulder height to each dog. Electric shocks were delivered through the floor of the boxes, but if the dog jumped over the barrier into the other half of the box, it would break a photocell beam and the shock would be terminated. In other words, dogs in all the conditions could escape from the shock. Seligman and Maier predicted that the dogs in the yoked control condition would be less likely to learn to jump the barrier than dogs in the other conditions, because the dogs in the yoked control condition had learned helplessness in Phase 1.

▶ **control group** A group which is used for comparison with an experimental group.

▶ **yoked control** A yoked control experiences the same physical events as a member of the experimental condition, but whereas the experimental condition is able to influence these events, the yoked control is not.

Seligman and Maier's paper is a report of two experiments. This summary deals only with the first.

Subjects and design

Twenty-four 'experimentally naïve' mongrel dogs were used, eight in each condition. A standard independent-measures (between subjects) experimental design was used, with one experimental condition and two control conditions. The three conditions were labelled 'escape', 'normal control' and 'yoked control'. The comparison of most interest was between the 'escape' and 'yoked control' conditions.

Procedure

Escape condition: Phase 1 – Each dog in the escape condition was suspended in a hammock with four holes for its legs. Attached to its two hind legs were electrodes through which the electric shocks were delivered. The dog's head was held in position by panels on either side. If the dog pressed either panel with its head the shock was terminated. Each dog received 64 shocks of a 6.0 mA magnitude. The shocks were delivered at random time intervals which varied between 60 seconds and 120 seconds (the mean interval was 90 seconds). If the dog failed to press a panel during any given shock, that shock would be terminated after 30 seconds. Each shock counted as one trial.

Escape condition: Phase 2 – After 24 hours the escape condition dogs were subjected to ten trials in the shuttle box. Each trial began with the lights in the box being switched off (the neutral stimulus). After ten seconds a shock was delivered through the floor of the box (the unconditioned stimulus). The shock could be terminated if the dog jumped the barrier which divided the box into two parts. If the dog jumped the barrier after the neutral stimulus had occurred and before onset of the shock, the shock was not delivered. Through the process of classical conditioning the neutral stimulus was to become a conditioned stimulus which signalled the onset of a shock. The time taken to escape was measured from onset of the neutral/conditioned stimulus. If the dog failed to escape after 60 seconds the shock was terminated and the next trial was begun. Trials were separated by a mean interval of 90 seconds.

Yoked control condition: Phase 1 – The dogs in this condition were placed in the same hammock apparatus as the escape dogs. They were treated in exactly the same way except that they were unable to terminate any of the 64 electric shocks. Each shock was of the same duration as the mean length of shock for the equivalent trial in the escape condition. Since the dogs in the escape condition learned to terminate the shocks more and more rapidly as the trials progressed, the duration of each successive shock in the yoked control condition gradually diminished.

Yoked control condition: Phase 2 – After 24 hours the dogs in this condition were subjected to ten trials in the shuttle box. The procedure was exactly the

▶ **independent-measures design** When a study involves comparing the scores from two or more separate groups of people.

▶ **neutral stimulus** A stimulus that has no meaning for a person or animal before the onset of conditioning.

▶ **unconditioned stimulus** A stimulus which automatically, or reflexively produces a response.

▶ **classical conditioning** A form of learning which involves the pairing of a neutral stimulus with a reflex.

▶ **conditioned stimulus** A stimulus which only brings about a response because it has been associated with an unconditioned stimulus.

same as for Phase 2 of the escape condition. After seven days the dogs in this condition that failed to learn to escape were tested again in the shuttle box, once more following the same procedure.

Normal control condition: Phase 1 – The dogs in this condition did not take part in Phase 1. They just relaxed and prepared for the onset of Phase 2.

Normal control condition: Phase 2 – The dogs in the normal control condition were subjected to ten trials in the shuttle box, following the same procedure as in the other two conditions.

Results

▶ **dependent variable** The thing which is measured in an experiment, and which changes, depending on the independent variable.

Seligman and Maier present various measures of the dependent variable. Dogs in the yoked control condition (those who had been unable to terminate the shock in Phase 1 of the experiment) took 48.22 seconds on average to escape from the shocks, whereas the dogs in the other two conditions took less than 27 seconds on average to escape. These differences in escape times were statistically significant ($p < .05$, Duncan's multiple-range test). In addition, three-quarters of the dogs in the yoked control condition failed to escape on nine out of the ten trials, whereas only 12.5 per cent of dogs in the normal control condition, and no dogs in the escape condition failed this number of times. Overall, the dogs in the yoked control condition were more likely to fail to escape than the dogs in the other conditions ($p < .05$, Duncan's multiple-range test).

Discussion

The failure of the dogs in the yoked control condition to exercise their potential control over the electric shock suggests that the notion of learned helplessness has some validity. The experience of these dogs in the first phase, when they had no control over what happened to them, seemed to interfere with their ability to learn what was evidently a fairly straightforward escape response. Even dogs from this condition that did happen to jump the barrier during a trial 'reverted to "passively" accepting shock' (p. 4) on subsequent trials.

Animal experiments are a very controversial feature of psychological research. Quite apart from the idea of delivering electric shocks to animals, the reader of the original paper may be shocked to discover that one dog in the yoked control condition died 'during treatment'. And the language of the paper does not convey especially warm feelings for the animals ('Three dogs were *discarded* from the Escape group' (p. 2, emphasis added).

Having said this, the ethics of psychological and animal research is no straightforward matter. Learned helplessness can be argued to be an important feature of human experience, especially for those who are socially, economically and politically disadvantaged. It may be, for example, that learning to be helpless is related to the phenomenon of institutionalization, whereby people who have been in long-stay hospitals and residential units appear to lose their individuality and capacity for self-direction. The phenomenon might occur because people in institutions have a very limited ability to control their own lives. Whatever they do, however they are, their life is still pretty much determined by the routines and demands of the institution. Seligman and Maier's work (which of course extends beyond just one simple study reported here) may provide valuable insights into the nature of institutionalization which could contribute to our knowledge of how to combat and reverse the process.

suggested answers → P. 480

Questions

1. In Phase 1 the trials in the yoked control condition were carried out after the trials in the escape condition. Why?

2. What do you feel about the use of animals in the psychology laboratory?

3. Give some examples of situations in which people might learn to be helpless.

Bashing Bobo

BANDURA, A. ROSS, D. AND ROSS, S.A. (1961)

Transmission of aggression through imitation of aggressive models.

Journal of Abnormal and Social Psychology, 63, 575–82.

Introduction

This study looks at how aggressive behaviour develops in children. It has attracted a lot of attention from a number of academic disciplines and is still quoted in many texts despite its age. There are two social issues that the study addresses. First, is aggression an innate feature of our behaviour? And to look at one particular aspect of this issue, can we say that male aggression towards women is a feature of 'natural' male behaviour, or is it learned? These questions have a bearing on how we develop social policies to deal with aggressive behaviour. The second issue, which follows on from the first, is: if aggression is learned then how is it learned?

Bandura's approach is an extension of behaviourism and basically sees people as being moulded by their life experiences. It looks at how we are affected by the rewards and punishments that we experience every day. Bandura is a leading figure in Social Learning Theory, which attempts to extend the concepts used in operant and classical conditioning to explain complex human social behaviour. Key concepts in this approach are reinforcement and imitation.

The study

▶ **behaviour (also spelt 'behavior')** Anything a person (or animal) does that can be observed and measured by a third party. Behaviour can be thought of as the public side of human life, in contrast to 'experience' (thoughts and feelings) which can be thought of as the private side.

▶ **aggression** A term used in several ways, but generally to describe negative or hostile behaviour or feelings towards others.

In this study, Bandura set out to demonstrate that if children are passive witnesses to an aggressive display by an adult, they will imitate this aggressive behaviour when given the opportunity. More specifically, the study was guided by the following predictions:

- Subjects exposed to aggressive models will reproduce aggressive acts resembling those of the models.
- The observation of subdued non-aggressive models will have a generalized inhibiting effect on the subject's subsequent behaviour.
- Subjects will imitate the behaviour of a same-sex model to a greater degree than a model of the opposite sex.
- Boys will be more predisposed than girls towards imitating aggression (p. 575).

Subjects

In the study, 36 boys and 36 girls aged between 37 and 69 months were tested. The mean age was 52 months. One male adult and one female adult acted as role models.

Design

The study had three major conditions: a control group, a group exposed to an aggressive model, and a group exposed to a passive model. The children who were exposed to the adult models were further subdivided by their gender, and

part II

▶**behaviourism** A school of thought which holds that the observation and description of overt behaviour is all that is needed to comprehend the human being, and that manipulation of stimulus–response contingencies is all that is needed to change human behaviour.

▶**punishment** According to behaviourist theory: anything that decreases the probability that a behaviour will recur in similar circumstances. More popularly: an aversive stimulus.

▶**Social Learning Theory** The approach to understanding social behaviour which emphasizes how people imitate action and model their behaviour on that of others.

▶**classical conditioning** A form of learning which involves the pairing of a neutral stimulus with a reflex.

▶**reinforcement** Any consequence of any behaviour that increases the probability that that behaviour will recur in similar circumstances. The term is usually used of learned associations, acquired through operant conditioning, but it may also be applied to other forms of learning.

▶**control group** A group which is used for comparison with an experimental group.

▶**imitation** Copying someone else's behaviour and specific actions.

▶**independent variable** The conditions which an experimenter sets up, to cause an effect in an experiment. These vary systematically, so that the experimenter can draw conclusions about changes in outcomes.

by the gender of the model they were exposed to. In other words there were three independent variables. A summary of the groups is shown in Table 4.2.

Table 4.2 *Bandura's eight experimental groups*

Control groups – 24 subjects Eight experimental groups (each with 6 subjects) ■ Aggressive model condition – 24 subjects ■ Non-aggressive model condition – 24 subjects			
Aggressive model condition			
6 boys with same-sex model	6 boys with opposite sex-model	6 girls with same-sex model	6 girls with opposite sex-model
Non-aggressive model condition			
6 boys with same-sex model	6 boys with opposite sex-model	6 girls with same-sex model	6 girls with opposite sex-model

This is quite a complicated design that appears to cover a lot of different possibilities. However, the number of children in each group is quite small, and the results could be distorted if one group contained a few children who are normally quite aggressive. The researchers tried to reduce this problem by pre-testing the children and assessing their aggressiveness. They observed the children in the nursery and judged their aggressive behaviour on four 5-point rating scales. The rating scales were:

(a) physical aggression;
(b) verbal aggression;
(c) aggression towards inanimate objects;
(d) aggressive inhibition.

A composite score for each child was obtained by adding the results of the four ratings. It was then possible to match the children in each group so that they had similar levels of aggression in their everyday behaviour. The observers were the experimenter (female), a nursery school teacher (female), and the model for male aggression. The study reports that the first two observers 'were well acquainted with the children' (p. 576).

A disadvantage of using rating scales in this way is that different observers see different things when they view the same event. This might mean that the ratings will vary from one observer to another. To check the inter-coder reliability of the observations, 51 of the children were rated by two observers working independently and their ratings were compared. The high correlation that was achieved ($r = .89$) showed these observations to be highly reliable, suggesting that the observers were in close agreement about the behaviour of the children.

Procedure

The children were tested individually. In Stage 1 they were taken to the experimental room, which was set out for play. One corner was arranged as the child's play area, where there was a table and chair, potato prints and picture

part ii

▸ **inter-coder reliability** A phrase which describes the extent to which two independent observers (coders/raters) agree on the observations that they have made. Also known as inter-observer reliability and inter-rater reliability.

▸ **correlation** A measure of how strongly two or more variables are related to each other.

▸ **reliability** The reliability of a psychological measuring device (such as a test or a scale) is the extent to which it gives consistent measurements. The greater the consistency of measurement, the greater the tool's reliability.

stickers, which were all selected as having high interest for these children. The adult model was escorted to the opposite corner where there was a small table, chair, tinker toy, mallet and Bobo (a 5-ft inflatable doll). The experimenter then left the room.

In the non-aggressive condition, the model assembled the tinker toys in a quiet, subdued manner, ignoring Bobo. In the aggressive condition the model started to assemble the tinker toys, but after one minute turned to Bobo and was aggressive to the doll in a stylized and distinctive way. The aggression was both physical (for example 'raised the Bobo doll, picked up the mallet and struck the doll on the head', p. 576), and verbal (for example, 'Pow!', and 'Sock him in the nose', p. 576). After ten minutes the experimenter returned and took the child to another games room.

In Stage 2, the child was subjected to 'mild aggression arousal'. The child was taken to a room with attractive toys, but after starting to play with them the child was told that these were the experimenter's very best toys and she had decided to reserve them for the other children.

Then the child was taken to the next room for Stage 3 of the study. The experimenter stayed in the room because 'otherwise a number of children would either refuse to remain alone, or would leave before termination of the session'. In this room there was a variety of toys, both non-aggressive (three bears, crayons and so forth) and aggressive toys (for example, a mallet peg board, dart guns, and a 3-ft Bobo). The child was kept in this room for 20 minutes, and their behaviour was observed by judges through a one-way mirror. Observations were made at 5-second intervals, giving 240 response units for each child.

The observers recorded three measures of imitation in which they looked for responses from the child that were very similar to the display by the adult model:

(1) imitative for physical aggression;
(2) imitative verbal aggression;
(3) imitative non-aggressive verbal responses.

They also looked at two types of behaviour that were incomplete imitations of the adult model:

(1) mallet aggression;
(2) sits on Bobo.

In addition, they recorded three types of aggressive behaviour that were not imitations of the adult model:

(1) punches Bobo;
(2) non-imitative physical and verbal aggression;
(3) aggressive gun play.

By looking at the results we can consider which children imitated the models, which models they imitated, and whether they showed a general increase in aggressive behaviour rather than a specific imitation of the adult behaviours.

Results

The data are summarized in Table 4.3. They show that:

- The children who saw the aggressive model made more aggressive acts than the children who saw the non-aggressive model.
- Boys made more aggressive acts than girls.
- The boys in the aggressive conditions showed more aggression if the model was male than if the model was female.
- The girls in the aggressive conditions also showed more physical aggression if the model was male, but more verbal aggression if the model was female.
- The exception to this general pattern was the observation of how often they punched Bobo, and in this case the effects of gender were reversed.

Discussion

One of the issues commented on by Bandura *et al.* is the effect that the gender of the model had on the children. They noted that the aggression of the female model had a confusing effect on them. For example, one of the children said, 'Who is that lady? That's not the way for a lady to behave. Ladies are supposed to act like ladies ...' (p. 581), and another child said, 'You should have seen what that girl did in there. She was just acting like a man. I never saw a girl act like that before. She was punching and fighting but no swearing' (p. 581). On the other hand, the aggressive behaviour of the male model fitted more comfortably into a cultural stereotype of appropriate behaviour. For example, one boy said, 'Al's a good socker, he beat up Bobo. I want to sock like Al' (p. 581), and one of the girls said, 'That man is a strong fighter, he punched and punched and he could hit Bobo right down to the floor and if Bobo got up he said, "Punch your nose". He's a good fighter like Daddy' (p. 581).

If we look back at the questions we raised in the background section of this summary, then what can we learn from the study? First, is aggression innate? Like all examples of the nature–nurture debate, it is very hard to get clear evidence one way or the other. This study shows that aggressive behaviour can be learned, but it does not offer any evidence on the question of whether some features of aggression are also innate. On the issue of male violence, it is worth noting that the children in this study already had an expectation that men will behave more aggressively than women. This was shown by the children's comments.

The second question was how is aggression learned? Bandura believes that we can learn by being witnesses to the behaviour of others, and his study offers some support for this idea. If this is so, then it would suggest that the regular viewing of violent behaviour on television programmes would encourage the learning of violent behaviour in the viewer. A later variation of the experiment

▶ **nature–nurture debates** Fairly sterile theoretical debates, popular in the 1950s, concerning whether a given psychological ability was inherited or whether it was learned through experience.

Table 4.3   *Mean aggression scores for experimental and control subjects*

Response category	Experimental groups				Control group
	Aggressive		Non-aggressive		
	Female model	Male model	Female model	Male model	
Imitative physical aggression					
Female subjects	5.5	7.2	2.5	0.0	1.2
Male subjects	12.4	25.8	0.2	1.5	2.0
Imitative verbal aggression					
Female subjects	13.7	2.0	0.3	0.0	0.7
Male subjects	4.3	12.7	1.1	0.0	1.7
Mallet aggression					
Female subjects	17.2	18.7	0.5	0.5	13.1
Male subjects	15.5	28.8	18.7	6.7	13.5
Punches Bobo					
Female subjects	6.3	16.5	5.8	4.3	11.7
Male subjects	18.9	11.9	15.6	14.8	15.7
Non-imitative aggression					
Female subjects	21.3	8.4	7.2	1.4	6.1
Male subjects	16.2	36.7	26.1	22.3	24.6
Aggressive gun play					
Female subjects	1.8	4.5	2.6	2.5	3.7
Male subjects	7.3	15.9	8.9	16.7	14.3

Source: Bandura, Ross and Ross (1961).

(Bandura *et al.*, 1963) showed the children the violent behaviour on a video rather than in real life, and found they were still likely to imitate the aggressive behaviour towards the Bobo doll.

There are, however, a number of reasons why we should be cautious about making too many connections between this study and the everyday experience of children. For example, we have no evidence about any long-term effects of the study, and also, it is very uncommon for children to be in a situation where they are alone with strangers. Much of their experience will be with people they know who will give their opinions on whatever is going on.

Questions

1. How is aggression measured in this study?

2. How else could it be measured?

3. What are the three independent variables?

4. What ethical guidelines does Bandura appear to break?

suggested answers
→ p. 480

Monkey talk

GARDNER, R.A. AND,
GARDNER, B.T. (1969)

Teaching sign
language to a
chimpanzee.

Science,
165, 664–72.

Introduction

Can we talk to the animals? This is a delightful possibility and a number of researchers have attempted to go beyond simple commands like 'sit' and 'die for the Queen', and tried to create a dialogue with another species. The most likely animals for success are the primates, and in particular the chimpanzee. The early attempts, however, by Kellogg and Kellogg (1933), and by Hayes (1950), to teach chimps to talk failed to show any language ability in the animals. It appeared that apes do not have the equipment to speak, so further attempts were made to teach other sorts of language to them.

The results of these later studies have fascinated the scientific community and the public, but there has not been much agreement on what they tell us. According to Gardner and Gardner, 'the results of project Washoe presented the first serious challenge to the doctrine that only human beings have language.' Lenneberg (1967), on the other hand, writes, 'there is no evidence that any non-human form has the capacity to acquire even the most primitive stages of language development.'

Before we look at the study, it is important to distinguish between language and communication:

- *Language*: A small number of signals (sounds, letters, gestures) that by themselves are meaningless, but can be put together according to certain rules to make an infinite number of messages.
- *Communication*: The way in which one animal or person transmits information to another and influences them.

Everyone agrees that animals can communicate with each other; the disagreement is over whether they can use something similar to human language to do this.

The study

The failure of the early studies to encourage chimpanzees to use speech sounds led the Gardners to look for a different mode of communication. The expressive qualities of a chimpanzee's gestures suggested that sign language might be effective. They chose to use American Sign Language (ASL), which has its own rules of use and, like other foreign languages, does not directly translate into English. Some of the signs are iconic (look like the concept) and some of the signs are arbitrary (look nothing like the concept). In this study, they did not use the additional 'finger spelling' of human signers to deal with uncommon or technical terms, so they had to use the signs that were available (for example, they translated psychologist as 'think-doctor'). ASL is in common use, and the Gardners reasoned that they could compare the progress of their chimp with the progress of a deaf child born to deaf parents.

For practical reasons, it was not possible to take a chimp from birth, and it was estimated that Washoe (named after the home county of the University of Nevada) was between 8 and 14 months old when she arrived. Chimps are usually totally dependent until the age of two years, partially dependent until four, reach sexual maturity at eight and full adult maturity between 12 and 16 years. The young age of Washoe meant that little progress could be made for the first few months. The environment for Washoe was designed to provide the minimum of restriction and the maximum of social stimulation. A human helper was with Washoe throughout her waking hours, and all the helpers were fluent in ASL.

Chimpanzees are remarkable imitators, and in the early interaction, Washoe was encouraged to imitate the gestures of the humans. She would be rewarded for her efforts with tickles! Later in the programme, when Washoe made an incorrect sign or a badly formed sign, then she would be encouraged to imitate the correct one. However, if she was pressed too hard for the right sign, Washoe sometimes became diverted from the original task, or ran away, or went into a tantrum, or even bit the tutor.

An example of *delayed* imitation is described by the Gardners. For some time they had been insisting that Washoe use a toothbrush to clean her teeth after meals (what for, goodness only knows!). They would sign the command to brush her teeth, and although she clearly did not like the procedure, she would submit to it. Later, on a visit to the Gardners' home, Washoe explored the bathroom, climbed on the sink, looked at the toothbrushes and signed 'toothbrush'. The importance of this was that it was the first time she had made this sign, and there was no obvious motivation for making the sign other than simply to identify the object. It is unlikely that she wanted the toothbrush or that she wanted to brush her teeth.

One of the striking features of human language acquisition is the babbling stage, when the baby makes many of the sounds of its language, but in no meaningful way. In the early stages of 'Project Washoe', the chimp did not appear to babble but as the project went on she made more and more sign-like gestures without any real meaning (the Gardners called this 'manual babbling'). They encouraged this babbling with smiles and claps.

The researchers used operant techniques like shaping (see the study by Skinner earlier in this chapter) to introduce new signs into Washoe's vocabulary, though it is fair to say that operant training is not a part of language acquisition in children. After learning a new sign like 'open' in one particular context, Washoe was able to generalize the sign to new contexts.

To start with, the researchers kept full records of Washoe's signs, but this recording became difficult as her vocabulary increased. After 16 months they introduced a recording system where they recorded a new sign only after three different observers had observed Washoe make it spontaneously (with no prompts other than 'what is it?') and in an appropriate context. This sign was accepted as being in the vocabulary if it appeared at least once each day for 15 consecutive days. At the end of the 22nd month of the project, Washoe used 30 signs that met these stringent criteria.

▶ **imitation** Copying someone else's behaviour and specific actions.

▶ **shaping** The 'moulding' of behaviour by the method of successive approximations, or by the naturally occurring contingencies of reinforcement delivered by the environment.

The researchers describe how Washoe came to differentiate new signs. For example, when she first learned the sign for 'flower' she would use it in a number of contexts (like when she found a tobacco pouch) to indicate 'smell'. She was shaped to use the new sign of 'smell' for the appropriate context though the Gardners note that she still made a number of errors with these two signs.

The most important, and controversial, observations centred around the combinations of signs. Naming objects and actions is one thing, but human language puts words together in certain structures that create complex meanings. Could Washoe combine her signs to create a simple grammar? In this paper, the Gardners report that Washoe was just starting to combine signs into simple two-sign combinations.

Discussion

The Gardners established that signs are the appropriate medium for two-way communication with a chimpanzee. However, it is clear that there are very real differences between Washoe's communications and the language of children. Aitchison (1983) suggests ten features of language that distinguish it from communication, including:

(1) arbitrariness of the symbols (the symbol is not like the object or the action it is describing);

(2) semanticity (the use of symbols to mean objects or actions);

(3) displacement (refers to things that are distant in time and space);

(4) spontaneous usage;

(5) turn-taking;

(6) structure-dependence (the symbols can be combined according to the rules of grammar).

Although Washoe used arbitrary symbols, and showed semanticity, the other features were far less evident in her signs.

One set of criticisms of the study came from one of the signers that the Gardners used to communicate with Washoe. This signer was a deaf person who used ASL as their main form of communication. They reported:

> Every time the chimp made a sign, we were supposed to write it down in the log. ... They were always complaining because my log didn't show enough signs.
>
> All the hearing people turned in logs with long lists of signs. They always saw more signs than I did. ...
>
> The hearing people were logging every movement the chimp made as a sign. Every time the chimp put his finger in his mouth, they'd say 'Oh, he's making the sign for DRINK,' ... When the chimp scratched himself, they'd record it as the sign for SCRATCH. ... When [the chimps] want something, they reach.

Sometimes [the trainers] would say, 'Oh, amazing, look at that, it's exactly like the ASL sign for GIVE!' It wasn't. (cited in Pinker, 1994, p. 337–8)

Another study, of a similar nature, was carried out by Terrace (1979) on a chimpanzee called Nim Chimpsky (named after the US linguistics expert, Noam Chomsky, who was very unimpressed by Washoe's performance). Terrace recorded, on tape, over 20,000 communications from Nim during a two-year period. When the data were analysed, a disappointed Terrace found some striking differences between Nim's communication and child language. First, there was no increase in the length of Nim's communications, whereas children show a steady increase in sentence length with age. Second, only 12 per cent of Nim's communications were spontaneous (the rest were prompted by the teacher), whereas children initiate more communications than they respond to. Third, the amount of imitation increased with Nim, whereas with children it declines as language develops. Fourth, and perhaps most important, Nim made frequent interruptions and did not seem to learn to take turns in communication, in stark contrast to the turn-taking skills of children.

The overall conclusion seems to be that it is possible to initiate simple communication with chimpanzees and to encourage them to use a number of signs to communicate a range of concepts. They do not, however, learn language in the same way that children do, and it seems unlikely that they ever will. As Noam Chomsky wrote 'It is about as likely that an ape will prove to have language ability as that there is an island somewhere with a species of flightless birds waiting for human beings to teach them how to fly' (cited in Terrace, 1979).

Questions

suggested answers
→ p. 480

1. Describe some examples of animal communication. How do these communications differ from human language?

2. Describe some forms of human communication that do not use language.

3. What are the strengths and weaknesses of the Gardners' case-study method of collecting information?

4. What do you think are the main difficulties in recording sign language in a chimp?

5. People usually do not interrupt each other in conversation. How do they know when to speak and when to be silent?

6. Try to invent an appropriate sign for 'psychologist'.

chapter **5**

COMPARATIVE
PSYCHOLOGY

▶ **ethology** The study of behaviour in the natural environment.

▶ **evolution** The development of bodily form and behaviour through the process of natural selection.

▶ **pecking order** A hierarchy first observed in chickens where the most dominant animal has preferential access to food, mating, videos etc.

THE first two papers in this chapter are in the ethological tradition of comparative psychology. Ethology is the study of animal behaviour in its natural habitat. The modern discipline of ethology dates from the early 1920s, and the concerns of that time still set the agenda for modern studies. The key questions of ethology are:

(a) What is the immediate cause of a behaviour?

(b) How has that behaviour developed in the lifetime of the animal?

(c) What is the function of behaviour (how does it enhance the survival of the animal)?

(d) Why is the function dealt with in this way?

So, ethologists look at behaviour from an evolutionary perspective which sees animals being designed by their ability to survive. Some body adjustments and some behaviour will make the individual more adapted to the local environment, and therefore more likely to mate and pass on their genes. Everything has a cause, and that cause is survival.

Ethologists have looked at a range of species and developed a number of concepts, some of which have drifted into everyday speech. One of the early concepts to develop centred around the stereotyped behaviour of animals in certain situations. The idea of the Fixed Action Pattern (FAP) describes the relatively fixed way that an animal will approach a particular task. The paper by Tinbergen (1952) describes the FAP of the stickleback when mating. Studies like this have been able to describe the FAPs of various animals and the simple signs or signals (sign stimuli) that precede these behaviours.

Another concern of the ethologists has been dominance hierarchies or pecking orders. Some animals show a social structure where some members of a group have prior access to resources. Sometimes it is food, sometimes it is mating. The hierarchy helps to maintain order in the group by reducing the number of conflict situations, and also helps to share out the available resources in such a way that the survival of the group is protected at the expense of the weaker (or unluckier) individuals. In this chapter, the study by Rawlins (1979) looks at the development of social behaviour in a monkey troop over a number of years. Although the environment is artificially constructed, it still provides one of the clearest accounts of monkey behaviour 'in the wild'.

The third study moves away from an ethological perspective, into the laboratory. Calhoun (1962) describes the behaviour of rats in a restricted laboratory environment, and looks at the development of social behaviour. It has been extensively quoted in discussions on the dangers of high-density living. Elsewhere in this text are two other papers on comparative psychology based on laboratory work. The study in Chapter 10 by Harlow (1959) describes his work on attachment with rhesus monkeys. The study by Rosenthal and Fode (1963; see Chapter 18) provides a remarkable demonstration of the experimenter effect, where the expectations of the person conducting the experiment can have an unintentional influence on the outcome of the study, even when the subjects of the study are laboratory rats!

Finally there is a summary of a study by Alexander and Hines (2002) that is embedded firmly in the traditions of evolutionary psychology. Evolutionary psychology seeks to explain behaviour (most importantly, human behaviour) by examining its evolutionary significance. It starts from the point of view that behaviours that people exhibit today relate to behaviours that evolved in humans for a reason – that is, to behaviours that have had an evolutionary function in the development of the human species in terms of its adaptations to its environments. Alexander and Hines take an observation about contemporary human behaviour (female–male differences in children's toy preferences) and subject it to the critical scrutiny of an evolutionary perspective.

There are two important issues to consider before looking at the studies. The first is anthropomorphism, which is the tendency to see human characteristics in the behaviour of animals. So some people might describe a dog as being 'brave' or a lemming as 'committing suicide'. The problem with the use of these human terms is that in people they imply a choice behaviour. Behaviour is brave when a person knows the possible dangerous consequences of their behaviour but continues with it regardless. Does a dog make this evaluation? Suicide is a choice to finish your own life, yet no one could suggest that lemmings wake up one morning and consider the possible alternatives before deciding their lives are futile and ending it all. Anthropomorphism is a danger when studying animals, and some of the studies in this book are guilty of attributing some human characteristics to their animal subjects.

The second issue to consider is Lloyd Morgan's canon. This refers to the different ways that we can explain animal behaviour. For example, if we see a cat getting out of Thorndike's puzzle box (described in the introduction to Chapter 4) we might think that it had an understanding of the mechanism of the box and 'knew' how to get out. Alternatively, it might just have learned which behaviours will be followed by its release. The first explanation presumes that the cat has some complex thought processes; the latter does not. Lloyd Morgan suggested that descriptions of animal behaviour should always use the lowest level of explanation possible, and we should not presume that animals have complex mental processes unless we are unable to explain their behaviour in any other way.

▶ **experimenter effects**
Unwanted influences in a psychological study which are produced, consciously or unconsciously, by the person carrying out the study.

▶ **anthropomorphism**
Attribution of human characteristics to animals.

The colony of monkeys

RAWLINS, R. (1979)

Forty years of rhesus research.

New Scientist, 82, 108–10.

Introduction

Ethology is the study of animals in their natural habitat. This would seem to be the most obvious place to investigate animal behaviour, but much of the early work on animals was carried out in laboratories. In fact, a lot of psychological research was conducted using specially bred strains of animals, usually rats, which would not be able to survive in their natural habitat. This study of artificially created animals in artificial environments gained a strange prominence in psychology for a number of years. The advantages of this sort of work are the high levels of control that are possible, and the ease and cost of the work. The disadvantages are more obvious.

The study of animals in their natural habitat, on the other hand, is difficult, costly and time consuming. Look at it this way, would you find it easier to work in a laboratory all day and go home in the evening, or spend six months in the middle of a rain forest trying to catch up with a troop of primates who hide from you and throw fruit at you?

It is only in the last 40 years that ethological studies have been able to provide us with much detailed information about the behaviour of animals. Remarkably, our knowledge about the behaviour of primates is still relatively light, though the article by Rawlins presents the evidence from a fascinating longitudinal study.

▶ **ethology** The study of behaviour in the natural environment.

The study

The small island of Cayo Santiago lies one mile off the coast of Puerto Rico in the Caribbean. A number of US academic institutions wanted a supply of primates for research, so it was decided to create a primate colony on Cayo Santiago. At the start of 1939, a total of 450 rhesus monkeys (captured in India) and 14 gibbons (captured in South East Asia) were released onto the island, having first been screened for tuberculosis, and marked with an identifying tattoo.

The first 18 months marked a period of adjustment. After a lot of fighting in which many of the monkeys died, a social organization developed and six social groups emerged. The gibbons did not fare so well. They competed with the rhesus monkeys for food and living space, and attacked people and monkeys. Eventually they were recaptured and sold. Once the gibbons had been removed, the researchers decided to concentrate on the rhesus monkeys and no further animals were added.

Two scientists, Carpenter and Tomlin, studied the monkeys and noted who made up the groups, how they behaved, what kind of hierarchies existed in the groups, and how they moved around the island. Other scientists studied mating, menstrual cycles and haematology.

During the Second World War (1939–45) this research was seen as non-essential, and so supplies were difficult to obtain. Over 450 animals were removed from the island for research on disease, and by 1944 only 200 monkeys were left. For the next ten years the island was mainly used as a resource of animals for medical research, but in 1956 a regular census was reintroduced, and a good record exists of the social organization of the monkeys from that time up to the present day. However, the haphazard selection of monkeys for research continued, and this made the study of social organization difficult since the social order of the troops was constantly being disrupted.

This changed in 1970 when the new scientist in charge ensured that the four main remaining social groups were left intact, and the research monkeys were taken from the rest of the population. This facilitated the start of long-term studies into social development in monkey troops. The island was attractive to researchers because of the ease of access from the major research institutions, the ease of getting around the island and the high visibility of the monkeys. However, the environment was not entirely natural to the monkeys and they had to be provided with food.

The social organization in 1979

In 1956, when the census was reintroduced, there were 150 animals in two groups, and in 1979 (when the paper was written) there were 610 monkeys living on the now reforested island.

The animals were divided into six social groups, ranging in size from 53 to 139 animals. A further six males were living a solitary existence. The monkeys were trapped once every year to tattoo new animals and take blood samples. The maternal line (who is the mother to each monkey) was known, though the paternal line could not even be guessed at because of the multiple matings of the females.

The daily activity of the animals has a clear rhythm. In the cool of the day, at first light, the animals look for food. During the heat they rest and groom each other, and as the heat subsides in the afternoon they feed and play before going up the trees to sleep at sunset. The grooming appears to have both a health function and a social function, and the observation of this activity, particularly who is grooming whom, gives some insight into the social structure of the troop.

▶ **matriline** A family tree based on the female line: that is, mothers, grandmothers, etc.

Each group is made up of a number of adult males and between two and four matrilines. The matrilines consist of an adult female, her adult daughters and all their juvenile offspring. Males leave the troop they were born in when they mature at around three to four years, but the females remain. The adult males sometimes move on to another troop, but they never return to the troop they were born into. The movement of the males reduces the chances of inbreeding.

In each troop the males and females have separate hierarchies. The hierarchies affect the access to food and grooming partners, and also limit the aggression in the troop. The animals have a developed system of signals for dominance, threat, defeat and subordinance, and these signals are part of the system for controlling aggression. The position of each individual in the hierarchies is established by fighting, but after the fight the position remains fixed for a considerable period of time. In general, the older males hold the highest positions in the hierarchy. Each matriline has a group rank, and all members of the top matriline appear to outrank all members of the other matrilines. Within the matriline the dominant individual is the mother. As the juvenile females reach puberty they immediately rise in status above their older sisters. This means that the mother is at the top of the hierarchy, followed by the youngest mature daughters. Young males take the rank of their mother until they leave the troop, when they have to establish themselves from scratch in the new troop (see Figure 5.1 for an outline of how the troops developed).

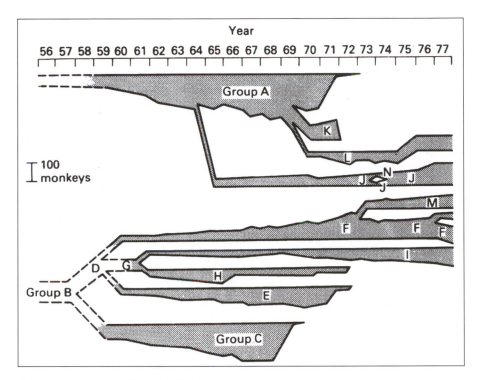

Figure 5.1   *A summary history of all the social groups*

The same general social structure can be observed in all six troops on the island, but there are considerable differences in the amount of friendship and fighting within each troop.

Discussion

The study of animal behaviour is valuable in its own right. There is always a pressure, however, to consider what parts of the study can be applied to human behaviour. In this case it must be noted that rhesus monkeys are not our closest 'relatives'. The primates that have the greatest biological similarity to people are chimps and gorillas, and these animals have very contrasting patterns of social organization. It is dangerous, then, to attempt any extrapolation to the social organization of people.

► **anthropomorphism**
Attribution of human
characteristics to animals.

Whenever we consider animals there is always some bias towards anthropomorphism. It is, however, very difficult to write about animal behaviour without making some reference to human behaviour and experience. The problem is how to prevent the inadequacies of language from obscuring the differences between people and animals. In this study, the struggle for dominance and the development of hierarchies seems to have a similarity to the behaviour of some people. However, the main difference is that people can choose their lifestyles (up to a point), and have created a wide range of different types of social organization. The connection of these social organizations to the behaviour of the monkeys on Cayo Santiago is, therefore, very limited.

Questions

suggested
answers
➤ p. 481

1. Identify some advantages and disadvantages of the longitudinal approach used in this study.

2. How could the researchers assess the dominance of a particular monkey?

3. In the original article, Rawlins writes 'it is the males who stir the genetic pot' (p. 110). What does this mean? And how do they do it?

4. What do you think are the important differences between Cayo Santiago and the natural environment of the rhesus monkeys?

5. What effects do you think these differences have on the behaviour of the rhesus monkeys?

A fishy tale

TINBERGEN, N. (1952)

The curious behaviour of the stickleback.

Scientific American,
187, 22–6.

▶ **evolution** The development of bodily form and behaviour through the process of natural selection.

▶ **pecking order** A hierarchy first observed in chickens where the most dominant animal has preferential access to food, mating, videos etc.

Introduction

Before the emergence of the theory of evolution, people believed that there was a clear distinction between human beings and animals. It was believed that the wonders of animal behaviour were due to instinct, and that it was the gift of reason that made human beings unique. The theory of evolution challenged this distinction and forced people to review their studies of both human beings and animals. It was no longer enough just to describe animal behaviour as instinctive, and a need developed to explore how animals behave in the way they do, and why.

The careful observation of different species led to the discovery of various social processes. For example, the Norwegian psychologist Schjelderup-Ebbe (1922, cited in Hayes, 1994, p. 897) described the pecking behaviour of chickens, and was able to demonstrate that they have a rigid hierarchy that was indicated by who pecked whom, and how often. The most dominant bird pecked all other birds. The next most dominant bird pecked all birds except the most dominant bird and, in turn, was pecked only by the most dominant bird. This pecking order has been observed in a number of other species, and various attempts have been made to apply the concept to human social behaviour.

There are a number of problems with the observation of animals, including practical ones of access. Tinbergen made the unlikely choice of the stickleback for study because it is small, relatively tame and does not react adversely to handling, probably because it depends on its spines for protection. It also displays some dramatic and intriguing behaviours. It was also the first creature he studied while at school.

If you are interested in the work of Niko Tinbergen (1907–88) then you could start by looking at his page on the Nobel Prize site, which gives a brief account of his life and interests.[1] He won the Nobel Prize for 'discoveries concerning organization and elicitation of individual and social behaviour patterns' in 1973 along with Konrad Lorenz and Karl von Frisch. The remarkable collaboration was interrupted by the Second World War, in which they were on different sides. Tinbergen was Dutch and spent much of the war as a hostage in a prison camp. Lorenz on the other hand was conscripted into the German army and spent some time in a Russian prison camp. The remarkable aspect of the collaboration was Lorenz's endorsement of the German Nazi Party and his scientific justification for what we now call ethnic cleansing. Tinbergen clearly did not share these views and it is testament to his humanity that he could look past this after the war and renew his collaborative work with Lorenz.

---

1. http://nobelprize.org/nobel_prizes/medicine/laureates/1973/tinbergen-autobio.html

The study

This study concentrates on the courtship and reproductive behaviour of the stickleback. In their natural habitat, the fish mate early in spring in shallow fresh waters. The mating cycle has a particular ritual which can be observed in the tank as well as the natural habitat:

▶ **territory** The space that is defended by a person or animal.

- The male leaves the school and creates a territory for itself from which it will drive any intruder, either male or female.
- The male builds a nest, digging a small pit in the sand, filling it with weeds, and boring a tunnel through it.
- The male then changes colour, from grey, to a bright red underside and a blueish-white top.
- The females have, meanwhile, changed shape and become bulky with 50 to 100 eggs.
- The male courts any approaching female with a zig-zag motion – the 'dance' continues until the female responds and swims towards the male with a 'head-up' posture.

IN THE FIRST STAGE of courtship the male stickleback (*left*) zigzags toward the female (*right*). The female then swims toward him with her head up. The abdomen of the female bulges with from 50 to 100 eggs

IN THE SECOND STAGE, seen from above, the male stickleback swims toward the nest he has built and makes a series of thrusts into it with his snout. He also turns on his side and raises his dorsal spines toward the female.

Figure 5.2 *The stages of mating in the stickleback*

- The male then swims towards the nest and the female follows.
- At the nest he makes a series of rapid thrust with his snout into the entrance.
- The female enters the nest – nose out one end, and tail out of the other.
- The male prods her tail with rhythmic thrusts and she lays her eggs; she then leaves the nest and the male swims in to fertilize the eggs.
- The whole ritual takes about one minute (see Figure 5.2).

The male may escort as many as five females through the nest and fertilize their eggs. Then his colour reverts to normal (as the mating drive declines) and he starts to drive away all other sticklebacks, including the females. The male guards the nest from predators and 'fans' the water over the nest to enrich the supply of oxygen to the eggs. The more developed the eggs become, the more oxygen they need and the longer the male spends each day ventilating them. After they hatch, the male keeps them together for a day before they become independent.

Tinbergen and his associates carried out a number of studies on this

IN THE THIRD STAGE, also seen from above, the female swims into the nest. The male then prods the base of her tail and causes her to lay her eggs. When the female leaves the nest, the male enters and fertilizes the eggs.

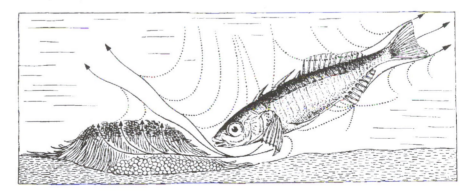

IN THE FOURTH STAGE the male 'fans' water over the eggs to enrich their oxygen supply. The dotted lines show the movement of a coloured solution placed in the tank: the solid lines, the direction of the water currents.

Source: Tinbergen (1952)

behaviour. They had noticed that the courting male would respond aggressively to red-coloured fish, and had even been observed to react aggressively when a red mail-van passed the window some 100 metres away. The team built some models of sticklebacks and painted them red, pale silver or green. They put them on wires, placed them in the tank and found that the fish would respond with some aggression to the green and silver models, but would respond most aggressively to the red models. They carried out similar studies to investigate the effects of shape, size and type of body movement on the rituals of the stickleback behaviour. Among the observations was that a female stickleback will follow a red model wherever it goes, and will attempt to enter a non-existent nest if the model is poked into the sand. Tinbergen concluded that the stickleback responds to sign stimuli – a few characteristics of an object rather than to the object as a whole. However, they would only respond when they were in the breeding season, and the sign stimuli had no effect at other times.

The researchers carried out a series of manipulations, including filling the sandpit of the male repeatedly, and castrating the male. In the case of the sandpit, the male kept re-digging the pit for a while but then continued with the nest building regardless of the missing pit. With castration, the first phase of courtship was left out of the ritual, but if the eunuch male was given a nest of eggs then it would vigorously fan it. This suggests a complex relationship between the internal drives to mate, and external sign stimuli.

When the male becomes territorial it becomes hostile to other sticklebacks, though very little fighting is observed. When two males meet at the border of their territories, they begin a series of attacks and retreats. Each takes the offensive in its own territory and the conflict see-saws back and forth. Neither fish touches the other, but they dart back and forth 'as though attached by an invisible thread' (p. 24). If the fighting becomes more intense, the fish become vertical and make jerky movements.

Tinbergen observed that when the fish were in a crowded tank where the territories were small and the fighting intense, then both fish began to dig in the sand. This behaviour appears to be irrelevant to the fight and seems to challenge the connection between sign stimuli and behaviour. However, other species display incongruous behaviour, and it may be that the animal is showing displacement activity – enabling it to release tension through an otherwise irrelevant action.

The theory of displacement was tested in a further experiment. A red model was placed in the male's territory, and when the male attacked it, the model was moved to hit the male. The fish retreated to the weeds, and when it returned it approached the model, and then adopted the vertical position. Tinbergen suggested that the escape drive and the attack drive are balanced, so the fish needs some displacement activity to resolve the conflict.

Discussion

Tinbergen asks the question about the usefulness of studying one animal in such detail. He points out some of the dangers but suggests that 'the many

▶ **territoriality** The name given to a set of behaviours which involve establishing and maintaining access to a particular area while refusing the same to potential competitors of one's own species.

▶ **displacement activity** Behaviour that is a substitute for the desired behaviour, for example, stroking the pet of someone you are attracted to.

years of work on sticklebacks, tedious as much of it has been, has been highly rewarding' (p. 26). The rewards include the observation of the sign stimuli, the discovery of the displacement activity and the observations of the interaction between internal drives and external signs. Tinbergen goes on to suggest that this interaction is likely to be a feature of mammal, and even human behaviour.

The strength of the work is in the detail of the observations and the identification of the various signs that stimulate ritualized behaviour. It is clear that the development of ritualized behaviour has survival value for species. What is less clear is how far we can extrapolate the ideas of sign stimuli, displacement activity, courtship, and territory to human behaviour.

Questions

suggested answers → p. 481

1. What methods does Tinbergen combine in this series of studies?

2. What sign stimuli does he identify in this study?

3. Suggest some examples of sign stimuli for people – simple signs that provoke stereotyped behaviour.

4. What are the differences between territorial behaviour in the stickleback and territorial behaviour in people?

5. Suggest some examples of displacement activity in people.

Rat City:
the behavioural sink

CALHOUN, J.B. (1962)

Population density
and social pathology.

Scientific American,
206, 139–48.

Introduction

If rabbits 'breed like rabbits', why isn't the world over-run with rabbits? It seems that, when left undis-turbed by human interference, animals manage to balance the size of their population to fit the environment they are living in. But what would happen to the behaviour of animals if the population increased in a restricted space?

The study of animal behaviour shows that most species have developed structures of social behaviour that enhance the survival value of the species. In some species which are fiercely territorial, such as the robin, there are rituals of behaviour that space out the territories of the birds to allow each territory an adequate food supply, and also prevent serious conflict between the individu-als. In other species that are more social, there are social structures that limit the size of each group.

Calhoun was interested to investigate what would happen if the environment was structured so that the animals could not disperse in their usual way.

The study

▶ **territoriality** The name given to a set of behaviours which involve establishing and maintaining access to a particular area while refusing the same to potential competitors of one's own species.

Six populations of laboratory rats (the domesticated white albino Norway rat) were studied in two series of three populations each. In the first series, each population began with 32 rats, and in the second series each population began with 56 rats. In all cases the rats were just past weaning and were equally divided between males and females. By the 12th month, all the populations had multiplied to the size of 80 adults, and after this the researchers removed the infants that survived birth and weaning in order to keep the populations steady.

The rats were placed in groups of equal size in each of the four pens that made up the apparatus. As shown in Figure 5.3, the apparatus was in the form of a square, but the separation of the pens by an electric fence, and the use of small bridges to move between them, effectively turned the environment into a row of four pens, with two end pens (with only one entrance) and two middle pens. The whole apparatus was 10 foot by 14 foot. The pens were complete living units and each one contained a drinking fountain, a food hop-per, and an elevated artificial burrow reached by a winding staircase. Calhoun estimated that each pen could comfortably hold 12 rats, which is the size of groups in which they are usually found. When the population reached 80 in the apparatus, then each pen would be likely to have 20 rats if they spread themselves out evenly (see Figure 5.3).

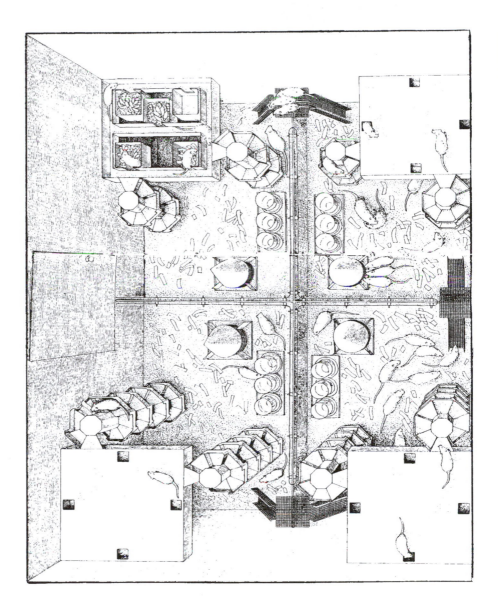

Figure 5.3 *Effect of population density on behaviour*[1]

Source: Calhoun (1962).

1. *Figure 5.3. Description* The effect of population density on the behaviour and social organization of rats was studied by confining groups of 80 animals in a 10 x 14 ft room divided into four pens by an electrified fence. All pens (numbered 1, 2, 3 and 4 clockwise from the door) were complete dwelling units. Conical objects are food hoppers; trays with three bottles are drinking troughs. Elevated burrows, reached by winding staircases, each had five nest boxes, seen in Pen 1, where top of burrow has been removed. Ramps connected all pens but 1 and 4. Rats therefore tended to concentrate in pens 2 and 3. Development of a 'behavioural sink', which further increased population in one pen, is reflected in Pen 2, where three rats are eating simultaneously. Rat approaching ramp in Pen 3 is an estrous female pursued by a pack of males. In Pens 2 and 3, where population density was highest, males outnumbered females. In Pens 1 and 4, a dominant male was usually able to expel all other males and possess a harem of females. Dominant males are sleeping at the base of the ramps in pens 1 and 4. They wake when other males approach, preventing incursions into their territories. The three rats peering down from a ramp are probers, one of the deviant behavioural types produced by the pressures of a high population density.

Results

Calhoun expected that sleeping groups would develop with around 13 to 27 in each. In fact, during the 10th to 12th months, when they looked at 100 sleeping groups, only 37 fell in this range. Thirty-three groups had fewer than 13 rats and 30 had more than 27. Only in the groups of expected size was the sex ratio equal. The smaller groups were most commonly made up of six females and two males, and the larger groups tended to be male dominated. The females distributed themselves equally over the four pens but the males were concentrated in the two middle pens.

The major cause of this concentration of males was the dominance fighting that created social hierarchies. These fights took place in all four pens, but in the two end pens it was possible for one male to take over the whole pen as his territory. Once dominance had been established, the male slept at the bottom of the ladder of the one entrance to the end pen. From this position he was able to keep all other males out, while allowing free access to females.

The account by Calhoun is very anthropomorphic in parts; for example, writing about the male rats in the end pens he says:

> he would sleep calmly through all the comings and goings of his *harem*; seemingly he did not even hear their *clatterings* up and down the wire ramp. His conduct during his waking hours reflected his dominant status. He would move about in a *casual and deliberate* fashion, occasionally inspecting the burrow and nest of his harem. (p. 143, emphasis added)

There were some other males in the end pens, but they were subordinate, remained hidden in the burrows most of the time and never attempted sexual activity with the females. Interestingly, when they did come out, they attempted to mount the dominant male who did not reject the advances.

In the end pens, the population was lowest and the mortality rate among the females and the infants was also low. The females built nests for the young and nursed them effectively. Half the infants born in these pens survived. The young in the middle pens did not fare so well; in the first series, 96 per cent died before weaning, and in the second series 80 per cent died before weaning. Females in the middle pens became progressively less effective at building nests and nursing their young, eventually failing to even attempt nest building. Infants were abandoned on the floor of the pen, where they died and were eaten by the adults. Females who lived in the middle pens received excessive attention from the males when they came into oestrus.

The social organization in the middle pens showed some large changes from the behaviour that is normally observed. Some distinct patterns emerged in the male behaviour, and Calhoun described how four types of male emerged:

(1) *Aggressive dominant males*: In every group of 12 or more males, one was the most aggressive and the most common victor in fights. However, this

▶ **anthropomorphism** Attribution of human characteristics to animals.

▶ **harem** Literally, a domestic arrangement where a powerful man uses his influence and wealth to have exclusive sexual access to a number of women; commonly (and incorrectly) used to describe the social organization of animals where a male mates with more than one female, who in turn only mate with that male.

rat was periodically ousted from his position, and a new rat emerged as the dominant animal. These rats were 'the most normal in our population' (p. 145), though even these were occasionally prone to bursts of attacking females and young.

(2) *Homosexual males*: Calhoun calls this group homosexual, though in fact they were just very sexually active, and would try and mount males, females not in oestrus, juveniles, and anything on four legs that squeaked. These animals rarely battled for status.

(3) *Passives*: These animals 'moved through the community like somnambulists [sleep walkers]' (p. 145). They ignored all the other rats of both sexes and all the rats ignored them. They did not even make advances to female rats in oestrus. They looked the healthiest because they were fat, sleek and did not have any scars or missing fur from fighting, 'but their social disorientation was nearly complete' (p. 145).

(4) *Probers*: These rats were hyperactive and hypersexual, though much more discriminating than the 'homosexual' rats. In time, many of them became cannibalistic.

Discussion

This is one of those studies in psychology that is commonly misreported. It is often claimed that the animals were left to breed at will (when in fact after the size reached 80 the young were removed), and that all the populations died out (when in fact they did not). In the study Calhoun claims that 'the evidence indicates that in time failures of reproductive function would have caused the colonies to die out' (p.139), but it is not clear what he bases this on, since as the size of the population decreased the pressure on space would have declined and the social organization might have returned to normal. Also, in his original observation of wild rats restricted in an enclosure of a quarter of an acre, the population grew to 150 and then remained stable.

It is very tempting to make connections between the breakdown in social organization of the rats in this environment, and the social problems of life in the city. However, there are some very real distinctions to be drawn. For example, human beings do not have species-specific patterns of 'nest-building' and child-rearing. Different cultures live in different domestic arrangements, some in fixed homes, others are nomadic. Childcare practices are varied and affected by cultural norms and changing fashions. In short we must be very careful when we try to extrapolate from a study like this to human behaviour.

Calhoun also carried out similar studies on crowding and found that rat populations stabilized at a certain number and that the rats commonly organized themselves into groups of around 12 individuals. This raises the question of whether each species has its own optimum group size. This brings us to Dunbar's Number which estimates the optimum group size. Dunbar (1993) suggests that there is a 'cognitive limit to the number of individuals with whom any one person can maintain stable relationships' and that this limit is related to the processing capacity in the brain. In other words, the bigger the brain the bigger the social group. He looked at social group size in a range of primate species and, by comparing this with their processing capacity, he was able to derive the optimum social group size for humans, and that number is 150. This number has been popularized and applied to business environments (for example, Gladwell, 2002) and to the study of Internet communities.

suggested answers
→ p. 482

Questions

1. What controls are used in this study?

2. What problems are there with the design of the study?

3. What is the problem with referring to one group of rats as homosexual? Why do you think Calhoun chose to use this term?

4. If you were writing an article for a newspaper about the problems of inner-city life, how could you use the findings of this study?

5. Give some examples of anthropomorphism from the text.

Just monkeying around

ALEXANDER, G.M. AND
HINES, M. (2002)

Sex differences
in response to
children's toys
in nonhuman
primates.

Evolution and
Human Behavior,
23, 467–79.

Introduction

If you were asked to explain why more girls than boys preferred to play with dolls, and why more boys than girls preferred to play with trucks, you would probably say that children are brought up in that way – not necessarily as a direct result of what parents do, but because of wider cultural norms and values that shape our gender identity. In other words you would probably argue that girls and boys, through socialization, quickly and robustly learn to prefer things that girls and boys are 'meant' to prefer. And you may very well be right.

But challenging received wisdom is one of the things that good psychological research can do. The exploration of alternative explanations for things that we think are already well explained is one of its most important roles. If nothing else, it encourages critical reflection and a healthy, questioning approach to the world around us.

The study

▶ **sex differences** A large body of psychological research exists which aims to document psychological differences between females and males.

The researchers who conducted this study set out to discover whether factors other than socialization could account for observed sex differences in toy preference. Specifically they were interested to discover whether more biological/evolutionary forces might be at work. To this end they observed the spontaneous behaviour of captive vervet monkeys when different toys were placed in their enclosure. Their reasoning was that other species are not subject to the same gendered socialization processes as humans. So if socialization is the only reason for sex differences in toy preference in children, they should not be able to observe any differences in the behaviour of male and female vervet monkeys towards toys with varying levels of gendered associations.

Subjects and materials

The animal subjects were 44 female and 44 male vervet monkeys from seven captive social groups housed in different enclosures at a US animal laboratory. The monkeys had distinctive markings, and independent observers were able to agree on the identification of most monkeys (Cohen's Kappa = .84). The age range of the sample was two months to 15 years.

Six toys were selected: two 'masculine' toys (a ball and a car), two 'feminine' toys (a doll and a cooking pot), and two 'neutral' toys (a picture book and a stuffed dog). The gender association of each toy was based on theoretical and empirical evidence from the existing literature (e.g. Maccoby and Jacklin, 1980).

▶ **independent variable** The conditions which an experimenter sets up to cause an effect in an experiment. These vary systematically, so that the experimenter can draw conclusions about changes in outcomes.

Design

The researchers employed a factorial design with two independent variables (IVs): the sex of the monkey (male or female) and the gender identification of the toy (masculine, feminine or neutral). Two dependent measures (DVs) were taken: an 'approach' score and a 'contact' score. The approach score was the amount of time that each monkey spent within two metres of a toy; the contact score was the amount of time that each monkey spent in contact with a toy. Although the authors characterize this study as an experiment, it could also be regarded as an example of a structured observational study.

Procedure

Each of the seven groups received one practice trial (to accustom them to the presence of the experimenters) and either one or two experimental trials. For each trial, the toys were placed one at a time in the group enclosure for five minutes. The order of the toy placement was randomized. The behaviour of the animals was videotaped, and later coded to give an approach score and a contact score for each animal in relation to each toy. The contact measure is the more important of the two dependent measures because the approach score mostly reflected behaviour that was unrelated to the toys (for example, passing within two metres of a toy when moving from one area of the enclosure to another). Results were analysed by means of a series of ANOVAs. The researchers point out that the sequential presentation of the toys is not the same kind of preference test as is characteristically used with human children, where all the toys are presented at once and the child chooses which one to play with. The inter-rater reliability between the independent observers was quite high (Kappa = .84).

▶ **ANOVA** An inferential statistic that can be used with interval-level data and that is capable of dealing with more than one independent variable at a time. The word is an acronym of ANalysis Of VARiance, and is conventionally written in capital letters. Probably the most widely used statistical technique in experimental psychology.

Results

Overall it was observed that male monkeys came into contact with toys more often than did the female monkeys, so raw scores were converted into individual percentage scores (a monkey's contact time with each toy, as a percentage of its total contact with all six toys). Figure 5.4 shows that the females spent a greater percentage of their total toy contact time with 'feminine' toys than did the males ($p < .01$). Conversely, the males spent a greater percentage of their total toy contact time with 'masculine' toys than did the females ($p < .05$).

These are findings that are based on between-group (female versus male) differences. The pattern is slightly different if looked at from a within-group perspective. Within the group of females a higher percentage of time was spent in contact with feminine toys than with masculine toys ($p < .01$). However, within the masculine group there was no significant difference in percentage of contact time spent with masculine and feminine toys.

The researchers also analysed their data in order to test for any effects of dominance rank or animal group (the data were pooled from seven different groups of vervet monkeys), and also to test for effects associated with whether the toys represented animate (dog, doll) or inanimate (pot, pan, book, car) things. These analyses suggested that these factors had no systematic effect on the findings.

▶ **inter-rater reliability** A phrase which describes the extent to which two independent observers (coders/raters) agree on the observations that they have made. Also known as inter-observer reliability and inter-rater reliability.

▶ **dominance rank** Differences in power that position the individual in a rank order of influence, and access to resources and mating.

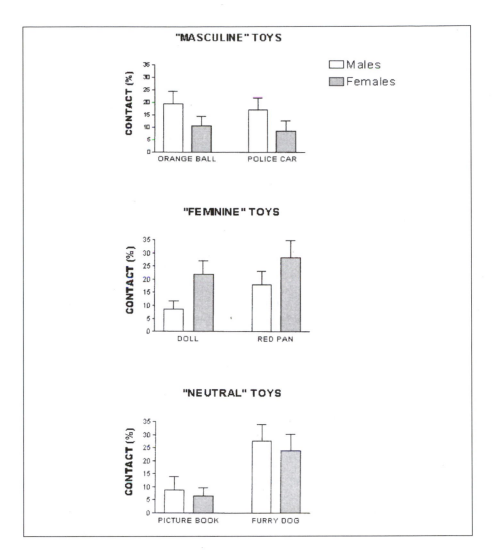

Figure 5.4 *Toy contact time¹*

Source: Alexander and Hines (2002)

Discussion

The findings indicate that sex differences in toy preference can be observed in vervet monkeys. The fact that these differences can apparently be observed in non-human species suggests that such differences do not have to be caused by socialization processes. The observed monkeys had had no previous opportunities to learn about the toys that were used in the study, and would have had no way of learning any 'gendered' associations of the toys. If the observations that were made in the course of this study are valid then the differences that they show require explanation by means of some mechanism other than socialization.

The authors of the study propose a number of possible explanations. For example, there may be specific object features that appeal differently to males and females, prior to any experience of sex-typed toys. Colour is one such feature, with a known preference among female rhesus monkeys for the 'reddish-pink' coloration of infant monkeys. In this study the face of the doll was pink and the cooking pot was red. A colour preference of this sort might be associated with nurturing, and may be one of the cues that elicits behaviours among females that promote infant survival. Equally, the ball and the car are objects that can be projected through space, and are associated with more active physical play. This type of play, in turn, might be particularly useful to males in preparation for hunting and gathering food.

The basic argument of the paper is that there may be factors underlying sex differences in toy preference that are now 'hidden' from view in humans by the all-enveloping blanket of socialization. But the origins of these differential preferences might lie in factors that have had some sort of significance in the survival and evolution of the human species.

It is important to pay attention to the logic of the argument in papers such as these. To say that sex differences in toy difference do not *have* to be caused by socialization processes is not the same as saying that these differences *are not* caused by socialization processes. This paper cannot, and does not argue that sex differences in toy preference are not caused by socialization processes. It does, however, show that other explanations are possible, and worthy of further investigation. In doing this it is playing a crucial role in challenging 'received wisdom'.

Questions

suggested answers ➤ p. 482

1. How might you design a study to work out whether the colour of the toys could influence the toy preferences of male and female monkeys?

2. The paper does not specifically say whether or not the observers who coded the monkeys' behaviour were blind to the experimental hypothesis. Indeed, it may be rather difficult to keep observers naïve to the experimental hypothesis when they are coding both the sex of the monkey, and the amount of contact between each monkey and different types of toys (it would not take much to guess that there was something going on about sex differences in toy preference when observing the amount of time male and female monkeys are in contact with a car or a doll). Why might you, as a critical reader of this paper, want to know more about how much the observers knew about the aims of the experiment?

3. What toys did you play with as a youngster? Were they 'gendered'? Why did you choose to play with these toys?

▶ **hypothesis** Experiments are designed to test one or more hypotheses. An hypothesis is a prediction of what will happen in an experiment. It is worded in such a way that the results of a well-designed experiment will clearly show whether the prediction is right or wrong.

chapter 6

BIO-PSYCHOLOGY

▶ **brain** Large grey thing at the top of your neck.

▶ **spinal cord** The bundle of nerve fibres that runs up the spine to the brain. It is the pathway by which the brain sends and receives neural messages to and from the rest of the body.

▶ **brain stem** The stem-like part of the brain at the top of the spinal cord. It controls all our involuntary muscles regulating the heartbeat, breathing, blood circulation and digestion.

▶ **cortex** The outermost layer of nerve tissue of the cerebral hemispheres.

HOW much is our behaviour and experience influenced, or controlled, by our biology? It is this question which physiological psychologists explore when they investigate how the brain works. Their studies concentrate on the structure and function of the nervous system, and, in particular, they look at how the brain is designed and how messages pass through the central nervous system.

The brain consists of three major layers which reflect our evolutionary development. At the top of the spinal cord is the brain stem, which appears to control the basic life support functions of the body. When someone is declared to be 'brain dead', then it is this part of the brain that is showing no signs of activity. On top of the brain stem is a large structure known as the cerebral cortex which appears to control the cognitive functions like thought and memory and also action (movement). In between the cortex and the brain stem is a collection of structures known as the limbic system, whose function is much less clearly known. However, they are thought to have some effect on emotions as well as on some cognitive processes.

Psychology textbooks often give a diagrammatic map of the brain which gives a summary of the findings from physiological psychologists. These diagrams present a 'car engine' model of the brain with different parts doing different jobs. For example, it has been possible to identify an area of the cortex that affects vision (the visual cortex) and an area that affects movement of the body (the motor cortex). There are, however, a number of problems with this naming of parts of the brain. First, there are large areas of the brain the functions of which are relatively unknown. Second, it is difficult to distinguish one area from another because some are no more than just a slight thickening of the tissue. Third, it is clear that the areas interact with each other, so a simple wiring diagram does not do justice to the complexity of the whole system.

Another issue to consider is reductionism. Reductionism is the attempt to explain complex behaviour in terms of simple causes. In the case of physiological psychology, it is the attempt to explain what we do and think and feel in terms of brain structure and brain chemicals. So a person in love may poetically think 'my heart goes ping when I think of you', but a physiological psychologist might describe the same experience as the

▶ reductionism An approach to understanding behaviour which focuses on one single level of explanation and ignores others. The opposite of holism.

firing of their love-neurones (made-up name). With this analysis, we seem to lose something of a very special human experience by reducing it to a series of chemical changes. On the other hand, however, the reductionist explanations are very plausible and this is shown by how often people are given chemicals (such as tranquillizers) to change their mood or their behaviour. Reductionist approaches are very useful in science because they allow us to bear down on a question and isolate key elements of the issues involved. For this reason it is the cornerstone of biopsychological research.

Bio-psychology (a.k.a. physiological psychology or neuroscience) suggests some answers to the big question for psychologists; what is a person? This approach suggests that we are biological machines, made up of cells and chemicals. The problem is that we do not experience our day-to-day lives as if we are machines. We experience ourselves as autonomous beings, capable of choice and self-direction. But if we argue that we do not act as biological machines, but have choice and free will, then where does this free will come from, and where does it reside? Bio-psychology can give us a number of fascinating insights, and can describe phenomena of the brain, but it is open to question what this all means. We can start to describe the machine but we do not know what brings it to life. It is like the story of Pinocchio.

We might be able to make the puppet but what would give it life? What would make it human?

The studies chosen for this chapter look at a range of issues in bio-psychology, but all of them highlight the interaction between physiological and psychological variables. The paper by Sperry (1968) looks at the phenomenon of people with a brain split in two. This challenges our notion of what a person is; does a person with two brains have two people inside their head? The study by Schachter and Singer (1962) explores what emotions are, and how we experience them. Their two-factor theory suggests an interaction between physiological and psychological variables. The study by Dement and Kleitman (1957) puts a scientific focus on questions that have puzzled philosophers for centuries; why do we sleep, and what is the purpose of dreams? The studies by Raine *et al.* (1997), and by Maguire *et al.* (2000) are examples of studies that use modern imaging techniques in order to examine the structure and function of the brain. The final paper by Melzack (1992) is a remarkable account of the phenomenon of the phantom limb, which is a relatively common experience for people with limb loss or limb damage. In these cases the person can still feel a missing or damaged limb even though it is not there.

A brain of two halves

SPERRY, R.W. (1968)
Hemisphere deconnection and unity in conscious awareness.
American Psychologist, 23, 723–33.

► **commissural tissue** Fibres that connect the two hemispheres of the brain.

► **epilepsy** A disorder of the brain characterized by excessive neural activity leading to mental and motor dysfunction.

► **lateralization of function** The distribution of some cognitive and motor functions to one hemisphere of the brain.

Introduction

'Your left hand doesn't know what your right hand is doing' is a saying used to convey the idea of disorganization. Strangely, some people experience exactly that feeling because the part of their brain that knows what one hand is doing really doesn't know what the other hand is doing. How could this be? The brain is divided into two relatively symmetrical halves; they are only relatively symmetrical because although they look the same they have very different functions. The split occurs from nose to back so the two halves are known as the right hemisphere and the left hemisphere. They are joined at the base of the hemispheres by commissural fibres, which are bundled into structures called 'commissures' (the corpus callosum, the massa intermedia, and the anterior commissure are the most important of these structures). If these fibres are cut, the two hemispheres of the brain become disconnected and have no internal means of communicating with each other.

The reason the fibres are sometimes cut by surgeons is to reduce the effects of epilepsy. When someone has a grand mal (major epileptic seizure) their brain cells fire excessively, and they start having uncontrollable movements and often lose consciousness. If these attacks are uncontrolled they can be life threatening because of the strain on the heart and the damage done to the person when they are unconscious. In some extreme cases the brain is 'cut in half' to contain the attack within one half of the brain. Modern medicine is much more likely to use medication to control epilepsy, though in extreme cases surgery is still used (see below).

The two halves of the brain do not carry out the same tasks, and so communicate with each other through the commissural fibres. In right-handed people the major functions of language are carried out in the left hemisphere. This division of tasks between the two sides is referred to as lateralization of function. It is very easy to get confused over right and left because many of the nerve fibres swap sides in the nervous system, so Table 6.1 gives a brief summary of the important functions described in this study.

Table 6.1 *Which hemisphere of the brain deals with sources of information?*

Function or stimulus	Part of brain
the RIGHT visual field	LEFT hemisphere
the LEFT visual field	RIGHT hemisphere
language	LEFT hemisphere
information from the LEFT hand	RIGHT hemisphere
information from the RIGHT hand	LEFT hemisphere
information from the LEFT ear	90% RIGHT hemisphere
information from the RIGHT hand	90% LEFT hemisphere
information from the LEFT nostril	LEFT hemisphere
information from the RIGHT nostril	RIGHT hemisphere

The study described here concerns Sperry's psychological tests on 11 patients who had their commissural fibres cut to control their epilepsy. Sperry had extensive experience of conducting brain research on animals though the operations were carried out by neurosurgeons. An account of the work is given in Sperry's speech when he received his Nobel Prize for Medicine in 1981.[1] There is film of the patients taken at the time of the operations and also some follow-up work 35 years after the initial operations.

The studies

The following sections provide an overview of a whole variety of controlled laboratory studies which have been carried out with people with hemisphere deconnection.

Subjects

The subjects in the studies summarized in Sperry's paper were 11 patients who had undergone 'the most radical disconnection of the cerebral hemispheres attempted thus far in human surgery' (p. 723). All had a history of advanced epilepsy, and the surgery was seen as a 'last resort' (p. 723). Sperry reports excellent therapeutic outcomes for two of the patients with regard to their epilepsy, and holds judgement on the success of the intervention in the remaining nine cases since they had only relatively recently undergone the surgery.

Design

▶ **natural experiments (also quasi experiments)** Studies in which comparisons are made between different conditions that come about through natural political, social, economic or demographic circumstances, rather than through direct manipulation of a variable by an experimenter.

▶ **case study** A detailed description of a particular individual or group under study or treatment.

There are a variety of designs used in the studies which are reported here, but overall the work carried out appears to have been a mixture of quasi-experiments and case studies. The quasi-experiments involved comparing the performance of the 11 subjects on various tasks with the performance of people with no inter-hemispheric deconnection. The case studies were extensive investigations of the 11 subjects themselves which aimed to pin down the effects of hemisphere deconnection, and thereby to address the question of how the hemispheres work in a 'normal' brain. Clinical case studies of people who have either accidentally, or for some therapeutic reason, experienced damage to specific areas of the brain are an important research method of the brain and behavioural sciences. They can be thought of as a kind of 'opportunistic' experimentation.

Procedure

Sperry used standard procedures for investigating lateralization of brain function. The requirements for such investigations are controlled laboratory conditions and specialized equipment which allow tasks to be set separately to the two hemispheres of the subject's brain via sight, sound, smell and touch.

---

1. You can read the speech at http://nobelprize.org/nobel_prizes/medicine/laureates/1981/sperry-lecture.html

The two hemispheres receive different visual information. However, it is not as simple as the left eye sending information to the left brain and so on. It is best described in the following way. Imagine looking straight ahead. Then the view to the right of your nose is the right visual field and the view to the left of your nose is the left visual field. The nerves of the visual system are arranged in such a way that the view of the left visual field goes to the right hemisphere of the brain and the view from the right visual field goes to the left hemisphere of the brain (see Figure 6.1).

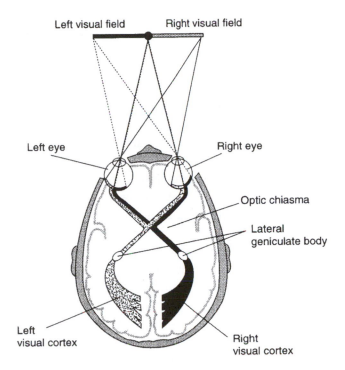

Figure 6.1   *Visual pathways in the brain*

An example of a standard task for investigating lateralization involves subjects responding to visual information that is sent to just one half of the brain. This is achieved by blindfolding one of the subject's eyes, instructing them to fixate with the seeing eye on a designated point in the middle of a screen, and then projecting the stimuli on either the left or right hand side of the fixation point for less than a tenth of a second.

Another example would be a tactile task in which the subject's hands are hidden from their own view. Again, information from stimuli that are presented to the left hand goes to the right hemisphere. Auditory and olfactory stimuli can also be presented to one side of the brain using various methods of blocking the unused ear or nostril. Note that in the case of sound about 10 per cent of the information goes to the same side of brain, the remaining 90 per cent going to the opposite hemisphere; and in the case of smell all the information goes to the same side of the brain (information from the left nostril is processed by the left hemisphere).

Results

Needless to say in a paper which summarizes a series of research studies there are a lot of results reported. This section will briefly describe a number of the findings.

Subjects who were presented with an image in one half of their visual field were only able to recognize the image as one they had already seen if it was presented again within the same half of the visual field. If the same image was re-shown to the other side of the brain, the person would respond as if they had never seen the image before.

Right-handed subjects were able to give good descriptions of any image that was presented to the right-hand side of the visual field, but reported that images displayed on the left-hand side were either not noticed or appeared as just a flash. However, the subjects were able to respond non-verbally to images presented on the left of the visual field, perhaps by pointing with their left hand to a related object. Remember that for right-handers (and also some left-handers) language is controlled by the left hemisphere.

This language-related effect could also be seen when two symbols were presented simultaneously, one on either side of the visual field. If the person was asked to draw with their left hand (shielded from their own view) what they had seen, they would draw the left-hand symbol. But when asked to say what they had just drawn the subject would say the name of the right-hand symbol!

The same effects were evident when the subjects were responding to tactile information from either hand. The left hand would seem to be unable to respond to any stimulus presented to the right hand. In addition, objects put in the subject's right hand could be named and described in words, whereas only appropriate non-verbal responses could be made to objects presented to the left hand.

The separation of function between the two hemispheres could be very clearly seen in tasks which involved parallel responses by both hands to two different stimuli presented simultaneously to the two sides of the visual field. The performance of 'normal' subjects was slowed down by the competing demands of the tasks, yet the people with hemisphere deconnection could actually perform these double tasks in parallel as quickly as they were able to perform one of the tasks on its own. Sperry is quick to point out, however, that although the patients did not appear to be particularly worse off mentally than people with intact inter-hemispherical connections, they were certainly not better off. Enhanced performances of the sort just described were only noted on very specific and highly unusual laboratory tasks.

Discussion

The numerous effects which Sperry reports add up to a convincing account of 'an apparent doubling in most of the realms of conscious awareness' (p. 724) for the deconnected patients. In many of the tasks that were set, it was evident that 'the second hemisphere does not know what the first hemisphere has

▶ **phenomenological**
Concerned with the person's own perceived world and the phenomena which they experience, rather than with objective reality.

been doing' (p. 726). Indeed, Sperry argues that the effects are easier to understand if one thinks 'of the mental faculties and performance capacities of the left and right hemispheres separately' (p. 727), rather than looking at the behaviour of each subject as a single individual. The different hemispheres seemed to have their own perceptions, their own memories and their own phenomenology.

In intact brains, lateralization of brain function is complemented by lines of communication across the hemispheres. For the patients described in this series of studies it appeared that the lack of communication across the hemispheres was, under normal conditions, compensated for by other information-disseminating strategies. For example, the patients could use speech as a means of telling the right hemisphere what was going on in the world of the left hemisphere. In the laboratory, subjects had to be prevented from talking as they performed tasks in order that this line of communication was also disconnected. So to the informal observer, and probably to the patients themselves, the dual lines of consciousness were most likely not noticeable and could only be isolated by Sperry and his colleagues under highly controlled, laboratory conditions. Indeed, Sperry argues that in general the deconnection of the hemispheres did not appear to affect the patients' intelligence or personality. The effects of the surgery did however show themselves in short-term memory difficulties, limited concentration spans and orientation problems.

Sperry ends by warning the reader that the results that he summarizes are imperfect generalizations:

> Although the general picture has continued to hold up in the main as described, it is important to note that, with respect to many of the deconnection symptoms mentioned, striking modifications and even outright exceptions can be found among the small group of patients examined to date. (p. 733)

One area of interest that has developed since Sperry's work has been work on 'anarchic' or 'alien' hands (see for example Marchetti and Della Salla, 1998, or Della Salla, 2005). This racy term introduces another phenomenon that might have some explanation in the split-brain studies. People with anarchic hands experience actions in one hand that they find difficult to control. So for example the rogue hand might suddenly reach out and steal somebody else's ice-cream.

Brain surgery has also developed since Sperry's work and in extreme life-threatening cases of brain damage or epilepsy surgeons can carry out an hemispherectomy (removing one hemisphere of the brain). This does not sound possible but it can be successfully performed and patients can recover quite remarkably (Kossoff *et al.*, 2003). The puzzle here is that if you remove, say, the left hemisphere then the patient should not be able to undertake actions controlled by that hemisphere (for example, moving their right hand). But commonly they can. The control centre has gone but the puppet keeps moving. It is interesting to speculate about what this might mean with regard to our current understanding of the brain's structures and functions.

suggested answers
→ p. 483

Questions

1. Why does the presentation of the visual stimuli need to be so brief (less than a tenth of a second)?

2. In the tactile tasks in which objects are presented to one hand, why is it important that the subject cannot see their own hand?

3. Why are people who have specific localized damage to areas of their brain so popular with researchers in the brain and behavioural sciences?

How do you feel?

SCHACHTER, S. AND
SINGER, J.E. (1962)

Cognitive, social
and physiological
determinants of
emotional state.

Psychological Review,
69, 379–99.

Introduction

How do you feel? It's a question that we are often asked, but always find difficult to answer. If you try to describe how you felt when you were angry or afraid or happy, you will probably use descriptions of bodily changes, for example, 'my legs turned to jelly' or 'I felt warm' or 'I had butterflies in my stomach' or 'my heart went ping'. We experience various bodily changes when we experience emotion, and there is clearly a strong connection between the reactions of our body and our feelings.

In 1890 William James proposed that these changes occur as a response to a stimulating event, and our experience of these changes is what we call emotion. The Danish psychologist Carl Lange suggested something similar around the same time, and so the idea became known as the James–Lange theory. The theory suggests, counter-intuitively, that we are afraid because we run away, and we are angry because we strike. This seems to be the wrong way round, since we would normally say that someone ran away because they were afraid. But it is easy to think of instances where the recognition of emotion does come after the bodily responses. If you trip on the stairs you automatically make a grab for the banister before you have a chance to recognize a state of fear. After the crisis is over, the emotion you feel includes the perception of a pounding heart, rapid breathing, and a feeling of weakness or trembling in your arms and legs.

In 1929 Walter Cannon produced a critique of the James–Lange theory that was, until recently, considered devastating. His objections included the observations that:

(1) The same changes in the internal organs occur in a range of emotional responses, so how can we tell anger from fear?

(2) Artificial changes in the state of the internal organs brought about by, for example, injections of adrenalin, do not produce the experience of emotion.

▶ **adrenalin** A hormone secreted by the adrenal glands, which causes an increase in blood pressure, release of sugar by the liver and a number of other physiological responses to threat.

Subsequent studies found some slight differences between the bodily responses to different emotions, but these differences were not enough to explain the very different experiences we have in different emotions. So psychologists started to look at the role of cognitive factors in the experiences of emotion.

The study

Schachter and Singer describe the work of Marañon (1924), who carried out an experiment to see whether stimulation of body changes by injections of adrenalin would produce feelings of emotion. About 70 per cent of subjects experienced physical symptoms such as a dry mouth or a pounding heart, but no emotion. The remainder reported experiences of emotion, but qualified their statements by saying that they felt 'as if' they were undergoing an emotional experience. Marañon also found that if he questioned his subjects about a painful event before the injection they were unlikely to respond emotionally, but after the injection they often became upset. This suggests that the physiological arousal brought on by the injection was not enough to produce emotion unless the person was provided with an appropriate cognition such as an upsetting memory

Schachter and Singer brought the available evidence together in their two-factor theory of emotion. The two-factor theory suggests that emotion comes from a combination of a state of arousal and a cognition that makes best sense of the situation the person is in. There are three propositions:

(a) If a person experiences a state of arousal for which they have no immediate explanation, they will label this state and describe their feelings in terms of the cognitions available to them. The same state of arousal could be labelled as 'joy' or 'fury' or 'jealousy' and so forth, depending on the situation the person is in.

(b) If a person experiences a state of arousal for which they have an appropriate explanation, then they will be unlikely to label their feelings in terms of the alternative cognitions available.

(c) In similar situations, a person will react emotionally or experience emotions only if they are in a state of arousal.

The procedure

The experimental test of the propositions required (a) the experimental manipulation of a state of physiological arousal, and (b) the manipulation of the explanation that an individual will give to this arousal. The subjects were told that the aim of the experiment was to look at the effects of vitamin injections on visual skills, and were asked if they would mind having an injection of suproxin (made-up name). If they agreed (and 184 out of 185 did), they were given an injection of either adrenalin (epinephrine) or a placebo. The effects of adrenalin are very similar to the effects of arousal of the sympathetic division of the autonomic nervous system (as in the fight or flight syndrome) – increases in blood pressure, heart rate, blood sugar level, respiration rate, and blood flow to the muscles and brain, with an accompanying decrease in blood flow to the skin. This is often experienced as palpitations, tremors, flushing and faster breathing. The effects begin after three minutes and last from ten minutes to an hour. Note that all the subjects thought they had received an injection of vitamins.

The subjects were then put into one of the four experimental conditions:

(a) *Ignorant*: subjects were given an adrenalin injection and not told of the effects of the drug.

(b) *Informed*: subjects were given an adrenalin injection and warned of the 'side effects' of the drug (hand shaking, heart pounding, dry mouth, etc.).

▶ **arousal** A general physiological state in which the sympathetic division of the autonomic nervous system is activated.

▶ **placebo** An inactive substance or fake treatment that produces a response in patients.

▶ **autonomic nervous system (ANS)** A network of nerve fibres running from the brain stem and spinal cord, which can activate the body for action, or set it into a quiescent state.

▶ **spinal cord** The bundle of nerve fibres that runs up the spine to the brain. It is the pathway by which the brain sends and receives neural messages to and from the rest of the body.

These subjects were therefore prepared for the effects of the adrenalin (although they thought these were to do with the suproxin).

(c) *Misinformed*: subjects were given an adrenalin injection and told to expect side effects but were told these would be numb feet and headache. These subjects would, therefore, not be expecting the effects of the adrenalin.

(d) *Placebo*: subjects were given an injection that would have no effect and were given no instructions of what to expect.

In the ignorant condition the subjects experience arousal without any obvious reason for it. The theory predicts that they will describe this arousal in terms of the situation they are in. The subjects in the informed condition on the other hand, will experience the same arousal but will have an obvious explanation for it (the adrenalin). Their experience, then, will not be affected by the situation they find themselves in. To test this out, the subjects were either put in a situation designed to produce euphoria or a situation designed to produce anger:

In the *euphoria* situation, the subject was left in a room for 20 minutes with a stooge 'to let the drug be absorbed before the vision test'. The stooge started to fool around in the untidy waiting room, playing 'paper basketball', airplanes, catapults, hoola-hoop and generally behaving in a very excitable way.

In the *anger* situation, the subject was left with the stooge for 20 minutes and asked to fill in a questionnaire. The stooge expressed displeasure at the injection and increasing displeasure at the questionnaire, which asked increasingly personal questions. The first few questions were inoffensive but later it asked 'Do you hear bells?', 'Do you bathe and wash regularly?', 'How many times a week do you have sexual intercourse?' (remember this was 1962 and sex hadn't been invented yet), and finally 'With how many men, other than your father, has your mother had extra-marital relationships – 4 and under, 5 to 9, or 10 and over?' (note you cannot answer 'none at all').

The study ran seven conditions as shown in Table 6.2.

Table 6.2   *The conditions in the Schachter and Singer experiment*

Euphoria	Anger
Informed	Informed
Ignorant	Ignorant
Misinformed	
Placebo	Placebo

Measurement

The researchers made observational measures of emotional response through a one-way mirror, and also took self-report measures from the subjects. The self-report questionnaire contained a number of mock questions but the crucial ones are shown in Table 6.3.

▶**self-report** A number of popular research methods are based on self-report: for example, questionnaires, interviews, attitude scales and diary methods. These are methods which rely on research subjects' accounts of their own experiences and behaviour.

Table 6.3   *The self-report rating scale used by Schachter and Singer*

1. How irritated, angry or annoyed would you say you feel at present?				
I don't feel at all irritated or angry	I feel a little irritated and angry	I feel quite a lot irritated and angry	I feel very irritated and angry	I feel extremely irritated and angry
2. How good or happy would you say you feel at present?				
I don't feel at all happy or good	I feel a little happy and good	I feel quite a lot happy and good	I feel very happy and good	I feel extremely happy and good

The subjects were all psychology students, and their health records were checked to make sure that the adrenalin would not have an adverse effect.

Results

The subjects who received the injections of adrenalin reported clear feelings of arousal in comparison with the placebo subjects. For the score of self-reported emotion, the irritation/anger score was subtracted from the happiness score to produce the data shown in Figure 6.2.

The scale is a measure of happiness minus anger, so in the euphoria situation the ignorant and the misinformed groups appear to experience the greatest happiness and least anger (as predicted) and in the anger situation the ignorant group experiences the least happiness and greatest anger (also as predicted).

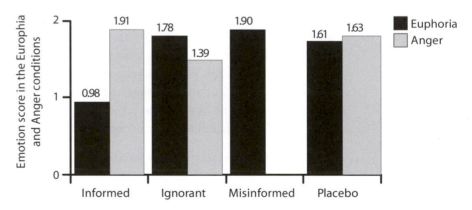

Figure 6.2   *Self-reports of emotion in the various conditions of the Schachter and Singer experiment*

Discussion

Perhaps because people wanted to believe the theory and perhaps because of the complexity of the experiment, no attempt at replication was made until 1979, when Marshall and Zimbardo failed to obtain the same results as the original study.

A closer inspection of the original study reveals a few problems:

(a) The differences between the groups of subjects were small and only became significant after a number of the subjects were discarded.

(b) Some of the subjects in the misinformed and the ignorant groups attributed their arousal state to the injection, saying, for example, 'the shot gave me the shivers'. This is a problem because these subjects were meant to have experienced arousal without an obvious cause.

(c) The results were presented as a measure of relative emotion – happiness minus anger – when in fact the self-reports of all the experimental subjects in both the euphoria and the anger situations were on the happy side of neutral. This shows that Schachter and Singer were unsuccessful in their attempt to induce anger.

(d) There was no measure of the subject's mood before the experiment.

(e) The misinformed condition was not reported in the anger situation.

The two-factor theory is a fascinating idea, and it seems clear that physiological changes and cognitive evaluations form part of our experience of emotion. Subsequent work has shown that the relationship is more complex than the two-factor theory predicts, and, for example the work by Valins (1966) on false-feedback showed that a person's belief about their physiological state will affect them regardless of their actual state. In one study Valins showed male students some pictures of semi-naked women (why are these studies never carried out the other way round?). The participants believed they had been wired up to record their pulse and were played the sound of a heartbeat through headphones. In fact the heartbeat they heard was not their own but had been prerecorded. Half of the participants heard the pulse increasing as they looked at the picture and half heard it decreasing. When the slide show was finished the participants gave attractiveness ratings for the women they had seen. As expected the participants who heard the heart rate increasing rated the women as more attractive. The subjects believed that they had been aroused by the slides and this affected their judgement of attractiveness. This effect of false-feedback has been replicated several times.

► **false-feedback** Providing inaccurate biological feedback to someone; for example, suggesting that their heart rate is lower than it really is to convince them that their anxiety level is low.

Questions

1. Briefly summarize the design of this experiment.

2. How did Schachter and Singer measure emotion?

3. Suggest some other ways that you could measure and record your own and other people's emotions.

4. What ethical concerns might there be with this study?

5. Do you think the results would have been different if they had not used students in their study?

suggested answers ➤ p. 483

To sleep, perchance to dream

DEMENT, W. AND KLEITMAN, N. (1957)

The relation of eye movements during sleep to dream activity: an objective method for the study of dreaming.

Journal of Experimental Psychology, 53, 339–46.

Introduction

We are at one and the same time fascinated and frightened by our dreams. Why do we have these strange images and stories during our sleep, and what do they mean? In this culture we are reluctant to discuss the content of our dreams in case they are seen to be a sign of a disturbed mind, so we often keep the products of our sleeping activity to ourselves. However, the topic remains fascinating for everyday conversation and also for scientific enquiry.

Empson (1989) draws together some information that shows how important dreams have been in other cultures and in the past of our own culture. A number of ancient texts, including the Bible, make repeated references to revelations that occur during dreams. The plays of Shakespeare have many references to dreams, some of which are prophetic; for example, the dream of Julius Caesar's wife predicts his death. This tells us something about the beliefs that Elizabethan audiences held about the nature and interpretation of dreams. In what is probably the most famous speech in a play Hamlet wonders whether to take his own life or not ('to be or not to be, that is the question') and in the speech he wonders whether death is an extension of sleep and, if so, whether dreams would continue in this endless state?

> ...To die, to sleep;
> To sleep: perchance to dream: ay, there's the rub;
> For in that sleep of death what dreams may come
> When we have shuffled off this mortal coil,
> Must give us pause: there's the respect
> That makes calamity of so long life. (*Hamlet*, 3.1)

▶ **unconscious mind** The part of our mind that is beyond our conscious awareness.

A more modern influence on our view of dreams was provided by Freud, who suggested that they are the product of our unconscious mind. We have certain unconscious wishes, and these wishes are expressed in our dreams. Often the nature of the wish is heavily disguised in the dream so that it does not alarm us. This view is probably most representative of the popular view of dreams today.

Until the work by Dement and Kleitman, very little was known about the frequency of dreaming, the length of dreams or the value of dreams for healthy sleep. Nathanial Kleitman was the first Western psychologist to concentrate on the study of sleep and is responsible for setting up the first sleep laboratory and carrying out a range of imaginative studies. One of these was to live in a cave for a month to investigate the effects of living to a different clock, rather than to the 24-hour one given to us by the movement of the earth around the sun. William Dement was a student of Kleitman's and together they discovered Rapid Eye Movement sleep (REM). Dement joined Stanford University (in the USA) in 1963 and has worked there ever since researching sleep and sleep disorders.

The study

▶ **correlation** A measure of how strongly two or more variables are related to each other.

Dement and Kleitman note that an earlier observation had shown that people have periods of prolonged rapid eye movements (REM) during sleep, and there seemed to be some connection with the occurrence of these periods and the experience of dreaming. It is possible to see the eyes of a sleeping person or animal move during these periods, without the use of sophisticated equipment. The study set out to look at three questions:

(1) Does dream recall correlate with periods of REM?
(2) Is there a correlation between the estimate of dream length and the time in REM?
(3) Is the type of eye movement related to the content of the dream?

Subjects

Seven adult males and two adult females were studied. Five were studied intensively, while minimal data were gathered from the other four just to confirm the findings of the main five.

Procedure

In a typical study, the subject reported to the laboratory just before their usual bedtime. They had been asked to eat normally but to avoid caffeine or alcohol on the day of the study. Two or more electrodes were attached near the eyes to record electrical changes, and hence movement of the eyes. Two or three further electrodes were attached to the scalp to record brain activity during

▶ **electroencephalogram** A method of recording the electrical activity of the brain.

the night. The electrodes were connected to an electroencephalograph (EEG) which amplified and recorded the signals.

At various times during the night the subjects were woken up to test their dream recall. The return to sleep usually took less than five minutes. The nine subjects were studied over a total of 61 nights, with a total of 351 awakenings which averaged out at 5.7 awakenings per night.

Results

All the subjects showed periods of REM every night. These periods occurred at regular intervals during the night, though each subject had their own pattern. The average gap between each REM period was 90 minutes, with individual norms varying between 70 minutes and 104 minutes. The length of the REM periods varied between 3 minutes and 50 minutes, and they tended to increase in length as the night progressed. The REM periods were accompanied by a particular pattern on the EEG of brain wave activity. The REM EEG was characterized by a low-voltage, relatively fast pattern.

The subjects were woken up by a doorbell ringing close to the bed. The subject then had to speak into a tape recorder near the bed, and to say whether they had been dreaming, and what was the content of the dream. In an attempt to eliminate the possibility of experimenter effects, the experimenter did not communicate with the subjects during the night. The subjects were only recorded as having dreamed if they were able to relate a coherent and relatively detailed description of the dream content. Table 6.4 shows the results of these awakenings, and the data are shown graphically in Figure 6.3. The results show that REM sleep is predominantly, though not exclusively, associated with dreaming, and N-REM (non-REM) sleep is associated with periods of non-dreaming sleep.

▶ **experimenter effects**
Unwanted influences in a psychological study which are produced, consciously or unconsciously, by the person carrying out the study.

Table 6.4 *The number of wakenings associated with recall or no recall of dreams after REM and non-REM sleep*

Subject	Rapid Eye Movements (REM)		Non-Rapid Eye Movements (N-REM)	
	Dream recall	No recall	Dream recall	No recall
DN	17	9	3	21
IR	26	8	2	29
KC	36	4	3	31
WD	37	5	1	34
PM	24	6	2	23
KK	4	1	0	5
SM	2	2	0	2
DM	2	1	0	1
MG	4	3	0	3
Total	152	39	11	149

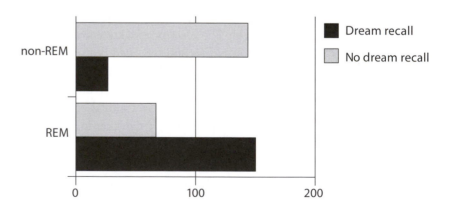

Figure 6.3 *The recall of dreams after REM and non-REM sleep*

Sometimes the subjects were awakened during periods of deep sleep (which is shown by a particular pattern of brain waves with no REM). On these awakenings the subjects were often bewildered and sometimes said they had been dreaming without being able to state the content of the dream. They also described a great variety of feelings, such as pleasantness or anxiety, but these feelings could not be related to any dream content.

A series of awakenings were carried out to see if the subjects could accurately estimate the length of their dreams. They were woken up either 5 minutes or 15 minutes into a REM period, and asked to say whether they thought the dream had been going on for 5 or 15 minutes. Table 6.5 shows that these estimates were fairly accurate.

Table 6.5 *Results of dream-duration estimates after 5 or 15 minutes of rapid eye movement*

Subject	5 minutes		15 minutes	
	Right	Wrong	Right	Wrong
DN	8	2	5	5
IR	11	1	7	3
KC	7	0	12	1
WD	13	1	15	1
PM	6	2	8	3
Total	45	6	47	13

It was also hypothesized that the REM represented the scanning of visual images and so a connection should be possible between the measurement of the REM and the content of the dream. The subjects were woken up to test this idea after some particular patterns of REM. The patterns were:

(a) mainly vertical eye movements;
(b) mainly horizontal eye movements;
(c) both vertical and horizontal eye movements;
(d) very little or no eye movement.

The recall of the dreams showed some relationship to the type of eye movements. For example, a person who was woken up after a series of vertical movements reported standing at the bottom of a cliff and operating a hoist, whereas a person woken up after some horizontal movements reported dreaming of watching two people throw tomatoes at each other.

Discussion

The study gives us a clear indication of a connection between REM and dreaming, though that relationship is far from being fully understood. The study formed the basis of much subsequent research which has been able to use more sophisticated equipment to build up a picture of the different patterns of brain waves that occur through a normal night's sleep.

A similar study by Goodenough *et al.* (1959) raises some questions about the connection between REM and dreaming. They questioned 60 people about the frequency of their dreams and then persuaded the eight most frequent

► **self-report** A number of popular research methods are based on self-report: for example, questionnaires, interviews, attitude scales and diary methods. These are methods which rely on research subjects' accounts of their own experiences and behaviour.

► **sleep deprivation** A lack of the necessary amount of sleep brought about by neurological or psychological or social causes, and creating a range of negative psychological and bodily effects. Sometimes used as a form of torture.

dreamers ('dreamed every night'), along with the eight least frequent dreamers to take part in laboratory recordings of their sleep patterns. When they woke the high dreamers from their REM sleep they reported dreams on 44 out of 49 occasions. They also reported dreams on half the awakenings during non-REM sleep. On the other hand, the self-reported low dreamers only reported dreams when woken during 19 out of 42 REM sleeps, and only seven out of 43 non-REM sleeps. So there would appear to be some large differences between individuals in the reports of dreaming during REM.

Dement and Wolpert (1958) tried to affect the content of dreams by providing some stimulation to the dreamers. They did this by playing a tone, or flashing a light or spraying them with cold water. A number of subjects incorporated the stimulation into their dreams and one, for example, dreamt about spilling a glass of water on himself. The matching of eye movements to the dream content has not received support in subsequent research and it appears that people who were blind from birth and newborn babies both show REM even though they may have poor, or non-existent, imaging skills.

Today there is a vast amount of sleep research being carried out and much of it is aimed at helping people with sleep disorders or who work shifts. A sleep disorder can be a serious psychological condition (see Griffith *et al.*, 1972, summarized in Chapter 8). There is also a down side to some of the work, as the disruptive potential of sleep deprivation has also been explored. Being deprived of sleep is a very distressing condition and it has been used to make prisoners 'more cooperative'. It has been used by the security services of many countries, who have deprived political prisoners of sleep by playing them loud heavy metal or children's music for long periods of time. According to the BBC website (2003), the Psychological Operations Company (Psy Ops) of the US Army said the aim was to break a prisoner's resistance through sleep deprivation and playing music that was culturally offensive to them. Sergeant Mark Hadsell, of Psy Ops, told *Newsweek* magazine:

> These people haven't heard heavy metal. They can't take it. If you play it for 24 hours, your brain and body functions start to slide, your train of thought slows down and your will is broken. That's when we come in and talk to them.

As well as heavy metal music the Psy Ops unit also use the theme tune from the children's programmes *Sesame Street* and *Barney the Dinosaur*. One US serviceman said 'In training, they forced me to listen to the Barney "I Love You" song for 45 minutes. I never want to go through that again' (BBC website, 2003).

suggested answers → p. 483

Questions

1. What do the results tell us about REM sleep?

2. What observations would you make about the subject sample?

3. What controls are used in the study?

4. What other controls can you suggest?

5. What are the main differences between sleeping in a laboratory and sleeping in your own bed?

6. Get someone to wake you up after you've been in REM sleep for 5 minutes. Record what you call them.

Murderers!

RAINE, A., BUCHSBAUM, M. AND LaCASSE, L. (1997)

Brain abnormalities in murderers indicated by positron emission tomography.

Biological Psychiatry, 42, 495–508.

Introduction

Are criminals different from law-abiding citizens and can we spot them? This question has a long, and not very proud, history in the social sciences. In the nineteenth century, Cesare Lombroso asserted that criminals had a particular appearance and a particular set of behaviours. He wrote:

The criminal by nature has a feeble cranial capacity, a heavy and developed jaw, projecting [eye] ridges, an abnormal and asymmetrical cranium – projecting ears, frequently a crooked or flat nose. Criminals are subject to [colour blindness]; left-handedness is common; their muscular force is feeble. (cited in Rose *et al.,* 1984, p. 53)

If only life was so easy! Outside of film drama, the notion of the ugly and identifiable criminal is not a reality. In fact, criminological research does not tend to find any physical or behavioural differences between people who engage in crime and people who do not. In a review of this issue, Stephenson (1992) suggested that it is not useful to try and divide the population into criminals and non-criminals, or even to divide criminals into persistent offenders and those who stop offending. Despite this, there continues to be a lot of interest in finding ways of identifying criminals, and thereby finding a probable cause which may be correctable.

A relatively new way of looking for differences between people is to examine patterns of brain activity through the use of imaging techniques. Figure 6.4 shows the kind of pictures that can be produced. There are four basic techniques that are currently used:

▶ **positron emission tomography (PET)**
Uses radioactivity to label blood, blood sugars or important neurotransmitters such as dopamine. The labelled substance is then injected into mugs (sorry, volunteers) while they lie in the scanner and carry out mental tasks such as problem solving. The scanner picks up the gamma rays emission to find out where the labelled substances are active in the brain. This requires a fair amount of computer processing because the PET scanner has to sift through around 7–8 million gamma-ray signals a second. PET scanning is the most established of the brain imaging techniques but requires massive investment.

▶ **dopamine** A neurotransmitter. Neurotransmitters are chemicals that carry information from one nerve cell to another.

PET (positron emission tomography) uses radioactivity to label blood, blood sugars or important neurotransmitters such as dopamine. The labelled substance is then injected into volunteers while they lie in the scanner and carry out mental tasks such as problem-solving. The scanner picks up the gamma-ray emissions to find out where the labelled substances are active in the brain. This requires a fair amount of computer processing because the PET scanner has to sift through around 7–8 million gamma-ray signals a second. PET scanning is the most established of the brain-imaging techniques, but requires massive investment.

MEG (magneto-encephalography) uses very sensitive sensors to pick up the faint magnetic fields generated by active nerve networks. In order to pick up these very weak magnetic changes, the MEG machines are exceptionally sensitive and can be affected by the movement of traffic in the street.

MRI (magnetic resonance imaging) uses a combination of powerful magnets and radio pulses to measure changes in oxygen levels and hence blood flows in the brain. The great advantage of the MRI technique is that these scanners

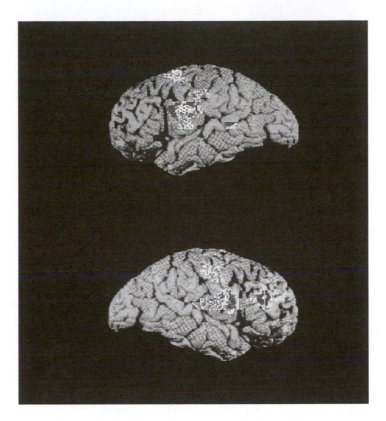

Figure 6.4 *Examples of the kind of pictures that can be produced through imaging techniques*

are relatively common in hospitals and can be converted for brain imaging without too much further expense.

fMRI *(Functional Magnetic Resonance Imaging)* The most substantial developments in scanning have come with the fMRI scan, which is the scan of choice for psychologists. The scans use MRI technology to measure the changes in the blood oxygen levels that are connected to neural activity in the brain or spinal cord. It gives a picture of what is happening in the brain rather than a picture of its structure. One major problem with fMRI is that the scanners are noisy, and the effects of this noise have to be taken into account when interpreting the data.

All four of these methods produce exciting and very visual results, and it is now common to see colour images of the brain with particular areas shaded to show different levels of activity. It is important, however, not to overestimate the quality of this evidence (see McCrone, 1995) as there are a number of problems with these sorts of data, for example:

- The creation of the colour images involves many steps and there are numerous ways for error or wishful thinking to creep in.
- A hotspot of brain activity could be due to excitatory nerves (the 'on switch') or inhibitory nerves (the 'off switch'), as the activity looks the same to the scan.

▶ **spinal cord** The bundle of nerve fibres that runs up the spine to the brain. It is the pathway by which the brain sends and receives neural messages to and from the rest of the body.

- There is evidence that as the brain becomes practised in a task, then the amount of nervous activity required to activate that task declines. It might be that the hotspots are not where the important activity is taking place but where the brain is struggling with something new.
- MRI scans are susceptible to very small movements and even a pulse in the forehead can contribute to false readings.
- MEG scans are notoriously difficult to interpret, and among the many problems is the common observation of activation centres outside the skull.

The general view, however, seems to be that we should not let concerns about the quality of the evidence and its interpretation spoil a good story, and there is no doubt that the imaging data of the brain tell a number of good stories. The study by Raine *et al.* is one of them.

The study

The study used PET scans to examine the brains of 41 people (39 males and 2 females) who were charged with murder and were pleading Not Guilty for Reasons of Insanity (NGRI), and compared them with 41 controls. All the NGRIs were referred to the imaging centre for legal reasons, such as to obtain evidence for the defence. The reasons for the referrals were:

▶ **schizophrenia** A mental disorder marked by some, or all of the following symptoms: delusions, hallucinations, incoherent word associations, inappropriate emotions or lack of emotions.

▶ **epilepsy** A disorder of the brain characterized by excessive neural activity leading to mental and motor dysfunction.

▶ **standard deviation** A measure of dispersion.

▶ **cortex** The outermost layer of nerve tissue of the cerebral hemispheres.

- schizophrenia (6 cases);
- head injury or organic damage (23);
- drug abuse (3);
- affective disorder (2);
- epilepsy (2);
- hyperactivity or learning difficulties (3);
- personality disorder (2).

The average age of the NGRIs was 34.3 years (standard deviation = 10.1). The controls were selected to match for age and sex, and the six NGRIs who were diagnosed as schizophrenic were matched with six other people with the same diagnosis but no history of murder. All the controls were further screened for their mental and physical health.

All of the participants were injected with a glucose tracer, required to work at a continuous performance task that was based around target recognition for 32 minutes, and then given a PET scan. The NGRIs were compared with the controls on the level of activity (glucose metabolism) in right and left hemispheres of the brain in 14 selected areas. The researchers looked at activity in six cortical areas (part of the cerebral cortex) and eight subcortical areas (brain structures below the cortex);

Cortical areas
- lateral prefrontal
- medial prefrontal

Subcortical structures
- corpus callosum
- amygdala

- parietal
- occipital
- temporal
- cingulate

- medial temporal lobe and hippocampus
- thalamus
- putamen
- globus pallidus
- midbrain
- cerebellum

The data were analysed using the multivariate technique MANOVA, which is a specialized form of the statistical procedure ANOVA.

Results

▶ **ANOVA** An inferential statistic that can be used with interval-level data and that is capable of dealing with more than one independent variable at a time. The word is an acronym of ANalysis Of VAriance, and is conventionally written in capital letters. Probably the most widely used statistical technique in experimental psychology.

The cerebral cortex is commonly described in terms of four areas or lobes: the frontal, parietal, temporal and occipital. In this study, compared to the controls, the NGRIs were found to have less activity in their prefrontal and parietal areas, more activity in their occipital areas, and no difference in their temporal areas.

The results from the subcortical areas found less activity in the corpus callosum (which joins the two halves of the brain; see Sperry, 1968, in this chapter). They also found an imbalance of activity between the two hemispheres in three other subcortical structures. In the amygdala and the hippocampus, compared to the controls, the NGRIs had less activity in the left side and more activity in the right side. Also, in the thalamus the NGRIs had more activity in the right side, though no difference in the left side.

Analysis of the data showed that the handedness of the participants had no effect on the results, and likewise, the ethnicity of the participants had no effect on the results. As over half of the participants were referred as a result of head injury or organic brain damage, a further test was carried out to see if there were any differences between them and the non-head-injury participants. The only differences that were found were in levels of activity within the corpus callosum.

Discussion

The authors argue that their research supports previous findings about the role of certain brain structures in violent behaviour. They suggest that the difference in activity in the amygdala (which is part of the limbic system) can be seen to support theories of violence that suggest it is due to unusual emotional responses such as a lack of fear. The authors also comment on the differences in corpus callosum activity between the NGRIs and the controls, and suggest this can be matched up to evidence of people with a severed corpus callosum which shows they can have inappropriate emotional expression and an inability to grasp long-term implications of a situation (Sperry, 1974).

It is important to note that the authors are cautious about the implications of their findings. They note that the findings:

- cannot be taken to show that violence is only caused by biology;
- do not show that NGRIs are not responsible for their actions;
- do not say anything about the causes of the brain differences;
- cannot be generalized from NGRIs to other types of violent offenders;
- cannot be generalized to other types of crime.

We would also add some further limitations to the conclusions of this study:

(1) Imaging techniques are still being developed and the data should be treated with caution.

(2) The task used by the participants before the scan is a general activity task and has no bearing on violent acts or even the decision to be violent. The relevance and appropriateness of this task is not obvious.

(3) NGRIs are not necessarily charged with murder because of a violent act. It is possible to murder someone with poison (not very violent) or even shoot them without any more violence than a finger press. There are no controls in this study for the level of violence used in the alleged murder.

(4) Even if there are clear differences between the brain scans of the NGRIs and the controls, these differences might be a result of the crime and its consequences rather than a cause of it.

Considering all the criticisms of the design of the study and the techniques used to collect the data, it is appropriate to be cautious about making any generalizations from the findings. The results show that we can use imaging techniques to find differences in brain activity between different groups of people. But deciding what these differences mean is another matter altogether. It is difficult to be sure in a study such as this whether the differences have indeed been accurately measured, whether the differences really do have the neurological implications that are proposed, and whether the subjects were divided up into meaningful groups in the first place. Given that data such as these could prove to have significant treatment consequences, it would be wise to remain circumspect about their real value.

It would also be wise to have reservations about the potential use of these data; that is in the possible identification of potential murderers. The pitfalls here can be explained by looking at sex differences. We know, for example, that in the UK girls do, on average, a little better than boys on verbal tasks. However, the difference is very slight, so if we were given the verbal test results of two children, one boy and one girl, but we did not know which test result went with which child, our chances of predicting the sex of the child just from the test result would be little better than sheer guesswork. In the same way, given the brain data of individuals similar to those from this study, the chances of identifying the potential murderer would also be very slight.

Adrian Raine is more optimistic about the potential of this research and said in a BBC programme in 2004:

There are now 71 brain imaging studies showing that murderers, psychopaths, and individuals with aggressive, antisocial personalities have poorer functioning in the prefrontal cortex – that part of the brain involved in regulating and controlling emotion and behaviour.

Literally speaking, bad brains lead to bad behaviour. ... One of the reasons why we have repeatedly failed to stop crime is because we have systematically ignored the biological and genetic contributions to crime causation. (BBC website, 2004)

It is fair to say that not everyone agrees with Raine. It is our view that imaging has a great potential for investigations into how the brain works. However, the history of psychology's attempts to investigate differences between groups of people (see Gould, 1982, in Chapter 9 of this volume) leads us to be very wary about any slight differences that can be found in an array of complex data. For the moment, studies like this one illustrate the techniques of brain imaging, and tell us an interesting story about individual differences that we would do well to treat cautiously.

Questions

1. What do the results tell us about the brain of a murderer?

2. What are the benefits and problems with using scanning techniques to investigate the brain?

3. Why do you think people commit murder?

4. If we could identify a potential murderer through a brain scan, what should we do about it?

suggested answers → p. 484

Mastermind

MAGUIRE, E.A., ET AL. (2000)

Navigation-related structural change in the hippocampi of taxi drivers.

Proceedings of the National Academy of Science, USA 97, 4398–403.

► **phylogenetic** To do with the evolution of a species. If a feature of an organism is said to be 'phylogenetically' old, it means that it appeared early in the species' evolutionary history.

► **amnesia** The loss of memory, usually through physical causes.

Introduction

London taxi drivers are renowned for two main things. They have an opinion on everything, and they really know their way around London. The first of these 'facts' is nothing more than a stereotype; the second happens to be true. And it is this second fact that makes them of great interest to psychologists who are interested in the structure and function of a small part of the brain called the hippocampus.

Humans have two hippocampi (a left and a right one) located in the medial temporal lobe (see Figure 6.5). This phylogenetically old brain structure is part of the limbic system and is thought to play an important role in the formation of new memories. Damage to this structure is associated with amnesia, particularly anterograde amnesia (difficulties with forming new memories). It is also thought to play an important role in relation to the retention of information about spatial relationships in the outside world, underpinning people's ability to navigate their way around their environment. One way of testing this is to see if differences can be detected in the hippocampi of people with particularly refined and extensive navigational skills when compared with the hippocampi of people who do not have such skills.

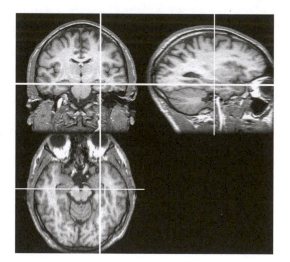

Figure 6.5   *Location of hippocampi*

Note: The crosshairs show the location of one of the hippocampi. In the top right hand image the head is facing to the right.

London taxi drivers undertake extensive training, known as 'being on the Knowledge', which lasts on average for two years. During this time they must acquire an internal representation of the sprawling complexity of the London road system. This is particularly difficult because unlike many capital cities the roads of central London are still based on a medieval street plan and not on the grid system so favoured by modern planners. The drivers then have to undertake a rigorous examination to test their ability to recall directions from this 'cognitive map', to ensure that when they get a fare they are able to transport their passenger(s) to the correct location by means of the most efficient route. This is even more sophisticated than modern satellite navigation devices because they can respond to traffic jams by changing their strategies. So, if one of the functions of the hippocampus is, indeed, to store spatial representations of the environment, then it should be possible to detect some kind of structural or functional difference between the hippocampi of London taxi drivers and the hippocampi of people who do not spend so much of their time undertaking tasks based on extensive spatial representations of the world around them.

▶ **independent-measures design** When a study involves comparing the scores from two or more separate groups of people.

The study

▶ **magnetic resonance imaging** Uses a combination of powerful magnets and radio pulses to construct an image of brain structures. Functional MRI (fMRI) requires participants to undertake some sort of task (without moving! – for example, watching a video or listening to audio stimuli) and measures changes in neural activity associated with the performance of that task. The great advantage of the MRI technique is that these scanners are relatively common in hospitals and can be converted for brain imaging without too much further expense.

Subjects and design

The study employed an independent-measures design. An experimental group of 16 right-handed male London taxi drivers who had been licensed for a minimum of 18 months (mean age 44 years, mean post-qualification taxi driving experience 14.3 years) was compared with a control group of 50 right-handed males who were not taxi drivers.

Procedures

Structural magnetic resonance imaging (MRI) scans of the subjects' brains were taken. This type of MRI constructs an image of the brain without requiring the subject to undertake any type of task (as is required for functional MRI). The images were then subjected to two kinds of analysis which aimed to provide measures of the size of different brain structures, and the relative density of grey matter within them.

Results

▶ **posterior** An anatomical term denoting the opposite of the anterior end of an organism. In terms of the human brain, this equates to the 'back' of the brain.

▶ **anterior** An anatomical term denoting the 'nose' end of an organism.

▶ **correlation** A measure of how strongly two or more variables are related to each other.

The *only* structures of the brain in which differences could be detected between the two groups (in terms of grey matter volume) were the left and right hippocampi. Specifically there was a greater volume of grey matter in the posterior hippocampi of taxi drivers than of control subjects; conversely the non-taxi drivers showed a greater volume of grey matter in the anterior hippocampi than did the taxi drivers (see Figure 6.6).

A correlational analysis, comparing length of taxi-driving experience with the measures of grey matter volume within the taxi-driving group, showed a significant positive correlation for the right posterior hippocampus ($r = 0.6$, $p < 0.05$), and significant negative correlation for the right anterior hippocampus ($r = -0.6$, $p < 0.05$). The more experienced the taxi driver, the greater the grey matter volume in their right posterior hippocampus tended to be (and the smaller the grey matter volume in their right anterior hippocampus).

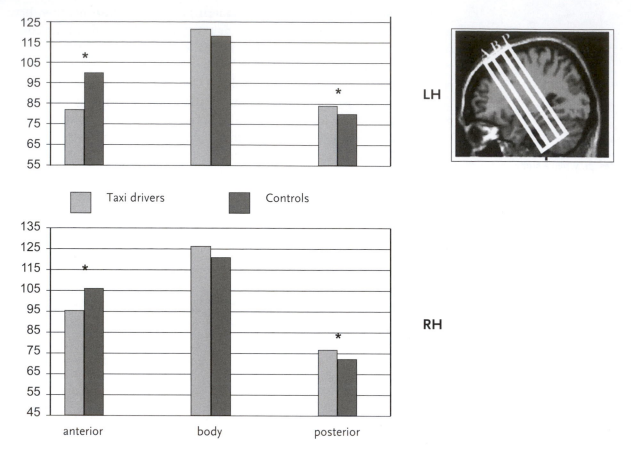

Figure 6.6 *Volumetric analysis findings*

Note: The orientation of the slices measured in the volumetric analysis with respect to the hippocampus is shown (top right inset). A, anterior; B, body; P, posterior. The upper figure shows the average relative size of these three areas of the left hippocampus for experimental and for control subjects. The lower figure shows the same data but for the right hippocampus. * There were significant differences (*p* < 0.05) in size for anterior and posterior areas for both left and right hippocampi, but no differences in the body area of the hippocampi.

Discussion

It seems that being a London taxi driver is associated with a specific distribution of grey matter in the hippocampus. Without further analysis, it would be unclear what this means. It might be that people with bigger posterior hippocampi are more likely to become taxi drivers. Or it might be that people who become taxi drivers develop bigger posterior hippocampi. The correlational analysis lends weight to the second interpretation, because it appears to be describing a process whereby length of service as a taxi driver is actually associated with a re-distribution of grey matter within the hippocampus. It is as if the day-on-day spatial processing that is required of London taxi drivers causes specific areas on the hippocampus to 'recruit' more neural circuitry. However, the researchers are clear that they are working at a relatively macroscopic level, so they can only speculate about the neural mechanisms that might underlie the different patterns of grey matter volume that they have observed.

Findings such as these are difficult to interpret unless they are viewed in the context of the entire body of literature within which they are embedded. If one were to look only at the design of this study in isolation, then one would have to question the validity of the researchers' interpretations of their observations. London taxi drivers may differ in all sorts of systematic ways from a group of non-taxi driving adults. Perhaps the extra grey matter in the posterior hippocampus relates to the physical activity of actually driving a car all day. Or maybe it relates to the skill of talking to someone who is sitting behind you, who you can only see in a mirror! These interpretations are probably less likely, but not out of the question. The point is that it is using this study *in concert* with other studies that allows the researchers to point towards navigation skills and highly developed spatial representations as the variables of interest here.

So the findings of this study are of interest for two main reasons. First, they lend support to the notion that the hippocampus deals with the kind of neural processing that is required for navigation around the environment. Second, they provide evidence of plasticity within the healthy adult brain: that is, evidence that the structure of the adult human brain can change in line with everyday activities, and in response to the demands of the environment. This has 'obvious implications for rehabilitation of those who have suffered brain injury or disease' (Maguire *et al.*, 2000, p. 4402).

▶ **plasticity** The capacity for change within a system. If a system is 'plastic' it is capable of change. Plasticity is a feature of the newborn baby's brain and the neural basis for development and learning.

Questions

suggested answers → P. 484

1. What related research questions could be addressed by undertaking similar studies, but with the following comparison groups? a) Retired taxi drivers versus age-matched controls; b) Expert musicians versus experienced taxi drivers; c) People who do poorly on tests of navigational skills versus age-matched controls; d) Expert chess players versus experienced taxi drivers.

2. Why does the correlational analysis lend support to the idea that being a London taxi driver actually causes a re-distribution of grey matter volume in the hippocampus?

3. What implications does the observation of plasticity in the adult brain have for rehabilitation in cases of brain injury or disease?

Where does it hurt?

Phantom limbs.
MELZACK, R. (1992)
Scientific American,
April, 90–6.

Introduction

Why do we feel pain? The answer to this question is nowhere near as straightforward as it might appear (see for example Melzack and Wall, 1985). The most obvious suggestion is that injury to the body causes tissue damage, which in turn causes the sensation of pain. However, there are a number of phenomena that challenge this simple notion. First, some people are born without the ability to feel pain, but this is very rare and also it is a health-threatening condition. More commonly, people report episodic analgesia for events when they are injured but do not feel the pain until some minutes or hours after the injury: the injuries range from minor abrasions to broken bones or even limb loss. Melzack *et al.* (1982) described how 37 per cent of people reporting to an emergency clinic with a variety of injuries reported no pain until some minutes or hours after the injury. He observed six characteristics of episodic analgesia:

▶ **analgesia** Lack of sensitivity to pain.

(1) The condition has no relation to the severity or the location of the injury.
(2) There is no simple relationship to circumstances – some of the injuries occurred during military combat, whereas others occurred in more mundane settings such as work.
(3) The victim can be fully aware of the nature of the injury but feel no pain.
(4) The analgesia is instantaneous.
(5) The analgesia lasts for a limited time.
(6) The analgesia is localized to the injury – the patient might experience no pain at the severed limb but complain about the needle prick for an injection.

A further challenge to the pain–tissue damage connection comes from the observations that we can have pain without injury. Many headaches have no known damage or explanation of cause. And some pain, for example that caused by small kidney stones, is out of all proportion to the injury. But the most dramatically puzzling thing of all is the experience of pain after healing, and, in particular, phantom limb pain. This occurs in people who have lost a limb, often in an accident, who still experience the presence of that limb (a phantom) and sometimes experience pain in it as well.

▶ **phantom limb** The name given to the phenomenon experienced by amputees of still feeling the limb as present and alive even though it has been surgically removed.

The study

The phenomenon of phantom limbs (see Figure 6.7) has been recorded for over a century, and their 'existence' raises a number of questions about how our senses work, and how we interpret sensory information. This paper provides a review of the evidence on phantom limbs and proposes a way of understanding this phenomenon.

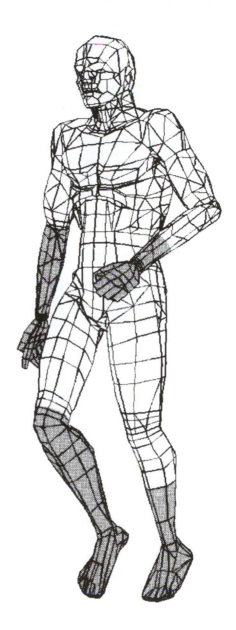

Figure 6.7 *Shaded areas represent the most common examples of phantom limbs*

Phantom limbs have the following remarkable features:

(a) A vivid sensory quality and precise location in space so at first people might try to walk on a phantom leg because it feels so real.

(b) In most cases a phantom arm will hang down at the side when the person sits or stands, but moves in coordination with other limbs when the person is walking.

(c) Sometimes it gets stuck in an unusual position, for example, one person had a phantom arm bent behind them, and could not sleep on their back because the limb got in the way.

(d) Wearing an artificial arm or leg enhances the phantom, and it often fills the extension like a hand fits a glove.

(e) Phantoms have a wide range of sensations including pressure, warmth, cold, dampness, itchiness and different kinds of pain (around 70 per cent of amputees suffer pain in the phantom).

(f) Patients perceive phantoms as an integral part of the body so even when a phantom foot is felt to be dangling in the air several inches below the stump and unconnected to the leg, it is still experienced as part of the body and moves appropriately.

(g) Phantoms are also experienced by some people with spinal injury, and some paraplegics complain that their legs make continuous cycling movements producing painful fatigue, even though their actual legs are lying immobilized on the bed.

Explanations of phantom limbs

▶ **neuroma** Nerve nodule which develops at a point where nerves have been cut.

▶ **spinal cord** The bundle of nerve fibres that runs up the spine to the brain. It is the pathway by which the brain sends and receives neural messages to and from the rest of the body.

An early explanation was that the cut nerve ends, which grow into nodules called neuromas, continue to produce nerve impulses which the brain interprets as coming from the lost limb. Working on this hypothesis, various cuts have been made in the nerve pathways from the neuromas to the brain in an attempt to remove pain. These cuts sometimes bring about short-term relief, but the pain usually returns after a few weeks, and the cuts do not remove the phantom. A further theory suggested that the source of phantom limbs was in the excessive spontaneous firing of nerve cells in the spinal cord that had lost their normal sensory input from the body. However, evidence from spinal injury patients shows that people with complete breaks in the spinal cord can still feel pain in the lower body. Therefore, the spinal cord cannot be the source of these sensations and phantoms.

▶ **cortex** The outermost layer of nerve tissue of the cerebral hemispheres.

▶ **thalamus** The sub-cortical structure in the brain which receives sensory information and relays it to the cerebral cortex.

A more recent approach has been to look for a cause in the brain, and in particular the sensory cortex and the thalamus. Although there is some evidence to support the role of these brain structures, Melzack concludes that this explanation cannot account for all the phenomena of phantoms, and that the simple 'electrical wiring diagram' approach to the brain will not provide the answers to this puzzle.

Melzack's model

Melzack suggests that the brain contains a neuromatrix, or network of neurons. This neuromatrix responds to information from the senses and also generates a characteristic pattern of impulses that indicate the body is whole and is also your own. He calls this pattern the neurosignature. It may be helpful to think of it as a mental hologram that builds up a picture of your body in the mind. If a limb is removed, the sensations cease from that region but the hologram is still created in the neuromatrix (sounds more like Star Trek than anything else).

The matrix has at least three major nerve circuits:

(a) Sensory pathways passing through the thalamus and sensory cortex.

(b) Emotional and motivational pathways passing through the limbic system.

(c) Pathways associated with the recognition of self, which is commonly thought to involve the parietal lobe of the cortex. Studies of people with damage to the parietal lobe have shown problems with their sense of self; for example some patients have been known to push one of their own legs out of bed because they were convinced that it belonged to a stranger.

Melzack offers the image of a musical piece. He suggests that the neuro-signature is like the basic theme of the orchestral piece. The collective sound changes as the instruments play their parts (the sensory input), but the product is continually shaped by the underlying theme (the neurosignature) which provides continuity for the work even as the details of its rendition change.

▶ **innate** Genetically pre-programmed.

Melzack suggests that the matrix is largely pre-wired (or innate), and offers the evidence that very young children can experience phantoms after amputation, and people born with limbs missing can experience vivid phantoms. The matrix also responds to experience, as shown by the gradual disappearance of some phantoms, though it is interesting to note that they can sometimes reappear years later.

Discussion

The phenomenon of phantom limbs creates a number of medical problems: for example, how to reduce the pain in parts of the body that do not exist. It also raises doubts about some major assumptions in psychology. One of these assumptions is that sensations are produced by stimuli affecting the senses, and that perceptions that occur without these stimuli are abnormal or hallucinations. However, phantom limbs tell us that the brain does more than just detect and analyse sensory inputs. It also generates perceptual experience, even when there are no sensory inputs. We do not need a body to feel a body.

▶ **perception** The process by which the brain organizes and interprets sensory information.

▶ **cognition** Mental processes. 'All the processes by which ... sensory input is transformed, reduced, elaborated, stored, recovered and used' (Neisser, 1967, p. 4).

This view has implications for how pain can be treated. Many people suffer long-term, debilitating pain, and the traditional approaches of surgery or large doses of medication have only produced limited relief. Modern techniques are making more use of cognitive and motivational approaches to pain relief with considerable success.

Perhaps one of the most remarkable discoveries about phantom limbs comes from Vijay Ramachandran (for example Ramachandran and Rogers-Ramachandran, 1996; see also his study on synaesthesia, summarized in Chapter 15). He invented a mirror box which can be used to give apparent movement to a phantom limb. For example if someone has a missing left arm, when they put their right arm into the mirror box they can see the mirror image of the right arm where their left arm should be (see Figure 6.8). When they move their right arm and watch the mirror image they commonly get the experience of moving their phantom limb. In this way a number of people have been able to relieve the discomfort in their phantom limbs.

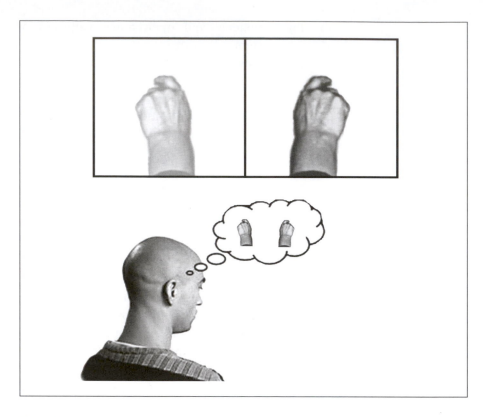

Figure 6.8 *Mirror box*

▶**reductionism** An approach to understanding behaviour which focuses on one single level of explanation and ignores others. The opposite of holism.

The phenomenon of phantom limbs highlights some problems with simple reductionist explanations of behaviour and experience (the attempt to explain all our complex feelings and behaviour in terms of simple biological responses). Maps of the brain that describe it like a car engine, saying which bits are responsible for which functions, are clearly too simplistic. The experience of pain appears to involve a complex interaction of sensory information, cognitive evaluations, and emotions. It will surely take a highly sophisticated model to make sense of this complex phenomenon.

Questions

suggested answers ➔ p. 485

1. What is the evidence that shows pain is not a direct result of tissue damage?

2. How can pain be measured?

3. Why is the inability to feel pain a health-threatening condition?

4. Remember a physically painful experience that you have had and list what made the pain worse and what made the pain better. Categorize the things you identify into cognitive, physiological and emotional factors.

part iii

DIVERSITY

▶ **aggression** A term used in several ways, but generally to describe negative or hostile behaviour or feelings towards others.

▶ **identity** The sense that you have of the sort of person you are.

▶ **gender** The inner sense of being either male or female.

▶ **personality** A distinctive and relatively stable pattern of behaviours, thoughts, motives and emotions that characterize an individual.

PSYCHOLOGY often makes generalizations about people: how people behave, how people think, and how people feel. Although some of these general statements are quite useful, they ignore the differences between groups of people, and between individual people. For example, if we wanted to talk about human aggression we might be able to say something about how all people show their aggression, but we would have to acknowledge the differences that exist. Some groups of people are much more aggressive than others; for example men are, on the whole, more aggressive than women, and army commandos are, on the whole, more aggressive than Buddhists. These are examples of groups that have different levels and styles of aggression. Also, within those groups there will be some individual differences. You might know some women who are very aggressive, and some men who are non-aggressive. The problem for psychology is to identify the features that we share with other people, and still acknowledge the differences between individuals.

The studies in this part have been selected to show how psychology has approached the issues surrounding diversity. One such issue which has

stimulated a considerable amount of research concerns identity – our sense of who we are. We have included two studies about our sense of ethnic identity (Hraba and Grant, 1970; Nobles, 1976) and three about our sense of gender identity (Diamond and Sigmundson, 1997; Koff, 1983; Kitto, 1989). Elsewhere in the text you will find other studies that ask difficult questions about identity. For example the report by Melzack (1992) on phantom limbs (described in Chapter 6) challenges our understanding of how we recognize and experience our own bodies, the report of multiple personality by Thigpen and Cleckley (1954) challenges our ideas about having a single and coherent identity, and the work of Loftus and Pickrell (1995) challenges the accuracy of the memories that we use to define our sense of identity.

Much of the psychology that is taught in British and US universities and colleges is fairly insensitive to cultural differences. However, the different cultures that exist within our societies, and around the world, do not share the same behaviours and social structures. As well as the two studies mentioned above we have included studies elsewhere in the text that specifically deal with issues of cultural diversity, including a comparison of childcare (Brazelton *et al.*, 1976), a study of culture-specific language (Labov, 1969) and perceptual judgements (Deregowski, 1972).

We also look at what psychologists refer to as abnormality. Some people have unusual thoughts and feelings, or display some unusual behaviour patterns. Sometimes we regard this as eccentricity and sometimes we regard this as a sign of mental ill-health. The judgement to make is whether someone is just being different, or whether they are being odd. The way we make this distinction is influenced by a range of factors including our culture, class, religion and general outlook on life. We have included four studies that look at the issues of defining abnormality and the treatment of people with a variety of mental health problems. Studies of abnormality are bound to be controversial because at the heart of them is an initial judgement to see a behaviour as 'mad' rather than 'a bit unusual'. They are also controversial

because of the treatments that are used. These treatments depend on the theory that is developed about the causes of the behaviour. If the theory states that the cause of the behaviour is a biological imbalance then the treatment will be biological, i.e. drugs. Unusual behaviours are also described elsewhere in the book for example a study on autism (Baron-Cohen *et al.*, 1997), a review of therapies (Smith and Glass, 1977) and an account of phantom limbs (Melzack, 1992).

Finally, in this part of the book, we look at some issues around individual differences. The measurement of personality is a common feature of everyday life in, for example, magazines and job selection. A cautionary tale about the use of personality questionnaires can be found in the paper by Forer (1949). A description of the development of a personality test is given in the paper by McCrae and Costa (1987) and also in the paper by Bem (1974). There is also a paper by Plomin and Daniels (1987) on the controversial issue of the inheritance of personality features.

chapter **7**

IDENTITY

▶ identity The sense that you have of the sort of person you are.

▶ scientific racism The use of bogus scientific arguments to enhance the power of one group of people over another.

THE psychology that you read in most texts is mainly about the experience and behaviour of White people. Psychology courses, conferences and textbooks do not pay much attention to the diversity of cultures that exist within Western societies and around the world. It is possible to find some reference to cross-cultural studies, but very often the societies under examination are studied by Western psychologists who can only give the perspective of an outsider. In an analysis of introductory textbooks Smith and Bond (1993) found that in common European texts less than 2 per cent of the cited research came from outside Europe and the USA, and in texts from the USA it was even more narrow in that less than 6 per cent of all cited research came from outside the writers' own country. This is remarkable given the diverse populations that live in the USA and Europe. It is also noted in both this country and in the USA that the experiences of people from minority groups are not well represented in psychology texts or psychology courses.

In this collection of studies we have chosen to look at two that say something about the experience of Black people within the Western world, and about Black identities. The study by Hraba and Grant (1970) replicates a classic investigation by Clark and Clark (1947), where children were asked to choose between White and Black dolls. Their results suggested a change in the consciousness of Black US children over the intervening 20 years. Clark and Clark's work probably had the greatest social impact of any research in psychology. It was crucial evidence in court cases that finally brought about a change in the law and a massive change in status for Black people in the USA. The paper by Nobles (1976) theorizes on Black identity and provides a framework for considering these issues. If you think that Nobles is overstating the case when he refers to scientific racism, then we refer you to an article in *The Psychologist*, the flagship journal of the British Psychological Society. In 1990, it published an overtly racist article by Rushton which attempted to mount a case for racial superiority. Scientific racism is sadly still a reality as dominant groups seek to explain their political power through bogus scientific arguments (see also Richards, 1998).

Elsewhere in the text there are some studies that deal specifically with cultural issues. The paper by Brazelton *et al.* (1976) in Chapter 10 deals with neonatal behaviour in different cultures, the paper by Deregowski (1972) in Chapter 14 looks at cultural variation in perception, and the paper by Labov (1969) in Chapter 12 looks at cultural differences in language. We also cover an article by Stephen Jay Gould in Chapter 9 on the uses of Intelligence Quotient (IQ) testing. He demonstrates how findings were perverted for political ends and used in support of racist views of White superiority.

A second aspect of identity that is covered in this chapter is gender. When the birth of a new baby is announced, the first question on everyone's lips is 'Is it a boy or a girl?' This is a very important question for people, and you will find that out if you refuse to give the questioner the answer. If you say 'Well, there is not a lot of difference between boys and girls at birth, so in order to stop you behaving towards the child in accordance with your gender stereotypes, I am not going to tell you, and the child's name is Chris', then you will create a surprising amount of resentment. The category of boy or girl is perhaps the most important categorization of your life.

Psychologists often make a distinction between sex and gender. Sex is seen as the biological differences between male and female whereas gender is defined as the 'psychological attributes, characteristics, and behaviours that are acquired within a social context and are related to the social meanings of sexual categories in a given society' (Williams, 1987, p. 135). Scientific beliefs about this distinction are fiercely held and they form the backdrop to the study by Diamond and Sigmundson (1997) about the boy who was raised as a girl. This case study gives us some evidence on the relationship between our identity and our biology, and it also provides an insight into the workings of science and shows how compassion can be buried under the weight of scientific ambition.

One difference between men and women that is very clear is the power and status they have in society. The study by Kitto (1989) shows how an apparently inconsequential bit of everyday language can affect our perception of people, and, in particular, diminish opportunities and respect for women. Koff (1983) uses an interesting projective technique to explore the experience of the important female life event of menarche. This study also relates to the power and status differential, since issues which are specifically of concern to women have characteristically been under-researched in psychology.

▶ **gender** The inner sense of being either male or female.

▶ **menarche** The onset of menstruation.

Black dolls and White dolls

HRABA, J. AND GRANT, G. (1970)

Black is beautiful: a re-examination of racial preference and identification.

Journal of Personality and Social Psychology, 16, 398–402.

Introduction

Very rarely in psychology does a piece of research have a dramatic, enduring positive impact on a nation. This study is an example of one that did. In 1939, Clark and Clark first reported their work on racial identification and preference in Black US children. They were interested in how racial awareness developed, and devised a novel test using dolls with different skin colour. Clark and Clark (1947) found that Black children preferred White dolls and rejected Black dolls when asked to choose which were nice, which looked bad, which they would like to play with and which were a nice colour. This suggested that Black children had negative attitudes towards themselves and their cultural background.

The political context to these studies was the USA's social policy towards Black people. By the start of the twentieth century slavery had been banned but new ways to oppress people had been created. Under a court ruling passed in 1896 it became legal to create a segregated society under the principle of 'separate but equal', and many parts of the USA used this principle to have separate buses, drinking fountains and schools for Black and White people. You will not be surprised to know that the facilities for Black people were poorer and so a legal battle was fought against the 'separate but equal' court ruling.

As they went from state to state challenging the policy of segregated education, Clark and Clark repeated their studies in each state and came to the same conclusions. They were able to show scientifically something that seems so obvious today – if you treat someone as inferior for long enough they end up feeling inferior. The battle ended up in the US Supreme Court and finally in 1954 the principle of 'separate but equal' was ruled illegal.

At first glance the doll studies of Clark and Clark seem quite slight, but don't be misled here. Big ideas can sometimes be demonstrated with relatively simple studies, and Clark and Clark were able to make some profound statements about self-identity from their studies. The results of this speeded up the emancipation of Black people in the USA and so can reasonably be said to be one of psychology's most important studies of the twentieth century.

The study we summarize here was carried out 30 years after the first doll studies by Clark and Clark. The intervening years had brought about some social changes in the USA. The 1960s saw the growth of the Civil Rights Movement (most famously, the leadership of Martin Luther King), and the influence of militant Black religious and political organizations and figures (most famously Malcolm X). This led to some improvement in the opportunities for Black people, and a change in their expectations. Since that time, Black people have made advances within US society and occupy an important place in the democratic structure. Despite this, Black people are still on average economically disadvantaged and still live with the experience and effects of racism.

▶**racism** Using the pervasive power imbalance between races/people to oppress dominated peoples by devaluing their experience, behaviour and aspirations.

The study

Hraba and Grant's study was a replication of Clark and Clark (1947), so they followed the same procedures as far as possible. The children were interviewed individually using a set of four dolls: two Black and two White, but identical in all other respects. The children were asked the following questions:

(1) Give me the doll that you want to play with.
(2) Give me the doll that is a nice doll.
(3) Give me the doll that looks bad.
(4) Give me the doll that is a nice colour.
(5) Give me the doll that looks like a white child.
(6) Give me the doll that looks like a coloured child.
(7) Give me the doll that looks like a Negro child.
(8) Give me the doll that looks like you. (p. 399)

Clark and Clark suggested that items 1–4 measured racial preference, items 5–7 measured awareness or knowledge, and item 8 measured racial self-identification. Hraba and Grant attempted to assess the behavioural consequences of racial preference and identification by asking the children to name the race of their best friends. They also asked the teachers for the same information.

The subjects were 160 children aged between 4 and 8 years who attended primary schools in Lincoln, Nebraska. Eighty-nine of the children were Black (60 per cent of the Black children attending school in Lincoln) and 71 were White. In the town of Lincoln at that time 1.4 per cent of the total population were Black, and in the five schools used in the study the proportions of Black children were 3 per cent, 3 per cent, 3 per cent, 7 per cent and 18 per cent. Also, 70 per cent of the Black children in the study reported they had White friends.

Results

The results provide a comparison of Hraba and Grant's data with that of Clark and Clark, and they also provide a comparison of the responses of Black children and White children.

Table 7.1 shows that, in the Lincoln study, Black and White children preferred the doll of their own 'race'. The White children were significantly more ethnocentric on items 1 and 2, there was no difference on item 3, and the Black children were significantly more ethnocentric on item 4.

The Clarks had found that Black children preferred White dolls at all ages, though this preference decreased with age. Hraba and Grant found that Black children at all ages preferred a Black doll and this preference increased with age. The Clarks had classified their subjects by skin colour into three categories: light (practically White), medium (light brown to dark brown), and dark (dark brown to Black). Hraba and Grant used the same criteria. The Clarks found that children of light skin colour showed the greatest preference for the White doll and the dark children the least. Hraba and Grant did not find this trend at all.

▶ **ethnocentrism** Being unable to conceptualize or imagine ideas, social beliefs, or the world from any viewpoint other than that of one's own particular culture or social group. The belief that one's own ethnic group, nation, religion, scout troop or football team is superior to all others.

Table 7.1 *Percentage responses to the doll questions*

Subject	Clark and Clark (1939) Blacks	Lincoln study (1969) Blacks	Lincoln study (1969) Whites
1 *'Play with'*			
White doll	67	30	83
Black doll	32	70	16
Don't know/no response			1
2 *'Nice doll'*			
White doll	59	46	70
Black doll	38	54	30
Don't know/no response			
3 *'Looks bad'*			
White doll	17	61	34
Black doll	59	36	63
Don't know/no response		3	3
4 *'Nice colour'*			
White doll	60	31	48
Black doll	38	69	49
Don't know/no response			3

For the remaining items on the test (items 5 to 8) Hraba and Grant obtained similar results to Clark and Clark. The children made few errors of racial identification or personal identification. They found that the race of the interviewer had no effect on the choices of either the Black or the White children. Also, there was no apparent connection for both Black and White children between doll preference and the race of friends.

Discussion

The results give a very different picture of doll preference in 1969 to doll preference in 1939. Hraba and Grant suggest a number of explanations for this discrepancy:

(1) Black people were more proud of their race in 1969 than they were in 1939.
(2) Children in Lincoln, unlike those in other cities, might have chosen Black dolls in 1939.
(3) The growth of organizations in the Black community might have enhanced Black pride.
(4) Inter-racial contact might create Black pride.

Whichever interpretation one follows (and after all it is difficult to say what children's preferences for dolls tells us about their self-identity), this replication highlights the fact that social psychological findings are inevitably the product of a particular point in history.

After the original doll studies were published, Mamie Phipps Clark continued her work at Columbia University where, in 1943, she became the first African-American woman and the second African-American (after her husband Kenneth Clark) in the University's history to receive a psychology doctorate. However, even after her ground-breaking work Phipps Clark had difficulty finding work as a psychologist. She described her frustration:

> Although my husband had earlier secured a teaching position at the City College of New York, following my graduation it soon became apparent to me that a black female with a Ph.D. in psychology was an unwanted anomaly in New York City in the early 1940's. (O'Connell and Russo, 2001. p. 271)

Mamie Phipps Clark and Kenneth Clark had to struggle against prejudice all their professional lives and it is sad that their work still does not receive much attention today. An attempt to correct this was made in 2001 when the American Psychological Association sponsored a conference on race and identity that led to a book on the legacy of Kenneth Clark (Philogene, 2004).

Psychology has a history of looking at behaviour and experience from a White perspective. Robert Guthrie (a student of Clark and Clark) found he was the only Black face in a sea of White when he enrolled on a masters course at a US university in 1955. Some years later he wrote the classic and brilliantly titled text *Even the Rat Was White*, which described the role of racial bias in the history of psychology, in the development of divisive theories and also in the failure to value the work of black psychologists.

▶**identity** The sense that you have of the sort of person you are.

Questions

1. How did the researchers measure racial identity in this study?

2. How else could you measure racial identity?

3. Why do you think the children in the Clark and Clark study preferred the White dolls?

▶ suggested answers p. 485

Black identity[1]

NOBLES, W.W. (1976)

Extended self: rethinking the so-called Negro self-concept.

Journal of Black Psychology, 2, 15–24.

▶ **Eurocentric** The tendency to view Europe as *the* main culture in human societies, and to negatively compare all other cultures to Europe.

▶ **evolution** The development of bodily form and behaviour through the process of natural selection.

▶ **innate** Genetically pre-programmed.

▶ **scientific racism** The use of bogus scientific arguments to enhance the power of one group of people over another.

▶ **eugenics** The political idea that the human race could be improved by eliminating 'undesirables' from the breeding stock, so that they cannot pass on their supposedly inferior genes. Some eugenicists advocate compulsory sterilization, while others seem to prefer mass murder or genocide.

▶ **drapetomania** The tendency of Black slaves in America to run away from the slave owners: this entirely sensible behaviour was defined as a form of mental illness by the slave owners, and given this label.

Introduction

The psychology that is presented in mainstream introductory textbooks is usually described as a psychology of people and behaviour. But what people? And how is that behaviour judged? It is fair to say that most European psychology courses are Eurocentric, and tend to describe the world from the viewpoint of White, educated, middle-class people. There are, of course, many other peoples in the world (and many others in Europe), and the way they construct their view of the world and their behaviour has a number of differences from the White Eurocentric account.

One particular group of people who are virtually invisible within mainstream psychology are Black people. The first point we have to consider is whether there is a need for a body of knowledge directed specifically to Black people, that psychology has so far failed to provide. Guthrie (1980) suggests that there is such a need and presents the following argument.

One of the major early influences on psychology was Darwinism and the theory of evolution. The scientists of the time tended to believe that human differences came from innate causes within people rather than environmental forces in society. The evolutionary approach was twisted to explain the superiority of certain groups in society. Darwin, in dismissing the intellectual abilities of women, wrote that the 'less highly evolved female brain [was] characteristic of the lower races, and therefore of a past and lower state of civilization' (in Miles, 1988). A considerable amount of scientific energy went into an attempt to show that some peoples are intellectually and morally superior to others. The 'evidence' produced does not stand up to scrutiny (for further discussion of this point see Gould, 1981). This scientific racism is at the heart of the eugenics movement (the attempt to selectively breed a 'superior' group of people) and the early work on individual differences.

Psychology is not politically neutral. It is always influenced by the society and the times it is written in. At its worst, it has been used to provide a scientific justification for oppressive practices. A much-quoted example is the diagnosis of the 'mental illness' drapetomania in Black American slaves. This condition was characterized by the irresistible urge to run away from the slave plantations. Today, we would not interpret the escape behaviour of slaves as a sign of mental disturbance.

Guthrie (1980) suggests that historical factors such as Darwinism and eugenics not only influenced early behavioural scientists, but also have a continuing effect on modern psychology. This effect makes it important to develop a psychology of Black people. One such contribution is the Afrocentric approach exemplified by the Nobles paper. The Afrocentric approach aims to dislodge Western civilization from its self-appointed position as the yardstick

1. Acknowledgement: Thanks to Patrick Hylton, Lincoln University for help in producing this summary.

by which every other culture is defined, and attempts to put the African factor at the centre of any research on Black people.

The paper

Nobles' account does not present any empirical research, but asks us to re-evaluate the standpoint of contemporary psychology. He suggests that the position of the social scientist is similar to that of the colonial master and his subject people. Table 7.2 shows the comparison between political and scientific colonialism.

▶**colonialism** Political oppression where one nation or culture dominates another one and, in particular, removes wealth from the dominated culture, believes it has a right of access into the dominated culture, and has a power base outside the dominated culture.

Table 7.2 *Similarities between political and scientific colonialism*

Colonialism manifested by	Political colonialism	Scientific colonialism
Removal of wealth	Exportation of raw materials and wealth from colonies for the purpose of 'processing' it into manufactured wealth and/or goods	Exporting raw data from a community for the purpose of 'processing' it into manufactured goods (i.e. books, articles, wealth)
Right of access and claim	Colonial Power believes it has the *right of access* and use for its own benefit anything belonging to the colonized people	Scientist believes she/he has unlimited *right of access* to any data source and any information belonging to the subject population
External Power Base	The centre of power and control over the colonized is located outside the colony itself	The centre of knowledge and information about a people or community located outside of the community or people themselves

Source: Nobles (1976).

Nobles suggests that the two most important themes in European/American science are:

(a)   survival of the fittest;
(b)   control over nature.

These themes are reflected in the European/American emphasis on 'competition', 'individual rights', 'independence' and separateness. In psychology this leads to an emphasis on individuality, uniqueness and difference.

By contrast, the themes of the African world view are:

(a)   survival of the people;
(b)   being one with nature.

These themes are reflected in the African values of 'cooperation', 'interdependence' and 'collective responsibility'. The psychological emphasis would then be on commonality, groupness and similarity.

These two approaches are summarized in Figure 7.1. Nobles argues that the lives of Black people in Europe and America are interpreted within the history and psychological framework of the European world view. To understand the psychology of Black people, he continues, it is necessary to interpret their behaviour and experience within an African perspective.

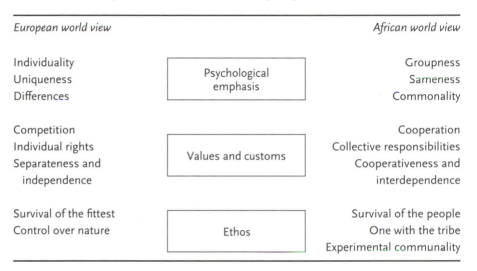

European world view		African world view
Individuality Uniqueness Differences	Psychological emphasis	Groupness Sameness Commonality
Competition Individual rights Separateness and independence	Values and customs	Cooperation Collective responsibilities Cooperativeness and interdependence
Survival of the fittest Control over nature	Ethos	Survival of the people One with the tribe Experimental communality

Figure 7.1 *Differences between African and European world views*
Source: Nobles (1976).

The tradition of European philosophy connects the notion of self with the experience of independence. The European self is believed to develop by establishing your uniqueness or separateness from other people. Your different-ness from other people is used to define your individuality. On the other hand, the African philosophical tradition views the self as being centred on the identity of the people, rather than individual differences. Nobles argues that in understanding the traditional African conception of self we must consider the belief that 'I am because We are, and because We are therefore I am'. A person's self-definition is dependent on the definition of the people.

▶ **identity** The sense that you have of the sort of person you are.

Discussion

The paper by Nobles provides a powerful criticism of the methods and the theories of contemporary Western psychology. It challenges the assumption that psychological theories and concepts can be applied to all people in all situations. The ideas presented in the paper make it essential to see Western psychology as being just one of many possible accounts of human behaviour and experience. Also, it is important to recognize that Western psychology is a product of the various cultural and historical influences that have formed society. In other words, it is not the detached and 'objective' science that it is often assumed to be.

The Afrocentric approach suggests that most of Western psychology should be rejected because it is culturally inappropriate for Black people. According to this view, it is as psychologically constraining and deforming as the shackles that were used to physically enslave Black people.

The Afrocentric approach is one opposing view to mainstream Western psychology. It is not without its critics, however, and perhaps the most controversial feature of the Afrocentric approach is the suggestion that the differences between peoples are biologically based. Nobles and Goddard (1984) write that Black Americans are 'African in nature and American in nurture' (p. 39).

The criticisms that are made of other attempts in psychology to explain differences between people in terms of genetics can also be used here. For example, it is not clear that we can define a political concept like race in biological terms. Also, the various attempts to disentangle the effects of nature and nurture in psychological qualities have had a remarkably unsuccessful history in psychology. One of the major problems is that the variation between individuals within a group is often so great that it makes the marginal differences between groups quite meaningless.

Another criticism of the approach concerns its attempt to describe the 'true' identity of Black people. This attracts the same criticisms that are made of other personality theories that attempt to fit people within a rigid framework developed by the researcher. An alternative approach is to allow people to describe their own experience within their own framework.

These criticisms challenge whether it is possible to define and measure the Afrocentric personality, but they do not challenge the central force of the argument which requires Western psychologists to re-evaluate their theories and data.

▶ **genetic** Biological inheritance.

▶ **race** Commonly used to refer to groups of people such as White people or Black people etc. It implies a genetic component to the differences between these groups, but research shows that the term 'race' has no biological validity and is best described as a political construct.

▶ **nature–nurture debates** Fairly sterile theoretical debates, popular in the 1950s, concerning whether a given psychological ability was inherited or whether it was learned through experience.

▶ **personality** A distinctive and relatively stable pattern of behaviours, thoughts, motives and emotions that characterize an individual.

Questions

suggested answers → p. 486

1. Think about the other areas of psychology you have studied and suggest which of them have been insensitive to cultural differences.

2. Take another study in psychology and imagine that it had used subject groups of different ethnic backgrounds. In what way do you think the results would have been different?

3. In your everyday life, think of examples of behaviour that show cooperation or collective responsibility (African self-image). Then think of examples of behaviour that show separateness or competition (Western view of self).

4. A common exercise for exploring self-concept is to try and give 20 answers to the question 'Who am I?' Start each answer with the phrase 'I am ....' How many of your answers refer to features of your personality (for example, generous), how many refer to groups that you belong to, and how many refer to things that you do? Have you described yourself by your differences from other people, or your connection to other people?

The boy who was raised as a girl: a psychological tragedy

DIAMOND, M. AND SIGMUNDSON, K. (1997)

Sex reassignment at birth: a long term review and clinical implications.

Archives of Pediatric and Adolescent Medicine, 151, 298–304.

DIAMOND, M. AND SIGMUNDSON, K. (1997)

Sex reassignment at birth: a long term review and clinical implications.

Archives of Pediatric and Adolescent Medicine, 151, 298–304.

Introduction: the back story

Some stories just jump out of the page at you and demand to be read. This is one of them. It is a story about a boy who was brought up as girl, and that line is often enough to make you want to read further. On one level it is a curious real-life story of one person's unusual upbringing and on another it is a story about science and how ordinary people can get lost in a scientific argument. If you want to take it a step further then it is also a story about stories, by which we mean it tells us about how stories develop in our society and how they are used and shaped by people with a point to prove (see Potter and Edwards, 1990, in Chapter 17).

The story is one of personal and scientific tragedy. It is a personal tragedy because of the distress it caused to the family at the centre of the story eventually leading to the early death of two of the central characters. It is also a tragedy for science in that it makes us even more suspicious of scientists and doctors and their intentions.

The paper we are summarizing here is a follow-up to a very influential case study in the medical and psychiatric literature. David Reimer[2] was born in rural USA in 1965 along with his twin brother Brian. When they were eight months they were both given a minor operation on their penis for medical reasons. The doctor made a mistake and burnt off David's penis. The parents were left with a dilemma of what was the best thing to do for their child. At the time it was not medically possible to replace the penis so the options were to bring up the boy without a penis or to bring him up as a girl. They were referred to Johns Hopkins Hospital in Baltimore where they met the world's leading sexologist, Dr John Money, and at this point their family tragedy collided with an international scientific dispute.

John Money was famous for his work on hermaphrodites (people born with the physical characteristics of both sexes) and had pioneered work on assigning them to one sex or the other. He claimed some success in this work and he also went further to claim that any child could be successfully brought up as a girl or a boy. He wrote:

> In place of a theory of instinctive masculinity or femininity which is innate, the evidence of hermaphroditism lends support to a conception that psychologically, sexuality is undifferentiated at birth and that it becomes differentiated as masculine or feminine in the course of the

▶ **sexologist** Someone who makes a systematic study of human sexuality.

▶ **hermaphrodite** A person who at birth has both male and female sexual characteristics and so cannot be unambiguously assigned to male or female.

▶ **innate** Genetically pre-programmed.

---

2. In the paper he is referred to as John because at that time he still wanted to remain anonymous. After the paper was published he was happy to reveal his name and so we are using that name in our summary. He was actually given the name of Bruce when he was born but he took the name David later in his life.

various experiences of growing up. (Money *et al.*, 1955, cited in Kitzinger, 2004, page 451)

In other words he is making a distinction between sex (our biology, our genitals, our chromosomes XY or XX) and gender (our sense of masculinity or femininity). Money was very confident that whichever sex a child was born as, he could assign them into the opposite gender and they could grow up to be healthy and adjusted adults. The problem was that he did not have any evidence for this and there was a growing challenge to this suggestion. Among the scientists who challenged Money was Milton Diamond, one of the authors of the study we are summarizing.

David Reimer's parents were persuaded by Money that the best option was to surgically change David into a girl and raise him as such. They agreed to this believing they had little choice and so created a unique psychological study on sex and gender. David's twin brother was, of course, the control of this study because he was genetically identical but being brought up as a boy. This had the potential to be the perfect test of Money's theory.

David's 'sex-reassignment' was the first ever carried out on a developmentally normal infant boy and there was considerable scientific curiosity about what happened. For many years the only source of evidence about the boys came from Money and his associates, who reported that the reassignment was successful. Money was featured in magazines on the topic and included a chapter on the case in his influential textbook *Man and Woman, Boy and Girl* (1972). One report said:

> The girl's subsequent history proves how well all three of them [parents and child] succeeded in adjusting to that decision. (Money and Tucker, 1973, p. 95, cited in Diamond and Sigmundson, 1997)

Nothing could have been further from the truth, and the true story came to light only when David Reimer was 30 years old. Milton Diamond had advertised each year in the scientific press for the doctors dealing with the twins to make contact so that he could review the case. Eventually in 1994 he was introduced to Reimer, who was shocked to learn that his case was being portrayed as a success and being used to promote the widespread use of sex change in cases of genital injury and hermaphroditism. Reimer agreed to participate in the follow-up study described here, which on publication created shock waves through the medical and psychological worlds.[3]

The study

The paper briefly outlines the background to the case and reviews the outcome by looking at the medical notes that were available, and by interviewing Reimer,

▸**gender** The inner sense of being either male or female.

▸**genetic** Biological inheritance.

3. The co-author with Diamond (H.K. Sigmundson) was the head of the psychiatry department to which David Reimer was referred. He was tracked down by Diamond and eventually persuaded to contact Reimer and report the case with Diamond (Colapinto, 2000).

his wife and his mother. The evidence is used to consider two postulates about sexuality that can be derived from Money's work.

Postulate 1: Individuals are psychosexually neutral at birth.

This postulate holds that we are not born with a strong sense of being male or female but can be encouraged into either gender. The evidence from this case challenges this view and the authors give several examples of how Reimer rejected the female role from a very early age despite the best efforts of his doctors and family.

Reimer's mother described one incident that was typical of Brenda/David's behaviour.[4] She described how when the boys were about 4 or 5 they were watching their father who was shaving and their mother who was applying makeup. Brenda applied shaving cream and pretended to shave. When she was corrected and told to put on lipstick and makeup like her mother, she said: 'No, I don't want no makeup, I want to shave' (p. 299).

Perhaps the most striking and most disruptive aspect of Brenda's behaviour was that she often stood to urinate. She was already rejected by the girls at school but this behaviour led to her being barred from the girl's toilets by the other girls. This led to further conflict and eventual expulsion from school.

At the age of 14, Brenda rejected any further hormone treatment designed to feminize her and decided to start living as a male. After some questioning from Reimer, his father revealed what had happened to him and why. In interview he recalled, 'All of a sudden everything clicked. For the first time things made sense and I understood who and what I was' (p. 300).

David Reimer took on his new name and started to live as a male and to deal with his physical handicap. When he lived as a female he had felt that his attitudes, his body and his behaviour were all at odds with each other. Back as a male, they became connected. When he was 25 he married a woman who was several years older than him and adopted her children.

Postulate 2: Healthy psychosexual development is intimately related to the appearance of the genitals.

This postulate holds that to develop as a well-adjusted male or a well-adjusted female you have to have genitals that look like our expectations of genitals. With regard to this case, the reasoning was that because David Reimer could not be given regular-looking male genitals it would be better to bring him up as a girl and use surgery to create something that looked like female genitals.

In interviews Reimer described how the doctors at Johns Hopkins Hospital made a big issue about his genitals and encouraged him to have surgery to become more female in appearance. He recalls thinking, 'Leave me be and then I'll be fine. ... It's bizarre. My genitals are not bothering me, I don't know why it's bothering you guys so much' (p. 301).

---

4. Another name issue; in the paper David's female name is given as Joan and the case is often referred to as John/Joan case. The real name that Reimer was given between the ages of 18 months and 14 years was Brenda.

The annual sessions with John Money involved David and his brother having to inspect each other's genitals and talk about a number of graphic sexual matters (this is described in more detail in Colapinto, 2000). Reimer was aware of what the doctors wanted of him but it did not fit with his experience of himself and he resisted all further surgery and tried as far as possible to avoid Johns Hopkins Hospital. On one occasion he was introduced to male-to-female transsexuals in order to convince him of the advantages of being female and having further surgery to create female-looking genitals. His response was to run off and hide on the roof of a nearby building.

Reimer recalled thinking that it was very small-minded of others to think that his personality could be summed up by the presence or absence of a penis saying:

> And I thought to myself, you know I wasn't very old at the time but it dawned on me that these people gotta be pretty shallow if that's the only thing they think I've got going for me; that the only reason why people get married and have children and have a productive life is because of what they have between their legs. (p. 301)

Reimer was always clear about his sexual preference and his first sexual partner was female. During his life he was approached sexually by males but reports that he was never attracted to them. The paper describes his responses to this questioning as being matter-of-fact and not homophobic.

Comments

The paper comments that it is rare for case studies to have long-term follow-ups, though in the case of sex reassignment this is obviously an important part of the evidence. The evidence presented in this paper provides a clear challenge to the postulates at the centre of Money's work. The authors are measured in their criticism of John Money and his associates (which is not the case in other reports of the case such as Colapinto, 2000) though they note that the treatment of David Reimer was based on postulates that did not have a body of evidence to support them. The sexual reassignment clearly failed and Reimer maintained his male identity in his behaviour, emotion and cognitions even when he was consistently told the opposite and encouraged to behave in female ways.

The failure of the treatment and its devastating effect on the Reimer family is a tragedy, but not necessarily an indictment of John Money. Scientists commonly go beyond what they know to try out new ideas and new treatments. Not all of these will work. The issue here is the response of the Johns Hopkins team when it was clear that the reassignment was not working. On top of this is the deliberate misrepresentation of the case until Diamond and Sigmundson followed it up. This misrepresentation led to many more operations being carried out. It also stole the story of his life from David Reimer, and created a false story for scientific consumption.[5]

▶ **personality** A distinctive and relatively stable pattern of behaviours, thoughts, motives and emotions that characterize an individual.

▶ **identity** The sense that you have of the sort of person you are.

---

5. A similar story theft happened with Christine Sizemore in the film *The Three Faces of Eve* described in Chapter 8.

Diamond and Sigmundson's paper had a dramatic effect on the medical community, and many people who had been given surgery based on the postulates described above were able to make better sense of their lives and tell their own stories. After the paper was published and Reimer appeared (in silhouette) on television he was introduced to a journalist by Diamond and agreed to tell his story in a way which identified him and gave a full account of his life experience (Colapinto, 2000). In it he described how when he first met Diamond and learned that other people had been given the same surgery, he was staggered and said, 'I figured I was the only one. And here Diamond tells me they're doing all these surgeries based on *me*. That's why I decided to cooperate with Mickey' (Colapinto, 2000, p. 208).

The paper was based on interviews in the mid-1990s and concludes by describing Reimer's reassignment back to being male as successful. It describes him as a mature and forward-looking man with a keen sense of humour and balance. He is described as being philosophical about what happened to him, though still bitter. That is the image that also comes through in Colapinto's book though he reports that Reimer could never forget his nightmare childhood and sometimes hinted that he was living on borrowed time (Colapinto, 2004). And so he was. In 2002 Reimer's twin brother Brian took his own life with an overdose of anti-depressants and David's life became more troubled after this. During the next two years he was made redundant and his explosive anger and periods of depression created tensions in his marriage. On 4 May 2004 he took his own life.

▶ **natural experiments (also quasi experiments)** Studies in which comparisons are made between different conditions that come about through natural political, social, economic or demographic circumstances, rather than through direct manipulation of a variable by an experimenter.

Questions

suggested answers ➔ p. 486

1. Why is this case described as a quasi-experiment?

2. What justification would the doctors offer for telling David Reimer for 12 years that he was a girl?

3. Who owns the story of a case study, the author or the subject? Why?

Mirror, mirror on the wall ...

KOFF, E. (1956)

Through the looking glass of menarche: what the adolesecnt girl sees.

In S. Golub (ed.), *Menarche*, pp. 77–86. Lexington, Mass: D.C. Heath.

Introduction

Growing up is not something that happens smoothly and gradually. There are events and changes that bring about a shift in the way we see the world and the way the world sees us. Half of the population have a clear sign of their growing maturity when they start to menstruate. The physical changes associated with the first menstruation (menarche) have been researched and described in some detail, but there have been relatively few studies of the psychological changes that accompany it.

Koff reports that some writers have suggested that menarche brings with it a number of changes in body image and sexual identification. They suggest the pre-menarcheal girl experiences difficulty in organizing and communicating her thoughts. The onset of menstruation is associated with a dramatic shift, and the post-menarcheal girl is seen to organize her thoughts and express herself more clearly. Interviews with post-menarcheal girls found that they experienced themselves as more womanly and began to reflect on their future reproductive roles. They also described more acceptance of their bodies as feminine, and a greater awareness of themselves as female.

Menarche usually occurs relatively late in the sequence of physical changes that occur in adolescence. In fact, girls can develop their secondary sexual characteristics and more feminine appearance as much as two years before menarche. Koff suggests, however, that the onset of menarche, which is a sharply defined event, is the key event around which girls make sense of the changes that are happening to them.

This article combines the results from two studies conducted by the author, both of which used projective techniques to explore the perceptions and feelings of the girls in the studies.

▶ **menarche** The onset of menstruation.

▶ **projective tests** Psychometric tests which involve providing the person with ambiguous stimuli, and seeing what meanings they read into them. The idea is that this will illustrate the concerns of the unconscious mind.

The studies

In the first study, girls from the seventh grade of a US school (approximately 12 years old) made drawings of male and female figures on two occasions about six months apart. The researchers were able to divide the girls into three groups:

(1) 34 girls were pre-menarcheal on both occasions;
(2) 23 girls were post-menarcheal on both occasions;
(3) 30 girls were pre-menarcheal on the first occasion and post-menarcheal on the second.

This is a quasi-experimental design since the groups selected themselves by their menarcheal status.

▶ **natural experiments (also quasi experiments)** Studies in which comparisons are made between different conditions that come about through natural political, social, economic or demographic circumstances, rather than through direct manipulation of a variable by an experimenter.

▶ **hypothesis** Experiments are designed to test one or more hypotheses. An hypothesis is a prediction of what will happen in an experiment. It is worded in such a way that the results of a well-designed experiment will clearly show whether the prediction is right or wrong.

The researchers collected the pictures and gave them a 'sexual differentiation score' (measuring how much the male and female drawings were distinguishable by their sex) using a previously developed scale. The hypothesis was that the pictures of the post-menarcheal girls would show greater sexual differentiation than the pictures of the pre-menarcheal girls. The researchers also recorded which picture, male or female, the girls drew first.

The three groups of girls were distinguishable by the types of drawings they produced. Figures 7.2 and 7.3 show an example of the drawings made by a girl who was pre-menarcheal on both occasions. These show a dramatic contrast with the pictures drawn by post-menarcheal girls, examples of which are shown in Figures 7.4 and 7.5. Perhaps the most interesting pairs of pictures are the ones drawn by girls who changed their menarcheal status between the two drawings, and an example of this is shown in Figures 7.6 and 7.7. The girls in the three groups were approximately the same age, in the same year at school and had experienced the same time gap between the two drawings. The key feature seems to be the menarcheal status of the girls.

Koff reports that, overall, the post-menarcheal girls drew pictures that showed more features of sexual differentiation. Also, among the girls who changed their menarcheal status, there was a significant increase in the sexual features drawn in their second pictures. Another finding was that post-menarcheal girls were more likely to draw their own sex first.

In a second study, Koff and her associates used a sentence-completion task to further investigate the perceptions of the girls. The subjects in this study were 16 pre-menarcheal and 18 post-menarcheal girls. They were given the cue sentence 'Ann just got her period for the first time' and were then asked to complete a number of other sentences. Some of the items received similar

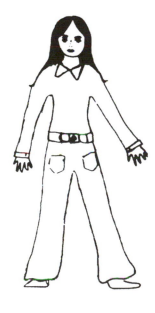

Figure 7.2 *Drawing by a pre-menarcheal girl,* **Figure 7.3** *Drawing by a pre-menarcheal girl,*
Time 1 *Time 2*

Figure 7.4 *Drawing by a post-menarcheal girl, Time 1*

Figure 7.5 *Drawing by a post-menarcheal girl, Time 2*

Figure 7.6 *Drawing by a girl whose menarcheal status changed over course of study – pre-menarcheal, Time 1*

Figure 7.7 *Drawing by a girl whose menarcheal status changed over course of study – post-menarcheal, Time 2*

responses from both groups of girls. For example, when asked to complete the sentence 'When Ann looked at herself in the mirror that night ...' the girls gave responses such as 'she felt more grown up', 'she thought she had changed', 'she thought she looked older'.

Some other items, however, did show some differences between the pre-menarcheal and post-menarcheal girls. For example, the sentence 'Ann regarded her body as ...' received a number of completions from pre-menarcheal girls about altered body image, such as 'more mature than it was', 'a woman's body', and 'different'. The post-menarcheal girls were less likely to make this sort of response, and some reported no change, for example 'she did before', or 'the same as yesterday'. The authors of this summary are unclear about how this observation fits with the results of the first study (and the original authors argue that it does), which indicated a changed perception of the woman's body in post-menarcheal girls.

Discussion

▶ **identity** The sense that you have of the sort of person you are.

The studies add weight to the suggestion that menarche is an important psychological event for a girl that acts as the turning point in her view of herself and her identity as a woman.

The paper raises a number of other important issues, not least of which is the relative lack of research into the psychology of women. It is quite remarkable that major life events such as menstruation or pregnancy have received so little attention by psychologists.

The study also uses the interesting method of projective techniques. The basic idea of a projective technique is to provide someone with a relatively bland stimulus and let them make of it what they want. Their response is likely to show some characteristics of their thoughts and feelings that they would otherwise find difficult to articulate. The drawings produced by the girls gave a dramatic representation of the effects of menarche, and it is very doubtful whether it would be possible to use interviews or questionnaires to give such a graphic illustration of the psychological changes taking place. Some psychologists might regard these sorts of qualitative data with suspicion since they do not have numbers attached to them.

▶ **qualitative data** Data which describe meaning and experience rather than providing numerical values for behaviour such as frequency counts.

The study was carried out on a relatively small sample of US girls, so without further empirical work we cannot generalize the findings to women with a different cultural background. Further studies that explore the experience of menarche in other cultures would give some insight into the processes by which women develop their female identity.

Questions

1. Why has psychology shown relatively little interest in the behaviour and experience of women?

2. What are projective techniques? What are the advantages and disadvantages of these techniques?

3. Try out the 'draw a female and male' test on your friends and family and look for any systematic difference between the responses.

suggested answers → p. 486

Gender reference terms: separating the women from the girls.

KITTO, J. (1956)

British Journal of Social Psychology, 28, 185–7.

Girls just want to have fun

Introduction

Does it matter what words we use to describe and label people? Feminist writers have argued that it does matter (see for example Lakoff, 1975). Their argument is that words do not just reflect our beliefs and attitudes, but actually play a part in forming and reinforcing those beliefs and attitudes. The use of the pronouns 'he', 'him' and 'his', for example, to refer to people (both women and men) is more than just a neutral, unimportant grammatical convention. It has the effect of putting men implicitly at the centre of anything that is spoken about, whilst 'backgrounding' women. The effect is subtle, but pervasive and powerful. Nowadays most social scientific publications require writers to use non-gender specific pronouns when referring to people.

The experiment summarized here was designed to investigate whether or not these kinds of subtle effects of language could be demonstrated empirically. Specifically, it set out to examine whether people's attitudes to an adult female could be affected by her being described either as a 'girl' or as a 'woman'. Should the tendency to describe adult women as 'girls' be seen as endearing and harmless? Or is there something more important and problematic going on when people do this?

▶ **attitude** A relatively stable opinion about a person, object, or activity, containing a cognitive element (perceptions and beliefs) and an emotional element (positive or negative feelings).

The study

The study involved subjects choosing which of two candidates was the more suitable for a hypothetical job. Each candidate was presented to the subjects by means of a reference which had apparently been written by her previous employer. One of the references referred to the candidate as a 'girl' and the other referred to her as a 'woman'. The subjects actually performed this task twice: once for a low-status job, and once for a high-status job. Kitto's hypothesis was that the candidates referred to as girls would be more likely to be thought suitable for the low-status job, and the candidates referred to as women would be more likely to be nominated as suitable for the high-status job.

▶ **gender** The inner sense of being either male or female.

▶ **hypothesis** Experiments are designed to test one or more hypotheses. An hypothesis is a prediction of what will happen in an experiment. It is worded in such a way that the results of a well-designed experiment will clearly show whether the prediction is right or wrong.

Subjects

Sixty-four subjects participated: 32 women and 32 men. No further details of subjects are given.

Design

This experiment used a two-condition repeated measures design. The independent variable was the term used to describe the candidate ('girl' or 'woman'); the dependent variable was measured by means of the subjects' judgements of the candidates' suitability for the particular jobs.

Procedure

▶ repeated measures design (also within groups) An experimental design where each subject carries out each condition of the experiment.

▶ independent variable The conditions which an experimenter sets up, to cause an effect in an experiment. These vary systematically, so that the experimenter can draw conclusions about changes in outcomes.

▶ dependent variable The thing which is measured in an experiment, and which changes, depending on the independent variable.

Each subject received two job advertisements. One was for a high-status job ('personal assistant for top executive'), the other for a low-status job ('helper/server in a café'). With each advertisement were references, ostensibly written by a former employer, for two candidates. For each job, one of the candidates was referred to as a 'girl', the other was referred to as a 'woman'. All four references were matched in terms of the personal qualities and abilities that were described for each candidate, the extent and relevance of the candidates' previous experience, and their age (all were 25). Each reference appeared an equal number of times in each of the two conditions; that is, for half the subjects reference A referred to the candidate as a girl, and for the other half of the subjects reference A referred to the candidate as a woman.

Each subject was required to choose, for each of the two jobs, which of the two candidates they thought was more suitable. The order in which the subjects made these decisions was randomized, so that some saw the high-status job advertisement and references first, and some saw the low-status job advertisement and references first. Subjects were also asked to give reasons for their decisions.

Results

▶ chi-square test An inferential statistic that can be used to show whether or not there is a statistically significant relationship between two categorical (nominal) variables. It can be thought of as the categorical equivalent of a correlation coefficient (which is used to look for relationships within ordinal or interval data).

▶ inferential statistics A way of using statistics to enable us to make inferences from data about relationships among variables, particularly with reference to cause and effect. This involves going *beyond* the data, hence the term 'inferential'. A contrast can be made with *descriptive statistics*.

▶ nominal scale The crudest level of measurement, which simply sorts people or things into categories (see also ordinal scale and interval scale).

Note that the measures in Table 7.3 are 'dependent'. In effect each subject appears in two cells in the table, so the chi-square test is not a suitable inferential statistic in this instance, despite the fact that a nominal scale of measurement is used. Kitto reports using a McNemar matched samples test (a chi-square test for dependent samples) to show a statistically significant relationship between the status of the selected job, and the description of the candidate ($p < .001$). Table 7.3 and Figure 7.8 show that the candidate labelled 'woman' tended to be chosen for the high-status job, while the 'girl' was more often selected for the low-status job.

Table 7.3 *Contingency table showing subjects' selections of candidates for high and low-status jobs*

	Low status	High status
Girl	40	18
Woman	24	46

Source: Kitto (1989).

About 40 per cent of the subjects reported having been aware of the usage of the embedded terms in the different references that they saw. Kitto labelled these subjects the 'aware' group and compared their pattern of responses with the 60 per cent of unaware subjects. Both groups showed the same preference for the girl for the low-status job and the woman for the high-status job. 'Thus the results cannot be explained as an artefact caused by a small number of subjects self-consciously making selections they thought the experimenter wanted' (p. 186).

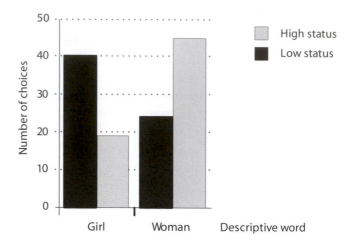

Figure 7.8 *The selection of 'girls' or 'women' for high and low-status jobs*

Discussion

The results support Kitto's hypothesis. The candidates referred to as girls were more likely to be thought suitable for the low-status job, whilst candidates referred to as women were more likely to be thought suitable for the high-status job.

The reasons that subjects gave for their decisions suggested that the inferences they made about the candidates were affected by the embedded terms 'girl' and 'woman'. For example, the subjects for whom the candidate was described as a 'woman' were more likely to give their reasons for choosing her in terms of her maturity, reliability and trustworthiness. On the other hand, the subjects for whom the candidate was described as a 'girl' were more likely to give their reasons for choosing her in terms of her youthfulness, vivaciousness and liveliness. The inferences tended to be positive for both embedded terms, but appeared to work against the person labelled as a 'girl' when it came down to assessing suitability for a responsible, high-status position.

The results certainly lend weight to the argument that the tendency to refer to adult women as 'girls' is more than just a harmless linguistic convention. Kitto argues that we should be aware of the subtle effects that language can have on our attitudes to others. The terms 'girl' and 'woman' are so frequently used in everyday life to label people that we may not notice the effects that they have on our perceptions of those people.

▶ **inference** Going beyond what we know to make an intelligent guess.

suggested
answers
→ p. 487

Questions

1. Why did each reference appear in each condition an equal number of times? That is, why did the same reference refer to the candidate as a girl for some subjects, and as a woman for other subjects?

2. It is very common in the English language to use 'he' to mean 'a person'. What other gender-specific terms can you think of that are used to describe people of both sexes?

3. Most of the inferences attached to the term 'girl' were positive ones. This seems to be a particularly interesting observation. Why?

chapter **8**

ABNORMALITY

▶ paranoia An irrational fear, suspicion or distrust of others.

WHEN music is discussed, everyone has an opinion. We like Tamla Motown music. But ask us what we like about it, and we struggle to analyse what we find exceptional in the songs. We can recognize the music, and we know how we feel about it, but we don't know how we recognize it.

People find it easy to make judgements of 'oddness' in other people. 'He's never been quite right, you know' is a familiar judgement from a street-corner conversation. In a similar way to our judgement of music we also find it hard to say what it is that may be odd about a person. And we would find it harder still to classify that oddness.

Psychological diagnosis is an attempt to classify oddness in people. It is a difficult process that is steeped in controversy. Observers often cannot agree on a diagnosis for a patient, and classifying a person can lead to the carers ignoring signs and symptoms that do not fall into the diagnostic pattern. Despite these problems, diagnosis is attempted because it has some benefits, one of which should be effective treatment.

The psychological diagnosis of abnormality has a long history. The Greeks, for example, recognized such diagnoses as senility, alcoholism, mania, melancholia and paranoia. The first comprehensive system of psychological disorders was created in 1896 by Emil Kraepelin (see Kraepelin, 1913). He believed that mental disorders have the same basis as physical ones, and that the same diagnostic principles should be applied: that is, the careful observation of symptoms. Other diagnostic systems were suggested by, among others, Eugen Bleuler, Adolf Meyer and Ernst Kretschmer. Clearly, though, the more systems in operation, the greater the opportunity for confusion. So in 1952 the *Diagnostic and Statistical Manual of Mental Disorders* (DSM) was developed and approved by the American Psychiatric Association. A revised version, DSM IV is widely used today. A diagnosis is arrived at using family resemblances. If you think of a big family that you know, then you will notice that most of the family members have some similar physical features, yet each member of the family is different from the others. It is a similar recognition process with mental disorders. Each person who has a particular condition has some similar features in their behaviour to other people with the same condition.

▶ **schizophrenia** A mental disorder marked by some, or all of the following symptoms: delusions, hallucinations, incoherent word associations, inappropriate emotions or lack of emotions.

▶ **multiple personality** A dissociative disorder in which one or more personalities exists in the same individual, and each personality is relatively integrated and stable.

▶ **behaviour therapy** The process of treating abnormal behaviour by looking only at the symptoms, and using conditioning techniques to modify them.

▶ **phobia** An anxiety disorder characterized by persistent fear out of proportion to the danger, a compelling desire to escape the situation, and a recognition that the fear is excessive.

One of the biggest controversies about psychiatric diagnosis is whether disorders are being *observed* and categorized by psychologists or whether the psychologists are actually *inventing* them. The current version of the DSM runs to 900 pages and describes more than 300 mental disorders. The DSM structures the way we think about life, behaviour and experience and defines many sorts of behaviour as mental disorders, some of which do not seem to deserve the label of mental disorder. For example it has a disorder called Oppositional Defiant Disorder, something you or I might well call 'being awkward', and another called Conduct Disorder, which might be called 'naughtiness' by someone else.

A diagnosis can be worth a lot of money. It can be worth money to the patient because if you want to sue an employer for causing your illness you have to have a diagnosis. It can also be worth a lot of money to the pharmaceutical industry because for every diagnosis there is a medication you can use. You might not be surprised to read that some of the main funders of DSM development are the pharmaceutical companies. The world thinks it is going mad because the drug companies tell it so, and psychologists collude in this nonsense. If you want to read more about this then we recommend you start with Kutchins and Kirk's (1997) book *Making Us Crazy*.

This chapter contains five studies that look at issues around abnormality and its treatment. The study by Rosenhan (1973) questions our ability to identify those with a diagnosable condition, from those with no such condition. The condition that was most commonly diagnosed in Rosenhan's study was schizophrenia, and that is the focus of the study by Griffith *et al.* (1972). The third study, by Thigpen and Cleckley (1954), describes the famous case of a young woman with a multiple personality. This condition still causes some controversy amongst psychologists, though it captured the public imagination through the film *The Three Faces of Eve*. The study by Lang and Lazovik (1963) examines treatment, looking at the effectiveness of behaviour therapy as a way of dealing with a phobia. The last study is by Mark Griffiths (no relation to the Griffith above), who is one of our colleagues at Nottingham Trent University. It was difficult to know where to place this study in the text. It fits everywhere and nowhere. It's about unusual cognitions so it could have fitted in the cognitive psychology section; it's about the behaviour of gambling so it could have fitted into the social psychology section; and it's about adolescent gamblers so we could have put it into the developmental psychology section. We decided to put it here in the abnormal psychology chapter because it frames the discussion as being about the extreme behaviour of pathological gambling. There was also a space here.

You don't have to be mad to work here. You don't even have to be mad to be in here ...

ROSENHAN, D.L. (1973)

On being sane in insane places.

Science, 179, 250–8.

Introduction

How do you know when someone is odd? What judgements do you make to assess someone as being not just 'different' but 'abnormal'? We make these judgements in everyday life, and it is necessary in a number of social situations to be able to identify 'abnormal' behaviour and to respond appropriately. Mental health workers have to make judgements about whether someone is psychologically 'abnormal' and needing specialized help. The definition and categorization of abnormality is both difficult and controversial, and the way we make these definitions varies between societies.

Rosenhan starts his paper with a simple question, 'If sanity and insanity exist, how shall we know them?' (p. 250). His study is designed to look at the categorization of abnormality and to question whether madness, like beauty, is in the eye of the beholder.

The study

The research question is: 'Do the salient characteristics that lead to diagnoses [of abnormality] reside in the patients themselves or in the environments and contexts in which observers find them?' (p. 250). This was tested in this study with the further question: 'If "normal" people attempt to be admitted to psychiatric hospitals, will they be detected as being sane, and if so, how?'

A number of 'sane' people (a graduate student, three psychologists, a paediatrician, a painter and a 'housewife' – Rosenhan's term) attempted to gain admission to 12 different hospitals in five different states in the USA. They telephoned for an appointment, and arrived at admissions complaining that they had been hearing voices. They said the voice, which was unfamiliar and the same sex as themselves, was often unclear but it said 'empty', 'hollow', 'thud'. These symptoms were chosen because they simulated an existential crisis (Who am I? What is it all for?) which could arise from concerns about how meaningless your life is. They were also chosen because there is no mention of existential psychosis in the literature.

The 'pseudopatients' gave false names and jobs (to protect their future health and employment records), but all other details they gave were true, including general ups and downs of life. After they had been admitted, the pseudopatients stopped simulating any symptoms, except possibly nervousness, fear of exposure as a fraud, and their inevitable reaction to the novelty of the situation. Each pseudopatient had been told they would have to get out by their own devices by convincing staff they were sane. They took part in

▶ **existential crisis** The realization that you are alone in your experience of the world, and that the only meaning your life has is the meaning you choose to impose on it.

▶ **psychosis** A mental state characterized by profound disturbances in reality testing, thought and emotion.

▶ **participant observation**
A method of study in which the investigator joins in the social process being observed.

ward activities, and spent time writing notes about ward staff and patients. This method is best described as participant observation, because the observers were attempting to get an 'insider' view of the social setting by becoming participants in that setting.

Results

▶ **schizophrenia**
A mental disorder marked by some, or all of the following symptoms: delusions, hallucinations, incoherent word associations, inappropriate emotions or lack of emotions.

All of the pseudopatients disliked the experience and wished to be discharged immediately. Not one of the pseudopatients was detected, and all but one were admitted with a diagnosis of schizophrenia. This diagnosis was made without one clear symptom of this disorder. They remained in hospital for 7 to 52 days (average 19 days), and were eventually discharged with a diagnosis of schizophrenia 'in remission'. Visitors to the pseudopatients observed 'no serious behavioural consequences'. Although they were not detected by the staff, many of the other patients suspected their sanity (35 out of 118 patients voiced their suspicions).

In a follow-up study, a teaching and research hospital which was aware of the first study was informed that during the next three months one or more pseudopatients would attempt to be admitted into hospital. Each staff member rated on a 10-point scale each new patient as to the likelihood of their being a pseudopatient. Table 8.1 shows a record of these ratings. Around 10 per cent were suspected by one psychiatrist and another staff member. However, no pseudopatients attempted to be admitted during the period, so the staff were rating their regular intake.

Table 8.1 *Judgements of all admission patients as to the likelihood that they are pseudopatients*

Number of patients judged	193
Number of patients confidently judged as pseudopatients by at least one staff member	41
Number of patients suspected by one psychiatrist	23
Number of patients suspected by one psychiatrist AND one other staff member	19

Source: Rosenhan (1973)

General observations

While the pseudopatients were in the psychiatric hospitals their normal behaviours were entirely overlooked or misinterpreted. For example, nursing records for three of the pseudopatients showed that the writing was seen as an aspect of their pathological behaviour: 'Patient engages in writing behaviour.' Rosenhan notes that there is an enormous overlap in the behaviours of the sane and insane. We all feel depressed sometimes, have moods, become angry and so forth, but in the context of a psychiatric hospital, these everyday human experiences and behaviours were interpreted as pathological. In another incident a psychiatrist pointed to a group of patients waiting outside the cafeteria half an hour before lunchtime. To a group of registrars (trainee psychiatrists) he suggested that such behaviour was characteristic of an oral-acquisitive syndrome. However, a more likely explanation would be that the patients had little to do, and one of the few things to anticipate in a psychiatric hospital is a meal.

The pseudopatients carried out a simple observation of behaviour of staff towards patients that illustrates the experience of being hospitalized on a psychiatric ward. The pseudopatients approached a staff member with a simple polite request, for example 'Pardon me, Mr/Ms/Dr X, could you tell me when I will be presented at the staff meeting?' Table 8.2 shows how the staff responded to this request. Rosenhan carried out a similar study in a university with students asking university staff a simple question. In the university study, nearly all the requests were acknowledged and responded to. This was not the case in the psychiatric hospital, where the pseudopatients were treated as if they were invisible.

Table 8.2   *Self-initiated contact by pseudopatients with psychiatrists, nurses and attendants*

Response	Percentage making contact with patient	
	Psychiatrists	**Nurses and attendants**
Move on with head averted	71	88
Makes eye contact	23	10
Pauses and chats	2	2
Stops and talks	4	0.5
NUMBER OF RESPONDENTS	13	47
NUMBER OF ATTEMPTS	185	1283

Source: Rosenhan (1973).

▶ **depersonalization** A dissociative disorder where the individual often feels cut off or unsure of their identity.

The overwhelming experience of hospitalization for the pseudopatients was one of depersonalization and powerlessness. The patients were deprived of many human rights such as freedom of movement and privacy. For example, their medical records were open to all staff members, regardless of status or therapeutic relationship with the patient. Personal hygiene was monitored and many of the toilets did not have doors. Some of the ward orderlies would be brutal to patients in full view of other patients but would stop as soon as another staff member approached. This indicated that staff were credible witnesses but patients were not.

Strangely, the pseudopatients were given a total of 2100 medication tablets, though only two were swallowed. The rest (2098) were either pocketed or flushed down the toilet. Often, when the pseudopatients visited the toilets to dispose of their tablets they found the medication of other patients which had already been placed there. As long as the patients were cooperative, then their behaviour went unnoticed.

The pseudopatients kept records of the amount of time the nurses stayed in the ward offices (around 90 per cent of the time), the number of times medical staff came onto the ward, and the amount of time spent with patients by the physicians. They noted that the total time a patient spent with psychiatrists, psychologists, registrars and so forth was, on average, under seven minutes per day.

Discussion

Rosenhan claims that 'It is clear we cannot distinguish the sane from the insane in psychiatric hospitals' (p. 257), though many would argue that this conclusion overstates the case. His study did, however, illustrate a failure to detect sanity, and, in the follow-up study, a failure to detect insanity. It also illustrated the depersonalization and powerlessness created by psychiatric hospitals.

Rosenhan points out that behaviour in the institution was systematically reinterpreted according to the expectations of the staff. These expectations were created by the labels of sanity and insanity. He suggests that instead of labelling a person as insane, it is more useful to discuss behaviours, the stimuli that provoke them and their correlates.

Rosenhan makes an interesting methodological point about the nature of participant observation. He notes that, although he and the other pseudopatients had very negative experiences in the psychiatric hospitals, their accounts do not describe the experience of real patients who did not have the comfort of believing that the diagnosis was false.

Not surprisingly, Rosenhan's article created a major storm when it was published. The most common argument was that faking symptoms for a medical condition would fool most doctors and therefore psychiatric diagnosis is no worse than medical diagnosis. For example Spitzer (1975) argued that,

> If I were to drink a quart of blood and, concealing what I had done, come to the emergency room of any hospital vomiting blood, the behaviour of the staff would be quite predictable. If they labelled and treated me as having a peptic ulcer, I doubt I could argue convincingly that medical science does not know how to diagnose that condition.

Despite these criticisms, Rosenhan's study has stood the test of time and still provides a challenge to our view about abnormal behaviour.

Questions

suggested answers → p. 487

1. What criteria were used to diagnose the pseudopatients as mentally disturbed?

2. List the similarities and differences between pseudopatients and 'real' patients.

3. List some behaviours that you regard as 'abnormal', and try to say why they are abnormal.

4. What criticisms can you make of the methods used in this study?

The Three Faces of Eve

THIGPEN, C.H. AND CLECKLEY, H. (1954)

A case of multiple personality.

Journal of Abnormal and Social Psychology, 49, 135–51.

Introduction

Our definition and understanding of 'abnormality' is affected by the culture we live in. Some explanations fit neatly into the general view of life that prevails in a particular culture at a particular time. Some phenomena, on the other hand, challenge our view of life and are regarded with much greater scepticism. The many 'supernatural' experiences that people report are an example of this. Religious visions, and visions of deceased loved ones are commonly reported but do not fit into our current explanations of the world. These experiences, therefore, become marginalized and ignored.

One relatively rare observation of abnormality is the person with multiple personalities. This condition is not to be confused with schizophrenia or other psychotic disorders since the sufferers do not show the disturbances of emotion, perception and reality testing associated with psychosis. The multiple personality challenges our view of people, and receives considerable scepticism as a result. Thigpen and Cleckley recognize this scepticism but suggest that their case study of a unique individual is evidence for the existence of this condition.

The condition is commonly referred to as Dissociative Identity Disorder, and is an extreme example of the common response to unpleasant situations of becoming dissociated. It is a common experience to feel as if you are not really there. Many of the reports of passengers trapped on the trains that were bombed in London in 2005 described a sense feelings of unreality and it seeming as if they were in a film (BBC website, 2005). We are able to cope with distressing situations by not being fully there, but what if that sense of not being there becomes extreme? This is the basis for Dissociative Identity Disorder, which was very rarely observed until the last 20 years when diagnosis has become much more frequent and much more controversial.

▶ **schizophrenia** A mental disorder marked by some, or all of the following symptoms: delusions, hallucinations, incoherent word associations, inappropriate emotions or lack of emotions.

▶ **psychosis** A mental state characterized by profound disturbances in reality testing, thought and emotion.

▶ **case study** A detailed description of a particular individual or group under study or treatment.

The case study

▶ **multiple personality** A dissociative disorder in which one or more personalities exists in the same individual, and each personality is relatively integrated and stable.

▶ **amnesia** The loss of memory, usually through physical causes.

▶ **hypnosis** A temporary trance-like state that can be induced in healthy individuals.

The patient (referred to as Eve White in the study) had been referred for therapy to one of the authors because of 'severe and blinding headaches'. She also complained of 'blackouts', though her family were not aware of anything that would suggest a real loss of consciousness or serious mental confusion. The patient appeared to have a number of complex, but relatively unexceptional marital conflicts and personal frustrations. She showed amnesia for a recent trip, and the therapists used hypnosis to restore that memory.

The first sign of anything unusual in the case was when a letter arrived some days after the hypnosis. It was written in a confident hand and concerned her therapy, but at the bottom of the page there was a childish postscript written in a different hand (see Figure 8.1). On her next visit Eve White denied sending the letter, though she remembered having begun one which she had

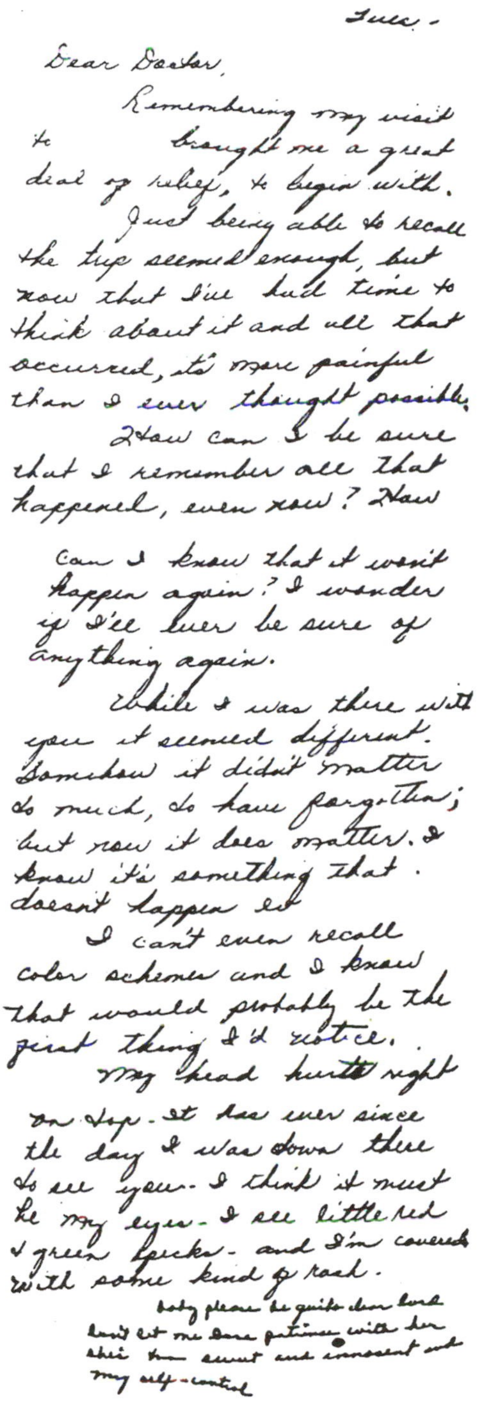

Tues.

Dear Doctor,

Remembering my visit
to   brought me a great
deal of relief, to begin with.

Just being able to recall
the trip seemed enough, but
now that I've had time to
think about it and all that
occurred, it's more painful
than I ever thought possible.

How can I be sure
that I remember all that
happened, even now? How

can I know that it won't
happen again? I wonder
if I'll ever be sure of
anything again.

While I was there with
you it seemed different.
Somehow it didn't matter
so much, to have forgotten;
but now it does matter. I
know it's something that
doesn't happen ed

I can't even recall
color schemes and I know
that would probably be the
first thing I'd notice.

My head hurts right
on top. It has ever since
the day I was down there
to see you. I think it must
be my eyes. I see little red
& green specks. and I'm covered
with some kind of rash.

baby please be quite dear lord
don't let one done patience with her
she too sweet and innocent and
my self-control

Figure 8.1 *Letter from Eve*

not finished. During the interview she became distressed and asked whether hearing an imaginary voice indicated that she was insane. She reported that she had on several occasions briefly heard a voice addressing her. During this conversation Eve White suddenly put both hands to her head as if in pain. After a tense moment of silence her hands dropped, and the therapist observed a 'quick, reckless smile'. In a bright voice she said: 'Hi there, Doc'!

The demure and retiring Eve White had changed into a confident and relaxed person, with a very different physical presence. She crossed her legs and 'the therapist noted from the corner of his awareness something distinctly attractive about them, and also this was the first time he had received such an impression' (p. 137). This new person 'had a childishly daredevil air, an erotically mischievous glance, a face marvellously free from the habitual signs of care, seriousness and underlying distress' (p. 137). The voice and language structure were different, and to the therapist it appeared to be an entirely different woman.

Over the next 14 months, a series of interviews totalling over 100 hours explored the behaviour and experience of Eve White and the other woman, Eve Black. Although Eve Black could sometimes appear unexpectedly, she could only be 'called out' by the therapists when Eve White was under hypnosis. Eve Black had been in existence since early childhood, and when she was 'out' Eve White was not aware of what was happening. In contrast, when Eve Black was not out she was aware of what was happening. This loss of awareness by Eve White, and the coming out of Eve Black to be mischievous, led to a number of incidents in childhood where Eve White was punished for wrongdoings she was unaware of. Some of these incidents, revealed during the therapy, were later substantiated in interviews with her parents and her husband.

Eve Black was irresponsible and shallow, looking for pleasure and excitement. She succeeded in concealing her identity from Eve White, and also from her parents and husband. She denied marriage to the man, whom she despised, and denied any relationship to Eve White's daughter. Her unpleasant behaviour, harshness and occasional acts of violence observed by the husband and parents were attributed to unaccountable fits of temper in a woman who was habitually gentle and considerate.

Both personalities were given a series of psychological tests with the following results:

IQ scores – White 110, Black 104;
Memory function – White was far superior;
Rorschach (ink-blot) – profile of Black far healthier; the personality of White was repressive, and Black was regressive.

During the therapy sessions it became clear that Eve Black had little compassion for Eve White, and could not be persuaded to help with the therapy. However, as Eve White became aware of the other personality she became able to prevent her 'getting out' on occasions, and so negotiation was necessary for Eve Black to get more time 'out'.

▶ **Rorschach test** A personality test made up of bilaterally symmetrical ink-blots. The test is designed to encourage the subject to project their unconscious fears and conflicts onto the ink-blots so that their description of what they see in the inkblots should shine some light on their unconscious.

As the treatment progressed, Eve White's headaches started to recur and she started to experience more 'blackouts'. Eve Black denied responsibility and said that she also experienced lack of awareness during these blackouts. The general state of mind of Eve White deteriorated and confinement was considered. It became easier for the therapist to call up whichever personality he wanted to examine, and childhood experiences were investigated under hypnosis. During one such episode, Eve White appeared to relax into a sleepy state. After a while her eyes opened and she stared blankly around the room before looking at the therapist and saying: 'Who are you?' It appeared that a third personality had emerged who called herself Jane. This new character had full awareness of the other two, but neither of them could be aware of her.

▶ **electroencephalogram**
A method of recording the electrical activity of the brain.

The three personalities were subjected to electroencephalogram studies (EEG: see the study by Dement and Kleitman, 1957, Chapter 6 of this volume), and it was possible to make a clear distinction between the readings of Eve Black and the other two personalities.

The therapy then continued of the three women in the same body. To the therapists, it appeared that Jane was the person most likely to bring a solution to the troubled mind, and that her growing dominance over the other personalities appeared to be an appropriate resolution. However, they point out that 'we have not judged ourselves as wise enough to make active decisions' about how the drama should develop, and they note the moral problems with 'killing' one or more of the personalities.

Discussion

What does this all mean? Could the therapists have been conned by a successful actress? They assert that the performance could not have continued so long and so consistently. Was the woman psychotic? The answer appears to be 'no', since she showed no other symptoms of psychosis. Thigpen and Cleckley ask us to judge whether they became so involved that they lost their sense of judgement and overdramatized the result.

▶ **personality** A distinctive and relatively stable pattern of behaviours, thoughts, motives and emotions that characterize an individual.

They remained convinced that they had witnessed three personalities within the same body. They noted that this observation created as many problems as it solved, not least of which was the question of what we mean by personality. In everyday speech we refer to dramatic changes in personality with phrases like 'he's a new man' or 'she's not herself' or 'he's been reborn'. So, maybe our personalities are not as fixed or stable as we like to believe.

Thigpen and Cleckley finished their account with a plea for psychiatry and psychology to consider a wider range of behavioural and experiential phenomena, even when they do not fit into established theories.

There is a further twist to this case study. Christine Sizemore (the real name of Eve) had always wanted to tell her own story but Thigpen had discouraged her from doing this because of the possible harm it would do her if she revealed herself to the world. A less charitable interpretation would be that he was also protecting his control over the story. According to Sizemore, she agreed to Thigpen and Cleckley preparing academic reports about her for discussion in scientific seminars, but she was not aware they were writing a book for publication to the general public.

Thigpen and Cleckley published their book of Eve's story and then sold the rights of it to Hollywood. When *The Three Faces of Eve* starring Joanne Woodward was premiered, Thigpen and Cleckley were the stars of the event, but Sizemore was advised to leave town to avoid distress and not to see the film. Joanne Woodward got an Oscar for playing Chris Sizemore, who got nothing, not even any recognition of her existence. The book and the film told of a successful therapy and a happy ending, but this bore little relationship to the truth. Some time later when she tried to write her own account, she discovered that Thigpen claimed to have a document signed by her giving him full rights over her story. In an ironic twist, Christine Sizemore's identity and life story had been taken over by her psychiatrists.

Eventually she collaborated with her cousin Elen Pitillo to reveal her identity(ies) to the world in 1977 with the book *I'm Eve*. Thigpen used all manner of stalling tactics to delay giving Sizemore rights to her own story, and in the end they went ahead without ever getting release from the contract held by the therapist. This text tells a very different story from Thigpen and Cleckley, a story which starts much earlier in her life, has many more identities and goes on much longer. It is also clear that the appearance of 'Jane' did not resolve the problems of split identity and she disappeared herself sometime later after becoming a disruptive influence.

Questions

suggested answers → p. 488

1. What were the main differences between Eve White and Eve Black?

2. What is the difference between multiple personality and schizophrenia?

3. Give some examples of the therapists' involvement with their patient.

4. What problems with the case-study method does this study highlight?

Paranoid humanoid

Dextroamphetamine: evaluation of psychomimetic properties in man.

GRIFFITH, J.D., CAVANAUGH, J., HELD, J. AND OATES, J.A. (1972)

Archive of General Psychiatry, 26, 97–100.

> **schizophrenia** A mental disorder marked by some, or all of the following symptoms: delusions, hallucinations, incoherent word associations, inappropriate emotions or lack of emotions.

> **delusion** False belief that typically originates from a misinterpretation but is firmly believed and strongly maintained in spite of contradictory proof or evidence.

> **hallucination** A sensory perception experienced in the absence of an external stimulus.

> **amphetamine** A central nervous system stimulant that increases energy and decreases appetite; used to treat narcolepsy and some forms of depression; commonly used recreationally.

The study

> **psychosis** A mental state characterized by profound disturbances in reality testing, thought and emotion.

Introduction

Schizophrenia is a psychiatric diagnosis that describes a wide range of experiences that commonly involve impairments in the perception or judgements of reality and often have a negative effect on the daily life of the individual. A person who experiences schizophrenia often shows disorganized thinking, and reports experiencing delusions or hallucinations, in particular auditory hallucinations. The rates of schizophrenia are declining in this country in some groups though rising in others (Picchioni and Murray, 2007). It is estimated that around 1 per cent of the population will experience episodes during their lifetime, and the prevalence of the disorder in any one year is between two and four in 1000. The prevalence rates are similar for men and women but it tends to show earlier in men, and is also more common in men (ONS, 2007).

As with all mental disorders the causes and treatments of schizophrenia are controversial. In the Western world where we commonly look first to medical explanations, the treatments are often chemical. The discovery of neuroleptic drugs in the middle of the twentieth century changed treatments for mental distress and eventually were a big factor in the closure of mental hospitals and the treatment of patients in the community.

Similarities between the behaviour of some types of drug users and people with schizophrenia has led to the idea that the neurochemical effects of certain drugs might mimic the kind of neurochemical mechanisms that underlie schizophrenia. Amphetamine drugs are of particular interest in this respect. They have been observed to be psychotomimetic (that is, capable of inducing psychosis in the user). And amphetamine psychosis 'can be very similar to acute paranoid schizophrenia' (p. 97).

The relationship between amphetamine psychosis and schizophrenia is potentially complex, however. The psychosis that is observably related to amphetamine usage might, in fact, be caused by other factors, such as sleep deprivation, or perhaps by a particular sensitivity to amphetamines within the physiology of the person. Or it may be that psychosis is only caused by amphetamines in those people who are already predisposed to schizophrenia. This study set out to pick apart the relationship between amphetamine drugs and psychosis by attempting to examine the 'pure' effects of amphetamine usage within a controlled setting.

One of the most striking features of this study is the attention that is necessarily paid to ethics. Subjects were to be recruited to take a drug that is known to be harmful. What's more, the doses were to be sufficiently high to make psychotic episodes likely. Therefore the researchers needed full, informed consent, from unpaid subjects, who were assured of proper monitoring and medical care throughout. Subjects were allowed to withdraw from the study at any time, for any reason. It was also decided to recruit subjects who had a previous history of amphetamine usage in order to minimize the chances of any of the subjects having an unexpected reaction to the drug.

Method

Nine adult subjects who had previously taken amphetamine drugs were recruited. Each subject was screened for physical and mental health problems, and hospitalized for the six weeks prior to the study in order to ensure that they took no alcohol or other drugs. The study design could best be described as a clinical case study, with multiple cases. The subjects received varying oral dosages (usually between 5 and 10 mg) of dextroamphetamine hourly, according their level of tolerance for the drug. This was designed to allow the drug to accumulate in the body over a period of days. They were monitored continuously, and their diet was carefully controlled. Various measures were taken, including:

(1)   tape-recorded interviews by psychiatrists;
(2)   clinical descriptions by the psychiatrists who monitored the subjects;
(3)   a symptom checklist;
(4)   self-reports of psychosis given retrospectively by the subjects;
(5)   various psychological tests and measures including IQ and projective tests.

For one week before the first administration of the amphetamine, a placebo was administered hourly and control observations and tests were conducted.

Results

The most striking effect of the drug, psychologically speaking, was the onset of extreme paranoia. In six of the subjects this occurred within one to five days. Overall, eight of the nine subjects became psychotic. Subjects started to believe that they had discovered the 'real' purpose of the experiment. One thought that the study was really set up to get him to hospital to treat his (imagined) terminal heart problem. Another thought that his ex-wife had hired someone to kill him. There were also reports of the feeling of being observed through hidden cameras and of being talked about on TV. One olfactory hallucination was reported, but no visual or auditory ones. Sleep patterns became irregular. All showed symptoms of depression by the time they had received 50mg of the drug, with a general loss of interest in everything, an irritability and a tendency to lie in bed. When the administration of the drug ceased the symptoms dissipated within 44 to 72 hours. All the participants were aware of what they had gone through and understood their experiences as drug induced, showing no long-term effects from the procedures.

▶ **sleep deprivation** A lack of the necessary amount of sleep brought about by neurological or psychological or social causes, and creating a range of negative psychological and bodily effects. Sometimes used as a form of torture.

▶ **case study** A detailed description of a particular individual or group under study or treatment.

▶ **projective tests** Psychometric tests which involve providing the person with ambiguous stimuli, and seeing what meanings they read into them. The idea is that this will illustrate the concerns of the unconscious mind.

▶ **paranoia** An irrational fear, suspicion or distrust of others.

Discussion

The results suggest a number of things about amphetamine psychosis. First, psychosis does not appear to be a rare outcome of amphetamine usage, as eight of the nine subjects were affected. Nor, by the same logic, does it or appear to be dependent on pre-disposing factors within a person. It is true, of course, that the sample in this study is small, and all the subjects had a history of drug usage, so strong conclusions cannot be drawn. Perhaps they all shared some sort of predisposing susceptibility to psychosis. The swiftness and the reliability of the onset of psychosis is nevertheless striking.

Stronger conclusions can be drawn about other factors. Sleep deprivation could not be regarded as a cause of the psychoses, nor could other factors such as multi-drug usage. The subjects had been kept free of other drugs for a period of time before the study, and the onset of extreme paranoia occurred so quickly that it could not reasonably be put down to sleep deprivation. Sleep disturbances were evidently a result of the drug usage. Taking all their observations into consideration the researchers conclude that high dosage amphetamine abuse is liable, in itself, to result in psychosis.

The researchers also compare and contrast the observed symptoms of the participants with the symptoms of acute paranoid schizophrenia. The paranoia that was observed was very like the paranoia associated with schizophrenia. However there was no sign of thought disorder in these subjects, neither were there any auditory or visual hallucinations. The researchers conclude that the amphetamine psychosis that resulted from small, frequent doses over a prolonged period should be considered more of a paranoid state, than a schizophrenic one.

Needless to say, the techniques used in this study are risky and expensive. They promise to shed light on the effects of long-term drug usage, and may be particularly useful in coming to understand the precise pharmacological effects of drugs such as amphetamines. A better understanding of these things may lead to a better understanding of conditions such as schizophrenia, and to better treatments. However the costs to subjects are potentially high, and rigorous ethical and medical safeguards need to be in place before studies of this sort can be undertaken.

An important postscript to this discussion is to note the impact of anti-schizophrenic drugs. If, as the above paper suggests, schizophrenia has a chemical basis, it is therefore likely that the condition can be alleviated through chemical means. The problem with this is that (a) things are never that simple, and (b) the drugs that are used have some very negative side effects. Anti-psychotic medication such as chlorpromazine has been used for the last 50 years to reduce the level of hallucinations and delusions experienced by people suffering from schizophrenia. The medication is relatively successful in reducing these symptoms (WHO, 2001) but some of the side effects are damaging and permanent. For example tardive dyskinesia develops in about one in five patients on the medication and leaves the person with unusual behavioural tics. Abnormal facial movements such as smacking lips, chewing, sucking and twisting the tongue can all be signs of tardive dyskinesia. Jerky, often purposeless limb movements are also characteristic signs. Approximately one person in five on anti-psychotic medication will experience tardive dyskinesia. It often persists after the treatment has stopped and cannot be treated (www.emental-health.com).

Questions

1. Why were the subjects not paid for their participation?

2. Subjects were allowed to withdraw from the study at any time and for any reason. This is good practice in psychological research, and required by British Psychological Society ethical guidelines. However the issue of withdrawal from this study is somewhat more complex than normal. Why?

3. Why was there a 'control' week involving the administration of a placebo?

suggested answers → p. 488

Experimental
desensitization
of a phobia.

LANG, P.J. AND LAZOVIK, A.D. (1963).

Fear today, gone tomorrow

Journal of Abnormal
and Social Psychology,
66, 519–25.

Introduction

Many people experience fears that seem to be irrational: for example, a fear of spiders or heights (the famous French philosopher Jean-Paul Sartre had a fear of being chased by a giant lobster). For some people the fear becomes so great that it interferes with their everyday life. These fears are often referred to as phobias, and psychologists have tried to explain how they develop and how they can be alleviated. One technique for alleviation is systematic desensitization, which is a behaviour therapy. The paper by Lang and Lazovik provides a good illustration of this therapy, and evaluates its effectiveness in treating snake phobias. A contrasting style of treatment (psychoanalytic psychotherapy) is illustrated in Chapter 11 of this book, which describes one of Freud's famous case studies.

The authors cite Wolpe (1958) as the originator of the therapy, which is usually discussed in connection with the theory of classical conditioning. The idea of systematic desensitization is that people with phobias are gradually taught to respond to the phobic object (or situation) with muscle relaxation rather than with fear. The procedures are described below, and are based on the notion of reciprocal inhibition: that is, the response of relaxation is incompatible with a response of fear (you cannot be both fearful and relaxed at the same time). So the stronger the relaxation response becomes, the more it inhibits the old fear response.

One criticism of behaviour therapies such as systematic desensitization comes from the psychoanalytic perspective. As Lang and Lazovik point out, behaviour therapists are not usually interested in the original causes of the phobia. They focus on treating and alleviating the behavioural symptoms. Psychoanalysts argue that, in treating only the symptoms, behaviour therapies leave the root causes of the problem untouched. So while the behavioural symptoms of, say, the snake phobia might indeed be alleviated, they will ultimately be replaced by another set of symptoms which have the same root cause. This is known as symptom substitution. The behaviour therapists counter with the argument that the so-called 'symptoms' are the problem, and that alleviating them will not necessarily lead to symptom substitution.

The study

This study has a simple experimental design in which a number of snake-phobic students were allocated either to one of two treatment conditions, or to one of two control conditions. The experimental subjects received desensitization therapy; the control subjects did not. A variety of measures were used to assess the effectiveness of the therapy, including a follow-up examination of

▶ **phobia** An anxiety disorder characterized by persistent fear out of proportion to the danger, a compelling desire to escape the situation, and a recognition that the fear is excessive.

▶ **systematic desensitization** A classical conditioning technique for reducing fear and anxiety by replacing it with a calm response.

▶ **behaviour therapy** The process of treating abnormal behaviour by looking only at the symptoms, and using conditioning techniques to modify them.

▶ **case study** A detailed description of a particular individual or group under study or treatment.

▶ **classical conditioning** A form of learning which involves the pairing of a neutral stimulus with a reflex.

the subjects' anxiety levels six months after the original investigation, and an assessment of whether any symptom substitution had occurred.

Subjects

Twenty-four snake-phobic students from the USA participated. They were selected on the basis of questionnaires and interviews which explored their susceptibility to the phobia. Only those judged to have a strong phobia (for example, those who reported an unpleasant response to seeing a snake) were included in the study. The assignment of subjects to the four conditions was done 'essentially at random, although an effort was made to balance roughly these groups in terms of intensity of fear and motivation to participate in the experiment' (p. 521). Five therapists were involved in the desensitization procedures, and each worked with between two and four of the experimental subjects.

Design

A four-condition independent-measures (between subjects) design was used, with two experimental conditions and two control conditions. The main independent variable was whether the subjects received a desensitization programme or not. The dependent variable was measured by making a direct observation of the subjects' behaviour when faced by a real-life snake (the 'Snake Avoidance Test'), and by getting subjects to rate the level of their fear when faced by the live snake.

Procedure

The two experimental groups both received a period of training and a period of desensitization. During the training phase of five 45-minute sessions, the subjects constructed an anxiety hierarchy. This was a list of 20 situations which involved snakes, and which were rank-ordered from 'most feared' to 'least feared'. For example, seeing a picture of a snake might have been an item towards the 'least feared' end of a subject's scale, whilst holding a snake would most likely have been towards the 'most feared' end. Each subject constructed their own personal hierarchy in consultation with their therapist. After the hierarchy had been completed, the subjects were taught deep muscle relaxation (Lang and Lazovik refer to the methods of Jacobson, 1938, in this regard), and then introduced to the process of hypnosis. All training and therapy was done on a one-to-one basis.

The desensitization phase involved eleven 45-minute sessions. During these the subjects gradually worked through their hierarchy of fears. The process started with hypnosis and deep muscle relaxation. The subjects were then instructed to imagine the least-feared item on their list. When they were able to do this without any fear response (when they could relax completely when imagining the situation described in the item) they moved onto the next item on the list. When they could relax whilst imagining this item, they progressed to the next, and so on, until they reached the most-feared item. They would only move to the next-most-feared item on the list if they had successfully learned to relax in response to the previous one. Of the 13 experimental subjects, seven completed 16 steps or more in their hierarchy, and six completed 14 steps or fewer.

The strength of each subject's phobia was tested in the following ways. The subject was brought into a room with a snake 15 feet away in a glass cage. An experimenter, who took no part in the other aspects of the study, encouraged the subject to come into the room, to approach the snake, and if possible to touch it or hold it. If the subject actually touched the snake they passed the Snake Avoidance Test. If they refused to touch the snake then they were asked to approach as near as they could, and the distance they ended up from the snake was measured. The score they were assigned on this basis was on a 19-point scale, with 1 indicating 'held snake', 2 indicating 'touched snake', 3 indicating 'approached to within one foot', 4 indicating 'approached to within two feet', and so forth, to 19 which indicated 'refused to enter room'. The higher the score, then, the stronger the avoidance of the snake. All subjects were asked at this point to rate the fear they were experiencing on a 10-point 'Fear Thermometer'. In addition, the subjects completed a Fear Survey Schedule (FSS) at the beginning and end of the experiment, and were interviewed by the experimenters. The FSS listed 50 phobias which were rated by the subjects on a 7-point scale according to their subjectively judged susceptibility to each fear. Snake phobia was included in this list. In Table 8.3 the sequence of events for each group of subjects is detailed. The 'Test' phases involved all the measures described in this paragraph. Note that 20 of the original subjects were retested after six months.

Table 8.3 *The Snake Avoidance Test: experimental design*

Group	Experimental procedures				
E1	Test 1	Training	Test 2	Desensitization	Test 3
E2		Training	Test 2	Desensitization	Test 3
C1	Test 1		Test 2	Desensitization	Test 3
C2			Test 2	Desensitization	Test 3

Source: Lang and Lazovik (1963)

Results

For the experimental subjects 'the percentage of increase [in numbers passing the test] from Test 2 to Test 3 yielded a t of 2.30, $p < .05$. A similar test of the control subjects was not significant' (p. 522). The scores for this measure are shown in Table 8.4. The therapeutic gains appear to have been maintained for most experimental subjects over the ensuing six months.

The average distance measures on the 19-point Snake Avoidance Test are shown in Table 8.5 and in Figure 8.2. Note that the average distance decreased between Test 2 and Test 3 for the experimental subjects, whereas the average distance increased for the control subjects. A 'change' score was computed for each subject, using a simple formula to calculate how much closer (or further away) the subject had stood on Test 3 than on Test 2. The positive average change score for the experimental groups indicates that they were standing (on average) nearer at Test 3 than at Test 2, whereas the minus score for the control subjects indicates the opposite. A Mann-Whitney U test showed statistically significant differences between the individual change scores of all the experimental subjects when compared with all the control subjects ($p < .05$).

Table 8.4 *Number of subjects who held or touched the snake during the avoidance test*

Group	N	Test 1	Test 2	Test 3
E1	8	1	1	5
E2	5	–	1	2
C1	5	0	0	0
C2	6	–	1	2
E1 and E2	13	–	2	7
C1 and C2	11	–	1	2

Source: Lang and Lazovik (1963).

Table 8.5 *Mean Snake Avoidance Test scores at Tests 2 and 3, mean change scores and the Mann-Whitney U test*

Group	Test 2	Test 3	Change score	U
Experimental	5.35	4.42	.34	34.5*
Control	6.51	7.73	−.19	

$* p < .05.$

Source: Lang and Lazovik (1963).

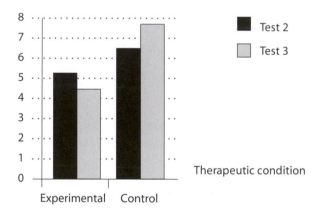

Figure 8.2 *Snake avoidance scores for the experimental and control groups at Test 2 and Test 3*

The subjects' self-ratings on the FSS and on the Fear Thermometer also indicated therapeutic gains for the experimental subjects in comparison with the control subjects, but no statistically significant differences across the groups were found.

Subjects who completed more than 15 items on their hierarchy during desensitization showed significantly greater therapeutic gains on 'nearly all measures employed in this experiment' (p. 523). These subjects also showed an overall decrease in self-reported phobic responses on the FSS.

Discussion

The measures used by Lang and Lazovik suggest that desensitization therapy is effective in reducing the intensity of snake phobias. Perhaps the most convincing data come from the Snake Avoidance Test, which gives a direct behavioural indication of the subjects' levels of fear. Of the 13 experimental subjects, seven were able to touch or hold the snake during Test 3, whereas of 11 control subjects only two were able to touch or hold the snake.

The fact that the experimental subjects who completed more than 15 items on their hierarchy showed an overall decrease in self-rated anxiety on a range of phobias (as measured by the FSS) suggests that, in this instance, symptom substitution was not taking place. Indeed this indicates (albeit somewhat weakly) that desensitization of one phobia may lead to a decrease in overall levels of anxiety. The six-month follow-up is a strong point of this study. It indicates that the therapeutic gains were not just temporary improvements.

As with all studies, a number of questions spring to mind in relation to the results. One of these has to do with the effects of demand characteristics on the behaviour of the subjects (see Orne, 1962, Chapter 18 of this volume). Presumably the experimental subjects knew they were receiving therapy, and were being compared with a group of control subjects who were not receiving therapy. One wonders whether this might have had some effect on the outcome measures, since all the subjects would have had a pretty clear idea of what was expected of them during each testing phase. And demand characteristics of the initial interviews and questionnaires concerning subjects' levels of snake phobia may also have played a part. If these measures had overestimated the levels of anxiety which each subject experienced in response to snakes, then the therapeutic 'gains' may not have been gains at all.

Nevertheless, one study cannot address all these issues, and the cases for and against the effectiveness of procedures such as systematic desensitization are ultimately built over a period of time, and over sequences of investigations. This study lends support to the proposition that systematic desensitization is an effective treatment for phobias.

▶ **demand characteristics**
Those aspects of a psychological study (or other artificial situation) which exert an implicit pressure on people to act in ways that are expected of them.

Questions

suggested answers → P. 489

1. Why does this study not necessarily mean that systematic desensitization, in itself, is an effective treatment of phobias?

2. What was the reason for having two experimental groups, when the only difference between them was that one group was tested prior to initial training, and the other group was not?

It could be you!
But it probably won't be

GRIFFITHS, M.D. (1994)

The role of cognitive bias and skill in fruit machine gambling.

British Journal of Psychology, 85, 351–69.

▶ **gambling** The act of staking money or something of financial value in the hope of winning (including the payment of a price for a chance to win a prize).

▶ **technological addictions** Non-chemical (behavioural) addictions which involve human–machine interactions. A behavioural addiction refers to a repetitive activity which becomes the single most important thing in a person's life. It is carried out to the neglect of everything else and is used as a reliable and consistent way of modifying mood. Tolerance to it builds up over time, and removal of the behaviour creates withdrawal symptoms. The behaviour compromises everything else in that person's life including their relationships, job and hobbies.

Introduction

Gambling is becoming a part of everyday life. Every day seems to bring a new opportunity to try and beat the odds. At one level it is the absurd television quizzes that ask you to text in your answer to the question 'What is the capital of France? (a) Paris, (b) Paris Hilton, (c) a cabbage.' Even if you're not sure about the answer you can redial the premium price number to cover all the options and ensure that you enter the lottery for the prize of a night out with Paris Hilton (answers b and c[1]) in Paris (answer a). The opportunities to gamble are endless and not surprisingly people in the UK are gambling more often and spending more money on it.

Why do people gamble? Do they think they are going to beat the odds and win? For most people in the population, gambling represents a casual and relatively rare occurrence; the odd pound on a big horse race like the Grand National or maybe on your football team to win a big game. Maybe you play the slot machines when you go to the seaside or when you have a few moments to kill. You'll probably lose your money but it is relatively harmless because it will not impinge on your daily life. But what if the gambling becomes important to you and you think about it all the time and spend whatever time and whatever money you have on the slot machines? This is more of a problem.

Griffiths has studied gambling and technological addictions for the last 20 years. This paper illustrates some of the research techniques that can be used to explore this behaviour and tries to tease out some of the characteristics that distinguish the casual gambler from the more regular ones. In particular it asks whether regular fruit machine players think differently to non-regular players. Wagenaar (1988) outlines some of the cognitive distortions that affect the cognitions (thought patterns) of gamblers. These include:

- *Illusion of control*: the belief that we can control chance events, for example being able to choose the winning numbers on a lottery (rather than just taking a lucky dip) or being able to throw the numbers you want on dice.
- *Flexible attributions*: where gamblers explain (attribute) their wins in terms of skill and their losses in terms of bad luck.
- *'Near wins'* (Gilovich, 1983): where gamblers transform a loss into a near win, for example, even though if the result was 2–1 in the football game and you bet on 2–0 you are no nearer getting a payout than if you bet on 6–0. A loss is a loss, even though it seems like you nearly won.

---

1. The authors would like to state clearly that they do not see any resemblance whatsoever between Paris Hilton and a cabbage and have only made the above comment for weak comic effect.

- *Hindsight bias*: the near universal tendency to believe you knew something all the time. For example, the number of people who now say they always believed the war in Iraq would turn into a humanitarian disaster is much bigger than the number who predicted it before the invasion (see also the study by Fischhoff *et al.*, 2005, in Chapter 2).
- *'The gambler's fallacy'*: the expectation that the probability of winning will increase with the length of an ongoing run of losses (Wagenaar, 1988).
- *Availability bias*: this occurs when judgements are made about chance events in terms of how easily the information comes to mind. For example we get lots of information about lottery winners but very little about the losers. Also, slot machines are designed to make a lot of noise when they pay out and no noise when they don't. We therefore have more information about the times when there is a win rather than the times when there is a loss, even though losing is much more common than winning.

The study

The focus of this study is regular fruit machine gamblers. It has been observed that regular users are aware they will lose all their money during a long run. It appears they are playing *with* money rather than *for* it and their intention is to stay on the machine for the longest possible time rather to take any money from it. Daley (1987) suggests that machine players gamble to buy time rather than to win money. They also see their gambling as a skilled behaviour rather than a game of chance. Modern fruit machines have special play features such as 'nudge' or 'hold' buttons which introduce an element of skill (or possibly just the illusion of skill).

The study looks at the following questions:

- Is the skill involved in playing fruit machines real or imagined?
- Do regular players show different thought patterns from non-regular players? In particular, do the regular players make more irrational judgements?
- How do regular and non-regular players describe their level of skill? In particular, will regular players be more skill-oriented in their descriptions?

Method

Sixty participants were recruited, all of whom had played fruit machines at least once in their lives. The non-regular users were recruited via a poster advertisement circulated in the local university and college campuses (15 males and 15 females) and the regular users were recruited through a regular gambler known to the author (29 males and 1 female).

The study was carried out in an amusement arcade to enhance the ecological validity of the data. Each participant was given £3 to gamble on a fruit machine which played at 10 pence a go, hence giving each player 30 free plays. Participants were asked to try and stay on the machine ('FRUITSKILL') for a minimum of 60 plays after which they were given the choice of keeping the winnings or playing on.

Participants were randomly allocated to either to the 'thinking aloud' or the 'non-thinking aloud' conditions. The thinking aloud participants were told to say out loud every thought that went though their heads when it went through. They were told not to censor anything and to keep talking as continuously as possible. They were not required to speak in complete sentences or to justify their thoughts.

The researcher recorded:

- total time on the fruit machine;
- total number of gambles;
- amount of winnings;
- result of every play.

In the 'thinking aloud' condition the responses were recorded via a lapel microphone and transcribed within 24 hours. All the participants took part in a semi-structured interview after playing the machine in which they were asked about their experience of playing the machine and, in particular, their perception of the skill involved and their personal level of skill.

Results

The results present a range of qualitative and quantitative analyses. In the measures of machine play, there were few differences between the regular and non-regular players. The regular users gambled faster (eight plays per minute compared with six plays per minute) and were able to make more plays for the same money (meaning they were slightly more successful) but they didn't stay on the machines any longer than the non-regular players.

For the 'thinking aloud' data, the researcher examined the responses of the 30 participants in this condition and then devised a set of coding categories. This coding system was made up of four categories of irrational comments and 27 categories of rational ones. Overall, the regular users made more irrational comments than the non-regular users (14 per cent v. 2.5 per cent). Only five of the categories showed a significant difference between the regular and non-regular users which can be summarized as follows:

- Regular users made more irrational comments in which they personified the machine, for example 'the machine likes me'.
- Non-regular users made more rational comments and asked more rational questions relating to confusion about the machine, for example, 'I don't understand this', and 'What's going on here?'.
- Regular users made more reference to the number system on the machine, for example, 'I got a "2" there'.
- Non-regular users made more miscellaneous utterances (over 25 per cent of everything they said), for example 'I think I'll get a bag of chips after playing this.'

The paper includes some examples of thinking aloud from the regular users to illustrate the range of cognitive bias. These include,

- *Hindsight bias*: 'I had a feeling it was going to chew up those tokens fairly rapidly ... I had a feeling it had paid out earlier because it's not giving me a chance' (page 360).
- *Flexible attributions*: 'This "fruity" is not in a good mood ... someone's obviously won out of this before' (page 360).
- *Illusions of control*: 'I'm only gonna put one quid in to start with because psychologically I think it's very important ... it bluffs the machine – it's my own psychology' (page 360).
- *Personification*: 'This machine doesn't like me ... ooh it does, it's given me a number ... hates me!! It's given me low numbers, I don't think it wants to pay out at all ... It probably thinks I'm a f**kwit – it's not wrong!!' (page 360).

The analysis of the post-play interviews shows that the regular users believe there is more skill in machine playing then the non-regular users and also that they believe they have those skills.

Discussion

▶ **cognitive behaviour therapy** Attempts to modify everyday thoughts and behaviours, with the aim of positively influencing emotions. It is based on the idea that how we think (cognition), how we feel (emotion) and how we act (behaviour) all interact together. Specifically, our thoughts determine our feelings and our behaviour. Therefore, negative and unrealistic thoughts can cause us distress and result in problems.

If it can be shown that the main difference between players and non-players is the way they think about the process then it might be possible to use cognitive behaviour therapy to help people reduce their gambling. In fact, just getting users to consider their own thought processes might well be a first step in the process. Griffiths reports that one of his participants subsequently stated that taking part in the study and reviewing his own 'thinking aloud' reports helped him to think differently about his gambling and eventually to stop playing the machines (Griffiths, 1993).

The method of thinking aloud is one way of trying to access the very private thought processes that we experience. If you ask people to think back after an event to describe how they were thinking, it is likely that will turn their thoughts into a coherent story and miss out many of the strange and irrational thoughts that fly by us all the time. In this study Griffiths was able to capture some of the flavour of gambling as a person gambles. It is obviously not a perfect method because it is inevitable that a person will inevitably still censor some of their thoughts. One of the problems Griffiths reports is that some of the gamblers left long silences of up to 30 seconds. He speculates as to this being due to their gambling being an automatic process that requires little thought although they might also have been 'in the zone' and so focused on what they were doing that any other activity was impossible.

There were some other problems with the data collection and analysis; for example, some of the regular users did not want to play on the chosen machine and instead chose to play on their favourite one. This means that some of the differences between the regular and non-regular players could be

▶**inter-coder reliability** A phrase which describes the extent to which two independent observers (coders/raters) agree on the observations that they have made. Also known as inter-observer reliability and inter-rater reliability.

explained by the difference between the machines rather than the difference between the players. Also, the coding system of 31 categories is so large that there are only a few comments in each category and the inter-rater reliability is reported as being low (though we are not given a value for it). A further issue is that the participants were initially given a stake for 30 plays and this may not have been enough to show the skill of the players, which might only become evident with extended play.

Studying real behaviour in real situations is always going to present problems for collecting and interpreting data. This study takes psychological analysis into the unlikely laboratory of an amusement arcade and provides us with some insights into the behaviour and thought processes of gamblers.

Questions

suggested answers
→ p. 489

1. If this study was carried out in a control laboratory rather than an amusement arcade, what differences would you expect in the results?

2. What criticisms can you make of the methods used in this study?

3. Try the 'thinking aloud' method yourself when you are doing something. A good example is to try this when you are driving. If you don't have a licence, then try it when you are making a fish-finger sandwich in the kitchen at home. It's harder than you think.

chapter 9

INDIVIDUAL DIFFERENCES

▶ **personality** A distinctive and relatively stable pattern of behaviours, thoughts, motives and emotions that characterize an individual.

▶ **intelligence** An inferred characteristic of an individual, usually defined as the ability to profit from experience, acquire knowledge, think abstractly or adapt to changes in the environment.

▶ **reliability** The reliability of a psychological measuring device (such as a test or a scale) is the extent to which it gives consistent measurements. The greater the consistency of measurement, the greater the tool's reliability.

▶ **validity** The question of whether a psychometric test or psychological measure is really measuring what it is supposed to.

THE study of individual differences within psychology is concerned with describing and explaining ways in which people differ, one from another. Key areas within this sub-discipline of psychology are personality and intelligence. And a key agenda of this sub-discipline is the development of reliable and valid methods for measuring personality and intelligence.

Personality is a collection of cognitions (thoughts) affective responses (emotions) and patterns of behaviour that are unique to a person. Psychologists have produced numerous scales that purport to measure different dimensions of personality and psychological attributes such as intelligence. However, the task of devising scales that accurately measure psychological constructs is a very difficult one, beset with potential hazards. The study by Forer (1949) in Chapter 18 of this book illustrates one of the problems we have to consider with psychometric tests. People can be very *gullible* when faced by expert opinion, and it is not very difficult to impress people with a few simple generalizations about their personality, especially when presented with the trappings of science. Forer suggests that we should be very

sceptical about the findings from personality tests.

One highly influential approach to the measurement of personality comes in the shape of the Big Five. This is not a reference to Take That before Robbie Williams' departure. Rather it is the notion that the diversity of humans can be adequately described with reference to five personality dimensions, each of which is potentially measurable. The study by McCrae and Costa (1987) examines the validity of this so called 'five factor model' of personality.

One dimension that we expect to define differences between people is their sex. Issues around sex and gender are discussed elsewhere in this text (Chapter 7) and in this chapter we describe an attempt to look at the dimension of gender. The study by Bem (1974) describes how a scale for measuring masculinity and femininity was developed and tested. The study highlights the complexity of test construction and the importance of relating measurement to theoretical ideas, in this case about gender.

The third 'study' presented in this chapter is actually a summary of a set of arguments from a book by Stephen Jay Gould (1981), set out in an article in

▶ **behaviour (also spelt 'behavior')** Anything a person (or animal) does that can be observed and measured by a third party. Behaviour can be thought of as the public side of human life, in contrast to 'experience' (thoughts and feelings) which can be thought of as the private side.

▶ **intelligence** An inferred characteristic of an individual, usually defined as the ability to profit from experience, acquire knowledge, think abstractly or adapt to changes in the environment.

▶ **psychometric tests** Instruments which have been developed for measuring mental characteristics. Psychological tests have been developed to measure a wide range of things, including creativity, job attitudes and skills, brain damage and, of course, 'intelligence'.

▶ **trait** A specific facet of personality.

▶ **genetic** Biological inheritance.

New Scientist in 1982. The arguments are far reaching, and have great significance within psychology, both methodologically and politically speaking. Gould reviews the history of efforts to measure intelligence and shows how poor the scientific grounding of some of these efforts has been, and how dangerous their effects can be. Psychology is not just an abstract discipline in which people come up with clever ideas for how to study things. Often the theories and techniques that psychologists develop have real consequences for real people, and not all of these consequences have been good.

The final paper by Plomin and Daniels (1987) in this chapter deals with the controversial issue of the inheritance of personality traits.

The reason the issue is controversial is because of the potential consequences of believing a quality to be inherited. Say, for example, we discovered that the differences between people in their singing ability could be mainly explained by genetic variation, then a government or commercial organization might try to selectively breed superior singers in an attempt to win the Eurovision Song Contest. Although this may be too horrible to contemplate, try to imagine what might happen if instead of singing ability we were talking about aggression or criminality or ugliness.

The Big Five

McCRAE, R.R. AND
COSTA, P.T. (1987)

Validation of the
five factor model
of personality
across instruments
and observers.

*Journal of Personality and
Social Psychology,*
52, 81–90.

▶ **personality** A distinctive
and relatively stable pattern
of behaviours, thoughts,
motives and emotions that
characterize an individual.

▶ **trait** A specific facet of
personality.

▶ **psychometric
tests** Instruments which
have been developed
for measuring mental
characteristics. Psychological
tests have been developed
to measure a wide range of
things, including creativity,
job attitudes and skills, brain
damage and, of course,
'intelligence'.

▶ **behaviour (also spelt
'behavior')** Anything a
person (or animal) does
that can be observed and
measured by a third party.
Behaviour can be thought
of as the public side of
human life, in contrast
to 'experience' (thoughts
and feelings) which can be
thought of as the private
side.

Introduction

Two central questions in the field of individual differences and
personality are: 'How many personality dimensions does it take
to adequately describe a person?' and 'What might these dimensions be?' Famously, Eysenck (1947) developed a trait model of
personality based on two dimensions: extraversion and neuroticism. Cattell in contrast developed a theory of personality based on 16
traits (the 16 PF; see Cattell *et al.*, 1970).

The question of how many traits/dimensions to have in a model is
largely a matter of what level of abstraction we want to work at in psychology.
Needless to say, at one extreme we might argue 'the more then merrier', and
propose personality theories that are based on hundreds of traits. In this way
we could produce rich, detailed descriptions of personalities. However, such
theories would lead to unmanageably complex psychometric tests that would
be of little practical use to anybody. One would also find that many of the traits
were actually quite similar, and might be better grouped together into more
fundamental 'factors'.

At the other extreme we might want to argue that only one personality
trait is important, and that if we want to understand human behaviour and
experience we just need to know about ... well, about what? Which is THE
personality trait that captures the human condition? And who should decide?

So somewhere between these two extremes lie theories that propose
descriptions of people based on a small number of dimensions. One principle that such theories follow is that of parsimony. This principle holds that
the number of dimensions that are used should be the smallest number
that adequately account for the available data. In recent years there has
been a lot of interest in models that are based on 'The Big Five' personality
dimensions, which is where McCrae and Costa's study comes in.

One particularly interesting feature of the Big Five model is that (like
Cattell's 16 PF) it is based on the 'lexical hypothesis'. The lexical hypothesis
expresses the view, usually attributed to Allport and Odbert (1936), that culturally important ways of thinking about personality differences are likely to be
encoded in the words of a language. So if we want to know what dimensions
of personality are important, we should carefully analyse the words that a language uses to describe personality traits. One way of doing this is to generate
lists of adjectives that describe personality, get lots of participants to use these
adjectives to rate people that they know, then subject these ratings to factor
analysis. Factor analysis is a statistical method for examining the relationships
among highly complex, detailed sets of things, in order to extract a simpler
set of core underlying 'factors'. When Norman (1963) undertook this task he
argued that five factors could best represent the richness and detail of English
language adjectives that describe personality traits.

The study

▶ **neuroticism** A personality dimension based on a person's measured susceptibility to neuroses.

The Big Five personality factors as used in this study are: neuroticism, extraversion, agreeableness, conscientiousness and openness to experience (in many 'Big Five' studies, the fifth factor is labelled 'culture' rather than 'openness').

- Neuroticism refers to the experiencing of negative emotions.
- Extraversion is about a lively engagement with the outside world.
- Agreeableness is about getting on with other people.
- Conscientiousness refers to the regulation of our behaviour.
- Openness to experience is concerned with curiosity and creativity.

The factors are dimensions, and a well-designed scale would 'place' each person at some point on each of these dimensions. So if a person was placed 'low' on the neuroticism factor, this would indicate that they do not typically experience negative emotions, do not worry a lot, and have a relatively calm approach to life. In theory it should not be possible to predict a person's score on any given factor from their score on any of the other factors, because the factors should be independent one from another (they should be *orthogonal*). For example, just because someone scores high on neuroticism, that should not allow us to make any inference about how they would score on agreeableness or extraversion. In practice models of personality can never fully live up to this ideal, and some level of relationship will always exist among the different factors. For example, there is a tendency for people who score high on neuroticism (who worry a lot about life) to score lower than others on extraversion (to be less inclined to be outward looking and highly sociable).

Materials and design

▶ **validity** The question of whether a psychometric test or psychological measure is really measuring what it is supposed to.

▶ **self-report** A number of popular research methods are based on self-report: for example, questionnaires, interviews, attitude scales and diary methods. These are methods which rely on research subjects' accounts of their own experiences and behaviour.

The study set out to test the validity of the five-factor model of personality by comparing ratings about the same target people from different sources of data, and from different instruments. The different sources of data that were used were self-reports, and peer ratings. The different instruments that were used were the NEO Personality Inventory (NEO-PI; Costa and McCrae, 1985) and an adjective-rating scale. The NEO-PI items are short statements that are rated by the respondent for accuracy (how well the item describes the target person). They were administered in a first-person (for self-report) and third-person (for peer ratings) format. The adjective-rating scale comprised 80 bipolar items that were rated on a 9-point scale according to which pole gave the best description of the target person. Each of the items 'load' on (contribute to) one of the five personality dimensions. Examples of these items are 'calm–worrying' (neuroticism), 'retiring–sociable' (extraversion), 'irritable–good natured' (agreeableness), 'careless–careful' (conscientiousness), and 'uncreative–creative' (openness to experience).

If similar patterns emerge from peer reports *and* from self ratings, using *two* different types of psychometric instrument, then this gives more support to the validity of the underlying model of personality than if just one source of data and one instrument is used.

Subjects and procedures

The target subjects who rated themselves and who were rated by peers were 118 women (age range 28–85, mean age 53.8 years) and 156 men (age range 29–93, mean age 59.9 years). These subjects came from a community sample of volunteers from a large-scale longitudinal study in Baltimore, USA. Each subject nominated up to four people known to them (not relatives) who could provide personality ratings of them. Of these nominees, 747 completed the rating task. The age range of peer raters was 19–87 years (mean age 54.2 years), and the average length of acquaintance with the target was 18.3 years (range 1–74 years).

The instruments were administered to the target subjects and to the peer raters over a period of 3 years 6 months. Both instruments produce five scores per subject, one for each of the Big Five dimensions. It is important to remember that the study aims to examine the validity of the five-factor model of personality, not to find out about individual participants. So results are expressed in terms of the overarching structure of the five factors, not in terms of participant scores.

> **▶ longitudinal study** A study which monitors changes occurring over a period of time.

Results

Two important findings from this study are as follows. First, peer ratings using the NEO-PI showed relatively high levels of agreement with the peer ratings using the adjective scale. The 722 raters generated one NEO-PI score and one adjective scale score for each target subject, on each of the five factors. These pairs of scores on each factor provided the raw data for five correlations (one correlation for each of the five factors), each of which produced coefficients greater than .70 ($n = 722$, $p < .001$). This shows a good level of inter-instrument consistency.

Second, peer ratings showed a relatively high level of agreement with self-reports. For those target subjects who had four peer raters, the aggregated scores of the four peers correlated at least at the level of $r = .48$ ($p < .001$) with the target subject's self-report on all five factors when measured by the adjective scale. Similarly high correlations were seen on four out of the five factors when the peer ratings were compared with the target subject's self-report on the NEO-PI scale (the agreeableness factor was the exception, with a statistically non-significant correlation of $r = .24$).

Discussion

The original study contains a considerable amount of detail about the patterns of findings, which mostly show a high level of concurrent validity between the different sources of ratings (peers versus self) and between the different instruments (the NEO-PI and the adjective factors). Assessing concurrent validity is one way of addressing the crucial question of whether the psychometric indicators that we use are really measuring what we think they are measuring (see pp 464–6, Chapter 19 [validity]). The two, separately developed psychometric scales both produce a picture of the structure of personality that is

▶ **concurrent validity** A method for assessing whether a psychometric test is valid (that is, really measures what it is supposed to) by comparing it with some other measure which purports to measure the same thing – also known as convergent or congruent validity).

▶ **criterion validity** A method for assessing whether a psychometric test is valid (that is, really measures what it is supposed to) by comparing it with some other measure. If the other measure is assessed at roughly the same time as the original one, then the type of criterion validity being applied is concurrent validity; if it is taken much later, it is predictive validity.

consistent with the proposals of the Big Five model. Equally, this picture emerges from both peer (third-person) and self (first-person) ratings. These findings go some way to giving confidence that the Big Five model is a useful one. At the very least they suggest that the indicators 'concur', in that they are measuring the same thing (whatever that 'thing' might be).

However, the stronger form of validity testing known as criterion validity was not addressed empirically in this study. Criterion (or predictive) validity refers to the extent to which the findings from these instruments map onto real-world patterns. One way of assessing this is to match personality profiles to occupation types. For example, the personality theory on which the Big Five model is based might predict that people with certain personality profiles are more likely to go into some types of occupation than they are to go into other types. Perhaps people who score high on agreeableness and on extraversion are more likely to go into professions that involve a lot of interaction with others. If robust relationships can be demonstrated between the scores from Big Five personality profiles (on the one hand) and some objective, real world criterion such as occupation choice (on the other), then that really would be strong evidence that the Big Five model is describing something of real psychological significance.

The attempt to describe and measure personality in terms of the five factors is an example of the quantitative approach. This method provides lots of data which can be used to generate all sorts of theories about differences between people and causes of behaviour and events. Health is one area where researchers have looked to see if certain patterns of personality are associated with disease (for example, Marshall *et al.*, 1994). The alternative approach is to look for the unique characteristics of each individual and avoid any attempt to reduce that individual to a series of numbers. This is the qualitative approach. There is a massive divide between the two approaches and adherents to the qualitative or quantitative camps commonly trade insults with each other in journals such as *The Psychologist* (for example, Shevlin, 2003).

Questions

1. What are the most important dimensions that you use in your thinking about and assessment of other people? What are your implicit 'Big Five' (or 'Big Four' or 'Big Six') factors?

2. What different kinds of 'validity' do psychologists assess when developing and using psychometric measures?

suggested answers → p. 490

BEM, S.L. (1974)

The measurement of psychological androgyny.

Journal of Consulting and Clinical Psychology, 42, 155–62.

Measuring masculinity and femininity

Introduction

Scales, tests and inventories are part of the psychologist's toolkit, and are of particular interest to psychometricians. The development of such measuring devices is an exacting process, and before they are used to measure anything in the real world their reliability and validity must be assessed. So it is quite common to see research studies which are devoted to the process of developing a particular scale. Such studies put the scale in question 'on the market' (if the reader is convinced by the processes of assessment which are reported), and allow future users to refer back to see how their measuring device was constructed and what its potential strengths and weaknesses might be.

Bem's famous article is a good example of such a study. It reports the development of a new scale for measuring psychological androgyny. The Bem Sex Role Inventory (BSRI) assesses the extent to which masculine and feminine traits co-exist in individuals irrespective of their actual sex. Here we will focus on the process of test development as reported in Bem's paper, but a very brief outline of androgyny is appropriate.

Bem challenges the traditional idea of femininity–masculinity, whereby people are either feminine or masculine. She also challenges the notion that femininity and masculinity are necessarily to do with being (biologically) female or male. She argues that 'dimensions of masculinity and femininity are empirically as well as logically independent' (p. 155), so that it is possible for someone to be both feminine and masculine ('androgynous') according to 'situational appropriateness' (p. 155). The development of the BSRI, which contains independent feminine and masculine scales, is the first step in the process of exploring these arguments.

▶ **psychometric tests** Instruments which have been developed for measuring mental characteristics. Psychological tests have been developed to measure a wide range of things, including creativity, job attitudes and skills, brain damage and, of course, 'intelligence'.

The study

Subjects

▶ **reliability** The reliability of a psychological measuring device (such as a test or a scale) is the extent to which it gives consistent measurements. The greater the consistency of measurement, the greater the tool's reliability.

Different subjects were used at different stages of the development of the inventory. In the 'item selection' stage, 100 Stanford University undergraduates (50 female, 50 male) acted as the 'judges' (see procedure section below). At the stage of 'psychometric analysis', 723 Stanford undergraduates (279 female, 444 male) and 194 junior college students (77 female, 117 male) were used as subjects. The junior college students were paid. Fifty-six of the Stanford undergraduates (28 female, 28 male) took part in the retest phase.

Design

This is a paper which documents the development of a psychological measuring scale. The process in this case involved two stages: item selection and
psychometric analysis. These stages are described in detail below.

Procedure

Item selection

Initially the author and some student assistants chose 200 words to describe
personality characteristics which they judged to be 'both positive in value and
either masculine or feminine in tone' (p. 156). One hundred undergraduate
'judges' were asked to rate all of these words on a 7-point Likert scale, according to how desirable each characteristic was in US society either for women
or for men. One set of 50 judges (25 female, 25 male) rated the desirability of
each characteristic for women ('In American society, how desirable is it for a
woman to be sincere?' p. 157). The other set of 50 judges (again, half female,
half male) rated desirability of each characteristic for men ('In American society, how desirable is it for a man to be sincere?' p. 157). If a word was rated by
men and women in both sets of judges to be significantly more desirable for
a woman, then it qualified as a potential 'feminine' item for the inventory. If
a word was rated by men and women in both sets of judges to be significantly
more desirable for a man, then it qualified as a potential 'masculine' item for
the inventory.

Twenty feminine items and 20 masculine items were selected (Bem does
not specify how this final selection was made) from those which qualified for
the final inventory. The inventory also includes 20 'neutral' items (neither
masculine nor feminine) which were incorporated as a measure of social
desirability effects in self-rating. The selection of and rationale for these
neutral items is described in detail by Bem, but is not covered in this
summary

Use of the inventory

When the inventory is administered, subjects are instructed to rate themselves on each of the 60 items using a 7-point Likert scale on which a score
of 1 denotes 'Never or almost never true' and a score of 7 denotes 'Always or
almost always true' (and so forth). A subject's Femininity (F) score is obtained
by adding up all the ratings for the 20 feminine items, and their Masculinity
(M) score is obtained by adding up their ratings for the 20 masculine items.
Subjects also receive an Androgyny (A) score.

The simplest way of calculating A is to subtract the M score from the F
score. The closer this number is to zero, the more androgynous the person.
High positive scores on A indicate a feminine sex-typed person, and high
negative scores indicate a masculine sex-typed person. Note that Bem suggests using a more sophisticated statistical test to calculate the A score but
acknowledges that the simple difference score between F and M can be used
instead.

Psychometric analysis

Once a measuring device has been assembled it must be tested for its psychometric properties. This is done by administering it to a large sample of the population which it is designed to measure, and noting various statistical properties of the data which emerge.

A vital step in this process is the assessment of the reliability of the measuring device. This involves examining the extent to which it gives consistent results. Bem did this in two ways. First she looked at the internal consistency of the scale. If the scale is internally consistent then a person who scores high on one masculine item will also be likely to score high on the other masculine items. Her analyses (see the statistical note below if you must) confirmed that the test was internally consistent.

The second kind of reliability Bem assessed was the test–retest reliability of the inventory. This gives an estimate of the extent to which the results of the BSRI are consistent over time. Fifty-six of the original 723 Stanford University undergraduate subjects completed the inventory for a second time four weeks after having done their first test. Their retest scores on each of the F, M and A scales were compared with their original 'test' scores by means of a correlation coefficient (signified by r). The correlations were sufficiently strong to allow Bem to claim a high level of test–retest reliability (for Femininity $r = .90$; for Masculinity $r = .90$; and for Androgyny $r = .93$).

The final statistical property that will be considered in this summary (Bem considers several in the original paper) is the relationship between the F and the M scales. Remember Ben's argument is that femininity and masculinity are 'empirically independent' dimensions. This means that people's scores on the F scale should show no consistent relationship with their scores on the M scale. Calculation of correlation coefficients for the F and M scores for the Stanford undergraduates showed values of nearly zero for r. This supports Bem's assertion of empirical independence for the two dimensions, because the nearer a value of r is to zero (irrespective of whether it is positive or negative), the smaller the relationship between the two variables which have been compared. When a test or scale can be shown to match up to a piece of theory in this way it is said to have a level of construct validity.

Results

The most important result of this process of development, aside from the population norms and various statistical properties, is the inventory itself.

For copyright reasons we are unable to show the items from the BSRI here.

We strongly recommend that you consult Table 1 (p. 156) of the original paper which shows the 60 items organized into three columns of 20; one column for masculine, one for feminine and one for neutral items. The items are mostly single words, although about a fifth are short phrases. The masculine column contains adjectives such as 'aggressive' and 'self-reliant'. The

---

▶ **internal consistency** If a test is internally consistent then the items in that test really are measuring the same thing (or same set of things). Note that this does not necessarily mean that they are measuring what they are meant to measure. In this respect, internal consistency has more to do with reliability than validity.

▶ **test–retest method** A system for judging how reliable a psychometric test or measure is, which involves administering the same test to the same people on two different occasions, and comparing the results.

▶ **correlation coefficient** A number between -1 and +1 which expresses how strong a correlation is. If this number is close to 0, there is no real connection between the two; if it is close to +1 there is a positive correlation – in other words, if one variable is large the other will also tend to be large; and if it is close to -1, there is a negative correlation – in other words, if one variable is large, the other will tend to be small.

▶ **construct validity** A method for assessing whether a psychometric test is valid (that is, really measures what it is supposed to) by seeing how it matches up with theoretical ideas about what it is supposed to be measuring.

feminine scale lists words such as 'compassionate' and 'understanding'. The neutral scale consists of items such as 'friendly' and 'jealous'.

Discussion

To say that a measuring device is reliable is to say that it produces consistent patterns of results. Assessing the reliability of an inventory like the BSRI is relatively straightforward, since most of the work can be done by means of standard statistical procedures. The evidence that Bem presents suggests that the BSRI does, indeed, give reliable results.

However once reliability has been assessed, the much harder task of considering validity appears. The extent to which a scale is valid is the extent to which it measures what it sets out to measure. For a scale to be valid it must firstly be reliable. But if a scale is reliable this does not in itself mean that it is valid. Imagine a ruler that is wrongly calibrated. It will give perfectly consistent results when used to measure things (it will be perfectly reliable), but the measurements will be invalid (and therefore useless). Unfortunately there are no easy statistical means for assessing validity. Sometimes the results of a scale are compared to the results of existing scales which are thought to measure the same thing. This is known as concurrent validity. Bem does in fact compare the scores of her subjects on the BSRI with their scores on two other existing masculinity–femininity scales which she administered to them at the same time. The relationship among the various scales was relatively weak, so Bem simply concluded that the scales were measuring different aspects of sex roles. This handy 'get-out clause' always exists in relation to estimates of concurrent validity.

▶ **concurrent validity** A method for assessing whether a psychometric test is valid (that is, really measures what it is supposed to) by comparing it with some other measure which purports to measure the same thing – also known as convergent or congruent validity).

To what extent, then, can the BSRI be said to be valid? That is, to what extent does the Femininity scale really measure femininity? And what about the M and A scales? One way of assessing the validity of the BSRI is to examine the way that the instrument was constructed in the first place. Certainly the care and attention to detail at the stage of item selection is one point in its favour. Bem did not just throw together 40 items that she felt were related to masculinity and femininity. Instead she involved a large number of other people in the selection process (at least 100 others), with the result that the final scales were built on a fair degree of social consensus; consensus that the 20 F items really were more desirable characteristics for women than for men in the USA in the 1970s, and likewise for the 20 M items.

But even if it was possible to demonstrate that the scales were valid there (in the USA) and then (in the 1970s), this could never ensure that they are valid here (wherever you are reading this) and now. Bem shows great awareness in her article that the BSRI is a culturally specific measuring device, by stressing that the items were assessed for desirability for men and women in the USA. She shows less awareness of the historical specificity of the BSRI, but of course this is something which is always easier to assess in retrospect.

Questions

suggested
answers
▶ p. 490

1. What are the limitations of using students as the subjects in this study?

2. Bem developed the BSRI in the USA in the 1970s. Why should we be cautious of using this instrument today outside the USA?

3. What does it mean to say that a test is reliable? What does it mean to say that a test is valid?

4. What different types of reliability do psychologists talk about?

Statistical note

▶ **alpha coefficient (Cronbach's Alpha)** A statistic which is used to give an estimate of reliability.

To measure the internal consistency of the scale, Bem calculated separate alpha coefficients (also known as Cronbach's alpha, and signified by α) for the Femininity scale and for the Masculinity scale. Coefficient α gives a measure of the internal consistency of the inventory. It works by assessing, statistically, the extent to which responses to the different items on a given scale relate to one another. For example, if the 20 items which make up the Masculinity scale really are all measuring a bit of masculinity then one would expect, on balance, to see a positive correlation among the scores for those items for each subject. In other words, if a given subject rates themselves as 7 on the item 'Acts as a leader', and we assume (as the BSRI does) that 'Acts as a leader' and 'Aggressive' are both measures of 'masculinity, then we would assume that they would be more likely to give themselves a high rating on 'Aggressive' than a person who had rated themselves as 1 on the 'Acts as a leader' item. Coefficient α gives a statistical estimate of the extent to which responses to items on a given scale really do relate one to another. Bem cites relatively high alpha values for both the Femininity and the Masculinity scales (α for F = 0.8; α for M = 0.86: like a straightforward correlation coefficient the maximum value for α is 1), and so was able to claim that they are reliable in the sense of being internally consistent.

Introduction

GOULD, S.J. (1982)
Mis-measuring intelligence
A nation of morons.
New Scientist
(6 May 1982),
pp. 349–52.

Intelligence is perhaps the most controversial topic in modern psychology. It has created furious debate throughout the twentieth century and continues to do so. The issue that creates this controversy concerns whether intelligence is inherited or not. Although this is the way the question is usually framed, the real debate is about whether the differences between individuals can be explained by genetic or environmental causes. You might well ask whether this matters at all, but the paper by Gould, which is a short article taken from his book *The Mismeasure of Man*, illustrates how this question can have large social consequences.

If we are going to investigate intelligence, then we need to be able to measure it. The first tests of intelligence were developed in France by Alfred Binet who started his scientific studies by examining the relationship between head size and intelligence. He discovered that there is no relationship between these two factors. He was later commissioned by the minister of public education to develop a technique to identify children in need of special education, and from this the intelligence test was born. The test was used to give an estimate of a child's mental age by comparing the child's performance on various tasks with the performance of children of various ages. It was later suggested that the mental age of the child should be divided by the chronological age to give an index of intelligence and so the notion of IQ was developed.

Intelligence Quotient (IQ) = Mental Age / Chronological Age x 100

Subsequently, the calculation of IQ has become more sophisticated. It is now based on norm referencing, or in other words it depends on calculating the average performance for your peers then comparing you against the average.

Binet believed that children who were in need of extra help could be identified by these tests, but he vigorously argued against the idea that intelligence is a fixed quantity that cannot be improved by further help. This approach got sadly lost in the translation of tests into the English language and in their transportation to the USA. In contrast to the approach of Binet, the fiercest supporters of intelligence testing became scientists who believed that individual differences are mainly due to genetic factors, and that a society should scientifically breed a superior group of people (this is referred to as eugenics). For example, Lewis Terman who introduced the IQ test to the USA while he was professor of psychology at Stanford University wrote:

> If we would preserve our state for a class of people worthy to possess it, we must prevent, as far as possible, the propagation of mental degenerates. (Terman, 1921, cited in Kamin, 1977)

▶ **intelligence** An inferred characteristic of an individual, usually defined as the ability to profit from experience, acquire knowledge, think abstractly or adapt to changes in the environment.

▶ **genetic** Biological inheritance.

▶ **Intelligence Quotient (IQ)** A numerical figure, believed by some to indicate the level of a person's intelligence, and by others to indicate how well that person performs on intelligence tests.

▶ **eugenics** The political idea that the human race could be improved by eliminating 'undesirables' from the breeding stock, so that they cannot pass on their supposedly inferior genes. Some eugenicists advocate compulsory sterilization, while others seem to prefer mass murder or genocide.

This is the basic eugenic argument, that scientists should identify the useless, the stupid and the weak, and prevent (or discourage) them from having children. In this way the general population will improve its genetic stock. The crude simplicity of this dogma appeals to some politicians who have used the bogus science to justify oppressive policies.

The article

The article describes one story in the development of intelligence testing. Psychologist Robert Yerkes was concerned to establish psychology as a 'hard' science, and thought that mental testing looked a promising route to achieve this. Unfortunately, in 1915, mental testing did not enjoy much credibility, so Yerkes tried to change this.

The outbreak of the First World War (1914–18) in Europe and the subsequent involvement of the United States brought about a massive mobilization of armies. Yerkes managed to persuade the US military to give mental tests to all army recruits, and as a result he was able to preside over the testing of 1.75 million people.

There were three types of test: literate recruits were given a written test called the Army Alpha, men who were illiterate or who failed the Alpha were given a pictorial test called the Army Beta, and failures on the Beta were to be recalled for an individual spoken examination. The Alpha had eight parts made up of the items we recognize today as characteristic of IQ tests, such as analogies, filling in the missing number, and unscrambling a sentence. The Beta test had seven parts including number work and the picture completion task shown in Figure 9.1. Each test took less than an hour and could be administered to large groups.

Yerkes asserted that the tests measured 'native intellectual ability' (cited in Gould, p. 349), in other words intelligence that was unaffected by culture and educational opportunities. But the level of cultural and educational knowledge required is clearly illustrated in the examples from the tests given below:

> Washington is to Adams as first is to ...
> Crisco is a: patent medicine, disinfectant, toothpaste, food product.
> Christy Mathewson is famous as a: writer, artist, baseball player, comedian.

There were a number of problems in the administration of the tests. In particular, many who were illiterate in English were still allocated to the Alpha test and so scored zero or near to zero. Yerkes had overestimated the level of literacy in the general population and so the queues for the Beta tests became very long, leading to the inappropriate reallocation of men to the Alpha test. Failures on the Alpha test were often not recalled to take the Beta test. This created a systematic bias in the test since recent immigrants who had a poor grasp of English, and Black soldiers who had not been given much, if any, formal education, were unable to score on the Alpha test. Another problem

Figure 9.1 *Part six of examination Beta for testing innate intelligence*

was that even the Beta test required the use of a pencil and the writing of numbers, and many men had never held a pencil in their lives. Gould outlines a number of other problems with the testing procedures which suggest that the data should be looked at with considerable scepticism. However, at the time, the results had a considerable impact, and by the end of the war some of the army camps were using the tests to screen people for officer training.

The tests generated a lot of interest, and by 1921, when Yerkes published his findings, he was able to refer to 'the steady stream of requests from commercial concerns, educational institutions and individuals for the use of army methods of psychological examining or for adaptation of such methods to special needs'. Mental testing and psychology had achieved the credibility that Yerkes wanted.

Gould reports that three 'facts' were created from the testing data:[1]

(1) 'The average mental age of White US adults stood just above the edge of moronity at a shockingly meagre 13. Terman had previously set the standard at 16' (p. 351). That is why the title of the article is 'A Nation of Morons', because the data suggested that the USA was just that.

(2) It was possible to grade European immigrants by their country of origin. According to the test results, the average man of many countries was a moron, with the fair people of Northern and Western Europe scoring higher than the Slavs of Eastern Europe and the darker people of Southern Europe.

(3) The average score of Black men was 10.4, which was considerably below the White average.

Although the 'finding' that the average US citizen was a moron caused some concern,[2] this was nothing compared to the response to the other two 'facts'. These were used to support the idea of genetic differences between races. Carl Brigham, one of Yerkes' colleagues, argued for a genetic explanation of data and proposed the racial superiority of Nordic people (from Northern Europe). He came up with some remarkable reasoning: for example, his explanation of the low average score of Jewish men despite the very many major accomplishments of Jewish scholars, statesmen and performing artists. Brigham argued that we notice the exceptional performance of some Jews (for example Einstein) because it is unusual against the performance of the average Jew.

This line of argument was threatened by two problems with the data. First, the immigration of different national groups had taken place at different times, and the most recent immigrants, and hence the least familiar with English, were the Slavs and the people from Southern Europe. So if literacy was having an effect on the test scores, then these people would be disadvantaged. Second, the data showed that the average score rose with the length of residence in the USA. This is a clear indication that the more experience a person had of the USA the higher their score was on the test, suggesting a cultural bias in the questions. Brigham, however, argued quite bizarrely that these data showed that the early immigrants were the brightest from each national group, and the subsequent immigrants were progressively more stupid.

So, despite the evidence, the eugenic argument took hold and one of the consequences of this was the passing of the Immigration Restriction Act in 1924 by the US Congress. The scientists who supported the eugenics argument lobbied the politicians and, according to Gould, 'won one of the greatest victories of scientific racism in American history' (p. 352). The Act set immigration quotas based on the US population in 1890 (over 30 years prior

► **race** Commonly used to refer to groups of people such as White people or Black people etc. It implies a genetic component to the differences between these groups, but research shows that the term 'race' has no biological validity and is best described as a political construct.

► **validity** The question of whether a psychometric test or psychological measure is really measuring what it is supposed to.

---

1. Gould means that three widely held beliefs were created by the data and many people came to see them as accurate statements of truth (facts) rather than partial interpretations of the evidence (opinion).

2. At this point UK readers must put their prejudices to one side and stop sniggering at this.

to the Act). This year was used as the benchmark because immigration from Southern and Eastern Europe had been relatively low before this date.

During the next 20 years, conditions deteriorated dramatically in Europe for Slavs and Jews as the Nazi governments enacted policies of 'racial purity' culminating in genocide. Gould tells how many people tried to flee the political oppression but were denied access to the USA. Estimates suggest that the immigration quotas barred up to 6 million people from Southern, Central and Eastern Europe, a number with some significance in the history of Europe.

Discussion

The article tells one chapter in the giant history of intelligence testing, and in no way attempts to provide a balanced view. It illustrates the human consequences of academic debates, and highlights the need to examine the political context of psychological theory.

One of the striking points to note is that the debate continues, though the evidence has become no more clear. There is no good evidence to support the view that group differences in IQ scores are due to genetic differences. The statistic that is commonly used to estimate the influence of genetics is heritability. This statistic estimates how much the variation *within* any given population is due to genetic factors. It does not, however, tell us about why two populations will differ and so contributes nothing to our understanding of this issue (see Rose *et al.*, 1984). It also fails to tell us anything about how much genetics affects the characteristics of an individual.

▶ **heritability** An estimate of the extent to which genetic individual differences contribute to individual differences in observed behaviour.

There is also a lack, even today, of a clear operational definition of intelligence, which tends to undermine any line of argument. Likewise the whole idea of 'race' defies definition, with the only sensible conclusion being that race is more a political construct than a biological one.

Problems like these make assertions about racial differences very difficult and, in fact, one of the leading psychometricians, Kline (1991) suggests that

> The only advantage in setting out the different scores on IQ tests of racial groups is to give ammunition to those who wish to decry them. It adds nothing to theoretical understanding or to the social or educational practice. (Kline, 1991, p. 96)

Finally, we need to consider how it is that IQ testing has gained such respectability and prominence despite an inability to define the quality it is measuring, and its use in the cause of scientific racism. The best answer must draw on the plausibility of the tests and the excessive respect given to psychologists and their claims (for an example of this, see the study by Forer in Chapter 18).

Questions

suggested answers ➜ p. 491

1. Identify the cultural and educational bias in the examples of the Alpha questions contained in the summary, and in the Beta items shown in Figure 9.1.

2. What is scientific racism?

3. What is intelligence? Try and list the skills that you associate with intelligent behaviour.

A brave new world

PLOMIN, R. AND DANIELS, D. (1987)

Why are children in the same family so different from one another?

Behavioral and Brain Sciences, 10, 1–16.

▶ **personality** A distinctive and relatively stable pattern of behaviours, thoughts, motives and emotions that characterize an individual.

▶ **genetic** Biological inheritance.

▶ **intelligence** An inferred characteristic of an individual, usually defined as the ability to profit from experience, acquire knowledge, think abstractly or adapt to changes in the environment.

▶ **behaviour (also spelt 'behavior')** Anything a person (or animal) does that can be observed and measured by a third party. Behaviour can be thought of as the public side of human life, in contrast to 'experience' (thoughts and feelings) which can be thought of as the private side.

Introduction

Were you born with your personal qualities of intelligence and personality or did you develop them? This fundamental question has been asked for centuries and during that time has generated more heat than light. The advances in our knowledge of inheritance and the discovery of the mechanisms of genetic transmission have intensified the debate rather than resolved it. The reason for the heat is that the various scientific answers point to various solutions to the problems of social living and some of these solutions are very disturbing.

An example of how this debate has raged in psychology can be found in the story of intelligence testing which is briefly discussed in the summary of the paper by Stephen Jay Gould (earlier in this chapter). To put the debate in its starkest form, if there are strong genetic components to a behaviour then we can change the occurrence of this behaviour in our society through genetic means such as selective breeding (eugenics) or genetic engineering. It is possible consequences like these that make reasoned discussion about these issues very difficult.

It is important to start by clarifying the central question. If we phrase it in the form 'is personality inherited?' then it does not really make sense. There are two points to make here,

(1) In order to have a personality we need to have the basic features of a human being (that is, a body and a brain), and these are formed from the genetic material we inherit. On the other hand, our personalities can only develop though an interaction with the environment because we will die unless we are nurtured. Even physical characteristic such as our height are formed by both genetic and environmental influences.

(2) People have a lot of characteristics in common, but in studies of personality, the psychologists are not concerned with the personality features we share but with the differences between one person and another.

Putting these two points together we can see that the central issue in behavioural genetics is not whether personality is inherited, but how much of the differences between people in their personalities can be attributed to genetics and how much can be attributed to the effects of the environment. The paper by Plomin and Daniels goes a step further by examining different aspects of environmental influence and attempting to assess how much they contribute to individual differences.

The paper

The paper by Plomin and Daniels is an extensive review of the evidence on the role of the non-shared environment (see below), and appeared in *Behavioral*

eugenics The political idea that the human race could be improved by eliminating 'undesirables' from the breeding stock, so that they cannot pass on their supposedly inferior genes. Some eugenicists advocate compulsory sterilization, while others seem to prefer mass murder or genocide.

behavioural genetics The study of the influence of genetics on a range of behaviours, most commonly personality and intelligence.

trait A specific facet of personality.

schizophrenia A mental disorder marked by some, or all of the following symptoms: delusions, hallucinations, incoherent word associations, inappropriate emotions or lack of emotions.

and Brain Sciences along with more than 30 reviews and comments on the article from other scientists. In this summary we will concentrate on the main article.

The article starts by pointing out that research in behavioural genetics rarely finds evidence that more than half of the differences between people in their complex behavioural traits can be explained by genetics. Therefore, for personality, psychopathology and cognition, the research suggests that most of the differences between people are due to environmental factors. Plomin and Daniels give the example of schizophrenia, which is commonly presented as a genetic condition even though the evidence points the other way. The evidence from close family members of people with schizophrenia is that the incidence is much lower than you would expect if the condition was largely under genetic control. This is a remarkable way to start a paper, because Plomin is so heavily associated with genetic explanations of behaviour.

Research designs

It is difficult to conduct research into the relative effects of genetic and environmental influences on people. The problem is that people who share genetic features (family members) commonly also share environmental features (same home or town or patterns of parental care). There are two basic designs that attempt to control for these features.

1 Adoption studies

adoption studies Studies designed to investigate the relative influence of environmental and genetic factors by comparing children in different family situations.

The basic logic of adoption studies is:

- people who are related (shared genetic inheritance) but adopted separately (different environment) will resemble each other only for genetic reasons, and
- people who are unrelated (no shared genetic inheritance) but adopted together (shared environment) will only resemble each other for reasons of shared environment.

2 Twin studies

twin studies Family-based studies that look for the relative influence of genetic and environmental factors on a range of social and cognitive qualities.

monozygotic twin A twin from the splitting of one fertilized ovum; commonly an identical twin.

Twin studies compare the resemblance of identical twins (monozygotic) with the resemblance of same-sex fraternal twins (dizygotic). Identical twins are genetically identical, whereas fraternal twins only share 50 per cent of their genes, like normal siblings. By examining the correlation coefficients of the similarity between these two sets of twins we can estimate the relative effects of environment and genetics.

It is worth noting that these designs are not without their critics and the evidence that comes from them is controversial.

The non-shared environment

Plomin and Daniels go one step further with the analysis of environmental influence and argue that we can categorize environmental influences into two parts:

► **correlation coefficient** A number between -1 and +1 which expresses how strong a correlation is. If this number is close to 0, there is no real connection between the two; if it is close to +1 there is a positive correlation – in other words, if one variable is large the other will also tend to be large; and if it is close to -1, there is a negative correlation – in other words, if one variable is large, the other will tend to be small.

(1) *Shared environment*: all environmental influences that make children in families similar to one another (for example being treated the same as our siblings by our parents);

(2) *Non-shared environment*: the influences that make family members different (for example, being treated differently to our siblings by our parents).

They show how the results from studies using the designs outlined above can be used to estimate these two types of environmental influence. The rest of the paper goes on to examine the nature and importance of the non-shared environment.

Plomin and Daniels review the evidence on the importance of the non-shared environment in the psychological measures of personality, psychopathology and IQ. In the research on personality they claim that genetic effects can be shown to account for less than 50 per cent of the differences between people. The rest of the differences, once the measurement error is removed, are mainly explained by the non-shared environment. Although they cite a large number of studies, one of the limitations of this evidence is that it mainly comes from pencil and paper questionnaires.

Plomin and Daniels' reading of the evidence of psychopathology comes to the same conclusion, and they suggest, for example, that sharing the same family environment with a schizophrenic relative does not increase your chances of developing the disorder. In the area of IQ, they further claim that the shared environment has no long-term effects on performance, though the non-shared environment accounts for between 40 per cent and 60 per cent of the differences between people.

So, if the variations between us are explained not by what we share in a family but by the differences in our experience, then what are these differences? It might be that the key experiences are unusual and unique events like accidents or good luck. Alternatively, there may be some systematic differences that can be examined and evaluated. Plomin and Daniels suggest the following list of items that might cause children in the same family to differ:

► **psychometric tests** Instruments which have been developed for measuring mental characteristics. Psychological tests have been developed to measure a wide range of things, including creativity, job attitudes and skills, brain damage and, of course, 'intelligence'.

- *Measurement error;* for example, the unreliability of psychometric tests.
- Non-systematic features of the non-shared environment; for example, accidents, illness, trauma.
- Systematic features of the non-shared environment:
  - Family composition; for example, birth order
  - Sibling interaction; for example, differential treatment
  - Parental treatment; for example, differential treatment
  - Extra-familial networks; for example, peers, teachers, television.

The scientific study of the non-shared environment is relatively recent, but there have been some attempts to measure its effect. An example of this is the Sibling Inventory of Differential Experience (SIDE), which has 11 sub-scales that measure aspects of sibling interaction, parental treatment and the peer group.

Plomin and Daniels argue that environmental influence is important but it acts differently from the way in which we usually think of it. In the case of the influence of parents, for example, the effect has little to do with the aspects of parenting that are common to all children in the family, and everything to do with the different ways in which the children are treated.

One of the complicating issues here is that using the same behaviour with two different people will not necessarily be perceived as giving them the same treatment. Saying 'well done' to one person can be encouraging and stimulating, and to another can be oppressive because of the expectation that they should continue to do well in the future. Questionnaire evidence shows that parents believe that they treat all their children similarly, but that their children experience differences in treatment. Observational evidence of parents, on the other hand, tells a different story and suggests that parents are very consistent in their behaviour towards their young children and infants.

Plomin and Daniels conclude the article by saying that:

> children in the same environment experience practically no shared environmental influence that makes them similar for behavioural traits. In other words, the effective environments of siblings are hardly any more similar than are the environments of strangers who grow up in different families. (p. 15)

Discussion

The sting of this article is in the tail. It starts out by emphasizing the role of environmental factors in a range of psychological variables (personality, psychopathology and IQ). These variables were the focus of heated debate over the best part of the twentieth century concerning the likely role of genetics. Arguments against the genetic explanations of psychopathology and personality can be found in Rose *et al.* (1984), and against the genetic explanations of intelligence in Kamin (1977). Plomin and Daniels start their argument by disarming the critics of genetic explanations with their statement about the role of the environment. If we leave on one side the casual way they suggest that about 50 per cent of differences in personality and intelligence can be accounted for by genetic explanations, we could view their paper as support for the role of social interventions in the development of personal and cognitive skills.

Sadly, this reading would be wrong. The authors divide environment into shared and non-shared, and by showing the importance of the non-shared environment they suggest that the shared environment has little or no effect on the differences in performance. Or to put it another way, the intentional attempts at nurturing by parents and teachers are far less important than the unintentional or accidental features of the process. This view is challenged by a number of the commentators to the Plomin and Daniels article in the notes that follow it (for example, Nyborg, 1987; Rose and Kaprio, 1987).

In the last part of the article the authors also start to speculate on whether the differences in people attributed to the non-shared environment are cause or effect. In other words, does the non-shared environment cause the differences or is it just another measure of the differences that already exist between people? You see, one possible explanation of the effects of the non-shared environment is that they are caused by genetic differences between individuals. Interestingly enough, Plomin and Daniels do not find any evidence to support this view.

Behavioural genetics will continue to be a controversial topic and it is likely to come to greater prominence as our knowledge about genetics increases. The moral and political questions it generates are unlikely to be easily resolved and people will need to deal carefully with the findings if we are to avoid actions that degrade sections of our society and subject them to inhuman or brutal treatments.

Questions

1. What is meant by the term behavioural genetics?

2. What would be the advantage of being able to control behaviour such as aggression through genetic engineering?

suggested answers → p. 491

part **iv**

DEVELOPMENTAL PSYCHOLOGY

DEVELOPMENTAL psychology is
sometimes understandably but
misleadingly thought of as child
psychology: understandably because
the major part of the literature in
developmental psychology is about
children; misleadingly because it gives
the impression that psychological
development stops as the child enters
adulthood. A truly comprehensive
developmental psychology should
concern itself with the whole lifespan of
human development. Having said this,
the studies summarized in this part
reflect the traditional preoccupation with
children. The studies that have been
selected for inclusion have been chosen
in order to give a fair reflection of the
literature as it is, rather than trying to
show how it should be.

Attachment is the subject of Chapter
10. Studies of attachment look at the
way in which babies and children bond
with adult caregivers, and focus on
the consequences of problems that
can occur during the course of this
complex process. Perhaps the most
famous name to be associated with
attachment is Bowlby, who popularized
the controversial notion of maternal
deprivation (Bowlby, 1951). His work is
not represented here, but the summaries
of Harlow (1959), Koluchová (1972),
Hodges and Tizard (1989b) and
Brazelton et al. (1976) provide a good
introduction to the area.

Chapter 11, on Classic Approaches,
includes work to do with two of the
all-time-great figures in developmental
psychology: Piaget and Freud.
Ironically, neither was a developmental
psychologist! Piaget's approach is
touched upon in the summary of Samuel
and Bryant's (1984) paper, which
provides a small methodological critique
of one of his research procedures.
Freud's case history of Little Hans
provides an insight into the influential
psychoanalytic approach to psychology.
And the inclusion of Watson and
Rayner's (1920) much-quoted study of
Little Albert ensures that the traditions
of behaviourism do not go unrecognized
in this volume. The last study is an
experimental study looking at the
theories of Russian psychologist Lev
Vygotsky.

Finally, Chapter 12 deals with the
development of communication. The
child's eventual mastery of language is
perhaps the single most impressive and
important achievement of childhood.
The first two studies in this chapter
show how language development can

▶ **attachment** The tendency
of the young of many
species to stay close to an
adult, usually the mother.

▶ **case history** A detailed
clinical description
of a person which
characteristically forms
the basis for some kind of
therapeutic intervention.

▶ **psychoanalysis** Freud's
theory of personality which
describes how human
behaviour is affected by
unconscious thoughts and
feelings.

▶ **behaviourism** A school of
thought which holds that the
observation and description
of overt behaviour is all that
is needed to comprehend
the human being, and that
manipulation of stimulus–
response contingencies is
all that is needed to change
human behaviour.

be traced right back to the moment of birth (and probably before). The final study of the chapter deals with the work of a sociolinguist, Labov, who looked at the issue of how to assess children's language competence, and made a series of methodological and political points that are relevant to the whole field of developmental psychology.

The studies that are included in this part are not the only ones in this book that relate to developmental psychology. In a very real sense all of psychology is developmental since it is the study of things (people and processes) which change and develop over the course of time. For too long psychology as a whole has tended to study static snapshots of people, frozen in time and space, and thereby has risked missing some things which lie at the very core of human existence.

chapter **10**

ATTACHMENT

▶ attachment The tendency of the young of many species to stay close to an adult, usually the mother.

▶ behaviour (also spelt 'behavior') Anything a person (or animal) does that can be observed and measured by a third party. Behaviour can be thought of as the public side of human life, in contrast to 'experience' (thoughts and feelings) which can be thought of as the private side.

ATTACHMENT refers to a strong emotional tie between two people. In developmental psychology, the term 'attachment' is often taken to mean the emotional tie between the infant and the adult caregiver. It is a popular belief in this culture that the emotional experiences we have in our early years will have an important effect on our adult behaviour and experience. This belief has received considerable support from some psychologists, for example John Bowlby.

In 1951 Bowlby produced a report for the World Health Organisation in which he suggested that 'mother love in infancy and childhood is as important for mental health as are vitamins and proteins for physical health' (see Bowlby, 1965, p. 240). The clear implication of this is that mothers are a crucial part of a child's development and that many of the problems of later life can be traced back to inadequate mothering. While it is clear that the evidence supports the value of a warm and stable emotional environment for a child, it does not support the notion that this environment must be created by the biological mother. The problem lies in the choice of the term 'mothering' to describe the process of caring for a child. A mother is a woman who gives birth to a child, whereas mothering is a collection of activities that can be carried out by anyone, though most commonly this person is the mother.

Bowlby presented a considerable amount of evidence that illustrated the negative effects of early experience. It showed that children brought up in institutions who were not given the opportunity to develop stable emotional bonds failed to thrive and develop in the same way as children brought up in family homes. Bowlby concentrated on the emotional bond with the mother, though there are many other features of the institutions that affected the development of the children. The report led to a change in the way that children are cared for in institutions and helped to raise the standards of childcare generally.

A lot has happened in the 50 years since Bowlby's initial report and in the UK the pattern of family life has gone through some radical changes. Research has also moved on and it is clear that there are considerable weaknesses in Bowlby's theory (e.g. see Tizard, 1986). Despite this there is general agreement that the theory still has some merit and that his work made a major contribution to the development of good childcare in the UK. In a recent review by the World

►**longitudinal study** A study which monitors changes occurring over a period of time.

Health Organization (2004) Bowlby's much quoted assertion about early nurturing (see above) was reworked as:

> Sensitive and responsive caregiving is a requirement for the healthy neurophysiological, physical and psychological development of a child. (p. 5)

Bowlby's work stimulated a lot of other research studies which have used a variety of methods in an attempt to broaden our understanding of attachment. Some work has looked at attachment processes in animals, and the first study in this chapter describes the famous (possibly infamous) work of Harlow (1959) with rhesus monkeys. Other rich sources of information are the various case studies of children brought up in severely deprived circumstances,

and the study by Koluchová (1972) is an example of this work. The third example of work in this field is the longitudinal study of Hodges and Tizard (1989b), which looks at the development of a number of children who spent their infancy in institutions before being adopted into families. Finally, we include a paper by Brazelton *et al.* (1976) that looks at cultural differences in the behaviour of newborn infants.

There are no simple answers or straightforward theories to describe any type of human relationship, least of all the relationships between children and their parents. Despite this, or maybe because of this, psychologists need to study attachment, because the everyday beliefs that we have about it affect the development of social policies which affect children's lives.

Can you hear me mother?

HARLOW, H.F. (1959)

Love in infant monkeys.

Scientific American, 200, 68–74.

Introduction

What is love? And how do we develop our bonds of affection? These are major questions for psychologists, though they have turned to some unlikely sources for the answer. One of these unlikely sources has been the field of comparative psychology and the work of Harry Harlow and his associates.

Harlow's work developed from an unfortunate accident that occurred in the primate colony he was responsible for. Harlow wanted to reduce infant mortality in the animals and create a sturdy and disease-free colony for use in various research programmes (Harlow and Harlow, 1962). He separated the animals from their mothers, and from all social contact, at birth and put them in a controlled and isolated environment. The primary objective of a reduced mortality rate was achieved, but at the cost of their psychological health and social competence. The monkeys sat in their cages and stared fixedly into space, circled their cages in a repetitive and stereotyped manner, clasped their heads in their hands and rocked, and developed self-injurious compulsive habits. Harlow suggested that it was possible to observe similar behaviour patterns in disturbed children and adults. When these monkeys were put together, they were unable to develop a characteristic social structure and, most remarkably, were totally unable to mate. They could make the right movements, but not in the right order! Any attempts to encourage mating produced vicious assaults. Some of the females were eventually impregnated but were unable to nurture their young and would just brush them off or would abuse them. Harlow and his team decided to investigate these phenomena, and in a famous series of experiments looked for the important factors in the development of affectional bonds and 'normal' social behaviour.

▸ **behaviour (also spelt 'behavior')** Anything a person (or animal) does that can be observed and measured by a third party. Behaviour can be thought of as the public side of human life, in contrast to 'experience' (thoughts and feelings) which can be thought of as the private side.

The study

Harlow observed that the isolated monkeys became quite attached to the gauze nappy pads that were placed on the floor of their cages. They showed some distress when the pads were removed once a day for cleaning, and the attachment seemed similar to a human baby's attachment to a teddy or a blanket. The researchers used this observation as a starting point for their experiments on the importance of nursing and body contact in the development of attachment.

The researchers made two surrogate mothers. One was a bare wire frame with a wooden head and a crude face. The other model had a covering of terry cloth over the frame and a more monkey-like face. They placed eight newborn monkeys in individual cages with equal access to both the cloth and wire 'mothers'. Four of the infants received their milk from one mother and four from the other. The milk was provided via a nursing bottle with a nipple protruding through the frame. The two models (Harlow continually referred

▸ **self-injurious behaviour** Behaviour which causes either physical or mental harm to the self. In extreme cases, self-injurious behaviour can become life threatening.

▸ **attachment** The tendency of the young of many species to stay close to an adult, usually the mother.

▸ **surrogate** Substitute

to the models as 'mothers', but this is not an acceptable description of them) proved to be physiologically equivalent; the monkeys in the two groups drank the same amount of milk and put on the same amount of weight. However, the models were not psychologically equivalent; all the monkeys spent more time clinging to the cloth model regardless of whether they were being fed by it or not.

The results showed the importance of bodily contact for young monkeys. Harlow went on to say:

> all our experience indicates, in fact, that our cloth covered mother surrogate is an eminently satisfactory mother. She is available 24 hours a day to satisfy her infant's overwhelming compulsion to seek bodily contact; she possesses infinite patience, never scolding her baby or biting it in anger. In these respects we regard her as superior to a living monkey mother, though monkey fathers would probably not endorse this opinion. (p. 70)

▶ **anthropomorphism**
Attribution of human characteristics to animals.

This strange mixture of anthropomorphism and stereotyped attitudes about the role of mothers and mothering probably give us more insight into contemporary attitudes than into the development of affectional bonds.

In the next phase of the study, Harlow subjected the monkeys to stressful situations to see how they would respond. In one example they were presented with a mechanical teddy bear (bigger than themselves) which walked towards them playing a drum. The monkeys who had been fed by the cloth model climbed onto this model to reduce their anxiety. The monkeys who had been fed by the wire model also went to the cloth model under this stress.

In another test, the monkeys were taken to a strange situation which was a much larger room than they were used to, and which contained a number of unfamiliar objects. The monkeys would 'hide' in the corner and cover their heads with their arms. However, if the cloth model was put in the room the monkey would rush to it and climb on it. Then it would start to explore the room using the model as a base. It would check out the objects one by one and return to the model continually. Harlow suggested that this response can also be seen in young children.

A final test involved giving the monkeys the opportunity to press a lever that opened a window. Previous research had shown that monkeys will do this just to look out, and will press the lever more often to view some stimuli (another monkey for example) than for others (a bowl of fruit perhaps). The experimental monkeys pressed the lever to look at the cloth model as often as they did to look at another real monkey. In contrast they showed very little interest in the wire model.

Other studies showed that the monkeys had a slight preference for a rocking model over a rigid model, though no preference for a heated model over a non-heated model. Also, if the monkeys were raised with the cloth model for five months, then separated from it for 18 months, they still showed the same level of attachment when they were reunited.

Discussion

Harlow, and a number of other researchers, saw this work as an important contribution to our understanding of human attachment. In particular, the work disputes the importance of feeding in the development of attachment (cupboard love), and at the time of these studies this was an important challenge to Freudian ideas about child development.

The objections to Harlow's conclusions are numerous and come, in part, from his own subsequent work (Harlow and Harlow, 1962). The monkeys who were 'reared' by the cloth 'mothers' but were otherwise kept isolated, still grew up to be socially inept. The 'mothering' provided by these models was woefully inadequate. However, monkeys that were kept with a cloth model in isolation from other monkeys, but who were allowed to play with three other young monkeys for one hour every day, grew up to be indistinguishable in their social behaviour from monkeys who had been reared by their natural mothers. The crucial ingredient for the healthy psychological development of the animals was by this account shown to be social contact, and not contact comfort, or even mothering.

Questions

suggested answers → p. 492

1. What are the major findings of the study?

2. What are the problems in making generalizations from this study to the behaviour of children?

3. What behaviours did Harlow notice in the monkeys that were similar to the behaviour of disturbed children?

4. What are the problems with using the terms 'mother' and 'mothering' in the observations of these monkeys?

5. How does Harlow's work make you feel? Was his treatment of monkeys justified?

Family life

HODGES, J. AND TIZARD, B. (1986)

Social and family relationships of ex-institutional adolescents.

Journal of Child Psychology and Psychiatry, 30, 77–97.

Introduction

One of the major questions which developmental psychologists have studied is whether or not there is a critical period in the first stages of human development, and, if there is, how long it extends after birth. By 'critical period' we mean a stage during which the child is highly 'malleable', when the occurrence of damaging experiences might have long-term (perhaps lifelong) consequences.

Koluchová's (1972) work (which is also summarized in this chapter) deals with this issue by means of a longitudinal case study. Hodges and Tizard's investigation, which is summarized here, is also longitudinal, but with a larger sample of children. Their subjects spent the first two years of their lives in institutional care, before being either adopted or returned to their biological parents. They were followed up and assessed at various stages until the age of 8 (see for example Tizard and Hodges, 1978), and were then reassessed for the purposes of this study at the age of 16. A comparison of this group of children with a matched group who had been with their families throughout their lives provides the basis for a quasi-experimental investigation which could potentially isolate some of the long-term effects of early institutional care, and which would thereby contribute to our understanding of the complex critical period issue.

▶ **longitudinal study** A study which monitors changes occurring over a period of time.

The study

Subjects

▶ **natural experiments (also quasi experiments)** Studies in which comparisons are made between different conditions that come about through natural political, social, economic or demographic circumstances, rather than through direct manipulation of a variable by an experimenter.

Thirty-nine children aged 16 were the subjects of this study. They had all been in institutional care until at least 2 years of age, at which point most of them had either been adopted or restored to biological parents. At the time of the study 23 of the children were with adopted families (the 'adopted' group), 11 were with their biological parents (the 'restored' group), and 5 were in institutional care. The paper focuses on 31 of the adopted and restored (that is, 'ex-institutional') children.

All of these children were the subjects of a longitudinal study which had followed their progress until they were 8 years old. The original sample had included 65 children at age 4, and 51 children at age 8. Relatively high rates of 'subject attrition' are a typical feature of longitudinal research.

Two comparison groups of children were established. One was drawn from the London area, and was made up of 16-year-old children who were matched one for one with the ex-institutional children on the basis of sex, position in the family, whether they were from one or two-parent families, and the occupation of their family's main breadwinner. The other comparison group comprised a same-sex school friend (of the same age) for each of the ex-institutional children.

Details of the subject sample are included in a companion article (Hodges and Tizard, 1989a) which needs to be read in conjunction with the paper summarized here.

Design

▶ **self-report** A number of popular research methods are based on self-report: for example, questionnaires, interviews, attitude scales and diary methods. These are methods which rely on research subjects' accounts of their own experiences and behaviour.

The study reported in this paper was part of a large-scale longitudinal investigation, the data for which were gathered by means of various self-report measures, interviews and assessment scales. The authors focus on comparisons among the various groups of subjects who participated in the study: the adopted group, the restored group and the comparison groups. They also compare the data from the 16-year-old ex-institutional children with data from the ex-institutional children at age 8.

Procedure

Five principal methods were used to collect data on all the adolescents (including those in the comparison groups):

(1) an interview with the adolescent subject;
(2) an interview with their mother (in some cases with their father present);
(3) a self-report questionnaire concerning 'social difficulties';
(4) a questionnaire completed by the subject's schoolteacher about the subject's relationships with peers and teachers;
(5) the Rutter 'B' scale: this comprises 26 items and is used for psychiatric screening.

Again, details of the assessment procedures are included in the companion article.

Results

A lengthy results section includes data on the following issues:

▶ **attachment** The tendency of the young of many species to stay close to an adult, usually the mother.

- attachment to parents;
- relations with siblings;
- showing affection;
- similarity and assimilation;
- confiding and supporting;
- disagreements over control and discipline;
- involvement in the family;
- peer relationships;
- specific difficulties with peer relations;
- special friends;
- relationships between attachment and peer relationships;
- relationships between current and earlier peer relations;
- overfriendly behaviour;
- relationships with teachers.

In many of these areas differences were apparent among the different groups in the study, but some of them are based on rather too few responses to be meaningful. At the end of the results section the authors summarize the main differences which they observed between the comparison groups and the ex-institutional group as a whole. These were:

(1) The ex-institutional adolescents were more often 'adult-oriented'. For example, teachers rated the ex-institutional adolescents as 'trying to get a lot of attention from adults' more often than the school comparison group ($p < .05$)' (p. 92). This continued a pattern that had been observed at the age of 8.

(2) The ex-institutional adolescents had a greater likelihood of encountering difficulties in getting on with peers. Table 10.1 shows that the ex-institutional teenagers were more likely than the matched subjects to be rated 'less popular than average' by their teachers (and slightly more likely to be rated 'more popular than average').

(3) The ex-institutional teenagers were 'less likely to have a special friend' (p. 92). There were statistically significant differences in this respect according to the accounts of the mothers ($p < .02$), and the accounts of the adolescents themselves showed the same basic pattern without reaching the level of statistical significance (see Figure 10.1).

(4) The ex-institutional group were 'less likely to turn to peers for emotional support if anxious' (p. 92).

(5) The ex-institutional teenagers were 'less likely to be selective in choosing friends' (p. 92). That is, they were somewhat more likely to be 'friendly with any peer who was friendly towards them, rather than choosing their friends' (p. 91), at least according to the parents' judgements.

Table 10.1   *Teachers' assessment of popularity with peers*

	Less popular than average	Average	More popular than average	Total
Ex-inst.	12 (39%)	12 (39%)	7 (23%)	31
Matched comparisons	4 (15%)	20 (74%)	3 (11%)	27
School friend comparisons	6 (21%)	18 (64%)	4 (14%)	28

(Ex-inst. *vs.* matched comparisons $p < .025$.)

Source: Hodges and Tizard (1989b).

Perhaps the most striking differences that the authors report were between the adopted adolescents and the 'restored' adolescents within the ex-institutional group. It appeared that the within-family relationships of the restored group were noticeably different from the within-family relationships of the adopted and comparison groups (indeed the adopted group and the comparison groups showed no major differences in terms of intra-familial relationships). These

▶ **intra-** As a prefix before any word, this means 'within'.

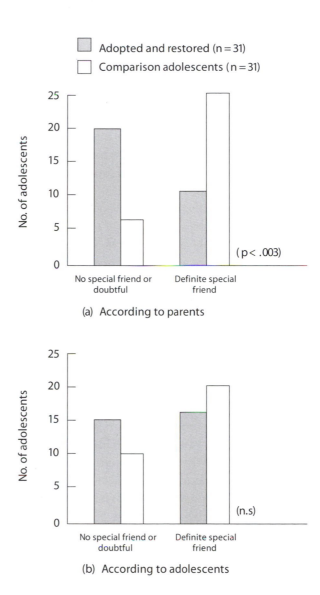

Adopted and restored (n = 31)
Comparison adolescents (n = 31)

(a) According to parents

(b) According to adolescents

Figure 10.1 *Number of adolescents with special same-sex friend*

differences were that the restored adolescents tended to be less attached to their mothers, showed less affection to their parents, identified themselves less with their parents, and had particular difficulties in getting on with their siblings.

Discussion

The study indicates that the adopted children were more able to overcome some of the problems of early institutional upbringing than the restored children, notably the problem of attachment to parents. The authors offer a plausible explanation for this. One of the features of institutional care is the lack of a single, stable caregiver, or pair of caregivers. Children in institutions have to spread their attachments rather thinly over a large number of people:

'By the age of 2, an average of 24 different caregivers had looked after them for at least a week; by 4, the average was 50' (Hodges and Tizard, 1989a, p. 53).

One might expect, then, that forming stable long-term attachments could be a problem for such children. However, Hodges and Tizard noted that the family environments into which the adopted children were subsequently integrated were more suited to counteracting this potential problem than the family environments of the restored children. The financial situation of the adoptive families was often better, they had on average fewer children to provide for, and the adoptive parents were particularly highly motivated to have a child and to develop a relationship with that child. The biological parents in Hodges and Tizard's sample seemed to have been 'more ambivalent about their child living with them' (p. 94).

It seems then, according to Hodges and Tizard's findings, that in terms of stable familial attachments, the negative experiences of early institutional upbringing can be overcome with the right environment and adequate resources. However, the children in this study were still only 16 years old, and it may be that in the longer term they could face problems with the sorts of stable attachments that come in later years outside the family environment. Indeed, the fact that there were differences between the whole ex-institutional group and the comparison groups with regard to relationships beyond the family (friendships and relationships with peers, for example) suggests that the long-term prognosis for them is far from clear.

Families are changing in the UK and so the questions for research psychologists are changing as well. It is estimated that one in three children will experience parental separation before the age of 16. Most of these children go through a period of unhappiness; many experience low self-esteem, behaviour problems, and loss of contact with part of the extended family. Children are usually helped by good communication with both parents, and most settle back into a normal pattern of development (Dunn and Deater-Deckard, 2001). Many children have experience of being in a step-family. Becoming part of a step-family seems to be helpful for younger children but to be harder for older children to adapt to (Hawthorne *et al.*, 2003). Older children seem to appreciate step-parents more when they act in a supportive and friendly way rather than being involved in discipline or control. In some ways research into these new families is likely to be more challenging than research into institutional care. We can all agree that institutional care is not the best arrangement for children but what if research found that step-parents are not very good either?

Questions

suggested answers ➤ p. 492

1. How might 'subject attrition' have biased the findings of this study?

2. Can the differences observed between the ex-institutional group and the comparison groups at 16 years of age definitely be put down to the early institutional experiences of the former?

Severe
deprivation
in twins:
a case study

KOLUCHOVÁ, J. (1972)

Emotional deprivation

Journal of Child
Psychology and
Psychiatry,
13, 107–14.

▶ **monozygotic twin** A twin
from the splitting of one
fertilized ovum; commonly
an identical twin.

Introduction

Koluchová's case study describes one of the most severe cases of childhood deprivation on record within the psychological literature. It is a brief, descriptive paper about a pair of Czechoslovakian identical (monozygotic) twin boys who were 'reared from age 18 months to 7 years in social isolation by a psychopathic stepmother and an inadequate father' (p. 114). The story is distressing, and shot through with human tragedy, despite the author's somewhat bald account. However, Koluchová manages to convey a sense of optimism about the development of the boys' lives subsequent to the period of deprivation. The author was part of a multi-disciplinary team which was involved with the children when they were admitted to hospital.

The boys' mother died after giving birth to them in September 1960, and for the first 11 months of their lives they lived in a children's home. By the age of 18 months they were again living with their father, his new wife and four other children, two of whom were their natural siblings. The authorities only became involved in 1967 after the father had taken the twins to a local paediatrician in order to obtain a certificate granting them exemption from entering primary school. 'Gradually it became clear that this was a case of criminal neglect' (p. 108) and a trial ensued. The twins had evidently been brought up in isolation from the rest of the family, unable to go outside or into the main family living room. Their room was unheated and they were periodically locked up in the cellar and beaten. By the time this paper was written the twins had begun to be able to talk about their early experiences, and their accounts matched with the story that had emerged during the court case.

The case of the children, who are referred to as P.M. and J.M., is of interest to psychologists for two reasons. First, psychologists are people, and human dramas such as this must be taken note of by the whole of society. Second, psychologists are scientists, engaged in the pursuit of knowledge about the human condition; knowledge which can be turned to good use in improving the quality of human life. Cases such as this, as tragic as they are, provide psychologists with the opportunities to further our understanding of 'normal' childhood development. By examining what appear to be the consequences of the twins' abnormal early experiences we may be able to make advances in our understanding of what constitutes 'normal' development, and further our understanding of what factors contribute to healthy psychological and physical growth. This strategy is a familiar one in abnormal and developmental psychology, and is used to compensate for the fact that formal experimentation cannot be undertaken into these sorts of areas, at least not with people (see Harlow, 1959, earlier in this chapter).

The study

part iv

▶ **Intelligence Quotient (IQ)** A numerical figure, believed by some to indicate the level of a person's intelligence, and by others to indicate how well that person performs on intelligence tests.

▶ **fine-motor skills** Skilled movements on a small scale, usually to do with the hands (e.g. writing, sewing, picking up small objects), in contrast to gross-motor skills which are movements on a big scale (walking, kicking, jumping).

▶ **cognition** Mental processes. 'All the processes by which ... sensory input is transformed, reduced, elaborated, stored, recovered and used' (Neisser, 1967, p. 4).

▶ **nature–nurture debates** Fairly sterile theoretical debates, popular in the 1950s, concerning whether a given psychological ability was inherited or whether it was learned through experience.

The effects of the children's five years and six months of social and emotional deprivation were very wide ranging. At age 7 they could hardly walk, had very poor fine-motor skills, and hardly any spontaneous speech. Their play skills were 'primitive', they were 'timid and mistrustful' (p. 109), their ranges of emotional expression were limited, and their IQs, had they been measurable, 'would have been within the range of imbecility' (p. 110). They were also unable to understand the meaning of pictures. Koluchová's assessment of their mental age was that they were functioning, on average, at the level of 3-year-old children.

After spending some time in a children's home and in a special school for children with learning difficulties, the twins moved into a permanent foster home and into a mainstream school. Their development from age 7 to age 10 appears to have been relatively rapid, for by that age the Wechsler Intelligence Scale for Children (WISC) showed that they were functioning intellectually at around average levels, with particular gains having been made on verbal components of the tests. It seems that a stable environment had compensated to some extent for the earlier extremes of deprivation, and although the author presents an uncertain prognosis for future development, there is an optimistic feel to the paper. We should note, however, that this account emphasizes cognitive and intellectual development. The emotional impact of such experiences will always be much less easy to assess, even though, as Koluchová asserts, 'the most severe deprivation ... was probably their poverty of emotional relationships and their social isolation' (p. 113).

During the court case it became essential for the prosecution to demonstrate that the children's disabilities at age 7 had been caused by deprivation rather than, as the stepmother had claimed, that they had been 'defective from birth' (p. 110). It is not entirely clear what evidence was used to do this. It may have been some combination of the records of the children's first institutional home which showed no evidence of disability up until 11 months of age, the testimony of neighbours who had noticed unusual things about the family, and the fact that the children's development did seem to speed up substantially after being taken into care. An important upshot of this is that it shows how difficult it is in principle to separate out the influences of nature and nurture, even in detailed investigations of individual cases.

Discussion

Case studies are noted for the richness of data which they produce, and the human dramas that they reveal can be engaging and moving. One of the most notable exponents of this brand of psychology is Oliver Sacks, whose text *The Man who Mistook his Wife for a Hat* (Sacks, 1986) stands as a classic. But case studies, like all other research methods, have their limitations. The reader of this paper can be left with the feeling that this is one person's account of a complex state of affairs in which the author has had considerable licence in choosing which aspects of the case to present. Much is made, for example, of the idea that the stepmother was the pivotal character in the story. The father is presented as rather slow and powerless, but less to blame for what happened. Since the reader's access to the case is controlled by Koluchová, one can only surmise what a different author might have made of this disturbing affair.

It is an interesting footnote that, when she revisited the case, Koluchová (1991) said that the condition of the boys 22 years after being taken in by their foster family proved the possibility of total reparation of even severe deprivational damage. They made remarkable progress over a number of years and caught up with their peers intellectually and emotionally. Both were drafted for national service and later married and had children. They are said to be entirely stable and enjoy warm relationships. One is a computer technician and the other is a technical training instructor (Clarke and Clarke, 1998).

A general problem with case studies like this is the balance between scientific interest and the welfare of the child. Getting the balance wrong can be damaging. For example, in a well-reported case from the USA, a girl called Genie had been kept in a back room strapped to a chair until she reached her teens. Sadly Genie's suffering did not come to an end when she was discovered, but continued at the hands of the scientific community. After her discovery, researchers struggled for access to the disturbed child and some were able to foster her, to help her development and also to facilitate the scientific observation. Distressingly, when the research money ran out, the fostering ended, and Genie then experienced a number of poor foster placements where she was abused and regressed to her non-communicative condition. Later, her mother was able to take more responsibility for her and sued the psychologists for excessive experimentation on the child. For a full account of Genie's story see Rymer (1993).

Questions

suggested answers ➔ p. 492

1. What sorts of biases might have entered Koluchová's account?

2. What conclusions can be drawn from this study about 'normal' childhood development?

3. How do psychologists try to establish a healthy balance between scientific interest and the welfare of the child in cases such as these?

The behaviour of newborn children in two different cultures

BRAZELTON, T.B., KOSLOWSKI, B. AND TRONICK, E. (1976)

Neonatal behaviour among urban Zambians and Americans.

Journal of Child Psychiatry, 15, 97–107.

▶ **neonates** New-born animals.

▶ **behaviour (also spelt 'behavior'** Anything a person (or animal) does that can be observed and measured by a third party. Behaviour can be thought of as the public side of human life, in contrast to 'experience' (thoughts and feelings) which can be thought of as the private side.

▶ **cross-cultural studies** Studies which examine psychological phenomena in people from more than one cultural background.

▶ **nature–nurture debates** Fairly sterile theoretical debates, popular in the 1950s, concerning whether a given psychological ability was inherited or whether it was learned through experience.

▶ **genetic** Biological inheritance.

Introduction

The question that this study set out to investigate was whether newborn babies (neonates) show differences in behaviour from one culture to another. As such, Brazelton *et al.* (1976) paper stands as an example of cross-cultural, developmental psychology. Cross-cultural work is a highly significant, yet somewhat neglected, feature of psychological research. Examining the first few days of the life of infants from different cultures promises to add to our understanding of what it is we are born with, and what it is that we learn: what role our genes play in our development, and what role the cultural environment plays. In other words, this kind of work can make a contribution to the pervasive nature–nurture debate.

However, it would be misleading to think that the findings of cross-cultural studies are easy to interpret in terms of the nature–nurture debate. For a start, it is difficult to disentangle the respective influences of culture and genes, because groups of people who have lived separately from each other for generations will differ both culturally and genetically. It would also be tempting to think that the behaviour of a newborn baby is solely the product of what it inherits from its biological parents. The thinking would then go that if differences are detected between infants from different cultures in the first few days of life, then these must be predominantly genetic in origin. But the story is much more complex than that. For a start, neonates are born into a culture which envelops them from the first moment of their life; and surely the way in which they behave in the second moment of their life will be influenced by what they experienced in the first. In fact culture exerts a powerful influence even *in utero* (whilst still in the womb). For example, Brazelton *et al.* highlight various cultural practices, set within a prevailing economic climate, that result in urban Zambian women eating a relatively low-protein diet during pregnancy. This has various consequences for the mother, including potential depletion of the uterus, which in turn has consequences for the early stages of the child's life.

Brazelton *et al.*'s paper reports an investigation into behavioural differences between a group of urban Zambian newborns, and urban North American newborns. The findings of differences between the two groups on certain measures are used to try to reason through the respective influence of genetic and cultural factors on early behaviour. Note that the two groups of infants differ both in terms of their genetic inheritance and in terms of their cultural environment, so differences between the groups may be due to either, or both, influences.

The study

Participants

Twenty infants were studied, ten Zambian and ten North American. The mothers of the US babies had been given no more than one injection of a mild muscle-relaxant during labour, otherwise the births were 'natural'. Furthermore, all the US babies were firstborn and were from middle-class families. The mothers of the Zambian babies had also experienced natural childbirths, but had all previously given birth to at least three children. Furthermore, the Zambian mothers were from the 'urbanized slums of Lusaka' (p. 99). All the babies, in both groups, were breastfed. No information is given about the sex of the babies.

Design

▶ **natural experiments (also quasi experiments)** Studies in which comparisons are made between different conditions that come about through natural political, social, economic or demographic circumstances, rather than through direct manipulation of a variable by an experimenter.

This is a structured observational study involving quasi-experimental comparisons between the two groups of neonates. Systematic observations of the infants were made using a set of formal scales. The scales were used to assign a score to each infant on each of a number of dimensions.

Procedure

▶ **inter-coder reliability** A phrase which describes the extent to which two independent observers (coders'/raters') agree on the observations that they have made. Also known as inter-observer reliability and inter-rater reliability.

The babies were measured in a variety of ways on the first, fifth and tenth days of their lives. The most important measure was the Neonatal Behavioral Assessment Scale (Brazelton, 1973). This scale measures infants on more than 24 dimensions to do with interactive, perceptual and motor abilities. Examples of these dimensions are: social interest in experimenter, motor activity, hand-to-mouth activity, alertness, following with eyes.

The first examinations were done in hospital, the follow-up observations on Days 5 and 10 were done in the babies' homes. The observations were shared among the three authors. Inter-observer reliability was checked and found to be at least .85 on all items for each pair of observers.

Results

▶ **intra-** As a prefix before any word, this means 'within'.

Day 1 assessments showed 'evidence of intra-uterine depletion' (p. 101) in each of the Zambian infants. Their skin was dry, their faces were wrinkled, and their birth weight was low (6 lbs, on average). The signs were those associated with placental dysfunction towards the end of pregnancy. Muscle tone and head control were poor, and the babies were described as 'limp and unresponsive' (p. 101). The US babies, in contrast, were heavier, and were immediately more active and responsive.

Figures 10.2(a–c) show all the dimensions on which the two groups scored significantly differently on at least one of the three assessment days. Figure 10.2a shows that on Day 1 the US infants scored significantly higher ($p < .10$ [sic]) on six dimensions than the Zambian infants: motor activity, tempo at height, rapidity of buildup, irritability, following with eyes and cuddliness. ('Tempo at height' and 'rapidity of buildup' are basically measures of activity and alertness.) Only two dimensions showed significant differences on Day 5 (this time with the Zambian infants scoring higher): rapidity of buildup and alertness (see Figure 10.2b). On Day 10 Zambian infants scored significantly higher on consolability, social interest and alertness, whilst the US infants scored higher on motor activity, tempo at height, rapidity of buildup, and defensive movements (see Figure 10.2c). There is one anomaly in the authors' reporting of results for Day 10: they write that the Zambian infants scored significantly lower than the US infants on reactivity to stimulation, whereas the data in the table that they display shows that the Zambian infants got a higher score on this measure (see Figure 10.2c).

In terms of the overall pattern of development described in the two groups, it is noteworthy that the scores of the US infants stayed relatively constant across the ten-day period of the study, while the scores of the Zambian infants on measures related to social attentiveness increased.

Discussion

The authors note that the most significant feature of their findings was the change in relative scores on certain measures across the two groups. On Day 1 the Zambian infants scored lower on a number of measures, mostly to do with alertness and activity. This they put down to the relatively stressed intra-uterine environment of the Zambian babies, resulting in early dehydration and an overall lack of energy. By the tenth day the Zambian group had started to score more highly than the US group on measurements of social interaction (for example, social interest, alertness).

The explanation they offer draws on the complex web of interrelationships among various genetic and non-genetic factors, though they focus on the latter. The stable scores of the US infants in the study probably reflected the good physiological environment they experienced in the womb during the later stages of pregnancy, in conjunction with their 'relatively nonstimulating environment' (p. 106) in the first ten days. The US babies all stayed in hospital for at least four days, and were most likely handled less than the Zambian infants. Mothers were encouraged to feed on a four-hourly schedule. The authors talk about the US mothers following the 'cultural emphasis in the United States on quieting the infant and protecting him from external stimulation' (p. 106).

In contrast, the increased scores of the Zambian infants from Day 1 to Day 5 most likely reflected 'recovery from a poor physiological environment' (p. 104), as they quickly began to be rehydrated and to receive nutrition by feeding from their mother. Thereafter, the increased social responsiveness of the Zambian babies may have been influenced by the more active, contact-oriented, stimulating child-rearing practices of the Zambian women. For example, Zambian infants are carried in a *dashica*, which secures them to their mother's hip. Not only does this encourage more frequent touching, it also allows the infant to see more of the (social) world than other modes of carrying. The Zambian babies were breastfed on demand, and slept in the same bed as their mother. Many other differences are also noted by the authors, who conclude that for

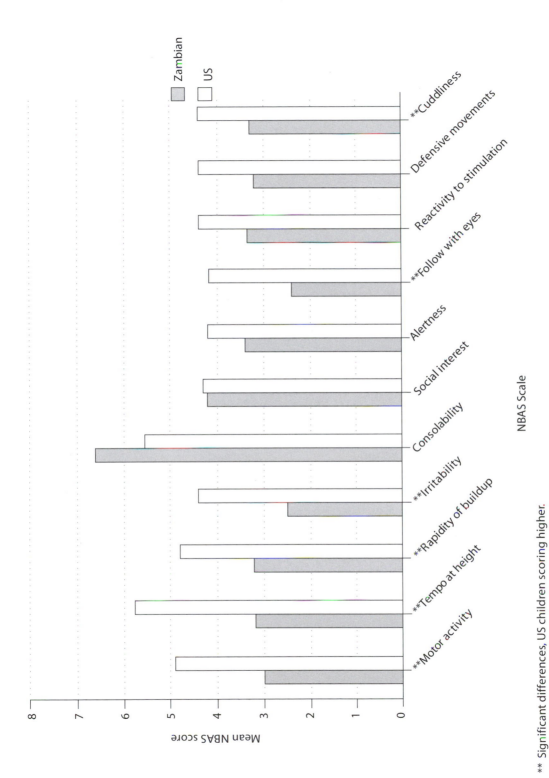

Figure 10.2a *Mean NBAS scores for Zambian and US infants on Day 1*

** Significant differences, US children scoring higher.

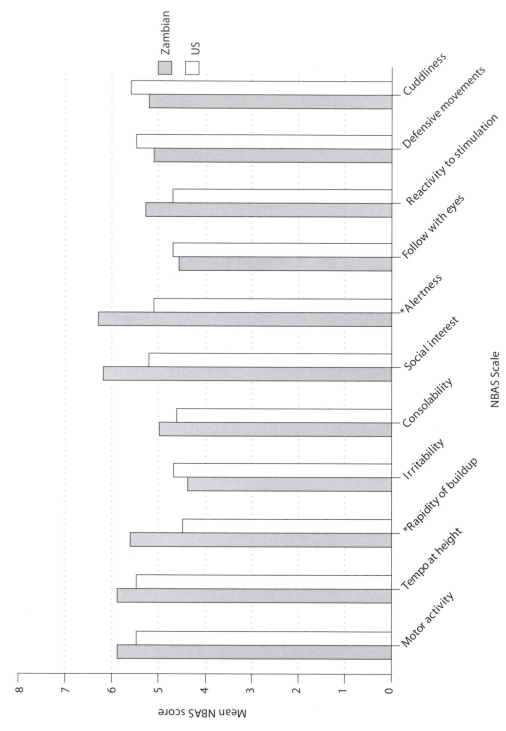

Figure 10.2b *Mean NBAS scores for Zambian and US infants on Day 5*

* Significant differences, Zambian children scoring higher. *?* Anomaly in original report.

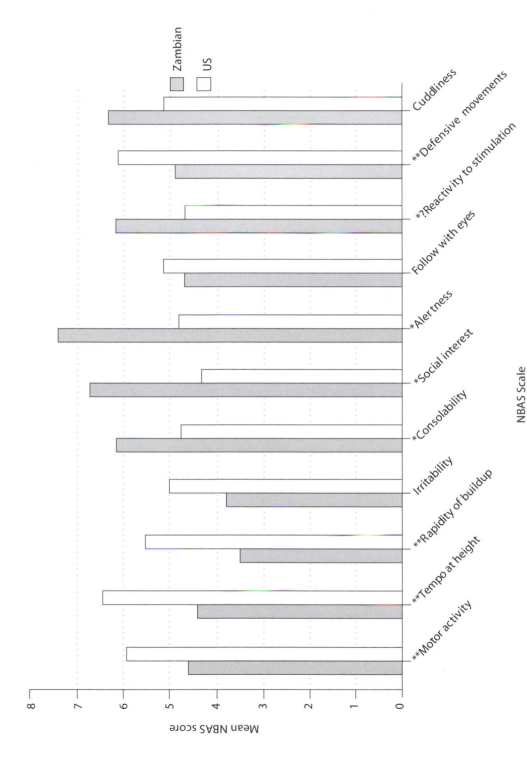

Figure 10.2c *Mean NBAS scores for Zambian and US infants on Day 10*

* Significant differences, Zambian children scoring higher. ** Significant differences, US children scoring higher. *? Anomaly in original report.

the US mothers 'there is no care practice that even approximates the Zambian mother's almost constant contact with her infant' (p. 106).

The comparison of the experiences of the newborns across the two cultures makes fascinating reading, and the authors certainly come up with some plausible connections between child-rearing practices and the different patterns of scores of the two groups on the various behavioural measures. However, interpretations linking the child-rearing practices with the behaviour must be made very cautiously. There are a number of important differences between the two groups, other than the broad cultural and genetic differences highlighted by the authors. Some of these are tackled in Question 1, below.

Questions

suggested answers → p. 493

1. What systematic differences are there between the women in the two groups other than cultural and genetic differences?

2. The inter-observer reliability estimates were made because the authors were afraid that they were 'becoming biased' (p. 100). What potential bias is there in these data, and why does the inter-observer reliability estimate not fully reassure us that this bias has been countered?

3. How could the source of bias identified in the answer to Question 2 be controlled against?

chapter **11**

THE CLASSIC APPROACHES

THERE are arguably three classic approaches in developmental psychology that represent three very different traditions in psychology. In this chapter we have decided to illustrate each approach with one study, though the influence of all three approaches appears throughout this volume.

One way of organizing our thinking about human development is to distinguish between different aspects of human psychology, namely affective, behavioural and cognitive aspects – what we feel (affective), what we do (behavioural) and what we think (cognitive). One task of developmental psychology, then, is to account for how children develop in these three different areas.

The work of Freud gives us some insight into the emotional (affective) development of children, and his theories have been very influential on Western culture and social policy during this century. The work of Bowlby (1965) on attachment, for example, is heavily influenced by Freudian theory. In this chapter we have chosen one case study from a number of lengthy studies published by Freud. This illustrates the methods that he used as well as the kind of insights that he offers us.

The second classic approach, covering the behavioural aspects of human development, is provided by behaviourism. The influence of the behaviourists on psychology as a whole has been far reaching, so it is essential to look at their work. Elsewhere in this book we have summarized studies about the shaping of behaviour (Skinner, 1960, Chapter 4), about the nature of reinforcement (Olds and Milner, 1954, Chapter 4), about behavioural therapies (Lang and Lazovik, 1963, Chapter 8), and about imitative learning from a Social Learning Theory perspective (Bandura *et al.*, 1961, Chapter 4). In this chapter we review a famous study about conditioning fear.

The most important theorist in the cognitive tradition is Jean Piaget, who became interested in how his own children developed their way of interpreting the world. He devised a range of delightful puzzles for children that highlight the unique characteristics of child thought. His approach is not without its critics, and the paper we have chosen, by Samuel and Bryant (1984), provides a re-evaluation of some of his tests, and gives a further insight into the way children think and make sense of the world.

▶ **affective** To do with feelings or emotions.

▶ **behaviour (also spelt 'behavior')** Anything a person (or animal) does that can be observed and measured by a third party. Behaviour can be thought of as the public side of human life, in contrast to 'experience' (thoughts and feelings) which can be thought of as the private side.

▶ **cognition** Mental processes. 'All the processes by which ... sensory input is transformed, reduced, elaborated, stored, recovered and used' (Neisser, 1967, p. 4).

▶ **behaviourism** A school of thought which holds that the observation and description of overt behaviour is all that is needed to comprehend the human being, and that manipulation of stimulus–response contingencies is all that is needed to change human behaviour.

▶**Social Learning Theory**
The approach to understanding social behaviour which emphasizes how people imitate action and model their behaviour on that of others.

Needless to say, these three aspects of development should never be thought of as separate things. People's thoughts, feelings and behaviour are all inter-related. And in the same way that these different aspects of development should not be treated as separate, one from another, so should the developing child not be treated as separate from other people. Development does not happen to an individual child in a vacuum. A developing child is part of a family, part of a society, part of a culture. A developing child has relationships with other children and adults. Understanding development is fundamentally about understanding the child as a social being. The final paper in this chapter reminds us of this perspective, taking as it does a Vygotskian, social constructivist perspective on development – a perspective that contrasts sharply in important respects with the work of Piaget.

Introduction

Analysis of a phobia of a five-year-old boy.

FREUD, S. (1909)

In *The Pelican Freud Library* (1977), Vol. 8, *Case Histories 1*, pp. 169–306.

I want a girl, just like the girl that married dear old Dad

If you had only heard of one psychologist before you opened this book, it was probably Freud. He has a unique place in the history of psychology and a unique place in the development of ideas in the twentieth century. His work provokes strong opinions both supporting and challenging his theories. In this book it is impossible to do justice to the theories or to represent the arguments for or against them. We will just try to give a flavour of Freud's approach which shows some of the strengths as well as some of the weaknesses.

One of the key themes of Freud's work is the importance of the first few years of life in the subsequent development of personality. He suggested that 'the boy is father to the man', meaning that our experiences in childhood have a crucial effect on our adult personality. He believed that children experience a lot of emotional conflict, and their future adjustment depends on how well these conflicts are resolved. Another theme within Freud's work concerns the unconscious mind, which is that part of our mind of which we are not aware. Freud believed that the unconscious contains all manner of unresolved conflicts and has a powerful effect on our behaviour and experience. He argued that many of these conflicts will show up in our fantasies and dreams, but the conflicts are so threatening that they appear in disguised forms, in the shape of symbols.

Freud was a practising therapist who developed his theories from his observations of his patients, and his reflections on his own experience. He wrote case histories in terms of his recollections and interpretations of the interviews and did not keep complete ongoing records.

The study that we have chosen for this book is unusual in two respects. First, it is the analysis of a child (Hans), and Freud usually dealt with adults. Secondly, the therapy was carried out by correspondence and interview with the boy's father, rather than with the child himself. The study gives some insight into how Freud viewed child development and how he interpreted the seemingly bizarre imagination of the child.

▶ **unconscious mind** The part of our mind that is beyond our conscious awareness.

▶ **case history** A detailed clinical description of a person which characteristically forms the basis for some kind of therapeutic intervention.

The study

The report is written in three parts: (a) the introduction, (b) the case history and analysis, and (c) the conclusions.

Introduction (pp. 169–84)

Freud reports how the analysis was conducted through his conversations and correspondence with Hans' father. He notes that it was the special relationship between father and son that allowed the analysis to progress and for the discussions with the boy to be so detailed and so intimate. The first reports of Hans are when he was 3 years old. At this age he developed a lively interest in his 'widdler' (penis), and also those of other people. On one occasion he asked 'Mummy, have you got a widdler too?'

The parents recorded numerous extracts of conversation with Hans which show his concerns and their attitude towards him. When he was about 3 years and 6 months old his mother told him not to touch his widdler or else she would call the doctor to come and cut it off. Around the same time, Hans' mother gave birth to his sister Hanna, and Hans was told that the stork had brought the baby. (It was common at that time – 1906 – to keep children ignorant of information about fertility, and so stories about babies being flown in by giant birds were commonly told to keep children quiet.)

Hans expressed jealousy towards his sister, though this diminished after a few months. His parents also recorded that Hans had considerable interest in other children, especially girls, and formed emotional attachments with them. Throughout this time, the main theme of his fantasies and dreams was widdlers and widdling.

Case history and analysis (pp. 185–259)

Just before Hans was 5, his father wrote to Freud about his son. He described the main problem as follows: 'He is afraid a horse will bite him in the street, and this fear seems somehow connected with his having been frightened by a large penis' (p. 185). From this time on, the father provided Freud with considerable detail of conversations with Hans, and together they tried to make sense of what the boy was experiencing and tried to resolve the fear of the horses. Freud noted that the fear of the horses had developed just after the child had experienced some anxiety dreams about losing his mother, and around the time he had been warned about playing with his widdler. Freud reasoned that the boy, who liked to get into bed with his mother, had a repressed longing for her, and had focused his libido on her.

One month later, the correspondence revealed that the phobia (which Hans refers to as his 'nonsense') was much worse. Hans' father made a connection between the phobia and Hans' interest in his widdler, so he said to him 'If you don't put your hand to your widdler any more, this nonsense of yours'll soon get better' (p. 193).

Hans' anxieties and phobia continued and he was afraid to go out of the house for fear of the horses (note that in the early twentieth century horses were used in many forms of transport, including freight carts, buses and cabs). One night, Hans told his father of a dream/fantasy which his father immediately summarized as follows:

> In the night there was a big giraffe in the room and a crumpled one: and the big one called out because I took the crumpled one away from it. Then it stopped calling out: and I sat down on top of the crumpled one. (p. 199)

▶ **libido** Freud's concept of internal motivational energy commonly taken to mean the sex drive.

▶ **phobia** An anxiety disorder characterized by persistent fear out of proportion to the danger, a compelling desire to escape the situation, and a recognition that the fear is excessive.

This dream/fantasy was interpreted by Freud and the father as being a reworking of the morning exchanges in the parental bed. Hans liked to get into his parents' bed in the morning but his father often objected (the big giraffe calling out because he had taken the crumpled giraffe – mother – away). Both Freud and the father wondered about the significance of the giraffe and whether the long neck was a symbol for the large adult penis, but Hans rejected this idea.

Hans was taken to see Freud, who asked him about the horses he was frightened of. Freud was interested by certain aspects of the description, for example the black bits around the mouth. He reasoned that the horse was a symbol for his father, and the black bits were a moustache. After the interview, the father recorded an exchange with Hans where the boy said 'Daddy, don't trot away from me!' (p. 207); bear in mind that we are dealing with an English translation from the original German text which makes some idioms sound rather odd.

Hans' fear of horses developed and he became particularly frightened about them falling over. He described an incident where he witnessed this happening (later verified by his mother). Throughout this analysis the parents continued to record copious examples of dialogue, and the father asked many leading questions to help the boy discover the root of his fear. For example:

> Father: When the horse fell down did you think of your daddy?
> Hans: Perhaps. Yes. It's possible. (p. 213)

Hans started to develop a particular interest in toilet functions, especially *lumf* (a German word denoting faeces). Hans had long discussions with his father about *lumf*, the birth of his sister, the colour of his mother's underwear and his liking for going into the toilet with his mother or the maid. He also describes his imaginary friend called Lodi who he had named after *saffalodi*, a German sausage. Hans's father pointed out to the child that the sausage looked a little like *lumf*, and Hans agreed.

During this period the fear of the horses declined and two final fantasies marked a change in Hans and an apparent resolution of his conflicts. First, he described a fantasy where he was married to his mother and was playing with his own children. In this fantasy he had promoted his father to the role of grandfather. In the second fantasy, he described how a plumber came and first removed his bottom and widdler and then gave him another one of each, but larger.

Discussion (pp. 260–303)

Freud divided his discussion of the case to offer three points of view.

Support for his theory of sexuality

Freud believed that children could provide valuable evidence, writing 'I do not share the view ... that assertions made by children are invariably arbitrary and untrustworthy' (p. 261). He saw the conversations with Hans as providing powerful support for his view that children have an interest in sexual

> ▶ **Oedipus complex**
> According to Freud: the conflict between a boy's desire for his mother, and the fear of punishment by castration for that desire by his father.

matters from a very early age. In particular, the case study provided support for his theory of the Oedipus complex in which the young boy wishes his father would go away so that he can have exclusive intimacy with his mother. Freud believed that much of Hans' problem came from the conflict caused by this desire. The final fantasy of being married to his mother supported this idea.

The nature of phobias

Freud noted that Hans' parents were determined from the very beginning of his illness that he was neither to be laughed at or bullied, but that 'access must be obtained to his repressed wishes by means of psychoanalysis' (p. 275). This appears to have been a successful strategy, though Freud wrote that therapeutic success was not the primary aim. The main aim of the therapy was to allow Hans to gain conscious control of his unconscious wishes, to undergo a journey of self-discovery.

Freud referred to Hans' recollection of seeing a horse fall down and reasoned that this event alone was not enough to explain the development of the phobia, even though it became the focus for his various anxieties. The real causes of phobias lie in the hidden conflicts of the unconscious mind. The implications of this line of thinking are far-reaching, particularly with regard to potential treatment. It would not be enough, in Freud's opinion, to treat the fear of horses directly, for this would only be tinkering with the symptoms of a deeper problem. One may be able to get rid of horse phobia by, say, a behavioural treatment, but symptom substitution would most likely occur, and the unconscious conflicts would simply manifest themselves in another form. It is worth contrasting Freud's ideas with the behavioural approach to treating phobias (Lang and Lazovik, 1963, Chapter 9 of this volume).

> ▶ **symptom substitution**
> The situation where the treatment and removal of one symptom is ultimately followed by the development of another symptom, because the cause of the disorder has not been dealt with.

Views on life and children

Freud starts this last section of the report by contesting the idea, inescapable for the reader, that Hans is in some way a very strange child. He points out that Hans was able to express fears and wishes that many children do not have the opportunity to articulate, and as a result had been able to resolve conflicts that would remain unresolved in other children. Freud notes that there is no sharp distinction between the neurotic and the normal, and that many people constantly pass between normal and neurotic states. He goes on to make some comments about education, suggesting that (in his time) it was largely concerned with controlling people rather than encouraging self-awareness. He suggests that psychoanalysis would be one way of helping someone to become 'a civilized and useful member of society' (p. 303).

Postscript

Thirteen years after the case study was published, 'Little Hans', at 19 years old, appeared at Freud's consulting room. He declared that he was fit and well and had suffered no troubles during adolescence. He had no recollection of the discussions with his father, and described how when he read his case history it 'came to him as something unknown' (p. 304).

Discussion

It is difficult not to be intrigued by this case study, but it is equally difficult not to be sceptical about some of the reasoning made by Freud and Hans' father. We will leave you to draw your own conclusions, though we do recommend that if you find the study at all interesting then you should read more of the case studies that appear in the collected writings of Freud. The Pelican Freud Library is a good place to start.

The case study of little Hans raises a number of issues that still provide some controversy today:

(a) *Reliability of child evidence*: Freud had no trouble in accepting the evidence of a child, and suggested that children are no more likely to tell lies than adults. This idea was not acceptable at the time, and it is only very recently that the evidence of children has been given much weight in situations such as police inquiries and court proceedings.

(b) *Disturbed behaviour should be treated rather than controlled*: Freud notes in the study that Hans' father asked him to emphasize the severity of Hans' symptoms so that readers of the study would not think that Hans should just have been given a 'sound thrashing' to solve his problem. We still have the debate today about whether children should be punished or helped for bad behaviour. Many people favour the 'help' approach (until, of course, some hoodies jump all over their car in a car park in Whitby, bless 'em).

(c) *Sexuality of children*: Freud sees Hans' talk about sexual and bodily matters as reflecting his perfectly normal interest and emotional involvement in these things. This was not a commonly held view at the time, though it is something that we are more likely to accept today.

When you read the report it is hard not to smile at some of the comments made by Hans, and the way they were dealt with by his father. For example, Hans had played happily for many months with his 'imaginary friend' Lodi, but his father discovered the source of the name (sausage, see above) and suggested that this sausage looked like *lumf*. His father was telling Hans that his imaginary friend was really a turd!

Questions

1. How do you think people show their unconscious wishes in their behaviour?

2. What criticisms can you make of Freud's method of collecting data?

3. What differences are there between the attitudes of Hans' parents and the attitudes of parents today?

4. Freud comments that education was largely concerned with controlling people rather than encouraging self-awareness. How has education today changed from that of Freud's time?

suggested answers → p. 494

The tale of Little Albert

WATSON, J.B. AND RAYNER, R. (1920) Conditioned emotional reactions. *Journal of Experimental Psychology;* 3, 1–14.

Introduction

Can fear be learned? This was the main question behind this study by Watson and Rayner. They wanted to demonstrate that behaviourist theory could be applied to humans. The study is usually described by referring to the concept of classical conditioning developed by the Russian physiologist, Ivan Pavlov. Pavlov studied the salivation response in dogs and noticed that food in the mouth will stimulate salivation. This natural link between stimulus and response is called a reflex. Pavlov presented his dogs with a neutral stimulus (such as a bell) before putting the food in their mouths. After this had been repeated a few times the dogs began to associate the bell with the arrival of the food and would salivate to the sound of the bell: they had learned a new stimulus–response (s–r) relationship (see Figure 11.1). Pavlov and Watson believed that a lot of human learning could be explained in terms of learned s–r relationships, and the study described below is often cited as an illustration of this.

▶ **behaviourism** A school of thought which holds that the observation and description of overt behaviour is all that is needed to comprehend the human being, and that manipulation of stimulus–response contingencies is all that is needed to change human behaviour.

▶ **classical conditioning** A form of learning which involves the pairing of a neutral stimulus with a reflex.

▶ **reflex** An automatic reaction to a stimulus: often inborn but can also be learned or modified by experience.

▶ **neutral stimulus** A stimulus that has no meaning for a person or animal before the onset of conditioning.

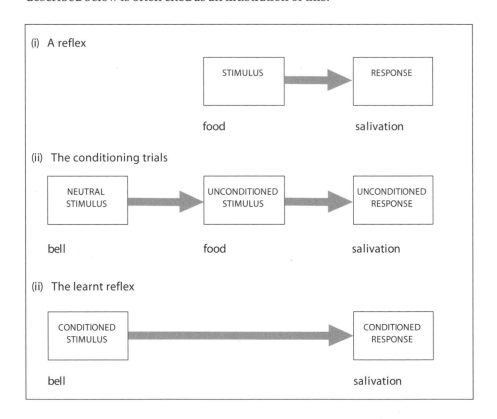

Figure 11.1 *Classical conditioning*

Watson and Rayner were specifically interested in whether our emotional responses can be conditioned using the principles outlined above. The idea is that by the time we are adults we have a very complex repertoire of emotional

> **unconditioned response**
> A response which occurs automatically to a particular stimulus, and doesn't have to be learned.

responses which can be elicited by all sorts of stimuli. Watson and Rayner believed that these complex s–r relationships are built upon a few basic unconditioned ones, through the processes of classical conditioning. Their study, which is one of the most famous (or perhaps infamous) in the history of psychology, involved conditioning an infant to respond with fear to the sight of a rat. In this case, they used the unconditioned response of fear to a loud noise.

The study

Subject

The subject of this investigation was an infant named Albert B. Little Albert (as he is now popularly known) was the son of a wet nurse in a children's home, and was 9 months old at the beginning of the study. 'He was on the whole stolid and unemotional. His stability was one of the principle reasons for using him as a subject in this test' (p. 1).

Design

> **baseline measures** Measures of performance or behaviour before the research intervention is made.

This was a single-case laboratory experiment which took place over approximately four months. Baseline behavioural observations were made in the first phase of the study. A 'treatment' phase followed, and subsequent behavioural observations were made to assess the effects of the treatment.

Procedure

At 9 months of age, Albert was tested with various stimuli to examine whether or not he exhibited a fear in response to them. Some of the neutral stimuli that were used at this stage were a white rat, a rabbit, a dog, a monkey, masks with and without hair, cotton wool and burning newspapers. They were demonstrably 'neutral' stimuli since none of them elicited anything like a fear response from the child. In fact, Albert's most common response was to play with the objects.

> **unconditioned stimulus**
> A stimulus which automatically, or reflexively produces a response.

> **behaviour (also spelt 'behavior')** Anything a person (or animal) does that can be observed and measured by a third party. Behaviour can be thought of as the public side of human life, in contrast to 'experience' (thoughts and feelings) which can be thought of as the private side.

The unconditioned stimulus which Watson and Rayner used in the baseline phase of the study was the sound made by striking a four-foot steel bar with a hammer, just behind the child. Naturally this sudden noise caused the child to cry, presumably through fear. At the age of eleven months and three days the conditioning process started. The white rat was presented to Albert. As he reached out to touch it 'the bar was struck immediately behind his head' (p. 4). The process was repeated once on the first day, and a further five times one week later. The conditioning was 'topped-up' with two more pairings 17 days later.

Twelve days after the first treatment a variety of stimuli were presented to Albert in order to examine the effects of generalization. These included his toy blocks, a rabbit, a dog, a fur coat and cotton wool. These were presented to Albert periodically during the next few sessions. The white rat was also presented periodically without the sound of the bar to test the extent and duration of the initial conditioning. Observations of the child's behaviour were made in the form of laboratory notes for each session. The results of the study are presented in the form of excerpts from these notes.

Results

The following are excerpts from the laboratory notes cited in the paper.

First treatment session

White rat suddenly taken from the basket and presented to Albert. He began to reach for rat with left hand. Just as his hand touched the animal the bar was struck immediately behind his head. The infant jumped violently and fell forward, burying his face in the mattress. He did not cry, however. (p. 4)

Just as the right hand touched the rat the bar was again struck. Again the infant jumped violently, fell forward and began to whimper. (p. 4)

Second treatment session (7 days after first)

When the rat nosed the infant's left hand, the hand was suddenly withdrawn. ... It is thus seen that the two joint stimulations given the previous week were not without effect. (p. 4)

Joint stimulation with rat and sound. Started, then fell over immediately to right side. No crying. (p. 4)

Rat suddenly presented alone. Puckered face, whimpered and withdrew body sharply to the left. (p. 5)

Third treatment session (12 days after first)

Blocks ... offered. Played readily with them, smiling and gurgling. (p. 5)

Rat alone. Leaned over to left side as far away as possible, then fell over. (p. 6)

Rabbit alone. The rabbit was suddenly placed on the mattress in front of him. The reaction was pronounced. Negative responses began at once. He leaned as far away from the animal as possible, whimpered, then burst into tears. (p. 6)

Dog alone. The dog did not produce as violent a reaction as the rabbit. The moment fixation occurred the child shrank back. (p. 6)

[The cotton wool] was placed on his feet. He kicked it away but did not touch it with his hands. (p. 7)

Fourth treatment session (17 days after first)

Rat alone. ... The response was much less marked than on the first presentation the previous week. It was thought best to freshen up the reaction by another joint stimulation ... just as the rat was placed on his hand the rod was struck. Reaction violent. (p. 7)

Rabbit alone. Leaned over to left side as far as possible. Did not fall over. Began to whimper but reaction not as violent as on former occasions. (p. 7)

On this same day ... Albert was taken into a large well-lighted lecture room belonging to the laboratory. ... The situation was thus very different from that which obtained in the small dark room. (pp. 8–9)

Rat alone. No sudden fear reaction appeared at first. The hands, however, were held up and away from the animal. (p. 9)

Follow-up session (1 month and 18 days after first treatment)

Santa Claus mask. Withdrawal, gurgling, then slapped at it without touching. When his hand was forced to touch it, he whimpered and cried. (p. 10)

Fur coat. Wrinkled his nose and withdrew both hands, drew back his whole body and began to whimper as the coat was put nearer. (p. 11)

Blocks. He began to play with them as usual. (p. 11)

The rat ... touched his hand. Albert withdrew immediately, then leaned back as far as possible but did not cry (p. 11)

Discussion

Albert's behaviour as recorded by Watson and Rayner does suggest that emotional responses to stimuli can be learned. Before conditioning, Albert was not afraid of the white rat; after conditioning (comprising seven pairings of noise and rat), he did appear to be afraid of it. The learned emotional response generalized to stimuli which had a similar appearance to the white rat, such as cotton wool, a rabbit and a Santa Claus mask. The conditioned emotional responses were maintained for over one month.

The study is cited very widely in psychological literature despite it being based on the evidence from one case. Interestingly, it is often incorrectly reported in many textbooks, with some adding a happy ending by suggesting that Albert's fear was deconditioned by Watson and Rayner. Harris (1979) reviewed the various descriptions of this study that appear in the psychological literature and suggested that the story of Little Albert has developed like a myth, with each generation of psychologists retelling the story to illustrate their own position.

Needless to say, the work carried out by Watson and Rayner would be quite unacceptable today. They intentionally caused their subject, a very young infant at that, to become distressed. The matter-of-fact recording of observations like Albert jumping violently and burying his face in the mattress show a curious detachment from what was clearly an upsetting experience for the child, and from what should have been an upsetting experience for the researchers. Their argument that Albert was sufficiently stable emotionally to withstand the procedures with no lasting effect is not convincing, especially in the light of their argument in another part of the paper that '[conditioned emotional responses] persist and modify personality throughout life' (p. 12). Furthermore, Albert left the hospital before any therapeutic strategies could be used to remove the conditioned emotional response.

A sensible evaluation of the study must take into account its historical and cultural context. We must bear in mind that at the beginning of the twentieth century there may have been a much greater faith than exists today in the capacity of science to provide answers to society's problems. Maybe Watson and Rayner believed that a greater good would come out of this child's distress, in terms of improved insights into the important issue of human learning, and in terms of developing treatments for people who show extreme and irrational emotional behaviour.

For the interested, one of Watson's many innovations in psychological research was to make extensive use of film recordings. He filmed some of the sessions with Little Albert and every so often they appear on YouTube. So get searching and you may well be able to see Watson, Rayner and Albert in action.

▶ **phobia** An anxiety disorder characterized by persistent fear out of proportion to the danger, a compelling desire to escape the situation, and a recognition that the fear is excessive.

Questions

suggested answers → p. 494

1. Why did the experimenters move Albert to a different room in the fourth session?

2. What behavioural strategy might the authors have used to reverse the conditioning which had occurred?

3. Watson and Rayner's methods were unacceptable by today's standards. What methods could we use instead to study things such as phobias?

Piaget's cognitive approach

SAMUEL, J. AND BRYANT, P., (1984)

Asking only one question in the conservation experiment.

Journal of Child Psychology, and Psychiatry 25, 315–18.

Introduction

How do children think? Are their thought processes just a scaled down version of adult thought processes, or are they altogether different? Swiss psychologist Jean Piaget (that's 'Jean' as in French for 'John') carried out some remarkable studies on children that had a powerful influence on our theories of child thought (see for example, Piaget, 1952). He argued that children's thinking is qualitatively different from the thinking of adults. For readable and interesting introductions to Piaget's work we suggest you try Donaldson (1978) and Boden (1979).

Piaget's theory of cognitive development suggests that children develop their ability to think through a series of maturational stages. In brief the child progresses through the:

(a) *Sensorimotor stage* – (birth to around 18 months), during which the child is learning to match their senses (what they see and hear, and so forth) to what they can do.

(b) *Pre-operational stage* – (18 months to about 7 years), during which the child is learning to use symbolism (and language in particular), and is developing some general rules about mental operations.

(c) *Concrete operational stage* – (7 to around 12 years), during which the child is able to use some sophisticated mental operations but is still limited in a number of ways; for example, the concrete operational child tends to think about the world in terms of how it is, and finds it hard to speculate on how it might be.

(d) *Formal operational stage* – (12 years and above), which is the most sophisticated stage of thinking and is mainly governed by formal logic.

Piaget said that the different quality of thought in these stages can be seen in the errors which children make with certain problems. He devised a number of ingenious tests of child thought to illustrate this different style of thinking. The most famous of these tests concern the pre-operational stage. In this stage Piaget said that children's thought has the following features:

(1) They are unable to conserve. For example, they do not appreciate that if you change the shape of an object it keeps the same mass.

(2) They are unable to *reverse* mental operations. If they have seen some action take place they can not mentally 'rewind the tape'.

(3) They rely on their *intuitions* about what they can see rather than what they can reason.

(4) They are perceptually egocentric, finding it difficult to imagine a view from any other viewpoint than their own.

▶ **cognition** Mental processes. 'All the processes by which ... sensory input is transformed, reduced, elaborated, stored, recovered and used' (Neisser, 1967, p. 4).

▶ **conservation** According to Piaget, the ability to recognize that a quantity remains the same even if it changes its shape.

▶ **egocentrism** The tendency to see things from your own personal perspective, to the exclusion of other possible perspectives.

An example of one of Piaget's tests is carried out with some Plasticine or child's modelling clay. The child is shown two lumps of Plasticine the same shape and size. The adult asks, 'Which one is bigger?' and the child replies 'They're both the same.' Then, in full view of the child, the adult rolls out one of the lumps of Plasticine into a sausage shape. The adult now asks the same question and many pre-operational children answer, 'The sausage is bigger'. Piaget believes that the child does not realize that the mass of the object stays constant (conserved) even though its shape has changed. If children at this developmental stage were able to 'rewind the tape' of the adult rolling out the clay, if they were able to reverse the adult's actions in their minds, they would realize that there was still the same amount of Plasticine. Because they cannot conserve and cannot mentally reverse the process, the children use their intuition to answer the question. One of the pieces of Plasticine looks bigger than the other, so they answer that it is bigger than the other.

The Plasticine example is a test of conservation of mass. Piaget used other tasks to explore number and volume conservation. Number conservation tasks involve lining up two rows of buttons. The rows have the same number of buttons each, and are of equal length, so that each button in one row is directly opposite and level with a button in the other row. The child is asked whether there are more buttons in one row or the other. The experimenter then bunches up one of the rows without removing any buttons. The child is asked again whether there are more buttons in one row than in the other. The child who cannot conserve number answers that the longer row now has more buttons.

Volume conservation tasks are done with two identical beakers each with exactly the same amount of fluid in them. The child is asked if one beaker has more fluid in than the other, or if they contain the same amount. The fluid from one beaker is then poured into a taller, thinner beaker (or into a shorter, fatter beaker), again without removing any of the liquid. The child is asked the conservation question again, and the non-conserving child answers that there is now more (or less) fluid in the different-shaped beaker.

The work of Piaget captured the imagination of developmental psychology and many students mounted expeditions to primary schools armed with Plasticine, counters and beakers to try out Piaget's tests. In the 1960s and the 1970s, these tests were thought to give real insight into the qualities and limitations of child thought. However, from the late 1970s onwards, there has been a growing body of evidence that suggests that Piaget's methods led to underestimation of the cognitive abilities of children.

The study

Samuel and Bryant devised their study to see whether children could really conserve after all, and whether the results that people usually obtain when they carry out one of Piaget's tests are due to the structure of the test rather than the limitations of child thought. They were particularly concerned with the way in which the traditional conservation task involved asking the child the same question twice. The traditional Piagetian procedure would start with a question like 'is there more Plasticine in this lump or in this lump, or are they the same size?' to which the child would answer 'they're the same size'. The experimenter would then deliberately alter the experimental materials in full view of the child (perhaps rolling one of the lumps into a sausage), and then repeat the first question. Now there are all sorts of reasons for suspecting that some children might interpret this whole procedure as meaning that the experimenter wants them to give a different answer to the question when it is asked for the second time. One such reason (you might think of others) has to do with the fact that children are only usually asked the same question twice when they have got the answer wrong the first time. So repeating the question might be leading the child to believe that 'they're the same size' was the wrong answer. In short, Samuel and Bryant were concerned that the failure of some children on the conservation task might be more to do with the demand characteristics of the research procedure (see Orne, 1962, Chapter 18 of this volume) than failure to reason logically.

For this reason, they designed a study in which half of their sample of children were only asked the conservation question once, after the materials had been altered by the experimenter. The other half of the sample were asked the conservation question twice, as in the standard Piagetian procedure. If, as they hypothesized, the 'one question' group of children tended to give more correct responses on the task than the 'two question' children, this would suggest that their concerns about demand characteristics were warranted.

Subjects

The subjects were 252 children from Devon, England, between the ages of 5 years and 8 years 6 months (8;6). The sample was divided into four age groups of 63 children each. The mean ages of the four groups were (i) 5;3 (ii) 6;3 (iii) 7;3 and (iv) 8;3.

Design

The main independent variable of interest was manipulated across three conditions:

(1) *Standard*: Samuel and Bryant carried out the conservation task in the way that Piaget described, asking the children about the size of the objects before and after the shape was changed.

(2) *One judgement*: In this condition they only asked the children about the size (or number, or volume) of the objects after the transformation.

(3) *Fixed-array control*: In this condition the children just saw the objects after they had been changed, and not before.

Children from each age group were allocated to one of the three conditions, giving an independent-measures design (each child only performed in one of the conditions), with equal average ages across the three conditions.

The researchers carried out mass, number, and volume conservation tasks

---

► **demand characteristics** Those aspects of a psychological study (or other artificial situation) which exert an implicit pressure on people to act in ways that are expected of them.

► **sample** The group of subjects used in a study: the selection of people, animals, plants or objects drawn from a population for the purposes of studying that population.

► **independent variable** The conditions which an experimenter sets up, to cause an effect in an experiment. These vary systematically, so that the experimenter can draw conclusions about changes in outcomes.

► **independent-measures design** When a study involves comparing the scores from two or more separate groups of people.

with each child. Each child was given four trials with each type of task, and the order of the tasks was systematically varied between the children.

Results

The researchers recorded whether the children made an error in judgement on any of the tasks. An error was recorded when they said that one lump was bigger than the other, or one row had more counters than the other, or one glass had more liquid than the other. The results are summarized in Tables 11.1 and 11.2, and in Figure 11.2.

Table 11.1 *Mean errors of judgement for all the tests (maximum possible error = 12; minimum possible error = 0)*

Age	Experimental condition		
	Standard	**One judgement**	**Fixed array**
5 years	8.5	7.3	8.6
6 years	5.7	4.3	6.4
7 years	3.2	2.6	4.9
8 years	1.7	1.3	3.3

Source: Samuel and Bryant (1984).

Table 11.2 *Mean errors of judgement for all ages (maximum possible error = 4; minimum possible error = 0)*

Age	Experimental condition		
	Standard	**One judgement**	**Fixed array**
Mass	1.5	1.2	1.7
Number	1.5	1.0	1.5
Volume	1.8	1.6	2.5

Source: Samuel and Bryant (1984).

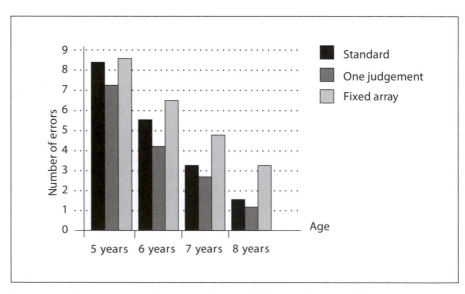

Figure 11.2 *Average number of errors made by the children (maximum possible error = 12; minimum possible error = 0)*

The researchers carried out a number of sophisticated statistical tests and drew the following conclusions:

(a) *Age*: There was a significant difference between every age group. Each group of children made fewer errors than all the groups that were younger than them.

(b) *Conditions*: The children made significantly fewer errors on the one judgement task than on the other two tasks. The children also made significantly fewer errors on the standard task than the fixed-array task.

(c) *Materials*: The children made fewer errors on the number task than on the other two tasks.

Discussion

The study confirms Piaget's observation that children will make errors in the conservation tasks he devised. However, the study also shows that children will make fewer errors in these tasks if the procedure is changed slightly. This shows that the reason for at least some of the errors is to do with the task itself rather than the way children think. Samuel and Bryant conclude that the important question is not whether children possess an intellectual skill, but how and when they decide to apply that skill.

The studies by Samuel and Bryant and other researchers that challenge the original theories of Piaget are sometimes described as having refuted Piaget's ideas. This is very far from the case, for basic insights from Piaget still hold good. Children have different thought processes from adults and these can be seen in the errors they make in cognitive tasks. In the above study, the children made conservation errors in all the conditions, and the frequency of these errors reduced with age. But one message that Samuel and Bryant's work leaves us with is the importance of paying close attention to the details of research procedures, for even minor alterations can have an effect on the results.

Questions

1. What do developmental psychologists mean by conservation?

2. Why do adults have problems carrying out studies on child thought?

3. Piaget believes that adult thought is very logical. Give some examples of adult thoughts that are not logical.

suggested answers ➜ p. 495

Vygotsky's social constructivist approach

WOOD, D., WOOD, H. AND MIDDLETON, D. (1978)

An experimental evaluation of four face-to-face teaching strategies.

International Journal of Behavioral Development, 1, 131–47.

Introduction

According to Piaget, the story of child development is a story about processes that go on within the child, and in transactions between the child and his or her environment (Piaget, 1976). Piaget's theory provides a classically *constructivist* perspective on development, whereby the maturing child constructs their knowledge and understanding of the world by acting within and on the world around them. The world that the child acts within and on includes (of course) other people. But from a Piagetian perspective, other people do not play an important causal role in the child's psychological development. As a result, Piagetian theory plays down the role of teaching and instruction in child development. Teachers can facilitate children's learning by creating appropriate settings and contexts – by organizing children's environments in ways that support their development – but essentially the same pattern of development would occur, with or without the teaching.

A different perspective on development is provided by Vygotsky (1962). His theory of child development places much more emphasis on the child as a social being. Hence Vygotsky's position as a *social constructivist*. For Vygotsky what goes on between people in interaction is at least as important, psychologically speaking, as what goes on within each person. From this perspective other people do play a causal role in children's psychological development. Vygotsky argues that the interactions a child has with adults and with other children shape the course of that child's development in fundamental ways. One upshot of this is that Vygotsky places more emphasis on the role of teaching and instruction than does Piaget. A helpful way of framing this essential difference between Piagetian and Vygotskian theory is to remember that Piaget emphasizes processes that go on *within* the child, while Vygotsky focuses on processes that go on *between* the child and other people.

The study

Working from a broadly Vygotskian perspective, the researchers set out to examine the relative effectiveness of different approaches to teaching. They had observed and described these approaches in a previous study of children who were receiving one-to-one instruction from their mothers while completing a construction task (Wood *et al.*, 1976). The approach that was of particular interest to them was one that they labelled 'contingent' teaching. Contingent teaching follows two simple rules:

(1) If the child succeeds on one step of the task, give less help when next intervening.

(2) If the child fails on one step of the task, give more help when next intervening.

If teachers follow these rules then their behaviour will be shaped to the child's moment-by-moment needs because their teaching interventions will be contingent on the child's level of mastery on each step of the task.

In order to study the contingent teaching strategy in a systematic way, the researchers operationally defined five different levels of intervention for a construction task (see Table 11.3). If the child fails on a step when Level 2 support is given (a 'specific verbal instruction') a contingent teacher will increase the level of support by offering the next intervention at Level 3 ('selection'). Likewise, if the child experiences success with a Level 2 intervention, then a contingent teacher will offer less support on their next intervention (Level 1).

Table 11.3 *Levels of intervention*

Level	
Level 1	General verbal encouragement (lowest level of intervention) – e.g. 'Good. What's next?'
Level 2	Specific verbal information – e.g. instructor tells child what to do next
Level 3	Selection – instructor finds or indicates the pieces that are needed next
Level 4	Prepared material – instructor places materials together so that child needs only 'finish off' that bit of the assembly (for example, by pushing pieces together)
Level 5	Demonstration (highest level of intervention) – instructor demonstrates one step of the construction by doing it for the child

Three other teaching approaches were identified from previous observations. These were labelled 'verbal' (the instructor relies almost exclusively on verbal instructions), 'demonstration' (the instructor relies on showing the child how to do the task) and 'swing' (the instructor swings from the lowest level of intervention to the highest level, contingent upon failure, and then back again). The study set out to compare the relative effectiveness of each of these four approaches to teaching children. The hypothesis was that contingent teaching would result in the best learning, because the interventions are targeted at the child's 'region of sensitivity to instruction' (Wood *et al.*, 1978, p. 133), right at the boundary between success and failure on any given aspect of the task.

▶ **learning** A change in behaviour, or the potential for behaviour, that occurs as a result of environmental experience, but is not the result of such factors as fatigue, drugs or injury.

Subjects, materials and design

Sixteen boys and 16 girls aged 3;0 to 4;0 participated. They were divided into four groups, and matched on age (to within one month) and sex. The same instructor worked one-to-one with each child, but varied the type of instruction given according to which group the child had been allocated. The different groups were labelled 'contingent', 'verbal', 'swing' and 'demonstrate' to reflect the four different teaching approaches that the instructor adopted. The task that the child worked on was a construction task, using building blocks that had to be assembled into a pyramid.

Procedure

Each child was settled into the experimental setting with their mother, and then allowed to familiarize themselves for a few minutes with the construction materials. After this the instructor worked individually with the child according to one of the four teaching approaches (depending on which group the child had been allocated to). This instruction phase resulted in the pyramid being fully constructed, whereupon it was dismantled and the child was asked to build it without help. A number of measures were taken during the independent building phase in order to measure the effectiveness of the child's learning (the dependent variable). The most important of these measures were an activity score (the total number of building operations, with each operation being a move such as putting two blocks together, or lining blocks up), and an outcome score (the total number of correct building operations). The outcome score was then divided by the activity score to give a measure of efficiency (such that a score of one would represent a perfect sequence of building operations, with no errors). The instructor's behaviour was also recorded to provide a measure of the extent to which they acted in accordance with the teaching approach laid down for each group of children.

The observational measures that were used were reported as having an inter-rater reliability score of 90 per cent or greater.

▶ **inter-coder reliability** A phrase which describes the extent to which two independent observers (coders/raters) agree on the observations that they have made. Also known as inter-observer reliability and inter-rater reliability.

Results

Children in the contingent group scored significantly higher on the outcome measure than children in all of the three other groups. They also scored significantly higher than the children in the verbal and swing groups on the activity score, and significantly higher than the children in the swing and demonstration groups on the efficiency score (see Table 11.4).

Table 11.4 *Scores for contingent, verbal, swing and demonstration methods*

Scores	Contingent	Verbal	Swing	Demonstration
Mean activity scores	37.5	20.9*	20.9*	24.5
Mean outcome scores	15.0	6.2**	4.0**	2.6**
Mean efficiency scores	0.44	0.25	0.19**	0.06**

$* \ p < 0.05$ $\quad ** \ p < 0.01$

Discussion

When it came to undertaking the building task independently, children in the contingent teaching group performed on average more building operations (activity score), achieved more correct operations (outcome score), and also achieved a higher proportion of correct operations (efficiency score) than most of the other children. The researchers conclude from this that 'patterns of instruction ... do have causal influences on the child's rate of learning' (Wood *et al.*, 1978, p. 143). In the contingent teaching condition there seemed to be something about the 'fit' between the child's behaviour and learning needs (on the one hand) and the adult's behaviour and instructional approach (on the other) that caused the learning to be more effective.

One crucial aspect of Vygotskian theory that is illustrated by this study is the notion of the Zone of Proximal Development (ZPD). A child's ZPD is the difference between what that child can do independently, and what they can do with the assistance of someone who is more able than them (an older child, for example, or a teacher or parent). For example, in the early stages of learning to read a child may be able to identify the letters on a page independently. But an adult is able to help the child put the letters together to form words that can be put together to make the story. So with adult help the child is able to 'read', whereas without adult help the child is only able to name letters. It is within this 'zone' that learning occurs, according to Vygotskian theorists, with children achieving things together with adults that they are not quite ready to achieve alone. One way of thinking about the contingent teaching approach that was used in this study is in terms of the ZPD: the contingent teacher was constantly adjusting their behaviour to keep it within that 'zone' between the child's current level of independent mastery of the task, and the level of mastery that was possible with adult support. Although the whole study is about a somewhat constrained construction task, the researchers argue that the principles that they have identified are basic principles of effective teaching and learning that apply generally to relationships between teachers and learners.

Of course one small experiment does not allow judgments to be made about the relative worth of Piagetian and Vygotskian theories. Piaget would be able to explain these findings just as adequately as would Vygotsky. The importance of this study is that it represents a body of work that places an emphasis on the causal role of teaching in development and learning, because it starts from the assumption that child development is, in essence, a social phenomenon.

Questions

suggested answers → p. 495

1. How might Piagetian theory explain these findings?

2. Identify two different strategies that the researchers might have used to ensure that the children in the contingent group did not turn out to perform best on the task simply because they were already better at the task than the children in the other conditions.

3. Think of a teacher who has inspired you, who has really helped you to learn. Did they just 'facilitate' the learning that would have happened anyway? Or did they 'cause' you to learn?

chapter **12**

COMMUNICATION

nature–nurture debates
Fairly sterile theoretical
debates, popular in the
1950s, concerning whether
a given psychological ability
was inherited or whether
it was learned through
experience.

innate Genetically
pre-programmed.

COMMUNICATION is a basic feature of
all living things. Human beings love to
communicate and devise all manner of
ways to get messages from one person
to another. We also communicate in a lot
of unconscious ways, and pass messages
about our intentions, our attitudes
and our emotions. We even invent
communications with things that can't
respond, like trees or our cars. The basic
ingredients of communication are a
sender, a message and a receiver, though
it is worth noting that the message which
the sender sends is often not the same
as the message the receiver receives.

Human beings are arguably unique in
possessing the ability to communicate
through language (though see the article
by Gardner and Gardner, Chapter 4 of
this volume, on language development
in chimpanzees). This language is
able to produce an infinite number of
messages, convey abstract ideas and
refer to events that took place years ago
and in other parts of the world. These
features distinguish 'language' from
'communication'. The latter usually has
a simple message that is located in this
place and at this time. Imagine a type of
non-verbal communication that says 'I
loved you last Thursday fortnight but I
feel a bit iffy about you today'. Your non-

verbal communication cannot convey
abstract messages of this sort with this
degree of precision, but your language
can.

So, a major question that has
occupied developmental psychologists
concerns how children learn the quite
remarkable skill of language. As with
most other areas of psychology, the
nature–nurture debate has been played
out in relation to language acquisition.
Skinner and Chomsky represent the
two opposing standpoints, with Skinner
asserting that language is learned (the
'nurture' position) and Chomsky arguing
for an innate linguistic capacity. The
first two studies reported in this chapter
(by Condon and Sander, 1974, and by
Fernald, 1985) reinforce the common-
sense notion that right from birth (and
probably from before birth), the human
skill of language emerges out of a potent
mixture of biological potential (nature)
and social context (nurture). The studies
look at how language is mixed in with
other communication skills such as
movement and rhythm, and how we are
able to adjust our language when we are
talking to infants. The third study (Bryant
et al., 1989) goes on to look at some of
these factors in relation to the crucial
communication skill of reading.

▶ sociolinguist A person who specializes in studying sociological aspects of language.

One political battleground in this field has been the area of educational performance and language style. An argument developed during the 1960s about the quality of language spoken in different social classes, with the basic proposition being that the standard English of the upper and middle classes is a superior form of language and conveys messages of greater sophistication than working-class talk. In order to highlight this important issue we have described one piece of the influential work of the sociolinguist Labov, who refutes these notions of linguistic superiority.

The dance of the neonates

CONDON, W.S. AND SANDER, L.W. (1974)

Neonate movement is synchronized with adult speech: interactional participation and language acquisition.

Science, 183, 99–101.

Introduction

In the 1960s and 1970s, W.S. Condon and Adam Kendon started to publish work on non-verbal behaviour and 'interactional synchrony' (see for example, Condon and Ogston, 1966, and Kendon, 1970). Their intriguing empirical work was suggesting that the body movements of interacting people are synchronized in an extraordinarily complex way. We appear to move in a sophisticated dance with someone even when we are not trying to do this. Furthermore, Condon and Kendon claimed that these body movements are coordinated with the rhythms of speech. The notion of interactional synchrony became a controversial issue in the literature of developmental psychology when Condon and Sander published the paper that is summarized here, claiming that the same sorts of synchronies between speech and non-verbal behaviour could be detected even in newborn babies.

The study

▶ **microanalysis** A detailed analysis of observational data, usually using film/video material played back at slow speeds.

▶ **neonates** New-born animals.

▶ **aphasia** Literally speaking, an absence of speech.

▶ **autism** A condition of social withdrawal characterized by (i) impairment in reciprocal social interaction, (ii) impairment in verbal and non-verbal communication, and in imaginative activity, (iii) a restricted repertoire of activities and interests.

▶ **schizophrenia** A mental disorder marked by some, or all of the following symptoms: delusions, hallucinations, incoherent word associations, inappropriate emotions or lack of emotions.

The study is based on a microanalysis of sound films of newborn babies (neonates) who were either being spoken to directly or were being played tape-recordings of adult human speech and other kinds of sounds. The authors were interested in whether the movements of newborn babies are synchronized with speech sounds in the same way that adults' movements seem to be. They cite evidence from Condon and Ogston (1966) that adult speakers coordinate their movements with their own speech (so called 'self-synchrony'), and that listeners coordinate their movements with the speech of speakers ('interactional synchrony'). Furthermore, they cite evidence from Condon and Brosin (1969) that people with disorders such as aphasia, autism and schizophrenia display 'marked self-asynchronies' (in other words a lack of coordination between their own speech and movement).

Condon and Sander's claim is that the coordination of speech and movement is so fine-grained that it happens at a level well beyond our normal conscious awareness. This is why the frame-by-frame analysis (a systematic microanalysis) of a permanent audio-visual record is necessary. The sound-film that the authors used yields 30 frames of film per second, and the detailed examination of these frames, going backwards and forwards again and again over the same short sequences, allows for the identification of complex features of behaviour and speech which we simply cannot perceive in real time.

The paper actually presents the findings of six studies, but for the purposes of this summary they will be treated as one.

Subjects

Sixteen neonates were studied. Fourteen of these babies were between 12 and 48 hours old, and two were 14 days old.

Design

▶ **structured observation**
A method of recording behaviour where the behaviours are pre-categorized into a limited framework.

This study is an example of a systematic and highly structured observation. The authors characterize their method as a 'frame-by-frame microanalysis of sound films' (p. 99), whereby very brief sequences of audio-visual records are inspected in great detail. Since the film record provides 30 frames per second, the observational analysis can be fine-grained. The study was designed to examine the relationships between human speech sounds and babies' movements.

Procedure

A total of approximately five hours of sound film was collected from the 16 participating babies, of which approximately one hour was suitable for analysis given that each baby spent large periods of time asleep! Fourteen of the neonates were filmed whilst lying in their crib, and two were held. The infants were filmed in a variety of contexts, including:

(1) being spoken to directly by an adult male speaking US English;
(2) being played an audio tape of an adult male speaking US English;
(3) being played an audio tape of disconnected vowel sounds;
(4) being played an audio tape of tapping sounds;
(5) being played an audio tape of an adult speaking Chinese.

Short sequences of the sound-film of each infant were inspected frame-by-frame, again and again. Changes in the direction and speed of movements of all the infant's moving body parts were recorded. Particularly crucial to the reported analysis was the identification of the frame numbers which marked changes in direction or speed of any of the moving body parts. The audio record was also 'segmented' in this fashion and frame numbers which marked speech boundaries between phonemes, syllables and words were identified. The extent to which changes of direction and speed in the movement of body parts coincided with speech boundaries was recorded and is summarized in the results section below.

▶ **phonemes** The basic units of sound in a language.

Results

Table 12.1 shows the way in which 93 per cent of the changes in speed and direction of movement of Baby E's body parts corresponded with the boundaries of speech segments within a 30-second period (892 frames of film). The much lower level of agreement between the movements of Baby C and the sound track of the adult talking to Baby E are shown in the row labelled 'Study 3' (the authors confusingly refer to their different analyses as different 'studies'). This suggests that this correspondence of movement and speech segments for Baby E was not just happening by chance.

Table 12.2 shows how 87 per cent of changes in speed and direction of Baby A's movements coincided with the boundaries of speech segments from the tape-recorded adult speaker. Note the much lower levels of synchronization (agreement) between the movements of Babies C and E, and disconnected vowel and tapping sounds.

Table 12.1 *Correspondence of infant movements with live speech*

Study	Total frames	Total discrepancies	Agreement (%)	Estimated range of agreement *
1	892	65	93	91.3–94.5
2	336	21	94	90.3–96.4
3	336	119	65	59.0–70.0

Baby E's motion segmentation was compared with the speech segmentation of the adult for the total sequence (Study 1) and for the first 336 frames only (Study 2). In Study 3, Baby C's motion segmentation during 336 frames of silence was compared to the first 336 frames of speech segmentation on the sound track of Baby E.
* This column gives, for $p = .025$, the maximum risks of overestimating the lower limit and of underestimating the upper limit for random samples having the percentage of misses in Studies 1 to 3.
Source: Condon and Sander (1974).

Table 12.2 *Correspondence of infant movements with recorded speech and non-speech sounds*

Study	Sound	Baby	Total occurrences	Total discrepancies	Agreement (%)
4	Speech (word boundaries)	A	146	19	87
5	Disconnected vowels	E	167	97	42
		C	124	51	59
6	Tapping sounds	E	27	15	44
		C	34	16	53

Source: Condon and Sander (1974).

Condon and Sander's original illustration of synchronized speech and movement is reproduced in Figure 12.1. The figure should be read from left to right and downwards rather like a musical stave. The speech is transcribed above each section of the figure ('come over an' see who's over here'), and is split into speech segments along the row headed 'phonetics'. Each line in the figure represents one body part moving, and the arrows denote when there is any change in speed or direction of movement in that body part. Note that the arrows occur at the boundaries of the speech segments (which are marked on the first 'stave' by vertical lines).

Discussion

The results show that the movement of the newborn babies was synchronized with adult speech sounds. That is, changes in direction and speed of moving body parts occurred precisely in coordination with the speech segments that the researchers had identified. The synchronization appeared to be just as strong when an unfamiliar language was played. Much lower levels of synchronization of movement were observed with ordinary rhythmic tapping sounds and with disjointed spoken vowel sounds. This seems to suggest that

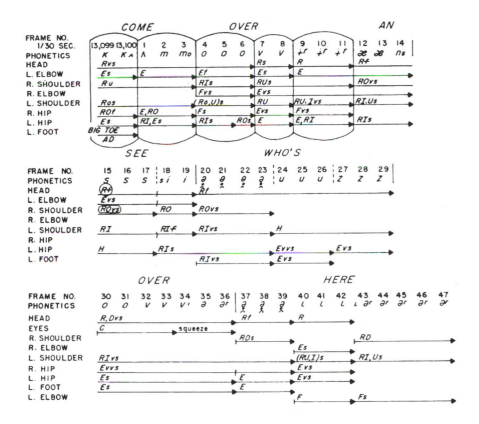

Figure 12.1 *Frame-by-frame microanalysis of sound and movement*
Two-day-old neonate moving synchronously with adult speaking, 'Come over an see who's
over here'. The transcription read vertically shows that the infant's configurations of movement
coincide with the articulatory segments of the adult's speech. Definition of descriptive
notation: F, forward or flex (depending on body part); H, hold; D, down; E, extend; C, close: RI,
rotate inward; RO, rotate outward; AD, adduct; and U, up. Lower case letters refer to speed: s,
slight: f, fast: and vs, very slight.

Source: Condon and Sander (1974).

babies, at birth, are somehow tuned into the sounds and structure of normal
adult speech. Perhaps we are born prepared in this way for the learning of any
language.

The authors are very clear that they have not simply observed 'responses'
on the part of the infants to the 'stimulus' of adult speech. They argue for a
much more sophisticated understanding of communication which focuses on
the enmeshment of interactions between babies and adults: a kind of interactional ballet. For example, they observed that the synchronies appear between
speech and movement when the baby is already moving. This suggests that
the speech sounds are not 'causing' the baby to move, and that the interactions
that they have studied must themselves be understood as part of a 'more macroscopic level of regulation and organization of the infant–caretaker system'
(p. 101). As such, the authors are clearly operating within an interactional level
of analysis.

They conclude with the following exciting speculation:

> If the infant, from the beginning, moves in precise, shared rhythm with the organization of the speech structure of his [sic] culture, then he participates developmentally through complex, sociobiological entrainment processes in millions of repetitions of linguistic forms long before he later uses them in speaking and communicating. By the time he learns to speak, he may have already laid down within himself the form and structure of the language system of his culture. (p. 101)

But before we get too carried away with the seductive qualities of this research it is important to bear in mind that Condon and Sander's findings remain controversial. Work on interactional synchrony has been criticized on a number of grounds (see Rosenfeld, 1981, for a useful critique of the literature). Some claim that the methods of frame-by-frame microanalysis are not sufficiently reliable (it is difficult for observers to agree when the changes in speed and direction of movement in a body part actually occur; McDowall, 1978a), and that the levels of synchrony reported by Condon and Sander occur so infrequently that they can be attributed to chance factors (if enough body parts are moving for enough of the time that someone is speaking, then some sequences of them will inevitably fall at the boundaries of speech segments; see McDowall, 1978b).

It is certainly the case that Condon and Sander did not provide an exhaustive account of their methods in this article. For example, it is evident that they were highly selective in choosing which sequences of analysed film they reported. But their methods and ideas have received support from a number of quarters (see for example, Austin and Peery, 1983, and Gatewood and Rosenwein, 1981) and the work remains intriguing and highly suggestive.

▶ **reliability** The reliability of a psychological measuring device (such as a test or a scale) is the extent to which it gives consistent measurements. The greater the consistency of measurement, the greater the tool's reliability.

Questions

suggested answers → p. 495

1. Why are the authors especially interested in the finding that there is 'a synchronization of infant movement organization with the articulatory segments of adult speech *as early as the first day of life*'? (p. 99; emphasis added).

2. Why is it so essential in this study to have a film record of the infants' movements?

3. What is the significance of the comparisons they made between US English speech sounds, Chinese speech sounds, disconnected vowel sounds and tapping sounds?

4. Why did they use taped speech sounds some of the time?

5. Two of the infants were held in one of the studies that the authors report: what problems might this cause in terms of interpreting results obtained from these two children?

Introduction

When adults talk to babies, they talk in a different way from how they talk to adults. They tend to adopt a tone of voice and style of expression which has been somewhat misleadingly labelled motherese. The label is misleading since all adults seem to talk in this way to babies, not just their mothers. Motherese is characterized by relatively high-pitched speech, and varied and exaggerated intonation; adult-to-adult speech tends to be lower in pitch, and more monotonous. It has been suggested that motherese actually plays an important role in the infant's development of language (Snow, 1979). Among other things, it is more interesting to the baby than adult-to-adult (or adult-directed) speech, and so engages their attention for longer. Presumably, the more a baby focuses on language, the more opportunity there is for learning. Fernald's study set out to discover whether babies prefer listening to motherese than to normal adult talk. If they do, this would give some support to the suggestion that motherese enhances the interactions between adults and infants.

It is not easy to find out what a baby likes listening to, because it is very difficult to tell exactly what a baby is listening to at any given moment in time. Babies do not have to move their heads in the direction of a sound in order to attend to it. One way of tackling this problem is to use operant techniques (for a description of these techniques see the study by Skinner, Chapter 4 of this volume). With operant techniques the baby has to do something to make a particular sound occur. Fernald cites Glenn and Cunningham's (1983) work in which babies had to learn to operate a switch which allowed them to listen to either one of two possible sounds. Once they had learned the basic skill, a measure of preference could be obtained by observing how long they spent listening to each sound.

The study

Fernald used a variation on this operant theme. She placed the infants in a room with one loudspeaker on each of the side walls. Out of one speaker could be played eight-second bursts of a woman talking to her own infant. Out of the other speaker could be played eight-second bursts of the same woman talking to another adult. In other words, motherese was played from one speaker, and adult-to-adult speech came from the other. The babies could cause an eight-second burst of speaking to come from one or other speaker by turning towards it. So if infants turned towards the motherese speaker, they would hear motherese. If they turned towards the adult-to-adult speaker they would hear adult-to-adult talk. Exactly how this worked is described in the procedure section, below.

Before the experimental trials, each infant was given four training trials. This was to show them that one type of speech sound was to come from one

Listen with mother

FERNALD, A. (1985)

Four-month-old infants prefer to listen to motherese.

Infant Behavior and Development, 8, 181–95.

▶ **motherese** A misleading label for the style of speech adults characteristically use when communicating with babies and very young children. It is misleading because all adults tend to use this style of speech, not just mothers. A more satisfactory label might be 'baby talk register'.

part IV

▶**hypothesis** Experiments are designed to test one or more hypotheses. An hypothesis is a prediction of what will happen in an experiment. It is worded in such a way that the results of a well-designed experiment will clearly show whether the prediction is right or wrong.

▶**repeated measures design (also within groups)** An experimental design where each subject carries out each condition of the experiment.

▶**dependent variable** The thing which is measured in an experiment, and which changes, depending on the independent variable.

side of the room and another type of speech sound was to come from the other. The first training trial consisted of the speaker on one side of the room playing one eight-second burst of either motherese or adult-directed speech. The infant's gaze would tend to be attracted by this sound, causing them to turn in the direction of the sound. If they did not turn, then the mother, whose lap the infant was sitting on, was instructed to swivel her chair to the side from which the sound came. The next training trial consisted of an eight-second burst of the other kind of speech (depending on what kind of speech had been played in the first training trial) from the other speaker. Again the infant would tend to turn in the direction of the sound. This whole process was repeated for the third and fourth training trials.

The difference between the training trials and the experimental trials was that in the experimental trials the infant had to turn in the direction of one of the speakers in order to cause speech sounds to be played from it, rather than just responding to the sounds as they had done in the training trials. Fernald's hypothesis was that the infants would turn more often in the direction which caused motherese to be played than in the direction that caused adult-directed speech to be played.

Subjects

The data come from tests on 48 four-month-old infants, 21 of whom were female, 27 of whom were male.

Design

▶**counterbalancing** A method of controlling against potentially confounding variables in experiments. Typically, counterbalancing is seen in action in repeated measures designs in an effort to control against order effects, and characteristically involves alternating the order in which subjects do the conditions of an experiment.

▶**confounding variable** A variable which causes a change in the dependent variable, but which is not the independent variable of the study.

▶**independent variable** The conditions which an experimenter sets up, to cause an effect in an experiment. These vary systematically, so that the experimenter can draw conclusions about changes in outcomes.

This experiment was based on operant techniques. It used a kind of repeated measures design in which the dependent variable was measured by counting the number of times out of 15 trials that the infant turned in the direction which caused a burst of motherese to be played.

Counterbalancing was used to control against two important and potentially confounding factors. These were:

- side of presentation of motherese (left or right);
- the order of presentation of motherese and ordinary adult speech in the training stage (motherese first or last).

Of the 48 infants, 12 heard motherese on the left, and heard it first in the training trials; 12 heard motherese from the right, and first in the training trials; 12 heard motherese from the left, and second in the training trials; 12 heard motherese from the right, and second in the training trials. So all possible combinations of left/right and first/second are accounted for in this factorial design. This ensures that if a tendency to turn in the direction of motherese is found, a sceptic cannot argue that this was only because motherese was always heard, say, on the left-hand side (and perhaps babies tend to prefer any sounds which are played on their left-hand side).

Procedure

▶ **factorial design** A form of experimental design involving more than one independent variable.

The laboratory was divided into two rooms. In the main room sat the mother with the infant subject on her lap. The mother wore headphones and listened to music throughout the experiment. In the adjoining room sat a judge and the experimenter. A one-way mirror separated the rooms, and a camera in the main room could be monitored by the judge in the adjoining room. The judge and the experimenter actually performed different tasks, but in the interests of a straightforward summary we will refer to them as the 'experimenters'.

On the wall directly in front of the child was a video camera, and just above this was a green light. Each trial began with the green light going on to attract the child's attention to the mid-line of the room. When the experimenters were satisfied that the child was looking at the green light (they could observe this by monitoring the picture from the video camera) the light was switched off. Nothing then happened until the child turned its head at least 30 degrees in one direction or the other. As soon as it did turn its head 30 degrees an eight-second burst of speech came from the speaker on the side of the room which it had turned towards. After the eight-second burst the sound would stop and the green light would then go on once again to attract the child's attention back to the mid-line of the room. The next trial was begun when the experimenters were satisfied that the infant was looking at the green light once more.

▶ **binomial test** An inferential statistic that is used when there is a simple 'either/or' outcome to a task (for example, either heads or tails, either right or left, either male or female). It tests to see whether there is any statistically significant bias in favour of one or other of the alternatives.

▶ **t-test** A statistical test that computes the likelihood of achieving a particular difference between the means of two sets of scores.

There are a number of important things to note about the procedure. First, for each trial no sound was heard from either side of the room until a 'criterion head-turn' of 30 degrees had spontaneously been made by the infant. The experimenters judged when this had occurred by monitoring the child's movements through the video camera, a task that they practised before the experiment began. Second, half the infants heard motherese from the right speaker and adult-to-adult speech from the left speaker, whilst half heard motherese from the left speaker and adult-to-adult speech from the right speaker. Third, the voice that the child heard was not their own mother's.

Results

Thirty-three out of the 48 infants turned more often in the direction that caused motherese to be played than in the direction that caused adult-directed speech to be played. A binomial test on the relative proportion of infants who turned most often in the direction of motherese compared with the proportion that turned most often in the direction of adult-directed speech showed the differences in these proportions to be statistically significant at the level of $p < .01$. A t-test showed that the mean number of head-turns in the direction of motherese (8.73) was significantly greater ($p < .05$) than the mean that would have been expected by chance (7.5).

Discussion

The data support Fernald's experimental hypothesis. Overall, the babies made more head-turns in the direction of motherese than in the direction of adult-directed speech. This suggests that, on average, the babies preferred to listen to the motherese speech sounds, and in turn this preference suggests that motherese may play a useful role in infant language development.

The evidence from this one study is, of course, not compelling. Just because infants appear to prefer to listen to this kind of speech does not necessarily mean that it actually helps their language development. Babies prefer to eat very sugary and salty foods, but this does not mean that these foods help their physical development. By four months of age, perhaps they are just more used to hearing motherese. Furthermore, some infants actually seemed to prefer adult-directed speech; two babies turned every time in the direction which caused adult-to-adult speech sounds to be played. However, the results of one research study should never be interpreted in isolation from the body of literature out of which it has emerged. Fernald's data should be considered within the context of other work which shows how particular features of motherese are well suited to the needs of the infant (see for example Snow, 1979). This bigger picture suggests that adults talk to babies in a way that may facilitate their language development.

suggested answers → p. 496

Questions

1. Why did the speech sounds on both sides of the room, whether adult-directed or motherese, come from the same woman speaker?

2. Why were the speech sounds not recorded from the infants' own mothers?

3. Why did half the babies hear motherese from the left, and half hear it from the right?

All the king's horses and
all the king's men ...

Nursery rhymes,
phonological skills
and reading.

BYRANT, P.E. BRADLEY, L. MACLEAN,
M. AND CROSSLAND, J. (1989)

Journal of
Child Language,
16, 407–28.

Introduction

'Ker-aah-tuh spells cat.' This is the intuitive explanation of how we read. We look at the components of the word (the letters), make the individual sounds, and combine them into the familiar sound of the word. It seems obvious, but it is not what we actually do. One everyday example will give an indication of the problem. If you have ever tried to proofread any of your own work you will know that mistakes are hard to spot. For example, if you made a typing error and wrote 'sivler' instead of 'silver' it is quite likely that you will miss it when you look back over the work for errors (Rawlinson, 1975). If you read using the 'Ker-aah-tuh' method then you would notice this error. In fact we are able to read text that is misspelled, as can be seen if you read the following text that has been circulated widely on the Internet:

I cdnuolt blveiee taht I cluod aulaclty uesdnatnrd waht I was rdanieg. Aoccdrnig to rsereach at Cmabrigde Uinervtisy, it deosn't mttaer in waht oredr the ltteers in a wrod are, the olny iprmoatnt tihng is taht the frist and lsat ltteer be in the rghit pclae. The rset can be a taotl mses and you can sitll raed it wouthit a porbelm. [Although the text refers to Cambridge University the original findings were by Rawlinson; see Rawlinson, 1999, or the *Guardian*, 2003.]

Reading is a complex task and it is still not clear exactly how we do it nor how we learn it. Psychological research has identified a number of factors that are important in the development of reading skills. The study by Bryant et al. looks at how one of the skills of spoken language – learning to recognize and use sounds – can have an effect on learning to read. Their study looks at how nursery rhymes aid the development of spoken and written language.

There has been considerable interest in the role of nursery rhymes in the development of children. Research has shown that:

- they are important in the interactions between parents and children;
- parents recite them to children as young as 3 months old;
- parents speak them in a strikingly distinct style;
- children choose to listen to nursery rhymes from a very young age.

One of the questions to consider is what kind of influence nursery rhymes have. Do they help semantic development (understanding meanings) or syntactic development (understanding grammar) or phonetic development (understanding the sounds of language)? It seems likely that they aid all three to some extent, but any effect they have is likely to be most pronounced in the domain of phonetic development. Two common features of nursery rhymes are rhyme (no surprise there), and alliteration (words that have the same initial sound, for example Goosey, goosey gander, or Jack and Jill). The researchers argue that a child who is sensitive to rhyme and alliteration must recognize that different words have common sounds. They suggest that this sensitivity to rhyme and alliteration may also aid the development of reading. An early report of the study described in this paper found that children with more knowledge of nursery rhymes performed better on simple tests of rhyme and alliteration. The subsequent work of this longitudinal study goes on to investigate whether this early advantage in language skills was maintained when the children learned to read.

▶ **longitudinal study** A study which monitors changes occurring over a period of time.

The study

The study is based on 64 children from a wide range of social backgrounds who were tested on five occasions over a three-year period. At the time of the first test the average age of the children was 3;4 (3 years, 4 months; range 2;10–3;9), and the last measures were taken when the average age was 6;3 (range 5;9–6;8). The first two measures were taken in the children's homes and the final three measures were taken at their schools:

(1) *Knowledge of nursery rhymes*: measured at the start of the project.
(2) *Phonological sensitivity*: a number of measures were taken at different times during the study, and they are reported under two headings:
    – rhyme detection;
    – phoneme (language sounds) detection.
(3) *Reading and spelling*: standardized tests of reading and spelling were given at age 5;11 and a further reading test was given at age 6;3.
(4) *IQ and vocabulary*: a standardized vocabulary test was given at age 3;4, and an IQ test was given at age 4;3. On both tests the children scored slightly above the population averages.

▶ **phonemes** The basic units of sound in a language.

▶ **Intelligence Quotient (IQ)** A numerical figure, believed by some to indicate the level of a person's intelligence, and by others to indicate how well that person performs on intelligence tests.

Results

▶ **correlation** A measure of how strongly two or more variables are related to each other.

▶ **hypothesis** Experiments are designed to test one or more hypotheses. An hypothesis is a prediction of what will happen in an experiment. It is worded in such a way that the results of a well-designed experiment will clearly show whether the prediction is right or wrong.

The results showed that knowledge of nursery rhymes correlated very strongly with rhyme detection ($r = .64$), phoneme detection ($r = 0.61$) and reading ($r = 0.59$). These correlations offer some support for the research hypothesis. However, the limitation with results like this is that they do not provide strong enough evidence on their own for the relationship between nursery rhymes, phonological skills and reading. It might be that some other factor, such as IQ, affects all three scores and can therefore explain the correlations described above.

The researchers used the statistical procedure of multiple regression to examine the data further. A regression analysis is one step on from correlation. In a regression with two variables we use one variable (the independent

▶ **independent variable** The conditions which an experimenter sets up, to cause an effect in an experiment. These vary systematically, so that the experimenter can draw conclusions about changes in outcomes.

▶ **multiple regression** Using the scores from more than one independent variable to predict scores of a dependent variable.

▶ **dependent variable** The thing which is measured in an experiment, and which changes, depending on the independent variable.

variable) to try to predict the score on the other (the dependent variable). For example, if we have two sets of scores for a group of workers where one is their aptitude test result, and the other is a measure of their performance at work, then we might want to know how well we can predict someone's performance at work from their aptitude score. If we can do this with some confidence then we can use the aptitude test to select the best people for the job. The regression analysis will tell us how confident we can be about our predictions on the basis of the aptitude test.

A multiple regression can deal with more than two variables and can either combine them or remove some in order to find the best predictor of the dependent variable. In this study, the dependent variable is reading at age 6;3 and the researchers want to remove all the variables, other than knowledge of nursery rhymes, that might have affected the reading scores. They used their regression analysis to remove the effects of (a) differences in age, (b) IQ, (c) vocabulary at age 3;4, (d) the mother's educational level, and (e) the sensitivity to rhyme at the age of 3;4. Once all these of variables had been controlled for it was possible to estimate the effect of nursery rhyme knowledge on subsequent reading skill, and the researchers found that there was still a significant relationship between these two variables.

The analysis of the data was extended to try to explore how nursery rhymes prepare children for reading. The researchers argued that nursery rhymes enhance a child's sensitivity to rhyme and alliteration and this increases their phonological sensitivity and eventually their reading. They derived two predictions from this hypothesis:

(1) Scores on the first test of nursery rhyme knowledge will predict later scores of phonological sensitivity.

(2) Nursery rhyme scores will not be related to reading if the effects of phonological sensitivity are controlled for.

The researchers carried out further multiple regression analyses on their data which provided support for these predictions.

They carried out one further analysis on their data which was a path analysis, and this showed there to be a number of possible predictive paths through the data. These paths are discussed by the authors in another of their papers (Bryant et al., 1990).

Discussion

Once all the complex analyses are stripped away, we are left with the finding that the informal learning of nursery rhymes by children at a very young age has an effect on their language skills such as rhyme detection and, later, their skills of reading. The authors conclude that the repetition of nursery rhymes to young children can make an important contribution to the development of reading skills in the child, and potentially the adult. A word of caution, however. Even the most sophisticated statistical procedures cannot guarantee that the cause–effect relationships examined in this type of study really exist. The authors have taken every effort to account for other interpretations of their data, but we have to acknowledge that there may be all sorts of variables outside their data that may also account for the patterns that they identify.

It is quite remarkable how such a simple test as 'knowledge of nursery rhymes' can have such a power to predict later performance. This ability to predict is relatively uncommon in the literature on language development. If we return to the question posed at the beginning of this review – How do we learn to read? – we can say that our skills of reading are developing long before anyone shows us a book, and the skills of spoken language are an important part of our ability to learn to read.

suggested answers → p. 496

Questions

1. From the information that has been given in this summary, think of one variable that has not been mentioned that may play a causal role with respect to both the extent of a child's knowledge of nursery rhymes, and their subsequent reading ability. Why is this such an important question to ask in relation to this study?

2. What nursery rhymes do you know? Look for some common features in them, or just have a laugh singing them to yourself.

Introduction

Talking proper

LABOV, W. (1969)

The logic of nonstandard English.

In P.P. Giglioli (ed.), *Language and Social Context*. Harmondsworth, England: Penguin. Originally in *Georgetown Monographs on Language and Linguistics*, 2, 1–31.

part iv

In this influential paper Labov, a sociolinguist, set out to challenge the basic principles of language deprivation theory. Deprivation theory (or deficit theory) had been used to explain the consistent trend of underachievement in schools among ethnic minority groups and working-class children, both in the United Kingdom and in the United States. The idea was that children from these backgrounds lacked some of the key language skills that enabled non-minority and middle-class children to succeed in schools. The empirical basis of the theory was the poor performance of these children (relative to their White and middle-class counterparts) on language assessments carried out by schoolteachers and researchers.

It is important to note from the outset that the relatively poor performance of these groups of children in their schoolwork and on language assessments at that time is not in dispute (see for example Scarr, 1981). Indeed, Labov reports data from a 1968 study which shows that the Black New York City children that he and his colleagues were working with lagged more than two years behind the national norm on reading tests. What is at stake in this article is what this all means. To deprivation theorists, the apparent deficit in language skills shown by Black and working-class children pointed to, and was caused by, a form of 'cultural deprivation' (Labov cites Deutsch et al., 1967, as leading proponents of this perspective). The homes of these children were supposed to have an impoverished linguistic environment which prevented them from developing the full range of verbal skills which enabled White middle-class children to succeed in school.

The work of the British educationalist Basil Bernstein (1959, 1960) was influential in this respect. Although it is unclear whether Bernstein really was a deficit theorist (Edwards, 1979), his work is strongly associated with this line of thinking. It was Bernstein who had framed the notion of restricted and elaborated linguistic codes (originally 'public' and 'formal' codes, respectively); the former being a rather concrete and limited form of language which was characteristic of working-class speakers; the latter a more symbolic and flexible way of speaking which was available to middle-class speakers. The restricted code was seen as being less useful, less powerful, less adaptive than the elaborated code, and was thought to be the result of the relationships and linguistic environment within the working-class household. Translated into the terms of deprivation theory, these ideas resulted in extreme assertions such as:

> the language of culturally deprived children ... is not merely an under-developed version of standard English, but is a basically non-logical mode of expressive behavior. (pp. 183–4, cited by Labov from the work of Bereiter et al., 1966)

The language of Black US inner-city children in particular was seen from this perspective as deficient in verbal skills and limited in its grammar. Labov's

▶ **sociolinguist** A person who specializes in studying sociological aspects of language.

▶ **deficit theory** A way of explaining educational failure among certain children by claiming that they, or their background, are somehow 'deficient'.

▶ **linguistic environment** A phrase used to describe the language that we hear and see around us.

▶ **restricted language codes** Ways of using language characterized by limited vocabulary, simple grammatical structures, and a heavy reliance on shared implicit meaning and paralinguistic cues.

▶ **elaborated language codes** Ways of using language characterized by extensive vocabulary, complex grammatical structure, and an attempt to make meaning verbally explicit.

article is specifically based on research with Black New York City children, but class issues are never far from the surface since they were 'children from urban ghetto areas' (p. 182). He contests vigorously and empirically two key related features of the language deprivation tradition. First he argues that these children are not deficient verbally. True, they perform poorly on tests of verbal skills, but there are, he asserts, important non-linguistic reasons for this. Second, he argues that the language of the Black New York City child is not inferior to the dominant English dialect of the United States; it is simply different (although this argument is not dealt with here). An important part of Labov's reasoning has to do with the shortcomings of the methods of investigation and assessment which have traditionally been used in this field. In this respect his arguments are relevant to the whole enterprise of social science.

Methodological considerations

▶ **qualitative data** Data which describe meaning and experience rather than providing numerical values for behaviour such as frequency counts.

Labov's methods could be described as qualitative. He avoided testing the children, preferring instead to involve them in informal discussions. He and his colleagues had learned from experience that:

> the social situation is the most powerful determinant of verbal behavior and ... an adult must enter into the right social relation with a child if he wants to find out what a child can do. (p. 191)

The relatively poor verbal performance of Black New York City children in previous studies had not been due to any spoken language deficit. Instead, it had been caused artificially by the inhibiting and intimidating social context of the traditional research procedures that had been used. These would often involve a White middle-class adult, who knew little of the children or of their worlds, asking unusual and (to the child) irrelevant questions.

The empirical work which lay behind this paper was carried out by an experienced Black interviewer who knew the children's neighbourhood well, and had insights into their interests and aspirations. The work with one particular 8-year-old child (Leon) is documented. To allow Leon to demonstrate his true verbal competence, the interviewer paid particular attention to the conditions under which the discussions took place. Four key strategies are specifically noted: having a supply of potato chips available; bringing along Leon's best friend; sitting on the floor (to reduce the height imbalance between adult and child and the implications of power that this can hold); using taboo words and discussing taboo topics. The aim was to make the research situation one in which Leon felt able to talk.

The data which emerge from such a research strategy are transcripts of discussions which allow the children's spoken language to be examined in some detail. Labov used the data to illustrate his argument that previous assessments of Black New York City children's language had seriously underestimated their verbal skills. He also used the data to show the structure and sophistication of the children's language, which is different from, but not inferior to, standard US spoken English. However, this latter argument is not covered in this summary.

Results and discussion

The following is an extract of a conversation between Leon and the interviewer (CR) before the strategies mentioned in the method section (above) were implemented:

CR: Well–uh–did you ever get into a fight with a guy?
Leon: Nope.
CR: That was bigger than you?
Leon: Nope.
CR: You never been in a fight?
Leon: Nope.
CR: Nobody ever pick on you?
Leon: Nope.
CR: Nobody ever hit you?
Leon: Nope.

▶**performance** This refers to what a person actually *does*, which for many reasons may not represent well what that person is really capable of (their 'competence').

▶**competence** Hypothetical notion of what a person is really capable of – what their true abilities are – which may not always be reflected in their 'performance'.

It is not difficult to see how Leon's monosyllabic performance in this situation could lead an interviewer to believe that his verbal skills were underdeveloped. But Labov argues, and goes on to demonstrate, that Leon's verbal performance in this situation is not a good measure of his verbal competence. Take, for example, the following exchange from the second session with Leon when the strategies mentioned above had been implemented:

CR: ... but I wanted you to tell me about the fight that you had.
Leon: I ain't had no fight.
⎰ Greg: Yes you did!   He said Barry,
⎱ CR: You said you had one! You had a fight with Butchie,
⎰ Greg: An' he said Garland ... an' Michael.
⎱ CR: an' Barry
⎰ Leon: I di'n'; you said that Gregory!
⎱ Greg: You did.
Leon: You know you said that!

Leon is still defensively trying to deny that he had been fighting, but the stilted monosyllabic talk has been replaced with an active and competitive verbal performance. In Labov's view, the reason for Leon's poor performance in the first meeting was nothing to do with Leon himself, but was instead to do with the social situation of that interview. Labov's more general point is that this type of social situation tends to be created whenever children are tested or assessed in some way at school. As a result, children like Leon were being systematically disadvantaged by having their true abilities underestimated. There are all sorts of ways in which underestimations of this type can be damaging. The belief that a child has poor verbal and intellectual skills may in the long run cause that child to have poor verbal and intellectual skills (Rosenthal and Jacobson, 1966).

Overall, Labov's article provides a convincing and dense refutation of the suggestion that cultural deprivation and verbal deficits lie behind Black (and working-class) children's problems in schools. The children that Labov studied were not deficient in verbal skills, and neither were they culturally deprived in the way that some psychologists had claimed. Indeed the idea that the causes of their problems should be looked for within the children, or within their home environment, or within their relationships with their parents, is typical of an ethnocentric and reductionist perspective; a perspective which is unfortunately taken too frequently by psychologists. For this reason it is important that the work of social scientists from disciplines other than psychology is familiar to psychologists. It is the sociologist who is more likely to point out that the problems faced by Black children in New York City schools arise from the experience of being Black and interacting with the institutions of a White society, and not from inadequate parenting or deficient intellect.

▶**ethnocentrism** Being unable to conceptualize or imagine ideas, social beliefs, or the world from any viewpoint other than that of one's own particular culture or social group. The belief that one's own ethnic group, nation, religion, scout troop or football team is superior to all others.

▶**reductionism** An approach to understanding behaviour which focuses on one single level of explanation and ignores others. The opposite of holism.

Questions

1. Labov's data are qualitative and taken from a limited sample of interviews with children. What objections could you raise with this approach?

2. How would Labov defend his research strategy against these objections?

suggested answers → p. 497

part V

COGNITIVE PSYCHOLOGY

COGNITIVE psychology is about mental processes such as remembering, perceiving, understanding and producing language, solving problems, thinking and reasoning. It is an area of psychology which deals with abstract, invisible things which are not easy to pin down and define. Try asking yourself the question 'What is thought?' Then, when you have answered that, go onto the next question, which is 'Where is thought?' The slipperiness of the notions that cognitive psychology deals with make it a particularly difficult area to study!

One of the most influential books in the development of cognitive psychology was Ulric Neisser's *Cognitive Psychology* (1967), which helped to make the ideas more prominent. For Neisser, cognition is 'All the processes by which ... sensory input is transformed, reduced, elaborated, stored, recovered and used' (p. 4).

One of the central concerns of cognitive psychology is with the question of how information gets processed by the brain. It is not difficult to see why this is such an important question. The ability to act in ways which are recognizably human depends upon the ability to make sense of the world in which we live. Our contact with that world is via our senses: sight, hearing, smell, touch and taste. But the data that are picked up by our senses are raw, and most require processing and interpretation if they are to be useful to us. Our actions are at least partly based upon the processing and interpretation that goes on, so understanding these cognitive processes can help us understand what we do. The quantity and variety of work that explores these issues is huge and, like all sciences, this work ranges from the highly theoretical (see, for example, the following summaries of the papers by Craik and Lockhart, 1972, and Searle, 1980) to the directly applicable (see the summaries of Loftus and Palmer, 1974, and Baron-Cohen *et al*., 1997).

Within cognitive psychology can be found all the standard dialogues and debates which are encountered in psychology as a whole. For example, should we study human cognition in highly controlled laboratory conditions (like Ebbinghaus, 1913) or would it be better to aim for a higher level of ecological validity at the expense of precision and replicability, as in Bartlett's work? The summary of Bartlett (1932) provides descriptions of these competing approaches. Should we always try and study cognitive phenomena by

▶ **ecological validity** A way of assessing how valid a measure or test is (that is, whether it really measures what it is supposed to measure) which is concerned with whether the measure or test is really like its counterpart in the real, everyday world. In other words, whether it is truly realistic or not.

▶ **self-report** A number of popular research methods are based on self-report: for example, questionnaires, interviews, attitude scales and diary methods. These are methods which rely on research subjects' accounts of their own experiences and behaviour.

▶ **nature–nurture debates** Fairly sterile theoretical debates, popular in the 1950s, concerning whether a given psychological ability was inherited or whether it was learned through experience.

▶ **maturation** A pre-programmed growth process based on changes in underlying neural structures that are relatively unaffected by environmental conditions.

▶ **perception** The process by which the brain organizes and interprets sensory information.

▶ **memory** The capacity to retain and retrieve information.

making direct observations of people's performance on tasks, or is it acceptable to rely on self-reports of cognition?

And what about the nature–nurture controversy? How many of our cognitive skills do we learn through experience, and how many just unfold through maturation on the basis of inheritance? Gibson and Walk (1960) addressed this issue in the famous 'visual cliff' study. Finally, how much influence does culture have on our cognitive processes? Do all humans think and perceive in the same way, or are there differences across cultural divides? Deregowski's (1972) paper on picture perception tackles this important issue. One of the remarkable lessons from cognitive psychology is that nothing is as it seems. Our memories do not make accurate records of events (Loftus and Pickrell, 1995) and we sometimes don't see what is right in

front of our eyes (Simons and Chabris, 1999).

In this part, we have included some studies that look at the issues of perception, memory and mind. There are also a number of studies in other parts of this book that can be included under the broad heading of cognitive psychology, for example, the papers on social judgements in Chapter 2, and the papers on communication in Chapter 12. Other papers in this text include Samuel and Bryant's (1984) investigation of child thought, and Bryant *et al.*'s (1989) study of the development of reading skills. The cognitive approach is currently the most influential area of psychology, and though it starts from the core topics contained in this chapter it has far-reaching theoretical and practical implications.

▶ **memory** The capacity to retain and retrieve information.

WE take our memory for granted until it fails us. Then we experience all kinds of irritating phenomena, such as the feeling that the thing we want to recall is on the tip of our tongue but we cannot quite remember it. On other occasions our memory will surprise us and we will recall unusual pieces of information or personal events for no obvious reason. Sometimes our memory plays tricks on us and we remember things that never happened. For example, do you have any memories of events where you can see yourself doing something? If, like many other people, you have 'memories' like this, then it is obvious that they cannot be an accurate record of what you perceived at the time, because you could not have seen yourself. Your memory has made the event into a mental 'home movie' and then sold it to you as a record of the event.

The study of memory is as old as the discipline of psychology, dating at least as far back as the work of Ebbinghaus in the 1880s (see Ebbinghaus, 1913). Indeed Ebbinghaus' investigations of his own memory are the starting point for our summary of one of Bartlett's influential studies (Bartlett, 1932). Bartlett is notable for trying to study the characteristics of everyday remembering,

rather than the abstract properties of experimentally induced memories.

There are two main traditions in the study of memory:

- the study of everyday experience;
- the experimental study of mental mechanisms.

The work of Ebbinghaus probably marks the beginning of the experimental tradition, and the work of Bartlett is an important marker in the study of everyday experience. The most commonly researched of these in psychology is the experimental study of mental mechanisms. This might seem a little disappointing because the interesting bits are the phenomena of everyday life. In fact, the cognitive psychologist Ulrich Neisser suggested that a basic principle of memory research was: 'If X is an interesting or socially significant aspect of memory, then psychologists have hardly ever studied X' (1982, p. 4). Neisser goes on to make a more remarkable claim when he says:

> I think that 'memory' in general does not exist. (Neisser, 1982, p. 12)

This sounds ridiculous because it is obvious that we remember things and can recall them, but the issue is whether there is really a thing we can call 'memory'. There does not seem to be any one part of the brain that controls memories, so thinking of memory as a mechanism like a hard drive on your computer is probably not helpful. In fact it does not help us to explain the phenomena of everyday memory, as we will see in the following studies, because it is clear we do not store and recall exact records of events. Far from it, we construct our memories and in so doing we distort them and in some cases invent them.

Craik and Lockhart's (1972) exposition of their levels-of-processing framework for memory research is an example of a paper which addresses a theoretical problem, and which is principally of interest to cognitive psychologists engaged in the study of mental mechanisms. Having said that, their emphasis on the process of 'remembering', rather than on the structure of 'memory', resonates with Bartlett's earlier analyses. In their study, Craik and Lockhart refer to the multi-store model of memory, and one feature of this model is the focus for the summary of the paper by Sperling

(1960) in Chapter 16. This research looks at sensory memory and uses ingenious techniques to investigate how large this memory store is and how long the memories last.

Loftus and Palmer's (1974) analysis of the accuracy of eyewitness testimony illustrates how cognitive psychology can be put to work in addressing important, real-life questions. People put a lot of faith in evidence supplied by eyewitnesses, both in the context of the courtroom and in the context of everyday conversations about events. The faulty memories of some of Loftus and Palmer's subjects suggest that the testimony of eyewitnesses should perhaps be regarded more sceptically.

Thirty years after the original studies on memory distortion Elizabeth Loftus is still carrying out work in this field and still producing results that challenge our beliefs about memory. The final paper in this collection introduces one of the fiercest and most emotionally charged disputes in cognitive psychology. Who would have thought that data from cognitive psychology experiments could be used in multi-million dollar law suites?

▶ **levels-of-processing theory** The idea that what determines whether information is remembered, and for how long, is how deeply it is processed – that is, thought about and linked with other information.

▶ **multi-store model** Model of memory that proposes distinct memory stores, including long-term memory and short-term memory.

Remembering pictures

BARTLETT, F.C. (1932)

Remembering:
A Study in
Experimental and
Social Psychology.
Cambridge:
Cambridge
University Press.

Introduction

The earliest systematic work on the psychology of memory was carried out at the end of the nineteenth century by Ebbinghaus (see Ebbinghaus, 1913). He undertook a range of highly controlled experiments to discover the characteristics of human memory. To control for past knowledge he studied how well meaningless material could be remembered and re-learned. He used 'nonsense syllables', comprising consonant–vowel–consonant (CVC) three-letter sequences, such as WUT or GEF. These are easy to say and they sound like words but they do not have a recognized meaning. The studies were methodical, and provided a wide range of findings which had a major influence on the way memory research was conducted and the type of theories that were developed.

Bartlett criticized Ebbinghaus' work on the grounds that, in attempting to avoid the difficult problem of past knowledge by using nonsense material, it confined itself to a very artificial situation, and therefore lacked ecological validity. He also suggested that Ebbinghaus concentrated too closely on the material that was being remembered, and ignored other important features like the attitudes and prior experience of the subject. In contrast, Bartlett's book describes a series of studies into the memory of meaningful material like stories (most famously 'The war of the ghosts') and pictures.

Bartlett used two main methods in his studies. In one (the method of repeated reproduction), a single person is asked to keep remembering the same material over a period of time. The changes in the remembering are analysed to discover any systematic distortions. In the second method (the method of serial reproduction), the material is reproduced by the first subject. This reproduction is seen by the second subject who then makes their own reproduction. This new reproduction is seen by the next subject and so on, resulting in a 'chain' of remembering. When we pass on material in a spoken form in this way it is sometimes referred to as a Chinese whisper (after a children's game), and you will know from experience how distorted a message can become as it passes from one person to another.

▶ **memory** The capacity to retain and retrieve information.

▶ **ecological validity** A way of assessing how valid a measure or test is (that is, whether it really measures what it is supposed to measure) which is concerned with whether the measure or test is really like its counterpart in the real, everyday world. In other words, whether it is truly realistic or not.

▶ **repeated reproduction** A method used by Bartlett where the subject is asked to keep remembering the same event or drawing in order to investigate the systematic changes that people make in their memories.

The study

▶ **serial reproduction** A method of examining the accuracy of memory by asking people to reproduce what they recall of a story, on several successive occasions.

In his studies on serial reproduction, Bartlett used three types of material; (1) folk stories, (2) descriptive passages of prose, and (3) pictures. The folk stories were used because of the range of social information they carry and the unusual quality of many of them. The prose passages were used as a contrast to the stories. In this summary we will look at the picture material.

The pictures were shown to subjects who were then given something to do for around 15 to 30 minutes before being asked to reproduce the drawing. Simple, but ambiguous, pictures were used and as many as 20 reproductions were collected for one chain.

Transformation to conventional representations

Whenever the material was meant to represent a common object but contained some unfamiliar features, then these features were transformed during the course of the serial reproduction. In the drawings shown in Figure 13.1, all the characteristics of the original drawing which have any peculiarity are lost. The face is tilted upwards immediately, becomes oval and then round, acquires eyes, a nose and a mouth, and becomes a conventional representation of a face. The face continues to have some elaborate features up until the title change on Reproduction 7, when the elaboration declines and disappears.

Elaboration

There were two frequent types of elaboration. In the first type, as the whole figure was gradually being transformed, certain relatively disconnected material was elaborated into some characteristic that naturally belonged to the new setting. In the second type, some details were simply enhanced.

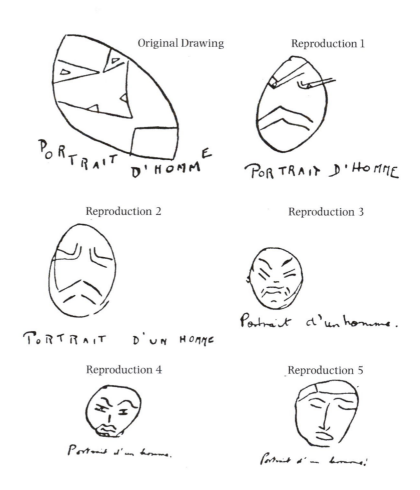

Figure 13.1 *Example of successive reproductions*

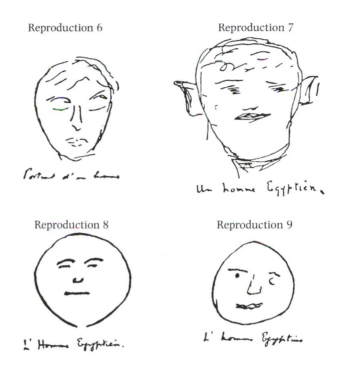

Reproduction 6

Reproduction 7

Portrait d'un homme

Un homme Égyptien.

Reproduction 8

Reproduction 9

L' Homme Égyptien.

L' homme Égyptien

Figure 13.1   *Continued*

Figure 13.2 is an example of the first type of elaboration. The drawing is a representation of the Egyptian 'mulak', a conventionalized reproduction of an owl, which may have been used as the model for our letter 'M'. The elaboration of certain features, for example the tail of the cat, can be seen to develop from the original sweep of the lines in the owl. However, by the tenth reproduction, the tail is actually sweeping in the other direction to the original drawing, and the cat has also acquired whiskers and a bow!

Simplification

Whenever there was a design which was not easily categorized (because it was odd or unfamiliar), there was a strong tendency to elaborate this into a recognizable form. Once in this form, the feature would then be simplified into a conventional example of this feature or form. If the chain continued, then elaboration developed from the new simplified drawing until it once again became ambiguous and started to simplify and change form again.

Naming

The verbal labels affected the reproductions of the drawings. One subject described their memorization of the mulak as follows:

I visualised throughout and gave names to the parts. I said to myself: 'a heart at the top, then a curve and a straight post down to a little foot at

Figure 13.2 *Example of successive reproductions*

the bottom. Between these two a letter W, and half a heart half-way up on the left hand side'. (p. 183)

This subject produced a drawing that followed this description but showed massive changes from the original picture.

Preservation of detached detail

When there was some detail that was detached from the main image and in a form that was representative (like decoration), then it tended to remain unchanged.

Discussion

▶ **schema** A mental framework or structure which encompasses memories, ideas, concepts and programmes for action which are pertinent to a particular topic.

Bartlett suggested that we base any learning on our existing schemas, which are ways of categorizing information in the world based on our past experience. When these conflict with what is being remembered, then distortions occur to make the material more in keeping with our world view, to make it fit into our existing schemas. Bartlett's argument is that learning and memory are active processes involving effort after meaning. The process of recall involves a constructive component, in that we use what we have retained, along with our existing schemas to re-create the original. The distortions, elaborations and simplifications that he observed in the serial reproduction of pictures support this perspective.

Bartlett's work was criticized as being too vague, and his predictions as being relatively un-testable. The following 40 years saw memory researchers concentrating on controlled laboratory studies using material of limited meaning. However, over the last two decades there has been a growing emphasis on meaningful material and how it is recalled in real-life situations.

Bartlett's studies on remembering make continued reference to the cultural context of material, and show an awareness that people with different experiences will interpret, memorize and recall the same material in very different ways. This was another feature that was ignored by psychologists for a number of years, and highlights the value of Bartlett's original studies.

suggested answers → P. 497

Questions

1. Identify some advantages of controlled laboratory studies of memory.

2. Identify some disadvantages of controlled laboratory studies of memory.

3. What are the main causes of distortion in memory according to Bartlett?

4. Try the method of repeated reproduction on yourself – find a picture in a book, and draw it from memory every day for two weeks. Only look at the previous day's drawings when doing each new one.

Models of memory

CRAIK, F.I.M. AND
LOCKHART, R.S. (1972)

Levels of
processing:
a framework
for memory
research.

*Journal of Verbal
Learning and
Verbal Behavior,
11, 671–84.*

▶ **multi-store model** Model
of memory that proposes
distinct memory stores,
including long-term memory
and short-term memory.

▶ **memory** The capacity
to retain and retrieve
information.

▶ **sensory buffer** Short-
acting memory store for the
sensory record of a stimulus.

▶ **forgetting** Loss of
information through
interference, decay,
displacement or a failure to
retrieve the information.

Introduction

Craik and Lockhart's theoretical paper set out to challenge the
widely accepted multi-store model of memory (see Atkinson
and Shiffrin, 1968), and to replace it with a new framework for
memory research centred on the concept of levels of processing. This summary of their paper gives a brief description of
the multi-store model, reviews Craik and Lockhart's objections
to it, and then examines their arguments in favour of the levels-of-
processing approach which they advocate.

The multi-store model

According to the multi-store model of memory, the three 'stores' which make
up memory (the sensory register, short-term memory, and long-term memory)
are differentiated one from another in terms of how much information they
can store, how long they can store it for, what format ('modality') they store
it in, if and how forgetting occurs, and also by their place in the sequence of
information processing that goes to make up memory.

The first store in the sequence is known as the sensory register. Incoming
information can enter this store without being attended to, and can be held (in
the case of visual information at least) for up to one second before it decays
spontaneously (see the following summary of the work by Sperling, 1960,
in Chapter 16). The information is probably stored in the same modality as
the input (Atkinson and Shiffrin, 1968); in other words, visual information
is stored visually, auditory information is stored acoustically and so forth.
This means that the information is relatively un-interpreted and is for a brief
moment a 'literal copy of [the] input' (Craik and Lockhart, 1972, p. 672). The
storage capacity of the sensory register is large, since a lot of information can
be taken in without ever being attended to.

The tiny fraction of the information in the sensory register which is attended
to then passes into the next store, known as short-term memory (STM). Craik
and Lockhart cite Peterson and Johnson (1971) who showed that information
in STM is stored in an acoustic format. STM traces have a duration of several
seconds: Peterson and Peterson (1959), for example, estimated the duration
to be 6–12 seconds, after which the memory trace decays. The most striking
characteristic of STM, however, is its limited capacity and the consequent ease
with which information held within it can be disrupted or displaced. Miller
(1956) estimated the total capacity of STM to be approximately seven chunks
of information, with a chunk being a unit of whatever material is being presented (letters, words, numbers, dates, phrases and so forth).

From STM the information passes into long-term memory (LTM), providing it has not been forgotten by decay or displacement. Long-term memory
may have a limitless capacity (can you imagine your long-term memory being
full?), and memory traces can last a lifetime. It is uncertain how forgetting

▶ semantic To do with meaning.

from LTM occurs, if indeed it does occur. There is general agreement that the information in LTM tends to be coded semantically. That is we store information in our LTM according to its meaning. Figure 13.3 shows the structure of the three-stage (multi-store) model.

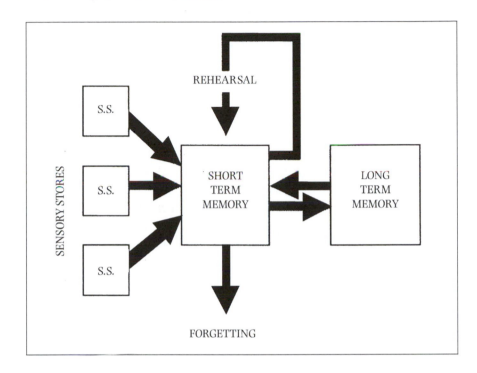

Figure 13.3 *Traditional multi-store model of short-term and long-term memory*

The problems with multi-store models

The core of Craik and Lockhart's objection to the multi-store model is that the characteristics which distinguish the stores from each other are poorly specified and appear to be too dependent on the research paradigms that have been used to investigate them. For example, the fragility of STM memories has been put down to limitations of capacity, but it is unclear whether this means storage capacity or processing capacity. That is, do we lose things from STM because bits of information get displaced by new bits of information, or is it because STM can only actively handle (process) small quantities of material at the same time? The psychologists who support the multi-store model have tended to favour the former (storage) interpretation, and dealt in 'numbers of chunks' that can be recalled from experimental tasks. Craik and Lockhart clearly favour the latter interpretation, as the phrase 'depth of processing' might indicate. They are also unhappy with the notion of a 'chunk' of information, for if STM really can deal with data at any level of abstraction (one moment dealing with seven physical features, the next moment coping with seven phrases), then it must be very flexible with regard to the format of data it can accept as input.

This latest point leads into another related objection, though before seeing what that objection is we need to take a step back temporarily. The whole rationale of the multi-store model rests on the stores being identifiably different in a number of respects. Of course all information has to be processed, and some stages of processing will come before other stages. So, as Craik and Lockhart point out, you can always put boxes round different stages in the sequence and call this stage 'the sensory register', this next stage STM, and this other stage LTM, but unless the different stages really are distinguishable one from another, above and beyond the simple observation that 'one comes before another', what is the point of having the boxes at all?

Now the objection that stems from this point is that gradually, through empirical work, the distinguishing features of the stages have been broken down. One example of this relates to how information is coded in each of the stores. Craik and Lockhart argue that originally the basis for discriminating between STM and LTM was established by Conrad (1964) and Baddeley (1966), who showed that coding in STM was primarily acoustic, and that coding in LTM was primarily semantic. However, STM has been shown to be able to accept other formats for information, including visual formats (the authors cite the work of Kroll *et al.*, 1970), and even semantic formats (they cite Shulman, 1970 and 1972, in support of this assertion). Indeed, if STM can work with chunks of information, such as meaningful phrases, then one would suspect that some semantic representation was being used. It is widely agreed that LTM works with semantically encoded information. So perhaps STM and LTM are not so different in this respect after all, in which case one major reason for naming them as separate stages is gone. On the basis of this, and other arguments, the authors propose that the multi-store model is not a useful model of memory.

The levels-of-processing framework

The levels-of-processing approach does away with the idea that memory is made up of a series of stores, and that information has to pass through each of these stores in turn (sequentially). According to the levels-of-processing framework, the initial analysis of incoming information is carried out in primary memory by a limited-capacity central processor. This processor can handle information very flexibly. The modality in which the information is handled is determined partly by the nature of the information itself, and partly by the purpose of remembering. In other words, if we are trying to remember the six figures in a telephone number for a few seconds while we dial, primary memory will handle the material in an acoustic or articulatory format (we will repeat the numbers to ourselves over and over again until we dial). If, on the other hand, we are listening to someone talk and trying to understand what they are saying, then the incoming data will surely be dealt with semantically. In fact primary memory, according to this theory, is virtually an attentional system. Craik and Lockhart's suggestion that some of the characteristics of memories are related to the function of those memories is a welcome one. The multi-store tradition dealt comparatively little with this issue, but one would surely expect that the nature of a memory will relate to the reason for attending to the to-be-remembered information in the first place.

The result of processing in primary memory is the memory trace. The key feature of the levels-of-processing approach is that the durability of the memory trace is affected by the depth at which the incoming information has been processed. Depth, in this context, has to do with the meaningfulness of the processing: the 'greater [the] degree of semantic or cognitive processing' (p. 675), the greater the depth. So if incoming information is processed semantically, it will tend to be remembered better (the resulting memory trace will be more persistent) than material that has just been processed according to, say, its physical features. A simple example might illustrate this point. If you listen to someone saying a sentence in your own language, you will be able to remember and repeat back what was said with relative ease, because you have been attending to the meaning of the words (deep processing). If on the other hand someone says the same sentence, but in a foreign language, you will have great difficulty in repeating what was said, because you will only have been able to attend to the sounds of the words (shallow processing of physical sound features). Notice that in this approach the capacity of primary memory is limited not in terms of storage (as in the multi-store model) but in terms of processing capacity. Information that is understandable and meaningful can be handled very efficiently by primary memory. But the same quantity of meaningless information, which can only be analysed in terms of its physical features, will be beyond its capabilities.

In support of their framework, Craik and Lockhart present a re-evaluation of existing data from empirical studies on incidental learning, selective attention, sensory storage, the serial position curve, repetition and rehearsal effects, and the distinction between STM and LTM. They show how the findings of these studies are compatible with their depth-of-processing approach. For example, in studies on incidental learning, subjects are asked to perform certain tasks on a set of experimental stimulus materials (a word list, for example). Tasks that have been used include crossing out all the vowels, copying down the words, rating words for pleasantness, finding rhymes for each word, estimating the frequency of the occurrence of the words in the English language. These are known as orienting tasks because they determine the way in which the subjects look at the material; in short they determine the way the material is processed. Once they have performed the required task, subjects are asked unexpectedly to recall the words they have been oriented towards. Subjects that performed a task which forced them to process the words semantically (estimating the pleasantness of the words, for example) are able to recall more words on average than subjects who performed tasks which forced them to process the words non-semantically (crossing out all the vowels, copying down the words, and so forth). In other words, the deeper the processing, the more durable the memory.

Conclusion

Craik and Lockhart summarize their basic position as follows:

▶ **incidental learning** Used in cognitive psychology to describe tasks in which subjects are asked to remember material that they did not expect to be asked to remember.

▶ **selective attention** The ability to direct our cognitive focus so that we pay attention to some stimuli and ignore or pay less attention to others.

▶ **serial position curve** A technique in memory research which looks at the effect of the position of a word in a list on the probability of it being recalled.

▶ **orienting task** This phrase is often used in connection with memory experiments. Orienting tasks are used in an attempt to get subjects to think about the stimulus materials in a certain way. In a word-list learning study, for example, some subjects might be oriented to think of the words in front of them as just collections of letters (perhaps by setting them the task of counting how many vowels there are) whilst other subjects are encouraged to think of the words in terms of their meanings (perhaps by getting them to fit the words together into sentences). Typically subjects' performance across orienting tasks is compared.

Specifically, we suggest that trace persistence is a function of depth of analysis, with deeper levels of analysis associated with more elaborate, longer lasting, and stronger traces. (p. 675)

In doing away with the various traditional memory stores they are not arguing anything particularly new or revolutionary. They rightly resist calling their approach a 'theory'. Instead they claim simply to have described 'a conceptual framework ... within which memory research might proceed' (p. 681). In this respect they have been successful, for their depth-of-processing framework has underpinned a large amount of research into memory processes. The quantity of work that an approach inspires is one indicator of its usefulness.

Questions

suggested answers ➜ p. 497

1. What are the three stores that make up memory within the multi-store model?

2. What are the most important ways in which the three stores are differentiated from each other?

3. What might be a suitable alternative word for depth (as in 'depth of processing')?

4. In an experiment with the following conditions, which condition would you expect to produce the best remembering for items on a word list? Rank order the conditions according to your expectations of subjects' performance on a recall task:

    – Condition (a): repeating the words over and over again;
    – Condition (b): thinking of bizarre visual images to go with each word;
    – Condition (c): putting the words into a sentence;
    – Condition (d): thinking of a rhyme for each word.

Eyewitness testimony

LOFTUS, E.F. AND PALMER, J.C. (1974)

Reconstruction of automobile destruction: an example of the interaction between language and memory.

Journal of Verbal Learning and Verbal Behavior, 13, 585–9.

Introduction

'I saw it with my own eyes, I can tell you exactly what happened.' This statement carries a lot of weight when we are trying to find out about an event. The evidence of eyewitnesses is a very important part of criminal trials, but is our memory as trustworthy as we believe it to be? The work of Bartlett (1932; see the first summary in this chapter) tells us that remembering is an inaccurate process that is distorted by expectations, values and cultural norms. So, can we really believe the evidence of our own eyes?

When we are describing an event, one of the possible causes of distortion might be the suggestions given to us by other people. In particular, they might suggest how we should remember the event through leading questions. A leading question is simply one that, either in its content or the way it is phrased, suggests to witnesses what answer is desired, or leads them to the desired answer. An example of a leading question in everyday conversation might be 'Do you like my new outfit?' This is not a request for serious evaluation of the cut, colour and style of the clothes, but a request for reassurance that we do not look stupid.

▶ **memory** The capacity to retain and retrieve information.

The first study

The 45 student subjects were shown seven film-clips of traffic accidents. The clips were short excerpts from safety films made for driver education. Following each clip, the students were asked to write an account of the accident they had just seen. They were also asked to answer some specific questions, the critical one of which was about the speed of the vehicles involved in the collision. There were five conditions in the study (each with nine subjects) and the independent variable was manipulated by means of the wording of the questions. The basic question was 'About how fast were the cars going when they ***** each other?' In each condition, a different word or phrase was used to fill in the blank. These words were; smashed, collided, bumped, hit, contacted. The results are shown in Table 13.1 and graphically in Figure 13.4. The data show that the phrasing of the question brought about a change in speed estimate.

▶ **independent variable** The conditions which an experimenter sets up, to cause an effect in an experiment. These vary systematically, so that the experimenter can draw conclusions about changes in outcomes.

Table 13.1 *Speed estimates used for the verbs used in the estimation of speed question*

Verb	Mean estimate of speed (mph)
Smashed	40.8
Collided	39.3
Bumped	38.1
Hit	34.0
Contacted	31.8

Source: Loftus and Palmer (1974).

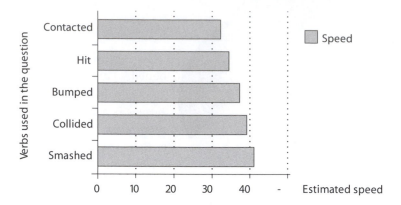

Figure 13.4   *Speed estimates for the verbs used in the witness question*

The second study

A similar procedure was used. The 150 student subjects saw a short (one minute) film which contained a four-second scene of a multiple car accident, and were then questioned about it. Fifty of the subjects were asked 'How fast were the cars going when they hit each other?'; 50 of the subjects were asked 'How fast were the cars going when they smashed into each other?'; and 50 of the subjects were not interrogated about the speed of the vehicles.

One week later, the subjects returned and, without viewing the film again, they answered a series of questions about the accident. The critical question was 'Did you see any broken glass?', which was part of a longer series of questions and was placed in a random position on each subject's question paper. There was, in fact, no broken glass in the film. Table 13.2 shows the responses of the students to this question, with the data shown graphically in Figure 13.5. These results show a significant effect of the verb in the question on the mis-perception of glass in the film.

Table 13.2   *Response to the question 'Did you see any broken glass?'*

	Verb condition		
Response	Smashed	Hit	Control
Yes	16	7	6
No	34	43	44

Source: Loftus and Palmer (1974).

Discussion

▶**demand characteristics** Those aspects of a psychological study (or other artificial situation) which exert an implicit pressure on people to act in ways that are expected of them.

There are two possible interpretations of the findings from Study 1. First, they could be due to a distortion in the memory of the subject created by the verbal label which had been used to characterize the intensity of the crash. Second, they could be due to response-bias factors, in which case the subject is not sure of the exact speed and adjusts his or her estimate to fit in with the expectations of the questioner (see Orne, 1962, on demand characteristics; Chapter 18 of this volume).

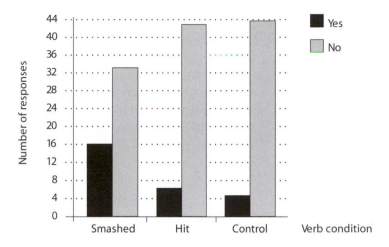

Figure 13.5 *Response to the question 'Did you see any broken glass?'*

In trying to account for the findings of the second study, Loftus and Palmer suggest that two kinds of information go into a person's memory of a complex event. The first is the information obtained from perceiving the event, and the second is the other information supplied to us after the event. In this case the 'other' information came from the speed question which had been posed to 100 of the subjects.

One of the difficulties with the finding that our memories are so susceptible to influence is that it contradicts our feeling that we are capable of recalling exact details of events. Neisser (1981) reported the case of John Dean, who gave eyewitness testimony at the Watergate hearings in the USA which eventually resulted in the resignation of President Nixon in 1974. Dean was reported to have an extremely accurate memory. He recounted conversations in very precise detail, and testified on oath that these were exactly what he had heard. There was no doubt that he, and others who worked with him, were convinced that he had an eidetic memory for detail.

Some time after Dean gave evidence, it was discovered that the President had been secretly taping all conversations in the White House. When these tapes were made public it was possible to compare Dean's testimony with an accurate record of what had been said. Interestingly, Dean's memory was found to be inaccurate in almost every detail, although his memory for the meaning of what had occurred in the conversation (the gist of it) was completely accurate. He had remembered what had been said, not by remembering the exact words which had been used, but by remembering what had really been meant. But he had no idea that his memories were not exactly the same as a tape-recording.

Although the laboratory studies on eyewitness testimony offer some clues to the way we remember events, there are some substantial differences between the content of the studies and the everyday activity of remembering. For example, when the subjects were giving their estimates of speed, they did not have any personal involvement in the judgement and had not taken any

▶ **eidetic memory**
'Photographic' memory – visual or acoustic memory which is so accurate as to be almost like a factual record.

part in the event. When we are telling a story about an event we have witnessed in everyday life, we often have some involvement in the people or the action, and we are often explaining our own behaviour as part of the action.

More recent experiments into the testimony of eyewitnesses have found that people can make errors when asked to identify people who might have taken part in a crime. In one experimental study participants were shown a low-quality surveillance video of a man and were told that he had shot a security guard. Then they were presented with five mug shots and asked to identify the criminal. It was an impossible task, because none of the five mug shots really matched the man in the video. Despite this, every one of the 350 participants picked out one of the mug shots as the man they had seen (Wells and Bradfield, 1998).

This sort of thing can and does happen in the real world. Perhaps witnesses who do not immediately recognize the perpetrator in a police line-up compare the five or six faces to their memory of the event and then choose the one that is closest. William Gregory went to prison in the USA for rape after being identified by two women. After eight years inside, the new science of DNA testing was able to show that he could not have committed the crimes and he was released (Fox News, 2006). Both of the women who identified Gregory insisted that he was their attacker after his release. The error rate of eyewitness identification is estimated to be only 5 in 1000 (Cutler and Penrod, 1995) but that is no consolation if you are one of the five.

Questions

1. What controls were used in this study?

2. What are the differences between laboratory studies of eyewitness testimony and the behaviour of eyewitnesses in everyday life?

3. List as many factors as you can that might influence your memory of an event.

4. What are the problems with using students in this study? Do you think there would have been different results with a different subject group?

suggested answers
→ p. 498

False or recovered memories?

LOFTUS, E.F. AND PICKRELL, J.E. (1995)

The formation of false memories.

Psychiatric Annals, 25, 720–5:

▶ **memory** The capacity to retain and retrieve information.

Introduction

You would not expect a debate about memory to be particularly controversial or heated, but the following one is. And it starts from a seemingly tame question: '*If you have a strong memory of an event can you be sure it actually happened?*' The simple and surprising answer to this question is 'no' and this has been recognized in psychology for a long time. For example Jean Piaget recalled an event from his childhood that he later discovered had not taken place. He wrote:

... one of my first memories would date, if it were true, from my second year. I can still see, most clearly, the following scene, in which I believed until I was about 15. I was sitting in my pram, which my nurse was pushing in the Champs Elysees, when a man tried to kidnap me. I was held in by the strap fastened around me while my nurse bravely tried to stand between me and the thief. She received various scratches, and I can still see vaguely those on her face. Then a crowd gathered, a policeman with a short cloak and a white baton came up, and the man took to his heels. I can still see the whole scene, and can even place it near the tube station. When I was about 15, my parents received a letter from my former nurse saying she had been converted to the Salvation Army. She wanted to confess her past faults, and in particular return the watch she had been given as a reward on this occasion. She had made up the whole story, faking the scratches. I, therefore, must have heard, as a child, the account of this story, which my parents believed, and projected it into the past in the form of a visual memory. (Piaget, 1962, cited in Loftus and Ketcham, 1994, pp. 76–7)

This is a remarkable story but it is not unique. It does not take much reflection on our own memories to realize that some of them are either elaborated or false. For example, you might have some memories of childhood events where you can see yourself and see what you did. At the time of the event you clearly could not see yourself. In your recollection of the event you have created a scene, a bit like a film, that puts you in the middle. It is not an accurate record of what you experienced at the time. Rather it is a reconstruction of the event, which at the very least includes a little bit of imagination.

The reason this issue has become so controversial in the last 20 years is because of the importance put onto memories of childhood in cases of child abuse. If a child is abused and is unable to report this until they are an adult then these memories can help to deal with a terrible wrong. If on the other hand, these memories are distortions or fabrications then a terrible wrong can be created. But why would anyone fabricate stories of child abuse?

The controversy comes from the use of imagination therapy, guided imagery and hypnosis with adults. These are therapeutic strategies for helping people to relive past events. But the techniques may involve suggestion, and the question that has been raised is whether the stories told by the patients in these types of therapy come from their memories or from the promptings of the therapists.

Elizabeth Loftus has been very prominent in challenging the stories that are told under these techniques and as a result has become a figure of great controversy. Recently, however, it is fair to say that the balance of opinion has swung behind her. Loftus (1997) cites the case of Nadean Cool who went for therapy in 1986 and during that therapy became convinced that she had repressed memories of being in a satanic cult, of being raped or having sex with animals, of being forced to eat babies and watch the murder of her 8-year-old friend. She came to believe that she had 120 different personalities, including children, angels and even a duck. Cool finally realized that the 'memories' were of events that could never have happened and she won a settlement against the therapist for $2.4 million. In another case a young woman came to 'remember' that her clergyman father had regularly raped her, sometimes while her mother had held her down. She also remembered being pregnant twice and being forced to abort herself. Later medical examination revealed that she was still a virgin and had never been pregnant. She also received a settlement of over $1 million against the therapist.

Loftus' work on memory (described in the previous summary) had already shown that our memories of events can be easily distorted. False information can be easily added into someone's recollection of an event. But is it possible to go further and implant memories of whole events that have never happened? Loftus set out to investigate this in a number of studies, one of which we summarize here.

The study

This is a small-scale study that investigates the possibility that false memories can be planted. The researchers recruited 24 participants (21 female, 3 male) with an age range between 18 and 53. They were recruited along with a family member who would be aware of the participant's early life. The second person was most commonly a parent or sibling and they were interviewed to discover three stories of events from the participant's childhood. They were also asked to provide information about a plausible shopping trip to a mall or department store and to confirm that the participant had not been lost during such a trip.

The participants were told they were taking part in a study of 'the kinds of things you may be able to remember from your childhood' (p. 721). They were mailed a five-page booklet that contained four short stories of events from their childhood. They were told that the stories had been provided by a relative. Three of the stories had, in fact, been provided by the relative but the fourth had been invented by the researchers. The false story was different for each participant but all contained the following elements: (a) lost for an extended period, (b) crying, (c) lost in a mall (shopping centre) or a department store at around the age of 5, (d) found by an elderly woman, (e) reunited with family.

The participant was asked to read the booklet with the stories and write what, if anything, they remembered of the events. After they returned the booklet they were interviewed within two weeks and again within a further two-week period. At the end of the second interview they were debriefed about the nature of the study and the deception that had taken place. They were then asked to guess which one of the stories was false.

Results

The 24 participants reviewed a total of 72 true stories and 24 false ones. They remembered at least part of 49 (68 per cent) of the true stories and this recall rate held constant through the two interviews. They also 'remembered' 7 (29 per cent) of the false stories, though in interview one of the participants changed her position and said she did not remember it. This left 6 (25 per cent) who judged the false event to be true and were able to provide some details of this 'event'.

The false event was described in less detail than the true events and the participants used fewer words on average (138 for the true story and 49.9 for the false one). At the debriefing 19 of the 24 participants correctly chose the 'lost in the mall' memory as the false story, but five incorrectly chose one of the other events.

Discussion

▶**false memory** Memory of an event that did not happen or a distortion of an event that did occur.

There have been many objections to this study and if it was the only piece of work on false memory then we would not be confident enough to make any generalizations about the phenomenon. There are, however, a range of other studies that confirm that memories can be created in this way.

One predictable comment about the study is that many people have actually been lost in their lives and the participants might have confused this experience with the false story. Loftus and Pickrell respond to this by pointing out that the participants were not asked to remember *any* event of being lost but a very *specific* experience on a shopping trip. Furthermore, the effect has also been shown to occur with memories for more unusual events such as childhood hospitalization or accidentally spilling a punch bowl at a wedding (Hyman *et al.*, 1995).

A strong attack on the ethics of the study was made by Crook and Dean (1999), who argued that a range of ethical guidelines had been broken by the researchers. It is important to say, however, that the study had been through the ethics committee of Washington State University. Perhaps more damning is the claim (also by Crook and Dean) that the results were exaggerated and misrepresented by Loftus and colleagues. This is harder to ignore because the study is relatively small-scale and a lot has been made of it. It is certainly the case that the study has nothing to say about how often and in what circumstances false memories can occur. It simply shows that it is possible to induce them in an experimental setting.

The work, however, has been supported by subsequent studies with much larger samples of participants, such as the work by Bernstein *et al.* (2005) on implanting memories of childhood food experiences. In another study by the authors, participants were told the research was on advertising and were asked to read advertisements for Disneyland. Half of the ads provided general information about the theme park and half specifically mentioned Bugs Bunny. The trick here is that Bugs Bunny does not live at Disneyland and the wascally wabbit (a Warner Brothers character) would be shown the door if he turned up. Despite this, a third of the participants who saw the Bugs Bunny advertisement 'remembered' that the events in the advertisement had actually happened to them. Many even expanded on the false memory, linking Bugs to Disneyland experiences not described in the advertisement. It appears that implanting false memories is a robust phenomenon.

Loftus' work has been judged by her peers to be outstanding and in 2003 she received the Award for Distinguished Scientific Applications of Psychology by the American Psychological Association, which is just one of numerous awards and honorary degrees she has received. She was named as one of the top 100 psychologists of the twentieth century in the *Review of General Psychology* and was the top-rated woman.

The false memory work remains important and disturbing. If we cannot trust our memories then how can we be sure about what has happened to us? Loftus and Pickrell comment that research on memory distortion has clearly shown that memories can be altered by suggestion. In fact we can come to 'remember' events that never occurred and in some cases never could have occurred. The research does not, however, give us the key to distinguish between real and false memories. Neither, it is important to add, does it deny the reality of child abuse, nor of adult recollections of child abuse. It just shows that these matters are complex. If true memories are judged to be false we risk denying a person's true experience; if false memories are judged to be true we risk involving other people in the sort of story that was constructed by Nadean Cool and her therapist. It's a tough call.

suggested answers ➔ p. 498

Questions

1. What ethical guidelines are particularly relevant to a study of this sort?

2. Why is this study so controversial?

3. Reflect on your childhood memories and see whether you can spot some parts of them that you have elaborated or even invented.

chapter **14**

PERCEPTION

▶ **perception** The process
by which the brain organizes
and interprets sensory
information.

▶ **cognition** Mental
processes. 'All the processes
by which ... sensory input
is transformed, reduced,
elaborated, stored, recovered
and used' (Neisser, 1967,
p. 4).

▶ **culture** The concept
of culture is difficult to
define though it refers to
the characteristic beliefs,
behaviours and sense of
identity that we share with a
group of people. Hofstede
(1980) identified four basic
dimensions which can be
used to compare them;
power-distance; *uncertainty-
avoidance, individualism,
masculinity–femininity.*

PERCEPTION has to do with the
taking in and making sense of the vast
array of sensory information that we
experience. Perception should not be
confused with sensation. Sensation
refers to the raw physical data which
impinge upon our senses. Perception
refers to the processes that occur in the
mind which convert these sensations
into a representation of the world
that we can make sense of. This is an
important issue to bear in mind because
perceptions are not, and should not be
thought of as, direct internal copies of
the outside world. Any given perception
is, in fact, a miraculous feat of cognition,
but one that happens so invisibly to us
that we do not appreciate how much
cognitive effort, how much internal
work and processing is really involved.
For example, consider Deregowski's
(1972) work on the three-dimensional
perception of pictures, summarized in
this chapter. People of Western cultures
tend to see pictures in three dimensions.
But of course pictures are really two-
dimensional representations of three-
dimensional scenes and objects. An extra
dimension is reconstructed by means of
internal cognitive processes.

One of the debates in the study of
perception is over the importance of

top-down or bottom-up explanations. A
bottom-up explanation is one that looks
at the sensations we obtain from the
environment and examines how we use
these to create our perceptions. Top-
down explanations look at the various
higher mental processes that affect the
way we perceive things. For example,
our expectations have an effect on what
we perceive, as shown in Figure 14.1. If
the figure is read from side to side then
the middle item appears to be the letter
'B', but if it is read from top to bottom it
appears to be the number '13'.

Figure 14.1 *The effect of context on the
perception of a simple shape*

So, which is it? It is neither and it is both,
and the interpretation depends on the
expectations we have of the figure as
well as its simple shape.

One aspect of perception that has
received considerable attention is the
question of how people use perceptual
cues to navigate themselves around the
complex 3-D environments in which they

live. One type of cue that is important in this respect is the sort that gives information about depth. These are the that help people to judge distances in three-dimensional arrays, and (hopefully) stop them from doing things like walking off cliff tops. Gibson and Walk's (1960) classic study of cognitive development examines the use of depth cues in the perceptual worlds of young human infants, and in some new born animals.

Another important perceptual skill is the ability to recognize people. Much work has been done on this topic in relation to the perceptual processes that underpin face recognition. However, in this book we look at a study that takes a slightly different approach, and which considers the cues that people use to identify others through their movements. In this study Kozlowski and Cutting (1977) were able to show that only minimal perceptual information is needed to identify a moving thing as a person.

Inventiveness of method is one distinctive feature of the psychological literature on perception. Perception comprises invisible, psychological processes, that cannot be directly observed, so psychologists have had to develop intriguing techniques that enable them to make inferences about these processes. One of these techniques, 'eye-tracking', is illustrated in the study by Carroll et al. (1992).

Walking off a cliff

GIBSON, E.J. AND
WALK, R.D. **(1960)**

The 'visual
cliff'.

Scientific
American,
202, 64–71.

Introduction

What does a newborn baby see when it first opens its eyes? This is a question which has puzzled philosophers and psychologists for many years, though unfortunately it is impossible to provide a full answer. The question is significant because it bears on the nature–nurture debate within the field of visual perception. Finding an answer might allow us to understand which of our perceptual abilities are inborn, and which abilities we have to learn.

There are a number of ways of investigating the nature–nurture question, though all of the methods produce evidence that is open to more than one interpretation. One of the methods is to investigate neonates and try to assess their abilities. Since neonates have had comparatively little opportunity for learning, it is reasonable to suggest that any abilities they have are inborn (see Condon and Sander, 1974, Chapter 12 of this volume). However, this method presents a few problems since neonates, and especially human babies, cannot do a lot. Also, just because a baby does not respond to certain visual stimuli does not mean that it does not see them or understand them. It might mean that it is unable to respond, or not in a suitable state to respond (the baby might be crying, or fretful, or nearly asleep).

One solution to this problem is to work with older babies who are better able to respond. This is the solution that Gibson and Walk chose in studying a sample of babies who could already crawl. The down side of this strategy is that babies are learning all the time, so data from these babies cannot contribute directly to the nature–nurture debate. But they do contribute to knowledge and understanding about the development of perceptual abilities, and the more we understand about these things, the more we are able to make sensible judgments about their origins. Furthermore Gibson and Walk also set about studying the behaviour of animal neonates which were only 24 hours old, and so some careful propositions about nature and nurture with regard to principles of perception can indeed be put forward.

A notable feature of this study is the use of an ingenious piece of apparatus. The 'visual cliff' which Gibson and Walk invented is made up of a thick piece of glass placed over a wooden box. Under the glass is a change of levels, as shown in Figure 14.2. The baby is placed in the middle of the glass, and its mother tries to get it to crawl either over the 'shallow' end of the apparatus or over the 'deep' end. If babies crawl over the shallow end but refuse to crawl over the deep end, then this suggests that they are able to perceive depth. If they crawl over the deep end, then either they have no depth perception, or they have rumbled the experimental apparatus, or they simply don't care any more.

The study

Gibson and Walk tested 36 infants ranging in age from 6 months to 14 months. They also tested a variety of animal neonates including lambs, chicks, rats, kittens and turtles.

▶ **nature–nurture debates**
Fairly sterile theoretical debates, popular in the 1950s, concerning whether a given psychological ability was inherited or whether it was learned through experience.

▶ **perception** The process by which the brain organizes and interprets sensory information.

▶ **neonates** New-born animals.

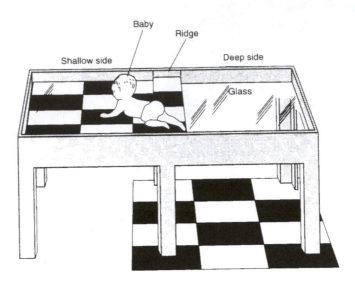

Figure 14.2 *The 'visual cliff'*

Children

Of the 36 children, nine stayed where they were and did not crawl in either direction. All of the 27 crawlers moved onto the shallow side at least once, and only three crawled over the deep side. Many of the infants crawled away from mother when she tried to encourage them to crawl over the deep side, and others stayed in the middle and cried. Some of the children peered through the glass and then backed away. Others patted the glass, yet despite this tactile reassurance still did not cross the 'cliff'. This suggests that babies that can crawl can also perceive depth.

Animals

Chicks tested at 24 hours after birth never made a mistake and always hopped onto the shallow side. Lambs and kids tested at 24 hours after birth always chose to go onto the shallow side. Rats went over the deep side as often as the shallow side. However, rats tend to use tactile cues when moving around (a common feature of nocturnal animals), and if the glass was lowered so that it was further away than the length of the rats' whiskers, then the rats used their visual sense and chose the shallow side 95 per cent of the time. Turtles chose the shallow side only 76 per cent of the time and chose the deep side 24 per cent of the time. These creatures, however, are aquatic and so have much less reason to fear depth. These results suggest that animals are able to discriminate depth as soon as they are able to move around, and this has obvious survival value.

Perception of depth is aided by a number of different 'depth cues' (pieces of information in the two-dimensional image that suggest depth). Gibson and

Walk continued their studies to look at two of these depth cues: pattern density and motion parallax.

Pattern density

▶ **pattern density** A visual depth cue. If you move away from a pattern such as a check, then the elements of the pattern get smaller as you move away and the pattern appears to get more dense.

If you move away from a pattern such as a check, then the elements of the pattern get smaller as you move away and the pattern appears to get more dense. Gibson and Walk put two different patterns either side of the middle section of the apparatus, but at the same depth. The only difference was the type of pattern. One pattern was a small check and the other pattern was a large check. If pattern density is an important cue then the animals will choose the large check side because the narrow check suggests depth. They found that rats chose the large check, but one-day-old chicks showed no preference. This suggests that, for some animals at least, this cue requires some learning.

Motion parallax

▶ **motion parallax** A visual depth cue. Objects and surfaces which are nearer to the viewer move more quickly within the field of vision than do objects and surfaces which are further away. Such differences in the relative movement of things within the visual field facilitate judgements of distance.

As the observer moves, nearer objects appear to move faster. A good example of this is the view from a moving train where telegraph poles at the side of the train track appear to move much faster than the trees in the distance. The relative speed of the objects gives us a clue as to how far away they are. Gibson and Walk investigated this cue by changing the pattern on the deep side so that it would produce the same image as the pattern on the shallow side. They did this by making the check bigger and more spaced out. Rats and chicks both continued to avoid the deep side, which suggests that they used the cue of motion parallax from a very early age.

Discussion

At first glance, the study suggests that some animals are born with the ability to perceive depth. However, the apparatus only allows the subjects to be tested after they start to move, and they might have already had some experiences that encouraged the learning of this skill. The most we can say about humans from this study is that babies as young as 6 months can perceive depth. In the end, then, this study leaves the question of whether this ability is inborn or learned unanswered.

Nevertheless, the visual cliff has provided interesting insights into factors which affect depth perception. Later work showed another important ingredient in the way children make sense of their perceptual world. Sorce *et al.* (1985) put 1-year-old infants on a visual cliff and got their mothers to wait at the other side. The mother was asked either to keep an expression of fear on her face, or to keep a happy and interested expression. The infants who saw the fearful face did not crawl across, but the infants who saw the happy face looked down to check the cliff again and then crawled over. If, however, the babies were put on a flat plane with no visual cliff, they crawled over without checking with mother. In this study, then, the babies used social information to back up their perception of the environment.

It is worth noting the practical and ethical problems with the study; in particular the failure of 25 per cent of the babies to respond at all, and the number of babies who appeared to become very distressed at the sight of their mother enticing them over a cliff.

suggested answers → P. 499

Questions

1. What are depth cues? And how many can you identify?

2. Give one piece of evidence from the study that suggests that some aspects of depth perception are innate.

3. Which pieces of evidence from the study suggest that some aspects of depth perception are learned?

4. What is the nature–nurture debate?

5. Why do psychologists explore the nature–nurture debate?

Why did the antelope cross the road?

DEREGOWSKI, J.B. (1972)

Pictorial perception and culture.

Scientific American, 227, 82–8.

Introduction

This is a review article which tries to answer the question 'do pictures offer us a lingua franca for intercultural communication?' (p. 82). In other words, are pictures seen and understood in the same way in different cultures? Are pictures a universal means of communication which transcend culture and language? The answer provided by Deregowski is 'no!', and is based on empirical work which dates back to the studies of Hudson (1960).

Hudson (1960) had noted difficulties among South African Bantu workers in interpreting depth cues in pictures. Such cues are important features of two-dimensional representations (pictures) of a three-dimensional world, for they convey information about the spatial relationships among the objects in the picture. A person using depth cues will extract a completely different meaning from a picture than will a person who is not using such cues.

On the basis of his observations, Hudson constructed a test of three-dimensional picture perception which was used in many parts of Africa with subjects from different tribal and linguistic groups. The test comprised several pictures which contained within them various combinations of three depth cues: familiar size, overlap and perspective. Familiar size refers to the cue whereby objects which are further away in the picture are drawn smaller than objects of the same size which are closer. The overlap cue is simply the effect of a nearer object obscuring parts of a more distant object. Perspective is given by the convergence of lines depicting edges which are parallel in the real world, but which appear to come together as they move into the distance. The classic example of this is the way that we draw a road or a railway line as it disappears into the distance.

The pictures were drawings of various combinations of the following elements: an antelope, an elephant, a person, a tree, a road, some hills and a flying bird. An example is given in Figure 14.3. The test involved showing the pictures to subjects and asking questions such as 'What do you see?', 'What is the man doing?', and 'Which is nearer, the antelope or the elephant?' The questions were asked in the subject's native language. Correct responses to the questions indicated that the person was interpreting the depth cues as intended, and resulted in them being classified as a three-dimensional perceiver. Incorrect responses were taken to indicate that the subject was seeing the picture in two dimensions.

Deregowski summarizes Hudson's findings as follows:

> The results from African tribal subjects were unequivocal: both children and adults found it difficult to perceive depth in the pictorial material.

▶ **culture** The concept of culture is difficult to define though it refers to the characteristic beliefs, behaviours and sense of identity that we share with a group of people.

▶ **perception** The process by which the brain organizes and interprets sensory information.

The difficulty varied in extent but appeared to persist through most educational and social levels. (pp. 84–5)

This summary is slightly at odds with Hudson's original data which show that the samples of schoolchildren that were tested showed much higher rates of three-dimensional perception than the adult samples. Some samples of adult subjects (57 illiterate Black mine labourers, for example) contained no three-dimensional perceivers (Hudson, 1960).

Further evidence that some subjects really were perceiving the picture in two dimensions was provided by a number of follow-up studies. One of

Figure 14.3 *Pictorial depth perception*
Pictorial depth perception is tested by showing subjects a picture such as the above illustration. A correct interpretation is that the hunter is trying to spear the antelope, which is nearer to him than the elephant. An incorrect interpretation is that the elephant is nearer and is about to be speared. The picture contains two depth cues: overlapping objects and known size of objects. The bottom illustration depicts the man, elephant and antelope in true size ratios when all are the same distance from the observer.

Source: Deregowski (1972).

these involved Zambian schoolchildren who had previously been labelled by Hudson's test as either two- or three-dimensional perceivers. Their task was to copy two figures. One of the figures was a straightforward trident shape. The other was the familiar trident illusion figure, in which the three prongs seem to merge into only two prongs at the handle (see Figure 14.4). Efforts to see this figure as a three-dimensional object cause perceptual confusion. The subjects had to lift a flap to see each figure, and could only draw when the flap was put down again and the figure was obscured from view. Those children who had been labelled as three-dimensional perceivers found the trident illusion figure harder to replicate and spent more time looking at it than they did at the ordinary trident. Two-dimensional perceivers spent the same amount of time looking at each of the figures.

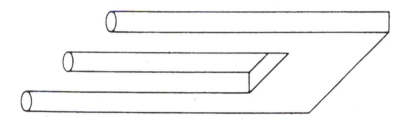

Figure 14.4 *Ambiguous trident*
The trident is confusing to observers who attempt to see it as a three-dimensional object. Two-dimensional perceivers see the pattern as being flat and are not confused.

Source: Deregowski (1972).

▶ **cross-cultural studies**
Studies which examine psychological phenomena in people from more than one cultural background.

Deregowski discusses other cross-cultural differences in picture perception. He notes, for example, the fairly consistent preference among African children and adults for split-type drawings over perspective-type drawings. Split-type drawings (see Figure 14.5) show all the important features of an object which could not normally be seen all at once from the same perspective. Perspective drawings give just one view of an object, with features that cannot be seen from that perspective not represented in the picture. He notes that in some cultures split drawing has been developed 'to a high artistic level' (p. 88), whereas in other cultures the perspective style is more common. The evidence that he draws on from art historians, anthropologists, and from the empirical work leads him to the conclusion that pictures are not a universal medium of communication, since they are perceived and produced in different ways by people of different cultures.

Discussion and evaluation

There is not enough cross-cultural work in psychology. For too long European and US researchers have conducted most of their empirical work in Europe and the USA, assuming that general principles of human behaviour and experience can be derived from such work. History and culture play such an important role in who and what we are that findings about people at one time

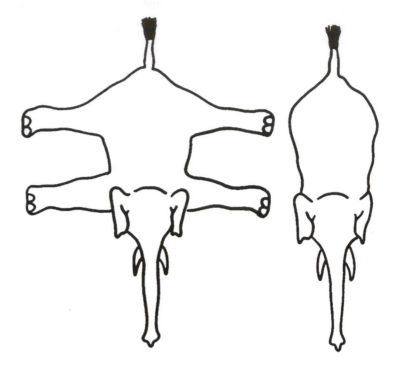

Figure 14.5 *Elephant drawing: split-view and top-view perspective*
The split-elephant drawing (left) was generally preferred by African children and adults to
the top-view perspective drawing (right). One person, however, did not like the split drawing
because he thought the elephant was jumping around in a dangerous manner.

Source: Deregowski (1972).

and in one place are unlikely to generalize very well to other people at other
times and in other places. The worrying side effect of this is that the longer
the literature of psychology remains so dominated by the perspectives of such
a small range of cultures, the more embedded becomes the notion that these
cultures are the norm, the yardstick against whom everyone else should be
compared. Cross-cultural psychology, whilst not the answer to the bigger
political issue of 'Whose psychology is it anyway?', at least keeps the important
issue of cultural diversity on the academic agenda.

As a piece of cross-cultural psychology, Deregowski's paper leaves one with
mixed feelings. On the one hand, the effort to address the question of cultural
differences in picture perception is worthy and interesting. As the author
points out in his opening paragraph:

> These differences merit investigation not only because improvement in
> communication may be achieved by a fuller understanding of them but
> also because they may provide us with better insights into the nature of
> human perceptual mechanisms. (p. 82)

On the other hand, there is the nagging feeling that somehow the Western interpretation and perceptual handling of pictures is implicitly privileged by the author. He does acknowledge the 'high artistic level' of split-style drawings, for example, but also suggests that children of all cultures produce this style of drawing at a certain stage of development. Is there an implication here that split-style drawing may represent a developmental stage of a culture, and that for the purposes of greater efficiency Western Cultures have grown out of this stage and into the more 'mature' perspective-style stage? Are we to infer that three-dimensional perception of drawings is more advanced than two-dimensional perception, rather than simply being a different interpretation of abstract symbols and conventional depth cues? This feeling of discomfort with the article is reinforced right from the start with some quotations from missionaries working in Africa at the turn of the twentieth century. For example:

> When all the people were quickly seated, the first picture flashed on the sheet was that of an elephant. The wildest excitement immediately prevailed, many of the people jumping up and shouting, fearing the beast must be alive, while those nearest to the sheet sprang up and fled. The chief himself crept stealthily forward and peeped behind the sheet to see if the animal had a body, and when he discovered that the animal's body was only the thickness of the sheet, a great roar broke the stillness of the night. (attributed to Mrs Donald Fraser, and cited by Deregowski, 1972, p. 82)

Whether this anecdote constitutes qualitative anthropological data, or whether it should be regarded as straight out of the dominant discourse of British colonialism is perhaps a matter for debate.

Questions

suggested answers → p. 499

1. In the trident test, children who had been labelled as three-dimensional perceivers found the trident illusion figure harder to replicate and spent more time looking at it than they did at the ordinary trident. Why does this suggest that they were, indeed, perceiving the figure in three-dimensions? Equally, children labelled as two-dimensional perceivers spent an equal amount of time looking at the two figures and did not find one figure harder to replicate than the other. Why does this indicate that these children were, in fact, perceiving in two dimensions?

2. What does ethnocentrism mean?

3. Why should we regard ethnocentrism as a problem in psychology?

Walk like a man ...

KOZLOWSKI, L.T. AND CUTTING, J.E. (1977)

Recognizing the sex of a walker from a dynamic point-light display.

Perception and Psychophysics, 21, 575–80.

Introduction

Recognizing people appears to be a very complex activity, even though we are able to do it with relatively little effort. We look at their clothes and their expression and their hairstyle, and a hundred and one other things to build up a picture of someone. The question is, however, do we need all this information? Can we recognize people, or some feature of a person, from a few very basic visual cues? The simple answer is 'yes'. Kozlowski and Cutting's (1977) investigation shows that we can recognize the sex of a person, just from the movement of points of light attached to their body.

Kozlowski and Cutting were building on research which showed that when lights are attached to various joints of a moving person, and the immediate environment is so dark that the person's body itself cannot be seen, observers have no difficulty in identifying the moving form as a human being. This is in itself surprising and interesting. What the observer actually sees is a set of lights moving in some kind of relation to one another. But what the person cannot help perceiving is a human form. Furthermore, in a previous investigation, the authors of this study found that observers could identify themselves and friends from such point-light sources. What they wanted to find out from this study was whether or not the sex of the person could be identified from these minimal visual cues. The paper reports five related experiments which together enable the authors to explore some of the properties of our perceptions of a walker picked out only by point-lights on joints.

▶ **perception** The process by which the brain organizes and interprets sensory information.

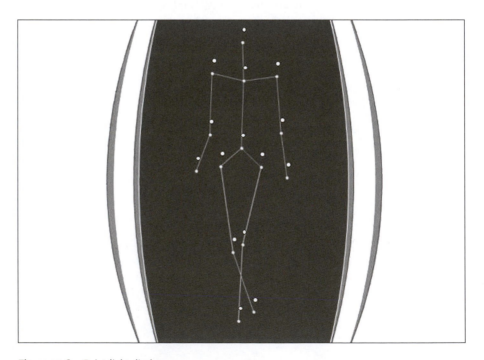

Figure 14.6 *Point light display*

The studies

Subjects

All the experiments used undergraduates as subjects. Their role was to watch video images and then respond as to whether the walker they were watching was male or female. Subjects participated in groups, and for experiments one and three they were paid. The number of subjects in each of the experiments was as follows:

Experiment 1:   30, 15 female, 15 male;
Experiment 2:   20, 10 female, 10 male;
Experiment 3:   30, 15 female, 15 male;
Experiment 4:   28, 18 female, 10 male;
Experiment 5:   259, 127 female, 132 male.

Design

▶ **binomial test** An inferential statistic that is used when there is a simple 'either/or' outcome to a task (for example, either heads or tails, either right or left, either male or female). It tests to see whether there is any statistically significant bias in favour of one or other of the alternatives.

The core of this study is the comparison of the pattern of subjects' actual judgements with the pattern that would be seen if the subjects were simply guessing. If, for example, 30 subjects all flipped a coin to decide on each of 100 trials whether to answer male or female, one would expect each model to be judged to be male about 50 per cent of the time, and to be judged female about 50 per cent of the time. A pattern of results such as this would indicate that subjects cannot tell the sex of the walker, and is referred to as performance 'at chance levels'. The greater the proportion of correct responses, in comparison to incorrect responses, the more confident we can be that subjects are doing more than guessing. The binomial test is used to decide whether the proportion of correct responses is sufficiently high to allow us to conclude that subjects can really identify the sex of the walker. A number of other comparisons were also made in the course of the five experiments. The important ones are summarized in the results section, below.

▶ **order effects** A set of confounding variables which must be controlled against in experiments that use repeated measures designs. In the simplest case of a two-condition experiment, if all the subjects do condition A first, then condition B, and (for the sake of argument) perform better in condition B, a sceptic can argue that this is nothing to do with the experimenter's manipulation of the independent variable, but is simply due to the subjects having practised on condition A, and improved by the time they did condition B (a practice effect, which is one kind of order effect). Counterbalancing controls against this confounding variable by alternating the order in which subjects do the conditions of an experiment.

Materials and apparatus

Video recordings of six people, three male and three female, were used. The models walked from left to right and back again in front of the camera, wearing reflective tape on their shoulders, elbows, wrists, hips, knees, and ankles. By adjusting the brightness and contrast of the video, the only things that could be seen were the lights. For Experiment 1, the full sequence of trials was recorded onto a second video, in random order, so as to control against order effects. Experiment 2 used still images taken from the videos. Experiments 3 and 4 used models who were walking with either greater than normal, or less than normal arm-swing (Experiment 3) and models who were either walking more quickly, or more slowly, than normal (Experiment 4). In Experiment 5, the configuration of point-lights was adjusted in order to find out if any joints are particularly important for identification of sex.

Procedure

In Experiment 1, groups of subjects viewed ten trials of each of six models, randomly pre-recorded on video. Each trial consisted of the model walking once from right to left, and once from left to right in front of the camera. The subjects could only see the point-light sources mounted on the six joints. Their task on each trial was simply to write down M or F according to their judgment about the sex of the walker. They also used a 5-point scale to rate how confident they were on each trial about their judgement. The procedures for subsequent experiments were broadly speaking the same, and any important differences are noted in the results summary below. Crucially, no feedback was given to subjects during any of the experiments about the correctness, or otherwise, of their responses.

Results

Five of the six walkers in Experiment 1 were identified correctly on the majority of trials. One of the women walkers was consistently mis-identified as a male. Overall, subjects made correct judgements on 63 per cent of the trials. If the mis-identified female model is excluded from the analysis, then nearly 69 per cent of judgements were correct. Subjects' confidence ratings showed a strong relationship to accuracy of judgement (see Figure 14.7). For those trials on which subjects judged themselves to be not at all confident, they performed at chance levels (only 55 per cent correct). For those trials on which they rated themselves as most confident, they averaged 87 per cent correct responses. In other words, subjects could tell when they could tell whether they were looking at a male or a female.

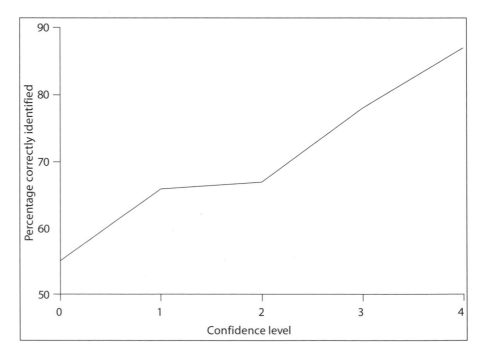

Figure 14.7 *Relationship between confidence of judgement and accuracy*

In Experiment 2, subjects had to try to judge the sex of the walker from static photos. Each walker had four photos taken of them. Subjects first of all had to guess what the pictures were of, since each one was in effect just a series of dots. They were then told that the pictures were of people walking, after which they sorted the images into two piles according to whether they thought each one to be of a male or a female. Only one of the 20 subjects guessed that the pictures represented people, with most thinking they were something like Christmas tree lights. Not surprisingly, when their sorting judgements were analysed they were found to be responding at chance levels. The static display gave no clues that the images were of people, let alone the sex of the people.

Experiments 3 and 4 examined the effects of different styles of walking on judgement of sex. This was an attempt to understand why one woman in Experiment 1 had been so consistently mis-identified. Analysis of her walking showed that she had the least pronounced arm-swing of the three females, and that she walked more slowly than the other two. Since the females walked on average with more arm-swing, and faster than the males, Koslowski and Cutting suspected that they may have identified two of the visual cues that subjects were using to make their judgements. So in Experiment 3, the models varied their arm-swing, and in Experiment 4 they varied their walking speed. However, the results simply showed that increasing and decreasing arm-swing, and increasing and decreasing speed, simply disrupted subjects' judgements, pushing them into chance levels of performance. In other words, increased arm-swing and increased speed of walking did not make it more likely that the walker would be judged as female. Unfortunately the researchers only looked at these two variables separately. They did not examine whether arm-swing and walking speed interact to affect judgement of sex. It is always quite possible in psychology for individual variables, when studied alone, to appear to have no effect, because their real impact is only observable when the operation of other variables is simultaneously taken into account.

In Experiment 5 the number and positioning of the point-light sources was manipulated. Table 14.1 shows the various combinations that were used on different trials. Remarkably, even on those trials where only the ankles were lit, subjects were still able to make better than chance judgements about the sex of the walker. Indeed, all the various combinations of lights enabled subjects to identify the sex of the walker. Upper body cues were found to be more effective than lower body cues. The authors conclude that 'any joint is sufficient and no joint is necessary for the recognition of a walker's sex' (p. 578). Unfortunately there is no mention of whether subjects were able to link the different images together. For example, the speed of a person's walking when only ankle joints were visible may have enabled subjects to link that person with their movement with the full configuration of lights (the same walkers were used for all the different light combinations). In other words, it may be the case that when the subjects were judging sex from just the ankle lights, they were in fact drawing on more information than the experimenters realized. Further investigation of this possibility would simply involve using different models for each of the different sets of light configurations. If subjects could guess someone's sex when the only example of them walking was with ankle lights on, then we could be more confident of this finding.

Table 14.1   *Percentage correct identification of sex of walker for seven point-light configurations*

Body portion		Female walkers		Male walkers		
		No. 1	No. 2	No. 4	No. 6	Mean
Lower body	A		61*	60*	39*†	54*
	HA		59*	55*	55	56*
	HNA		62*	42*†	62*	55*
Upper body	SER	53	62*	65*	65*	61*
	SERH	59*	69*	69*	84*	70*
Full body	SERHA	59*	72*	66*	72*	67*
	SERHNA	60*	77*	67*	78*	70*
Mean		58*	66*	60*	65*	

Key: A = Ankles, H = Hips, N = Knees, S = Shoulders, E = Elbows, R = Wrists,
* = $p < .05$, two-tailed, † = Results in the opposite direction

Discussion

The observation that an array of moving lights on a walker's joints is enough to allow us to perceive a person is in itself fascinating. This insight is used in the design of modern computer graphics. Lights are fixed to the joints of a person who is then filmed carrying out a range of movements. This information is put into a computer and used to generate the realistic movement of virtual characters in computer games and some films.

The additional insight, from this paper, that the sex of the person can be identified from a simple array of lights is equally intriguing. The authors speculate about a 'grammar' of movement, which we might be tuned into. When this is contravened by asking people to walk more quickly, or swing their arms more, the movement becomes ungrammatical, and normal interpretation is disrupted. The notion of a grammar underlying human behaviour is one that has been used by a number of psychologists to explain the phenomena that they observe. Condon and Sander (1974, Chapter 12 of this book) also spoke in these terms when trying to explain their finding that babies move in coordination with the sounds of adult speech.

Just like the grammar of your own native language, the grammar of walking and moving remains invisible in the course of everyday usage. You use the rules of language all the time but you would be hard pressed to say what they are. The language metaphor is useful in that it suggests a path for further research, using manipulations of the point-light source method to find out when observers' ability to interpret the lights breaks down. What sequences of movement are grammatical? What sequences are ungrammatical? Investigations of these sorts of questions can help us to pick apart some of the meanings of human behaviour which we are only aware of at a deeply subconscious level.

Questions

suggested
answers
→ p. 499

1. Why are the authors so keen to point out that no feedback was given to subjects about their performance during the experiments?

2. Can you think of any examples of everyday human cognition when we are able to 'fill in the gaps' of an incomplete stimulus, to make sense of it as a whole (as subjects were clearly doing in this study)?

3. Do you think we would be able to recognize other species, or perhaps mechanical objects, using the same type of point-light stimuli? Do you think other species could recognize their own kind in the same way?

Are you having a laugh?

CARROLL, P.J., YOUNG, J.R.
AND GUERTIN, M.S. (1992)

Visual analysis
of cartoons:
a view from
the far side.

In K. Raynor (ed.)
Eye Movements and
Visual Cognition:
Scene Perception
and Reading,
pp. 444–1.
New York:
Springer-Verlag.

▶ **perception** The process by which the brain organizes and interprets sensory information.

▶ **cognition** Mental processes. 'All the processes by which ... sensory input is transformed, reduced, elaborated, stored, recovered and used' (Neisser, 1967, p. 4).

▶ **eye-tracking** A technique used in cognitive science in which a camera focuses on one or both eyes and records their movement as the viewer looks at some kind of stimulus.

▶ **humour** Any form of entertainment or human communication which creates feelings of amusement or which makes people laugh or feel happy.

Introduction

Cognitive psychology specializes in the study of 'invisible' processes. Perception, memory, thought and so forth cannot be directly observed or measured. So if cognitive psychologists want to study these things, then they have to work by way of inference. The way they do this is sometimes framed in terms of the 'black box' model of cognition. In this model the black box represents the human mind, which cannot be seen into. Psychologists try to infer what is going on in there by observing what goes into the box (the stimuli that are experienced by the person) and what comes out of the box (how the person behaves). They then make inferences about what must be going on in the box in order to make sense of the relationships they observe between the input and the output. For example, in the visual cliff experiment (see p. 331), Gibson and Walk were trying to examine cognitive processes within very young infants. They created a set of stimuli (the visual cliff) and observed the infants' behavioural responses to those stimuli (staying on the 'shallow' side of the cliff). In order to explain this they inferred that the infants were able to perceive depth. Note that depth perception is an invisible, hypothetical construct that cannot be observed, but that is necessary to explain the infants' behaviour. The tradition of working in this way came partly out of the failure of behaviourism in its attempts to show that there are direct relationships between input (S) and output (R) that can be explained without recourse to the notion of a 'black box' (a mind).

Psychologists have developed numerous techniques for studying invisible processes in the human mind in this way. One of these is eye-tracking. Eye-tracking technology is capable of giving moment-by-moment information about exactly where on a given display a person is looking. Careful examination of looking behaviour is a powerful way of making inferences about what thought processes are going on. For example, eye-tracking techniques can be used to study the cognitive processes that support reading, by looking in detail at the way in which a reader's eyes move forwards and backwards across lines of text (see Figure 14.8).

The authors of this study used eye-tracking to examine cognitive processes that support humour. What kinds of information processing lie behind our perception of something as 'funny'?

The study

Suls' (1972) theory of humour suggests that the experience of 'getting' a joke depends on two stages. In the first stage the joke-teller sets up deliberately

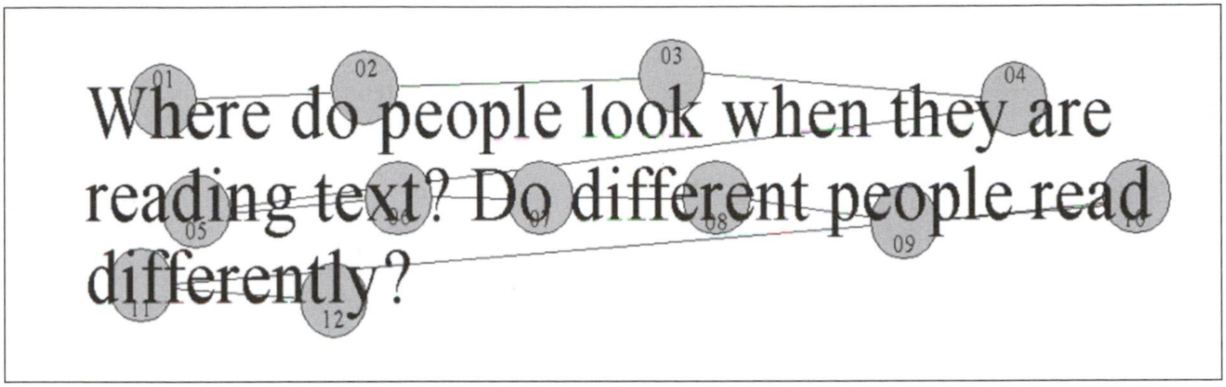

Figure 14.8 *An example of a scan path for someone reading*
Note: The text is displayed on a screen and the participant is asked to read it. When they have finished, information about their fixations can be plotted over the image. In this example each circle represents one fixation, and the small numbers indicate the sequence of the fixations.

misleading expectations in the mind of the listener. In the second stage, the denouement, a punch line is delivered that contravenes these expectations. The experience of 'getting-it' corresponds to the moment when the apparent conflict between the two stages is resolved in the mind of the listener, by reframing the information that they had been given in the first stage. According to Suls the reason that the 'why do birds fly south?' joke is funny (and it is, hilariously) is because the structure of the question leads one to focus on the information that the birds are going south. The punch-line contravenes that expectation by focusing on the mode of transport. If you do not already know the punch line to this joke, ask someone you know who is very old.

Carroll *et al.* set out to study this phenomenon in a structured way by tracking the eye movements of students while the students looked at still, single frame cartoon images with captions. For each cartoon the image and the caption were displayed separately, in sequence, to parallel the two-stage process described by Suls. This is because the humour in the cartoons comes from an incongruity between the image and the caption, rather like the incongruity between the body of a joke and its punch line. The aim of the study was to describe in fine detail the looking behaviour of the students, and to see what could be inferred from this behaviour about the cognitive processes that underpin the experience of 'getting the joke'. The original paper describes two related experiments, but this summary will only deal with one.

Subjects, apparatus and design

▶ **independent-measures design** When a study involves comparing the scores from two or more separate groups of people.

The 18 student subjects were divided equally across one of two conditions in this independent-measures design experiment. The task was to look at each of 24 cartoons from Gary Larson's *The Far Side*. Nine students saw the image first, then the caption; nine saw the caption first, then the image. An SRI Dual Purkinje eye tracker was used to track the students' looking behaviour.

Procedure

Students in the 'image first' condition, were shown a cartoon image and instructed to press a button as soon as they felt they had enough information, whereupon eye-tracking of the *image* stopped and the caption for the image was displayed. They then pressed the same button to indicate when they had understood the joke, and eye-tracking of the *caption* stopped. The reverse procedure was used for the students in the 'caption-first' condition. The rationale for this was as follows. The item that was seen first by each subject (whether it was the caption or the image) should be processed rather straightforwardly as it represents stage one of Suls' model, where there is not yet any incongruity. At some point during presentation of the second item (the image or the caption) stage two processing should start, whereby the incongruity becomes apparent, and the subject sets about processing the stimulus in order to reconcile that incongruity. Therefore, any systematic differences between the processing of items that were seen second, in contrast to the items that were seen first, may be attributable in part to the second-stage processing identified by Suls' theory.

Data were analysed by measuring fixations and saccades for the image stimulus. Fixations refer to measurable periods of time when a subject's gaze remains focused within a certain pre-defined area of the stimulus display. This shows that the subject is looking at something and implies that they are processing it. The number and duration of fixations were recorded. Saccades refer to quick lateral movements of the eye, made between fixations. The magnitude of these saccades (in terms of the 'distance' that the eye is shown to move across the stimulus display) are measured. The most important measures for this study related to fixations on the image.

▶ **fixation** Ability of the eye to focus on one point.

▶ **saccades** Eye movements used to quickly relocate the eyes from one position of gaze to another.

Results

The only statistically significant difference between the two conditions on the main measures employed is in terms of mean fixation duration; pictures that were viewed as the second item (in the 'caption-first' condition) were associated with longer fixation durations.

The differences in fixation duration were analysed further in a most interesting way. The mean fixation duration was calculated for each successive fixation, so the mean of all subjects' first fixations was calculated, then the mean of all subjects' second fixations and so forth.

Apart from the first fixation, the means stay rather similar across the two conditions until fixation six (approximately 1.5 seconds into the task, though this will differ from subject to subject). Subsequently the fixations on the image in the caption-first condition (for those who saw the image after the caption) are on average longer than those in the picture-first condition.

Discussion

The finding that there were statistically significant differences in mean fixation duration across the experimental conditions is, in itself, of limited interest, because it is quite difficult to say what it means. The real importance of this finding is that it gave the researchers an indication of how to explore their data further. As a result of this further exploration they discovered that the differences in fixation duration emerged at a certain point in the task (see Figure 14.9). This makes the findings much more intriguing.

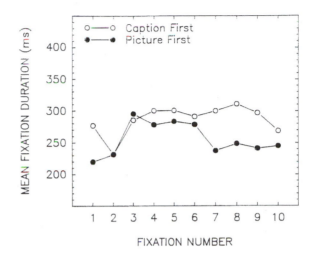

Figure 14.9 *Mean fixation durations for the first ten fixations on the picture portions of the cartoons in Experiment 1*

Note: Subjects in the caption-first condition had already read the captions, whereas those in the picture-first condition had not yet seen the captions. Each data point represents nine subjects each viewing 24 cartoons.

Length of fixation is one indicator of internal processing. In this situation the different behaviour of the subjects after fixation six probably indicates different internal cognitive processes. Consider the different cognitive tasks that the subjects in each condition are doing. In the picture-first condition, they are simply looking around the picture taking in the different elements, trying to remember its layout so that they will be able to interpret the caption which they are about to see. Their fixations are on average shorter than those in the caption-first condition, notably from fixation seven onwards. In contrast the subjects in the caption-first condition have a different task to perform. They have already seen the caption, developed an initial expectation of what is going on, and are now inspecting the picture in order to work out what the joke is. The pattern of fixation durations that these subjects show is interpreted by the researchers to mean that for the first six fixations (approximately 1.5 seconds) the subjects are orienting themselves to the picture that has just been presented to them. Subsequently they are trying to figure out something which is cognitively quite demanding, hence their fixations becoming longer in duration. They are looking in more detail at certain specific areas of each picture in an effort to reconcile the expectations that they built up from the caption with the information that they are now getting from the image. In terms of Suls' theory of humour, the transition from fixation six to seven is the transition from stage one to stage two processing. The researchers suggest that in these moments we are observing the subjects 'getting the joke'.

Carroll *et al.*'s study provides a good example of the use of eye-tracking in the study of cognitive processes. The researchers were able to observe relationships between the 'input' to the black box (in this case the stimuli of words and pictures, presented in different ways) and 'output' from it (the looking behaviour of the subjects). They were then in a position to make inferences about what cognitive processes were probably going on inside the black box (the subjects' minds), in order to make sense of the input–output relationships that they observed. Needless to say these inferences, though plausible, require further testing. One thing that would need to be done is to use other observational techniques with other joke formats to see whether similar patterns of processing can be inferred.

Questions

suggested answers → p. 500

1. Why are terms like 'probably', 'indicates', 'interpreted by the researchers to mean' used so much in the discussion section of this summary?

2. Why should other observational methods and other joke formats be used to test the interpretations of the researchers?

3. Why don't elephants like penguins?

chapter **15**

MIND AND THOUGHT

▶**cognition** Mental processes. 'All the processes by which ... sensory input is transformed, reduced, elaborated, stored, recovered and used' (Neisser, 1967, p. 4).

▶**hypothesis** Experiments are designed to test one or more hypotheses. An hypothesis is a prediction of what will happen in an experiment. It is worded in such a way that the results of a well-designed experiment will clearly show whether the prediction is right or wrong.

▶**autism** A condition of social withdrawal characterized by (i) impairment in reciprocal social interaction, (ii) impairment in verbal and non-verbal communication, and in imaginative activity, (iii) a restricted repertoire of activities and interests.

▶**theory of mind** The understanding we have that other people have their own thoughts and beliefs about the world, which may differ from our own thoughts and beliefs.

THE first two studies in this chapter address important philosophical issues to do with the nature of the mind. The remarkable thing about human beings is that we are able to reflect on our own experience and describe this experience to each other. One of the puzzles that emerges is that even when we know about how the brain works and we can describe our cognitive processes, we still cannot account for our unique personal experience of the world. We are all aware that we have a mind, but what is it and how does it work? The first study in this chapter (Baron-Cohen *et al.*, 1997) tests the hypothesis that people with autism have difficulties in understanding what is going on in the minds of others. The authors were able to show that adults with autism tend to do less well on a 'theory of mind' task than matched control participants. A well-developed theory of mind (something that is so taken for granted that people are not even aware of having one) may be an essential component of effective interaction and communication among people.

In a completely different vein, and a more theoretical one at that, Searle (1980) took issue with certain ideas that have emerged from the field of artificial intelligence about the nature of the mind. The key question here is whether computers can think and whether they can be like people. This is a common theme in science fiction which blurs the distinction between people and machines. The classic silent film *Metropolis* explores this idea and suggests that technology will one day make us unable to tell the difference between a human being and a mechanical copy. Numerous films (for example, Ridley Scott's cult classic *Blade Runner*) since then have returned to this theme, which challenges us to consider, among other things, whether we are just a rather sophisticated biological robot.

Some psychologists suggest that it is possible for machines to mimic human thought, and computer programmes have been developed which at first glance show some of the signs of thought. Searle, however, challenges this view and argues that computers can be a good tool for studying thinking, but cannot in themselves actually think. This remains an important argument because of the growing influence of computers in cognitive science, and their impact on how we think about the mind.

▶ **artificial intelligence (AI)**
Computer systems which are able to 'learn' and to produce the same kinds of outcomes as are produced by human thinking.

▶ **cognitive science** A multidisciplinary approach to studying artificial intelligence and similar phenomena, bringing together psychologists, linguists, information scientists and others.

▶ **synaesthesia** A mixing of the senses. For example a synaesthete might hear colours, see sounds, and taste tactile sensations.

The third study in this chapter looks at how human thought is structured. When we think, how do we connect one idea with another, and how do we recognize the meanings of words? The model suggested and tested by Collins and Quillian (1969) is an attempt to describe how our thought processes are structured. Following on from this, an engaging final study in this chapter looks at people whose thought processes appear to be structured in unusual ways. Ramachandran and Hubbard (2001) present findings from a set of innovative tests that shed light on the intriguing topic of synaesthesia.

Autism and theories of mind

BARON-COHEN, S., JOLLIFFE, T., MORTIMORE, C. AND ROBERTSON, M. (1997)

Another advanced test of theory of mind: evidence from very high functioning adults with autism or Asperger Syndrome.

Journal of Child Psychology and Psychiatry, 38, 813–22.

Introduction

Children and adults with autism have difficulties interacting with others, they also have difficulties communicating with others, and they tend to engage obsessively in a restricted range of activities. Various attempts have been made to discover the origins of autism and to identify a core deficit which can account for the typical range of behavioural symptoms of the syndrome. Bettelheim's (1967) psychoanalytic approach focused (unhelpfully) on poor parenting; Tinbergen and Tinbergen's (1983) ethological work directed attention towards interactions within families; and Lovaas (1979) took the typical behaviourist line and suggested that we should concentrate on the symptoms of autism rather than look for any underlying cause. In contrast to all these, the study summarized below emerged from a social-cognitive approach to understanding autism.

According to Baron-Cohen *et al.* (1985), the core feature of autism has to do with a characteristic way of understanding other people (hence the label social-cognitive). They argue, specifically, that children with autism do not develop a theory of mind (Premack and Woodruff, 1978) in the same way as do typically developing children. That is, many children with autism struggle to understand the notion that people, including themselves, have thoughts and beliefs about the world. Because this is such a taken-for-granted kind of understanding in everyday social life, the full implications of not having an adequately developed theory of mind are not immediately obvious. But the more you think about it the more you realize that social relationships and social interactions are based upon people's beliefs about other people's beliefs. For one thing, this ability to mind-read allows us to anticipate what other people are likely to do. Furthermore, effective communication between two people depends upon each person having a good sense of what the other is thinking. In fact if we could not conceive of other people's thoughts and beliefs, social interactions would become literally meaningless.

How can we investigate a person's theory of mind? How can we find out whether or not someone is able to understand the notion that other people have beliefs? One answer is to set up a task for subjects on which they can succeed only if they are able to attribute a belief state to another person. One of the most well known examples of such a task is the 'Sally–Anne' test, or the 'unexpected transfer task' (see Wimmer and Perner, 1983), which is a so-called false-belief task. The child subject is seated behind a desk opposite the experimenter. On the desk are two dolls, Sally and Anne. Sally has a basket in front of her, Anne has a box. The test unfolds as follows. Sally takes a marble and hides it in her basket. She then 'goes for a walk' and leaves the room.

▶**autism** A condition of social withdrawal characterized by (i) impairment in reciprocal social interaction, (ii) impairment in verbal and non-verbal communication, and in imaginative activity, (iii) a restricted repertoire of activities and interests.

▶**psychoanalysis** Freud's theory of personality which describes how human behaviour is affected by unconscious thought and feelings.

▶**ethology** The study of behaviour in the natural environment.

▶**behaviourism** A school of thought which holds that the observation and description of overt behaviour is all that is needed to comprehend the human being, and that manipulation of stimulus–response contingencies is all that is needed to change human behaviour.

► **social cognition** The way that we think about and interpret social information and social experience. In developmental psychology, the term refers to a theory of cognitive development which states that social interaction is the most important factor in a young child's cognitive development.

► **theory of mind** The understanding we have that other people have their own thoughts and beliefs about the world, which may differ from our own thoughts and beliefs.

Whilst she is away, and therefore unknown to her, Anne takes the marble out of Sally's basket and puts it in her own box. Sally returns and the child is asked the question 'where will Sally look for her marble?' The correct response is to point to or name Sally's basket; that is, to indicate that the child knows that Sally believes the marble to be somewhere where it is not. The incorrect response is to point to Anne's box.

The only way to succeed in this task (other than by luck) is to attribute a belief to Sally. The child has to be able to appreciate that Sally has beliefs about the world which can differ from their own beliefs, and which happen in this case not to be true (hence the label 'false-belief task'). Typically developing children can usually succeed on the task by the age of about 4. But when Baron-Cohen *et al.* (1985) tested children with autism (with an average verbal 'mental age' of more than 5 years) they found that 80 per cent of them failed the test. This study led to a mass of research on theory of mind and autism, much of which suggests that children with autism do indeed have difficulties with reading what is going on in the minds of others.

The study

► **hypothesis** Experiments are designed to test one or more hypotheses. An hypothesis is a prediction of what will happen in an experiment. It is worded in such a way that the results of a well-designed experiment will clearly show whether the prediction is right or wrong.

► **Tourette Syndrome** A neurological disorder that develops in childhood and is characterized by unwanted and uncontrolled movements and vocal tics.

One question that emerges from the research on theory of mind in children with autism is 'What about adults with autism?' Are the apparent difficulties that children with autism have with theory of mind tasks symptomatic of pervasive difficulties with mind-reading that are also experienced by adults with autism? Attempts to address this question experimentally have had limited success because theory of mind tasks have traditionally been designed to show what typically developing *children* can do. Some of the more complex tasks – so-called second-order theory of mind tasks (that involve the subject reasoning about what one person thinks that another person thinks, thus reading through two minds) – are still passed by most typically developing children by the age of 6 years. What is needed is a set of more adult oriented tasks that test for more subtle theory of mind effects.

The task that was used in the current study is the 'Eyes Task', developed for use with adults by Baron-Cohen (1995) as a measure of the ability to read the 'language of the eyes'. The task measures the subject's ability to interpret a person's mental state from a static picture of their eyes. It uses a forced-choice format whereby subjects have to chose one or other of two opposing terms that best describes the mental state expressed by the eyes (for example, 'relaxed or worried', 'calm or anxious', 'friendly or hostile'). The researchers hypothesized that adults with autism would perform less well on the task than would adults with Tourette Syndrome and 'normal' adults.

Subjects

Three groups of adults were selected: 16 with 'high functioning' autism (n=4) or Asperger Syndrome (n=12), with a mean IQ of 105 and an average age of 28.6 (range 18–49); 50 'normal' age-matched control adults, 25 of each sex, with a mean age of 30 (range 18–48; no IQ measures were taken for this group); and ten adults with Tourette Syndrome, with a mean IQ of 103.5 and a mean age of 27.77 (range 18–47).

Design

▶ **natural experiments (also quasi experiments)** Studies in which comparisons are made between different conditions that come about through natural political, social, economic or demographic circumstances, rather than through direct manipulation of a variable by an experimenter.

This was a straightforward quasi-experiment whereby the three experimental conditions were defined by the three groups of subjects who participated. The dependent measure was the score on the Eyes Task. Two control tasks were also used. One of these involved asking subjects to identify the gender of the person in the picture (the 'gender' task), and one involved making judgments about basic emotional expressions from full-face pictures (the 'emotion' task).

Materials

The Eyes Task was constructed by taking pictures from magazine images and making them into a standard size and format (see Figure 15.1), such that each one displayed the same area around the character's eyes. A panel of four judges generated a target word and a semantic opposite word for each of the 25 pictures. These were then tested on a separate panel of eight judges, who agreed unanimously on all of the target words.

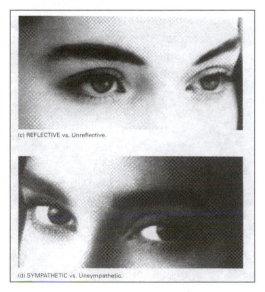

(c) REFLECTIVE vs. Unreflective.

(d) SYMPATHETIC vs. Unsympathetic.

Figure 15.1 *The eyes test*
The forced-choice pair of descriptions were randomized in terms of left–right presentation, and offered in identical case and font. For clarity here, the correct description is in upper case.

Procedure

The pictures were presented in a standardized format (see Figure 15.1) for three seconds each, along with the appropriate forced-choice mental-state terms. The experimenter asked of each picture "Which word best describes what this person is feeling or thinking?" Subjects could score a maximum of 25.

Results

Subjects in the autism/Asperger Syndrome group performed less well than subjects in both of the comparison groups (subjects with Tourette Syndrome, and 'normal' subjects) on the Eyes Task (see Table 15.1). These differences in performance were statistically significant at the level of $p < .01$. There were no differences across the three groups on the 'gender' control task. Furthermore, all subjects reached a ceiling level of performance (getting every question correct) on the 'emotion' control task.

Table 15.1 *Performance on the Eyes Task*

	Autism/Asperger Syndrome (n = 16)	'Normal' (n = 50)	Tourette Syndrome (n = 10)
Mean	16.3	20.3	20.4
SD	2.9	2.63	2.63
Range	13–23	16–25	16–25

Discussion

The results of the study lend support to the notion that adults with autism experience some difficulties with the Eyes Task, relative to matched control subjects. If we accept the Eyes Task as providing a subtle measure of theory of mind, then we can go on to interpret this as evidence that people with autism may continue to experience challenges with reading the minds of others into adulthood. The fact that the subjects with autism performed as well as the other subjects on the two control tasks indicates that their poorer performance on the Eyes Task was not to do with more basic perceptual problems when working with images of eyes (all the subjects were equally good at identifying the gender of the subject), nor was it to do with the recognition of basic emotions in others. The poorer performance on the Eyes Task seems to suggest that the subjects with autism had some difficulties in reading the thoughts and feelings of the characters in the pictures. Note how cautiously these interpretations are phrased here. It is rather common to read careless statements about people with autism 'lacking' a theory of mind, or about people with autism being 'unable' to mind-read. This simply is not the case, and is a major misinterpretation of the meaning of the evidence that has accrued through psychological research.

The authors also carried out an interesting comparison of females versus males in the 'normal' control condition. They expected to find that women were better at the eyes task than men, and this is indeed what they found. The differences they observed were statistically significant at the level of $p < .01$. This prediction follows on from evidence about gendered cognitive styles, suggesting that while men tend to prioritize 'systematizing' (analytical thinking, logical data-driven thought) women tend to prioritize 'empathizing' (thinking of others). The observation that people with autism may prioritize systematizing over empathizing in their dealings with the world around them has led to

▶ **cognition** Mental processes. 'All the processes by which ... sensory input is transformed, reduced, elaborated, stored, recovered and used' (Neisser, 1967, p. 4).

the suggestion that autism is an expression of a kind of extreme 'maleness' (see the 'extreme male brain theory of autism', Baron-Cohen, 2002).

The hypothesis that children and adults with autism have difficulties in understanding other minds has received support from a number of different sources, and stands as a plausible core feature of autism. It sits comfortably with the strong consensus among experts that the causes of autism are organic (that is, that autism is caused by some sort of physical damage to the central nervous system). However, extreme caution must always be exercised in interpreting the findings of studies that are undertaken with populations of people whose worlds may be very different to the worlds of the researchers (see for example the work of Labov, in Chapter 12). The researchers may, inadvertently, come to misinterpret behaviour that they observe because they are seeing it from the perspective of non-autistic people, rather than from the perspective of people with autism. It is particularly important that we proceed cautiously here, because this kind of research may have important consequences for our attitudes to, and beliefs about, people with autism (Grayson, 2006). Readers who are interested in the topics of autism and theory of mind are referred to the excellent books by Frith (2003) and Happé (1994), but are mostly encouraged to read some of the wealth of material that continues to be published about autism by people with autism.

Questions

suggested answers → p. 500

1. How important do you think a theory of mind is for everyday social interaction?

2. How might we decide whether the Eyes Task is really a test of theory of mind?

3. Why were adults with Tourette Syndrome included in this study?

4. There are a number of labels used in this study: 'high functioning', 'normal', 'autism', 'Tourette Syndrome'. How do these labels make you feel?

I'm sorry Dave,
I can't do that

SEARLE, J.R. (1980)

Minds, brains
and programs.

*Behavioral and
Brain Sciences,
3, 417–57.*

▶ **artificial intelligence
(AI)** Computer systems
which are able to 'learn'
and to produce the same
kinds of outcomes as
are produced by human
thinking.

▶ **cognition** Mental
processes. 'All the processes
by which ... sensory input
is transformed, reduced,
elaborated, stored, recovered
and used' (Neisser, 1967,
p. 4).

Introduction

The aim of those who work in the field of artificial intelligence (AI) is to build and programme computers to behave 'intelligently'. One area of AI has focused on programming computers to 'understand' natural language inputs. Natural language, in this context, means the sort of language that people use in their everyday lives, as opposed to the highly structured and inflexible language of computer programming. Some workers in the field wish to achieve artificial natural language understanding for the sake of it, simply because it would be useful if we could converse with computers without having to learn the obscure commands that are currently required. Others wish to find out more about how humans understand language by building computer models which allow them to test key aspects of their own theories.

Boden (1977) gives a detailed description and analysis of key natural language understanding programmes, including Weizenbaum's ELIZA, Winograd's SHRDLU and Schank's SAM. All of these programmes are able to handle various kinds of natural language inputs. ELIZA was able to respond to a user's input as if it were a non-directive psychotherapist. SHRDLU could converse about a virtual toy-blocks world. SAM was able to answer questions about, and provide synopses of, short stories that it had been told. But the question which springs to mind in relation to all of these programmes is, 'Do they really understand the language?' It is the issue of understanding that Searle tackles in this famous article.

Searle begins by distinguishing between two positions within the field of artificial intelligence: strong AI and weak (cautious) AI. The weak AI position holds that the computer is a very useful and powerful tool for studying cognition. Computer programmes can be written which put into practice theoretical models of cognitive processes. The performance of these models can be studied and compared with human performance. The models themselves are susceptible to detailed critical analysis because the discipline of writing a working computer program requires the model-builder to be precise and explicit about every detail of their theory. Searle has no argument with the weak AI position.

The strong AI position, on the other hand, holds that 'the appropriately programmed computer really is a mind, in the sense that computers given the right programs can be literally said to *understand* and have other cognitive states' (p. 417; emphasis as in original). Whereas weak AI operates on the assumption that computer models are only *simulating* cognition and understanding, strong AI assumes that the models are *duplicating* cognition and understanding. The Chinese Room *Gedankenexperiment* (thought experiment), which Searle describes in this paper, challenges the claims of strong AI.

Procedure

Thought experiments are a non-empirical form of investigation widely used in philosophy. The idea is that a mental scenario is constructed, and then the full implications of every element of that scenario are thoroughly thought out, taking each line of reasoning to a logical extreme. The Chinese Room is one such thought experiment, and a simplified version of it is described below.

The best way of thinking about the Chinese Room scenario is to imagine yourself as the central character. You are locked in a room on your own and given (perhaps through a letterbox in the door) a card with a Chinese character on it (see Figure 15.2). You understand no Chinese, so the character just looks like a complex squiggle. In the room you have a pile of other cards which have Chinese characters on them. You also have a set of instructions, written in English (which you do understand), and these tell you how to match up the symbol that has just been posted through the door with one of the symbols in your own pile. The matching that you do is based on the distinctive patterns and shapes of the symbols which are described in the English instructions. You then post the correct symbol from your pile back out of the letterbox in the door. This sequence of events is repeated again and again, and gradually you are able to perform the whole process pretty quickly.

Figure 15.2 *Examples of Chinese characters*

Now, in artificial intelligence terms the person outside the room who is posting in the Chinese symbols is the computer user, you are the computer's central processor, the Chinese symbols which come in to the room are questions, the symbols which you post out of the room are answers, and the English instructions are the computer program. To the user, who is a native Chinese speaker, it appears that you are able to understand Chinese, since the answers you give to the questions happen to be sensible and appropriate. In fact the answers you give are indistinguishable from the answers that a native Chinese speaker might give. However, if you have imagined yourself into this scenario it should be clear to you that you do not understand Chinese. All you have done is followed some rules which tell you how to manipulate certain symbols on the basis of a rather straightforward pattern-matching exercise.

Discussion

▶ **Turing test** In the Turing test a subject communicates via computer keyboard with two 'people' who are hidden from view; one of these people is a real person, and the other is a computer program. If the subject cannot reliably identify which is the computer and which is the person, then the computer program has passed the test and can be said to be able to think and understand.

One of the targets of Searle's thought experiment was the **Turing test** (Turing, 1950), which was proposed as a hallmark test of whether a computer could think and understand. In the Turing test a subject communicates via a computer keyboard with two 'people' who are hidden from view: one of these people is a real person, and the other is a computer program. If the subject cannot reliably identify which is the computer and which is the person, then the computer program has passed the test and can be said to be able to think and understand.

The Chinese Room scenario suggests that the ability to make responses in a language which are indistinguishable from those of a native speaker is not, in itself, sufficient to demonstrate *understanding*. Under certain circumstances ELIZA can pass the Turing test. But when it is revealed how the program works it becomes clear that its use of rather unintelligent pattern-matching strategies (rather like the ones you use in the Chinese Room) in no sense amounts to understanding. Searle argues that the Turing test, which is 'unashamedly behavioristic and operationalistic' (p. 423), does not provide a measure of understanding.

Searle's original article is complex, dealing as it does with difficult philosophical issues such as intentionality and the causal powers of the brain. It is rounded off by a number of invited peer commentaries which challenge and develop his ideas. Searle is allowed the last word with a lengthy rejoinder to his critics. His conclusion:

> I conclude that the Chinese room has survived the assaults of its critics. The remaining puzzle to me is this: why do so many workers in AI want to adhere to strong AI? Surely weak AI is challenging, interesting, and difficult enough. (p. 456)

suggested
answers
→ p. 501

Questions

1. One of the most entertaining thought experiments was dreamed up by Dennett (Hofstadter and Dennett, 1981). Imagine having your brain removed by keyhole surgery, placing it in a life-sustaining solution in a glass container (like one sees in science-fiction films), and replacing all the severed nerve connections by means of mini radio transmitters (this takes a bit of imagination!). Your body then moves to the other side of the room and looks at your brain (you can still see because your eyes have been reconnected via the radio transmitters). Now ask yourself the question 'where am I?' Are you over there, or over here, and who, in any case, is doing the asking? If your body commits a murder which bit of you should be locked up? (Safety note: don't try this at home, kids.)

2. What does Searle mean when he asserts that the Turing test is 'behaviouristic'?

3. What famous film is our title for this summary taken from?

COLLINS, A.M. AND QUILLIAN, M.R. (1969)

Retrieval time from semantic memory.

Journal of Verbal Learning and Verbal Behavior, 8, 240–7.

Is it a bird, is it a plane ...?

Introduction

We take our long-term memory so much for granted in our everyday lives that we tend to underestimate its sophistication, and focus instead on the relatively few lapses of memory that we experience. It is not so much the huge capacity of it that is remarkable, so much as its flexibility and efficiency. Consider our memory for facts (bearing in mind that this is just one aspect of memory). How can we carry so much information around with us, and retrieve it so quickly just when we need it? One thing is for sure, we do not explicitly store everything that we know. Consider the following facts about dogs. You would say that you 'know' all of the following, but how much of this is likely to be stored in our memory as 'facts about dogs'?

(1) Dogs are animals.
(2) Dogs have brains.
(3) Dogs live in Portugal.
(4) Dogs do not fly.

▶ **memory** The capacity to retain and retrieve information.

Maybe we could make a case for arguing that Example 1 is a fact that is somehow explicitly stored in our memory of 'dog'. But it would be extremely inefficient if everything we knew about dogs (such as in Examples 2 and 3) had to be stored explicitly with 'dog'. In fact Example 4 illustrates that this would not simply be inefficient, it would be literally impossible. Could you imagine a type of memory that contained explicit facts about everything that was not true of everything? People are not footballs. London is not in Norway. The moon is not a banana. ...

The issue that we are dealing with here is one of representation. How is knowledge represented mentally in a form that allows for such flexibility of use? This is the question that Collins and Quillian set about trying to answer in this study. They were particularly interested in word meanings, and how these are represented in semantic memory. The basis of their model was that each word is represented by a node which contains pointers (links) to other nodes that represent other related words. These nodes and links form a network which is organized in a hierarchy. They give the example of the node for 'canary', which would contain a pointer to 'bird' (denoting its category, or set), and pointers to 'sings' and 'is yellow' (denoting two of its properties). It is the position of any given node within this network of pointers/links which gives it its meaning. Figure 15.3 illustrates the structure of part of such a system.

▶ **cognitive economy** Models of human cognition should adhere to this principle which suggests that our cognition is so efficient that the underlying structures and processes must be economically organized (in other words, don't make the models too complicated). This is an example of the rule of parsimony.

The model conforms to the principles of cognitive economy (see Rosch *et al.*, 1976). In other words it maximizes the knowledge base of the system,

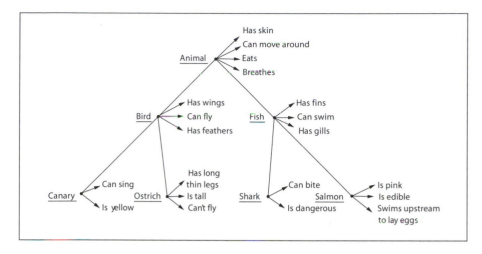

Figure 15.3   *Illustration of the hypothetical memory structure for a three-level hierarchy*

▶**inference** Going beyond what we know to make an intelligent guess.

while minimizing redundancy. It does this by enabling the crucial process of inference. That is, we know that a canary breathes, for example, not because that property is stored explicitly with canary, but because we know a canary is an animal, and that animals breathe. In other words we can infer that fact from the network of nodes and connections which form our semantic representation of this domain. Note that this means the property 'breathes' does not need to be redundantly represented for every single animal. This model can explain how we can 'know' things (about dogs, for example) which are not stored as explicit facts in our memory.

In Collins and Quillian's model there are two types of relations encoded in the network. Set ('S') relations have to do with the hierarchy of categories in the network. The statement 'a canary is a bird' expresses the fact that canary belongs to the set called 'bird', which is one level up in the hierarchy. 'A canary is an animal' is a similar type of sentence, only this time crossing two layers of the hierarchy. The other kind of relation is the *property* ('P') relation. Property relations are statements about the characteristics of the thing represented by a node. 'A canary can sing' is a property relation which is encoded on one layer of the hierarchy. 'A canary can fly' is a similar type of sentence, except that one layer of the hierarchy has to be crossed to be able to infer that because a canary is a bird, it must be able to fly.

One prediction from this model is that when searching our semantic memory in order to verify a statement, the more layers of the hierarchy you have to cross, the longer it should take to verify the statement as true or false. Collins and Quillian's study set out to test this prediction by presenting subjects with simple sentences about various hierarchically organized domains of knowledge. The sentences were constructed either as 'S' or 'P' type sentences. Some of them involved crossing two layers in the hierarchy (S2: A canary is an animal; P2: A canary eats), some involved crossing one layer (S1: A canary is a bird; P1: A canary can fly), and some involved within-layer judgements (S0: A canary is a canary; P0: A canary is yellow). So, two-layer sentences should take longer to verify than one-layer sentences, which in turn should take longer than within-layer sentences. In addition, 'S' type sentences should be quicker to verify than 'P' type sentences, because they involve no 'sideways' search of properties.

The study

Subjects

▶ **hypothesis** Experiments are designed to test one or more hypotheses. An hypothesis is a prediction of what will happen in an experiment. It is worded in such a way that the results of a well-designed experiment will clearly show whether the prediction is right or wrong.

Twenty-four employees of a company participated in three experiments. Due to technical difficulties the data from five subjects in Experiment 3 had to be excluded. This meant that the overall, pooled data that are reported in the paper come from 19 subjects in all. All subjects were naive as to the nature of the experiment and the hypotheses.

Design

▶ **independent variable** The conditions which an experimenter sets up, to cause an effect in an experiment. These vary systematically, so that the experimenter can draw conclusions about changes in outcomes.

▶ **dependent variable** The thing which is measured in an experiment, and which changes, depending on the independent variable.

The paper reports on three experiments, the data from which were pooled into a single set. For clarity they will be summarized as one experiment, because the only difference between them was in the manner in which false sentences were constructed, and this will not be dealt with here. The experiment used a repeated measures 2 x 3 factorial design (that is, there were two independent variables, one with two conditions and one with three conditions). The first independent variable was to do with the kind of relation stated within the sentence. This had two levels: property relation (P) or set relation (S). The second independent variable was to do with the number of layers that the sentence moved through in the semantic hierarchy. This variable had three levels: within-layers (0), across one layer (1), and across two layers (2). The 2 x 3 design gives six conditions in all: P0, P1, P2, S0, S1, S2. The dependent variable was measured in terms of the subjects' reaction times.

Materials and apparatus

▶ **repeated measures design (also within groups)** An experimental design where each subject carries out each condition of the experiment.

▶ **factorial design** A form of experimental design involving more than one independent variable.

A computer was used to display the sentences, and the subjects' responses were timed by means of a two-button (true or false) response box. Overall, 352 sentences were used from four different subject areas, although no subject read more than 224. The sentences were generated by the researchers, using 'is', 'has', and 'can' for property (P) sentences, and 'is' for set (S) sentences. An illustration of the sorts of sentences used in one of the hierarchies is given below:

P0	An oak has acorns.
P1	A spruce has branches.
P2	A birch has seeds.
S0	A maple is a maple.
S1	A cedar is a tree.
S2	An elm is a plant.

Two people who were not otherwise involved in the experiment generated the sentences independently from the researchers, using prompts such as 'tennis is_____'. 'Only in one case ... was their choice clearly not synonymous' (p. 243). An equal number of false S and P sentences were also generated.

Procedure

Subjects were presented with one sentence at a time and, as quickly and as accurately as possible, had to judge whether the sentence was true or false. Each sentence was displayed for two seconds, and was followed by a blank screen for two seconds until the next sentence appeared. The speed of presentation of the sentences was constant, irrespective of the speed of the subjects' responses. Each subject had 32 practice sentences before the experiment proper started. The sentences were randomly ordered, and contained equal numbers of true and false sentences of type $P0$, $P1$, $P2$, $S0$, $S1$ and $S2$. Data analysis was by means of a two-way related ANOVA.

Results

▶ **ANOVA** An inferential statistic that can be used with interval-level data and that is capable of dealing with more than one independent variable at a time. The word is an acronym of ANalysis Of VAriance, and is conventionally written in capital letters. Probably the most widely used statistical technique in experimental psychology.

Figure 15.4 shows the means for the six conditions across all trials for all subjects. Set (S) type sentences were more quickly verified than property (P) type sentences. This difference was statistically significant at the level of $p < .01$. Furthermore, two-layer (2) sentences took longer to verify than one-layer (1) sentences, which in turn took longer to verify than within-layer (0) sentences. These differences were also significant at the level of $p < .01$.

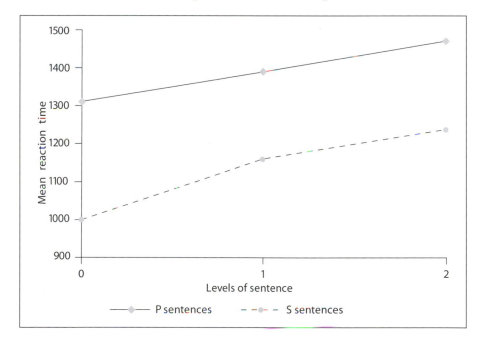

Figure 15.4 *Mean reaction times for different types of sentence*

Discussion

The data are clearly supportive of the Collins and Quillian hierarchical model of semantic memory. The hypothesis relating to speed of verification for set type sentences versus property type sentences was supported. In addition the hypothesis relating to movement across different layers of the hypothetical hierarchy was also supported. Interestingly, Collins and Quillian also predicted that the two lines in Figure 15.4 would be straight and parallel. This is because it should take a certain amount of time to move across one layer in the hierarchy, and the same amount of time again to move across a further layer. This should apply whether one is retrieving set information or property information. Five of the six mean scores fit this predicted pattern. The mean that stands out as not fitting this pattern is for S0. The authors explain that this may have been because S0 is a special kind of sentence involving repetition of a word ('A canary is a canary'). Subjects reported that they did not even really need to read these sentences, but could respond quickly on the basis of simple pattern matching. This may have been the cause of the quicker than expected reaction times in this condition.

This type of model has been highly influential in research on semantic memory. It went on to be developed and revised by Collins and Loftus (1975) in their work on spreading-activation, which shifted emphasis away from the notion of hierarchical organization, and focused more on the number, length and strength of links between nodes. These ideas are somewhat dated now, particularly with the advent of superior computational possibilities. However, models of human memory still tend to be based on some notion of networks of connections among nodes, and all must deal with the powerful human capacity for inference.

Questions

suggested answers → p. 501

1. Why was it necessary to use a computer to run this experiment?

2. What is the point of building computational models of human cognitive processes?

3. Draw up your own hierarchical network of a domain which is of interest to you (for example, sport, music, animals, psychological research methods).

Hearing colours, tasting shapes

RAMACHANDRAN, V.S. AND HUBBARD, E.M. (2001)

Psychophysical investigations into the neural basis of synaesthesia.

Proceedings of the Royal Society of London, 268, 979–83.

▶**synaesthesia** A mixing of the senses. For example a synaesthete might hear colours, see sounds, and taste tactile sensations.

▶**memory** The capacity to retain and retrieve information.

Introduction

Does everyone see the world in the way that you do? Do they see the same colours and hear the same sounds? The simple answer is 'no', and people with synaesthesia experience the world in quite an unusual way.[1] Synaesthesia (also spelt synesthesia) is a most intriguing condition that is experienced by a small number of people. It involves the mixing up of the senses, such that sounds are 'seen', or sights are 'smelt'. Our title for this summary comes from a paper in *Scientific American* by Ramachandran and Hubbard (2003), and captures the unusual sensory juxtapositions that people with synaesthesia seem to experience. The paper that we actually summarize here is also by Ramachandran and Hubbard, but it is an earlier paper of theirs, from 2001.

There are three main perspectives on synaesthesia. First there is the proposal that it is really a form of rather vivid memory. Perhaps a taste was strongly associated in one person's childhood with a particular shape, through some sort of classical conditioning, so that that person now 'remembers' that taste when they see the shape. Second is the suggestion that it is actually a form of metaphor. The person who describes a colour when they hear a particular note on the piano is really just creatively conveying their inner experience through words. They do not directly perceive the colour, but it captures something about the sound that is real for them, rather in the same way that great writers and poets are able to convey aspects of experience to their audience:

> King Claudius
> Though yet of Hamlet our dear brother's death
> The memory be green, and that it us befitted
> To bear our hearts in grief (*Hamlet*, Act 1, Scene 2)

Third, and perhaps the most intriguing perspective, is that synaesthesia is a 'genuine sensory phenomenon' (Ramachandran and Hubbard, 2001, p. 979). When synaesthetes report tasting a shape it is because they really are tasting it; not just remembering, and not just being creative. The researchers who authored this paper make it quite clear that it is this perspective that they favour, and the study they report on is one that is designed to test their views empirically.

---

1. Some artists and composers claimed to experience synaesthesia. For example the abstract expressionist painter Vasily Kandinsky attempted to make visual representations of music. If you check out his paintings you can see what he was trying to do.

The study

▸**grapheme** The symbol that represents a number or a letter. The word 'grapheme' contains eight graphemes, two of them the same.

If you cover a white sheet of paper with lots of the number grapheme '5' (written as a number, and in black), and then change some of those 5s to 2s, the 2s will be quite difficult to spot, because the shape of the numerals are so similar (they are potentially mirror images of one another). If you arrange the 2s into a specific shape that is embedded within the mass of number 5s, it should be very hard to see that shape. Of course if the 2s and the 5s were written in different colours, then it would rather easy to see the shape that the 2s make (see Figures 15.5a and 15.5b).

a)

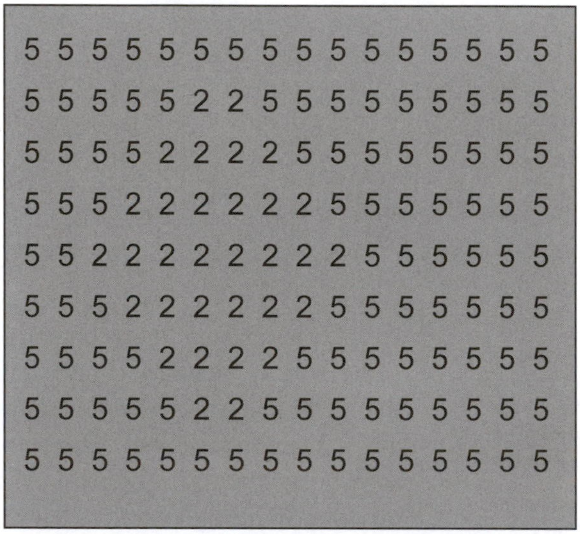
5 5 5 5 5 5 5 5 5 5 5 5 5 5 5 5
5 5 5 5 5 2 2 5 5 5 5 5 5 5 5 5
5 5 5 5 2 2 2 2 5 5 5 5 5 5 5 5
5 5 5 2 2 2 2 2 2 5 5 5 5 5 5 5
5 5 2 2 2 2 2 2 2 2 5 5 5 5 5 5
5 5 5 2 2 2 2 2 2 5 5 5 5 5 5 5
5 5 5 5 2 2 2 2 5 5 5 5 5 5 5 5
5 5 5 5 5 2 2 5 5 5 5 5 5 5 5 5
5 5 5 5 5 5 5 5 5 5 5 5 5 5 5 5

b)

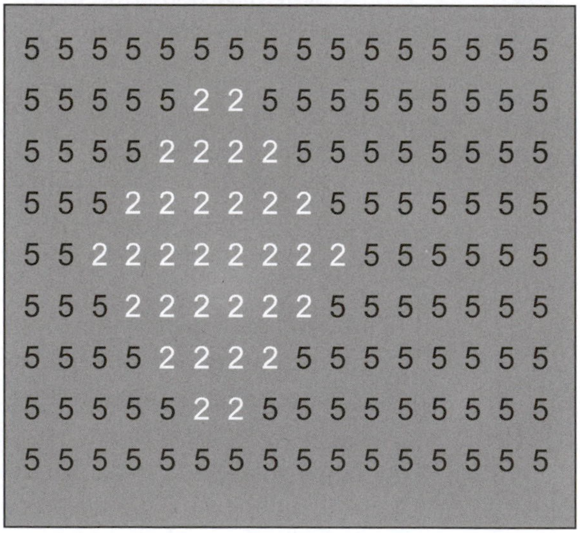
5 5 5 5 5 5 5 5 5 5 5 5 5 5 5 5
5 5 5 5 5 2 2 5 5 5 5 5 5 5 5 5
5 5 5 5 2 2 2 2 5 5 5 5 5 5 5 5
5 5 5 2 2 2 2 2 2 5 5 5 5 5 5 5
5 5 2 2 2 2 2 2 2 2 5 5 5 5 5 5
5 5 5 2 2 2 2 2 2 5 5 5 5 5 5 5
5 5 5 5 2 2 2 2 5 5 5 5 5 5 5 5
5 5 5 5 5 2 2 5 5 5 5 5 5 5 5 5
5 5 5 5 5 5 5 5 5 5 5 5 5 5 5 5

Figure 15.5 *'Pop-out' task*
Note: In the original, the numbers 2 in Figure 15.b were shown in red; here we have shown them in white.

Now suppose that you were a synaesthete who sees different numbers as different colours (you might be, of course!). If your synaesthesia was a genuinely *sensory* phenomenon, then you should be able to see the embedded pattern in the black and white version of the task (Figure 15.5a) just as readily as most non-synaesthetes see it in the multi-coloured version (Figure 15.5b). If on the other hand what you were really experiencing was some sort of memory or metaphor, rather than a real sensation, then it should be no easier for you to see the embedded pattern in the black and white version of the task than it would be for non-synaesthetes. This study reports on a set of tasks like this that were undertaken with two synaesthetes in order to explore what kind of a phenomenon synaesthesia really is.

Methods

The two subjects (referred to as J.C. and E.R.) were colour-number synaesthetes. They both 'saw' different colours for different numbers, and one of them at least saw different colours for different letters as well. Their performance on a set of tasks was compared with 20 control subjects who were not synaesthetes. The tasks that were used were as follows:

(1) Displays of numbers were constructed in tabular form, with seven columns and five rows (see Figure 15.6). The numbers were evenly spaced. They were selected so that they would 'group' perceptually by shape either in rows or in columns. If they grouped by shape in rows (as do the 3s and the 8s in Figure 15.6a), then the columns were designed to invoke distinct, alternating colours for the synaesthetes. If they grouped by shape in columns then the rows were designed to stand out as alternating colours for the synaesthetes. If the synaesthetes' experience of 'coloured' numbers was truly perceptual, then the matrices should appear to them to be organized according to 'colour' rather than shape. Different matrices were constructed for each synaesthete to reflect their colour-number connections. For example, Figure 15.6(b) shows how the display might look to one of the synaesthetes who saw different shades of red for the numbers 3 and 7 (shown here in white type), and different shades of green for the numbers 8 and 0. The synaesthetes and control subjects all undertook 144 trials on this perceptual grouping task, judging on each trial whether the numbers grouped in rows or columns.

(2) The second task, also a perceptual grouping task, used sets of numbers and letters. Each display comprised a set of distractor (background) letters or numbers, with one of four embedded shapes (a square, diamond, triangle or rectangle) formed out of a specific letter or number hidden within them. The different letters or numbers for each display were chosen to create specific colour contrasts for each of the synaesthetes. For example, in Figure 15.7 the Hs were seen as green by one of the synaesthetes, while the Ps and Fs were seen as red and yellow respectively. Control subjects should find the shape formed by the H extremely difficult to see. A series of these stimulus screens were displayed to the synaesthetes and to the

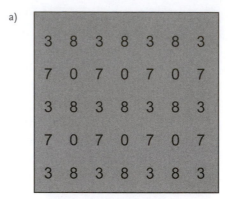

Figure 15.6 *Ramachandran and Hubbard's experiment for syaesthetes*
Note: In Figure b, in the original test the numbers shown in white were coloured red, and the black numbers were coloured green

control subjects. Each screen was displayed for one second, after which the subject had to identify which of the four shapes they had seen by pressing one of four keys on a keyboard.

(3) The third task involved displaying a letter that moved outwards, into peripheral vision, while the synaesthete stared at a fixation point in the middle of a display screen. The control subjects were not used in this task.

Results

For Task 1, J.C. reported 91 per cent of the trials as grouped in a way that was consistent with his colour associations, rather than by number shape. Control subjects, in contrast, grouped roughly 50 per cent of the trials by shape, indicating that there was no strong perceptual grouping effect working for them either way. E.R. reported 87 per cent of her matrices as grouped according to her colour associations, while the control subjects reported groupings that were consistent with grouping by shape ($p < .001$). In both cases the findings clearly suggest that the synaesthetes were 'seeing' the stimulus numbers as colours.

The two synaesthetes (81 per cent correct) performed significantly better on

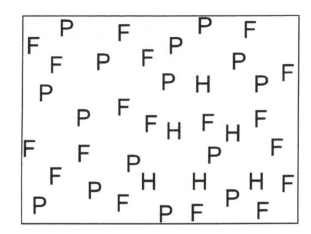

Figure 15.7   *The second task: a matrix of Hs forming a triangle shape embedded in a background of distractors*

Note: Normals find it difficult to detect the triangle. Synaesthete J.C. did so easily (for him the Hs were seen as green, the background Fs were seen as yellow and the Ps were seen as red).

Task 2 ($p < .05$) than did the control subjects (59 per cent correct), indicating that the synaesthetes were better able to see the embedded figure.

For the third task it was noted that the synaesthetes did not see colour if the numbers were presented a certain distance away from their point of fixation, within their peripheral vision. At this distance the subjects could still identify the numbers, but the colour experience did not occur. The researchers argue that if the synaesthesia was a kind of memory, or metaphor, it should not be affected by where the number is within a person's field of view: 'memories ordinarily show positional invariance' (Ramachandran and Hubbard, 2001, p. 981).

Discussion

The findings from these intriguing experiments indicate that the two synaesthetes experience colour as a real, physical sensation when seeing numbers. That is, they are not just experiencing vivid memories. Nor are they simply describing their experience by means of visually rich metaphor. They are actually seeing the colours that they report.

This is rather interesting because it suggests a physiological basis for synaesthesia, and has implications for a general understanding of how the brain is 'wired'. Ramachandran and Hubbard argue that one highly plausible explanation of the phenomenon is that it results from cross-wiring of different adjacent areas of the brain that typically deal with different perceptual tasks. In the case of colour-number synaesthesia the areas of the brain that process colour (on the one hand) and number graphemes (on the other) are next to each other in the fusiform gyrus (see Figure 15.8). If these areas are cross-wired that could explain why seeing a number grapheme causes the sensation of seeing a colour.

Why would such cross-wiring occur? There are a number of possibilities. Very early brain development in infancy is associated with rapid growth and

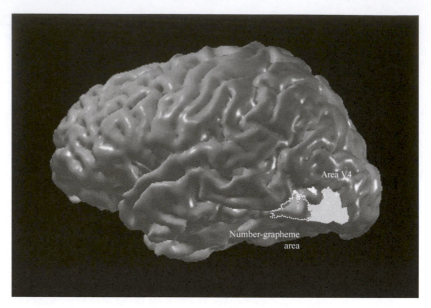

Figure 15.8 *Schematic showing that cross-wiring between area V4 and the number-grapheme area in the fusiform gyrus might be the neural basis of grapheme-colour synaesthesia*

Note: These can be seen in the lower right area of the image; area V4 is shown in lighter shades, and the number-grapheme area is the area within the dotted line (after Rickard *et al.*, 2000). Area V4 was defined by the use of standard functional magnetic resonance imaging methods.

▶ **synapses** Connections between nerve cells

with a proliferation of synapses. It may be that in the growing brain there is lots of connectivity across (what will become) different specialized pathways such that input from the different senses is not clearly differentiated in the infant (Stetri, 1987). In other words, synaesthesia may be a stage of typical development! Thereafter, there is a period of 'pruning', during which the overall connectivity within the brain *decreases*. It is thought that this decrease in connectivity is very important, and is associated with the increasing specialization of neural pathways (for the different senses, for example) that the child is learning to use (see Mareschal *et al.*, 2004). Synaesthesia in adults may be a result of 'faulty' pruning, with some unusual cross-pathway connectivity preserved. Furthermore there may be a genetic basis to this. Both the synaesthetes in this study had parents who were also synaesthetes.

Questions

suggested answers ➔ p. 502

1. Design a task to test whether a form of 'taste' synaesthesia (let's say 'tasting shapes') is a real perceptual process, as opposed to a vivid memory, or rich metaphor.

2. Design a task to test whether a form of auditory synaesthesia (let's say 'hearing colours') is a real perceptual process, as opposed to a vivid memory, or rich metaphor.

chapter **16**

ATTENTION

'WHY don't you pay attention?' someone barks at you. But don't they realize how difficult it is to pay attention when there are so many things to listen to or watch? The perceptual world is full of changing stimuli. Sounds, shapes, colours and smells wash around us all the time and the teacher still expects us to keep attending to her lecture on the life cycle of the gnat. What is she on?

To make sense of the world we have to select things from complex arrays of stimuli. If we did not do this we would be overwhelmed by the vast amount of sensations we experience. This selection means that we miss most things and attend to a small proportion of the world around us. We have to prioritize what is important and what is not. So when we are driving we try to attend to all the things that might affect our smooth progress along the road. It is accepted that we can only attend to so many things at one time and that is why the use of mobile phones while driving has been banned in the UK (see for example Strayer et al., 2003).

One of the puzzles of attention is illustrated in 'the cocktail party effect' which refers to the phenomenon of being able suddenly to tune in to a conversation to which you were not attending. You are standing in one group of people and if you were asked what was being said elsewhere you would say that you did not know. So how is it then that if another group mentions your name that you can suddenly switch your attention?[1] If you were not listening to their conversation how did you manage to hear this one word? You must have been filtering the information in some way to see if anything interesting came up so that you could switch over your attention if required. This is a very canny trick and it is not obvious how we manage to pull it off.

You can observe how strong this phenomenon is by placing a tape recorder next to yourself in a crowded room. Listen to the conversation for a while and then play back the tape. It would not sound anything like what you heard. On the tape will be a confusion

---

1. The naming of this as the 'cocktail party effect' says something about the psychologists who did the work as neither of the authors of this text has ever been to a cocktail party or even knows what one is.

of voices and it will be difficult to pick out any one thread of conversation but when you were there you heard the conversation without the buzz of noise and without the confusion. This filtering is the mental trick we call attention.

Early experimental work on attention was carried out on air-traffic controllers. They were experiencing two key problems. The first was having to apply intense concentration to the relatively boring task of staring at a screen and looking for changes. This is referred to as sustained attention, and the studies (for example Mackworth, 1950) found that performance at tedious tasks gets worse over time. As a result air-traffic controllers were given short shifts at the screens to minimize errors. In the early days of air travel the air-traffic controllers also had to communicate with the pilots over loudspeakers in the control tower. This meant that they had to select the voice of the pilot they were dealing with and ignore the others that were coming over the loudspeakers. This was the problem of selective attention that Colin Cherry (1953) set out to explore. Cherry devised a dichotic listening technique to investigate selective attention. This technique delivered a different message to each ear and it was the job of the listener to track one message and ignore the other. Theses studies provided some evidence on what it is possible to attend to and how much we can process of the unattended message.

In this chapter we have selected three papers that illustrate some of the remarkable phenomena of attention. The first study by Sperling (1960) shows that we are able to respond to much more sensory information than we might suppose. The second paper by Gray and Wedderburn (1960) is an example of the dichotic listening technique devised by Cherry. This illustrates further complexity in the way we are able to select messages to attend to. The final paper by Simons and Chabris (1999) is a modern classic that you probably will not believe when you read it. Fortunately there is a website to go to to check it out. In brief the study shows that if we are focusing our attention on one part of the visual world it is possible to miss massive changes in another part.

▶ **selective attention** The ability to direct our cognitive focus so that we pay attention to some stimuli and ignore or pay less attention to others.

▶ **dichotic listening** A procedure where different stimuli are presented to each ear simultaneously.

Now you see it, now you don't

SPERLING, G. (1960)

The information available in brief visual presentations.

Psychological Monographs, 74 (No. 11. Whole no. 498)

▶**multi-store model** Model of memory that proposes distinct memory stores, including long-term memory and short-term memory.

▶**sensory buffer** Short-acting memory store for the sensory record of a stimulus.

▶**iconic memory** The sensory memory for visual information.

▶**evolution** The development of bodily form and behaviour through the process of natural selection.

▶**cognition** Mental processes. 'All the processes by which ... sensory input is transformed, reduced, elaborated, stored, recovered and used' (Neisser, 1967, p. 4).

Introduction

According to the conventional multi-store model (Atkinson and Shiffrin, 1968), human memory comprises three different types of store: the sensory register, short-term memory, and long-term memory (see the summary of Craik and Lockhart, 1972, Chapter 13). Sperling's paper deals with the characteristics of the first of these stores, the sensory register, and examines how it deals with visual stimuli. The sensory register for visual information is often referred to as iconic memory.

Information from our environment is sensed by receptor cells, which respond to different types of physical energy: light, sound, heat and so forth. Patterns of receptor cell activation are stored for very brief periods of time as a sensory trace. These brief traces of receptor cell activity are what cognitive psychologists refer to as the sensory register, and can be thought of as the first stage of memory. It may be that in an evolutionary sense this relatively simple form of remembering was the first step in the development of those higher-order cognitive processes that we call memory.

One function of the sensory register is to enable the processing of complex stimuli, something people do every second of every day. Interpreting the meaning of patterns of receptor cell activity is a complex computational problem, particularly since these patterns are constantly changing. For example, when you see something (or hear something, or feel something, or smell something) it takes time and cognitive resources to process what it is that you have seen (or heard, or felt, or smelt). The sensory register acts as a kind of buffer, or temporary storage bin, that can hold unattended bits of the stimuli available for a fraction of a second, whilst the attended-to bits of the stimuli are processed.

It is probably the characteristics of iconic memory which allow cine film to work. Cine film appears to present a continuous moving image, when in fact it is a series of still shots put together in a way that gives the illusion of continuous movement. Between each individual frame of a film is a gap. If it was not for iconic memory, which maintains the receptor cell activity for a brief duration after the actual visual stimulus has disappeared, we would see these gaps. As it is, the gap is covered over by the 'memory' of the previous frame, until that memory is overwritten by the next frame. The result is the experience of continuity.

But how can the characteristics of such a fleeting kind of memory be investigated? Sperling set about this task by presenting research subjects with very brief exposures to visual stimuli. The questions that his work begins to address are:

(1) How long is information stored in iconic memory?

(2) In what format is information stored?

(3) How does forgetting happen?

The study

Subjects

> **forgetting** Loss of information through interference, decay, displacement or a failure to retrieve the information.

The data were collected from five subjects who each took part in 12 sessions, three per week. Four of the subjects were students, the fifth was one of Sperling's colleagues. It is interesting to note that, unlike most psychological research, Sperling wanted subjects who knew what the research was about, and who were practised at the tasks he set them. During the 12 sessions the subjects took part in seven experiments, over the course of which each subject did hundreds of trials.

Design

> **repeated measures design (also within groups)** An experimental design where each subject carries out each condition of the experiment.

The paper reports on all seven experiments. The basic design principle that Sperling was following throughout was repeated measures. In other words, he was always interested in comparing the scores of each subject on one task (condition) with their own performance on other tasks (conditions). In fact, the comparisons he makes stretch across the experiments he conducted (for example, the performances of subjects in Experiment 1 were compared with their performances in Experiment 3). Indeed, many of his key findings are extracted from these cross-experiment comparisons.

Materials and apparatus

> **tachistoscope** Apparatus for presenting brief visual displays.

The main piece of apparatus was a two-field tachistoscope (t-scope). A t-scope can make visual stimuli appear for very brief, precisely timed durations. For most of the experiments reported here an exposure time of 50 msec (one twentieth of a second) was used. The fact that it was a two-field t-scope simply means that it was capable of projecting two separate images (perhaps one immediately after the other) on each trial.

The stimuli that were presented in this way were cards with capital letters (and sometimes numbers) written on them. The letters were about 1 cm high, and were all consonants. They were arranged in various formats, according to the needs of the particular tasks. Typical arrangements are shown in Figure 16.1. Over 500 cards were used in order to prevent subjects learning the letters on any given card.

Procedures

The precise details of what subjects did changed from experiment to experiment, but the basic procedure was as follows. Working individually, the subjects were asked to stare (fixate) on a cross that was displayed where the stimulus material was about to appear. When they were ready, they clicked a button. This caused the stimulus card to be presented 0.5 seconds later. As soon as subjects received the cue to respond (which was sometimes immediately after

Type of display	3/3	4/4	3/3/3

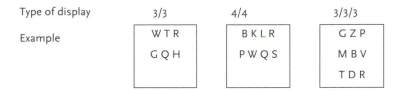

Figure 16.1 *Typical stimulus materials*

the image had been displayed, and sometimes after a tone) they wrote down all the stimulus items that they could remember in a response grid, guessing where necessary. Whenever the task was changed either within or across the experiments, the subject received two or three practice trials to familiarize themselves with the new procedures. It is difficult to tell from Sperling's paper exactly how many trials were involved for each subject in each experiment, but the number ranged from over 40 in Experiment 2, to over 215 in Experiment 1.

Trials were scored according to whether letters were recalled in the correct position on the response grid. Data analysis was by means of descriptive statistics, such as mean number of letters recalled by each subject, for each trial, on each type of task (in other words, for each trial of each condition). Sperling reported summaries of the findings from individual subjects separately. This is unusual in experimental work.

The individual experiments: results

This section gives brief descriptions of the experiments, including an outline of Sperling's findings and the implications of these findings. Only the first six experiments will be included because Experiment 7 is relatively unimportant for this summary.

Experiment 1: immediate memory

In this experiment subjects were simply asked to recall as many letters as they could from 12 different types of stimulus material. The complexity of the stimulus material ranged from cards with 3 letters to ones with 12 letters. As can be seen from Figure 16.2 subjects tended to get an average of 4 letters on each trial no matter how many letters were displayed. The overall average recall was 4.3 letters per trial.

This result suggests there is some kind of upper limit on the amount of material that can be remembered from very brief visual displays. However, the amount that can be recalled may not be the same as the amount that is available in the sensory register, because by the time subjects get to writing their answers down, the short-term memory bottlenecks have already begun to operate.

Experiment 2: exposure duration

This experiment showed that recall was not related to the length of exposure of the stimulus materials. In other words, recall performance stayed constant

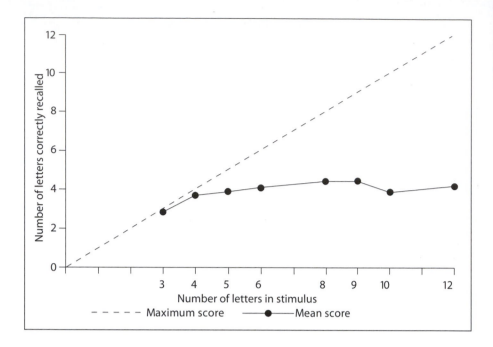

Figure 16.2 *Mean recall for full report*

across exposure durations of between 15 msec (0.015 of a second) and 500 msec (half-a-second). This simply shows that the 50 msec exposure duration used by Sperling was as good as any other brief exposure time he could have chosen.

Experiment 3: partial report

Sperling was interested to see if there was more information in the sensory register than subjects were able to report in Experiment 1. To investigate this he used an extremely well-thought-through technique, known as partial report. Subjects saw an array of letters in, say, a 3/3 format (three on the top row, three on the bottom) or a 4/4 format. Immediately after the stimulus had disappeared a tone was sounded. If the pitch of the tone was high, the subjects had to report back on the top line of letters. If the pitch of the tone was low, they had to report back on the bottom line of letters. Notice that the tone came after the stimulus disappeared, so it was not possible for subjects to look at the actual line of letters once they had heard the tone. Any information they were able to recall was therefore from their iconic store. Furthermore, the choice of tone was randomly selected, so if you tried to second guess which tone would appear and focus on one of the lines you would be likely to guess correctly only 50 per cent of the time and therefore would not improve your overall score. Later on in this experiment subjects also did 3/3/3 arrays (three rows of three letters) and 4/4/4 arrays (three rows of four letters), and a tone of middling pitch was introduced to signify the middle row.

This procedure produces a genuinely random sample of each set of

▶**random sample** A way of selecting a sample where every person from the defined population has an equal chance of being chosen.

stimulus materials. Because of this Sperling was allowed to assume that whatever proportion of letters was recalled correctly from the specified row could also have been recalled from the unspecified row(s). So, if the subjects were able to recall 75 per cent of the line it is reasonable to suggest they would have been able to recall 75 per cent of any line and hence 75 per cent of the total display.

Using this technique, Sperling was able to show that there was more information available within the iconic store than was demonstrated by subjects in the 'full report' task of Experiment 1. In the 3/3 trials, after two complete sessions, the average number of letters available to subjects was 5.6 out of 6. For the 4/4/4 stimulus materials, the average number of letters available was 9.1 out of 12. The mean scores for all subjects for all the displays are shown in Figure 16.3.

Experiment 4: decay of available information

The partial report procedure allowed Sperling to examine how long information remains available in the sensory register. This was done simply by delaying the recall cue. In the previous experiment the recall cue had been given immediately after the stimulus display. In this experiment the timing of the recall cue was used as the independent variable, and was systematically adjusted so that subjects performed in the following conditions: 00 msec delay, 150 msec delay, 300 msec delay, 500 msec delay (half a second), 1000 msec delay (one second). There was also a condition with a recall cue which came 50 msecs before the exposure. Nine-letter (3/3/3) and 12-letter (4/4/4) stimulus materials were used.

▶ **independent variable** The conditions which an experimenter sets up, to cause an effect in an experiment. These vary systematically, so that the experimenter can draw conclusions about changes in outcomes.

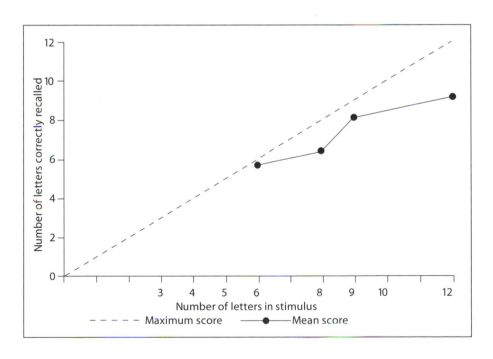

Figure 16.3 *Mean recall for partial report*

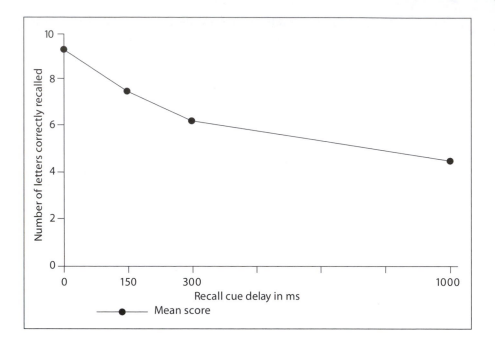

Figure 16.4 *Mean recall for partial report with delayed recall cue*

Figure 16.4 shows the average recall across subjects for the 4/4/4 trials. One subject did not do any of the 150, 300 or 500 msec trials, so the figures presented are averages for four subjects only. Two of these subjects did not do the 500 msec trials, so no average figure is given for that condition.

The figure displays the characteristic 'forgetting curve'. Immediate partial recall (0 msec delay) shows that approximately 9 of the 12 letters are available in the iconic store. This information appears to decay rapidly, so that at 300 msec only six letters are still available. After one second the number of letters available has fallen to the same level as for full report (Experiment 1). In other words, with the one-second delay, after processing the four or five letters that were immediately available to them, the subjects were unable to return to the iconic store to 'pick up' additional information, because that information had by then deteriorated. This is the basic type of evidence that psychologists have used to argue that the iconic store can store information for up to one second, and that if it is not processed further within that time, it will decay and be forgotten.

Experiment 5: some exposure parameters

The most important finding of this experiment was that a 'non-informational, homogenous, bright, post-exposure field' (p. 12) decreased the quantity of information available to the subjects from their iconic store. Correct recall was approximately halved in the condition where a bright post-exposure field was displayed for approximately one second after the stimulus field. This suggests that the information in iconic memory is stored visually, and that forgetting can be caused by 'overwriting' as well as by decay.

Experiment 6: letters and numbers

In this experiment a 4/4 L and N array (4 letters and 4 numbers jumbled up across two rows) was used. Different sounding tones were used to indicate whether the subject was to recall letters or numbers. The results showed that partial report based in this way on category (rather than on physical position, as in Experiment 3) produced only fractionally better recall than full report. In contrast, partial report by row showed that over seven out of the eight items were in fact available in the subject's iconic store. This suggests that the information is held in the iconic store in a pre-categorical, veridical form. This is a literal copy of the visual stimulus which has not yet been processed for meaning. It is possible to read off information like the spatial arrangement of the letters directly from the iconic store (because in a sense the subject can still 'see' it). This makes partial report by row relatively easy, because the subject can ignore the row(s) that have not been cued. But it is not possible to read off semantic information (whether a particular collection of lines and curves is a letter or a number) directly from the iconic store. In other words, the subject cannot simply ignore letters if they are cued to recall numbers, because they need to process the stimuli before they can tell whether they are letters or numbers. By the time they have done this for three or four items (and decided to discard, say, two of them, because they turn out to be letters), any unattended parts of the stimulus array will have decayed.

Discussion

Sperling's work has been influential in terms of both its method and its results. Tachistoscopic presentations of visual stimuli for very brief durations are an established method of investigation in this area. And the findings that Sperling presents in this paper still represent a bedrock of scientific knowledge about iconic memory. These findings have contributed to the conventional understanding that iconic memory has the following characteristics:

(1) Iconic memory can hold much more information than can be attended to and processed further. Most of the information in iconic memory is simply forgotten before we are even aware of it (Experiments 1 and 3).

(2) Information can persist in iconic memory for, at most, one second. If it is not attended to in that time for further processing, it is forgotten (Experiment 4).

(3) Information is stored in iconic memory in the form of a literal, un-interpreted copy of the original stimulus. Sometimes it is referred to as 'pre-categorical' for this reason (Experiments 5 and 6).

(4) Forgetting in iconic memory is by means of decay (Experiment 4) and by means of information being overwritten by incoming stimuli (Experiment 5).

Sperling's study was a remarkable breakthrough at the time of publication, both for what he discovered and for the methods he devised. He started the work on sensory memory in 1957 as part of his doctoral studies when George Miller (see Chapter 18 of this volume) arranged for him to borrow a tachistoscope. In 1988 Sperling was given the Distinguished Scientific Contribution Award by the American Psychological Association for his work on cognition (Anon, 1989).

Questions

suggested answers
→ p. 502

1. Why were only consonants used on the stimulus cards?

2. From your understanding of Experiment 6, what would you predict would be the outcome of an experiment with a 4/4/4 format of stimulus letters, 4 of which were coloured red, 4 of which were coloured black, and 4 of which were coloured green (with the different colours jumbled randomly across the rows and with different tones to cue recall by colour)?

3. Can you think of an example of the auditory sensory register (so called echoic memory) in operation?

GRAY, J.A. AND WEDDERBURN, A.A.I. (1960)

Grouping strategies with simultaneous stimuli.

Listening with one ear

Quarterly Journal of Experimental Psychology, 12, 180–4.

Introduction

Psychological research is often stimulated by a pressing practical need to understand some aspect of human behaviour. Sometimes this means that a series of research studies are carried out 'in the field': that is, in the actual settings in which the behaviour in question needs to be understood. This approach can increase the ecological validity of the research. But field studies are notably complex, and do not afford the same level of control over extraneous variables that can be achieved in laboratory-based work. A good example of applied research conducted in the laboratory is Gray and Wedderburn's (1960) investigation into selective attention. In order to see what their work applies to, we need to look at the research tradition in which they were working.

In the 1950s Broadbent was researching the attentional load on air-traffic controllers. Air-traffic control is renowned as an occupation which requires people to divide their attention across many competing sources of information, and to select certain types of information for further processing. Although air-traffic controllers are highly skilled and practised at this kind of information-processing, it can be assumed that the basic cognitive processes involved are a feature of everyday human cognition. For example, in the age of the television it is a common experience to try to listen to a conversation and the TV at the same time. It is impossible to give our full attention to both sources of information, and many of us have been caught out attending rather too carefully to the football results and not sufficiently carefully to a family conversation.

Broadbent set out to study these cognitive processes in the laboratory, under highly controlled conditions. One of the procedures that he used was known as dichotic listening. This is where subjects hear different auditory stimuli simultaneously in each ear. It is impossible for subjects to attend directly to all the incoming stimuli at once, so the procedure provides an opportunity to examine how this kind of informational overload is managed. A typical experiment using what Broadbent (1954) termed the split-span procedure would run as follows. The subjects wear stereo headphones, and they hear three numbers in one ear, and simultaneously hear three different numbers in the other ear.

The pairs of numbers are separated by about half a second. As soon as the three pairs of numbers have been heard, the subject tries to recall them either by speaking them out loud, or by writing them down. For half the trials they must recall 'by ear'. This means that they must recall all the numbers heard in one ear first, followed by all the numbers from the other ear. For the other half of the trials they must recall 'by pair'. This means that they must recall the first pair of numbers first, the second pair second, and the third pair last. See Figure 16.5 for an illustration of the procedure.

Intuitively we might expect the 'by pairs' recall to be easier, because it asks for recall in the order that the numbers were presented. In fact, subjects find

▶**fieldwork** Research which is conducted outside the laboratory.

▶**ecological validity** A way of assessing how valid a measure or test is (that is, whether it really measures what it is supposed to measure) which is concerned with whether the measure or test is really like its counterpart in the real, everyday world. In other words, whether it is truly realistic or not.

▶**selective attention** The ability to direct our cognitive focus so that we pay attention to some stimuli and ignore or pay less attention to others.

▶**cognition** Mental processes. 'All the processes by which … sensory input is transformed, reduced, elaborated, stored, recovered and used' (Neisser, 1967, p. 4).

▶**split-span procedure** Experimental procedure in which the participant is presented with two sets of stimuli simultaneously, one to each ear, and must divide their attention between them.

Correct recall 'by ears' = '358 914' or '914 358'
Correct recall 'by pairs' = '39 51 84' or '39 15 48'

Figure 16.5 *The split-span procedure*

▶ **sensory buffer** Short-acting memory store for the sensory record of a stimulus.

▶ **echoic memory** The sensory memory for sound.

the 'by ears' recall easier, and score more highly in that condition. Broadbent's interpretation of this finding was the catalyst for Gray and Wedderburn's project. Broadbent concluded that information is selected for further processing on the basis of its physical characteristics. In the split-span procedure the relevant physical characteristic was the input channel of the information: that is, which ear the information was being fed into. Broadbent argued that this information can be used to select one input channel (one ear) to attend to. The information from the attended channel is passed on for further processing to a limited capacity processor (short-term memory). The information from the unattended channel can then often be retrieved from the sensory buffer, where it is stored briefly in a kind of echoic memory (see Sperling, 1960, in Chapter 15 for more about sensory memory).

This model fits Broadbent's findings because in the 'by ears' condition, subjects only have to switch once from the attended channel to the sensory buffer (that is, after they have processed the information from the attended channel/ear). The 'by pairs' recall, in contrast, involves processing one item from the attended channel/ear, then switching to the sensory buffer to 'pick up' the unattended to item (from the other ear), then back again to the attended channel, then back to the sensory buffer ... by which time the information in the sensory buffer has probably decayed, and recall is consequently poorer.

The crucial point here is that Broadbent was arguing that information is selected for further processing on the basis only of its physical characteristics. In the split-span procedure the spatial location of the information (which ear it is being heard by) is the physical characteristic used by subjects. Other physical characteristics that can be used to select attention are things like the volume, pitch and rhythm of the auditory stimuli. Crucially this does not include the meaning of any incoming stimulus. It was Broadbent's view that at this early stage of information-processing the meaning of the incoming information was not yet accessible. For someone to understand what a piece of information meant, they first had to select it to attend to, and according to Broadbent they selected it on the basis of its physical characteristics.

Gray and Wedderburn set out to challenge the idea that we select what to attend to on the basis of the physical characteristics of the message. They argued that in the split-span procedure subjects have little choice but to make their selection on the basis of the physical characteristics of the stimuli, since the only way of making any discrimination is on the basis of which ear the information is heard in (all the stimuli are spoken by the same voice). So they decided to give the subjects another competing way of discriminating among the incoming stimuli. They decided to mimic the split-span procedure, using three numbers and three words. One ear would hear number–word–number. The other ear would simultaneously hear word–number–word. Furthermore, the three words would make a meaningful phrase (like 'there she goes'). Note that to pick up on the meaning of the phrase subjects must switch from one channel to the other and back again. According to Broadbent's model, subjects should still find it easier in this experiment to recall all the items from one channel (ear) before the other. If, however, subjects are able to use the meaning of the phrase to facilitate their recall, then this suggests that they are able to select material to attend to on something other than purely physical characteristics of the incoming stimuli.

Method

Subjects

▶ **dichotic listening** A procedure where different stimuli are presented to each ear simultaneously.

The subjects in this experiment were 15 undergraduates, five female and ten male. They had no experience of dichotic listening procedures.

Design

There was no formal experimental design reported in this paper. Gray and Wedderburn simply set their subjects a task, and observed how they performed it. Subjects were divided into two groups, and given slightly different instructions, but the comparison between the two groups was itself not an independent variable of any great importance. Although described as an experiment, it may be technically more accurate to call this a systematic observational study. One reason that this paper has been chosen for this book is because the researchers were undergraduates when they performed the study, and because it is published in a top journal, albeit in a 'Shorter Articles and Notes' section.

▶ **independent variable** The conditions which an experimenter sets up, to cause an effect in an experiment. These vary systematically, so that the experimenter can draw conclusions about changes in outcomes.

Materials and apparatus

The stimulus materials were played on a two-channel (in other words 'stereo') tape-recorder, and each channel was heard by one ear only. The stimuli for each trial comprised six items, including three numbers and three words. In one ear the information went number–word–number, and at exactly the same time the information in the other ear was word–number–word (see Figure 16.6). There was a half-second gap between each simultaneous pair of

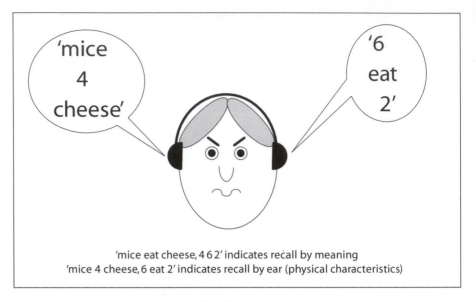

'mice eat cheese, 4 6 2' indicates recall by meaning
'mice 4 cheese, 6 eat 2' indicates recall by ear (physical characteristics)

Figure 16.6 *Gray and Wedderburn's dichotic listening task*

stimulus items, and a 13-second gap between each trial so that subjects could write down their responses. The three words made a phrase. Some of the phrases that were used were 'mice eat cheese', 'who goes there', 'my old flame', 'dear aunt Jane'. The numbers were generated from a table of random numbers, with no repetition within a trial.

Procedure

Subjects were divided into two groups, with seven in Group 1 and eight in Group 2. Group 1 were simply told that they would hear digits and words played to them. Group 2 were told that the words would make a phrase. Apart from that, all subjects undertook the same tasks under the same conditions. They were instructed to recall as many of the six stimulus items as they could for each of ten trials, by writing the items down after each set of six had been played. They were asked not to 'reshuffle' the items in their head or on the paper. The researchers wanted to know in what order the items would be recalled. The side of presentation of the stimuli was alternated so that for half the trials the first item presented to the left ear was a number, and for the other half of the trials it was a word.

In order to analyse the data, each subject's response for every trial was categorized 'according to strict conventions' (p.182) into one of three categories: 'ear', 'meaning' and 'indeterminate'. The 'ear' category referred to trials where the stimuli which had been presented to one ear were recalled before the stimuli that had been presented to the other ear. The 'meaning' category was for those trials in which recall was based on the three-word phrase. 'Indeterminate' referred to trials where it was unclear what strategy had been used to recall the items. The researchers simply report descriptive statistics relating to the levels of accuracy associated with each recall strategy.

Results

Most subjects used both 'ear' and 'meaning' methods of recall, though recall grouped by meaning was the preferred strategy for most subjects (see Table 16.1, column 2). Column 3 in Table 16.1 shows the percentage of trials in each of the three recall categories, for both groups of subjects: 37 per cent of Group 1's trials were recalled by meaning (21 per cent by ear), and 56 per cent of Group 2's trials were recalled by meaning (18 per cent by ear). Column 4 shows the percentage of items recalled correctly for those trials recalled by ear and for those recalled by meaning: for both groups recall by meaning produced greater accuracy, particularly for Group 2. Column 5 shows the number of lists which were perfectly recalled either by ear or by meaning, and, in parentheses, the number of subjects who achieved a perfect recall for at least one trial: all eight subjects in Group 2 achieved at least one perfect recall grouped by meaning.

Table 16.1   *Efficiency of performance in relation to method of grouping during recall*

Method of grouping for recall	Number of subjects with a recall preference	Percentage of trials in each recall category	Percentage of items recalled correctly	Number of trials with all six items correctly recalled
Group 1				
Ear	4	21	68	5 (1 subject)
Meaning	6	37	70	1 (1 subject)
Indeterminate	–	42	–	4 (1 subject)
Group 2				
Ear	5	18	66	1 (1 subject)
Meaning	8	56	87	21 (8 subjects)
Indeterminate	–	26	–	–

Discussion

▶ **inferential statistics** A way of using statistics to enable us to make inferences from data about relationships among variables, particularly with reference to cause and effect. This involves going *beyond* the data, hence the term 'inferential'. A contrast can be made with *descriptive statistics*.

The data show that recall organized by meaning is more effective than recall organized by ear. Since no inferential statistical tests were reported it is not possible to say whether this is a statistically significant effect. However, this is not so important here. Gray and Wedderburn were interested in whether recall by meaning was possible. By showing that it is at least as effective as recall by ear, they have a finding which challenges Broadbent's single-channel theory of attention. Broadbent's model would have predicted that recall should have been easier by ear, because that is still the key physical characteristic which should enable some items to be processed, and others to be held in the sensory buffer. By introducing a different 'difference' within the stimuli for each trial, a difference that was based on meaning rather than on any physical characteristics of the items, this investigation was able to challenge the notion that meaning only comes after attentional processes have selected information for further processing.

suggested
answers
→ p. 503

Questions

1. Broadbent regarded the ear in which a sound is heard as a physical property of a spoken auditory stimulus. What other physical properties of speech can you think of?

2. How ecologically valid is this study?

3. Try and think of some everyday examples of where you listen to or watch two messages at once. How do you do it? What unusual features of this process can you identify?

Introduction

Monkey business

SIMONS, D.J. AND CHABRIS, C.F. (1999)

Gorillas in our midst: sustained inattentional blindness for dynamic events.

Perception, 28, 1059–74; available at http://viscog.vp.uiuc.edu/reprints/simons videos available at http://viscog.beckman.uiuc.edu/media/Banyard_Grayson.html.

Some pieces of research have that special quality that first makes you laugh and then makes you think. This is the main criteria for being awarded an IgNobel Prize (http://improbable.com/ig/).[1] Some of the prizes are awarded with a touch of irony. For example the Royal Navy was awarded the 2000 Peace Prize for ordering its sailors to stop using live cannon shells, and to instead just shout 'Bang!' Some prizes, however, are awarded for sound pieces of research such as the study by Simons and Chabris, which is a scientific demonstration of a remarkable phenomenon. It is something that you would not believe unless you had seen it, or in this case, not seen it.

The phenomenon they investigated concerns our perceptual lapses where we do not notice something or someone that is right in front of our eyes. For example we sometimes find it difficult to spot changes in familiar images, which is often referred to as change blindness. When a partner spends a considerable amount of time and a bucketload of money on their new look, they expect some admiring comments when they meet you. If you do not notice the change and so ask 'have you paid the gas bill?' or 'do you know who scored for Forest at the weekend?' then they are disappointed and tell you that your failure to notice shows you do not care and that they are wasting their life with you. While both of these propositions might well be true there is actually a much better explanation for your failure to notice the new look. Next time you end up in a domestic dispute like this, remember to employ the change blindness defence.

Another type of perceptual lapse concerns our ability to focus on one part of our perceptual field and so not notice some important features elsewhere. This is referred to as inattentional blindness. For example, you might go into a crowded restaurant and be so focused on finding somewhere to sit that you miss one of our friends waving at you in the corner. When they confront you with your apparent rudeness later, you have a job explaining yourself.

The problem as stated in Simons and Chabris' paper is that the richness of our visual experience leads us to believe that our visual representations will include and preserve the same amount of detail as the original experience. We have a strong belief in the accuracy of our perceptions and memories, and we are reluctant to accept that they are not always accurate representations (see also the paper by Loftus and Pickrell on false memories). Simons and Chabris review the studies on inattentional blindness (the failure to perceive or remember visual items that we are not attending to) to draw out what we know about this phenomenon.

▶**change blindness** A phenomenon of visual perception where large changes within a visual image or scene are not detected by the viewer.

▶**inattentional blindness** The failure to perceive or remember visual items that you are not attending to.

---

1. These prizes, which are given out each year, are a balance to the Nobel Prizes which have been awarded every year since 1901 for achievements in physics, chemistry, physiology or medicine, literature and for peace (http://nobelprize.org/).

The key work that the researchers used as a stimulus for their study was carried out by Ulrich Neisser and colleagues about 30 years ago. In the design of one study (Neisser and Becklen, 1975) participants were asked to look at recordings of two separate events at the same time. In one event two people were playing a hand-slapping task and in the other three people were passing a basketball. In the conditions we are interested in here, participants were asked to follow and respond to one of the tasks. While they were doing this an unexpected event (such as losing the ball in the basketball task) happened in one of the tasks. Around 50 per cent of the participants showed no indication of having seen the unexpected event and even participants who did notice it were often unable to describe any details of it.

In later work on the basketball game task, participants were asked to watch a video of two teams passing the ball and to press a key every time members of one team made a pass. During this task a woman with an umbrella walks across the screen and is visible for four seconds (the unexpected event). Only six out of 28 participants reported seeing the woman even when directly questioned about her after the task. This experimental design has been used in other studies (Neisser, 1979), with the variation of superimposing the umbrella-woman onto the video of the basketball action. The interesting point from this variation is that it shows that the inattentional blindness does not come from being focused on events elsewhere. The umbrella-woman is still often missed even when the basketball passes right through her on the video so the viewer stares right through her image and does not see her.

The study

Simon and Chabris use a variation of Neisser's umbrella-woman technique to investigate four questions about inattentional blindness. They look at whether the likelihood of noticing the unexpected event is affected by:

- the difficulty of the task the participants are asked to do;
- whether the images are superimposed or whether the scene is filmed as one event;
- the nature of the unexpected event;
- whether the unexpected event and the attended event are similar or not.

Observers

There were 228 participants in the study, most of whom were students. They either volunteered or were given small inducements to take part. In the analysis 36 of the participants were excluded from the data for a variety of reasons, including not doing the task correctly and being aware of the experimental design before they did the study.

The videos

There were four videos, each of which was 75 seconds long. Each video showed two teams (wearing white shirts or black shirts) of three players who moved around in front of three elevator doors passing a basketball to each other either by throwing or bouncing. After 44–48 seconds one of two unexpected events occurred. Either a tall woman holding an umbrella walked left to right across the screen (Umbrella-woman condition), or a smaller woman in a gorilla suit (Gorilla condition) walked through the basketball players in the same way (see Figure 16.7, and you can see the video at the link given in the title panel of this summary). In both cases the unexpected event took about five seconds.

Figure 16.7   *The unseen gorilla*

Source: D.J. Simons and C.F. Chabris (1999). Gorillas in our midst: sustained inattentional blindness for dynamic events. *Perception*, 28, 1059–74. Figure provided by Daniel Simons.

There were two styles of video. In one condition the white team, black team and unexpected event were all filmed separately and then superimposed on each other so you could see them all at the same time (Transparent condition). In the other condition all seven actors were filmed at the same time (Opaque condition).

The participants were tested individually and watched one of the videos. They were either told to pay attention to the team in white (White condition) or the team in black (Black condition). Half of them were told to keep a mental note of the total number of passes made by the team (Easy condition) and the other half were told to count the number of bounce passes and the number of thrown passes by the attended team (Hard condition).

This all sounds much more complicated than it is, so we have summarized the design in Table 16.2, which shows just how logical and straightforward the study is.

After the video the participants were asked a series of questions starting with 'While you were doing the counting did you notice anything unusual on the video?' followed by questions that attempted to prompt recall of the unexpected event. However none of the participants that replied 'no' to the first question gave a different response to the prompts, so the recorded data deal with the first question only.

Table 16.2 *The design of the experiment*

Unexpected event	Style of video	Team attended to	Type of task
Umbrella-Woman	Transparent	White	Easy
			Hard
		Black	Easy
			Hard
	Opaque	White	Easy
			Hard
		Black	Easy
			Hard
Gorilla	Transparent	White	Easy
			Hard
		Black	Easy
			Hard
	Opaque	White	Easy
			Hard
		Black	Easy
			Hard

Results

Overall there were 192 viewings of a video, and across all conditions 54 per cent noticed the unexpected event, which shows a remarkable level of inattentional blindness. Table 16.3 shows the percentage breakdown of people seeing the unexpected event in each condition.

Table 16.3 *Percentage of participants noticing the unexpected event in each condition*

	Easy task		Hard task	
	White team	Black team	White team	Black team
Transparent				
Umbrella-woman	58	92	33	42
Gorilla	8	67	8	25
Opaque				
Umbrella-woman	100	58	83	58
Gorilla	42	83	50	58

When you combine the conditions you get the following summaries; more observers noticed the unexpected event in the:

- Opaque condition (67%) than the Transparent condition (42%);
- Easy condition (64%) than the Hard condition (45%);
- The Umbrella-woman condition (66%) than the Gorilla condition (43%);
- Gorilla condition when asked to concentrate on the Black team (58%) than the White team (27%).

Discussion

The main findings can be summarized as follows:

(a) When people are focused on a monitoring task about half of them will fail to notice an unexpected event. The researchers went a step further and ran a new version of the Gorilla condition where the gorilla stopped in the middle of the screen looked to camera and pounded its chest before walking off. Only half of the participants in this new condition noticed the gorilla.

(b) The phenomenon of inattentional blindness is robust and can be observed in a range of conditions and video formats.

(c) The level of inattentional blindness depends on the difficulty of the monitoring task.

(d) Observers are more likely to notice unexpected events if they are visually similar to the events to which they are paying attention. So the participants who were watching the basketball players in black shirts were more likely to see the gorilla (which was black) than those watching the white-shirted team.

One of the remarkable observations was that of the 88 people who did not see the unexpected event, none of them remembered the gorilla or umbrella-woman when they were specifically asked about or even told about it. In fact many had to be shown the video to prove to them that the event occurred, with some expressing their surprise by saying 'I missed *that*?!'

Phenomena like this create interesting problems for cognitive psychologists as they try to explain first what is going on and second why. In the discussion Simons and Chabris explore the factors that might be most important in understanding inattentional blindness and also explaining change blindness. On an ethical note the authors reassuringly record at the end of their paper that 'No animals were harmed in the making of the videos.'

Questions

1. The study uses students as participants. Is this important and if not why not?

2. What is the difference between change blindness and inattentional blindness?

3. Try to think of some everyday examples of change blindness and inattentional blindness.

suggested answers → p. 504

vi

PSYCHOLOGICAL METHODS

▶ discourse analysis A
method of studying human
experience by analysing
the things people say
to one another, and
how they express them,
both symbolically and
behaviourally.

▶ qualitative data Data
which describe meaning
and experience rather than
providing numerical values
for behaviour such as
frequency counts.

▶ quantitative data Data
which focus on numbers
and frequencies rather than
on meaning or experience.

IN some ways this whole text is about
psychological methods so why have this
section? The simple answers are first that
we wanted to emphasize some aspects
of the research process, and second that
we couldn't fit some of these studies in
elsewhere.

In Chapter 17 we consider some ways
of dealing with data, both qualitative
and quantitative. Some methods attract
adherents to the extent that they use
the method almost to the exclusion
of all others. In this case the method
becomes less a technique that you
choose to use when appropriate and
more a way of looking at the world. One
such method is the qualitative method
of discourse analysis, the introduction
of which in UK psychology is commonly
attributed to Potter and Edwards. We
include one of their papers. We include
another qualitative paper that takes
the more frequently used technique of
thematic analysis to look at the way
that people with AIDS make sense of
their condition (Weitz, 1989). As further
examples of quantitative techniques we
look at meta-analysis (Smith and Glass,
1977), which combines data from many
studies on the same topic. We also
look at the development of a
psychological scale to estimate the

level of stress in an individual (Holmes
and Rahe, 1967).

There are a number of potential fault
lines that run through psychology. Some
of these challenge our interpretations
of research studies. Human behaviour
and experience are very complex, and
anything we do or anything we say can
have numerous interpretations. When
we conduct studies we commonly have
an hypothesis in mind and, because we
are only human, we hope to get results
that go along with our expectations.
This means that we commonly see what
we want to see and fail to see things
that challenge our initial ideas. This
experimenter bias is only one of the
problems with research because our
participants are also likely to collude
with us. They might want to be 'good
participants' and help us to get the
results we want. As psychologists we
are in danger of unconsciously writing
a script for our participants to respond
to. If we do this then what we observe is
our 'play' rather than the real life we were
hoping for. In Chapter 18 we deal with
these and other issues of potential bias
in the way that we interpret our data.

The final chapter is different from all
the rest in that it does not contain any
summaries of research. What it does

instead is to summarize the main points in psychological research and to cross-reference them to the studies in the preceding 18 chapters.

Psychological research is a work in progress. We are still trying to find better ways to explore human behaviour and experience. Sometimes psychologists come up with new fancy pieces of equipment such as the eyetracker (see Carroll et al., 1992, in Chapter 14) and sometimes they are able to carry out experiments with grand designs (see Reicher and Haslam, 2006, in Chapter 3) and sometimes they will use very simple tricks to explore complex neurological events (see Ramachandran and Hubbard, 2001, in Chapter 15). Perhaps the most difficult thing to do is to get the right question and frame it in such a way that we can investigate it.

When we look at the findings of scientific research we are often in awe at what has been discovered and the technology that has been used to discover it. Sometimes we do not fully understand what was done or how the results were analysed. In these cases we have to rely on the experts to tell us what is what. Unfortunately they don't always get it right, sometimes because they make mistakes and sometimes because they are trying to mislead us. The more we know about how data are collected and interpreted, the less likely we are to be misled by experts. That is the point of this chapter and also one of the main reasons for this book.

chapter **17**

ANALYSING
DATA

> **qualitative data** Data which describe meaning and experience rather than providing numerical values for behaviour such as frequency counts.

> **discourse analysis** A method of studying human experience by analysing the things people say to one another, and how they express them, both symbolically and behaviourally.

> **quantitative data** Data which focus on numbers and frequencies rather than on meaning or experience.

IN this chapter we have chosen to focus on studies that have a particularly interesting approach to dealing with research data. The first two studies are both examples of analysing qualitative data (see Chapter 19, Section 1). The first one is by Potter and Edwards (1990) and uses the method of discourse analysis. Despite its name, discourse analysis is not just a method for dealing with data. It actually represents a tradition of enquiry within the social sciences based on a range of theoretical assumptions about communication and interaction between people. The paper we describe here concerns a political event in the 1990s when Nigel Lawson was Chancellor of the Exchequer in a Conservative government led by Margaret Thatcher.

The second paper by Weitz (1989) describes extensive interview research with people who had been given a diagnosis of AIDS. One way to explore people's responses to an event such as an illness is to give them a battery of tests and see how their scores on them are different from the scores of people without the illness. This approach can give us some valuable information but the answers we get are restricted by the

questions we ask. If, on the other hand, we use relatively unstructured interviews then our participants can set the agenda and describe the story as they see it. This is what Weitz set out to achieve, and in so doing she is able to give some unique insights into how people respond to chronic illness.

The next two papers illustrate ways of dealing with quantitative data. The first shows how a measuring tool can be developed. In this case there is an attempt to create a scale to measure stress. We have an intuitive judgement of 'load' when it comes to stress, by which we mean that as individuals we have an idea of how events will put some stress on us and the more events that happen to us the greater that sense of stress will become. One way of measuring stress, then, is to identify all the stressful events that happen to you, quantify their effect, and calculate the total 'load'. This is the approach that Holmes and Rahe (1967) adopted.

The final paper is an example of a meta-analysis (see Chapter 19, Section 2). Meta-analyses seek to answer a research question by combining all the pre-existing data sets within the literature that bear on that question, and re-analysing them together. They are rather like reviews of the current state of knowledge about a topic, but with a strongly empirical approach. They take a step back from a body of research on a topic and ask 'what, overall, does it all mean?'

Discourse analysis

POTTER, J. AND EDWARDS, D. (1990)

Nigel Lawson's tent: discourse analysis, attribution theory and the social psychology of fact.

European Journal of Social Psychology, 20, 405–24.

▶ **discourse analysis** A method of studying human experience by analysing the things people say to one another, and how they express them, both symbolically and behaviourally.

▶ **attribution theory** A social psychological theory which looks at how people understand the causes of their own, and other people's, behaviour.

Introduction

Potter and Edwards write in the area of discourse analysis, an approach to social psychology which takes a critical view of traditional social psychology and which emphasizes the role of language (discourse) in everyday life. The term discourse analysis is used in a variety of ways to describe a variety of things; here it refers to the kind of psychology advocated by Potter and Wetherell (1987).

Discourse analysts challenge the common-sense view that language is a purely descriptive medium used to convey information about the real world. They argue that language actually shapes (constructs) the real world, and our views of it. Their ideas may have far-reaching implications for how social psychology should be done. One of the most influential traditions in social psychology, attribution theory, has come in for especially heavy fire from discourse analysis. In this summary we will deal with just one of discourse analysis' criticisms of attribution theory: a criticism concerning method, which leads into a more general theoretical argument. The empirical work reported by Potter and Edwards focuses on this particular issue.

Attribution theory (see for example Jones et al., 1972; also Nisbett et al., 1973, and Chapter 2) is concerned with discovering the way that we come to conclusions about the causes of our own and other people's behaviour. The usual research procedure of attribution theory involves the presentation of 'vignettes' to research subjects. The vignettes (mini-stories) give brief descriptions of pieces of social behaviour. Typically, certain features of the description are systematically manipulated across conditions to create an experimental design. Subjects are asked to judge what caused the behaviour in each vignette, and the effects of the manipulations of the descriptions on the resulting causal judgements are observed.

It is not necessary to understand any more about attribution theory to follow the following critique (though more knowledge would, of course, help!). The vignettes supposedly supply the subjects with certain 'facts' about the situation in question. From these facts, the subjects make inferences about the causes of whatever was done by the characters in the story. The attribution researcher is interested in the inferences that the subjects make. Because the vignettes are descriptive and 'factual' they are thought to 'stand for' the situations they describe. In other words, subjects' interpretations of the vignettes are equivalent to what their interpretations would have been had they actually witnessed the events described.

The problem with this, according to discourse analysis, is that the 'facts' of the story are treated by the researcher as a problem-free bit of the whole exercise. They are treated as 'given', as though the person who wrote the vignette had no control over them. They are just gathered together in a neutral description of 'what really happened', and are of no particular interest in themselves.

What is of interest to the attribution theory researcher is how the subjects then go on to interpret the causes of 'what really happened'.

Discourse analysis points out that this whole process is based on a fundamental misapprehension of the relationship between words and reality. For a start, social behaviour is a very complex thing, so any short description of a piece of it must, in principle, rely on a selection of facts. This means that the writer of the vignette has already decided for the reader (in this case, for the research subject) what is and what is not relevant. And decisions about the relative relevance of different things are subjective and value-laden. The writer has also, for that matter, decided what constitutes a 'fact' in the first place. As the empirical work of Potter and Edwards in this paper shows, what does and does not constitute a fact is in itself open to argument and interpretation; 'what really happened' in any given slice of social behaviour is itself a matter of opinion.

So, discourse analysis argues that the vignettes that are used in attribution theory research are not just neutral descriptions of some piece of social behaviour. They are already loaded with meanings and implications by the selection of facts that the writer has chosen for inclusion, and by the things that the writer has chosen to present as facts. For these reasons they cannot just stand for reality, as they are but one version of events. The judgements that the subjects make about the causes of the behaviour described in the vignettes cannot be seen as equivalent to the judgements they would have made if they had directly witnessed the events in question, for those judgements have already been constrained by the version of events that has been imposed upon them.

The argument takes on a greater significance when we realize that the principles that Potter and Edwards are talking about apply just as much to real-life descriptions of events. Every day we encounter other people's versions of events, in the press, on the television, when we are gossiping and so forth.

On the basis of these versions, we form our own points of view about the events that have been described. What discourse analysis is arguing is that in forming our own points of view we should be aware that the descriptions we are receiving are never just neutral, factual descriptions of how things really happened. They are always someone's version of what happened. Furthermore, it is generally the case that people want their version of events to be believed, especially when the events in question are important and controversial. The upshot of this is that people will frame their version of events in the most believable and convincing way that they can. And one of the most effective ways of doing this is to make it sound as though they are just giving us a neutral unbiased account of the 'facts'! The empirical work presented by Potter and Edwards in this paper is a study of how people organize and structure their versions of events to try to make them appear factual and credible. They call this the study of factual discourse.

The study

The methods of discourse analysis involve the interpretation of texts. The texts that are typically used are detailed transcripts of naturally occurring talk, although any kind of text can be subjected to a discourse analysis. The materials that Potter and Edwards used in this study were newspaper articles and *Hansard* (a written record of the talking done within the British House of Commons). The analysis concerned a dispute which took place in Britain in the 1980s between a senior government minister and a group of journalists. The dispute arose from a briefing session in which Nigel Lawson (then Chancellor of the Exchequer, see Figure 17.1) reportedly briefed ten journalists on an idea to apply means-testing to benefits for old-age pensioners. When the idea was reported in the press, the Chancellor denied having floated it, accused the journalists of having produced 'a farrago of invention' (Hansard, 2 November 1988, cited in Potter and Edwards, p. 411), and argued that their accounts of the meeting were factually incorrect. So the core of the dispute was about what really happened at the briefing meeting, about what really were the facts of the matter. Potter and Edwards' study examines the way in which each side in the argument framed their version of events to make it appear as the more believable. Note that the data they use are textual, and that the texts are real ones, as opposed to ones that have been created in the laboratory.

Figure 17.1   *Nigel Lawson looking for a conspiracy*

Source: Popperfoto.

The focus of Potter and Edwards' analysis is on the notion of 'consensus' and on how this notion is used rhetorically (that is, how it is used in people's arguments) to make a version of events credible. The journalists' side of the story is grounded on the question 'how could ten journalists all have simultaneously misunderstood what Nigel Lawson was saying?' As the *Guardian* put it:

[In Nigel Lawson's view] the reporters, it seemed, had unanimously got it wrong. Could so many messengers really be so much in error? It seems doubtful. (cited in Potter and Edwards, p. 412)

The way in which the journalists and the papers for whom they worked were trying to convince the public that their account of events was truthful was to claim that ten independent witnesses all agreed on what the Chancellor had said. People tend to find this kind of argument convincing. Potter and Edwards highlight how the point is strengthened in the style of writing in the extract from the *Guardian* above. The use of the term 'so many' functions to make the consensus appear very big (and all the more convincing for that). They also suggest that the term 'unanimous' is used to emphasize the strength of consensus, which again has the function of making the journalists' account sound convincing and factual.

Nigel Lawson, however, continued to deny this apparently convincing consensus account given by the journalists. In his arguments, he redefined the 'consensus' among the journalists as 'collusion'; the fact that the journalists all agreed on what was said at the meeting did not mean that their account was correct. On the contrary, it meant that they must have got together after the meeting and colluded to create the story:

> Mr. Lawson: ... they went behind afterwards and they thought there was not a good enough story and so they produced that ... (*Hansard*, 7 November 1988, cited in Potter and Edwards, p. 416)

In a sense, the fact that so many agreed unanimously and to such a great extent was being used by Nigel Lawson to strengthen his case that there was collusion against him. The unspoken implication might be 'how often do ten genuinely independent journalists agree this much on anything (without having cooked it up among themselves)?' The title of Potter and Edwards' paper comes from Susan Crosland's commentary in the *Sunday Times* (13 November 1988):

> Nobody can say the Chancellor of the Exchequer is not a bold man. Who else would invite 10 senior journalists to his home for a briefing and then state that when his guests departed they went into a tent to concoct a 'farrago of invention'? (cited in Potter and Edwards, p. 106)

Discussion

The facts of the matter are clearly at the core of the dispute in this political incident. So any written or verbal account of the incident can only be a version, which would in the normal course of events be subject to refutations by other competing versions. This is in contrast to the attribution theory experiments, where the version of events given to subjects is not open to refutation; it is taken as factual and given. Yet, surely the inferences that a subject makes would depend entirely upon which version they happened to be presented with.

The facts of the matter about any given event do not speak for themselves. Facts can be presented in many different ways to support many different lines of argument. In this instance the fact that there were ten journalists present at the briefing is used by both sides to support their own case; the one argument based on consensus, the other on collusion and conspiracy. Discourse analysts argue that we have repertoires of argumentative techniques (rhetorical strategies) which we use, often very subtly and skilfully, to convince others that our version of an event is the one they should believe. One of these techniques is to argue that you are presenting a purely factual account.

Politicians' talk generally provides good examples of factual discourse which is used in an attempt to convince others of the truth of their version of events. It is sometimes referred to as 'spin'. However, it is not just politicians that do this sort of thing. Discourse analysis argues that this is something that you and I also engage in all the time in our everyday lives. The analysis points to the importance of language in everyday social life, and suggests that we take a more sophisticated view of the relationship between events (on the one hand) and people's accounts of events (on the other).

The authors' analysis of the different sides of the argument, and the rhetorical strategies that both sides used to support their own case is more extensive than indicated above. The function of this summary has been to give a working introduction to discourse analysis, and its challenging perspective on social psychological research.

Questions

suggested answers → P. 504

1. Discourse analysts typically work in great depth with data that have been collected from a relatively small number of sources. What might some of the strengths and weaknesses of their approach be?

2. What is the central concern of attribution theory?

3. The text makes the claim that everyone engages in 'factual discourse which is used in an attempt to convince others of the truth of their version of events'. Try to recall a recent situation in which you gave a 'version of events' to someone else. How did you present the 'facts' in order to persuade the other person that you were telling the truth?

AIDS and uncertainty

WEITZ, R. (1989)

Uncertainty and the lives of persons with AIDS.

Journal of Health and Social Behavior, 30, 270–81.

Introduction

AIDS (see Table 17.1) was always going to be different to other diseases. It made us discuss taboo topics like sex and drugs, it made us watch embarrassing television demonstrations of how to put a condom on a carrot, and it made us accept that the only protection from it is to change our behaviour. Doctors have got no cures to offer, but psychologists have studied behaviour for over a century so surely they can tell us something. The health threat posed by AIDS presented psychology with a very real challenge and provoked a large body of research.

The research into AIDS has raised a whole range of issues including how much we know about what people actually do, and how we can research issues of personal behaviour. In this particular study, Weitz was interested in how people who had developed AIDS managed to deal with the disorder and how they made sense of their lives. She decided to use extensive interviews with a relatively small number of people and from her data she derived some themes that tell us something about the experience of having AIDS, and also give some general insights into how people deal with chronic disease.

Table 17.1 *AIDS*

AIDS stands for Acquired Immune Deficiency Syndrome.

HIV stands for Human Immunodeficiency Virus.

It is generally believed that AIDS is caused by HIV. It attacks one type of white blood cells – the T helper lymphocytes – reduces the competence of immune system, and makes the body vulnerable to attacks by malignancies and infections.

If someone is infected with HIV they can continue without any symptoms for several years. Alternatively, they might develop a number of symptoms including swollen glands, weight loss, diarrhoea, fever and fatigue. This collection of symptoms are referred to as AIDS Related Complex (ARC).

The diagnosis of AIDS also requires identification of malignancy or infection not associated with a healthy immune system.

The study

> **cognition** Mental processes. 'All the processes by which ... sensory input is transformed, reduced, elaborated, stored, recovered and used' (Neisser, 1967, p. 4).

This study concentrates on the issue of uncertainty, which has been recognized as crucial for chronically and terminally ill people, and as a major source of stress in their lives. The feeling of uncertainty occurs when someone lacks a cognitive framework to understand their condition or situation, and when they cannot predict outcomes of their behaviour or condition. Few people tolerate uncertainty well, and they deal with it in a variety of ways. Two basic coping strategies have been identified:

(a) *Vigilance*: where people try to research possible diagnoses and so predict how their condition will develop, and

> **coping** The process of managing external or internal demands that are perceived as taxing or exceeding a person's resource.

(b) *Avoidance*: where people try to protect themselves against unpleasant knowledge by attributing symptoms to less harmful conditions, and not seeking medical advice.

These strategies create frameworks that allow the people to explain their situation to themselves and increase their sense of personal control.

Method and sample

> **sample** The group of subjects used in a study: the selection of people, animals, plants or objects drawn from a population for the purposes of studying that population.

> **population** In the context of research methods in psychology this refers to the total set of potential observations from which a sample is drawn.

> **Kaposi's sarcoma** Disfiguring skin cancer found, most commonly in around 10 per cent of people who develop AIDS.

Between July 1986 and March 1987, Weitz interviewed 25 residents of Arizona (USA) who had AIDS or AIDS-related complex (ARC). Four to six months after the initial interview 13 were re-interviewed (two declined to participate further, two had moved without leaving a forwarding address and eight had died or suffered brain damage in the interim). The interviewees were mainly men who described themselves as homosexual or bisexual, plus two heterosexual women who were intravenous drug users.

Respondents all referred themselves to the study from support projects or from the gay community. The sample was compared against populations of people with AIDS, and it was found that on issues of religion, geographical location and mode of transmission, the sample was representative of the population. However, the sample under-represented people with Kaposi's sarcoma, people of colour, and older people.

Each interview lasted from two to five hours at the respondent's or the interviewer's home. From the vast amount of material gathered from these interviews, Weitz was able to identify seven themes in the respondents' descriptions of their situations.

Results

> **people of colour** A term used (mainly in the United States) to refer to people who are not White and European. It is used to include people from Asia, and Hispanics, as well as Black people.

The findings are summarized under seven questions which are each the source of some uncertainty:

(1) *Will I get AIDS?* Fear of contracting AIDS is a big issue for gay and bisexual men. Among the respondents some assumed they had the infection long before diagnosis, whereas others developed theories that reduced their personal risk. Obtaining a test for the presence of HIV ought to reduce some uncertainty, but all except two of the respondents had initially declined to take a test. They reasoned that if they tested positive then it would increase their uncertainty and increase their sense of stigma. A positive test would not tell them if or when they would develop AIDS, so they would, in fact, be worse off than not knowing. They avoided the test until it was quite clear that they had developed AIDS.

(2) *What do my symptoms mean?* The symptoms of AIDS build up gradually, and it is possible to blame the symptoms on a variety of causes. For example, several men blamed their night sweats and exhaustion on the Arizona heat, and others confused their AIDS symptoms with the side effects of drug use. When the symptoms continued, the respondents found themselves in a position experienced by many people who develop chronic illnesses such as multiple sclerosis. They were anxious about their symptoms, but did not have the social support for adopting a sick role because they had not received a diagnosis.

(3) *Why have I become ill?* The respondents had all tried to come up with a reason for their illness, and although some had integrated it into religious experience (for example, believing that AIDS was a test from God), most of them had underlying attributions of personal guilt. On the whole, they blamed their promiscuity, homosexuality, lack of forethought, or drug use, but they were still left with the question 'Why me?'

(4) *Will I be able to function tomorrow?* In common with many other chronic disorders, AIDS causes unpredictable flare-ups and remissions. This made it very difficult to plan anything, even as simple as going shopping with someone the following Tuesday, because they did not know how they would feel on that day. As a consequence they tended to avoid plans, both long and short-term, to avoid disappointment.

(5) *Will I be able to live with dignity?* Fear of death is minimal compared with the fear of what life may become. In particular, the respondents feared neurological impairment (which is common in people with AIDS), and disfigurement by Kaposi's sarcoma (which occurs in 10 per cent of people with AIDS). They especially feared the unusual illnesses whose effects they could not predict one respondent said:

> I'm not [as] afraid of getting infections from people as I am from inanimate objects like fruits and moldy tile ... I know what a cold is like. ... [It's] something I have experienced. I've never experienced a mold infection. (p. 277)

(6) *Will I be able to 'beat' AIDS?* Can we beat death and live forever? The simple answer is 'no', but it did not stop the respondents from wondering whether God or medicine would be able to cure them. They reported various behaviours that they hoped would preserve or improve their health. These included prayer, a change of diet, exercise and attempts to enhance the will to live. Some had also managed to illicitly obtain experimental drugs that were being used in trials that were attempting to find a cure for AIDS.

(7) *Will I be able to die with dignity?* The uncertainty about how prolonged their final days would be led some of the people with AIDS to sign living wills to prevent physicians keeping them alive by extraordinary means, and some had made plans to commit suicide.

Weitz acknowledges that uncertainty is a central problem for people with many disorders, but she believes that it will have a particularly large impact on people with AIDS. This is because:

(a) They are more likely to know before diagnosis that they are at risk.

(b) They are likely to feel guilt over behaviours that led to the illness, such as drug use or sexual choices.

(c) They have difficulties in obtaining accurate diagnosis.

(d) They have difficulty in predicting the effects, since AIDS causes more extensive and less predictable physical and mental damage than other illnesses.

(e) Since it is a new disease, people with AIDS are more likely to lack answers to questions about treatment and prognosis.

Weitz goes on to draw some policy implications, including the suggestion that care workers should consider using the technique of stress inoculation. Janis (1983) suggests that people handle stress most effectively if they feel they are in control of their lives. To this end stress inoculation involves:

(1) giving people information about what to expect, which is realistic but which still allows them to maintain optimism;

(2) encouraging people to identify possible actions that can help them to survive and to find internal and external resources that allow them to take those actions;

(3) helping people to develop their own plan for responding to the situation.

▶ **stress inoculation** The suggestion by Janis that people handle stress most effectively if they feel they are in control of their lives. To achieve this, he proposes 'stress inoculation' in which people: (1) are given information about what to expect which is realistic but which still allows them to maintain optimism, (2) are encouraged to identify possible actions that can help them to survive and to find internal and external resources that allow them to take those actions, and (3) are helped to develop their own plan for responding to the situation.

Discussion

The study uses a very small sample of people but produces findings that appear to have some general relevance to health psychology. An important methodological comparison to make is between these relatively unstructured interviews and the tightly controlled questionnaires that are used for investigating aspects of personality (see McCrae and Costa, 1987 in Chapter 9) or judgements of risk (see Fischhoff et al., 2005, in Chapter 2). The comparison is between quantitative data (the scores from the questionnaires), and qualitative data (from Weitz's interviews). The qualitative data are clearly more difficult to obtain and also more difficult to interpret, but give an opportunity for the researchers to explore the complex experiences of the people they are studying.

▶ **quantitative data** Data which focus on numbers and frequencies rather than on meaning or experience.

▶ **qualitative data** Data which describe meaning and experience rather than providing numerical values for behaviour such as frequency counts.

Questions

suggested answers → p. 504

1. Why were people with the disfiguring Kaposi's sarcoma and people of colour missing from the sample?

2. What are the problems with this type of qualitative research?

3. Look at Question 3 under the heading 'Results' (above). What other disorders might involve a sense of guilt in the people who develop them?

Life is stress

HOLMES, T.H. AND
RAHE, R.H. (1967)

The Social
Re-adjustment
Rating Scale.

Journal of
Psychosomatic
Research,
11, 213–18.

Introduction

What are the events and experiences that affect our level of stress, and how can we measure the stress level on an individual? This is the question that Holmes and Rahe tried to address with their Social Re-adjustment Rating Scale. The scale looks at the stresses caused by major life events (the sort of events that we experience as difficult to deal with) and is based on previous research which had found that some social events that required a change in lifestyle were associated with the onset of illness.

The paper describes the development of the Social Re-adjustment Rating Scale. This involved the collection of data which aimed to quantify the stress created by different events.

The study

▶ **Social Re-adjustment Rating Scale** Holmes and Rahe's attempt to quantify stressors by giving a stress value to a number of major life events.

▶ **sample** The group of subjects used in a study: the selection of people, animals, plants or objects drawn from a population for the purposes of studying that population.

An opportunity sample of 394 people (details are shown in Table 17.2) completed a pencil and paper test. The test consisted of 43 life events 'empirically derived from clinical experience'. The subjects were given the following written instructions (instructions (b) and (c) are paraphrased):

(a) Social re-adjustment includes the amount and duration of change in one's accustomed pattern of life resulting from various life events. As defined, social re-adjustment measures the intensity and length of time necessary to accommodate to a life event, *regardless of the desirability of this event* (p. 213).

(b) Rate the events according to the amount of adjustment you think they require. Give your opinion of the average degree of re-adjustment necessary rather than the extreme.

(c) The first event on the list, 'marriage', is given an arbitrary value of 500. Look at each of the other events and consider whether it requires more or less re-adjustment than marriage, and whether it will take more time or less time to re-adjust. Give a number to each of the other events based on the 500 for marriage.

Results

▶ **correlation** A measure of how strongly two or more variables are related to each other.

The Social Re-adjustment Rating Scale is shown in Table 17.3. The values were calculated from the average score given to each event, divided by 10. So the value for marriage, which was given to the subjects as 500, therefore became 50.

The researchers compared the responses of the different groups of people in their sample and found a startling degree of agreement. They calculated 16 correlations to compare the different groups and all but one showed an agreement of $r > 0.9$. The exception was the comparison of White subjects with Black subjects, where the correlation was $r = 0.82$. Overall, then, it appears that the evaluation of stress is fairly constant across many groups of US society tested by Holmes and Rahe.

Table 17.2 *Characteristics of the sample*

Group	Number in group
Male	179
Female	215
Age <30	206
Age 30–60	137
Age >60	51
Single	171
Married	223
Lower class	71
Middle class	323
White	363
Black	19
Oriental	12
Protestant	241

Discussion

To measure your personal stress score, tick off the events that have occurred to you in a given time, usually 12 months or 24 months, and add up the re-adjustment values. A number of studies, by Holmes and Rahe in particular, have shown a connection between high ratings and subsequent illness and accident, though according to Sarafino (1994) the correlation between rating and illness is only about $r = 0.3$ which is not a very strong relationship.

There are a number of problems with this method of measuring stress. For example, how commonly do the life events in the scale actually occur? A study of nearly 2800 adults by Goldberg and Comstock (1980) used a modified version of the scale and found that 18 per cent of subjects reported five or more events, while 15 per cent reported experiencing none of the events in the prior year (this seems hard to believe since one of the events is 'Christmas'... Even more remarkable is the value of 12 given to Christmas. Surely it should be at least 6 squillion). The number of events increased with the number of years of schooling, and, for adults, decreased with age from early adulthood to old age. It is debatable whether the scale can pick up these population differences and measure stress effectively for all people.

Other criticisms concern the items in the scale which are vague or ambiguous. Also, some of them will have greater value for some groups in society rather than others. There is also the issue of individual differences in our ability to cope with stressful events. It is worth noting, however, that the measurement of psychological phenomena is a singularly difficult enterprise, and it is usually easier to come up with criticisms of existing attempts than to devise better ways of doing things.

The stressful-life-event approach to stress and illness generated a considerable amount of research, not least because the Social Re-adjustment Rating Scale developed by Holmes and Rahe provides a relatively straightforward way of measuring stress. It also conforms to everyday notions of the effect of dramatic events in our lives. In accounts of personal experience recorded in

▶**population** In the context of research methods in psychology this refers to the total set of potential observations from which a sample is drawn.

Table 17.3 *Social Re-adjustment Rating Scale*

Rank	Life event	Mean value
1	Death of spouse	100
2	Divorce	73
3	Marital separation	65
4	Jail term	63
5	Death of close family member	63
6	Personal injury or illness	53
7	Marriage	50
8	Fired at work	47
9	Marital reconciliation	45
10	Retirement	45
11	Change in health of family member	44
12	Pregnancy	40
13	Sex difficulties	39
14	Gain of new family member	39
15	Business re-adjustment	39
16	Change in financial state	38
17	Death of a close friend	37
18	Change to different line of work	36
19	Change in number of arguments with spouse	35
20	Mortgage over $10,000	31
21	Foreclosure of mortgage or loan	30
22	Change in responsibilities at work	29
23	Son or daughter leaving home	29
24	Trouble with in-laws	29
25	Outstanding personal achievement	28
26	Wife begins or stops work	26
27	Begin or end school	26
28	Change in living conditions	25
29	Revision of personal habits	24
30	Trouble with boss	23
31	Change in work hours or conditions	20
32	Change in residence	20
33	Change in schools	20
34	Change in recreation	19
35	Change in church activities	19
36	Change in social activities	18
37	Mortgage or loan less than $10,000	17
38	Change in sleeping habits	16
39	Change in number of family get-togethers	15
40	Change in eating habits	15
41	Vacation	13
42	Christmas	12
43	Minor violations of the law	11

Source: Holmes and Rahe (1967).

news reports, it is not unknown for people to say how a particular event, such as unexpected bereavement or desertion by a loved one, has 'shattered my life'. An alternative approach to measuring stress was proposed by Kanner et al. (1981), who argued that the minor stressors and pleasures of everyday life might have a more significant effect on health than the big, traumatic events assessed by the Holmes and Rahe scale, particularly in view of the cumulative nature of stress.

Kanner et al. (1981) developed a scale to explore these small events, which they called the Hassles and Uplifts Scale. They administered the checklist to a 100 middle-aged adults once a month for ten months. The Hassles scale was found to be a better predictor of psychological problems than life-event scores, both at the time and later. Scores on the Uplift Scale, however, only seemed to relate to symptoms in women.

Questions

suggested answers → p. 505

1. Identify three items in the scale that are likely to have different values for men and women, and say why.

2. Identify three items in the scale that are likely to have different values for people of different ages, and say why.

3. The scale was devised in the USA in 1967. What differences would you expect if you made up a similar scale today?

4. What other causes of stress, other than major life events, can you think of?

Introduction

Do psychotherapies work? That is, do people with psychological problems get better as a result of receiving therapy? And which types of therapy work best? There are so many varieties, such as behavioural (see Lang and Lazovik, 1963, and Chapter 8 of this volume), psychodynamic (see Freud, 1909, and Chapter 11 of this volume), humanistic (Rogers, 1951), transactional (Berne, 1968) and Gestalt (Perls, 1969), and that is only a selection.

Many evaluation studies have been carried out which look at the question of the effectiveness of various kinds of therapy. But, as with all areas of the psychological literature, the findings are scattered among hundreds of different volumes of different journals. Smith and Glass' paper is an attempt to draw together the results of these disparate studies. They collated the data from a large number of primary publications (375 studies in all) and attempted to draw general conclusions about psychotherapy from the patterns that were revealed. This investigative strategy is known as secondary research or meta-analysis.

Shrink-wrapped: the choice of therapist

SMITH, M.L AND GLASS, G.V. (1977)

Meta-analysis of psychotherapy outcome studies.

American Psychologist, 32, 752–60.

The study

Subjects

In a sense the subjects of this meta-analysis were all the subjects of the 375 original studies, estimated to be some 50,000 in number, divided across experimental and control conditions. All were clients of psychotherapists. The average age of clients in the original studies was 22 years, and they received on average 17 hours of therapy.

Design and procedure

The authors identified 375 studies of the effectiveness of psychotherapy within the psychological literature. All the studies selected had a quasi-experimental design. That is, they were based on comparisons between treated and untreated groups, or between groups receiving different kinds of therapy.

For all the studies at least one effect size was calculated. This was a numeric representation of 'the magnitude of the effect of therapy' (p. 753) as shown by each of the 375 primary studies. For some studies there were several outcome measures, so overall 833 effect sizes were calculated (see the statistical note below).

The effect sizes of each study were then taken as values of the dependent variable (the effectiveness of psychotherapy). These values were then related systematically to a variety of independent variables, the most important of

▶ **behaviour therapy** The process of treating abnormal behaviour by looking only at the symptoms, and using conditioning techniques to modify them.

▶ **psychodynamic** Dealing with psychological forces that influence the mind and behaviour.

▶ **humanistic** The humanistic approach to personality asserts that the most important feature of human beings is how they achieve their sense of self and how they actualize their potential.

► **natural experiments (also quasi experiments)** Studies in which comparisons are made between different conditions that come about through natural political, social, economic or demographic circumstances, rather than through direct manipulation of a variable by an experimenter.

► **effect size** When psychologists detect significant differences in the performance of subjects in experimental conditions they talk about having 'got an effect'. The bigger the differences, the bigger the effect size.

► **dependent variable** The thing which is measured in an experiment, and which changes, depending on the independent variable.

which were level of treatment (the basic treatment versus no treatment comparison), and type of therapy (psychodynamic, Adlerian, eclectic, transactional analysis, rational–emotive, Gestalt, client-centred, systematic desensitization, implosion, behaviour modification). It is these two independent variables which are examined in the results section below.

The details of the various statistical manipulations in this study are pretty impenetrable, so only two basic findings are dealt with. The reason for the complexity of the statistical procedures is the need to cope with data that have been collated from completely different studies with different designs and measurement procedures. Within each primary study important variables such as the experience of the therapist(s), length of therapy, original diagnosis of the clients' problems, and length of time between treatment and evaluation would have been controlled for. You would expect all these variables (and probably many others) to have significant effects on the efficacy of the therapy. But across the different studies no such control exists, so various statistical procedures are used to try and adjust the data to allow for such variables, and to examine how much effect they may have had on the overall findings of the secondary analysis.

Results

► **rational–emotive therapy** A form of psychotherapy which mixes rational argument with positive reward systems.

The results relating to both independent variables (level of treatment and type of therapy) are reported in terms of comparisons of means and standard deviations of effect sizes.

Level of treatment (treatment versus no treatment)

► **systematic desensitization** A classical conditioning technique for reducing fear and anxiety by replacing it with a calm response.

► **implosion therapy** A form of behaviour therapy based on 'overkill', in which the person is continually faced with the feared stimulus until their fear dies down.

► **independent variable** The conditions which an experimenter sets up, to cause an effect in an experiment. These vary systematically, so that the experimenter can draw conclusions about changes in outcomes.

► **standard deviation** A measure of dispersion.

► **median** The middle score in a set.

The mean effect size for the treated group (approximately 25,000 subjects who received some kind of therapy) fell 0.68 of a standard deviation above the mean effect size of the untreated group. This means that the average client in the treated group (the client that experienced the median size of therapeutic effect) was better off than 75 per cent of the untreated control subjects.

Additionally only 99 of the 833 effect sizes (12 per cent) were negative (meaning that in this small number of cases the clients were on average worse off than before the therapy).

Type of therapy

By comparing the average effect sizes for subjects who had received different kinds of therapies with the average effect sizes for control subjects, the authors were able to draw up a league table (or rank ordering) of the effectiveness of ten different therapies. This rank ordering is shown in Table 17.4. The higher the value in the right-hand column of Table 17.4, the greater the estimated effect of the therapy; the nearer the value in that column gets to 50, the smaller the difference between the treated and untreated groups, hence the smaller the effect of the named therapy.

Table 17.4 *Rank ordering of ten types of therapy*

Type of therapy	Median treated person's percentile status in control group
Systematic desensitization	82
Rational-emotive	78
Behaviour modification	78
Adlerian	76
Implosion	74
Client-centred	74
Psychodynamic	72
Transactional analysis	72
Eclectic	68
Gestalt (N.B. based on only 8 measures)	60

Source: Smith and Glass (1977).

Discussion

Smith and Glass concluded from their meta-analysis that psychotherapies do work. That is, more people improved in one way or another, having been through a course of therapy, than would have improved spontaneously with no treatment.

The rank ordering of the different therapies is interesting, but by Smith and Glass' own admission should not be taken too literally, since there was no way of controlling against important confounding variables. For example, systematic desensitization came out 'top', but this may have been due to the fact that systematic desensitization deals with more easily 'treatable' problems than, say, Gestalt psychotherapy. Smith and Glass' data supports this notion by showing that fear and anxiety reduction is more readily achieved through therapy than is personal change and 'adjustment'; desensitization deals with the former, Gestalt psychotherapy with the latter.

The final comparison that Smith and Glass made was between behavioural therapies (implosion, systematic desensitization, behaviour modification) and non-behavioural therapies (psychoanalytic, Adlerian, client-centred, rational–emotive, eclectic, transactional analysis). Their conclusion was that there are 'negligible differences in the effects produced by different therapy types' (p. 760).

It is fair to say that the use of meta-analysis can create as many problems as it solves. One problem that it attempts to solve is the inevitable one of relatively small sample sizes in individual studies. When all the studies that have been carried out in an area are combined, the resulting data can be said to come from a huge sample. However, differences in design and measurement across the studies mean that in many respects the study is not comparing like with like, so care is needed in interpreting the findings. Having said that, if care *is* taken at the interpretation stage, then the literature can surely benefit from studies such as these that try to step back from the detail of individual studies, and take a look at the bigger picture of what can be learned from a large body of work.

▶ **confounding variable** A variable which causes a change in the dependent variable, but which is not the independent variable of the study.

▶ **sample** The group of subjects used in a study: the selection of people, animals, plants or objects drawn from a population for the purposes of studying that population.

Statistical note

Smith and Glass calculated the effect size for each study by taking the mean difference between the treated subjects and the control subjects on the outcome measure of the study, and dividing this by the standard deviation of the control group on the outcome measure.

Questions

suggested
answers
→ p. 505

1. What particular problems are faced in researching the effectiveness of psychotherapies?

2. Although Smith and Glass's conclusions look very convincing, having been based on a detailed analysis of hundreds of studies with thousands of subjects, what factors might still have biased the overall pattern of findings in favour of the case for psychotherapy?

chapter **18**

ISSUES IN
RESEARCH

NOTHING is ever simple. Research is no exception and there are numerous pitfalls on the road to scientific discovery. In this chapter we present five papers that raise some troubling questions about psychological research and throw some doubt on the findings of other studies in this book. It is impossible to carry out the perfect research study because there will always be some variables you have not accounted for or responses that you did not anticipate. Therefore there are some key issues that we should look out for when we evaluate psychological studies.

We start by looking at the excellent account of demand characteristics by Orne (1962). Every situation we are in creates some social demands for us. People are great problem solvers and we are always trying to figure out what is expected of us. At the pantomime we are ready to shout 'Behind you!', in the doctor's waiting room we are happy to sit quietly and during the seminar we try to look interested whether we are or not. Most of the time we are good judges of when we should laugh with people, commiserate with people or just listen to them. People read the social situation and act accordingly. But what if this is what participants are doing in

psychology experiments: just acting in accordance with their sense of what the researcher wants them to do? What then can researchers really learn?

The second paper looks at the issue of who psychologists choose to do their studies on. You might imagine when you open a psychology text and it talks about 'people' that it is referring to all people or at least a wide range of people. Unfortunately this is not the case and the article by Sears (1986) shows that in the mid-1980s the bulk of psychological research was being conducted on undergraduate students, many of them psychology students. This does not matter if these students are representative of the general population, but Sears challenges this and therefore questions the conduct of psychological research in general.

The problem is not just about the use of students. In some texts when the authors allow the reader to believe the research is about 'people' it is, in fact, about animals. In their review of this issue Domjan and Purdy (1995) report a number of examples including the following paragraph from an introductory text:

> long after people have recovered
> more or less normal behaviour

▶ **demand characteristics** Those aspects of a psychological study (or other artificial situation) which exert an implicit pressure on people to act in ways that are expected of them.

▶ **population** In the context of research methods in psychology this refers to the total set of potential observations from which a sample is drawn.

following brain damage, they may relapse in old age. An old person's behaviour may deteriorate, eventually ending up about the same as it was just after the damage. (Kalat, 1993, p. 113)

The problem with this report is that the research used as evidence is a study conducted on laboratory rats (Schallert, 1983). The criticism here is not of the original research but of the way in which it is reported, especially in textbooks.

The third paper describes a demonstration of the gullibility we all have to experts. The basic definition of a television expert is someone who can state the mind-snappingly obvious as if they are discovering the Holy Grail. We appear to be strangely mesmerized by these statements and often suspend our common sense when we listen to them. Forer's (1949) paper is a classic that shows how a list of simple statements can be used to create an illusion of personal knowledge and scientific credibility. This is a trick that has been used for centuries by fortune tellers, mediums and other charlatans, but is it

now being used by psychologists? Forer challengers us to be sceptical of some psychological tests and to consider whether they are more than just smoke and mirrors.

The paper by Rosenthal and Fode (1963) shows the power of expectation on the outcome of research. This study defines the research problem we know as the 'experimenter effect', which roughly translates as the tendency to get the results we are hoping for or that we expect to see.

The final paper in this chapter, and also in the book, is very different from any of the others. It does not present any empirical work but is a moral call to the profession. It was made by George Miller (1969) as his presidential address to the American Psychological Association over 30 years ago but it is still challenging today. The basic issue is this: if psychologists can do even a fraction of what they claim in their attempts to change the ways people think, feel and behave, then they ought to be pretty sure that the changes they are making are able to bring some benefit to the world in which we all live.

► **experimenter effects**
Unwanted influences in a psychological study which are produced, consciously or unconsciously, by the person carrying out the study.

Demand characteristics

ORNE, M.T. (1962)

On the social psychology of the psychological experiment: with particular reference to demand characteristics and their implications.

American Psychologist, 17, 776–83.

Introduction

One problem with studying people is that their behaviour and experience change as a result of being studied. This means that we can never be certain in psychological research that we are finding out about how people really are. This holds true for all research methods to a greater or lesser extent, but it is particularly true of experimental methods. Orne's paper looks at why this might be the case. His review article begins with a brief discussion of some of the social psychological characteristics of the psychology experiment. It moves on to a discussion of demand characteristics, examining what they are, how they might affect research findings, and what can be done about them. The paper includes a number of references to both informal and formal psychology experiments conducted by Orne and his colleagues.

The psychological experiment as a social situation

▶ **demand characteristics**
Those aspects of a psychological study (or other artificial situation) which exert an implicit pressure on people to act in ways that are expected of them.

> The experimental situation is one which takes place within the context of an explicit agreement of the subject to participate in a special form of social interaction known as 'taking part in an experiment'. (p. 777)

Orne's first point is that the psychological experiment, involving as it does an interaction between experimenter(s) and subject(s), should be regarded as a social situation. In other words, a psychology experiment always takes place in a particular social context. In everyday life we expect people's behaviour to be affected by the social contexts in which they find themselves. For example, imagine being in a pub, a church, a football ground and a shopping centre.

If someone bumps into you in the shopping centre, you are likely to say 'Well really!', but at a football ground you wouldn't even notice it. In a lecture theatre if you put your hand up, you may get to ask a question. Do the same thing in an auction house and it might cost you. Orne argues that the psychology experiment is not exempt from this principle: the behaviour of subjects in an experiment will be affected by the social context created by that experiment.

One feature of any social context which can be expected to have an effect on behaviour is the relationship between the people involved. In an experiment, the proceedings are dominated by the experimenter–subject role relationship. There are characteristics of this relationship which make the psychological experiment a particularly potent and rather unusual social situation.

For example, within this role relationship experimenters find themselves with an unusual degree of power over their subjects. This is partly because in agreeing to take part in an experiment in the first place the subject:

implicitly agrees to perform a very wide range of actions on request without inquiring as to their purpose, and frequently without inquiring as to their duration. (p. 777)

Orne gives the following examples of subjects' 'remarkable compliance' (p. 778) to the demands of an experimenter. They are taken from informal pilot experiments which he and his colleagues carried out. The first involved a psychologist asking a few acquaintances for a favour. When they agreed they were asked to do five press-ups. Their reaction tended to be to ask 'why?' – with a degree of puzzlement. Another group of acquaintances were asked if they would take part in an experiment. When they agreed they were asked to do five press-ups. Their reaction tended to be to ask 'where?' This suggests that people are prepared to do things as subjects that they would not normally be prepared to do in other social contexts.

The second example of compliance is startling. Subjects were set a task which involved them making 224 additions of random digits on each of 2000 sheets of paper. Their watches were taken away and the experimenter told them to continue working until they were told to stop. 'Five and one-half hours later, the experimenter gave up!' (p. 777), amazed at the unquestioning diligence of the subjects. In a variation on this task, subjects were instructed to do the calculations on each sheet, then to tear up their answer sheet into at least 32 pieces before continuing with the next one, which was also to be torn up (and so forth). Again subjects tended to continue for several hours at this completely senseless task, simply because they were 'doing an experiment'.

Orne argues that one reason for people's willingness to do things in an experiment that they would not normally do otherwise is their desire to be 'good' subjects. Generally speaking, subjects want to help the experimenter do a good experiment; we all like to be involved in things which are successful. In addition, since a large proportion of psychological studies are carried out on students, the subject population may also tend to share the goals and values of experimenters in terms of the quest to further human knowledge and thereby to make a positive contribution to society.

▶ **population** In the context of research methods in psychology this refers to the total set of potential observations from which a sample is drawn.

What are demand characteristics?

▶ **hypothesis** Experiments are designed to test one or more hypotheses. An hypothesis is a prediction of what will happen in an experiment. It is worded in such a way that the results of a well-designed experiment will clearly show whether the prediction is right or wrong.

The totality of cues which convey an experimental hypothesis to the subject become significant determinants of subjects' behaviour. We have labelled the sum total of such cues as the 'demand characteristics of the experimental situation'. (p. 779)

The insight that the psychology experiment is a kind of social situation is an important one, since it reminds us that the subjects of psychological research are usually people. People do not just passively respond to things that happen to them. They actively try and make sense of what is happening, and act in accordance with their sense-making. There is no reason to assume that people in experiments are any different in this respect from people in any other kind of situation. This implies that subjects will tend to try and understand what is going on in the experiment that they are in, and their behaviour will be affected by whatever understanding they come to.

The most important thing that subjects will try to understand in an experiment is 'what is this person (the experimenter) trying to find out from me?' In other words, 'what is the experimental hypothesis?' Orne argues that subjects will automatically use whatever cues are available in the experimental situation in order to try and work out the experimental hypothesis. The cues can come from a variety of sources, such as the wording of instructions, the manner of the experimenter, the experimenter's known area of research (remember that many psychology experiments are done with students on the experimenter's course!), and so forth. The procedure is another source of information for the subject: if a test is given twice with some intervening treatment, even the dullest college student is aware that some change is expected, particularly if the test is in some obvious way related to the treatment (p. 779).

We all want to know what is expected of us in social situations, and we tend to act in accordance with our understandings of those expectations. The experimental hypothesis is literally an expectation of how subjects will act in the experimental situation. If subjects come to know the hypothesis, then their behaviour will tend to support it.

The point that Orne is trying to make is that the behaviour of subjects in experiments is a function of two different kinds of variables:

(a) those which are traditionally defined as experimental variables;
(b) the perceived demand characteristics of the experimental situation (p. 779).

If experimenters are not careful they may interpret their findings as being a consequence of their manipulation of the independent variable(s), when in fact the data have been artificially produced by the demand characteristics of the situation. Mix the power of the experimenter with a large helping of subject compliance, add some desire to be a good subject, season with some active sense-making, and you have a recipe for a self-fulfilling prophecy.

Orne gives examples of demand characteristics in operation in the findings of psychological research from his own fields of interest: sensory deprivation research and research into hypnosis. He cites one of his own studies (later published by Orne and Scheibe, 1964) which shows some of the dangers. One group of subjects were told they were in a sensory deprivation study. They undertook a series of tasks, signed release forms and were left on their own in a room which had some visible trappings of sensory deprivation (including a red 'panic' button) for four hours. However, the experimenters had not created any sensory deprivation at all. Another group of subjects were told they were control subjects in a sensory deprivation study. They did the same series of tasks and sat in the same room for four hours (only with the panic button removed). Both sets of subjects then repeated the original tasks. The performance of the subjects who thought they had undergone sensory deprivation had

> ▶ **independent variable**
> The conditions which an experimenter sets up, to cause an effect in an experiment. These vary systematically, so that the experimenter can draw conclusions about changes in outcomes.

> ▶ **self-fulfilling prophecy**
> The idea that expectations about a person or group can become true simply because they have been stated.

> ▶ **sensory deprivation** The cutting out of all incoming sensory information, or at least as much of it as possible. Sometimes used as a method of torture.

> ▶ **hypnosis** A temporary trance-like state that can be induced in healthy individuals.

deteriorated significantly on a number of the measures in comparison with the control group.

The subjects in the sensory deprivation condition appeared to have a very good idea, at least subconsciously, of the way they were expected to behave. Their behaviour promptly confirmed these expectations. Orne argues that many of the results of sensory deprivation (and hypnosis) studies could have been produced not by sensory deprivation (or hypnosis) but by demand characteristics: that is by people behaving in the way that they believe they are expected to.

What can be done about demand characteristics?

> It is futile to imagine an experiment that could be created without demand characteristics. One of the basic characteristics of the human being is that he will ascribe purpose and meaning even in the absence of purpose and meaning. In an experiment where he knows some purpose exists, it is inconceivable for him not to form some hypothesis as to the purpose, based on some cues, no matter how meagre. (p. 780)

When experimenting on people, demand characteristics are unavoidable, because people will always try to make sense of things. The most popular way of counteracting any systematic influence of such factors in an experiment is by means of deception. Experimenters put a lot of effort into concealing the true purpose of their experiment from their subjects by trying to convince them that they are really studying something completely different. Milgram's work (in Chapter 1 of this volume) is one notable example of this strategy. But deception has its own drawbacks. There are ethical problems with misleading people, and, besides, many people (especially psychology students) know that experimenters will try to deceive them, and will inevitably try and work out the true purpose of the investigation.

Orne's preferred method of dealing with demand characteristics is to encourage experimenters to be aware of their potential impact on research studies, and to suggest some strategies for assessing what this impact might be. If we can come to understand which aspects of subjects' behaviour are affected by demand characteristics, then we should be able to assess more accurately which aspects are affected by the bona fide experimental variables.

One strategy that Orne recommends is a kind of simulation exercise based on a combination of pre- and post-experimental enquiry. A group of subjects (drawn from the same population as the subjects in the experimental and control conditions) are told about the experimental procedures and asked to guess the hypothesis. They are then asked to behave in a way that they believe subjects would behave after having been given the experimental treatment, only without actually receiving the treatment. If the behaviour of these subjects correlates with the behaviour of subjects who had received the real experimental treatment, then there is a possibility that that behaviour has been produced by the demand characteristics of the situation.

Orne's basic message is that when the subjects of our research are people, we should be aware that they are active sense-makers rather than passive responders. This awareness should affect the way that research is designed and the way in which findings are interpreted.

suggested answers → P. 506

Questions

1. Demand characteristics are regarded as a source of 'artefact' in behavioural research. What does the word artefact mean in this context?

2. How can the behaviour of people in demonstrations of stage hypnosis be explained by demand characteristics?

3. Look at some of the other studies in this volume and try to identify any demand characteristics. Can the results be explained by these demand characteristics? Look especially at the quotation from page 779 of Orne's paper about giving a test twice 'with some intervening treatment'. How does this relate to Samuel and Bryant's (1984) investigation of conservation in children (see Chapter 11 of this book)?

Introduction

Psychology is regarded as the scientific study of human behaviour and experience. It attempts to make generalizations about how people behave, what influences that behaviour, and how people make sense of their experience. However, in their studies, whom do psychologists use to test their theories? There is considerable diversity in human behaviour and experience, so is this diversity taken into account when studies are designed and conducted? When a study is designed, it is important to state the target population of people under investigation which, for example, might be 'residents of Nottingham', or 'young people between the ages of 16 and 19'. Once we have stated the target population, we can set about selecting a sample of that population. A good, representative sample allows us to generalize our results from the sample back to the population. The study by Sears looks at the samples that are used in social psychology studies, and assesses how much we can generalize about people on the basis of these studies.

Who are psychology's subjects?

SEARS, D.O. (1986)

College sophomores in the laboratory: influences of a narrow data base on psychology's view of human nature.

Journal of Personality and Social Psychology, 51, 513–30.

The study

▶**population** In the context of research methods in psychology this refers to the total set of potential observations from which a sample is drawn.

▶**sample** The group of subjects used in a study: the selection of people, animals, plants or objects drawn from a population for the purposes of studying that population.

Sears reports that in the years after the Second World War (1939–45), social psychology used a wide range of subjects in its studies and a variety of locations. The prevailing feeling was that it was important to conduct studies both in the field and the laboratory. However, from the 1960s onwards, a trend developed for laboratory experiments which used the most available subjects – college students. Sears looked at the major journals in social psychology for the years 1980 and 1985 to discover what were the chosen samples and chosen locations of the published research. The results are shown in Figure 18.1 and Table 18.1.

The results show that the bulk of psychological research has been carried out on a very narrow subject base of students, and, in particular, psychology students. One explanation for this might be that the prestigious journals that Sears studied have a particular policy towards publications that encourages authors to send in laboratory-based studies. To test for this, Sears looked at other publications by the same authors in different journals. The 1980 *Psychological Abstracts* provided 237 entries by the same authors from a wide variety of journals. The analysis of these articles showed very few differences from the original analysis, and suggested that the results were not peculiar to the mainstream journals.

Another feature to consider might be whether these types of studies are very important in psychology. It might be that the work that has the greatest impact is not presented in these journals. However, Sears describes a study by

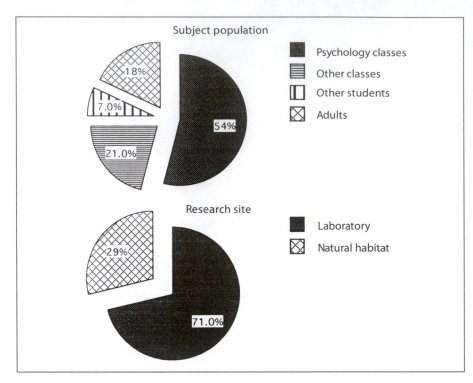

Figure 18.1 *Subject population and research sites in social psychology articles in 1980*

Table 18.1 *Subject population and research sites in social psychology articles in 1980 and 1985*

	1980	1985
Subject population		
American undergraduates	75	74
Psychology classes	54	51
Other classes	21	23
Other students	7	8
Adults	18	17
Research site		
Laboratory	71	78
Natural habitat	29	22
Combined		
Undergraduate/lab	64	67
Adult/natural habitat	15	13
Number of articles		
Total	333	187
Empirical and codeable	301	178

Source: adapted from Sears (1986).

Findley and Cooper (1981) who coded the articles cited in the most commonly used textbooks in social psychology. They found that in these textbooks the overall proportion of cited studies that used students as subjects was 73 per cent. So the curriculum of psychology courses contains the same subject bias as the literature as a whole. Sears goes on to look at other data which suggest that, up to 1960, psychologists used adults who were not students in about half of their studies, but since then there has been a consistent dependence on data from students.

Sears considers whether this subject bias presents any problems for social psychology. He notes that one of the potential hazards is the need to test concepts that have been developed in the laboratory in a real-life setting to see if they apply. An example of this is provided by the study of Piliavin et al. (1969, described in Chapter 1), who found that the laboratory-developed concept of diffusion of responsibility did not apply to their studies of bystander intervention on a New York commuter train.

College students are not very representative of the general population. They come from a narrow age range and are predominantly at the upper levels of educational background and family income. The 17 to 19-year-old young people who make up the majority of subjects in psychology studies have been shown to have a number of unique characteristics which Sears summarizes as follows:

(a) Their self-concept is unlikely to be fully formed.
(b) Social and political attitudes are less crystallized than in later life.
(c) They are more egocentric than older adults.
(d) They have a stronger need for peer approval.
(e) They have unstable peer relationships.

Also, college students differ systematically from other people of the same age:

(f) They are pre-selected for competence at cognitive skills.
(g) They are selected for compliance to authority.
(h) Their social and geographical mobility leads to enhanced instability in peer relationships.

It is difficult to disentangle the effects of the choice of subjects from the choice of location. Laboratory studies seem likely to have further effects including:

(i) Creating a cognitive set in the subjects, since they are often conducted as part of the students' course.
(j) Creating a set to comply with the authority.
(k) Isolation of the subject from the support of his or her peers to minimize 'contamination' of the individual's responses.

Sears provides an extensive review of modern psychology and shows how its concerns and findings have largely been led by the peculiar features of the

▶ diffusion of responsibility The idea that people are less likely to intervene to help someone who seems to need it if there are others present, because they perceive responsibility as being shared between all present, and therefore see themselves as being less responsible personally.

▶ bystander intervention The issue of when and under what circumstances passers-by or other uninvolved persons are likely to offer help to those who look as though they need it.

▶ egocentrism The tendency to see things from your own personal perspective, to the exclusion of other possible perspectives.

▶ set In psychology, commonly refers to perceptual set which is a preparedness (or expectation) to see particular forms or patterns.

US undergraduate. (He comments on several of the studies included in this text, including Asch, 1955; Bem, 1974; Milgram, 1963; Nisbett et al., 1973 and Schachter and Singer, 1962.) He suggests there are four main consequences for psychology:

(1) Psychology tends to view people as having a weak sense of their own preferences, emotions and abilities; they are compliant, their self-esteem is easily damaged, their attitudes are easily changed, and they are relatively unreflective.

(2) Material self-interest, group norms, social support and reference-group identification play little role in current research in the USA (though some European psychology is addressing these issues).

(3) Psychology views people as dominated by cognitive processes rather than emotional ones.

(4) Psychological theories treat people as highly egocentric.

He writes:

> To caricature the point, contemporary social psychology, on the basis of young students pre-selected for cognitive skills and tested in isolation in an academic setting on academic tasks, present the human race as composed of lone, bland, compliant wimps who specialize in pencil and paper tests. The human being of strong and irrational passions, of intractable prejudices, who is solidly embedded in tightly knit family and ethnic groups, who develops and matures with age, is not that of contemporary psychology; it does not provide much room for such as Palestinian guerrillas, southern Italian peasants, Winston Churchill, Idi Amin, Florence Nightingale, Archie Bunker, Ma Joad, Clarence Darrow, or Martin Luther King. (p. 528)

Discussion

The study produced a damaging critique of modern psychology. Perhaps surprisingly, it is not cited in many introductory psychology texts. There are a number of ways of responding to the challenges that Sears' article poses. For example, we could decide to confirm the results of studies conducted on students by repeating the study with a different population of participants. You might imagine that, since the paper by Sears was published, psychologists would have followed this course of action. Sadly, this has not been the case and a review of British psychology by one of the authors found a very similar pattern of research subjects to that observed by Sears (Banyard and Hunt, 2000).

The selection of students is not the only problem with sample selection. A recent study (Carnahan and McFarland, 2007), brilliant in its simplicity, has thrown some doubt on the interpretation of the Stanford Prison Experiment (SPE; see Haney et al., 1973, described in Chapter 3). The study looked at whether people who volunteer for certain types of psychological study are different from regular volunteers. In this example, students were recruited for 'a psychological study of prison life' using a virtually identical newspaper advertisement to the one used in the Stanford Prison Experiment, or for a 'psychological study' (an identical ad minus the words 'of prison life'). When they turned up for the study the students were given a battery of psychological tests. Those who had responded to the 'prison life' advert scored higher on measures of characteristics that might predispose them to be abusive (such as aggressiveness, authoritarianism, Machiavellianism, narcissism and social dominance) than those who had responded to the straightforward 'psychological study' advert. The former also scored lower on characteristics that might inhibit aggression such as empathy and altruism.

The point for the SPE is that it was not just the role that made the guards behave in the way they did. It is important to acknowledge that only certain sorts of people will seek out that sort of role in the first place. This observation has some implications both for our understanding of the SPE and also for our understanding of abuse carried out in real-life settings.

The question it leaves us with is 'what value are the data and theories of modern psychology?' A cynic might be inclined to dismiss much of psychology after reading this paper, but, on the other hand, you might be motivated to try to evaluate the biases in the studies and mentally adjust for them. It might also be worth speculating on the likely effects of changing the location or the subjects for a number of important studies.

Questions

suggested answers → p. 506

1. Why do psychologists use student subjects in their studies?

2. Why do psychologists tend to use laboratories in preference to conducting field studies?

3. Take one of the other studies in this text and speculate on the effects of carrying out the same procedure on a different subject group, for example, factory workers, or time-share salespeople.

Introduction

People appear to have a restless quest for information about themselves. We seek the advice and insight of fortune tellers, friends, counsellors and psychologists. The unfortunate truth is that we tend to neglect our usual critical skills when we deal with the information we receive.

An example of this comes from the work of Furnham and Varian (1988), who looked at how people predict and accept their own scores on psychological tests. In their first experiment, undergraduates tried to predict their own scores and also the scores of a friend on the EPI (the Eysenck Personality Inventory, which claims to measure how extravert and neurotic a person is). They were fairly good at this. Then some other undergraduates were given false feedback (in other words, incorrect results) after completing the EPI. They were more likely to accept positive feedback as accurate than negative feedback, even though it did not have any connection with their actual scores. The results of the first study suggest that we are quite good at predicting the outcomes of personality tests. However, the results of the second study suggest that when the outcomes of the test contradict our predictions, we are inclined to believe the test rather than our own evaluations.

This leads us to a discussion of the Barnum Effect (so named after the famous US showman). In brief, the Barnum Effect refers to a powerful tendency to believe information given to us about our personal qualities. This is used to good effect by fortune tellers, astrologers, handwriting experts, life coaches, mediums and various other contemporary shamans. If the 'expert' can say what people are prepared to accept, and can phrase it in such a way that it implies some intimate insight, then there is a good living to be made.

How gullible are you?

The fallacy of personal validation: a class-room demonstration of gullibility.

FORER, B.R. (1949)

Journal of Abnormal and Social Psychology, 44, 118–21.

▶ **Eysenck Personality Inventory** A psychometric scale for measuring neuroticism and extraversion.

▶ **neuroticism** A personality dimension based on a person's measured susceptibility to neuroses.

▶ **extraversion** A general tendency towards outgoing, social behaviour.

The study

▶ **Barnum Effect** Describes the fact that a carefully worded description of an individual's personality will often be uncritically accepted as valid if presented in sufficiently broad and general terms.

Forer points out that virtually every psychological trait can be viewed to a greater or lesser extent in everyone. This means that when we read a textbook on abnormal psychology we see a connection to our problems and experience; the 'oh, I'm sure I've got that' syndrome. We make this mistake because we lack a reference point for critical comparison, in that we do not know what other people are experiencing. For example, if we read that people with a 'Bashful Syndrome' (made-up name) are unsure of themselves in social situations, then we believe it could be us. This is because everyone is sometimes unsure in social situations, but the feeling only becomes noteworthy if you are very unsure of yourself. And you can only make this judgement by comparing yourself with other people and evaluating your unsureness as greater than theirs. This lack of a reference point for comparison makes us vulnerable to statements about ourselves that require a comparison to other people.

Some psychological tests, and psychological therapies, have used *personal validation* to back up the procedure. Personal validation asks the subject or client to say whether he or she agrees with the assessment of the therapist or tester. If they agree, it is seen as evidence for the validity of the test or therapy. However, it seems that people are vulnerable to agreement with certain sorts of comparative statements, so their agreement with the results of the test or therapy is affected by their belief in the test or therapist.

Procedure

Forer tested this observation on his introductory psychology class. During a lecture, he described his Diagnostic Interest Bank (DIB) to his students. In the manner of all the best con tricks, this whetted the appetite of the class and they persuaded Forer to let them take the test (the first rule of a successful con is to appear reluctant!). The class were given the test and told they would receive their personal profiles after the data had been analysed. One week later, each student was given a typed personality sketch with their name on it. The students had requested secrecy and this was encouraged by Forer.

Before the sketches were passed to the students, instructions were given to first read the sketches, and then to turn the papers over and complete the following steps:

▶ **personality** A distinctive and relatively stable pattern of behaviours, thoughts, motives and emotions that characterize an individual.

(a)   Rate on a scale of 0 (poor) to 5 (perfect) how *effective* the DIB is in revealing personality.

(b)   Rate on a scale of 0 to 5 the degree to which the personality sketch reveals *basic characteristics* of your personality.

(c)   Turn the paper again and check each statement as *true or false* about yourself, or use a question mark if you cannot tell.

When the students looked at their personality sketch they saw 13 statements. If, however, they had looked at the sketch of any of their colleagues they would have seen the same 13 statements. The universal sketch consisted of the following items:

(1)   You have a great need for other people to like and admire you.

(2)   You have a tendency to be critical of yourself.

(3)   You have a great deal of unused capacity which you have not turned to your advantage.

(4)   While you have some personality weaknesses, you are generally able to compensate for them.

(5)   Your sexual adjustment has presented problems for you.

(6)   Disciplined and self-controlled outside, you tend to be worrisome and insecure inside.

(7)   At times you have serious doubts as to whether you have made the right decision or done the right thing.

(8)   You prefer a certain amount of change and variety and become dissatisfied when hemmed in by restrictions and limitations.

(9)   You pride yourself as an independent thinker and do not accept others' statements without satisfactory proof.

(10) You have found it unwise to be too frank in revealing yourself to others.

(11) At times you are extraverted, affable, sociable, while at other times you are introverted, wary, reserved.

(12) Some of your aspirations tend to be pretty unrealistic.

(13) Security is one of your major goals in life. (p. 119)

After they had completed their assessment of the DIB and the personality sketch, the students were debriefed about the study. Forer writes that 'it was pointed out to them that the experiment had been performed as an object lesson to demonstrate the tendency to be overly impressed by vague statements and to endow diagnosticians with an unwarrantedly high degree of insight.' This was Forer's justification for the deception of his subjects.

Results

The results of completing steps A and B are shown in Table 18.2. The results of completing step C are shown in Table 18.3. The distribution of 'true', 'false' and 'uncertain' responses for each statement is shown in Figure 18.2. The data show an overwhelming acceptance of the phoney feedback. Table 18.3, for example, shows that 28 out of 39 accepted ten or more of the statements as true. Table 18.2 shows that 38 out of the 39 subjects gave the DIB a rating of at least 4 out of 5 in terms of its effectiveness in revealing personality. The analysis of the responses to individual items in the DIB shows that only items 5, 12 and 13 received more than four 'false' responses (see Figure 18.2).

Table 18.2 *Distribution of ratings*

Ratings	0	1	2	3	4	5	N
(a) DIB	0	0	0	1	25	13	39
(b) Sketch	0	0	1	4	18	16	39

Source: Forer (1949).

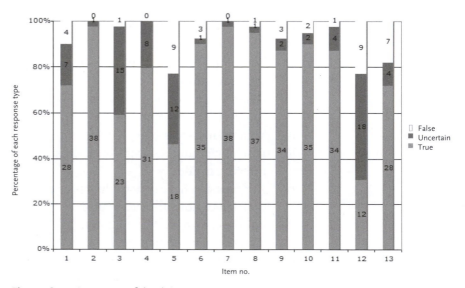

Figure 18.2 *Acceptance of sketch items*

Table 18.3 *Number of responses accepted as 'true' by each participant in step (c)*

Number true	5	6	7	8	9	10	11	12	13	N
Frequency	1	0	0	5	5	10	9	7	2	39

Source: Forer (1949).

Discussion

The study suggests that the method of personal validation of therapeutic procedures and personality tests is unsatisfactory. The students in this demonstration found that they were susceptible to agreeing with messages about themselves from a seemingly credible source.

If we look at a number of personality tests, we can interpret the popularity of these tests as another example of the Barnum Effect. As long as the test provides a plausible, largely positive description that relies on comparisons with the behaviour and experience of other people, then it is likely to be believed.

Questions

suggested answers
→ P. 506

1. Who are the most plausible sources of information about ourselves? In other words what kinds of people do we tend to believe?

2. The subjects in this study were students. How might the results have been different if the study had been carried out on a different subject group?

3. Forer justifies his deception of his students. Do you think this justification is sufficient?

4. Try this demonstration out on someone else, maybe after pretending to read their palm. Do be sure to tell them what it was all about afterwards.

Dull rats and bright rats

ROSENTHAL, R. AND FODE, K.L. (1963)

The effect of experiment bias on the performance of the albino rat.

Behavioral Science, 8, 183–9.

Introduction

One of the most important effects to control against in psychological experimentation is the effect of experimenter bias. Experimenters can all too easily find what they are looking for (support their own hypotheses) by inadvertently influencing the way in which their subjects behave. Quite how such bias happens is unclear, since the most troublesome forms of it happen outside of our awareness. But the chances are it is something to do with the experimenter's expectations of how the subjects in the different conditions will behave; people have a tendency to live up to (or down to) the standards that are expected of them (Rosenthal and Jacobson, 1966). Experimenter effects (another term for experimenter bias) are a source of artefact in behavioural research, meaning they can be the cause of artificial, non-valid findings (see also the summary of Orne's paper on demand characteristics above).

The study

▶ **hypothesis** Experiments are designed to test one or more hypotheses. An hypothesis is a prediction of what will happen in an experiment. It is worded in such a way that the results of a well-designed experiment will clearly show whether the prediction is right or wrong.

▶ **experimenter effects** Unwanted influences in a psychological study which are produced, consciously or unconsciously, by the person carrying out the study.

The authors of this study set out to examine whether or not experimenter effects can occur in studies of animal behaviour. They led their student subjects to believe that they were acting as experimenters and gave each one of them five rats which were to be trained over a period of days on a maze task (see Figure 18.3). In one condition, a group of students were led to believe that their rats had been specially bred to be 'maze-bright'; in the other condition the students were informed that their rats were 'maze-dull'. In fact, there was no difference between the groups of rats, which had all been randomly selected from the same stock. The only differences were in the minds of the student 'experimenters'. If any consistent differences in performance in the rats could be detected across the two conditions, those differences must have been caused by the expectations that the students had of their rats.

Subjects

Twelve students taking a course in experimental psychology in a US university acted as subjects in this experiment as part of their course requirements. None of them had any experience in working with animal subjects. In addition, 60 rats aged between 64 and 105 days old, which had no experience of a T-maze, were used. Throughout the paper the authors refer to the human subjects as 'experimenters' (because that is what the subjects thought they were) and to the rats as 'subjects'. We, on the other hand, will refer to the students as the subjects.

The rats were divided into 12 groups, such that every group had a similar mean age. There were two males and three females in each group. 'Several days before the beginning of the experiment [the rats were] placed on a 23-hour food deprivation' (p. 184).

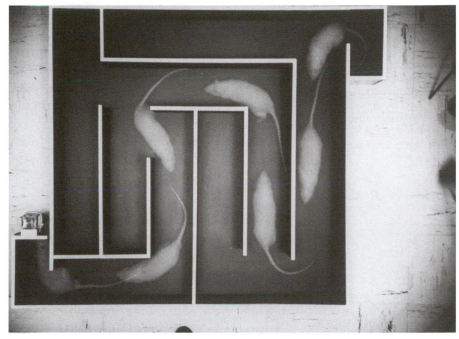

Figure 18.3   *Rat in a maze: the T-maze used in this study was simpler than the one illustrated here.*

Design

The study used a basic two-condition independent measures experimental design, with subjects' beliefs about the relative ability of their group of rats as the independent variable. Subjects were sorted into pairs according to their estimates of how much they expected to like working with the rats, and then each pair of subjects was split at random across the two conditions. Subjects in one condition believed they were working with maze-bright rats; in the other condition subjects believed they were working with maze-dull rats.

The dependent variable was the mean number of correct responses per rat per day over a five-day period. Other data were also collected, including mean response times for correct responses, and some self-assessment scores from questionnaires that the subjects completed.

Procedure

Subjects were told that the groups of rats with which they would be working had been bred over a series of generations to be either maze-bright or maze-dull. Maze-bright rats would show 'learning during the first day of running. Thereafter performance should rapidly increase' (p. 184). Maze-dull rats should show 'very little evidence of learning' (p. 184). The subjects were led to believe that the aim of the exercise was to give them experience in handling rats, and to give them experience in 'duplicating experimental findings' (p. 184).

▶reinforcement Any consequence of any behaviour that increases the probability that that behaviour will recur in similar circumstances. The term is usually used of learned associations, acquired through operant conditioning, but it may also be applied to other forms of learning.

Each subject was given a group of five rats labelled either maze-bright or maze-dull according to which condition the subject had been assigned. Needless to say, the rats had actually been divided into maze-bright and maze-dull groups at random.

Subjects were instructed to run their rats ten times for each of five days on a T-maze. The rats had to learn to discriminate between one arm of the maze which was painted white, and the other which was painted dark grey. Running to the darker arm was always reinforced; whilst running to the white arm was never reinforced. The arms were interchangeable, and swapped round at random, so that the rats could not just learn to run in a given direction. The subjects (believing they were experimenters!) recorded success rates per rat per day, time taken for every correct response, and also some post-experimental data on their feelings about their rats and how they had interacted with them.

Results

The data show that the rats that were believed to be maze-bright made, on average, more correct responses each day than the rats that were believed to be maze-dull (Table 18.4 and Figure 18.4). The correct responses of the maze-bright rats were on average quicker than the maze-dull rats on each of the five days (Table 18.5). Furthermore, the rats in the maze-bright condition showed a consistent trend of improvement in terms of number of, and speed of, correct responses over the five-day period. The performance of the maze-dull rats did not improve every day in this way.

Table 18.4   *Number of correct responses per rat per day*

Day	Maze-bright	Maze-dull	t	p (one-tailed)
1	1.33	0.73	2.54	.03
2	1.60	1.10	1.02	ns
3	2.60	2.23	0.29	ns
4	2.83	1.83	2.28	.05
5	3.26	1.83	2.37	.03
Mean	2.32	1.54	4.01	.01

ns = not significant
Source: Rosenthal and Fode (1963).

Table 18.5   *Mean time in minutes required to make a correct response*

Day	Maze-bright	Maze-dull	t	p (one-tailed)
1	3.13	3.99		ns
2	2.75	4.76		ns
3	2.05	3.20		ns
4	2.09	2.18		ns
5	1.75	3.20		ns
Mean	2.35	3.47	3.50	.02

ns = not significant
Source: Rosenthal and Fode (1963).

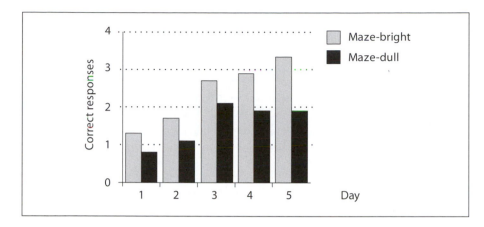

Figure 18.4 *Average number of correct responses per rat per day*

In the post-experimental questionnaire, subjects in the maze-bright condition reported higher levels of cleanliness, tameness, brightness and pleasantness in their rats than did subjects in the maze-dull condition. The former also made higher estimates of how often they handled their rats, and how gentle they had been with them.

Discussion

▶ **double-blind control** A form of experimental control which aims to avoid self-fulfilling prophecies, by ensuring that neither the subjects nor the experimenter who carries out the study are aware of the experimental hypothesis.

▶ **self-fulfilling prophecy** The idea that expectations about a person or group can become true simply because they have been stated.

▶ **placebo effect** An inactive substance or fake treatment that produces a response in patients.

The results certainly seem to indicate that the experimenter effect is alive and kicking in studies of animal behaviour. And if rats can be affected by human expectations, how much more powerful are experimenter effects likely to be in studies of human behaviour?

Experimenter bias can have some very serious consequences in scientific tests such as drug trials. If the person administering the drug has an expectation of how it will work, the patient might well behave accordingly. One way of dealing with this is the double-blind design, which conceals the experimental hypothesis from the person actually carrying out the experiment as well as from the subject. Alternatively, the person conducting the experiment is not permitted to know which conditions subjects have been allocated to. In this way the experimenter cannot have relevant and biasing expectations. This technique is commonly seen when a new drug is being tested against a placebo. None of the people who administer the drugs or who assess the health of the people taking the drugs know at any stage who is receiving the real thing and who is receiving the placebo.

Questions

suggested
answers
→ p. 507

1. How do you think the experimenter effect worked in this case? If the experimenters' expectations really did lie behind the differences in performance in the two groups, how might these expectations have been communicated to the rats?

2. Why were the subjects led to believe that the point of the whole exercise was to give them practice in handling rats and in duplicating experimental findings?

3. What are your feelings about animal research? For example, how did you respond to reading about the '23-hour food deprivation'?

Introduction

Why do we do psychology? The most obvious answer is 'to find out stuff'. This is also the answer we would give to similar questions about other subjects. But why do we want to find out stuff? What will we do with all the stuff that we find out? If we are finding out stuff about the weather, say, then there seems no problem in wanting to understand it, predict it and, if possible control it. This is what science does.

The weather gives us a simple example of science that on the surface at least has no obvious moral problems associated with it. But what if we study the atom and learn how to release the energy from it and so create the science of the atomic bomb? All of a sudden some moral questions have come into our work because the science will have some very powerful consequences for people. Should we do this research and, if we do, who should have the knowledge we discover?

Psychological research has not developed any weapons of mass destruction but it does throw up some difficult moral questions, so it is important to consider what we want to achieve from our studies. J.B. Watson (see Chapter 11) set the agenda for modern psychology when he wrote the following:

> The interest of the behaviorist in man's [sic] doings is more than the interest of the spectator – he [sic] wants to control man's reactions as physical scientists want to control and manipulate other natural phenomena. It is the business of behavioristic psychology to be able to predict and to control human activity. (Watson, 1930, p. 11)

If we follow Watson's suggestion we can use psychology to change the world. This is fantastic as long as (a) it needs changing in the first place, and (b) we change it for the better rather than for the worse. There is also the issue of who is going to do the changing, who gets changed and who decides what change is 'for the better'. Presumably the changing will be done by psychologists, and the people being changed will be those who are judged by psychologists to need changing. You can see the problem here, especially if those being changed are quite happy as they are.

The paper

George Miller was elected in 1969 as the President of the American Psychological Association and this paper is his Presidential Address. Miller starts his paper by noting that 'the most urgent problems of our world today are the problems we have made for ourselves' (p. 1036). At the time he gave the address the USA government was drifting deeper and deeper into military action in Vietnam against the peasant army of Vietnamese people, at considerable cost to both sides (55,000 US soldiers and in excess of 1.5 million

Vietnamese dead; Pilger, 1989). If these sorts of modern-day problems have been made by people then if we want to solve them we need to know a bit more about people. This is where psychology comes in. And if psychology can help with our problems then it should try to do so. Miller suggests that our obligations as citizens (rather than as scientists) means that if we have something of practical value to contribute, we should make every effort to ensure that it is implemented.

Miller starts his discussion by looking at the role of the American Psychological Association (well, it was his Presidential Address), and notes that in its constitution it is committed to 'advance scientific interests and inquiry and the application of research findings to the promotion of human welfare' (p. 1064). The problem with the idea of promoting human welfare is that it is not clear what this means. What is human welfare? How can we promote it? Are we talking about the greater human good in which case some individual rights might be compromised for the benefit of the wider society? Or are we talking about the welfare of every individual? Miller suggests that general statements about 'promoting human welfare' are little more than a sincere declaration that our heart is in the right place.

Revolutionary potential of psychology

Miller argues that psychology has the potential to be one of the most revolutionary activities ever developed by people. He writes 'if we were ever to achieve substantial progress toward our stated aim – toward the understanding, prediction and control of mental and behavioural phenomena – the implications for every aspect of society would make brave men tremble' (p. 1065). On the bright side, of course, psychology rarely lives up to the hype and nothing that it has done so far is very revolutionary. Psychologists might have developed psychometric tests, conditioned reflexes, factor analysis and psychoanalysis, but these hardly match up to the developments in other sciences such as gunpowder, the steam engine, computers, atom bombs, the contraceptive pill and so forth.

Miller argues that we are looking in the wrong direction if we are waiting for the great discoveries and applications to appear. He argues that the revolution will come in how we think of ourselves:

> I believe that the real impact of psychology will be felt, not through the technological products it places in the hands of powerful men, but through its effects on the public at large, through a new and different public conception of what is humanly possible and humanly desirable. (p. 1066)

Miller uses the example of Freudian theory. He suggests that the practical application (the therapy) has only had a limited impact, but the theory itself has changed the way we think about ourselves in the Western World. This is the type of change that happened when it was discovered, in other branches of science, that our planet is not the centre of the universe, and when it became accepted that our ancestors were fairly hairy and lived in trees. Such theories and discoveries change the way people see themselves. Psychology has the same potential to change our view of who we are and what we can be.

Miller goes on to explore the tricky issue of control. If we can control behaviour, in what circumstances should we do it? He comes to the conclusion that in contrast to 'control':

> understanding and prediction are better goals for psychology and for the promotion of human welfare because they lead us to think, not in terms of coercion by a powerful elite, but in terms of the diagnosis of problems and the development of programmes that can enrich the lives of every citizen. (p. 1069)

Giving psychology away

Miller notes the growing need for psychological services and writes that there are not enough psychologists to meet that need. He goes on to say 'the people at large will have to be their own psychologists and make their own applications of the principles we establish' (p. 1071). This has implications for how we deal with scientific knowledge. If we follow one path then psychologists will discover things about people, hold onto that knowledge and therefore become experts (knowing things that most people do not) and then will be able to use that expert status to sell their services and control the use of 'the knowledge'.

Miller proposes a different path when he writes 'our responsibility is less to assume the role of experts and try to apply psychology ourselves than to give it away to the people who really need it' (p. 1071). If we follow this path then we make psychological knowledge freely available (open source?) so that the general public can have a better view of who they are and what choices they have. In this way the control issue is about using psychology to allow the ordinary individuals to have more control over their own behaviour and hence their own lives. Miller finishes his paper by saying:

> I can imagine nothing that we could do that would be more relevant to human welfare, and nothing that could pose a greater challenge to the next generation of psychologists than to discover how best to give psychology away. (p. 1074)

Discussion

A lot has happened in the years since Miller's paper but the issues are still relevant. You might argue that some aspects of psychology are being given away all the time on the various television shows about human relationships that have turned us all into amateur therapists. The American Psychological Association makes a considerable amount of material available for general consumption (go to their website at www.apa.org) and they are certainly making an effort to give some psychology away.

Not everything is rosy in the garden of course and it is self-evident that psychology has sometimes been used by the few to exploit the many. Take

▶sleep deprivation A lack of the necessary amount of sleep brought about by neurological or psychological or social causes, and creating a range of negative psychological and bodily effects. Sometimes used as a form of torture.

▶phobia An anxiety disorder characterized by persistent fear out of proportion to the danger, a compelling desire to escape the situation, and a recognition that the fear is excessive

▶sensory deprivation The cutting out of all incoming sensory information, or at least as much of it as possible. Sometimes used as a method of torture.

the use of psychology in advertising and shop design to encourage greater spending and consumption, often by people who cannot afford it. We could also point to the use of psychology in warfare. This raises all sorts of moral questions. You might argue that if you wage war with psychology rather than with guns then less people will get killed and this might be a good thing, but the history of psychological warfare is not so benign (for a review see Watson, 1980, or Ronson, 2005).

A recent issue for psychologists to deal with has been the interrogation techniques at the US-run prisons in Iraq (most famously Abu Ghraib) and Guantanamo Bay. Psychologists have been involved in these techniques and the American Psychological Association has been challenged to rule them unethical. In 2006 the Association adopted a resolution that unequivocally condemned any involvement by psychologists in torture or cruel, inhuman or degrading treatment or punishment in any setting. Unfortunately it left its members with a get-out clause because it allows psychologists to still participate in national security interrogations. The problem with this is the abuse during these interrogations of specific psychological methods, including sleep deprivation, stress positioning, exploitation of phobias, forced nakedness, sensory deprivation, religious degradation and isolation. Both the American Psychiatric Association and the American Medical Association have banned their members from supporting interrogation processes, leaving many psychologists wondering why the American Psychological Association has not yet adopted a similar stance (Wessells, 2006).[1]

Questions

suggested answers ➤ p. 507

1. Try to think of psychology's great findings. What do you think are its greatest discoveries and inventions? If your list is a bit short then ask your teacher or a paid-up psychologist. Give them a list of successes in the other sciences like the human genome, the micro-chip, the moon landing, the mobile phone and then ask for psychology's equivalents. It never fails to wind them up.

2. If you were going to give psychology away, what do you think would be the most useful things for people to be given?

---

1. The British Psychological Society is reluctant to comment on issues such as this because it is keen to protect its status as a learned society, but if you go to the BPS website you will find a clear statement against the use of torture by psychologists (www.bps.org.uk).

chapter **19**

METHODOLOGY: HOW DOES PSYCHOLOGICAL RESEARCH GET DONE?

Chapter overview

This chapter is about the methods which psychology researchers use to collect data, and the ways in which they set about using their data to answer research questions. It is also about the business of reading and evaluating research. It provides a relatively straightforward overview of methodological issues in psychology, with links to summaries from the rest of the book to illustrate the concepts that are introduced. In this respect the chapter is completely self-contained, because all the examples are drawn from the studies we have summarized. We have found this style of learning to suit many people: instead of exploring methodological issues in the daunting abstract detail of a standard 'research methods' text, we briefly describe an issue or a concept, and straight away refer to one of the summaries, so that you can immediately see actual examples of the ideas. We would suggest that when you come to a bit of this chapter that you do not fully understand, you follow up on the summaries that are referred to in that section, in order to see in practice what we are talking about. To help you find the summaries, each time one is mentioned the relevant page numbers will be displayed alongside the text.

The chapter is structured in the following way. The first section is a discussion of the various kinds of data that researchers deal with in the course of empirical inquiry, with a focus on the differences between qualitative and quantitative data. The second section is an overview of different types of research methods used in psychology. The third section picks up on a number of key methodological themes, and in doing so provides some ideas about how to read and critically evaluate research papers. In this chapter, words and phrases that are listed in the glossary are still highlighted in bold, but the glossary entries are not listed in the margins.

Section 1: Data and data analysis

The academic discipline of **psychology** is grounded on empirical inquiry. Empirical inquiry is any kind of research which involves collecting data. Most of the summaries in this book concern empirical studies, although there are some that do not (see Searle, 1980, and Nobles, 1976, for two examples of non-empirical papers). Generally speaking, psychologists will not accept something to be the case unless they are able to point to empirical evidence in the literature. This reliance on evidence is what makes psychology a social science.

▶ **Searle (1980)** See pages 358–361

▶ **Nobles (1976)** See pages 177–180

A quick scan through the results sections of the summarized papers should be enough to show that psychology deals in data of all shapes and sizes. It is inevitable that an overview will not be able to do justice to the richness and complexity of this domain. The aim of this book, however, is to give an accessible starting point for thinking about methods and methodology, rather than to provide a definitive account of these things. Our objective is to provide a **set** of concepts that can be used to enhance your understanding of psychological research, and which will help you to evaluate it critically.

Qualitative and quantitative data

Our starting point for thinking about data is the distinction between qualitative and quantitative data. Qualitative data are about 'qualities' of things. They are descriptions, words, meanings, pictures, texts and so forth. They are about what something is like, or how something is experienced. Good examples of studies included in this book which are based on the collection of qualitative data are Koff (1983) and Weitz (1989). Koff collected and analysed drawings in order to try to discover what the onset of **menstruation** is like for adolescent girls. Weitz interviewed people who had **AIDS** to find out about their experiences of the disease and its consequences for their lives. Note that the studies which deal predominantly with qualitative data are in the minority in this book. This reflects the predominance of quantitative data in psychological research.

▶ **Koff (1983)** See pages 186–189

▶ **Weitz (1989)** See pages 406–409

Quantitative data are about 'quantities' of things. They are numbers, raw scores, percentages, means, **standard deviations** and so forth. They are measurements of things, telling us how much of something there is. Most of the studies in this book deal with quantitative data. For example, Bales (1955) quantified the proportion of particular kinds of communicative acts in decision-making **groups** (see Table 3.1 in Chapter 3), whilst Holmes and Rahe (1967) constructed a scale to measure the stresses caused by a variety of **life events** (see Table 17.3 in Chapter 17).

▶ **Bales (1955)** See pages 65–68

▶ **Holmes and Rahe (1967)** See pages 410–413

Sometimes people refer to research as being either qualitative or quantitative. This is a shorthand way of referring to different traditions of enquiry within the discipline. However, it can be misleading, for it implies that certain methods inherently produce certain kinds of data. For example, **experiments** are usually referred to as quantitative and textual analysis is usually described as qualitative. Experiments, however, can produce qualitative data as well as numbers. Milgram (1963) described the **behaviour** of his participants in some detail (qualitative data), as well as measuring the extent to which they were prepared to comply with the demands of the experimenter (quantitative data). Conversely, a method such as **participant observation**, which is usually associated with qualitative descriptions of a social setting from within that setting, can also yield quantitative data. Rosenhan (1973) collated numerical data from the participant observers (the **pseudopatients**) about the ways in which medical staff responded to patients. For this reason it is more accurate to use the terms **qualitative** and **quantitative** in their more restrictive sense (as we do in this chapter), to refer to 'data', rather than 'research' or 'method'.

Of course the decision of whether to collect qualitative or quantitative data (or both) in the course of a piece of psychological enquiry is a research design decision, which depends entirely on what it is that you are trying to find out. In other words, the type of data that are collected depend upon the nature of the research question. Generally speaking, if the research question is about meanings and experiences, or if it is about something that is relatively complex that is best looked at as a whole, then methods which produce qualitative data tend to be used. Haney et al. (1973) set about trying to capture the experiences of prison life. They sought to study the whole prison environment, as one large, complex set of psychological and sociological phenomena. The research resulted in a rich, detailed, 'thick' description of life within their **simulated** prison, with little emphasis on measurement. This is in contrast to the recent prison study by Reicher and Haslam (2006) that made extensive use of quantitative measures to back up the data they collected from **observations** and interviews.

If, on the other hand, the research question has a more restricted focus, and is about people's behaviour, or some psychological phenomenon that can be inferred from behaviour, then methods which generate quantitative data tend to be used. For example, Kitto (1989) asked the highly focused question of whether an applicant described as a girl is more or less likely to be offered a job than an applicant described as a woman. The data she collected reflected the simplicity of this question, and are reported in terms of the proportion of participants who judged each candidate (one of whom was described as a girl, the other as a woman) as suitable for particular types of job. Note that other aspects of this research would lend themselves to more complex, qualitative enquiry. For example, Kitto might have collected qualitative data to address the question of what it feels like for adult women to be referred to as 'girls' in different settings, or to examine the issue of how this kind of language is used day-to-day in office environments.

▶ **Milgram (1963)** See pages 12–17

▶ **Rosenhan (1973)** See pages 196–199

▶ **Haney et al. (1973)** See pages 69–73

▶ **Reicher and Haslam (2006)** See pages 74–80

▶ **Kitto (1989)** See pages 190–193

Question

1. What kind of data (qualitative or quantitative) were collected in each of the following studies, summarized in this book?

▶ **Labov (1969)** See pages 301–304

(a) Labov (1969);

▶ **Festinger and Carlsmith (1959)** See pages 31–36

(b) Festinger and Carlsmith (1959);

▶ **Hodges and Tizard (1989b)** See pages 250–254

(c) Hodges and Tizard (1989);

▶ **Lang and Lazovik (1963)** See pages 209–213

(d) Lang and Lazovik (1963);

▶ **Rosenhan (1973)** See pages 196–199

(e) Rosenhan (1973).

Suggested answers ➡ p. 507

Operational definition

Although most research in psychology uses quantitative data in order to measure things of interest, it is by no means easy to do this well. Psychologists are interested in all sorts of phenomena: **aggression**, happiness, depth **perception**, **memory**, pain, **prejudice**, **intelligence**, and so on and so forth. The problem is that most of the things we are interested in are unobservable, and therefore cannot be measured directly. We can, however, measure how people behave. So, if we want to know about some unseen psychological process, we have to select observable behaviours which 'represent' that process, and measure them instead. It is then up to the researcher to argue that the measurements of those observable behaviours are a valid representation of the invisible thing which is the real topic of the investigation.

The behaviour we choose to observe and record is called the operational definition of the invisible thing that we are really trying to study, and selecting the best operational definition is trickier than it sounds. We might, for example, think it would be rather easy to measure aggression: simply count the number of 'aggressive behaviours' that the research participants exhibit. But what counts as an 'aggressive behaviour'?

Question

2. What behaviours would you use to represent (or, 'operationally define') aggression?

Suggested answers ➡ p. 507

You can probably come up with quite a long list which includes things to do with physical violence to people and objects, and things to do with various kinds of verbal and non-verbal behaviour. One problem is the sheer number of things that we might count as aggressive. This is because aggression can be exhibited behaviourally in numerous ways. But there is an additional layer of complexity to deal with. This is because any given behaviour can be aggressive in one context, and not in another. In other words, the same behaviour can mean different things, at different times, in different settings, and even between different people. Slapping can be a sign of aggression. It can also be a sign of fear, disapproval, **humour**, self-defence, musicianship, achievement (high fives), a behavioural disorder, a poor aim, sexual pleasure. What any given behaviour means in any given setting is a matter of interpretation, and it is this that makes measurement in psychology such a difficult process. Look at Bandura et al. (1961) and think about the quality of their operational definition of aggression.

One of the best known, and most controversial, operational definitions of a hidden psychological construct is the IQ test, a measure of intelligence. There are a number of reasons why some people argue that the IQ test is not a valid operational definition of intelligence. One reason is that the test measures our performance, whereas the construct of intelligence is really to do with competence (ability). We might be very clever but perform poorly on the test because we were in a bad mood, or because the test was in a foreign language, or because it had a cultural bias in it (see Gould, 1982). And in any case, is the collection of mental puzzles that makes up an IQ test a good measure of intelligence in the first place? It might just measure 'puzzle-solving ability'. For all these reasons it is possible to argue that a person's behaviour on an IQ test might not validly represent their intelligence.

In attempting to prevent studies from getting unmanageably complex, psychologists sometimes use very simple measures to represent very complex things. The study by Tajfel (1970) is concerned with the highly complex issue of prejudice, but measures it using a bizarre task of asking schoolchildren to select a pair of rewards for two other unknown children who either have the same taste in abstract expressionist painters or not. The point of the study is to show that prejudice can be created on the simplest of pretexts, but the issue at stake here is whether the simple behaviour of the research participants bears much resemblance to the complex set of prejudiced stereotypes and **attitudes** that people hold in everyday life.

The key thing for the discerning reader of psychological research is to consider the quality of the chosen operational definitions used in a study, and to ask whether or not the measurements taken really do allow us to draw conclusions about the psychological phenomena they are supposed to represent.

Levels of measurement

How do we measure behaviour? A key notion here is the idea of levels of measurement. Psychologists use a wide range of measurement techniques. At the simplest level, they use categories to code behaviour. For example, the study by Hraba and Grant (1970) used a doll selection task to explore children's sense of racial **identity**. The behaviour that was measured was simply whether the children selected a Black doll or a White doll as the one they would like to play with. A similar example of this measurement technique can be seen in the study by Fernald (1985), where babies' preferences for particular types of speech sounds were measured by whether they moved their heads to the left or to the right. This type of measurement-by-categorization is called a **nominal scale**. As you look through this text you will find a surprising number of

▶ **Bandura et al. (1961)** See pages 103–108

▶ **Gould (1982)** See pages 230–235

▶ **Tajfel (1970)** See pages 46–50

▶ **Hraba and Grant (1970)** See pages 173–176

▶ **Fernald (1985)** See pages 293–296

▶ **Gibson and Walk (1960)** See pages 331–334

studies that use this relatively simple level of measurement, for example Gibson and Walk (1960), crawl/don't crawl; Harlow (1959), cloth model/wire model; Kitto (1989), high-status/low-status job.

A more sophisticated version of the nominal scale can be seen in the studies by Bales (1955) and by Bandura et al. (1961). In these studies the researchers observed complex social behaviour using a checklist of behaviours. Every time they observed a particular behaviour, the observers entered it on the checklist so that a record could be made of how frequently each behaviour occurred.

One level up from the categories of the nominal scale are scales that assign scores to people or things, and thereby allow them to be rank ordered (from least to most or vice versa). An example of this is the study by Holmes and Rahe (1967), which used this technique to devise a stress scale. They asked people to rate how stressful they found a series of events so that they could give a numerical value to each event. This scale can be used to measure the level of stress in groups of participants, allowing all participants to be rank ordered from least stressed to most stressed. Another example of this approach to measurement can be found in the study by Schachter and Singer (1962) where they attempted to estimate how emotional the participants were feeling. They asked their participants to estimate their emotional state on two five-point scales, one of which measured happiness and one of which measured anger or irritation. Again, on the basis of these measurements, they were able to rank order the participants in terms of their emotional states, and compare the scores from the different groups. This type of measurement is called an ordinal scale, because it puts things in a (rank) order.

A still more sophisticated measurement technique is to use a scale of measurement that has fixed intervals between its units. For example, scales that use units such as metres or seconds fall into this category. The difference between scores of 2 and 4 seconds is exactly the same as the difference between scores of 3 and 5 seconds: that is, 2 seconds. If we go back to the measurement of emotion by Schachter and Singer (1962), on the other hand, we cannot be confident that the interval between a happiness score of 3 and 5 is the same as the interval between a happiness score of 2 and 4. The problem is that we do not know what one unit of emotion looks like, whereas we can accurately define what one second is. These more sophisticated measures that use scales with fixed intervals are called, with startling originality, **interval scales**. An example of the use of this type of measurement scale can be seen in the study by Rosenthal and Fode (1963), where they measured the time taken by a rat to complete a maze.

As ever in psychology, there are hidden complexities when it comes to deciding what type of measurement is being used. For example, an IQ test (see Gould, 1982) is probably best thought of as an ordinal scale, because we cannot be confident about the units of an IQ test in the way that we are confident about units of time. However, the downside of this is that it restricts the type of statistical tests that can be used with the data. There is, therefore, a pressure to view a number of psychological measures as interval scales so that the researchers can use a full range of statistical tests.

Question

3. What level of measurement best describes the following examples?

(a) Lang and Lazovik's (1963) data on their 19-point snake avoidance test;

(b) Kitto's (1989) data about whether the 'girl' or 'woman' would be most suitable for the job;

(c) Samuel and Bryant's (1984) data on whether children got a **conservation** question right or wrong;

(d) Collins and Quillian's (1969) data on reaction times.

Suggested answers → p. 507

Data analysis

Raw data are never reported in psychological research papers. The data have always been subjected to some sort of analysis. The analysis that is undertaken depends upon the type of data that have been collected, and the reason that they have been collected in the first place. In other words, decisions about data analysis are made at the design stage of a study, and are determined by the aims of the research. Data analytic strategies can be thought of on a dimension which ranges from 'very straightforward' at one end to 'highly complex' at the other.

At the straightforward end of data analysis are those strategies that simply involve collation and summarization. For quantitative data this might involve the use of simple descriptive statistics, such as measures of central tendency and percentages. Descriptive statistics do just what they say they do: they describe the data. They tell us things like the mean score of participants, the range of scores, the proportion of participants who achieved a certain score, and so forth. Essentially, descriptive statistics help us to see patterns and relationships in the actual data collected. Straightforward analytic strategies for qualitative data include sorting units of textual data into categories. Weitz (1989) gives us an example of this in the way that she identifies seven themes from the transcribed interviews with people with AIDS.

As a general rule, simpler forms of data analysis are appropriate when we are using our data to describe something. The word 'simple' should not be interpreted in a pejorative sense here. Careful, systematic description of phenomena is a vital step in the process of scientific discovery. Note that even an apparently straightforward descriptive collation and summarization of qualitative data is already a complex and demanding analytic process.

More sophisticated styles of data analysis tend to be used when the aim is to make **inferences** which go beyond the actual data collected. An example of this in a study which uses qualitative data is provided by Potter and Edwards (1990). In this study they use an approach known as **discourse analysis**. This involves a detailed analysis of relatively small amounts of transcribed text as

► **Lang and Lazovik (1963)** See pages 209–213

► **Kitto (1989)** See pages 190–193

► **Samuel and Bryant (1984)** See pages 277–281

► **Collins and Quillian (1969)** See pages 362–366

► **Weitz (1989)** See pages 406–409

► **Potter and Edwards (1990)** See pages 401–405

a means of reasoning through a complex set of propositions about our social world. In relation to quantitative data, if researchers have studied a genuinely representative sample of a specified population, then they are allowed to infer that the patterns they see in the data from the sample also apply to the population from which the sample was drawn. Later on in this chapter, when experimentation is dealt with, we will look briefly at another kind of statistical inference which is used to provide causal explanations of psychological phenomena.

Question

4. A multiple choice question. At what stage in the research process should the details of data analysis be worked out?

(a) when the data have all been collected and you can see what the whole set look like;

(b) whilst the data are being collected, so that you can see what they are going to look like;

(c) before you've even thought of the research question, because you know what kind of analysis you are good at;

(d) during the very first stages of research design, well before any data are collected, but after the research question has been clearly established.

Suggested answers → p. 508

Section 2: Research methods and designs

In this section we give an overview of the kinds of methods that psychologists use in their research. For ease of reference the ideas are divided into subsections, but it should be noted that these divisions are simply meant to increase the readability of the text. In reality there are countless overlaps and blurred distinctions in the forthcoming paragraphs, which mean that if you think about things for too long, everything will tend to merge into one enormous, headache-inducing mess. As your understanding of psychological research develops, you will be increasingly able to pick the whole domain apart in your own way, and to construct your own picture of what is going on.

Experiments

Probably the most widely used method in psychological research is the experiment. An experiment is basically a **structured observation** involving the systematic manipulation of one or more **independent variables**, and the measurement of the effect of the manipulation on a **dependent variable**. It is held that experiments enable us to pick apart causality. In other words, experiments enable us to find out about the causes of things. One common mistake in the early stages of finding out about psychological research is carelessly to refer to every research study as 'an experiment'. This is wrong. Experiments are one kind of research method, which have a particular structure and logic to them.

One of the many examples of experiments in this text is Loftus and Palmer's (1974) work on leading questions. They were interested in whether an eyewitness's memory for an event could be affected by questions about the event. In order to study this they systematically manipulated the wording of a particular question so as to create different experimental conditions (or treatment conditions). In one condition, participants who had seen a film of a car accident were asked about the speed of the two cars that 'contacted' each other, whilst in another condition participants who had seen the same film were asked about the speed of the two cars that 'smashed' each other. Everything else, aside from the exact wording of these questions, was kept the same for all participants in all conditions. The experimenters recorded the participants' responses to the question, and found that the speed estimates of the group who had been asked the more dramatic question were on average 10 mph higher than the estimates of the other group. Because everything else had been kept the same for the different groups apart from this one thing, they were able to conclude that the wording of the question caused the speed estimates of one group to be higher than the other. After all, what else could have caused this difference to occur?

For the record, the different wordings of the question represented Loftus and Palmer's manipulation of the independent variable (the thing that does the causing), and the speed estimates were a measurement of the dependent variable (the speed estimates, according to this experiment, depended on what question the participant was asked).

► **Loftus and Palmer (1974)**
See pages 321–324

Question

► **Rosenthal and Fode (1963)**
See pages 434–438

5. In Rosenthal and Fode (1963) what was the independent variable and what was the dependent variable?

Suggested answers ➜ p. 508

The starting point for an experiment is an **hypothesis**. An hypothesis is a prediction about what will happen in the experiment. It is worded in such a way that a well-designed experiment will show the prediction to be either right or wrong. The hypothesis is formulated on the basis of a theory. If the prediction is found to be right (if the hypothesis is supported by the data), then this lends support to the theory. If the prediction is found to be wrong (if the hypothesis is not supported by the data), then this puts a question mark against some aspect of the theory. Of course, one experiment is never enough either to support or refute an entire theory.

► **Tajfel (1970)** See pages 46–50

For example, Tajfel (1970) reasoned, on the basis of his theory about prejudice, that simply being a member of a group was enough to cause people to **discriminate** against members of another group. So he set up an experiment whereby boys were allocated to different groups on some entirely arbitrary basis. They then had to allocate rewards for some trivial reason (a) to members of their own group (own-group condition), and (b) to members of a different group (different-group condition). Tajfel's prediction was that the boys would tend to allocate higher rewards to members of their own group than to boys from other groups (even though the groupings were essentially meaningless). The data from the experiment showed that Tajfel's prediction was correct, and he was able to 'accept' his hypothesis. This therefore stands as one piece of evidence which supports an aspect of Tajfel's theory about prejudice. Bear in mind that evidence can always be interpreted in different ways: whether Tajfel's data really support his theory depends on a critical analysis of whether the experiment was an appropriate way to test his theory.

Hypothesis testing

We use **inferential statistics** to test experimental hypotheses. The question we ask of the data is essentially always the same, and that is: 'Assuming my hypothesis is incorrect, what is the probability that the results I have obtained could have occurred by chance?' The inferential tests give us an estimate of that probability, and if it is very low then we are inclined to reject the 'chance factors' explanation and infer that our hypothesis is, in fact, correct. For example, in the study by Seligman and Maier (1967) on **learned helplessness**, the dogs in the helpless condition took on average 48 seconds to escape from the test situation whereas the other dogs took less than 27 seconds. There was less than a 5 per cent probability ($p < .05$) of obtaining this difference in the average scores by chance. Another way of putting this is that there were statistically significant differences between the scores for the different conditions. So the researchers were able to claim that their hypothesis had been supported, confident that the helpless condition really was having an effect on the dogs' behaviour.

▶ **Seligman and Maier (1967)**
See pages 99–102

There are a wide range of inferential statistical tests that can be used to estimate the probability that differences in scores across experimental conditions could have occurred by chance. The choice of tests depends on the design of the study and the type of data that have been collected. The tests go under a number of weird and wonderful names, such as the Mann-Whitney U test, and Page's L trend test, though our favourite is Roy's Largest Root.

The reader will not be surprised to discover that there is a lot more to this statistics and hypothesis testing malarkey than is written here. In this chapter we are trying to introduce you to the basic principles behind research. If you want to explore these issues in greater depth then we recommend that you pick up one of the many texts on behavioural statistics, though if you start to enjoy it we recommend you seek professional help.

Experimental design

There are two basic ways of designing an experiment. One way is to compare the performance of people in one condition with their own performance in another condition. Kitto (1989) provides an example of this. Participants received a reference for each of two job applicants for a high-status job. One applicant was referred to as a girl in her reference (the 'girl' condition), the

▶ **Kitto (1989)** See pages 190–193

other applicant was referred to as a woman (the 'woman' condition). Each participant's performance was measured on a nominal scale (see above) in terms of whether they judged the girl or the woman as more suitable for each job. Since each participant took part in both conditions (that is, saw both types of reference) Kitto was effectively comparing their performance in one condition with their own performance in the other, predicting that they would usually judge the woman to be more suitable than the girl for the high-status job. This is called a repeated measures design, also known as a within-subjects design. Actually Kitto's study was somewhat more complex, but this captures the underlying design principle.

Repeated measures designs are a good way of conducting an experiment. Because each person is compared against themselves, the design automatically controls for differences in the individuals taking part in the study. Kitto could have used different people in each condition. One group would then see the 'girl' reference, and the other group would see the 'woman' reference. They could then say whether or not they would offer their applicant the job, and those judgements would be compared across the two groups. This type of experiment is called an **independent measures** design, also known as a between-subjects design. One problem with this is that any differences that emerged might be nothing to do with the main experimental manipulation (the use of the **gender** references). They might simply be due to the tendency of one group of participants to be tougher than the other group on job applicants.

The main drawback with a **repeated measures** design is that if a person has taken part in one condition of the experiment it may well affect their performance in another condition. For example, if you look at the study on **imitating** aggression by Bandura et al. (1961), then you will see that if a child has been exposed to the aggressive model in one condition, it would not make sense subsequently to expose the same child to the passive model, because you will not know whether the aggressive model is still having an effect on the behaviour of the child. As a result of this problem, psychologists commonly use different groups of people for each condition of the study (independent measures), and compare the performance of these groups. If participants are randomly assigned to the different conditions then we are allowed to assume that any pre-existing differences among the participants will even out across the different groups.

There are a number of variations on these two core designs but the logic remains the same: we are either comparing the performance of one group of people in one condition with a separate group of people in another condition (independent measures), or we are comparing the performance of each person in one condition with their own performance in another condition (repeated measures).

▶ **Bandura et al. (1961)** See pages 103–108

Extraneous and confounding variables

The core principle, whichever basic design is chosen, is to make sure that the only systematic difference between the conditions of an experiment is that

▶ **Loftus and Palmer (1974)**
See pages 321–324

which is brought about by the manipulation of the independent variable. As mentioned above, the only difference between the conditions in the Loftus and Palmer (1974) experiment on leading questions was the change of word in the target question. Experimenters recognize that there are many things that affect the behaviour of participants. These things are collectively referred to as extraneous variables. These can be to do with environmental conditions (light, noise, heat and so forth), the characteristics of the participants (their emotional state, their sex, their age and so forth), the characteristics of the task (the instructions given by the experimenter, the way stimulus materials are presented and so forth). In fact the list is literally endless.

All these things are fine so long as they are either held constant, or randomized across the conditions of the experiment. They only become a problem if any of them differ systematically across the conditions and 'align' themselves with the experimenter's manipulation of the independent variable. For example, if Loftus and Palmer had 18-year-old participants in the 'contacted' condition, and 50-year-old participants in the 'smashed' condition, then the differences that they observed in the speed estimates might have been due to the age differences of the participants, rather than the wording of the question. Maybe, a sceptic could argue, older people simply tend to give higher estimates of speed than younger people. If this does happen, then we say that one of the extraneous variables (in this example, the variable of age) has become a **confounding variable**, because it confounds (messes up) the experimenter's attempts to interpret the findings of the experiment in the intended way. Extraneous variables are inevitable. **Confounding variables** are bad! Therefore a large part of the trick of designing a good experiment is to prevent extraneous variables from becoming confounding variables. This is what is meant by experimental control.

Question

6. Why are some extraneous variables dealt with by randomization?

Suggested answers ➡ p. 508

Issues with experiments

▶ **Piliavin et al. (1969)** See pages 18–23

Before we move on, there are two more issues which are worth a brief mention. First, a common misconception about experimentation is that it is something that is done in a laboratory. This is not necessarily the case. An experiment is about logic, not location. Work can be carried out in laboratories that has nothing to do with experimentation, and equally, experiments can be conducted in the strangest of places. The study by Piliavin et al. (1969) on the urban underground railway has all the features of a true experiment. The experimenters were able to manipulate the variables they wanted to investigate, and in doing so created four experimental conditions in which the behaviour of participants could be observed. The advantage of this kind of field experiment is its direct relationship with the real world, something that is said to add to its **ecological validity** (see Section 3, below). An advantage of experimentation in the laboratory, on the other hand, is that it is easier to achieve a more comprehensive level of control over other variables that have the potential to affect the behaviour of the participants.

Second, you will see that in many of the experiments in this text the researchers investigate the effects of more than one independent variable at a time. Such experiments are known as **factorial designs**, and are used to increase the explanatory power of the study. Again, Piliavin et al. (1969) is a good example. Two independent variables (or factors) were manipulated: the ethnic background of the person in need of help (Black or White) and the extent to which the person in need of help was responsible for their situation (drunk or visually impaired). It was hypothesized that the speed and amount of help offered would depend on these two factors.

▶ Piliavin et al. (1969)   See pages 18–23

Quasi-experiments

In a true experiment the experimenter directly manipulates the independent variable, usually by means of **random assignment** of participants to different experimental conditions. This is not always possible, so we sometimes take advantage of pre-existing differences between people in order to create what look like experimental conditions. This is known as a quasi-experimental (or '**natural-experimental**') design. It is something that has the logical structure of an experiment, except that the manipulation of the independent variable has not been directly in the control of the experimenter. For example, the study by Raine et al. (1997) looks at the differences in the brains of people found guilty of murder compared with ordinary people. The researchers were unable, for **ethical** reasons, to randomly assign volunteer participants to the two conditions ('If you draw an even number out of the hat, then you need to go off and commit a few murders – those of you who draw an odd number can go and make the tea – we'll meet back here later and have a look at your brains'). So instead they capitalized on people's pre-existing status as either 'murderer' or 'not murderer'. In a similar way, participants can be divided on the basis of their ethnic background (Hraba and Grant, 1970), or early life experience (Hodges and Tizard, 1989b), or age (Samuel and Bryant, 1984) or sex (Alexander and Hines, 2002).

A particularly neat example of this technique can be seen in the study by Koff (1983), where she studied young women on two occasions. Between the two occasions some of the young women reached **menarche** (started their periods). Koff had three groups of young women to compare: those who had reached menarche before the study began, those who had not reached menarche by the end of the study and those who changed status during the study. She had not allocated her participants to their respective groups (a true experiment) but she was still able to use these naturally occurring changes to divide the young women into three groups (quasi-experiment) and make some inferences about the effects of menarche on identity.

It is held that causal relationships are harder to establish by means of quasi-experimentation than by means of experimentation proper. Note that

▶ Raine et al. (1997)   See pages 152–157

▶ Hraba and Grant (1970) See pages 173–176

▶ Hodges and Tizard (1989b) See pages 250–254

▶ Samuel and Bryant (1984) See pages 277–281

▶ Alexander and Hines (2002)   See pages 129–132

▶ Koff (1983)   See pages 186–189

quasi-experimental comparisons are very common in psychology, and are used in conjunction with all sorts of methods, such as questionnaires, **observational studies**, and even the sorts of studies, like Koff's, which rely on qualitative data.

Observational studies

Participant and non-participant observation

All psychological research arguably starts with observation. Furthermore, our ability to describe and analyse the behaviour and experience of ourselves and others is an essential ingredient of everyday life. Good authors of fiction are able to describe behaviour and experience in ways that give a rich understanding of the people in their books. Psychologists also want to obtain rich understandings, but they commonly prefer to achieve that not through extensive prose but through the systematic recording of behaviour.

▶ **Rosenhan (1973)** See pages 196–199

The study by Rosenhan (1973) describes the observations of eight people who were admitted to a psychiatric hospital after (falsely) complaining of hearing voices. The study gives a flavour of being a patient in a psychiatric facility, and highlights how difficult it is to judge whether a behaviour is sane or insane. This kind or research is commonly referred to as participant observation because the observers took part in the setting they were observing. An example of non-participant observation, whereby observers take a more detached **role**, is provided by Rawlins' (1979) analysis of a colony of rhesus monkeys. In this **ethological** study the researchers observed the mating patterns, the social hierarchies, and the rhythms of daily life of the monkeys. The result was a rich picture of monkey behaviour that allows comparisons to be drawn with other species, including our own.

▶ **Rawlins (1979)** See pages 115–118

There is no clear line between participant and non-participant observation; it is more helpful to view these as the two poles of a participation dimension rather than as two separate categories. There are very few studies in which the observers are completely separate from the people they are observing, and few studies in which they fully participate. In the Rosenhan study, although the observers got themselves admitted to the psychiatric hospital, they were not in the same position as the patients because they believed that they were sane, and they knew that they could be released and return to their regular life when they wanted to. Similarly, it would appear that Rawlins' (1979) work is a non-participant observation since none of the observers joined the monkey groups. However, in this study the researchers were involved in the development of the colony by removing some monkeys, by checking them for their health, and by providing them with food on a regular basis. They were thereby intervening, if not exactly participating, in the social lives of the monkeys.

▶ **Rawlins (1979)** See pages 115–118

Question

7. What sorts of ethical considerations would you expect to have to address in participant and non-participant observational research?

Suggested answers ➜ p. 508

Structured and unstructured observation

The above two observation studies are relatively unstructured in the way they record behaviour. Some psychological studies, though, take a very structured approach to observing behaviour. Bales (1955) developed a very detailed observation framework that codes the behaviour of people in groups. Condon and Sander (1974) used an equally detailed system for recording the second-by-second movements of newborn babies. Observers are usually trained over a considerable period of time before using such frameworks, because they have to be used reliably. In other words, independent observers must be capable of using the same framework to observe the same behaviour, and come up with the same findings (see the section on inter-observer reliability, below). As a rule, structured observational methods are associated with the collection of quantitative data, while unstructured observational methods are associated with the collection of qualitative data.

Question

8. What are the relative advantages and disadvantages of structured and unstructured observational methods?

Suggested answers ➡ p. 509

Self-report methods

Experiments and observational studies typically provide us with a third-party analysis of behaviour, one which is constructed completely from the 'outsider' perspective of the researcher. This is only likely to give us one part of the picture as far as human psychology is concerned, given that a crucial feature of the human condition is our ability to reflect on our own behaviour and experience. So psychology researchers also use methods which set out to explore participants' own perspectives on things. Sometimes these methods genuinely try to take as their starting point the perspective of the participant, as is usually the case in semi-structured interviewing and in collaborative, **humanist** style research (see Weitz, 1989, for example). More frequently, they are about getting participants' responses to researcher-defined items and questions (see McCrae and Costa, 1987, for example). All these approaches we have lumped together under the generic heading 'self-report methods', though note that getting participants' responses to things like questionnaire items is frequently a component of observational and experimental studies (see our discussion of Schachter and Singer, 1962, in relation to levels of measurement, in Section 1 of this chapter).

Questionnaires and surveys

Perhaps the most favoured tool of the social scientist is the questionnaire. It is used to find out what people think, feel and do. Questionnaires are designed to draw out information from people in a manner which will allow the researcher to make generalizations about the topic. This is actually quite a difficult task, and questionnaires can be easily affected by bad design or bias. A **survey** is commonly a very short and highly structured questionnaire that is given to a large group of people.

► **Bales (1955)** See pages 65–68

► **Condon and Sander (1974)** See pages 288–292

► **Weitz (1989)** See pages 406–409

► **McCrae and Costa (1987)** See pages 221–224

► **Schachter and Singer (1962)** See pages 141–145

Response rates to questionnaires vary with the type of sample, and with the population concerned. A sample that is highly motivated and interested in a topic will obviously produce a higher response rate than one which is uninterested. The technique used to administer the questionnaire itself will also produce variation in response rate, with responses to postal questionnaires being lowest, and responses to telephone questionnaires highest. There are also some factors which have been shown to increase response rates, such as using follow-up queries, providing incentives to respondents (such as a prize draw or free ball-point pen) and, most importantly of all, increasing the ease of reply. As a general rule, the harder a questionnaire is to answer, the lower the response rate will be.

Two of the studies in this volume that used questionnaires are those by LaPiere (1934) and Hodges and Tizard (1989b). The study by LaPiere used the questionnaire to investigate attitudes to Chinese people among hotel and restaurant owners in the USA. The Hodges and Tizard study used questionnaires to find out about the behaviour and experience of ex-institutional children.

▶ **LaPiere (1934)** See pages 43–45

▶ **Hodges and Tizard (1989b)** See pages 250–254

Questionnaires have an appeal to social researchers of all kinds, including psychologists, because they allow a researcher to gather a large amount of information in a relatively short space of time. They also have a more serious advantage in that they allow the investigation of 'hidden' behaviour and experience. For example, sexual behaviour is socially invisible (in most cases), and our imagination, dreams and ambitions are also not open to public scrutiny. The skilful use of questionnaires allows investigation of many types of invisible behaviour and experience in large samples of people; although the more intensive investigations of this aspect of human life have tended to involve interviews rather then surveys.

Interviews

Interviews vary in the amount of structure they impose on the situation. Highly structured ones may be little more than spoken questionnaires. At the other end of the spectrum, semi-structured interviews can allow for an open-ended description of experience. The study by Weitz (1989), for example, used detailed interviews lasting from two to five hours to investigate the thoughts and feelings of people with AIDS. These sorts of interviews aim to allow people to describe their behaviour and experience in their own terms. This is in contrast to questionnaires and surveys where participants usually have to use the questioner's terms and concepts to describe their experience. Semi-structured interviews, which yield essentially qualitative data, are clearly more difficult to analyse, and more difficult to draw generalizations from, but they may offer a greater insight into people's personal worlds.

▶ **Weitz (1989)** See pages 406–409

Non-verbal methods

The main way we communicate is through words, and psychologists commonly use words as the medium for their exploration of behaviour and experience. Some things are difficult to express in words, such as our beliefs or our feelings, so it can sometimes help to be a little more inventive in our methods of investigation. In this volume there are two examples of studies that use picture drawing techniques to investigate psychological issues. The study by Koff (1983) asks young women to draw a picture of themselves, and this picture is used to infer something about the sense of identity that the young woman holds. On a very different issue, the study by Bartlett (1932) uses a picture drawing technique to investigate the systematic distortions that occur in memory over time. Methods such as these can be particularly useful when research participants have difficulties with use of the spoken or written word, as for example with young children, or people with severe learning difficulties.

▶ **Koff (1983)** See pages 186–189

▶ **Bartlett (1932)** See pages 311–315

Analysis of pre-existing materials

Meta-analysis

▶ **Smith and Glass (1977)**
See pages 414–417

Meta-analysis allows us to interpret and make sense of the findings of collections of studies that all deal with the same topic. An example of a meta-analysis in this volume is the study by Smith and Glass (1977), who moved into the controversial area of psychotherapy to evaluate how effective various therapies are. They used evidence from 375 studies on the effectiveness of **therapy**, including data from over 50,000 people. This is a particularly useful kind of research, because it is one way of trying to get hold of the bigger picture in relation to a given topic; something that is not always easy when dealing with a disparate set of studies which have accumulated over the years, and which are distributed across a variety of journals. The major challenge with meta-analysis is how to work systematically with different studies which were carried out by different researchers, using different measures, on different samples. Smith and Glass' approach was to calculate a standard **effect size** for each of the studies, to give some indication of how effective each therapy was in comparison with no therapy at all. Interestingly enough, there was little to choose between the therapies, all of which showed some overall positive effect. However, one must evaluate the outcome of such analyses with the notion of publication bias (see Section 3 of this chapter) in mind.

Analysis of text and other media

Not all research is done with live subjects. There are a whole range of psychologically interesting questions that can be answered by close analysis of cultural artefacts such as text, art, music, films, novels, newspaper reports and so forth. These tend to be questions which are broadly of interest to social psychologists. For example, a popular undergraduate research project is the investigation of sex role stereotypes in TV advertising. Such projects are based around structured observations of TV advertisements, looking at the different roles which are assigned to men and women. The idea is that analysis of these sorts of materials might give us some information about prevailing attitudes and behaviour. One example of a study based exclusively on textual materials is Potter and Edwards (1990), who analysed an important political event through the written media of British parliamentary records (*Hansard*) and

▶ **Potter and Edwards (1990)**
See pages 401–405

newspaper articles. Other examples of textual analysis in this book are those which analyse texts that have been generated by research participants.

Just like with observational studies, textual analysis can range from the highly structured approach of content analysis, which involves formal **categorization** and the counting of frequencies of things in texts (particular words, phrases, ideas and so forth), to the relatively unstructured approaches of qualitative data analysis (Weitz, 1989) and discourse analysis (Potter and Edwards, 1990), which tend to deal with bigger units of meaning, and which are not concerned with formal categorization or counting.

Correlational designs and regression

Psychologists sometimes get a mass of data, and want to know whether there are any patterns in it. They employ a variety of statistical procedures to find out. The first mental testers accumulated a lot of data from the scores of people they tested using a whole range of instruments. They wanted to know if the performance on one test was connected with performance on another. Two mental testers, Spearman and Pearson, developed tests of correlation to measure how connected these sets of scores were. A correlation will give you a value for the statistic r of between -1 and +1. This describes the degree to which the variables are related, and the direction of that relationship. The closer the value is to -1 or +1, the more related the variables are. A **regression** analysis is one step on from correlation. There is more information about regression in Bryant et al. (1989) who used the technique to show that the use of nursery rhymes with pre-school children had a positive effect on their reading performance when they were older.

Case studies

Some psychological research does not concern itself with large numbers of participants, as is usually the case with experiments or observational studies. Instead, it focuses on single cases: a technique known as the **case study** method. A single case does not have to mean just one single person. It might be a family, a social group, a company or even a nation. Case studies can be extremely useful, because they can allow the researcher to investigate something in great detail, and do justice to the complexity of the thing that they are trying to study. They have their limitations, though, not the least of which is our **uncertainty** about how unique any given case is. In other words, it is unclear how far it is possible to generalize findings from one case to another.

In this volume we have included a number of examples of case studies including Koluchová (1972), Thigpen and Cleckley (1954), Watson and Rayner (1920), Freud (1909), Sperry (1968), Diamond and Sigmundson (1997) and Ramachandran and Hubbard (2001). The Koluchová study looks at the exceptional case of the twin boys brought up in horrendous conditions, the Sperry study looks at the behaviour of people who have had their brains cut into two for medical reasons, and Ramachandran and Hubbard consider the fascinating phenomenon of **synaesthesia**.

Case studies are among the most engaging parts of psychology, and when

▶ **Weitz (1989)** See pages 406–409

▶ **Potter and Edwards (1990)** See pages 401–405

▶ **Bryant et al. (1989)** See pages 297–300

▶ **Koluchová (1972)** See pages 255–257

▶ **Thigpen and Cleckley (1954)** See pages 200–204

▶ **Watson and Rayner (1920)** See pages 272–276

▶ **Freud (1909)** See pages 267–271

▶ **Sperry (1968)** See pages 135–140

▶ **Diamond and Sigmundson (1997)** See pages 181–185

▶ **Ramachandran and Hubbard (2001)** See pages 367–372

reading this text people often choose to read the case studies first. We can learn a lot from exceptional cases, because they may throw light on how things work in unexceptional cases. For example, we can use the work of Sperry to see what people with hemisphere deconnection can and cannot do, and thereby make inferences about the normal role of the **commissural fibres** which connect the two halves of the brain.

The case study is an example of the idiographic approach to research. The idiographic approach is concerned with building up our knowledge on a case-by-case basis. In this way we learn about a large number of psychological things from a relatively small number of cases. This we contrast with the nomothetic approach, which is to do with studying a small number of things ('variables') spread across a relatively large number of cases. For example, Freud's idiographic work deals with all sorts of psychological phenomena, including memory, emotion, development, relationships, sexuality, language and so forth. The picture he weaves shows the interrelationships among all these things, and how they might work together to make up a whole person. The nomothetic model, on the other hand, focuses on one of these phenomena at a time (for example memory, or in fact a sub-area of memory) and tries to a derive a robust understanding of it by studying how it works in lots of different people. In a sense, the idiographic approach tackles psychology by studying people, whereas the nomothetic approach tackles it by studying variables. It is the latter approach that dominates contemporary psychology.

Psychometric testing

The term **psychometric** means 'measuring the mind', though many psychometricians would be very uncomfortable with a term such as 'mind'. A psychometric test is a task or set of tasks that can be given in a standard format to an individual, and which produces a score for each respondent, or which sorts each respondent into a category. It can involve almost any activity. Most commonly, for reasons of practicality, it involves filling in a questionnaire. Tests are used to measure **cognitive** functions (IQ tests: see Gould, 1982) **personality** (McCrae and Costa, 1987), mood (see Schachter and Singer 1962), stress (see Holmes and Rahe, 1967), and many other qualities. Psychometric tests are extensively used in everyday life and you are likely to come into contact with them from time to time.

▶ **Gould (1982)** See pages 230–235

▶ **McCrae and Costa (1987)** See pages 221–224

▶ **Schachter and Singer (1962)** See pages 141–145

▶ **Holmes and Rahe (1967)** See pages 410–-413

There are a number of important issues with psychometric tests, including their **reliability** and **validity** (see Section 3, below). A further issue concerns their **standardization**. The idea of standardization rests on the principle that abilities, both mental and physical, are distributed throughout a population according to a normal distribution curve. This curve describes a set of scores where a few people obtain extreme high scores, a few people obtain extreme low scores, and most people score around the average. If we assume the scores are normally distributed then we can make judgements about the relative performance of any individual using the statistics of standard deviation and z-scores.

Standardizing a test involves establishing how the scores of this test are distributed among the population, and making sure that the test, if administered to enough people, will produce a normal distribution. This involves testing large numbers of people and establishing what the normal scores for those types of people might be. From this, it is possible to develop population norms, which identify what would be an average score, what would be above average, and what would be below average. So standardization, at least in theory, allows us to judge how typical, or uncommon, someone's result is.

Psychometric tests are extensively used in research, because they offer the possibility of providing an agreed-upon measure of the things in which we are interested, and which therefore provide data which can be compared directly across different studies. We can use, for example, the 'Big Five' personality measures of McCrae and Costa (1987) to see how people with different **personality types** cope with different events, or perform different tasks. They are also relatively easy to administer, and provide straightforward quantitative data. It is important to remember, however, that they are using a limited number of responses to represent very complex cognitive, emotional and social qualities. And because they have all the trappings of science, and the weight of professional psychologists behind them, they may sometimes lead people into having a little too much faith in them (see Forer, 1949).

▶ **McCrae and Costa (1987)**
See pages 221–224

▶ **Forer (1949)** See pages 430–433

Longitudinal and cross-sectional studies

Psychologists commonly carry out their studies over a very limited time, often in a few minutes. In this way cross-sectional studies take a snapshot of behaviour. As we know from our holiday snaps, pictures never tell us the whole story. Photographs give us a dramatic frozen image whereas a video gives us the richness (and tedium) of ongoing action. Sometimes psychologists want to go beyond the snapshot and look at the ways in which behaviour and experience change over the course of time. For this they use **longitudinal studies**.

Longitudinal studies are, of course, particularly important in developmental psychology, because they focus on development itself. They can help us to understand the long-term consequences of certain types of behaviour and experience. For example, Koluchová's (1972) research gives us an insight into the developmental consequences of emotional deprivation in early childhood. Hodges and Tizard's (1989b) paper is part of a longitudinal project which charts the development of children who had been in institutional care until at least 2 years of age. Longitudinal designs are clearly expensive and time consuming, and one of the major difficulties, as shown in Hodges and Tizard, is participant attrition (that is, you inevitably end up a study with less participants than you started with). But such designs are the only way of addressing a number of key questions in psychology. How else can we know about things like the implications of early childhood experience for later development, other than by following children through periods of their lives? It is also true to say that people have an enduring fascination with stories which unfold over the course of time, as shown by the popularity of biographies and autobiographies, which are of course a kind of longitudinal case study.

▶ **Koluchová (1972)** See pages 255–257

▶ **Hodges and Tizard (1989b)** See pages 250–254

It is all very well collecting data, but how confident can we be of our findings? All measurement has some error in it, as any of you who have measured your bathroom floor before buying the tiles for it will know (by the way, if anyone wants about 30 cork tiles please get in touch). Psychologists try to make their measures as accurate and error free as possible and they consider a number of issues when they do this.

Reliability

One of the most important quality control checks in psychological research is to check the reliability of our measurements. Another word for reliability is consistency. If we are using a measurement technique we need to know whether it will give us consistent results. If we measure someone on a scale on a Wednesday afternoon, we hope to get the same results as if we had done the measurement on a Friday morning. It would remarkable if we got exactly the same result because all forms of measurement have an element of error in them, but we hope this error is relatively small. Psychologists use a number of techniques for assessing reliability including:

(a) *Test–retest reliability*: In this case we administer the measure to a group of people on two occasions and compare the two sets of scores using a correlation coefficient. A high correlation coefficient (one that is, by convention, above $r = 0.8$) indicates that the scores of the participants have remained relatively stable across the two administrations. Note the efforts that Bem (1974) put into establishing the **test–retest** reliability of the androgyny scale.

▶ **Bem (1974)** See pages 225–229

(b) *Internal reliability*: In this case we compare people's scores on two parts of the same scale to see how similar the scores are. This is also known as **split-half** reliability. If the whole scale is measuring the same thing (as it should be) then a person's score on one half should be similar to their score on the other half. If people score differently on two parts of a scale that are meant to be measuring the same thing, then we should be concerned about the quality of that scale (this would be rather like measuring an object with one end of a tape measure, and then getting a different reading when we used the other end of the tape measure to measure the same object). The statistical note at the end of the Bem (1974) summary develops this notion further.

▶ **Bem (1974)** See pages 225–229

(c) *Inter-observer reliability*: (also known as inter-tester/**inter-coder**/inter-rater reliability): This is simply a check that different users of the scale can get similar results from it. Two suitably qualified people should be able to administer the same scale to the same group of people, and get consistent scores from them. Equally, when using an observational schedule or checklist, observers who are working independently one from another should be able to get the same pattern of recorded observations as each other. The three authors of the Brazelton et al. (1976) study shared the

▶ **Brazelton et al. (1976)** See pages 258–264

► **Condon and Sander (1974)**
See pages 288–292

observations of their infant participants, and were able to demonstrate an inter-observer reliability level of at least .85 between each pair of observers: in other words, the independent observers agreed on at least 17 of every 20 observations made with their observation schedule. If independent observers cannot agree on a high percentage of the observations that they make, then the usefulness of the observations is called into question: see the Condon and Sander (1974) study of **neonate** behaviour, and the criticism which McDowall (1978a) made of the research.

Question

9. What are some of the difficulties in trying to apply the concept of reliability to the study of people?

Suggested answers ➜ p. 510

Replication

Associated with the notion of reliability is the concept of replication. It is a tenet of science that findings of empirical work should not be trusted unless they can be replicated. This means that an independent researcher should be able to copy the procedure of a given research study, and obtain the same pattern of results. This is why it is so important to be explicit about the details of how a research study was conducted. Sometimes replications are exact: in other words, they are conducted in exactly the same way, with the same type of participant sample. More usually they are designed slightly differently to ► **Samuel and Bryant (1984)**
See pages 277–281 tackle some vulnerable part of the original procedure. For example, Samuel and Bryant's (1984) study of conservation is part replication (of a classic Piagetian procedure) and part critique.

Validity

Reliability is only half the story. The second major aspect of quality control in relation to measurement is validity. A measurement technique is said to be valid if it measures what it claims to measure. Note that this is related to, but not the same as, the notion of reliability. For a measure to be valid it must first of all be reliable (it cannot be valid if it gives inconsistent measurements of the same thing), but it must also have other properties.

For a start it is possible to have a perfectly consistent (reliable) measure, which is perfectly consistently rubbish. For example, we might develop a measure of intelligence which involves measuring the circumference of a person's head, and then converting the resulting measurement into an IQ score. This would give high levels of test–retest reliability and inter-observer reliability (though the split-half technique gets a little messy). But it would not, ► **Schachter and Singer (1962)** See pages 141–145

► **Gould (1982)** See pages 230–235

► **McCrae and Costa (1987)** See pages 221–224 validly, measure intelligence. So the critical reader of psychological research must consider whether a happiness scale measures happiness (Schachter and Singer, 1962), and whether an IQ test measures intelligence (Gould, 1982), and whether 'five factor' personality scales measure personality (McCrae and Costa, 1987). This is exactly the same issue that was raised under the heading 'Operational definition' in the first section of this chapter.

There are a number of ways in which researchers try to examine the validity of their operational definitions and measures, including:

(a) *Face validity*: This simply means asking the question of whether, 'on the face of it', this measure looks valid. Do the items on the scale appear to measure what they purport to measure? Needless to say, this is a rather weak form of validity, only one step up from the legendary 'it seemed like a good idea at the time, sir' justification, which you can probably recall from your school days.

(b) *Concurrent validity*: A test has concurrent validity (a.k.a. congruent/convergent validity) if it can be shown to produce scores which are comparable to another separately developed test which purports to measure the same thing. So, if you were developing a measure of **extraversion**, you would probably try to demonstrate its concurrent validity with **Eysenck's Personality Inventory** (EPI), which also gives a measure of extraversion. To do this you would administer your test and the EPI to the same group of participants, and then correlate the two sets of scores. The higher the correlation (that is, the stronger the similarity between the scores of the two measures), the greater the concurrent validity. Of course this does not ultimately show that your test measures what it says it measures, because we cannot be certain that the one you compare it against actually measures what it says it measures. However, it is probably a step in the right direction.

(c) *Construct validity*: A test is said to have construct validity if it provides a good reflection of its own theoretical underpinning. For example, if your theory is that the psychological entity you are measuring is a biologically fixed **trait**, then you would usually expect to see a normal distribution of scores if you measure enough people on it. If you are able to give empirical evidence of this normal distribution, you can claim a level of construct validity. Similarly Bem's (1974) measure of androgyny is based on the theory that femininity and masculinity are separate characteristics which are independent from each other (orthogonal). She was able to show that there was, indeed, no systematic relationship between her participants' scores on these dimensions when measured with her sex-role inventory, and so was able to claim a good relationship between the measure and its underpinning theory: in other words, construct validity.

(d) *Criterion validity*: Also known as **predictive validity**. Perhaps the strongest test of validity is to compare the measure with some real-world benchmark. For example, if you have a scale that purports to measure leadership ability, you could administer it to all the employees in a company, without knowing who is who, and then try to predict who are the managers. If you can identify the managers better than you could just by guessing, then you can claim a level of criterion (predictive) validity for your measure. Raine et al. (1997) could potentially establish the predictive validity of their brain scanning techniques by scanning the brains of a large **random sample** of people and predicting which ones would

▶ **Bem (1974)** See pages 225–229

▶ **Raine et al. (1997)** See pages 152–157

be most likely to become murderers. If, in the fullness of time, their predictions were shown to be better than guesswork, then this would give a level of criterion validity to their measures. Consider for a moment, however, the ethical and moral implications of this idea.

(e) *Ecological validity*: Whether a study has high or low ecological validity is a critically evaluative judgement about the extent to which the research procedures involved relate to everyday human life. A study which examines the behaviour or experience of people in their natural settings is said to have high ecological validity (that is, high direct relevance to real life: see Rosenhan, 1973, for example). Studies which take place under highly controlled, artificial conditions (in a laboratory, for example) are said to be low in ecological validity (see Sperling, 1960).

▶ **Rosenhan (1973)** See pages 196–199

▶ **Sperling (1960)** See pages 375–382

Question

10. In terms of the relationship between the concepts of reliability and validity, we can say that reliability is a necessary but not sufficient condition for validity. What is meant by this?

Suggested answers ➔ p. 510

Quality control and qualitative data

The conventional procedures for assessing reliability and validity in research that uses quantitative data are relatively well rehearsed in research methods textbooks. Researchers who deal with qualitative data are under no less of an obligation to demonstrate that their findings are trustworthy, but do not have recourse to the traditional statistical procedures for doing this. They are often less concerned with the pure notion of reliability as described above, preferring instead to rejoice in the richness, diversity and changeability of human behaviour and experience. But validity is something that has to be tackled squarely. The methods that are used vary from one research tradition to another, and the story is too involved to be tackled here. Suffice it to say that the secret of doing good research, whatever tradition you are working in, is to be aware of the range of quality control procedures that are used within that tradition, and to be prepared to face the legitimate question of the sceptic, which is, in essence, 'Why should I believe your findings?'

Sampling

Psychologists use a range of sampling techniques. The type which is often presented as the ideal is a random sample, which is defined as a sample in which any member of the population has a genuinely equal chance of being selected. That sounds easy enough, but really, it is extremely difficult to obtain a truly random sample of any but the most restricted of populations. How would you go about getting a truly random sample of, say, British 15-year-olds? You could not just ask for volunteers, because only certain types of 15-year-olds would be likely to volunteer in the first place, and besides, where would you place the advert? The issue of sampling is important, because we have to know who the findings of any given study are meant to apply to. Really, we are only

► **Sears (1986)** See pages 425–429

meant to generalize findings from the particular sample of participants in a study to the population that they are meant to represent. The fact that many studies use students as participants (see Sears, 1986, and the section below on sampling biases) means that we have to be cautious in our interpretation of the findings of much psychological research.

Because of the difficulties of achieving a truly random sample, many researchers use a quota sampling system instead. Quota sampling involves looking at the population, and classifying it into categories. Then a sample is drawn which consists of some participants from each category, in roughly the same proportions as they occur in the population. One special kind of quota sampling is known as stratified sampling. In this the population is divided into strata (layers) like social class or family income, then a set number of people from each layer is chosen for the study.

Sometimes, too, the population is not easy to contact. Identifying illegal drug users, for instance, is not something which can be done by looking down a list. In this case, a researcher might use a technique known as snowball sampling: asking existing contacts to tell their friends about the study and ask them to get in touch with the researcher. In practice, though, what many researchers (and almost all psychology students) use is an opportunity sample, which essentially consists of taking their sample from people that they have the opportunity of studying (this is usually your parents, friends and family pets).

Incidentally, in this chapter we refer to the people from whom data are collected in the course of psychological research as 'participants', rather than 'subjects'. This is in line with the British Psychological Society's view that the label 'subject' can sometimes be a little demeaning. However, in the rest of the book we use the terms that the authors of the original papers themselves used. By and large this means that in the rest of the book we talk about research subjects.

Sources of error

Artefact: demand characteristics, experimenter effects and reactivity

Artefact in psychological research refers to findings that are artificial: findings that only tell us how participants behave in psychological research studies (when what we really want to know about is how they behave in their everyday lives). Particularly common sources of artefact are **demand characteristics**, **experimenter effects** and **reactivity**. The summary of Orne (1962) outlines the key issues to do with demand characteristics. His basic argument is that participants of psychological research studies will behave in accordance with their own efforts to understand the situation in which they find themselves, and their own interpretation of the 'demands' of that situation. Since the participants' understandings of the demands of the setting are likely to be at odds with the researcher's understanding, this may lead to misinterpretations of the participants' behaviour. In other words, the researcher may interpret the participants' behaviour as meaning one thing, when in fact it means

► **Orne (1962)** See pages 420–424

► **Samuel and Bryant (1984)**
See pages 277–281

► **Labov (1969)** See pages
301–304

► **Labov (1969)** See pages
301–304

► **Gould (1982)** See pages
230–235

► **Forer (1949)** See pages
430–433

► **Milgram (1963)** See pages
12–17

► **Asch (1955)** See pages
7–11

► **Haney et al. (1973)** See
pages 69–73

► **Nobles (1976)** See pages
177–180

► **Kitto (1989)** See pages
190–193

► **Watson and Rayner (1920)**
See pages 272–276

► **Rosenthal and Fode (1963)**
See pages 434–438

something completely different. For example, the study by Samuel and Bryant (1984) shows how the results that Piaget achieved in his tests were partly due to the way the children were interpreting the setting and the demands of the tasks, rather than a reflection of their true intellectual competence (which was Piaget's interpretation).

The broader point about the effect of the social context on the behaviour of participants is also tackled head on by Labov (1969). What we must remember is that psychological research involves participants entering into a social relationship with researchers. The behaviour of the participants is partly a function of that social relationship (as is the researchers'), just as everyone's behaviour is always partly a function of the social relationships that they are in. Sometimes psychology has ignored this, believing that we can somehow distil a pure form of behaviour from participants, so long as sufficient control is exerted over the research setting. There are obviously many dimensions of social relationships that can be considered in terms of the effect they have on behaviour, but one that is worth paying particularly close attention to in this context is the dimension of power. This is not the context to develop a full-blown thesis about the impact that the inevitable imbalance of power in the researcher–participant relationship has had on the literature of psychology. But we suggest you read all psychological research with questions about power in the back of your mind. In terms of this book, all of the following summaries have something to say about this issue, either explicitly or implicitly: Labov (1969), Gould (1982), Forer (1949), Milgram (1963), Asch (1955), Haney et al. (1973), Nobles (1976), Kitto (1989), Watson and Rayner (1920).

Experimenter effects are examined, and indeed demonstrated empirically, by Rosenthal and Fode (1963). Their finding that even the behaviour of rats can be influenced by the expectations of experimenters has far-reaching implications for psychological research, both in terms of design principles, and in terms of the interpretation of research findings. There is in psychological research, as in everyday life, a powerful tendency to find what you are looking for: the self-fulfilling prophecy. Incidentally, this is something that can affect all types of psychological research, not just experiments, so the label 'experimenter' effect is somewhat misleading.

Question

11. How can researchers deal with the issue
of experimenter effects?

Suggested answers ➜ p. 510

Reactivity refers to the idea that the act of observing or measuring something can affect the thing that is being observed or measured. In other words, in studying something, we change it. This is particularly true in research on human behaviour. We all know that we behave differently when we are being observed. This is a somewhat intractable problem for psychologists, because we usually want to know what people are like in their everyday lives, not just

▶ **Thigpen and Cleckley (1954)** See pages 200–204

what they are like when they believe that some aspect of their behaviour is being measured. For example, one of the difficulties in interpreting Thigpen and Cleckley's (1954) case study on **multiple personality** comes from the question of whether the behaviour of the subject (Eve White) was being influenced by being studied. At one extreme, it is possible that she was pretending: in other words, it is possible that her behaviour was completely to do with being observed. More realistically, it may be that some aspects of her behaviour and experience were enhanced or hidden away. These more subtle reactivity effects may be just as troublesome for psychological research as outright pretence, and considerably harder to detect.

Question

12. How can researchers deal with the issue of reactivity?

Suggested answers ➤ p. 510

Sources of bias

Publication bias

There is a potential distortion in the psychological research literature, which comes from the way research studies are chosen for publication. Researchers and editors prefer positive results. They prefer studies which 'reach significance'. This means that studies which show no differences between experimental conditions are less likely to become part of the literature. This is a serious problem, because studies which show no effects can be just as important as studies that do show an effect. Students, too, experience this with practical work, and often express disappointment when a practical exercise 'fails to work'. This disappointment is misplaced, because a statistically non-significant finding can be just as important as a statistically significant one in providing scientific information. Indeed, there is an extremely important distinction to be made between 'statistical significance', on the one hand, and real 'significance' (as in 'this finding is meaningful'), on the other. For example, let's say that a researcher has designed an attitude survey to measure differences in attitudes to smoking between smokers and non-smokers. The findings are very likely to be statistically significant, with smokers having a much more positive attitude to smoking than non-smokers. But they will never be significant in any other sense of the word, because they are so mind-numbingly obvious. Statistical significance is not everything in this life!

Ethnocentric sampling bias

Ethnocentrism refers to the tendency to see things from the point of view of your group, to overvalue the people and things that are part of your group, and to devalue the people and things that are not part of your group. In psychology, ethnocentrism means that psychologists give undue prominence to people like themselves. An analysis of introductory textbooks by Smith and Bond (1993) found that they mainly cited work by researchers from the USA. In a fairly standard text by Baron and Byrne (1991), 94 per cent of the 1700 studies mentioned were in fact from the USA. In a British text (Hewstone et al., 1988) about 66 per cent of the studies were from the USA, 32 per cent were European and under 2 per cent came from elsewhere in the world. These books are by no means exceptional, and the studies they selected reflect the places where psychological research is conducted.

So, psychological research is mainly conducted by the people of the USA and Europe, and they mainly study themselves. This means that the psychology in our textbooks is the psychology of the USA and Europe, but it is by no means clear whether the behaviour these peoples display is the same behaviour we can expect in other cultures and other lifestyles. This means we have two possible sources of bias: (a) researchers mainly study their own culture, and (b) researchers find it difficult to interpret the behaviour and experience of people from other cultures.

In this volume, we have tried to reflect how psychology has developed and what its main concerns are. This means we are really reflecting the concerns of western psychology, and looking at people from a very narrow perspective. It is important to acknowledge that we have *a* perspective rather than *the* perspective on people and their behaviour. We include a few studies in this volume that deal with issues of diversity, for example Brazelton et al. (1976), Stigler and Stevenson (1992), Nobles (1976), and Hraba and Grant (1970).

Other sampling biases

One of the studies summarized in this text highlights an underlying sampling problem in psychology. Sears (1986) found that over half of all published research was conducted on psychology students, and of the remainder a further quarter was conducted on other students. Those of you who have seen films such as *Animal House* will realize that being a student is not necessarily representative of the rest of your life. There is a further problem here in that the students who volunteer for studies might not be representative of the student populations, further biasing the sample. For example Carnahan and McFarland (2007) found that students who volunteered for a 'a psychological study of prison life', in response to newspaper advertisements had different personality characteristics to students who responded to an advertisement that was exactly the same except for the absence of the phrase 'prison life'. It seems that volunteers select the type of study they want to take part in.

Another source of bias is gender. Many studies are constructed from a male point of view; also, many studies have used male participants rather than female for reasons that are not at all clear. As you look through the studies in this text you might be surprised how many use just men or boys but make generalizations to people as a whole. For example, the studies by Milgram (1963), Asch (1955), Festinger and Carlsmith (1959), Sherif (1956) and Tajfel (1970) all use just male participants. It is hard to find studies that just use female participants unless like Koff (1983) they are looking at an identifiably female issue.

▶ **Brazelton et al. (1976)** See pages 258–264

▶ **Nobles (1976)** See pages 177–180

▶ **Hraba and Grant (1970)** See pages 173–176

▶ **Sears (1986)** See pages 425–429

▶ **Milgram (1963)** See pages 12–17

▶ **Asch (1955)** See pages 7–11

▶ **Festinger and Carlsmith (1959)** See pages 31–36

▶ **Sherif (1956)** See pages 60–64

▶ **Tajfel (1970)** See pages 46–50

▶ **Koff (1983)** See pages 186–189

Ethics

The ethical guidelines of the British Psychological Society (2006) state that in the conduct of their research, psychologists should always consider the following:

- *Consent*: Have the subjects of the study made an informed decision to take part? Have the parents of child subjects given informed consent to the research procedures? Have payments been used to induce risk-taking behaviour?
- *Deception*: Have the subjects been deceived? Was there any other way to carry out the study other than by using deception? Have the procedures been approved by other psychologists?
- *Debriefing*: Have the subjects been effectively debriefed? Has any stress caused by the procedures been removed?
- *Withdrawal from the investigation*: Are the subjects clear that they can withdraw from the study at any time without penalty or scorn?
- *Confidentiality*: Participants in psychological research have the right to expect that information they provide will be treated confidentially.
- *Protection of participants*: Investigators must protect participants from physical and mental harm during the investigation.
- *Observational research*: Unless the participants give their consent to being observed, observational research must only take place where those observed could normally be expected to be observed by strangers.
- *Giving advice*: Psychological advice must only be given if the psychologist is qualified in the area that the advice is requested in.
- *Colleagues*: Psychologists should take action if they believe that any of the above principles are being violated by a colleague.

▶ **Seligman and Maier (1967)**
See pages 99–102

▶ **Olds and Milner (1954)**
See pages 95–98

Note that there are also guidelines which relate to the use of animals in psychological research. There are a number of studies in this book in which the treatment of animals appears to have been less than humane (see Seligman and Maier, 1967, and Olds and Milner, 1954).

Ethics are socially agreed rules about what we think is acceptable and unacceptable behaviour. As such, they change over time. It is interesting to note that some studies that may appear very unethical to the readers of this text (for example, Milgram, 1963) were endorsed as ethical at the time of the study by psychologists and the wider scientific community. It is also interesting to note what is not included in the ethical principles. For example, the guidelines are about how you do research rather than what you study. It can be argued that work that degrades people, for example, should not be acceptable, such as work that is racially or sexually oppressive.

▶ **Milgram (1963)**   See pages 12–17

These ethical principles offer a framework for the conduct of research. They do not, however, address issues of the consequences of the research. Will the results of the investigation have a harmful or beneficial effect on our society, and the individuals within it? George Miller made a plea for the development of psychology in his presidential address to the American Psychological

Association in 1969. He entitled his address 'Psychology as a means of promoting human welfare', and his paper is summarized in Chapter 18. In it, he suggests that we should 'give psychology away'. Rather than trying to develop a psychological technology to control people, Miller believes that psychology should present 'a new and different conception of what is humanly possible and humanly desirable'. He goes on to say that we should think 'not in terms of coercion by a powerful elite, but in terms of the **diagnosis** of problems and the development of programs that can enrich the lives of every citizen'. This seems to us to be a rather good way of thinking about psychology. Perhaps you could reflect, whilst reading the summaries of the studies in this book, on whether you feel that the discipline lives up to Miller's vision.

SUGGESTED ANSWERS

Part I Social Psychology

1. Social Influence

Eight out of ten owners said their cats preferred it

▶**conformity** The process of going along with other people – that is, acting in the same way that they do.

1. The features that enhanced conformity include the use of strangers rather than friends, the choice of students as research participants, and the meaningless nature of the task.

2. I conform to a range of social norms: for example, behaving politely with people even when I don't like them, trying to appear reasonably presentable in public, eating with a knife and fork, and so forth.

3. Positive aspects of conformity include the reduction in social conflict, and the greater predictability of people and situations. Negative aspects include not thinking for yourself and a loss of individuality.

▶**ecological validity** A way of assessing how valid a measure or test is (that is, whether it really measures what it is supposed to measure) which is concerned with whether the measure or test is really like its counterpart in the real, everyday world. In other words, whether it is truly realistic or not.

4. The central criticism is that the study is not true to life (not ecologically valid). In particular the subjects had no emotional involvement in the task and the study was carried out in an unusual social context.

Be a good boy and do as you are told

▶**demand characteristics** Those aspects of a psychological study (or other artificial situation) which exert an implicit pressure on people to act in ways that are expected of them.

1. There are numerous possible explanations including the location of the study, the demand characteristics of the study, the social obligations put on the subjects, the unusual nature of the task they were performing, and the tendency for people to accept the commands of people in authority.

2. Advantages for the individual include less aggravation and more acceptance. Advantages for society include greater social order.

3. Disadvantages for the individual include less control of your own behaviour, and doing things you don't want to do. Disadvantages for society include a lack of dissent and therefore no pressure for social change.

▶ **behaviour (also spelt 'behavior'** Anything a person (or animal) does that can be observed and measured by a third party. Behaviour can be thought of as the public side of human life, in contrast to 'experience' (thoughts and feelings) which can be thought of as the private side.

4. You name them! The major ones include the deception about the true purpose of the study and the distress caused to the subjects. Also it was not made clear to the subjects that they could withdraw at any time, and they were offered financial incentives to behave in ways they might not approve of.

5. Milgram did not intend to cause distress and was surprised about the results. Also, the authors of this text believe that the Milgram study has made an important contribution to our understanding of human behaviour.

Going underground

1. The major problems are to do with control, ethics and authenticity.

2. The advantages are that you can observe people engaging in natural behaviour rather than responding to experimental requests in a restricted environment, and as a result the outcome is much less predictable and also more relevant to general discussions about human behaviour and experience.

3. We are not told the answer to this, so we can only speculate. A reasonable speculation is that the researchers were too embarrassed, scared or ashamed to conduct this themselves. The students wanted to earn some money and maybe had fewer social inhibitions.

4. The major problems come from the possible distress caused to the travellers, the deception of the travellers, and the possibility that the incident could have precipitated a nasty confrontation.

5. Just think of what people do in cities and how they live, and that should provide a whole range of questions that psychologists might be interested in. For example, one of the major leisure pastimes at the moment is shopping, and people spend hours looking at products that they might never buy.

Walk on by

1. The chief advantage is that they give a very accurate record of statements that people make publicly when they are usually trying to give their best account of an event. There is a lot of detail in them and the questioning from the barristers means that much of the possible ambiguity is clarified. The main disadvantage is that the witnesses are not speaking entirely freely because they are trying to present themselves in a reasonable light while probably being very nervous in an intimidating courtroom.

2. Family links are seen as very important in this society and we are incline to let people sort out their family business by themselves. People who try to intervene are commonly not thanked for their efforts. This is despite the fact that families are the most dangerous place to be – you are more likely to be abused, assaulted or bullied by a family member than by anyone else.

3. Some markers for a 'domestic' are, (i) the people do not appear to be

strangers, (ii) the person being targeted does not run away, (iii) the argument contains some personal content.

4. This is one for you to decide. In this text we have made the decision not to name the young woman from the New York assault but to refer to the Liverpool assault using the name of the victim. Feel free to disagree.

2. Social Judgements

Changing our minds

▶ **cognitive dissonance** The tension produced by cognitive imbalance – holding beliefs which directly contradict one another or contradict behaviour. The reduction of cognitive dissonance has been shown to be a factor in some forms of attitude change.

1. The answer to Question 2 has, on the face of it, nothing to do with the cognitive dissonance hypothesis. If, nevertheless, the same pattern of differences across the conditions was observed in the responses to this question, it would indicate that there was something else going on in the experiment instead of (or as well as) the expected cognitive dissonance effects. It would indicate that there was some more general difference across the conditions than the one intended by the experimenters.

2. This is so that the research can be replicated (exactly) to check the reliability of the reported results. The more unusual the research methods, the more detailed the account needs to be, because the reader is likely to be unfamiliar with the procedures that were used.

▶ **hypothesis** Experiments are designed to test one or more hypotheses. An hypothesis is a prediction of what will happen in an experiment. It is worded in such a way that the results of a well-designed experiment will clearly show whether the prediction is right or wrong.

Is she really going out with him?

1. In this study the task of the coder was to decide whether each reason given was situational or dispositional. Coding is a somewhat subjective process, and consequently can be unreliable. An independent coder allows the investigator to assess the level of 'inter-rater' (or 'inter-coder 'or 'inter-observer') reliability in their coding scheme. The greater the agreement between the different coders, the higher the inter-rater reliability of the coding scheme. The independent coder was not allowed to know the experimental hypothesis, so that there could be no systematic biasing of their coding in favour of the experimental hypothesis. This is to guard against the self-fulfilling prophecy of experimenter effects (see Rosenthal and Fode, 1963, Chapter 18 of this volume).

▶ **experiment** A form of research in which variables are manipulated in order to discover cause and effect.

▶ **reliability** The reliability of a psychological measuring device (such as a test or a scale) is the extent to which it gives consistent measurements. The greater the consistency of measurement, the greater the tool's reliability.

2. Nisbett et al. would predict that most of your explanations should be situational. Try to think of dispositional alternatives for each situational explanation that you have written.

I'm not prejudiced, but ...

1. For example, I have an attitude that we should protect the environment, but I never manage to take my newspapers or bottles to the recycling centres. Also I have an attitude that exercise is a good thing but I rarely exercise.

▶ **situational attribution** A reason for an act or behaviour which implies that it occurred as a result of the situation or circumstances that the person was in at the time.

2. There are numerous possible reasons including the opportunity to act on your attitude, habit, the behaviour might be too sensible or boring, it might take too much effort, or some of your attitudes might conflict with each other.

▶dispositional attribution
When the cause of a particular behaviour is thought to have resulted from the person's own personality or characteristics, rather than from the demands of circumstances.

▶inter-coder reliability A phrase which describes the extent to which two independent observers (coders/raters) agree on the observations that they have made. Also known as inter-observer reliability and inter-rater reliability.

▶experimenter effects Unwanted influences in a psychological study which are produced, consciously or unconsciously, by the person carrying out the study.

▶attitudes A relatively stable opinion about a person, object, or activity, containing a cognitive element (perceptions and beliefs) and an emotional element (positive or negative feelings).

3. The methodological problems include the Chinese people not knowing about the study, their American accents, the general lack of controls and the 50 per cent return rate on the questionnaires (though in truth this is quite a good return for postal questionnaires).

The minimal group studies

1. It is worth noting that teenage boys are perhaps the most competitive groups of people in our society. They are at an age when people take part in more games, and are part of a competitive education system. The choice of subjects clearly enhanced the results, and it would be interesting see what results would be found in a study on people, say, in a retirement home.

2. A harder question than it appears. You would probably say that you are a member of your family group, friendship group, your class or work group, but it is difficult to go much beyond that. However, it is very easy to know who is on your side, rather than not on your side, even though it is not always easy to identify the group to which you both belong.

Shock and awe

1. **(a)** *Availability*: people tend to judge the likelihood of an event happening by how easily they can think of an example.

   (b) *Hindsight*: people tend to integrate new observations into their memories and not realize that they have done so. This gives them the 'gift of hindsight'.

   (c) *Emotion*: if people feel scared or uncomfortable they can use this to 'colour' the event they are judging.

   (d) *Experience*: the things that happen to you or people close to you will affect judgements of risk.

2. For a start people have different levels of knowledge about the events, they might respond to the questionnaire with other people rather than alone, and they might say what they think they ought to say (to support the war effort for example) rather than what they really think.

3. Social Interaction

The robber's cave

▶ethnocentrism Being unable to conceptualize or imagine ideas, social beliefs, or the world from any viewpoint other than that of one's own particular culture or social group. The belief that one's own ethnic group, nation, religion, scout troop or football team is superior to all others.

1. Competition leads to conflict which leads to ethnocentrism.

2. (a) Observations of behaviour, (b) friendship choices, (c) the target practice judgements.

3. The distress to the children, the lack of informed consent, the inability to leave the study, etc.

4. Competing groups include sports teams, sports supporters, work groups, gangs, political parties and so forth.

5. The advantages include the spontaneous behaviour of the children, and the ability to generalize the results to other social situations involving children.

The mother (and father) of all groups

1. The sequence of acts can be examined. One important criticism of social psychology has been that it tends to present a rather static view of human interaction, when in fact one of the key features of human interaction is the way that it unfolds over the course of time. Obtaining data on the sequence of events in his studies allowed Bales to examine the typical stages of decision-making within groups. The methods he used in this respect are known as 'sequential analysis' (see Bakeman and Gottman, 1986).

2. First there is the complexity of the thing that is being observed. There may be too much going on within the group to be recorded by one observer, though it should be noted that a skilled observer will be able to 'see' and record a lot more than a novice. The second reason might be that any kind of research in psychology requires the researcher to address the issue of reliability. In this context, one thing Bales would need to establish is the level of inter-observer reliability that was achieved. In order to make this estimate he must have at least two observers, working independently, doing exactly the same observational task. The records of these two independent observers can then be compared. The more similar their records are, the higher the level of inter-observer reliability in the study. If necessary, the comparison can be made statistically by means of a correlation coefficient. If there is not sufficient agreement across the two observers the observation schedule may need altering, or the observers may need more training.

3. The behaviour of the group members might have been altered by their awareness of being observed. It is important that we, as readers of the study, know this so that we can properly evaluate the study. There are no easy ways around this problem of reactivity in psychological research; often the only thing we can do is be honest and open about our research procedures, and allow for these inevitable difficulties in our interpretations of our findings.

4. We leave this for you to answer. But bear in mind that the function of a group will have an important impact on its structure and behaviour.

The prison simulation

1. The prisoners became immersed in their roles so that the prison became very real to them; they became passive and dependent and they behaved in degrading ways towards each other.

2. One argument says that the study was ethically sound because it went through various ethics committees. But the luxury of hindsight suggests that there were a number of ethical violations, including the deception about the arrest, the distress to the prisoners, and their failure to realize that they could leave the study whenever they wanted.

3. Your choice, but we would suggest the 'Milgram Defense', which is that the results illuminate our understanding of human behaviour and the distress caused in the study is justified by this outcome.

▶ **correlation coefficient**
A number between -1 and +1 which expresses how strong a correlation is. If this number is close to 0, there is no real connection between the two; if it is close to +1 there is a positive correlation – in other words, if one variable is large the other will also tend to be large; and if it is close to -1, there is a negative correlation – in other words, if one variable is large, the other will tend to be small.

▶ **reactivity** A term used to describe the way in which the behaviour of research subjects can be affected by some aspect of the research procedure. Most commonly it is used to describe the way in which the behaviour of someone who is being observed is affected by the knowledge that they are being observed.

▶ **role** A social part that one plays in society.

4. Students were chosen because of their availability and their willingness to carry out something like this for a relatively small amount of money. However, as the study by Sears (see Chapter 18 of this volume) suggests, students may behave in very different ways from other adults.

5. Conventions for dealing with what is, and what is not acceptable, in published media are intriguing. The 'bleep' in TV programmes, when quite often the word can be lip-read; the asterisk in printed media documents when it is quite clear what the original word is; the red stars that obscure key parts of the body in red-top newspapers. One can learn a lot about a culture from studying the threshold between 'acceptable' and 'unacceptable'.

Tyranny

1. Permeability, legitimacy and cognitive alternatives.

2. One answer would say 'none' because there were so many ethical safeguards in place. You might argue that the television version of the study involved considerable editing and hence could have misrepresented the position of some of the participants.

3. His stated objection is that his prison simulation was so unethical that it should not be replicated. This study, however, was not a replication and had ethical safeguards. The only other reason for the objection would be to preserve his SPE brand. This is about marketing and not science.

4. One main problem is that television has a certain format for documentaries and it will force any story into this repetitive format. It goes like this:

    (a) The problem is set up and the viewer is introduced to the key players.

    (b) To start with everything goes fine with a few potential hurdles in the future.

    (c) Everything goes pear-shaped and the key players are filmed in tears, often by themselves on their own 'diary-cam'.

    (d) There is a resolution and some form of happy ending is presented. The viewer switches off feeling that they have been informed; they have felt some tension and anxiety but they have been reassured by the end of the programme. This format is almost impossible to challenge so any psychology programme is likely to be distorted to fit this. The big problem is that not all stories have happy endings, and not all problems are resolved.

    Other major problems are to do with the motivation of the programme makers and the participants. Balanced science does not always make an entertaining programme. Do the programme makers want to tell the full, complex, yet slightly boring story? Or do they want to attract a large audience?

Small world and getting smaller

1. The case for will concentrate on the evidence that some of the chains were able to be completed in six hops or less. The case against will concentrate

on the large number of chains (the majority) that were not completed. In fact, one of the targets was never found.

2. The more visible you are the more likely you are to be found in a small world study. By visible we mean the number of social contacts you have. So, anyone in a large workplace is more visible that someone who works at home. Also someone at school is more visible than an elderly housebound person.

Part II Biological and Comparative Psychology

4. Learning

The flight of the killer pigeons

▶ **shaping** The 'moulding' of behaviour by the method of successive approximations, or by the naturally occurring contingencies of reinforcement delivered by the environment.

1. By means of shaping using positive reinforcement.

2. Pigeons have better visual acuity, better vigilance skills and less fatigue at the task. They are smaller, cheaper to use and have no emotional involvement with the task.

3. You're on your own here, but if you believe that a war can be justified, and if you believed that the use of animals might prevent further loss of life, then you could argue for using animals in this way. However, this argument depends on the importance you put on human life over animal life.

▶ **positive reinforcement** In operant conditioning, strengthening learned behaviour by direct reward when it occurs.

4. Coastguard spotters looking for life rafts in a vast expanse of ocean, or maybe as quality control inspectors looking for the dodgy potato on a conveyor belt.

What's your pleasure?

1. You're on your own with this one.

2. You might think that they bring about some or all of the following: euphoria, relief, warmth, happiness, exhilaration, sense of personal fulfilment, bodily relaxation. In the context of this study, it is perhaps more interesting to think of the physical responses. Do you think it is plausible that all the different experiences of pleasure bring about the same bodily changes and come from the same pleasure centres? There is a connection here to the paper by Schachter and Singer (1962) in Chapter 6.

3. Without pleasure centres we would probably not bother to carry out the behaviours that keep us and our species alive. If a baby did not get pleasure from sucking and eating it would probably not bother to eat enough. And think what a nightmare going out with someone is. If we weren't driven by some major pleasure centres we would probably sit at home playing computer games all day rather than putting ourselves through the agonies of dating.

4. The answer is clearly, yes. The excessive pursuit of rewards can lead to behaviours that are damaging either socially or physically. These behaviours include excessive gambling, excessive drinking, excessive drug use, excessive exercise.

5. You need to make your own mind up about this kind of issue.

Learning to be helpless

▶ **yoked control** A yoked control experiences the same physical events as a member of the experimental condition, but whereas the experimental condition is able to influence these events, the yoked control is not.

1. Because the dogs in the yoked control condition had to receive, on average, the same overall duration of electric shocks in Phase 1 as those in the escape condition. If they had not, then any differences across the two groups in Phase 2 could have been attributed to the different amounts of electric shock administered in Phase 1. The dogs in the escape condition could terminate the shocks, so their performance had to be measured first in order to know how long each shock should last on each trial for the dogs in the yoked control condition.

2. When considering a question like this, try not to think in 'slogans'. Questions relating to the ethics and morality of psychological research are never quite as straightforward as they are sometimes made to appear.

3. A good example might be unemployment. The unemployed often experience multiple rejections in their search for work, and they can come to believe that the problem is something to do with them rather than their situation. In this circumstance they may well learn to be helpless and believe there is nothing they can do to get work.

Bashing Bobo

▶ **aggression** A term used in several ways, but generally to describe negative or hostile behaviour or feelings towards others.

▶ **self-report** A number of popular research methods are based on self-report: for example, questionnaires, interviews, attitude scales and diary methods. These are methods which rely on research subjects' accounts of their own experiences and behaviour.

1. In the pre-test of the children, aggression was measured using four 5-point rating scales: (a) physical aggression, (b) verbal aggression, (c) aggression towards inanimate objects, and (d) aggressive inhibition. During the experiment, a checklist was used with eight categories (see procedure section) making 240 observations at five-second intervals over a period of 20 minutes.

2. There are a number of methods of measuring aggression including physiological measures of arousal, and self-report measures.

3. Aggressiveness/non-aggressiveness of the model; sex of the child; sex of the model.

4. There is no mention of informed consent from parents, and given the high level of distress in the infants it is unlikely that it was obtained. Also the children were not able to leave when they liked, and were coerced into continuing with the study even when they wanted to leave.

Monkey talk

1. For example, a dog bark is an immediate response to something happening now. Dogs cannot bark to tell a story about something that happened last Tuesday. Another example is bird song which can convey such things as threat, or the position of the bird or the mating ambitions of the bird, but it is very stereotyped and limited in the range of things it can communicate.

2. People can communicate, for example, by touch, by tone of voice, by the way they walk, and by a whole range of non-verbal communication techniques.

3. The strengths are the level of detail and the depth of understanding they achieve with Washoe. The disadvantages include their tendency to over-

generalize from their one-animal case study, and from their emotional involvement with Washoe, which maybe clouds their judgement about the chimp's true abilities.

4. The difficulties include the speed of movement of the chimp's hands, the tendency of chimps to move around their environment at high speed, and the difficulty in recognizing when a sign has been made.

5. There may be all sorts of linguistic and non-linguistic cues which signal when someone is about to hand over the conversation to their communication partner. Obvious ones are to do with intonation, pauses and gaze.

6. Keep it clean.

5. Comparative Psychology

The colony of monkeys

1. Advantages include the richness of the data, and the opportunity to see development over time. The disadvantages include the time taken to collect data and the difficulty in collecting it. An ambitious longitudinal study is not always a good career move for an academic because of the potentially long gap between beginning the work and publishing it!

2. For example, which matriline it belonged to, whom it groomed and who groomed it.

3. Inbreeding (mating with family members) tends to bring out any genetic weaknesses that exist within a family. The survival and the development of a species depends on matings between unrelated individuals, so that the genetic weakness is thinned out and genetic variations develop. In the case of these monkeys, the males only mate outside the troop they were born in.

4. The differences include the closeness to water, the relative lack of trees in the early days of the colony, the protection from predators and the provision of food.

5. Your answers here will be speculative and no better than ours, but we suspect that the presence of predators (for example) would change the structure of the troops and make them more cohesive and less competitive.

A fishy tale

1. Ethological observation, and experiment.

2. The sign stimuli include colour of the fish, shape of the fish, orientation of the fish and movement.

3. For example, the sight of blood creates a sense of shock, a smile creates a feeling of warmth, and a baby's cry produces a feeling of concern.

4. The major difference is that all sticklebacks behave like this and all male sticklebacks will make these nests in the breeding season. It is not possible for a group of sticklebacks to get together one year and say 'I'm fed up of this territorial nonsense, let's form an anarcho-syndicalist collective for this mating season.'

5. For example, going out for a walk when you are angry so that you avoid an argument; doing the washing up instead of getting on with your essay.

Rat City: the behavioural sink

1. The controls include the type of animal, the structure of the environment, the steady supply of food and water and the removal of the young after the population's size reached 80 animals.

2. The main problems are the artificial environment and the artificial species (laboratory rats are specially bred and would be unlikely to survive in a natural environment).

3. The rats were hypersexual, and part of their activity was homosexual, but the description of them as homosexual suggested that they exclusively chose to mate with other males. The choice of the term probably tells us more about Calhoun's attitudes than it does about the rats.

4. The study could be used to illustrate the human problems associated with the inner city, such as increased levels of child abuse and child neglect, the high incidence of personal crime such as assault, the concentration of mental ill health and social pathology, also the high incidence of male aggression, and the general breakdown of social order. But bear in mind that connections between the rats and city life are very slight, if they exist at all.

5. For example, 'harem', 'homosexual', and 'somnambulist'.

Just monkeying around

1. You could employ a factorial design in which half of the 'masculine' toys were coloured 'reddish-pink', and half were coloured yellow, blue or green (these have been shown to be less preferred by female monkeys), while half of the 'feminine' toys were coloured 'reddish-pink' and half were coloured yellow, blue or green. If, on average the females preferred the 'feminine' toys, then this would not be related to their colour. If on the other hand the females preferred the 'reddish-pink' toys, then this would indicate that colour is playing a role.

2. Knowledge of the experimental hypothesis might influence the observations that were made (see Rosenthal and Fode, Chapter 18, on experimenter effects), particularly in a setting where observational judgments could not always be agreed upon by independent observers (Kappa = .84, indicating that there was *some* level of disagreement between observers on the observations that were recorded). For example, there may have been some inaccuracy in the recording of the sex of the different monkeys (the identity of different monkeys may have been confused from time to time on the video tape if the observers did not know the monkeys well) and it is possible that some judgments as to the sex of the monkey were actually influenced by the monkeys' behaviours – including which toys they contacted more! It would be interesting to ask the authors of the paper about this issue, in order to discover more about how they dealt with it.

3. How easy do you find it to accept evolutionary explanations of your

behaviour? How much of your behaviour do think has been 'shaped' by socialization processes?

6. Bio-Psychology

A brain of two halves

1. The short presentation of the stimulus ensures that there is no time for automatic eye movements which would 'spread' the information across both sides of the visual field and therefore across both sides of the brain.

2. Because any visual information will be transmitted to both sides of the brain, unless it can be restricted to one side of the field of vision (which can only be achieved when very brief visual displays are used: see Answer 1, above).

3. Examining the behavioural consequences of certain kinds of brain damage may help researchers to make inferences about the normal functions of the damaged areas of the brain, by documenting what things the brain-damaged subject is unable to do. Since researchers cannot deliberately cause brain damage in people, in order to perform quasi-experiments they must rely on the opportunistic study of people who have experienced damage 'naturally'. Note that researchers have felt able to cause intentional brain damage in animals in order to carry out such experiments.

▶ **inference** Going beyond what we know to make an intelligent guess.

▶ **natural experiments (also quasi experiments)** Studies in which comparisons are made between different conditions that come about through natural political, social, economic or demographic circumstances, rather than through direct manipulation of a variable by an experimenter.

▶ **independent-measures design** When a study involves comparing the scores from two or more separate groups of people.

▶ **independent variable** The conditions which an experimenter sets up, to cause an effect in an experiment. These vary systematically, so that the experimenter can draw conclusions about changes in outcomes.

How do you feel?

1. Independent-measures design. The independent variables are the information about the adrenaline injection given to the subjects, and the situation they are put in (euphoria situation or anger situation).

2. Observation of behaviour, and self-report by questionnaire with a single value of emotion arrived at by taking the anger rating from the happiness rating.

3. For example, a checklist of bodily experiences such as knee tremble, clammy skin, etc., or by using other self-report scales about experiences such as warmth, or anxiety or excitement, etc.

4. The major violation of ethical standards is the deception of the subjects.

5. It is likely the results would be very different. See the study by Sears in Chapter 18 for some suggestions of what these differences might have been.

To sleep, perchance to dream

1. The results tell us something about the relationship of REM with the experience of dreaming, but there are big variations between individuals.

2. The sample is restricted and so generalization is suspect. The sample is all adult, mainly male, rather small, and culture specific. On the last point it might be interesting to look at the relationship between REM and dreaming in a culture where dreams are talked about more openly.

3. The controls include the location, using the usual sleeping time of the subjects and asking them to avoid stimulants and depressants.

4. The interesting point here is the tension between the need for control and the need to create a situation as near to everyday life as possible. Rather than suggesting further controls, it might be useful to look at how to create a more ecologically valid design.

5. Consider factors such as familiarity, privacy and a change in night-time habits.

Murderers!

1. Arguably not a lot. People commit murder for a range of reasons. If we take it to its most basic, we have a body and a person standing over it. The person standing over it might have been cleaning a gun before it accidentally went off, or they might have come home to find their partner in bed with the whole cast of *Friends*, or they might be a soldier in action. The decision to call the act murder is a legal or social decision, and the decision to end the life of another person can be triggered by a wide range of events and emotions. It is unlikely that we can isolate the cause of murder and then attach it to a particular brain function.

2. The main benefit is that we no longer have to wait until someone dies before we examine their brain. The scan allows for a wide range of non-intrusive studies. The disadvantage is that the evidence is hard to interpret and the pretty pictures may confuse as much as illuminate mental processes.

3. There are a wide range of circumstances in which one kills another, for example for vengeance, or out of anger, or for money, or in response to an order from a superior. The point of this question is to consider whether it is likely to be connected to a simple brain structure. When the motivation for the act can be so different it would seem unlikely that it is always connected to one area in the brain. It is reasonable to suggest that aggression might be biologically influenced, but are all murders an act of aggression?

4. This is a tricky one. The above answers should tell you that the authors do not think this will be possible, but if it were, it would raise all manner of ethical dilemmas about the rights of the potential murderer and the rights of the society they lived in.

Mastermind

1. a) Are the apparent changes in brain structure observed by Maguire et al. relatively permanent, or would the brain structure revert to 'normal' without day-on-day activity?

   b) Is the re-distributed brain structure really a function of navigational expertise, or simply a function of any kind of expertise?

   c) Do people who are poor navigators have lower volumes of grey matter in the posterior hippocampus?

   d) Does the posterior hippocampus support different kinds of expertise in spatial memory, or is it primarily to do with navigating around a complex large-scale environment?

2. It is one thing to argue that an increased volume of grey matter in the posterior hippocampus predisposes people to go into professions such as taxi-driving. This interpretation of the researchers' findings (the one that they reject) is at least plausible because one might expect people to go into professions that suit their particular cognitive strengths. But it is somewhat harder to argue that different levels of grey matter volume predispose people to become taxi drivers *for a specific number of years* (such that the larger the volume of grey matter in your hippocampus the more likely you are to become a long-standing taxi driver) – which is what one would have to argue to account for the findings of the correlational analysis in this way. Note, however, that this interpretation is not ruled out.

3. The property of plasticity in the adult brain means that brain damage (through injury or disease) does not in principle need to be regarded as irreversible.

Where does it hurt?

1. (a) Pain without injury, (b) injury without pain, (c) pain out of proportion to injury, and (d) the phenomenon of phantom limb pain.

▶ **phantom limb** The name given to the phenomenon experienced by amputees of still feeling the limb as present and alive even though it has been surgically removed.

2. Measurement of pain usually involves self-report methods. For example, the McGill Pain Questionnaire (see Melzack and Wall, 1985), which has items on the location, strength and type of pain experienced by the respondent.

3. Pain is usually an adaptive response. In other words it is useful to us to know when our body is being damaged so that we can take steps to allow healing, or to prevent further damage. If you could not feel pain you would not know to drop the plate which is burning hot and which would, as a result, seriously damage your hand. Athletes who use painkillers to perform whilst they are injured risk making things much worse because they are overriding their body's natural defence mechanisms.

Part III Diversity

7. Identity

Black dolls and White dolls

1. By examining the answers that were given to their Question No. 8.

2. A difficult question, though Patrick Hylton, from Lincoln University, works on this to produce accounts of Black identity using interviews and Q-sorts.

3. One possible answer could be the lack of appropriate Black role models at that time. If you look at any old films made between 1930 and 1945 then you will see very few Black actors, and when they do appear they are usually playing the parts of villains or servants. Although there are

now many more models for Black children, it is remarkable how blinkered our everyday culture can be. For example, on a day-to-day level, in the 1970s it was still very difficult in this country to buy Black dolls, or birthday cards with Black children featured in the pictures. It could be argued, additionally, that the scarcity of Black dolls in the 1930s would have made the dolls that Clark and Clark used appear 'unusual' and hence less appealing to all the children.

Black identity

1. The answer depends on your knowledge of psychology, but the obvious areas to consider are any dealing with social relationships, such as attachment, or attraction, or conformity, or non-verbal communication, or aggression or emotional expression. One of the classic areas is language development. See the summary of Labov's paper in Chapter 12 for his account of some of the real consequences of cultural insensitivity.

2. This is actually a very difficult exercise unless you have some first-hand experience of a non-European culture. We suggest asking someone with that experience to consider this question with you.

3. Examples of cooperation can be found in family life (sometimes, though not at washing-up time), also in team games or any activity that requires a group of people. The most obvious examples of individual competition come from education, where we are always being compared against our peers and there is little or no incentive for cooperation.

The boy who was raised as a girl: a psychological tragedy

1. There is a difference between the two boys (brought up as girl/brought up as boy) that can be treated as an independent variable. It has not been manipulated by the experimenter but we can treat it *as if* it has. We can therefore treat the study *as if* it is an experiment – hence we call it a quasi-experiment.

2. We can only presume that (a) they thought it was for the best of the child, and (b) they trusted the experience and authority of John Money. It is a tough moral question to consider in what circumstances we would lie to someone. People are commonly lied to about their health, for example their life expectancy. Sometimes this is done to protect the ill person and sometimes (more often?) to protect the person telling the lie.

3. We would argue that anyone has a right to own their personal story. The laws of copyright are different, however, as are the conventions of science. David Reimer's story was 'owned' for years by the scientist who published accounts on his development without him knowing. Likewise Christine Sizemore's ('Eve' – see Thigpen and Cleckley in Chapter 8) story was owned and exploited by her therapist to the point of him blocking her telling the story herself.

Mirror, mirror on the wall ...

1. The most obvious reasons are that the subject of psychology, and the

▶ **attachment** The tendency of the young of many species to stay close to an adult, usually the mother.

general scientific community, have tended to be male dominated. Also, it is difficult to carry out empirical studies on experience, hence the use of projective tests in this study.

▶ **projective tests**
Psychometric tests which involve providing the person with ambiguous stimuli, and seeing what meanings they read into them. The idea is that this will illustrate the concerns of the unconscious mind.

2. The aim of a projective technique is to provide someone with a relatively bland stimulus and let them make of it what they want. The theory is that a person's response is likely to show some characteristics of their thoughts and feelings that they would otherwise find difficult to articulate. The major advantage is the information that can be obtained about thoughts and feelings, and the high level of personal disclosure that can occur. The main problem is getting people to agree on what this information means.

Girls just want to have fun

1. If reference A, for example, had always referred to the candidate as a woman, and the candidate described by that reference had been picked most often for the high-status job, a sceptic could have argued that the description of the candidate in reference A was simply better than in the other references, and that the choice actually had nothing to do with the terms 'woman' and 'girl'. Although all four references were very carefully matched (so that the description in one should not be better than any of the others), the technique of changing which references used the term 'girl' and which used the term 'woman' for each subject gives an extra level of experimental control.

2. Some examples: man, mankind, chairman.

3. One familiar male justification for using 'pet' names and labels to address and refer to women (such as 'love', 'dear', 'the girls' and so forth) is that they are endearing, friendly, positive terms. This may be the case (it certainly is not always the case). But Kitto's work suggests that even if the terms are meant well, they still may be contributing to sexual inequality.

8. Abnormality

You don't have to be mad to work here ...

1. Just the self-report of hearing a voice say 'empty' or 'thud'.

2. The similarities include that they have reported feeling unwell, and they have been hospitalized. The differences include the knowledge of the pseudopatients that they are really faking it, and that some people on the outside know this.

3. For example, you might think that being too unhappy to go to work is an abnormal behaviour, or always wearing a bow tie even when you are spending the day at home is unusual. If you make a list of behaviours such as these that you regard as unusual or abnormal, then you could look for some common properties in your list so that you can define what it is that you think abnormal behaviour is made up of.

4. One major criticism is the deception of the hospital staff. Another major criticism asks us to imagine what would happen if we went to a casualty

department and complained of stomach ache. How would we be treated? Perhaps Rosenhan was being particularly hard on psychiatric hospitals, especially when it is important for them to play safe in their diagnosis of abnormality because there is always an outcry when a patient is let out of psychiatric care and gets into trouble.

The Three Faces of Eve

1. Eve White was withdrawn and inhibited, whereas Eve Black was confident, relaxed, erotic and mischievous.

2. Schizophrenia is a psychotic condition in which people have disturbances of emotion, perception and reality testing. Although schizophrenia is commonly thought to involve a split personality, this is not the case at all. The most striking signs of schizophrenia are the hallucinations (often auditory) that people experience, and the failure to distinguish perceptions that originate in the environment (stimulation from outside the person), from perceptions that start inside the person.

3. The moment that Eve Black appears can be seen in a different way to that described by the therapist. He describes how he noticed Eve's legs for the first time, and notices that she appears erotic to him. He describes this as a change in her personality, but it also signals a change in his perception of her.

4. We have to ask whether this study is unique to the relationship between Eve and her therapists or whether we can generalize it to other cases.

▶ **perception** The process by which the brain organizes and interprets sensory information.

▶ **personality** A distinctive and relatively stable pattern of behaviours, thoughts, motives and emotions that characterize an individual.

Paranoid humanoid

1. If subjects are paid to participate, it calls into question the extent to which they are able to give full and proper consent. Money might tempt people into agreeing to take part when participation is not in their best interests, especially if they really need the money. Their judgement in giving informed consent might be compromised. This parallels the major debate within medical ethics about whether live organ donors should be paid. On the one had, payment would increase the availability of donated organs to the benefit of those who need transplants. On the other hand, the less well off you are, the more you might be tempted to donate an organ because of your need for money, and there is something very discomforting about the notion of people needing to sell parts of their body to survive.

2. If the subjects 'choose' to withdraw during this kind of psychotic study they may have made it difficult for the medical staff to give them the proper care and monitoring that they needed. Subjects could end up in difficulties, with no help available, on the basis of a decision that they made while under the influence of consistent doses of amphetamines.

3. The most important reason for this was to guard against the demand characteristics of the study. Subjects knew that they were to receive dextroamphetamine and that they were likely to experience psychosis. It could be that this knowledge in itself would affect their behaviour,

quite apart from any effect of the real drug. The control week allowed the researchers to assess the behaviour of the subjects when they only *thought* they were taking the drug.

Fear today, gone tomorrow

1. Because although the treatment groups were compared with non-treatment groups, in an effort to rule out the influence of spontaneous remission, the fact that the control groups received no treatment at all means that the 'desensitization/no desensitization' variable was not the only variable that differed across the experimental and control conditions. The most notable confounding variable in this respect was the fact that the experimental groups received a therapy and the control groups received no therapy. So the results may only indicate that therapy (in general) is effective against snake phobia; perhaps any old therapy would have had the same effects as systematic desensitization. It may, for example, just have been the time and interest of another person (which is necessarily given in the course of desensitization) that helped the experimental subjects to overcome their fear, not the desensitization process per se.

2. This allowed the authors to examine (a) the effects of the pre-therapy training itself, and (b) the effects of repeated exposure to the feared object:

    (a) If the subjects in Experimental Group 1 ('E1' in Tables 9.4 and 9.5) had made all their improvement between Tests 1 and 2, rather than between Tests 2 and 3, then this would have indicated that the pre-therapy training was having the therapeutic effect, rather than the desensitization itself. Note that this did not happen. No more subjects in E1 passed Test 2 than passed Test 1.

    (b) If the subjects in E1 had improved significantly more than the subjects in Experimental Group 2 (E2) by the time they undertook Test 3, then the desensitization process itself might not have been responsible for the change. It might have been the fact that subjects in E1 had been forced to see a live snake twice already (they had had 'repeated exposure' to the snake during Tests 1 and 2), whereas the subjects in E2 had only received one such exposure (during Test 2). This interpretation would have been further supported had subjects in control group one improved more than subjects in control group two. Check that you understand why.

It could be you! But it probably won't be

1. A laboratory is relatively sterile environment that probably calms people down. By contrast an amusement arcade provides a massive amount sensory stimulation in terms of sounds, sights and smells. It winds up the machine player and puts them into a different physiological and psychological state. In the laboratory you might expect the player to use the machine with less energy and excitement, to use it more slowly and to give up sooner.

► **control group** A group which is used for comparison with an experimental group.

► **confounding variable** A variable which causes a change in the dependent variable, but which is not the independent variable of the study.

► **phobia** An anxiety disorder characterized by persistent fear out of proportion to the danger, a compelling desire to escape the situation, and a recognition that the fear is excessive.

► **systematic desensitization** A classical conditioning technique for reducing fear and anxiety by replacing it with a calm response.

2. All psychological methods have their problems because we are trying to find out what people are feeling and why they are behaving in the way they do. In the end we can only make inferences about these questions because we can't take direct measures. In this study we are making the assumption that the different reports given by the regular and non-regular players during think-aloud trials reflect the way they are thinking and not just the way they talk about things.

9. Individual Differences

The big five

▶**face validity** Whether a test or measure looks on the surface as though it probably measures what it is supposed to.

1. The dimensions that we use to 'sort' other people into groups (and we do do this, one way or another) depend very much on what is important to us, and on our life experiences. For example, if spirituality is an important part of your experience, you will most likely make implicit judgments about others based on an assessment of their spirituality. If you have been let down in the past in important ways by others, then a dimension based on trustworthiness might be very important to you. Or maybe you assess people in terms of a more relative dimension, such as 'like me/not like me'. Do the personality dimensions that we use directly describe other people? Or do they, more subtly, describe us?

▶**concurrent validity** A method for assessing whether a psychometric test is valid (that is, really measures what it is supposed to) by comparing it with some other measure which purports to measure the same thing – also known as convergent or congruent validity).

2. Face validity, concurrent (convergent) validity, construct validity and criterion (predictive) validity. See Section 3, Chapter 19.

Measuring masculinity and femininity

▶**construct validity** A method for assessing whether a psychometric test is valid (that is, really measures what it is supposed to) by seeing how it matches up with theoretical ideas about what it is supposed to be measuring.

1. Remember that the 'subjects' in this study were actually used in the development of the BSRI. Tests and scales (and inventories) can only legitimately be used on members of populations from which they have been developed. This may mean that the BSRI is only able to tell us about gender identity in students, unless it can be shown that students are representative of some wider population(s).

▶**criterion validity** A method for assessing whether a psychometric test is valid (that is, really measures what it is supposed to) by comparing it with some other measure. If the other measure is assessed at roughly the same time as the original one, then the type of criterion validity being applied is concurrent validity; if it is taken much later, it is predictive validity.

2. Because notions of femininity and masculinity differ from culture to culture, and change over the course of time. This means that even if Bem had developed a valid measure of these constructs there is no guarantee that it will generalize across time and place. You should have noticed that Questions 1 and 2 touch upon very similar themes.

3. A reliable test is one that gives stable and consistent scores. A valid test is one that measures what it purports to measure. Make sure that you understand this distinction and that you can use these important terms appropriately.

▶**gender** The inner sense of being either male or female.

4. Test–retest reliability; internal consistency; inter-observer reliability; split-half reliability; parallel-forms reliability. Try and find out what these different labels mean. Most of them are covered in Section 3 of Chapter 19.

Mis-measuring intelligence

► **reliability** The reliability of a psychological measuring device (such as a test or a scale) is the extent to which it gives consistent measurements. The greater the consistency of measurement, the greater the tool's reliability.

► **validity** The question of whether a psychometric test or psychological measure is really measuring what it is supposed to.

► **test–retest method** A system for judging how reliable a psychometric test or measure is, which involves administering the same test to the same people on two different occasions, and comparing the results.

► **scientific racism** The use of bogus scientific arguments to enhance the power of one group of people over another.

► **intelligence** An inferred characteristic of an individual, usually defined as the ability to profit from experience, acquire knowledge, think abstractly, or adapt to changes in the environment.

1. The first question refers to US Presidents. Washington was the first and Adams was one of the others, and his place in the order of Presidents is the answer to this question. So if you do not know your US history you cannot score on this question. Crisco is a consumer product and if you are very poor then you might not have come across it. Christy Mathewson was a baseball player and you have to know about sports to get this. Picture 15 in the Beta Test, for example, refers to ten-pin bowling, and Picture 18 is a gramophone.

2. Scientific racism refers to the attempt to justify the political power of some groups (usually nation states) by seeking to show the superiority of this group over others. Science was also used to justify male power over women and early studies produced 'evidence' about the smaller size of female brains and hence their 'diminished' intellectual power.

3. Tricky question, but you might think that some of the following are examples of intelligent behaviour: scoring high on a maths test, solving a crossword puzzle, playing a defence-splitting pass in football, being able to empathize with someone. On the other hand you might regard the following as examples of unintelligent behaviour: burning the toast again, forgetting to take your wallet when you go out, buying a timeshare apartment after receiving a 'hard sell'. The general point to be drawn from this exercise is that the notion of intelligence is applied to such a wide range of behaviours that it is very hard to believe that it is just one quality.

A brave new world

1. It is taken to mean the exploration of the genetic influence on behaviour. Of course it is interesting to note that there is not a companion discipline called 'behavioural environment'. This suggests that certain answers are being sought rather than others, and those answers emphasize the role of genetics.

2. The obvious answer to this would be that we could remove aggression from the world, so people could stop being afraid of each other and nations would stop going to war with each other. There is a flip side to this, however, and it can be argued that aggression is not the issue, it is how we control it. Imagine a football match without any aggression (sadly, the authors have seen a few of these). It might be that aggression is the source of ambition and determination and courage. Do we want to remove these qualities from people? It is also worth noting that genetic influence is very complex and the interactions between the different individual components are not known. If you alter one component it is not clear what the various knock-ons will be.

10. Attachment

Can you hear me, mother?

1. In monkeys, social isolation from birth will create severe psychological and social disturbance.

2. First, the isolation experienced by the monkeys does not happen to children, even in extreme cases (see the summary of Koluchová in this chapter). Second, patterns of human social behaviour are very different from those of the monkey.

3. Harlow observed that the monkeys sat in their cages and stared fixedly into space, engaged in repetitive and stereotyped movements, and developed self-injurious behaviour. All of these sorts of behaviours and habits can be observed in some disturbed children and adults.

4. Neither term is effectively defined by Harlow. The models were not 'mothers' and they provided very little 'mothering' and so the use of these terms confuses what is happening to the monkeys, and encourages us to make connections to human behaviour that may not exist.

> ▶ **self-injurious behaviour**
> Behaviour which causes either physical or mental harm to the self. In extreme cases, self-injurious behaviour can become life threatening.

Family life

1. We can never know this, but it may be that the families who refused access to their children at age 16 (this was one of the causes of the subjects dropping out of the study) were more likely to be having child-rearing problems than those who agreed to take part once again. This would have the effect of making the findings rosier than they might otherwise have been.

2. No. One plausible competing explanation (and there are many more) is that the families which took in an extra child (whether by adoption or by having a child restored) at a relatively late stage in that child's development might have been affected in some unusual way by that event, and that whatever this effect was it may have somehow fed back into the child's subsequent upbringing. In other words there may have been things going on in these families after the child had been (re-)placed which could equally well have accounted for the authors' observations, and which had nothing to do with the child's early institutional experience. Plausible competing explanations for findings are a characteristic of quasi-experiments.

Emotional deprivation

1. One obvious one may relate to the optimism of the paper. We all need others to think we are doing a good job, and there is no reason to suspect that Koluchová is exempt from this very human need. Is it not possible, then, that some aspects of this case might have been presented in a way that shows the author in a good light? Or maybe this particular case was selected for presentation to a wider audience because things seemed to work out comparatively well (whereas less successful interventions have

gone unreported)? No offence is intended to the author in this respect. We simply want you to think critically about all aspects of psychological research.

2. The first part of your answer to this question should be a statement that only very tentative conclusions can be drawn from one case study! The paper does suggest that it may be possible to compensate quite effectively in later life for early developmental problems. By the age of 7 the twins had spent over five years in highly deprived conditions, yet by the age of 11 they were operating at a mental age roughly equal to their chronological age (intellectually, at least). In a small way this challenges the notion that there is a 'critical period' in early childhood during which time our abilities and personality are 'fixed'.

3. By adhering to established ethical guidelines which emphasize the rights of people who participate in psychological research.

The behaviour of newborn children in two different cultures

1. Firstly, the Zambian women had had at least three children prior to the ones that were observed in this study, whereas all the US babies were firstborn. This may have a whole variety of effects, including increased ease of feeding for the Zambian women, higher levels of child-rearing confidence in the Zambian women, and an entirely different family structure for the newborn to experience. Secondly, the US women were identified as middle-class, whereas the Zambian women lived in a 'semirural urbanized slum area' (p. 99). So it appears that there were systematic socio-economic class differences between the groups as well. Both the birth-order and class differences constitute confounding variables in this study, because they may in themselves account for the observed differences in behaviour across the groups of infants.

2. The most significant source of bias in these data is likely to be a kind of experimenter effect (see Rosenthal and Fode, 1963, in Chapter 18 of this volume). The fact is that the people who did the observations were the researchers themselves, and so they were fully aware of the research question, and fully aware of any expectations they might have had collectively about their observations. The inter-observer reliability checks go some way to addressing this, but do not really provide a watertight defence against the researchers' expectations affecting their own observations. The reason for this is that a high level of inter-observer reliability only tells us that the observers agree on their observations. But what if they are all expecting the same changes to occur in one of the groups? They may all, inadvertently, bias their observations in the same way, thus maintaining a high level of inter-observer reliability, whilst systematically biasing the findings of the study.

3. The most effective way of controlling against experimenter effects is to get someone who does not know the research question (or hypothesis) to collect the data. If this is done properly the researchers' expectations about what they are likely to find cannot influence what they actually do

find. The problem with this study is that the sorts of observations that Brazelton et al. made are rather specialized and require a relatively high level of clinical experience if they are to be done properly. It is often difficult to find people who are sufficiently well experienced in these sorts of procedures who do not also know what the research is about.

11. The Classic Approaches

I want a girl, just like the girl, that married dear old Dad

1. This is an important theme in Freud's work. He believed that we have unconscious wishes and fears which we repress, but which still affect our thoughts, feelings and behaviour. One outlet for these wishes is through dreams, another is through slips of the tongue (Freudian slips – when we say what we really mean but did not intend to say).

2. What data, you might ask? There are no quantitative data, only his reflections and interpretations of the interviews, so we have no way of checking his analyses. Having said this, there is a growing acceptance of qualitative data, like Freud's, in psychology today.

3. Difficult to say because of the great variation in parental attitudes within any society. However, Hans' father feels the need to explain why he didn't give Hans a 'good thrashing', and within today's attitudes that seems a little strange. Also, Hans' father seems to be concerned that Hans shouldn't play with his widdler. We can but hope that this particular parental hang-up is dying out.

4. Not a jot.

▶ **quantitative data** Data which focus on numbers and frequencies rather than on meaning or experience.

▶ **qualitative data** Data which describe meaning and experience rather than providing numerical values for behaviour such as frequency counts.

The tale of Little Albert

1. To examine whether the fear response generalized to other situations. That is, was Albert afraid of the rat itself, or was he afraid of the rat-in-that-particular-room? The reported response in the new room did appear to be less pronounced than previous responses, leading to the experimenters 'refreshing' the conditioning once again. This indicates to the reader that perhaps there was an element of situational specificity in the original conditioning, although the authors do not comment on this.

2. Systematic desensitization (see Lang and Lazovik, 1963, in Chapter 8 of this volume).

3. Perhaps the single most important method for studying this kind of phenomenon is the clinical case study. Case studies can provide detailed analyses of conditions which have occurred 'naturally' (in other words conditions that have not been created by experimental interventions). The case study is a stock method of abnormal psychology, and usually has the key advantage of being part of a therapeutic intervention. In other words, the point of the case study is not only to find out about the condition in question, but also to provide a sound basis for treatment. A number of case studies have been summarized in this book (for example, Freud, 1909; Koluchová, 1972; Thigpen and Cleckley, 1954).

Piaget's cognitive approach

1. The ability to appreciate that changing the appearance of something does not affect its critical attributes (such as mass, volume or number).

2. The basic problem is to do with communication: do the children understand the question or the task they are given in the way that the adult intends? Can they communicate their thoughts effectively? Also, does their limited attention span affect their performance on the task?

3. For example: (a) buying a ticket on the National Lottery and expecting to win; (b) having an extra drink on a Friday night and thinking that you won't regret it in the morning.

Vygotsky's social constructivist approach

1. A Piagetian theorist might hold that the contingent teacher is organizing the learning environment in such as way as to facilitate the child's own learning, rather than causing something fundamental to change in the child's ongoing development.

2. The researchers might have randomly allocated the children to each group, which would allow them to assume that prior ability on the task was equally matched across the four conditions. Alternatively the researchers might have screened the children before the experiment on a different construction task, taken a measure of each child's ability, and then matched the children across the groups such that the average ability of the children in each group was equal. The researchers do not specify which of these methods they used.

12. Communication

The dance of the neonates

1. It suggests that what we are dealing with here is an inborn ability.

2. There are a number of reasons for this. One is that the phenomenon that Condon and Sander were studying (if indeed it exists) is so complex and dynamic that to detect it at full speed as it happens is impossible. Only laborious work checking each individual frame of a film record allows us to see precisely how movements are coordinated with one another, and how these movements might be coordinated with speech.

3. The fact that the babies synchronized their movements with a spoken language (Chinese) which they could not possibly have heard before (even in the womb) suggests that there may be certain features of speech sounds which are common to more than one (maybe to all?) language(s). The fact that the babies did not synchronize with just any rhythmic sounds suggests that there is something special about the rhythms of speech which babies are able to attend to. Since learning language is one of the most important things any baby must do, there would be clear advantages to being able to 'tune in to' speech.

4. One reason is to exclude the possibility that the speakers were inadvertently coordinating their speech with the babies' movements.

5. The adults who were holding the children will have been moving with the rhythms of the speech, and the babies in turn may have been coordinating their movements with the adults' movements.

Listen with mother

1. If the speech sounds on each side of the room had come from different speakers, and the infant had shown a preference for one or other side, then this might have been attributable to a preference for a particular speaker, rather than for a particular style of speaking.

2. The research was trying to establish whether there is something inherently appealing about motherese, irrespective of who is speaking.

3. So that any preference that was shown across the sample of babies as a whole could not be attributable to a general right/left bias in an infant population.

All the king's horses ...

1. How about a variable such as the quality of the relationship between parents and their child? Perhaps two of the side-effects of good relationships between parents and children are (1) that the children read more nursery rhymes when they are younger, and (2) tend to become better readers when they are older. By this account knowledge of nursery rhymes and later reading ability might be conceived of as 'epiphenomena' of 'high quality parent–child relationships'. In other words, it's not the knowledge of nursery rhymes that causes the enhanced reading ability – both these things are, in fact, caused by something else. It may be that Bryant et al. deal effectively with this potential argument, in which case it would be relatively easy to think of another (what if degrees of mild hearing impairment were associated with more restricted knowledge of nursery rhymes, and less well developed reading ability in later years ...?).

The question is an important one because we are dealing here with correlational research, and in this context we must always be cautious of arguing for causal relationships between variables. If the authors of this study are right, that better knowledge of nursery rhymes at a certain age enhances reading ability at a later age, then parents would be able to cause their children to get better at reading by exposing them to more nursery rhymes at the age of 3. But if a sceptical position, such as outlined in the preceding paragraph, were to be right, then simply increasing the amount of nursery rhymes read at 3 years of age would have no effect on later reading (unless the reading of nursery rhymes caused a better relationship to develop between the parent and the child, which in turn caused improved reading ability).

Note that the arguments in this answer are entirely speculative. We are not trying to argue in favour of, or against, the findings of Bryant et al.'s paper. We are simply encouraging readers to ask 'what if' questions about research papers, for it is this appropriate level of informed scepticism that is the engine behind further research studies.

▶ **motherese** A misleading label for the style of speech adults characteristically use when communicating with babies and very young children. It is misleading because all adults tend to use this style of speech, not just mothers. A more satisfactory label might be 'baby talk register'.

▶ **population** In the context of research methods in psychology this refers to the total set of potential observations from which a sample is drawn.

2. Isn't it remarkable that you can still recite or sing these rhymes? They are very simple, very rhythmic, full of similar sounds and very memorable. Furthermore (although this has little to do with reading development) one striking feature of nursery rhymes is how violent some of them are. The issue of where nursery rhymes come from, what they represent, and how and why they are maintained within a culture, is an interesting sociological and psychological question.

Talking proper

1. We could ask how typical Leon is of other Black children in New York. Do the data from one 'case' really permit the far-reaching sociological arguments presented by Labov? And how selective has Labov been in the excerpts of data which he presents in his paper (he presents a little, but not much more, than is cited in this summary)? The short sequences of talk between CR and Leon do seem to fit well with Labov's ideas; but do they fit a little too well? How are we to know as readers whether the reported bits of data are really representative of all the unreported bits of data?

2. In response, Labov might argue that his ideas have emerged out of extensive research experience, only a small bit of which can be documented in any one article. The data that he reports in this paper are used to illustrate his ideas, and the case study of Leon helps to bring the whole subject to life in an engaging and concrete way.

Part V Cognitive Psychology

13. Memory

Remembering pictures

▶ **inference** Going beyond what we know to make an intelligent guess.

▶ **memory** The capacity to retain and retrieve information.

▶ **schema** A mental framework or structure which encompasses memories, ideas, concepts and programmes for action which are pertinent to a particular topic.

▶ **sensory buffer** Short-acting memory store for the sensory record of a stimulus.

1. The main advantages are the ability to make causal inferences, the clear and unambiguous responses of the subjects and the opportunity for replication.

2. The main disadvantages are that laboratory tasks rarely correspond to the everyday use of memory, and they commonly use meaningless material which the subject has no emotional involvement with.

3. In these studies on pictures, Bartlett found that people made the following systematic errors: (a) transformation to conventional representations, (b) elaboration, (c) simplification, (d) naming, and (e) preservation of detached detail. These errors may result from the structure of our pre-existing schemas. In his other studies, Bartlett found that attitudes and cultural expectations could also have a substantial effect on our memory.

Models of memory

1. The sensory register, short-term memory and long-term memory.

2. The three stores differ in terms of: how much information they can store, how long they can store information, what modality they store information in, and how (indeed if) forgetting occurs.

3. 'Meaningfulness' is perhaps the best alternative (if a little clumsy). It reminds us that the more we work with meanings when we are attending to something, the deeper the processing; the less we work with meanings, the shallower the processing.

4. The most likely rank ordering is probably (b)(c)(d)(a), with subjects in condition (b) performing best, and subjects in condition (a) performing worst. (c)(b)(d)(a) would also be a plausible rank ordering. Remember that this question is best answered empirically. Why not conduct a study yourself to find out the answer!

Eyewitness testimony

1. The controls include the age of the subjects, the use of video and the location of the experiment. All subjects were asked the same questions (apart from changes in the critical words), and the position of the key question in the second study was randomized.

2. In laboratory studies people get ready to remember something. In real life we often realize we have witnessed 'an event' only after it is all over. Another difference is that in laboratory studies we have no incentive to either remember or forget what we saw. On the other hand, real-life events bring their own incentives. Famous in British gangland history is the event where Ron Kray went into the Blind Beggar public house in East London and shot a member of the rival Richardson gang. Witnesses to the event had very hazy memories about what happened.

3. For example, food, alcohol, emotions, environment, who you were with, what the event meant to you, and so forth.

4. Students are used to remembering useless information, and are unusually good at memory tasks compared with other people (see the study by Sears in Part V for more information).

False or recovered memories?

1. There is a particular problem here if you actually plant a memory in someone's mind. What if they forget about the experiment but still remember the 'lost in the mall' event?

2. Apart from the multi-million-dollar law cases that confirm the power of this work, there is the belief we have about memories. We commonly take people at face value and so if an adult says they were abused as a child we are inclined to believe them. This is such a powerful issue, in fact, that we would have to feel very confident of our position if we were going to challenge them. If the person telling us the story is convinced they are telling the truth, the problem gets even harder. In a number of cases, people have been guided during therapy to invent extreme and bizarre memories of childhood abuse. It has been possible to challenge some of these. The controversial bit comes from the difficult truth that if there is no corroborative evidence there is no way of distinguishing a false memory from a real one.

3. Not thought of any? Well think harder. Can you see yourself in any of

your 'memory movies' or memory images? If you can then you must have elaborated it because you didn't see yourself at the time.

14. Perception

Walking off a cliff

1. Depth cues are visual information that help us build up a three-dimensional picture in the mind. Examples are the relative size of objects, height in the visual plane, superimposition of objects, pattern density, perspective lines and motion parallax.

2. There are a number to choose from, including the choice by the neonate chicks of the shallow side of the visual cliff rather than the deep side.

3. Three babies crawled over the deep side of the cliff. It also appears that the cue of pattern density has little effect on neonates.

4. The nature–nurture debate explores how much of our behaviour and experience is pre-programmed (innate) and how much of it is acquired through experience.

5. The reason why psychologists explore the nature–nurture debate is because it might give us some clues to one of the big questions in psychology: 'What is a person?' Are individuals and their societies made by their biological make-up, or are they moulded by their environment? There is, of course, a third approach which is to suggest that although we are influenced by biology and the environment, we, in fact, invent ourselves.

Why did the antelope cross the road?

1. The trident illusion only occurs if the viewer is trying to interpret the figure as three dimensional. If the viewer is not trying to interpret it as a three-dimensional figure, then it should be no harder to copy than the ordinary trident, for under these circumstances both figures are just 'lines on a page'. If, on the other hand, viewers are trying to see the figures in three dimensions, then they will be confused by the illusory figure, but not by the ordinary figure. The confusion would cause copying the illusory trident to be harder, and also mean that they would need to look at the illusory figure more in order to copy it accurately.

2. Ethnocentrism refers to the notion of regarding one's own culture as the norm against which other cultures should be compared. It means in effect being unable to see things from the perspective of other people's cultures. It is related to the notion of egocentrism, which refers to one person's inability to see things from another person's perspective.

3. We hope that you can answer this important question for yourself.

Walk like a man ...

1. No feedback was given, because if subjects were told whether they had guessed right or wrong on a particular trial, it might have been possible for them to learn the correct response. The researchers were not interested in whether subjects can learn to do this. They wanted to know

▶ **pattern density** A visual depth cue. If you move away from a pattern such as a check, then the elements of the pattern get smaller as you move away and the pattern appears to get more dense.

▶ **motion parallax** A visual depth cue. Objects and surfaces which are nearer to the viewer move more quickly within the field of vision than do objects and surfaces which are further away. Such differences in the relative movement of things within the visual field facilitate judgements of distance.

▶ **neonates** New-born animals.

▶ **nature–nurture debates** Fairly sterile theoretical debates, popular in the 1950s, concerning whether a given psychological ability was inherited or whether it was learned through experience.

▶ **egocentrism** The tendency to see things from your own personal perspective, to the exclusion of other possible perspectives.

whether the percept of 'sex of walker' is inherently available to observers from the minimal information provided by the point-light display on joints. They found that it was.

2. There are an infinite number of examples of this kind of processing. When we see an object partially obscured by another object, we do not have any difficulty in recognizing the half-visible thing for what it is. This is because we are able to use our experience of the world to make inferences, which allow us to go beyond the information that is directly available to our senses. Another example is listening to someone speak. We do not hear every syllable that is uttered, but it usually feels as though we do, because we are so expert at filling in the gaps according to our understanding of the meaning of what the person is saying.

3. In essence these are empirical questions, which can only be answered by conducting properly controlled research studies. Perhaps you could suggest a research design to address these questions?

Are you having a laugh?

1. This is because the cognitive processes that the researchers are trying to study can only be inferred. They can say for sure that fixations were of such and such a duration, and occurred in this and that pattern. But they can only infer the cognitive processes that underlie those observations.

2. When a set of findings comes from one type of data collection technique and from one type of experimental setup, it is always possible that those findings are to do with some arbitrary feature of the technique or task rather than being to do with the thing that is being investigated. We cannot be sure, from this one study, that the longer fixation times in the caption-first condition were anything to do with humour. They might, for example, have been to do with some general visual processing effect of seeing words followed by pictures. If extended processing times associated with 'getting the joke' can also be inferred from other data collection techniques and other joke formats – if the findings can be replicated and 'triangulated' – then we can be more confident that what we are observing is related to the humour.

3. Because they can't get the wrapper off.

15. Mind and Thought

Autism and theories of mind

1. Think about the following event which one of the authors witnessed when writing this summary: Two people were standing in a bus queue next to me. Person A asked person B 'When's it due?' Person B answered 'Five to', to which person A replied (in a worried voice) 'You're joking'. Understanding this exchange is apparently straightforward. But one of the preconditions for our understanding is an ability to appreciate that, before asking person B about the next bus, person A probably believed that there was one coming some time before 'five to'. In making sense

▶ theory of mind The understanding we have that other people have their own thoughts and beliefs about the world, which may differ from our own thoughts and beliefs.

of the brief interaction we are already using our own theory of mind. Imagine trying to make sense of this if you found it difficult to infer what was going on in someone else's mind. Furthermore, B would only be able to make sense of A's question by assuming that A was waiting for, and talking about, a bus. Again this may appear obvious, but notice that this very assumption is another act of everyday mind-reading. Incidentally, we could have illustrated this point with virtually any piece of conversation or social interaction.

2. We might compare the results of the Eyes Task with the results of other tests that purport to measure theory of mind, in order to establish their concurrent validity. In this study Happé's 'Strange Stories' was also used to measure theory of mind, though the results of these measures are not reported in the paper. Ultimately, whether or not a task measures theory of mind depends upon its 'fit' with the literature on the subject.

3. The idea of including a group with Tourette Syndrome is that, like autism, it is an organic condition that has its origins in childhood. If the group with autism performs differently to the group with Tourette Syndrome and the 'normal' group, then this suggests that the difference in performance is to do with the autism, rather than just being to do with childhood-onset organic disorders in general.

▶ autism A condition of social withdrawal characterized by (i) impairment in reciprocal social interaction, (ii) impairment in verbal and non-verbal communication, and in imaginative activity, (iii) a restricted repertoire of activities and interests.

4. 'High functioning' is a somewhat value-laden label, which of course has to be juxtaposed with 'low functioning'. It is difficult to imagine being a member of a group of people labelled as 'low functioning'? You yourself may have been given a label such as 'autistic' or 'Tourettes' or 'dyslexic'. How does the use of the term 'normal', to describe a group of people, make you feel? In this summary we have put 'normal' in inverted commas. Does that help? We're not sure.

I'm sorry Dave, I can't do that

1. Dennett used this thought experiment as a springboard for discussing the relationship between mind and body. I'm afraid we cannot provide a one-paragraph answer to these sorts of questions!

2. He is making the point that simply focusing on the observable behaviour of a computer (the Turing test focuses on the observable output of the computer) cannot tell us anything very important about how a computer works. Behaviourists were criticized on the same grounds: you cannot tell very much about how a person 'works' from simply studying their behaviour.

▶ behaviourism A school of thought which holds that the observation and description of overt behaviour is all that is needed to comprehend the human being, and that manipulation of stimulus–response contingencies is all that is needed to change human behaviour.

3. Stanley Kubrick's science-fiction masterpiece *2001: A Space Odyssey*. The 'speaker' is HAL, the spaceship's computer, which conducts natural language conversations with the crew. The sophistication of HAL in this respect is one of the most fictional aspects of the film (see Boden, 1977).

Is it a bird, is it a plane ...?

1. The most important function of the computer was to record the reaction times. Bear in mind that the timings are in milliseconds (thousandths of

seconds), so the actual differences in reaction times detected between the different sentence types are, in reality, tiny. The only way of obtaining timings with the precision necessary to detect such small differences is to use a computer. The computer also carries with it additional advantages, such as the capacity to standardize the way in which sentences are presented to subjects.

2. There are a number of reasons for trying to model human cognition on a computer. Perhaps the most important of these is that it forces cognitive psychologists to be explicit about the details of their theoretical models. It is one thing to draw a few boxes on a page, with some arrows pointing from one to the other, and claim that we have established a model of, say, human memory. It is quite another thing to construct a working version of that model on a computer. One of the most important lessons we have learned in the course of the last few decades of computational modelling is just what incredibly sophisticated information processors human beings are. We have learned this by discovering how difficult it is to get computers to do things that people do effortlessly: most notably, the difficulties in getting computers to understand a natural language input.

Hearing colours, tasting shapes

1. You could compare the performance of the 'taste' synaesthetes with the performance of control participants on the following discrimination task. Give all the participants shapes to feel under blanket (so they cannot be seen). The task would be to identify these shapes as quickly as possible. Needless to say different shapes with different associated tastes would need to be used. All the participants would do the task under two conditions: 1) a control condition, while consuming a neutral tasting drink such as water; 2) an experimental condition, while consuming a strong tasting substance. One would hypothesize that if the taste synaesthesia is a real perceptual phenomenon the discriminatory performance of the synaesthetes should be more disrupted by the strong tasting substance than would the performance of the control participants. Requiring the participants to consume different flavoured drinks can be thought of as a kind of 'interference' task. The task should interfere more with the synaesthetes' performances than with the non-synaesthetes' performances.

2. Use the same sort of task as above, but this time with a colour discrimination task. Think about the kind of interference task that you would use to try to disrupt any kind of discrimination that was going on through sound, rather than through sight.

16. Attention

Now you see it, now you don't

1. Consonants were used in order to minimize the probability of subjects making words out of the rows of letters. Because of the way that people

can deal with chunks of information, it may be considerably easier to remember

T O R K
G R A F
A P L E

than to remember

T R L K
G R Z F
W P L Q

Note, however, that it is impossible to stop human research subjects from finding meaning in any set of arbitrary stimulus materials.

2. Since the colour of the letters is part of their visual, physical make-up, the results of this experiment should be similar to the results of the 'partial report by row' experiment (Experiment 3). Given that information is stored as a literal copy of the stimulus, the colour of the letters should be available to subjects in their iconic store, so it should be possible for them to ignore those letters which are not the cued colour. In other words the colour or position of the letters is available in the sensory register, because these are physical characteristics of the stimuli. However, semantic characteristics of the stimuli (such as whether they are letters or numbers) are not directly available without further processing.

3. One example is this. You are talking at a party, and listening attentively to someone, when you overhear a snippet of interesting gossip from a conversation that has been going on behind you, but which you have not been attending to. Momentarily you put your current processing on hold (trying not to convey this to the people who you are meant to be listening to!) and 'inspect' your auditory store to interpret what it was you heard, which has been buffered there and which will be lost if you do not process it further. Does this sound familiar?

Listening with one ear

1. Things like volume, pitch, rhythm, accent, intonation. These physical characteristics are often referred to as 'prosodic' features of speech.

2. Ecological validity refers to the ease with which a piece of research can be related to everyday behaviour and experience. It would be fair to say that Gray and Wedderburn's study is rather low on ecological validity, since it was conducted under unusual conditions, and used relatively meaningless arrays of stimuli. For example, when do we ever hear one word exclusively in one ear, and a different word exclusively in the other ear in everyday life? Note that the judgment that a study is low in ecological validity is a critically evaluative judgment, not a condemnation.

3. One unusual feature is commonly called the 'cocktail party effect'.

Basically, it refers to the experience we have in a room of people who are all talking. We are able to focus on one conversation and exclude the others even though we are not able to move our ears to pick up the sound better. This is canny enough, but if one of the other conversations contains a word that is interesting to us, like our name, then we suddenly switch our attention without moving a muscle to listen in to the more interesting conversation. The problem for cognitive psychologists is: how did we hear the interesting word if we were not listening to the conversation?

Monkey business

1. When you are demonstrating the existence of a phenomenon like inattentional blindness it is not important to have a representative sample. If we wanted to know how many people in the adult population experienced this then representativeness would be more important, but the issue here is that a large proportion of the students experienced the phenomenon and it is likely that all people experience it sometimes.

2. Change blindness is a phenomenon of visual perception where large changes within a visual image or scene are not detected by the viewer; inattentional blindness is the failure to perceive or remember visual items that you are not attending to

3. Clearly the weapons inspectors in Iraq experienced inattentional blindness and so were unable to see the weapons of mass destruction even though they must have been staring them in the face. Talking of faces, I didn't notice when one of my colleagues shaved off his rather full beard until over a term later (change blindness).

Part VI Psychological Methods

17. Analysing Data

Discourse analysis

▶ **discourse analysis** A method of studying human experience by analysing the things people say to one another, and how they express them, both symbolically and behaviourally.

1. The resulting analyses can be insightful and challenging. Because discourse analysts often focus in great detail on very small sections of their data, their conclusions tend to be persuasive, and they avoid the superficiality that some psychology suffers from. On the other hand, one is always left wondering how legitimate it is to generalize from their analyses, given the relatively small number of data sources that are typically used.

▶ **attribution theory** A social psychological theory which looks at how people understand the causes of their own, and other people's, behaviour.

2. Attribution theory is concerned with the causes of human behaviour. Specifically, it examines the way in which people come to conclusions about the causes of their own behaviour and of the behaviour of others.

AIDS and uncertainty

1. It is likely that people with a disfigurement will be more shy of any social company, and will therefore become more invisible to the outside world. The term 'people of colour' is used by US writers to refer to people who

are not White English-speaking Americans, so it includes Black people and Hispanics and people from Asia. One reason for their absence from the study might be due to a different level of social support within their own communities.

2. One of the problems is that the study cannot readily be replicated because it is so detailed and so personal. Other problems are to do with the time it takes to collect the information, and to do with the reliability of participants' accounts.

3. Many health problems have some guilt attached to them, especially those that are perceived, rightly or wrongly, as the person's own fault. But when it comes down to it, we have probably all experienced guilt at having to take time off work or to cancel an arrangement because of illness, even when we really are unwell. Guilt is often not a rational response.

Life is stress

1. Item 12: Pregnancy, Item 23: Son or daughter leaving home, and Item 26: Wife begins or stops work, will all be different experiences for men and women for relatively obvious reasons.

2. Item 7: Marriage, and Item 10: Retirement, are clearly age-related. Marriage at 70 and retirement at 30 will be very different experiences from marriage at 30 and retirement at 70.

3. The scale is centred on family life, and one of the major changes over the last 30 years has been the growth in the number of people not living in small family units.

4. There are numerous events that can create stress, for example your favourite football team being relegated (or selling its top player to Manchester United), getting a bad mark at college, falling out with your best friend, losing your favourite teddy bear, etc.

Shrink-wrapped: the choice of therapist

1. How do you measure outcomes? That is, how do you measure how much 'better' someone has got after therapy? If people do seem to get better how can you be sure that this improvement is due to the therapy and not due to spontaneous remission (in other words, how can you be sure that they would not have got better anyway)? These are not insurmountable problems, so think how they can be addressed in the design of studies.

2. You would suspect that most published studies would show a positive effect in favour of psychotherapy. There may be two major reasons for this. First, the people who are most interested in the effectiveness of psychotherapy would be practitioners who have a stake in showing its effectiveness. Second, publication of evaluation studies is biased in favour of studies which show statistically significant differences between treated and untreated groups. That is, studies which show no significant differences will tend not to get published as readily as those that do show such differences. Furthermore, it is unlikely that many studies would ever show statistically significant negative effects of therapy (Smith and Glass

▶ **effect size** When psychologists detect significant differences in the performance of subjects in experimental conditions they talk about having 'got an effect'. The bigger the differences, the bigger the effect size.

stated that 12 per cent of their effect sizes were negative). These observations do not invalidate Smith and Glass's conclusions, and are probably in themselves contestable. But it is always important to think critically about what you are being told when you read psychological studies.

18. Issues in Research

Demand characteristics

▶ **artefact** An artificial finding that has been produced by some aspect of the research procedures, and which therefore does not really tell us anything relevant to the actual research question. For example, research participants who know that they are being observed may behave very differently from normal. This effect is known as 'reactivity', and is one form of artefact.

▶ **hypnosis** A temporary trance-like state that can be induced in healthy individuals.

1. Some kinds of behavioural outcomes of experiments can be artificially produced by the research procedures that have been employed, rather than by the manipulation of the independent variables. Artefact in this context denotes false, artificial, misleading findings about human behaviour, which tell us a bit about how people behave in experiments, but not much about how they behave in more normal situations. In such cases the ecological validity of the research is said to be low. Experimenter bias is another source of artefact which is dealt with in this book (see the study by Rosenthal and Fode later in this chapter).

2. It can be argued that people have an idea about how they should behave under hypnosis. Most people have seen others who have apparently been hypnotized, and know the kinds of things that are expected of a hypnotized person. The behaviour of people in hypnosis stage-shows may be attributable to them acting out these expectations (responding to the demand characteristics of the situation), rather than to any real effects of hypnosis. Orne has conducted much research into hypnosis and demand characteristics (see Orne, 1966).

Who are psychology's subjects?

1. Basically, because they are there! Students are readily available to researchers (who often lecture in higher education establishments). Because of the power dynamics within the lecturer–student relationship, students are very likely to 'volunteer' their help. Indeed, in many contexts it is a course requirement that students act as research subjects.

▶ **fieldwork** Research which is conducted outside the laboratory.

2. Again, the obvious answers are to do with ease and speed. There is considerable pressure in universities to produce publications. Research grants are allocated on the basis of the amount of published material produced by researchers. Therefore it is financially advantageous to publish as many articles as possible, and it is easier and quicker to conduct and report laboratory-based studies. Fieldwork, on the other hand, takes more time, and although it might well produce findings which are very useful, it is unlikely to produce as many publications and therefore will attract less money. As 'Deep Throat' says in *All the President's Men* when the journalists are trying to unravel a political conspiracy, 'follow the money'.

How gullible are you?

1. The sorts of people we believe when they tell us something about ourselves are doctors, scientists, experts, teachers, psychologists and so forth.

▶**psychometric tests** Instruments which have been developed for measuring mental characteristics. Psychological tests have been developed to measure a wide range of things, including creativity, job attitudes and skills, brain damage and, of course, 'intelligence'.

2. Older people might be less gullible (see the previous study in this chapter by Sears); they also might be more defensive about personality tests, and less trusting of psychologists.

3. Up to you to decide. I suspect his students learned a valuable lesson about the value of psychometric tests even though they were deceived along the way.

Dull rats and bright rats

1. Possibly through the gentleness and frequency of handling. Rosenthal and Fode suggest that animal handlers perhaps give 'an extra pat or two for good performance, a none-too-gentle toss into the home cage for poor performance' (p. 188). Perhaps the mood of the experimenter is transmitted through the medium of skin temperature, or muscle tension.

2. This is an illustration of the so-called single-blind design. Subjects are not permitted to know the true purpose of the experiment, or the experimental hypothesis, in case they themselves inadvertently (or deliberately) bias the results.

Why psychology?

1. Some people might argue that IQ tests are a great achievement, or Bowlby's attachment theory, or psychoanalysis, or behaviour therapy but it is difficult to come up with an equivalent of the microchip or antibiotics.

2. We think the most important thing to be given away is the information that will help every person to understand their behaviour and experience better and to also understand other people better. It's not too much to ask.

19 . Methodology: How Does Psychological Research Get Done?

1. **(a)** qualitative
   (b) quantitative
   (c) quantitative
   (d) quantitative
   (e) a mixture of quantitative and qualitative.

2. Perhaps: physical violence towards another person, physical violence to an object, physical violence to another person mediated by an object, shouting, swearing, adopting an aggressive stance (e.g. standing too close to another person), particular gestures (remember these can be highly culturally specific), staring, use of particular words and phrases ...

▶**ordinal scale** The most common level of measurement in psychological research, which involves assigning scores to people or things such that they can be rank ordered on the basis of those scores from most to least (or vice versa). Unlike interval scales, the raw data have to be converted into straightforward rank orderings before any further statistical procedures can be undertaken, because the size of the interval between the raw scores is meaningless (see also nominal scale and interval scale).

3. **(a)** Ordinal: a scale on which we are not quite sure whether the gap between a score of 18 and 19 is the same as the gap between 11 and 12. Note that this scale is to some extent associated with a measure of distance. If it had been purely a measure of distance, it would have been an interval scale.

   (b) Nominal: simple categorization of responses into one of two categories, according to whether the girl or the woman was chosen for each job.

▶interval scale As a rule
the most sophisticated
level of measurement used
in psychological research,
involving scales that are
based on properly calibrated
units of measurement.
Interval scales can be used
to measure people or things,
and enable researchers to go
beyond crude judgements
about the rank ordering
of scores. This is because
the intervals between the
scores from such a scale
are meaningful (unlike the
intervals between scores on
an ordinal scale). See also
nominal scale and ordinal
scale.

▶nominal scale The crudest
level of measurement,
which simply sorts people
or things into categories
(see also ordinal scale and
interval scale).

(c) Nominal: simple categorization of responses into one of two categories, right or wrong. Note that nominal data can be aggregated across participants to give ordinal data for groups of people.

(d) Interval: any kind of timing is an example of interval data, because we know that the difference between 100 ms and 200 ms is the same as the gap between 1300 ms and 1400 ms.

4. The answer is (d). Data analysis should be regarded as a core feature of research design. In reality some of the other strategies are taken. Strategy (a) can be a complete disaster, because there is nothing worse than getting a whole set of data in, then realizing that there is no way of analysing it sensibly. Strategy (c) is relatively common in practice (even though in theory it does not make much sense) because people often have favourite ways of doing things.

5. The independent variable (the variable that the researchers manipulated) was the subjects' (who thought that they were experimenters) expectations of their rats. Some subjects were led to have high expectations of their rats, and some were led to have low expectations. This manipulation created two conditions. The dependent variable was the rats' performance on the maze tasks. The researchers predicted that high expectations would cause the rats to perform better on maze tasks than would low expectations.

6. There is a two-part answer to this. The first part is to do with the fact that not everything can be controlled exactly by an experimenter. Certainly they can control things like the heating and lighting, and make those things the same for everybody. But they cannot control the individual characteristics of the participants. They cannot, for example, control people's emotional state. Some of their participants may be happy, and alert, others may be tired and a bit down. So what can be done about these things?

Well that brings us to the second part of the answer. Those things that cannot be kept exactly the same (those things that cannot be exactly matched) across the experimental conditions are allowed to vary randomly. To continue with the example of emotional state, if we allocate participants at random to the different conditions in an independent-measures design experiment, we are allowed to assume that for every happy, alert person in one condition, there is likely to be an equally happy, alert person in the other condition. We cannot be sure that this is the case, but we are allowed to assume it is. In this way, the differing emotional states of the participants are unlikely to have any systematic effect on any measured differences in scores between the conditions, and so would not constitute a confounding variable.

7. Most of the key ethical issues relating to participant and non-participant observation have to do with whether the observations are being made covertly or not. Covert observation is one way of dealing with problems of reactivity (people's behaviour being affected by the knowledge that they are being observed: see the section on artefact in this chapter). But is

it OK to observe people, and record their behaviour, when they do not know you are doing this? The consensus in the research community is that it is OK to observe people covertly as long as they are in public settings where they could expect to be being observed by others as a normal part of everyday life.

All this means that covert participant observation is rather problematic from an ethical point of view. Participant observation really implies some level of observation in non-public settings (being a member of a group means being more than just a casual passer-by). Furthermore, in participant observation the researcher is actively intervening in the lives of the people who are being observed, simply by virtue of 'participating'. If the group who are being observed have given their informed consent to this process occurring (that is, if the observation is not being done covertly), then this is probably acceptable. Nowadays there would have to be a pretty compelling scientific reason for a covert participant observation to be passed by a research ethics committee.

8. Unstructured observation can result in a rich, detailed and insightful analysis of a particular setting. Because observers are not constrained by checklists, they are free to notice and to explore anything to do with the research question. This is particularly useful for exploratory studies, when it is not possible to anticipate exactly what needs observing in advance. However, unstructured observations can become rather unmanageable, precisely because they are not constrained by tightly defined checklist definitions of what to (and, thereby crucially, what not to) observe. One result of this is that the data that are collected, often in the form of large quantities of field notes, can be difficult to analyse systematically. Furthermore, it is difficult to replicate unstructured observations, or to demonstrate their reliability, because different observers may simply focus on different aspects of the settings in which they are working.

▶ **structured observation** A method of recording behaviour where the behaviours are pre-categorized into a limited framework.

Structured observational studies, on the other hand, can be replicated by observers who are properly trained in the usage of the relevant observational schedule/framework. They are easier to constrain, since the schedule defines what should be, and what should not be, observed. The data are also recorded in a more analysis-friendly format. But structured methods also have their limitations. Since the role of the observational framework is to determine what should be observed, observers may systematically miss important things because they are not on their checklist. Observers with a checklist may not be particularly sensitive to the setting that they are in, because they are committed to their preconceptions of what is important to record. Furthermore, because structured observational schedules are not a good way of recording rich and interesting observations (they are better for doing things like counting frequencies of behaviours, and recording timings) they risk trivializing the research question.

9. Another word for reliability is consistency. A reliable measuring instrument should give a consistent measurement of the object that it is measuring. When the 'object' of the measurement is a person, then a

number of interesting factors come into play. Most obviously, people change. In the long term they grow and develop. In the short term it is true to say that people can change from week to week, from day to day, even from moment to moment. So psychological measuring devices are trying to do the equivalent of cutting a 3-year-old child's hair: they are trying to cope with something that will not sit still. If inconsistent measurements are obtained on, for example, a test–retest procedure, it is unclear whether the measuring device is at fault, or whether that device has simply been sensitive to changes that have taken place in the 'object' being measured between the first and second test.

Furthermore, people have a choice about how to respond to the conventional measuring devices of the psychologist, which are usually scales made up of questions or statements. People can choose to lie, they can choose to conceal certain things or to emphasize certain other things. This is quite unlike the bathroom floor, which cannot help but respond with the same measurement again and again (and we still get it wrong!). On a test–retest of a given personality scale, for example, it may be that any consistency that is detected between a person's responses on the two administrations is more to do with them remembering how they responded the first time, rather than anything to do with their personality.

10. Reliability is a necessary condition for validity. This means that for a test to be valid, it must first of all be reliable. It must give consistent measurements, otherwise it cannot be valid.

Reliability is not a sufficient condition for validity. This means that there is more to validity than just consistency of measurement, as illustrated in the 'head circumference as a measure of intelligence' example. In other words, showing that a test is reliable is one thing, but this does not necessarily mean that it is valid. For a test to be valid it must actually measure what it says it measures.

11. Double-blind procedures can be used. These involve ensuring that the people who are collecting the data do not know the research question/hypothesis. Alternatively, if they know the hypothesis, then information about which condition of an experiment each participant is in can be concealed from them. In this way the people collecting the data cannot have any expectations about how any given participant should behave, or at least no expectations that could systematically affect the outcome of the study.

12. One way of dealing with the issue of reactivity is to conduct research covertly. If people do not know they are being observed, then they cannot be affected by the observation. However, this strategy raises a whole raft of ethical issues. A more ethically acceptable way is for researchers to acknowledge the influence of reactivity in their data, and to interpret their findings accordingly.

▶ **validity** The question of whether a psychometric test or psychological measure is really measuring what it is supposed to.

▶ **double-blind control** A form of experimental control which aims to avoid self-fulfilling prophecies, by ensuring that neither the subjects nor the experimenter who carries out the study are aware of the experimental hypothesis.

GLOSSARY

ability tests Psychometric tests which are designed to measure what someone is already able to do, as opposed to what they might be able to learn in the future.

Acquired Immune Deficiency Syndrome (AIDS) AIDS is an infectious disease, most likely caused by a virus, that attacks the immune system making the host vulnerable to a variety of diseases that would be readily controlled by a healthy immune system.

action research A method of undertaking social research which acknowledges that the researcher's presence is likely to influence people's behaviour, and so incorporates the researcher's involvement as a direct and deliberate part of the research, with the researcher consciously acting as change agent.

addiction Often seen as a medical condition, for example 'Dependence on a drug, resulting in tolerance and withdrawal symptoms when the addict is deprived of the drug.' (Rosenhan and Seligman, 1989, page 685). Alternatively it can be seen as a set of behaviour with common features. Griffiths (1995) suggests that addictive behaviours have six components; *salience, euphoria, tolerance, withdrawal symptoms, conflict, relapse.*

adoption studies Studies designed to investigate the relative influence of environmental and genetic factors by comparing children in different family situations.

adrenaline A hormone secreted by the adrenal glands, which causes increase in blood pressure, release of sugar by the liver and a number of other physiological responses to threat.

affective To do with feelings or emotions.

aggression A term used in several ways, but generally to describe negative or hostile behaviour or feelings towards others.

AI See *artificial intelligence.*

alarm reaction A term used to describe the series of physiological responses brought about by the activation of the sympathetic division of the autonomic nervous system.

alpha coefficient (Cronbach's Alpha) A statistic which is used to give an estimate of reliability.

altruism Acting in the interests of other people and not of oneself.

amnesia The loss of memory, usually through physical causes.

amphetamine A central nervous system stimulant that increases energy and decreases appetite; used to treat narcolepsy and some forms of depression; commonly used recreationally.

analgesia Lack of sensitivity to pain.

ANOVA An inferential statistic that can be used with interval-level data and that is capable of dealing with more than one independent variable at a time. The word is an acronym of ANalysis Of VAriance, and is conventionally written in capital letters. Probably the most widely used statistical technique in experimental psychology.

anterior An anatomical term denoting the 'nose' end of an organism (see also *posterior*).

anthropomorphism Attribution of human characteristics to animals.

anxiety hierarchy Constructed in the course of desensitization, and comprising a rank-ordered list of those stimuli which produce fear in a phobic person.

aphasia Literally speaking, an absence of speech.

arousal A general physiological state in which the sympathetic division of the autonomic nervous system is activated.

artefact An artificial finding that has been produced by some aspect of the research procedures, and which therefore does not really tell us anything relevant to the actual research question. For example, research participants who know that they are being observed may behave very differently from normal. This effect is known as 'reactivity', and is one form of artefact.

artificial intelligence (AI) Computer systems which are able to 'learn' and to produce the same kinds of outcomes as are produced by human thinking.

attachment The tendency of the young of many species to stay close to an adult, usually the mother.

attitude A relatively stable opinion about a person, object, or activity, containing a cognitive element (perceptions and beliefs) and an emotional element (positive or negative feelings).

attribution The process of giving reasons for why things happen.

attribution theory A social psychological theory which looks at how people understand the causes of their own, and other people's, behaviour.

authoritarian personality A collection of characteristics found by Adorno to occur together, implying a rigid approach to moral and social issues.

autism A condition of social withdrawal characterized by (i) impairment in reciprocal social interaction, (ii) impairment in verbal and non-verbal communication, and in imaginative activity, (iii) a restricted repertoire of activities and interests.

autonomic nervous system (ANS) A network of nerve fibres running from the brain stem and spinal cord, which can activate the body for action, or set it into a quiescent state.

aversion therapy A technique of behaviour therapy which involves associating unpleasant stimuli with things that are to be avoided.

Barnum Effect Describes the fact that a carefully worded description of an individual's personality will often be uncritically accepted as valid if presented in sufficiently broad and general terms.

baseline measures Measures of performance or behaviour before the research intervention is made.

behaviour (also spelt 'behavior') Anything a person (or animal) does that can be observed and measured by a third party. Behaviour can be thought of as the public side of human life, in contrast to 'experience' (thoughts and feelings) which can be thought of as the private side.

behaviour shaping A process whereby novel behaviour can be produced through operant conditioning, by selectively reinforcing naturally occurring variations of learned responses.

behaviour therapy The process of treating abnormal behaviour by looking only at the symptoms, and using conditioning techniques to modify them.

behavioural genetics The study of the influence of genetics on a range of behaviours, most commonly personality and intelligence.

behaviourism A school of thought which holds that the observation and description of overt behaviour is all that is needed to comprehend the human being, and that manipulation of stimulus–response contingencies is all that is needed to change human behaviour.

binomial test An inferential statistic that is used when there is a simple 'either/ or' outcome to a task (for example, either heads or tails, either right or left, either male or female). It tests to see whether there is any statistically significant bias in favour of one or other of the alternatives.

blogosphere All weblogs or blogs; weblogs have many connections and bloggers read others' blogs, link to them, reference them in their own writing, and post comments on each others' blogs.

Bobo Inflatable doll used by Bandura in studies on aggression.

body image The way we imagine ourselves to look.

brain Large grey thing at the top of your neck.

brain stem The stem-like part of the brain at the top of the spinal cord. It controls all our involuntary muscles regulating the heartbeat, breathing, blood circulation and digestion.

bystander intervention The issue of when and under what circumstances passers-by or other uninvolved persons are likely to offer help to those who look as though they need it.

case history A detailed clinical description of a person which characteristically forms the basis for some kind of therapeutic intervention.

case study A detailed description of a particular individual or group under study or treatment.

categorization The first stage in the process of social identification, which involves grouping other people into social categories or sets. Research shows that such categorization in itself, even if based on minimal criteria, can lead to a strong bias in favour of the ingroup.

change blindness A phenomenon of visual perception where large changes within a visual image or scene are not detected by the viewer.

chi-square test An inferential statistic that can be used to show whether or not there is a statistically significant relationship between two categorical (nominal) variables. It can be thought of as the categorical equivalent of a correlation coefficient (which is used to look for relationships within ordinal or interval data).

classical conditioning A form of learning which involves the pairing of a neutral stimulus with a reflex.

cognition Mental processes. 'All the processes by which ... sensory input is transformed, reduced, elaborated, stored, recovered and used' (Neisser, 1967, p. 4).

cognitive behaviour therapy Attempts to modify everyday thoughts and behaviours, with the aim of positively influencing emotions. It is based on the idea that how we think (cognition), how we feel (emotion) and how we act (behaviour) all interact together. Specifically, our thoughts determine our feelings and our behaviour. Therefore, negative and unrealistic thoughts can cause us distress and result in problems.

cognitive development States that social interaction is the most important factor in a young child's cognitive development.

cognitive dissonance The tension produced by cognitive imbalance – holding beliefs which directly contradict one another or contradict behaviour. The reduction of cognitive dissonance has been shown to be a factor in some forms of attitude change.

cognitive economy Models of human cognition should adhere to this principle which suggests that our cognition is so efficient that the underlying structures and processes must be economically organized (in other words, don't make the models too complicated). This is an example of the rule of parsimony.

cognitive maps Mental images about where things are. People develop cognitive maps as they get to know a town or an institution; rats develop one as they explore mazes.

cognitive science A multidisciplinary approach to studying artificial intelligence and similar phenomena, bringing together psychologists, linguists, information scientists and others.

colonialism Political oppression where one nation or culture dominates another one and, in particular, removes wealth from the dominated culture, believes it has a right of access into the dominated culture, and has a power base outside the dominated culture.

commissural tissue Fibres that connect the two hemispheres of the brain.

commune A group of people living together and sharing everything.

competence Hypothetical notion of what a person is really capable of – what their true abilities are – which may not always be reflected in their 'performance'.

compliance The process of going along with other people – that is, conforming – but without accepting their views on a personal level.

computational modelling The process of modelling human cognitive processes on computers.

computer simulation The attempt to develop computer programmes which will replicate human processes such as skill learning or problem-solving.

concrete operational stage Piaget's third main stage of cognitive development during which the child is able to use sophisticated mental operations, but in a limited way.

concurrent validity A method for assessing whether a psychometric test is valid (that is, really measures what it is supposed to) by comparing it with some other measure which purports to measure the same thing – also known as convergent or congruent validity).

conditioned response A learned response which is produced to a conditioned stimulus.

conditioned stimulus A stimulus which only brings about a response because it has been associated with an unconditioned stimulus.

conformity The process of going along with other people – that is, acting in the same way that they do.

confounding variable A variable which causes a change in the dependent variable, but which is not the independent variable of the study.

consciousness The awareness of your own thoughts and feelings, and awareness of external stimuli.

conservation According to Piaget, the ability to recognize that a quantity remains the same even if it changes its shape.

consonance In the sense used in this book, this is the opposite of 'dissonance' (see *cognitive dissonance*).

construct validity A method for assessing whether a psychometric test is valid (that is, really measures what it is supposed to) by seeing how it matches up with theoretical ideas about what it is supposed to be measuring.

constructive memory The idea that in recalling an event we mentally reconstruct it from a series of cues.

control group A group which is used for comparison with an experimental group.

cooperation Acting together, in a coordinated way at work, leisure, or in social relationships, in the pursuit of shared goals, the enjoyment of the joint activity or simply furthering the relationship.

coping The process of managing external or internal demands that are perceived as taxing or exceeding a person's resource.

correlation A measure of how strongly two or more variables are related to each other.

correlation coefficient A number between -1 and +1 which expresses how strong a correlation is. If this number is close to 0, there is no real connection between the two; if it is close to +1 there is a positive correlation – in other words, if one variable is large the other will also tend to be large; and if it is close to -1, there is a negative correlation – in other words, if one variable is large, the other will tend to be small.

cortex The outermost layer of nerve tissue of the cerebral hemispheres.

cost–reward analysis Cognitive judgement based on assessment of the relative rewards or costs of following a particular course of behaviour.

counterbalancing A method of controlling against potentially confounding variables in experiments. Typically, counterbalancing is seen in action in repeated measures designs in an effort to control against order effects, and characteristically involves alternating the order in which subjects do the conditions of an experiment.

courtship Behaviour preceding mating.

criminology The study of crime and criminal behaviour.

criterion validity A method for assessing whether a psychometric test is valid (that is, really measures what it is supposed to) by comparing it with some other measure. If the other measure is assessed at roughly the same time as the original one, then the type of criterion validity being applied is concurrent validity; if it is taken much later, it is predictive validity.

cross-cultural studies Studies which examine psychological phenomena in people from more than one cultural background.

cultural deprivation A construct which has been used to explain educational failure among members of certain classes. Read the summary of Labov's work in Chapter 12.

culture The concept of culture is difficult to define though it refers to the characteristic beliefs, behaviours and sense of identity that we share with a group of people. Hofstede (1980) identified four basic dimensions which can be used to compare them; *power-distance*; *uncertainty-avoidance, individualism, masculinity–femininity.*

cyber-identity A social identity that people create on the Internet. Some people prefer to use their real names but many users create pseudonyms and reveal varying amounts of personal information which might or might not be accurate.

deconstructionism Originally a form of literary criticism, but more recently recognized for its value in philosophy Developed by the French philosopher Jacques Derrida, it is a set of ideas which challenge our common-sense assumptions about the nature of language and its relationship to the world around us.

deductive approach A research strategy in which theory is used to guide the collection of data which are then used to test propositions from that theory. See *inductive approach* for a description of an alternative strategy.

defence mechanisms Protective strategies that the mind uses to defend itself against unwelcome or disturbing information.

defensible space Clearly bounded or semi-private areas that appear to belong to someone.

deficit theory A way of explaining educational failure among certain children by claiming that they, or their background, are somehow 'deficient'.

deindividuation A state of awareness where a person develops a changed sense of personal identity which, in particular, leads to a reduced sense of personal agency (feeling that you are in control of your behaviour). The development of the state of deindividuation is often a response to conditions in the social environment.

delusion False belief that typically originates from a misinterpretation but is firmly believed and strongly maintained in spite of contradictory proof or evidence.

demand characteristics Those aspects of a psychological study (or other artificial situation) which exert an implicit pressure on people to act in ways that are expected of them.

denial A coping strategy/Freudian defence mechanism where distressing facts are eliminated.

dependent variable The thing which is measured in an experiment, and which changes, depending on the independent variable.

depersonalization A dissociative disorder where the individual often feels cut off or unsure of their identity.

desegregation The political policy of mixing up peoples; in particular the policy in the USA in the 1960s of encouraging inter-racial mixing.

diabetes Type I diabetes (also called, insulin dependent diabetes mellitus) involves a complete failure of the pancreas, and requires insulin replacement by injection. Type II diabetes (or non-insulin dependent diabetes) is far more common, and in this condition individuals retain some endogenous insulin and are able to maintain homeostatic glycemic control through diet, weight management and oral medication.

diagnosis The process of categorizing illness by examining signs and symptoms.

diary method A way of studying what human beings do in everyday life by asking them to note down specific items of information at regular intervals, or on appropriate occasions.

dichotic listening A procedure where different stimuli are presented to each ear simultaneously.

diffusion of responsibility The idea that people are less likely to intervene to help someone who seems to need it if there are others present, because they perceive responsibility as being shared between all present, and therefore see themselves as being less responsible personally.

discourse analysis A method of studying human experience by analysing the things people say to one another, and how they express them, both symbolically and behaviourally.

discrimination The behavioural expression of prejudice.

displacement A cognitive alteration of reality that involves replacing the true object of your emotions with someone who is more innocent and less threatening.

displacement activity Behaviour that is a substitute for the desired behaviour, for example, stroking the pet of someone you are attracted to.

dispositional attribution When the cause of a particular behaviour is thought to have resulted from the person's own personality or characteristics, rather than from the demands of circumstances.

dissonance See *cognitive dissonance*.

dominance rank Differences in power that position the individual in a rank order of influence, and access to resources and mating.

dopamine A neurotransmitter. Neurotransmitters are chemicals that carry information from one nerve cell to another.

double-blind control A form of experimental control which aims to avoid self-fulfilling prophecies, by ensuring that neither the subjects nor the experimenter who carries out the study are aware of the experimental hypothesis.

Down's syndrome A syndrome of behaviours and physical characteristics that is the result of having 47 rather than 46 chromosomes.

drapetomania The tendency of Black slaves in America to run away from the slave owners: this entirely sensible behaviour was defined as a form of mental illness by the slave owners, and given this label.

DSM – IIIR Published in 1987, it is the revised third edition of the *Diagnostic and Statistical Manual of Mental Disorders* developed by the American Psychiatric Association.

dyslexia The problems of poor reading skills are often grouped under the term 'dyslexia' though there is considerable dispute about whether such a condition actually exists. One review of the research (Stanovich, 1994) suggests that the term means no more than 'poor reader'.

echoic memory The sensory memory for sound.

ecological validity A way of assessing how valid a measure or test is (that is, whether it really measures what it is supposed to measure) which is concerned with whether the measure or test is really like its counterpart in the real, everyday world. In other words, whether it is truly realistic or not.

effect size When psychologists detect significant differences in the performance of subjects in experimental conditions they talk about having 'got an effect'. The bigger the differences, the bigger the effect size.

egocentrism The tendency to see things from your own personal perspective, to the exclusion of other possible perspectives.

ego-defence mechanisms See *defence mechanisms*.

eidetic memory 'Photographic' memory – visual or acoustic memory which is so accurate as to be almost like a factual record.

elaborated language codes Ways of using language characterized by extensive vocabulary, complex grammatical structure, and an attempt to make meaning verbally explicit.

electroencephalogram A method of recording the electrical activity of the brain.

emasculation Removing a man's sense of his masculinity.

empathic role taking Putting yourself into someone else's shoes and seeing things from their perspective. The ability to do this depends upon having a sufficiently developed theory of mind.

empathy In client-centred therapy, the accepting and clarifying of the client's expressed emotions.

encephalograph Method for recording electrical activity in the brain.

epilepsy A disorder of the brain characterized by excessive neural activity leading to mental and motor dysfunction.

equal status contact One of the suggestions to reduce racism, is to encourage contact between peoples where they experience themselves as having equal status.

estrus The portion of the estrous cycle when the female is sexually active.

ethics A set of rules designed to distinguish between right and wrong.

ethnocentrism Being unable to conceptualize or imagine ideas, social beliefs, or the world from any viewpoint other than that of one's own particular culture or social group. The belief that one's own ethnic group, nation, religion, scout troop or football team is superior to all others.

ethology The study of behaviour in the natural environment.

eugenics The political idea that the human race could be improved by eliminating 'undesirables' from the breeding stock, so that they cannot pass on their supposedly inferior genes. Some eugenicists advocate compulsory sterilization, while others seem to prefer mass murder or genocide.

Eurocentric The tendency to view Europe as *the* main culture in human societies, and to negatively compare all other cultures to Europe.

event recorder A device used in observational research for recording the occurrence of (and if necessary the duration of) behaviours.

evolution The development of bodily form and behaviour through the process of natural selection.

excitatory nerves Activity in excitatory neurons makes it more likely that connected neurons will fire.

existential crisis The realization that you are alone in your experience of the world, and that the only meaning your life has is the meaning you choose to impose on it.

expectancy effect A label to describe the way in which one person can effect the behaviour of another person simply by having expectations of that person. For example, it may be the case that having low expectations of a child in school can actually contribute to that child performing poorly.

experiment A form of research in which variables are manipulated in order to discover cause and effect.

experimenter effects Unwanted influences in a psychological study which are produced, consciously or unconsciously, by the person carrying out the study.

expert systems Artificial intelligence systems designed to provide human experts with an extended information source, to aid them in making decisions.

external locus of control The feeling or belief that events are caused by situations or by others, and cannot be influenced by oneself.

extinction (also extinguished) The weakening of behavioural responses due to the absence of reinforcement (operant conditioning), or the absence of the unconditioned stimulus (classical conditioning).

extraversion A general tendency towards outgoing, social behaviour.

eye-tracking A technique used in cognitive science in which a camera focuses on one or both eyes and records their movement as the viewer looks at some kind of stimulus.

Eysenck Personality Inventory A psychometric scale for measuring neuroticism and extraversion.

face recognition unit A hypothetical information-processing unit in the mind which is involved in identifying known people by their faces.

face validity Whether a test or measure looks on the surface as though it probably measures what it is supposed to.

factor analysis A method of statistical analysis which examines inter-correlations between data in order to identify major clusters of groupings, which might be related to a single common factor.

factorial design A form of experimental design involving more than one independent variable.

false memory Memory of an event that did not happen or a distortion of an event that did occur.

false-feedback Providing inaccurate biological feedback to someone; for example, suggesting that their heart rate is lower than it really is to convince them that their anxiety level is low.

feedback Knowledge about the effectiveness of one's performance on a task or set of tasks. Feedback appears to be essential in most forms of learning, and is more effective if it is immediate.

feminist research Mary Gergen (1988) suggested the following as the main themes of feminist research: (1) Recognizing the interdependence of experimenter and subject; (2) Avoiding the decontextualization of the subject or experimenter from their social or historical surroundings: (3) Recognizing and revealing the nature of one's values within the research context; (4) Accepting that facts do not exist independently of their producer's linguistic codes; (5) Demystifying the role of the scientist and establishing an egalitarian relationship between science makers and science consumers.

field experiment A study that follows the logic of an experiment, but is conducted in the outside world rather than the laboratory.

fieldwork Research which is conducted outside the laboratory.

fine-motor skills Skilled movements on a small scale, usually to do with the hands (e.g. writing, sewing, picking up small objects), in contrast to gross-motor skills which are movements on a big scale (walking, kicking, jumping).

fixation Ability of the eye to focus on one point.

fixation point Visual point that a person stares at.

forgetting Loss of information through interference, decay, displacement or a failure to retrieve the information.

formal operational stage Piaget's final stage of cognitive development where the child develops formal logic at around the age of 12.

frustration-aggression hypothesis The idea that frustrating circumstances or events, in which someone is prevented from reaching or achieving a desired goal, can produce aggression. Goals in this context do not need to be specific: for example, oppressive or impoverished social circumstances may frustrate a goal of leading a secure and comfortable life.

g The abbreviation for 'general intelligence': a kind of intelligence which is supposed to underpin all different types of mental operations, as opposed to more specific types of talents or aptitudes; also a spot.

gambling The act of staking money or something of financial value in the hope of winning (including the payment of a price for a chance to win a prize).

GAS See *general adaptation syndrome*.

gedankenexperiment Thought experiment.

gender The inner sense of being either male or female.

general adaptation syndrome The process of physiological adaptation to long-term stress, resulting in lowered resistance to illness and other negative outcomes.

genetic Biological inheritance.

grapheme the symbol that represents a number or a letter. The word 'grapheme' contains eight graphemes, two of them the same.

grooming Behaviour associated with cleaning the skin that has health, appearance and social functions; either of oneself or of others.

group dynamics The behaviour, feelings and cognitions of people within a group.

group In psychology, usually more than two individuals.

hallucination A sensory perception experienced in the absence of an external stimulus.

harem Literally, a domestic arrangement where a powerful man uses his influence and wealth to have exclusive sexual access to a number of women; commonly (and incorrectly) used to describe the social organization of animals where a male mates with more than one female, who in turn, only mate with that male.

hassles Minor irritations.

helplessness See *learned helplessness*.

heritability An estimate of the extent to which genetic individual differences contribute to individual differences in observed behaviour.

hermaphrodite A person who at birth has both male and female sexual characteristics and so cannot be unambiguously assigned to male or female.

homeostasis A state of physiological balance or equilibrium in the body.

Human Immunodeficiency Virus (HIV) Human Immunodeficiency Virus is the virus that is believed to cause AIDS by attacking the immune system.

humanistic The humanistic approach to personality asserts that the most important feature of human beings is how they achieve their sense of self and how they actualize their potential.

humour Any form of entertainment or human communication which creates feelings of amusement or which makes people laugh or feel happy.

hypnosis A temporary trance-like state that can be induced in healthy individuals.

hypothesis Experiments are designed to test one or more hypotheses. An hypothesis is a prediction of what will happen in an experiment. It is worded in such a way that the results of a well-designed experiment will clearly show whether the prediction is right or wrong.

iconic memory The sensory memory for visual information.

iconic representation Coding information in the mind by means of sensory image, usually, though not always, visual ones.

identification As used in Freud's theory – the process by which someone internalizes the characteristics, values, attitudes, mannerisms, etc. of another person.

identity The sense that you have of the sort of person you are.

ideology A set of overriding political or philosophical beliefs which govern the assumptions of a particular culture or society.

imaging techniques Visual representations of electronic activity in the brain.

imitation Copying someone else's behaviour and specific actions.

impeccable trivia Clever, precise, replicable but not about anything of any importance (see *cognitive psychology*).

implosion therapy A form of behaviour therapy based on 'overkill', in which the person is continually faced with the feared stimulus until their fear dies down.

inattentional blindness The failure to perceive or remember visual items that you are not attending to.

incidental learning Used in cognitive psychology to describe tasks in which subjects are asked to remember material that they did not expect to be asked to remember.

independent measures (also between subjects, different subjects) An experimental design in which a different group of subjects perform each condition of the experiment.

independent-measures design When a study involves comparing the scores from two or more separate groups of people.

independent variable The conditions which an experimenter sets up, to cause an effect in an experiment. These vary systematically, so that the experimenter can draw conclusions about changes in outcomes.

inductive approach A research strategy in which theory is derived ('induced') from the data. See *deductive approach* for a description of an alternative strategy.

inference Going beyond what we know to make an intelligent guess.

inferential statistics A way of using statistics to enable us to make inferences from data about relationships among variables, particularly with reference to cause and effect. This involves going *beyond* the data, hence the term 'inferential'. A contrast can be made with *descriptive statistics*.

information processing A mechanical model of cognitive activity.

ingroup A group you define yourself as belonging to.

inhibitory nerves Activity in inhibitory neurons makes it more less that connected neurons will fire.

innate Genetically pre-programmed.

instinct theories The name given to the suggestion that the reasons why people do things or act in certain ways is because they are driven by some kind of inborn pressure, or 'instinct'.

institutionalization A pattern of experience and behaviours associated with people in institutional settings, in particular a lessened sense of personal agency.

intelligence An inferred characteristic of an individual, usually defined as the ability to profit from experience, acquire knowledge, think abstractly, or adapt to changes in the environment.

Intelligence Quotient (IQ) A numerical figure, believed by some to indicate the level of a person's intelligence, and by others to indicate how well that person performs on intelligence tests.

interaction effect The result of at least two independent variables operating simultaneously on subjects' behaviour.

inter- As a prefix before any word, this means 'between'.

inter-coder reliability A phrase which describes the extent to which two independent observers (coders/raters) agree on the observations that they have made. Also known as inter-observer reliability and inter-rater reliability.

intergroup rivalry Competition between different social groups, which can often lead to powerful hostility.

internal attribution The judgement that a behaviour or act is caused by sources within the person – that is, their character, personality or intentions. This is also known as dispositional attribution.

internal consistency If a test is internally consistent then the items in that test really are measuring the same thing (or same set of things). Note that this does not necessarily mean that they are measuring what they are meant to measure. In this respect, internal consistency has more to do with reliability than validity.

internal locus of control The belief that important life events are largely caused by one's own efforts, abilities etc. as opposed to being caused by external circumstances.

inter-observer reliability *see inter-coder reliability.*

interpersonal Literally 'between persons', this term is used to describe actions or occurrences which involve at least two people affecting one another in some way.

interval scale As a rule the most sophisticated level of measurement used in psychological research, involving scales that are based on properly calibrated units of measurement. Interval scales can be used to measure people or things, and enable researchers to go beyond crude judgements about the rank ordering of scores. This is because the intervals between the scores from such a scale are meaningful (unlike the intervals between scores on an ordinal scale). See also *nominal scale* and *ordinal scale.*

intra- As a prefix before any word, this means 'within'.

intuitive thought Thought that predominantly uses the evidence from our senses.

irrational judgements Ones that are not supported by observation and do not appear logical.

jigsaw groups Technique used by Aronson to encourage group cohesion and the acceptance of outsiders.

Kaposi's sarcoma Disfiguring skin cancer found, most commonly in around 10 per cent of people who develop AIDS.

lateralization of function The distribution of some cognitive and motor functions to one hemisphere of the brain.

Law of Effect The learning principle that actions which have a pleasant effect on the organism are likely to be repeated.

learned helplessness The way that the experience of being forced into the role of passive victim in one situation can generalize to other situations, such that the person or animal makes no effort to help themselves in unpleasant situations even if such effort would be effective.

learning A change in behaviour, or the potential for behaviour, that occurs as a result of environmental experience, but is not the result of such factors as fatigue, drugs or injury.

learned reflex The end result of classical conditioning.

levels-of-processing theory The idea that what determines whether information is remembered, and for how long, is how deeply it is processed – that is, thought about and linked with other information.

libido Freud's concept of internal motivational energy commonly taken to mean the sex drive.

life events Major events that happen to an individual such as marriage, pregnancy, unemployment, relegation.

Likert scale Widely used in questionnaire studies and attitude surveys as the means by which subjects give 'ratings' in response to closed questions. The scale can be any size (often it is from 1–5 or 1–7), and each point on the scale is assigned a verbal designation. For example, on an attitude survey using a 5-point Likert scale, a rating of one might represent 'strongly agree', a rating of five might equal 'strongly disagree', a rating of three might equal 'neither agree nor disagree', and so forth.

linguistic environment A phrase used to describe the language that we hear and see around us.

living wills A legal document that prevents medical staff from keeping an individual alive by extraordinary means (not allowed in the UK).

Lloyd Morgan's canon This refers to the different ways that we can explain animal behaviour. For example, if we see a cat getting out of Thorndike's puzzle box (described in the introduction to Chapter 4) we might think that it had an understanding of the mechanism of the box and 'knew' how to get out. Alternatively, it might just have learned which behaviours will be followed by its release. The first explanation presumes that the cat has some complex thought processes, the latter does not. Lloyd Morgan suggested that descriptions of animal behaviour should always use the lowest level of explanation possible, and we should not presume that animals have complex mental processes unless we are unable to explain their behaviour in any other way.

locus of control Where control of what happens is perceived to come from. An internal locus of control means that the person sees it as coming from within themselves – so they are largely in control of what happens to them, or at least in a position to influence it. An external locus of control means that it is perceived as coming from sources outside of the person, and so is not something which the individual can influence.

longitudinal study A study which monitors changes occurring over a period of time.

LTM The common abbreviation for long-term memory.

magnetic resonance imaging Uses a combination of powerful magnets and radio pulses to construct an image of brain structures. Functional MRI (fMRI) requires participants to undertake some sort of task (without moving! – for example, watching a video or listening to audio stimuli) and measures changes in neural activity associated with the performance of that task. The great advantage of the MRI technique is that these scanners are relatively common in hospitals and can be converted for brain imaging without too much further expense.

magneto encephalography Uses very sensitive sensors to pick up the faint magnetic fields generated by active nerve networks. In order to pick up these very weak magnetic changes the MEG machines are exceptionally sensitive and can be affected by the movement of traffic in the street.

matriline A family tree based on the female line: that is, mothers, grandmothers, etc.

maturation A pre-programmed growth process based on changes in underlying neural structures that are relatively unaffected by environmental conditions.

median The middle score in a set.

medical model The approach to understanding abnormal behaviour adopted by members of the medical profession, for example psychiatrists.

memory The capacity to retain and retrieve information.

menarche The onset of menstruation.

menstruation The cyclic loss of blood by a woman, from her uterus (womb) when she is not pregnant. Menstruation generally occurs every four weeks after a woman has reached sexual maturity and prior to menopause.

mental representation A theoretical model of how we hold information in the brain.

microanalysis A detailed analysis of observational data, usually using film/ video material played back at slow speeds.

minimal group paradigm An approach to the study of social identification which involves creating artificial groups in the social psychology laboratory on the basic of spurious or minimal characteristics (for example, tossing a coin), and then studying the ingroup/outgroup effects which result.

mnemonics Strategies for helping people to remember information, usually involving cues such as rhyme or imagery.

monozygotic twin A twin from the splitting of one fertilized ovum; commonly an identical twin.

moral development The development of moral reasoning in children and adults concerning judgements of what is 'right' and what is 'wrong'.

moral reasoning Using cognitive processes to make judgements about right and wrong.

motherese A misleading label for the style of speech adults characteristically use when communicating with babies and very young children. It is misleading because all adults tend to use this style of speech, not just mothers. A more satisfactory label might be 'baby talk register'.

motion parallax A visual depth cue. Objects and surfaces which are nearer to the viewer move more quickly within the field of vision than do objects and surfaces which are further away. Such differences in the relative movement of things within the visual field facilitate judgements of distance.

MRI scans *see magnetic resonance imaging.*

multiple personality A dissociative disorder in which two or more personalities exist in the same individual, and each personality is relatively integrated and stable.

multiple regression Using the scores from more than one independent variable to predict scores of a dependent variable.

multi-store model Model of memory that proposes distinct memory stores, including long-term memory and short-term memory.

natural experiments (also quasi-experiments) Studies in which comparisons are made between different conditions that come about through natural political, social, economic or demographic circumstances, rather than through direct manipulation of a variable by an experimenter.

nature–nurture debates Fairly sterile theoretical debates, popular in the 1950s, concerning whether a given psychological ability was inherited or whether it was learned through experience.

negative reinforcement Encouraging a certain kind of behaviour by the removal or avoidance of an unpleasant stimulus.

neonates New-born animals.

neuroma Nerve nodule which develops at a point where nerves have been cut.

neuromatrix According to Melzack, network of neurons that responds to information from the senses and also generates a characteristic pattern of impulses that indicate the body is whole and is also your own.

neurosis A mental disorder where the patient commonly suffers from anxiety but remains in touch with reality.

neuroticism A personality dimension based on a person's measured susceptibility to neuroses.

neutral stimulus A stimulus that has no meaning for a person or animal before the onset of conditioning.

nominal scale The crudest level of measurement, which simply sorts people or things into categories (see also *ordinal scale* and *interval scale*).

non-shared environment The influences that make family members different (for example, being treated differently to our siblings by our parents).

normative Representing the norm; typical.

obedience Complying to the demands of others, usually those in positions of authority.

observation In its broadest sense this is the core of psychological research.

It is not just 'observational studies' that are based on 'observing'. On the contrary all empirical work is by definition grounded in the act of observation. Experimenters observe the behaviour of their subjects, interviewers observe the spoken responses of their subjects, discourse analysts observe the texts with which they are working, and so forth.

observational study A study which involves simply watching and recording what happens, rather than intervening and causing changes.

Oedipus complex According to Freud: the conflict between a boy's desire for his mother, and the fear of punishment by castration for that desire by his father.

olfaction The sense of smell.

omission A type of reinforcement regime where behaviour is shaped through continuous reinforcement except when unwanted behaviours occur. The technique of time-outs is sometimes referred to as an omission procedure.

operant conditioning The process of learning identified by B.F. Skinner, in which learning occurs as a result of positive or negative reinforcement of an animal or human being's action.

opinions Commonly used as a synonym for attitudes.

order effects A set of confounding variables which must be controlled against in experiments that use repeated measures designs. In the simplest case of a two-condition experiment, if all the subjects do condition A first, then condition B, and (for the sake of argument) perform better in condition B, a sceptic can argue that this is nothing to do with the experimenter's manipulation of the independent variable, but is simply due to the subjects having practised on condition A, and improved by the time they did condition B (a practice effect, which is one kind of order effect). Counterbalancing controls against this confounding variable by alternating the order in which subjects do the conditions of an experiment.

ordinal scale The most common level of measurement in psychological research, which involves assigning scores to people or things such that they can be rank ordered on the basis of those scores from most to least (or vice versa). Unlike interval scales, the raw data have to be converted into straightforward rank orderings before any further statistical procedures can be undertaken, because the size of the interval between the raw scores is meaningless (see also nominal scale and interval scale).

organic An organic condition is one that has a biological/physiological basis, as opposed to something like a neurosis, that is purported to have a psychogenic basis. Note 'organic' (biological/physiological) does not necessarily mean 'genetic'. Losing a leg in an accident results in an organic condition that is nothing to do with genetic predisposition.

orienting task This phrase is often used in connection with memory experiments. Orienting tasks are used in an attempt to get subjects to think about the stimulus materials in a certain way. In a word-list learning study, for example, some subjects might be oriented to think of the words in front of them as just collections of letters (perhaps by setting them the task of counting how many vowels there are) whilst other subjects are encouraged to think of the words in terms of their meanings (perhaps by getting them to fit the words together into sentences). Typically subjects' performance across orienting tasks is compared.

outgroup A group you define yourself as not belonging to.

paranoia An irrational fear, suspicion or distrust of others.

participant observation A method of study in which the investigator joins in the social process being observed.

pathology of power According to Zimbardo: the syndrome of oppressive behaviour that develops in people given the opportunity to exert personal power over another individual.

pattern density A visual depth cue. If you move away from a pattern such as a check, then the elements of the pattern get smaller as you move away and the pattern appears to get more dense.

pecking order A hierarchy first observed in chickens where the most dominant animal has preferential access to food, mating, videos etc.

peer group A group of people who are considered to be the equals of, or like, the person concerned.

people of colour A term used (mainly in the United States) to refer to people who are not White and European. It is used to include people from Asia, and Hispanics, as well as Black people.

perception The process by which the brain organizes and interprets sensory information.

perceptual acuity Visual resolution or clarity.

performance This refers to what a person actually *does*, which for many reasons may not represent well what that person is really capable of (their 'competence').

person recognition A key phrase used to label studies which look at the cognitive processes involved in recognizing other people. Understanding how we are able to recognize others is a non-trivial task, as has been shown by early attempts to get computers to recognize people.

personal constructs Individual ways of making sense of the world, which have been developed on the basis of experience. Personal construct theorists argue that getting to understand the personal constructs which someone applies to make sense of their experience is essential for effective psychotherapy, as well as for effective interaction in day to day living.

personal space The physical distance which people like to maintain between themselves and others. This varies according to their relationship with and attitude to other people, and according to norms and contexts.

personality A distinctive and relatively stable pattern of behaviours, thoughts, motives and emotions that characterize an individual.

personality type A simple of classification of people into narrow stereotypes, for example extravert.

PET scans see *positron emission tomography.*

phantom limb The name given to the phenomenon experienced by amputees of still feeling the limb as present and alive even though it has been surgically removed.

phenomenological Concerned with the person's own perceived world and the phenomena which they experience, rather than with objective reality.

phobia An anxiety disorder characterized by persistent fear out of proportion to the danger, a compelling desire to escape the situation, and a recognition that the fear is excessive.

phenomes The basic units of sound in a language.

phylogenetic To do with the evolution of a species. If a feature of an organism is said to be 'phylogenetically' old, it means that it appeared early in the species' evolutionary history.

placebo effect An inactive substance or fake treatment that produces a response in patients.

plasticity The capacity for change within a system. If a system is 'plastic' it is capable of change. Plasticity is a feature of the newborn baby's brain and the neural basis for development and learning.

pleasure centres Areas of the brain identified by Olds and Milner (1954) that when stimulated have strong reinforcing properties.

pluralistic ignorance The tendency for people in a group to mislead each other about a situation; for example, an individual might define an emergency as a non-emergency because others are remaining calm and not taking action.

population In the context of research methods in psychology this refers to the total set of potential observations from which a sample is drawn.

population norms A set of scores for a particular population (for example, females aged 18–24) which establishes the normal range of scores for that population, on a particular psychometric test or measure. Tables of populations norms are used to judge whether an individual's test result is typical for their population group or not.

positive reinforcement In operant conditioning, strengthening learned behaviour by direct reward when it occurs.

positron emission tomography (PET) Uses radioactivity to label blood, blood sugars or important neurotransmitters such as dopamine. The labelled substance is then injected into mugs (sorry, volunteers) while they lie in the scanner and carry out mental tasks such as problem solving. The scanner picks up the gamma rays emission to find out where the labelled substances are active in the brain. This requires a fair amount of computer processing because the PET scanner has to sift through around 7–8 million gamma-ray signals a second. PET scanning is the most established of the brain imaging techniques but requires massive investment.

posterior An anatomical term denoting the opposite of the anterior end of an organism. In terms of the human brain, this equates to the 'back' of the brain.

post-traumatic stress disorder An anxiety disorder resulting from experience with a catastrophic event beyond the normal range of human suffering, and characterized by (a) numbness to the world, (b) reliving the trauma in dreams and memories, and (c) symptoms of anxiety.

predictive validity A method of assessing whether a psychometric test is valid (that is, really measures what it is supposed to) by seeing how well it correlates with some other measure, which is assessed later, after the test has been taken.

prejudice A fixed, pre-set attitude, usually negative and hostile, and usually applied to members of a particular social category.

pre-operational stage Piaget's second main stage of cognitive development where the child's ability to reason is limited by their difficulty in mentally manipulating symbols.

projective tests Psychometric tests which involve providing the person with ambiguous stimuli, and seeing what meanings they read into them. The idea is that this will illustrate the concerns of the unconscious mind.

pro-social Any behaviour intended to help or benefit another person, group or society.

pseudo experiment See *natural experiments*.

pseudopatient In Rosenhan's study, the name given to people who feigned mental ill health.

psychiatrist A person who trains as a doctor and then specializes in mental disorders.

psychoanalysis Freud's theory of personality which describes how human behaviour is affected by unconscious thought and feelings.

psychoanalyst Therapist who is trained in psychoanalysis and employs its methods in treating emotional disorders (commonly with a beard and a central European accent).

psychodynamic Dealing with psychological forces that influence the mind and behaviour.

psychogenetic A psychogenetic condition is one that is held to have no physiological basis (in contrast to an organic condition), and that is based in instead on 'psychological' factors (such as a neurosis).

psychology The scientific study of experience and behaviour. Psychology draws together systematic studies of experience and behaviour using a wide range of methods, and focusing on many different angles and levels of experience.

psychometric tests Instruments which have been developed for measuring mental characteristics. Psychological tests have been developed to measure a wide range of things, including creativity, job attitudes and skills, brain damage and, of course, 'intelligence'.

psychosis A mental state characterized by profound disturbances in reality testing, thought and emotion.

punishment According to behaviourist theory: anything that decreases the probability that a behaviour will recur in similar circumstances. More popularly: an aversive stimulus.

qualitative data Data which describe meaning and experience rather than providing numerical values for behaviour such as frequency counts.

quantitative data Data which focus on numbers and frequencies rather than on meaning or experience.

quasi-experiment See *natural experiments*.

race Commonly used to refer to groups of people such as White people or Black people etc. It implies a genetic component to the differences between these groups, but research shows that the term 'race' has no biological validity and is best described as a political construct.

racism Using the pervasive power imbalance between races /people to oppress dominated peoples by devaluing their experience, behaviour and aspirations.

random assignment Allocating subjects to experimental conditions by using chance, such as a toss of a coin.

random sample A way of selecting a sample where every person from the defined population has an equal chance of being chosen.

rating scale See *Likert scale*.

rational–emotive therapy A form of psychotherapy which mixes rational argument with positive reward systems.

reactivity A term used to describe the way in which the behaviour of research subjects can be affected by some aspect of the research procedure. Most commonly it is used to describe the way in which the behaviour of someone who is being observed is affected by the knowledge that they are being observed.

reductionism An approach to understanding behaviour which focuses on one single level of explanation and ignores others. The opposite of holism.

reflex An automatic reaction to a stimulus: often inborn but can also be learned or modified by experience.

regression Technique for predicting scores on one variable given the values from another.

reinforcement Any consequence of any behaviour that increases the probability that that behaviour will recur in similar circumstances. The term is usually used of learned associations, acquired through operant conditioning, but it may also be applied to other forms of learning.

reinforcement contingencies The conditions under which positive or negative reinforcement are given.

reliability The reliability of a psychological measuring device (such as a test or a scale) is the extent to which it gives consistent measurements. The greater the consistency of measurement, the greater the tool's reliability.

REM Rapid eye movements during sleep.

repeated measures design (also within groups) An experimental design where each subject carries out each condition of the experiment.

repeated reproduction A method used by Bartlett where the subject is asked to keep remembering the same event or drawing in order to investigate the systematic changes that people make in their memories.

repertory grid technique A system for eliciting personal constructs and showing how individuals use them to interpret their experience.

repression A coping strategy in which a person forces unwanted thoughts or feelings out of their conscious awareness into their unconscious.

restricted language codes Ways of using language characterized by limited vocabulary, simple grammatical structures, and a heavy reliance on shared implicit meaning and paralinguistic cues.

role A social part that one plays in society.

Rorschach test A personality test made up of bilaterally symmetrical ink-blots. The test is designed to encourage the subject to project their unconscious fears and conflicts onto the ink-blots so that their description of what they see in the inkblots should shine some light on their unconscious.

saccades Eye movements used to quickly relocate the eyes from one position of gaze to another.

sample The group of subjects used in a study: the selection of people, animals, plants or objects drawn from a population for the purposes of studying that population.

schema A mental framework or structure which encompasses memories, ideas, concepts and programmes for action which are pertinent to a particular topic.

schizophrenia A mental disorder marked by some, or all of the following symptoms: delusions, hallucinations, incoherent word associations, inappropriate emotions or lack of emotions.

scientific racism The use of bogus scientific arguments to enhance the power of one group of people over another.

selective attention The ability to direct our cognitive focus so that we pay attention to some stimuli and ignore or pay less attention to others.

self-actualization The making real of one's abilities and talents: using them to the full.

self-concept The idea or internal image that people have of what they themselves are like, including both evaluative and descriptive dimensions.

self-efficacy beliefs The belief that one is capable of doing something effectively. Self-efficacy beliefs are closely connected with self-esteem, in that having a sense of being capable and potentially in control tends to increase confidence. But the concept is often thought to be more useful than the generalized concept of self-esteem, since people may often be confident about some abilities, or in some areas of their lives, but not in others.

self-esteem The evaluative dimension of the self-concept, which is to do with how worthwhile and/or confident the person feels about themselves.

self-fulfilling prophecy The idea that expectations about a person or group can become true simply because they have been stated.

self-injurious behaviour Behaviour which causes either physical or mental harm to the self. In extreme cases, self-injurious behaviour can become life threatening.

self-report A number of popular research methods are based on self-report: for example, questionnaires, interviews, attitude scales and diary methods. These are methods which rely on research subjects' accounts of their own experiences and behaviour.

semantic To do with meaning.

sensory buffer Short-acting memory store for the sensory record of a stimulus.

sensory deprivation The cutting out of all incoming sensory information, or at least as much of it as possible. Sometimes used as a method of torture.

sensory mode The route by which information comes to the brain; for example, through vision, hearing, smell.

sensory-motor stage The first of Piaget's stages of cognitive development where the infant learns to connect its sensations to its actions.

serial position curve A technique in memory research which looks at the effect of the position of a word in a list on the probability of it being recalled.

serial reproduction A method of examining the accuracy of memory by asking people to reproduce what they recall of a story, on several successive occasions.

set In psychology, commonly refers to perceptual set which is a preparedness (or expectation) to see particular forms or patterns.

sex differences A large body of psychological research exists which documents differences between females and males.

sexism Using the pervasive power imbalance between men and women to oppress women by devaluing their experience, behaviour and aspirations.

sexologist Someone who makes a systematic study of human sexuality.

shaped behaviour Behaviour that has been moulded by the method of successive approximations.

shaping The 'moulding' of behaviour by the method of successive approximations, or by the naturally occurring contingencies of reinforcement delivered by the environment.

shared environment All environmental influences that make children in families similar to one another (for example being treated the same as our siblings by our parents).

shuttle box Piece of equipment used by behaviourists to measure learning in animals, in which an animal commonly has to learn to jump from one side of the box to the other in order to avoid an electric shock.

siblings Brothers and sisters.

sign stimuli A simple sign provokes the response of a fixed action pattern.

simulation A method of investigation where the participants act out a particular scene or pattern of behaviours.

situational attribution A reason for an act or behaviour which implies that it occurred as a result of the situation or circumstances that the person was in at the time.

six degrees of separation The theory that anyone on the planet can be connected to any other person on the planet through a chain of acquaintances that has no more than five intermediaries. The theory was first proposed in 1929 by the Hungarian writer Frigyes Karinthy in a short story called 'Chains'.

sleep deprivation A lack of the necessary amount of sleep brought about by neurological or psychological or social causes, and creating a range of negative psychological and bodily effects. Sometimes used as a form of torture.

small-world problem The idea that everyone in the world can be connected through a very short chain of acquaintances.

social cognition The way that we think about and interpret social information and social experience. In developmental psychology, the term refers to a theory of cognitive development which states that social interaction is the most important factor in a young child's cognitive development.

Social identity theory An approach which states that the social groups and categories to which we belong are an important part of our self-concept, and therefore a person will sometimes interact with other people, not as a single individual, but as a representative of a whole group or category of people. There are three basic psychological processes underlying social identification which are categorization, social comparison and self-concept.

Social Learning Theory The approach to understanding social behaviour which emphasizes how people imitate action and model their behaviour on that of others.

social norms Socially or culturally accepted standards of behaviour, which have become accepted as representing how people 'ought' to act and what is 'normal' (that is, appropriate) for a given situation.

Social Re-adjustment Rating Scale Holmes and Rahe's attempt to quantify stressors by giving a stress value to a number of major life events.

social support The perceived comfort, caring esteem or help which an individual receives from other people or groups of people.

socialization The processes whereby a person learns the moral standards, codes of conduct, role expectations and role performances in their society.

social-learning See *Social Learning Theory*.

sociolinguist A person who specializes in studying sociological aspects of language.

somnambulist A sleep walker.

spinal cord The bundle of nerve fibres that runs up the spine to the brain. It is the pathway by which the brain sends and receives neural messages from the rest of the body.

split-half method A system for judging how reliable a psychometric test is which involves splitting the test into two, and administering each half of the test to the same people, then comparing the results.

split-span procedure Experimental procedure in which the participant is presented with two sets of stimuli simultaneously, one to each ear, and must divide their attention between them.

S-R learning See *stimulus–response learning*.

standard deviation A measure of dispersion.

standardization (a) The process of making sure that the conditions of a psychological study or psychometric test are always identical: (b) the process of establishing how the results of a psychometric test will usually come out in a given population, by drawing up sets of population norms: and (c) the process of comparing a new psychometric test with older, more established measures of the same thing.

stimulus An external environmental event to which an organism responds.

stimulus–response learning The name given to the behaviourist approach to learning, which viewed it as a simple association between an external stimulus and the behavioural response, denying any cognitive or mental processing.

STM The abbreviation used for short-term memory, or memory which lasts for only a few seconds.

stress experience How we perceive the situation and the experiences we are having. The experience of stress is affected by our cognitive appraisal of the situation that we are in, so stress is not inevitable. We might easily see an event as exciting rather than stressful.

stress inoculation The suggestion by Janis that people handle stress most effectively if they feel they are in control of their lives. To achieve this, he proposes 'stress inoculation' in which people: (1) are given information about what to expect. which is realistic but which still allows them to maintain optimism; (2) are encouraged to identify possible actions that can help them to survive and to find internal and external resources that allow them to take those actions; and (3) are helped to develop their own plan for responding to the situation.

stress response Physiological changes, such as autonomic arousal, which occur as a result of stress.

stressors Environmental changes that can induce a stress response.

structured observation A method of recording behaviour where the behaviours are pre-categorized into a limited framework.

successive approximations From the vocabulary of behaviourism, this refers to behaviours that are increasingly similar to a target behaviour.

superordinate goal A goal that over-rides existing goals.

surrogate Substitute.

survey A technique of collecting opinions from large numbers of people, generally involving the use of questionnaires.

symptom substitution The situation where the treatment and removal of one symptom is ultimately followed by the development of another symptom, because the cause of the disorder has not been dealt with.

synaesthesia A mixing of the senses. For example a synaesthete might hear colours, see sounds, and taste tactile sensations.

synapses Connections between nerve cells.

syntax The rules of grammar.

systematic desensitization A classical conditioning technique for reducing fear and anxiety by replacing it with a calm response.

tachistoscope Apparatus for presenting brief visual displays.

task-oriented leaders Leaders who focus explicitly on the tasks which have to be done by the team, and who show little or no interest in interpersonal concerns within it, unlike relationship-oriented leaders.

taxonomy A set of categories.

technological addictions Non-chemical (behavioural) addictions which involve human–machine interactions. A behavioural addiction refers to a repetitive activity which becomes the single most important thing in a person's life. It is carried out to the neglect of everything else and is used as a reliable and consistent way of modifying mood. Tolerance to it builds up over time, and removal of the behaviour creates withdrawal symptoms. The behaviour compromises everything else in that person's life including their relationships, job and hobbies.

temperament The stable aspects of the character of an individual, which are often regarded as biologically based, and as providing the basic dispositions which interact with the environment to develop personality.

territoriality The name given to a set of behaviours which involve establishing and maintaining access to a particular area while refusing the same to potential competitors of one's own species.

territory The space that is defended by a person or animal.

test–retest method A system for judging how reliable a psychometric test or measure is, which involves administering the same test to the same people on two different occasions, and comparing the results.

thalamus The sub-cortical structure in the brain which receives sensory information and relays it to the cerebral cortex.

theory of mind The understanding we have that other people have their own thoughts and beliefs about the world, which may differ from our own thoughts and beliefs.

therapy The treatment of an individual by physical or psychological means.

T-maze A piece of equipment used by behaviourists to measure learning in animals, so called because it has one choice point for the animal and so resembles a T.

Tourette Syndrome A neurological disorder that develops in childhood and is characterized by unwanted and uncontrolled movements and vocal tics.

trait A specific facet of personality.

transsexual An individual whose gender identity does not match the sex that was assigned to them at birth.

***t*-test** A statistical test that computes the likelihood of achieving a particular difference between the means of two sets of scores.

Turing test In the Turing test a subject communicates via computer keyboard with two 'people' who are hidden from view; one of these people is a real person, and the other is a computer program. If the subject cannot reliably identify which is the computer and which is the person, then the computer program has passed the test and can be said to be able to think and understand.

twin studies Family-based studies that look for the relative influence of genetic and environmental factors on a range of social and cognitive qualities.

Type A behaviour pattern A pattern of behaviour characterized by (1) an intense, sustained drive to achieve your personal (and often poorly defined) goals, (2) a profound tendency and eagerness to compete in all situations, (3) a persistent desire for recognition and advancement, (4) continuous involvement in several activities at the same time that are constantly subject to deadlines, (5) habitual tendency to rush to finish activities, and (6) extraordinary mental and physical alertness.

Type B behaviour pattern A pattern of behaviour which is the opposite of Pattern A – characterized by the relative absence of drive, ambition, urgency, desire to compete, or involvement in deadlines.

tyranny 'An unequal social system involving the arbitrary or oppressive use of power by one group or its agents over another' (Reicher and Haslam, 2006, p. 2).

uncertainty The feeling of uncertainty occurs when someone lacks a cognitive framework to understand their condition or situation, and when they cannot predict outcomes of their behaviour or condition.

unconditioned response A response which occurs automatically to a particular stimulus, and doesn't have to be learned.

unconditioned stimulus A stimulus which automatically, or reflexively produces a response.

unconscious mind The part of our mind that is beyond our conscious awareness.

universal grammar The cognitive structures of language that are observed in all known human languages and which are therefore said to be universal.

uplifts Minor events that produce a raising of a persons mood.

validity The question of whether a psychometric test or psychological measure is really measuring what it is supposed to.

verbal deprivation hypothesis The idea that children who do not experience extended forms of language may suffer cognitive deficits as a consequence.

vicarious reinforcement A form of reinforcement said to occur when an individual observes someone else being rewarded for a particular behaviour.

War on Terror The rhetorical centrepiece of US foreign policy in the early years of the twenty-first century; refers to unlimited military action against undefined people in undefined places with undefined ideas, loosely described as 'the bad guys'.

wet nurse A woman who breast feeds another woman's child.

yoked control A yoked control experiences the same physical events as a member of the experimental condition, but whereas the experimental condition is able to influence these events, the yoked control is not.

zone of proximal development (ZPD) A Vygotskian concept describing the difference between what a child can achieve on a task alone and what that child can achieve on the same task with help.

REFERENCES

Adorno, T.W., Frenkel-Brunswik, G., Levinson, D.J. and Sanford, R.N. (1950). *The Authoritarian Personality*. New York: Harper.

Aitchison J. (1983). *The Articulate Mammal: An Introduction to Psycholinguistics*. London: Routledge.

Alexander, G.M. and Hines, M. (2002). Sex differences in response to children's toys in nonhuman primates. *Evolution and Human Behavior*, 23, 467–79.

Allport, G.W. (1958). *The Nature of Prejudice*. New York: Anchor.

Allport, G.W. and Odbert, H.S. (1936). Traitnames: a psycho-lexical study. *Psychological Monographs*, 47 (no. 211).

Anon. (1989). Biography of George Sperling. *American Psychologist*, 44, 626–8.

Asch, S.E. (1955). Opinions and social pressure. *Scientific American*, 193, 31–5.

Atkinson, R.C. and Shiffrin, R.M. (1968). Human memory: a proposed system and its control processes. In K.W. Spence and J.T. Spence (eds), *The Psychology of Learning and Motivation*, Volume 2, pp. 89–197. New York: Academic Press.

Austin, A.M.B. and Peery, J.C. (1983). Analysis of adult–neonate synchrony during speech and nonspeech. *Perceptual and Motor Skills*, 57, 455–59.

Azibo, D.A.Y. (1996). *African Psychology in Historical Perspective and Related Commentary*. Trenton, N.J.: Africa World Press.

Baddeley, A.D. (1966). How does acoustic similarity influence short-term memory? *Quarterly Journal of Experimental Psychology*, 20, 249–64.

Bakeman, R. and Gottman, J.M. (1986). *Observing Interaction: An Introduction to Sequential Analysis*. Cambridge: Cambridge University Press.

Bales, R.F. (1955). How people interact in conferences. *Scientific American*, 192, 31–5.

Bandura, A., Ross, D. and Ross, S.A. (1961). Transmission of aggression through imitation of aggressive models. *Journal of Abnormal and Social Psychology*, 63, 575–82.

Bandura, A., Ross, D. and Ross, S.A. (1963). Imitation of film-mediated aggressive models. *Journal of Abnormal and Social Psychology*, 66, 3–11.

Banyard, P. and Flanagan, C. (2006). *AS Core Studies: Psychology*. Hove: Psychology Press.

Banyard, P. and Hayes, N. (1994) *Psychology: Theory and Application*. London: Chapman and Hall.

Banyard, P. and Hunt, N. (2000). Reporting research: something missing? *The Psychologist*, 12 (2).

Baron, R.A. and Byrne, D. (1991). *Social Psychology: Understanding Human Interactions*, 6th Edition. Boston: Allyn and Bacon.

Baron-Cohen, S. (1995). *Mindblindness: An Essay on Autism and Theory of Mind*. Cambridge, Mass.: MIT Press.

Baron-Cohen, S. (2002). The extreme male brain theory of autism. *Trends in Cognitive Sciences*, 6, 248–54.

Baron-Cohen, S., Jolliffe, T., Mortimore, C. and Robertson, M. (1997). Another advanced test of theory of mind: evidence from very high functioning adults with autism or Asperger Syndrome. *Journal of Child Psychology and Psychiatry*, 38, 813–22.

Baron-Cohen, S., Leslie, A.M. and Frith, U. (1985). Does the autistic child have a 'theory of mind'? *Cognition*, 21, 37–46.

Bartlett, F.C. (1932). *Remembering: A Study in Experimental and Social Psychology*. Cambridge: Cambridge University Press.

Baumrind, D. (1964). Some thoughts on the ethics of research: after reading Milgram's 'Behavioural study of obedience'. *American Psychologist*, 19, 421–3.

BBC website (2003). Sesame Street breaks Iraqi POWs. Available at http://news.bbc.co.uk/1/hi/world/middle_east/3042907.stm (accessed July 2007).

BBC website (2004). 'Biological key' to unlocking crime. Available at http://news.bbc.co.uk/1/hi/programmes/if/4102371.stm (accessed July 2007).

BBC website (2005) Reliving the London bomb horror. Available at http://news.bbc.co.uk/1/hi/uk/4346812.stm (accessed December 2005).

BBC website (2007). No charge for sat-nav rail driver. Available at http://news.bbc.co.uk/1/hi/england/6430859.stm (accessed March 2007).

Becker, M.H. and Rosenstock, I.M. (1984). Compliance with medical advice. In A. Steptoe and A. Mathews (eds), *Health Care and Human Behaviour*, pp. 135–52. London: Academic Press.

Bem, S.L. (1974). The measurement of psychological androgyny. *Journal of Consulting and Clinical Psychology*, 42, 155–62.

Berne, E. (1968). *Games People Play: The Psychology of Human Relationships*. Harmondsworth: Penguin.

Bernstein D.M., Laney, C., Morris, E.K. and Loftus, E.F. (2005). False memories about food can lead to food avoidance. *Social Cognition*, 23, 11–34.

Bernstein, B. (1959). A public language: some sociological implications of a linguistic form. *British Journal of Sociology*, 10, 311–26.

Bernstein, B. (1960). Language and social class. *British Journal of Sociology*, 11, 271–76.

Bettelheim, R. (1967). *Empty Fortress: Infantile Autism and the Birth of Self*. New York: Free Press.

Blass, T. (2004). *The Man Who Shocked the World: The Life and Legacy of Stanley Milgram*. New York: Basic Books.

Boden, M.A. (1977). *Artificial Intelligence and Natural Man.* Brighton: Harvester Press.

Boden, M.A. (1979). *Piaget.* London: Fontana.

Bowlby, J. (1951). *Maternal Care and Mental Health.* Geneva: World Health Organisation.

Bowlby, J. (1965). *Child Care and the Growth of Love,* 2nd edn. London: Penguin.

Brazelton, T.B. (1973). *Neonatal Behavioral Assessment Scale.* London: Heinemann.

Brazelton, T.B., Koslowski, B. and Tronick, E. (1976). Neonatal behavior among urban Zambians and Americans. *Journal of Child Psychiatry,* 15, 97–107.

British Psychological Society (2006). *Code of Ethics and Conduct.* Leicester: BPS.

Broadbent, D. (1954). The role of auditory localization in attention and memory span. *Journal of Experimental Psychology,* 47, 191–196.

Brown, R. (1988). Intergroup relations. In M. Hewstone, W. Stoebe, J. Codol and G. Stephenson (eds), *Introduction to Social Psychology: A European Perspective,* pp. 381–412. Oxford: Blackwell.

Bryant, P.E., Bradley, L., Maclean, M. and Crossland, J. (1989). Nursery rhymes, phonological skills and reading. *Journal of Child Language,* 16, 407–28.

Bryant, P.E., MacLean, M., Bradley, L.L. and Crossland, J. (1990). Rhyme and alliteration, phoneme detection, and learning to read. *Developmental Psychology,* 26 (3), 429–38.

Calhoun, J.B. (1962). Population density and social pathology. *Scientific American,* 206, 139–48.

Cannon, W.B. (1929). *Bodily Changes in Pain, Hunger, Fear and Rage.* New York: Appleton.

Carnahan, T. and McFarland, S.G. (2007). Revisiting the Stanford Prison experiment: could participant self-selection have led to the cruelty? *Personality and Social Psychology Bulletin,* 33, 603–14.

Carroll, P.J., Young, J.R. and Guertin, M.S. (1992). Visual analysis of cartoons: a view from the far side. In K. Raynor (ed.), *Eye Movements and Visual Cognition: Scene Perception and Reading,* pp. 444–61. New York: Springer-Verlag.

Casarett, D., Fishman, J.M., MacMoran, H.J., Pickard, A. and Asch, D.A. (2005). Epidemiology and prognosis of coma in daytime television dramas. *British Medical Journal,* 331, 24–31.

Cattell, R.B., Eber, H.J., and Tatsuoka, M.M. (1970). Handbook for the Sixteen Personality Factor Questionnaire (16 PF). Champaign, Ill.: Institute for Personality and Ability Testing.

Cherry, C.E. (1953). Some experiments on the recognition of speech, with one and with two ears. *The Journal of the Acoustical Society of America,* 25 (5), 975–9.

Chomsky, N. (1957). *Syntactic Structures.* The Hague: Mouton.

Clark, K.B. and Clark, M.K. (1947). Racial identification and preference in Negro children. In T. Newcomb and E. Hartley (eds), *Readings in Social Psychology,* pp. 169–78. New York: Holt.

Clarke, A.M. and Clarke, A.D.B. (1998). Early experience and life path. *The Psychologist,* 11, 433–36.

Colapinto, J. (2000). *As Nature Made Him: The Boy Who Was Raised As a Girl*. New York: HarperCollins.

Colapinto, John (2004). Gender gap: what were the real reasons behind David Reimer's suicide? *Slate Magazine*, 3 June. Available at http://slate.msn.com/id/2101678/ (accessed 15 February 2007).

Collins, A.M., and Loftus, E.F. (1975). A spreading-activation theory of semantic processing. *Psychological Review*, 82, 407–428.

Collins, A.M. and Quillian, M.R. (1969). Retrieval time from semantic memory. *Journal of Verbal Learning and Verbal Behavior*, 8, 240–247.

Colman, A.M. (1987). *Facts, Fallacies and Frauds in Psychology*. London: Unwin Hyman.

Concar, D. (1994). Prisoners of pleasure. *New Scientist*, 1 October, 26–31.

Condon, W.S. and Brosin, H.W. (1969). Micro linguistic-kinesic events in schizophrenic behavior. In D.V.S. Sankar (ed.), *Schizophrenia: Current Concepts and Research*, pp. 812–37. Hicksville, N.Y.: PJD Publications.

Condon, W.S. and Ogston, W.D. (1966). Sound film analysis of normal and pathological behavior patterns. *Journal of Nervous and Mental Disease*, 143, 338–47.

Condon, W.S. and Sander, L.W. (1974). Neonate movement is synchronized with adult speech: interactional participation and language acquisition. *Science*, 183, 99–101.

Conrad, R. (1964). Acoustic confusions in immediate memory. *British Journal of Psychology*, 55, 75–84.

Costa, P.T. and McCrae, R.R. (1985). *The NEO Personality Inventory Manual*. Odessa, Fla.: Psychological Assessment Resources.

Craik, F.I.M. and Lockhart, R.S. (1972). Levels of processing: a framework for memory research. *Journal of Verbal Learning and Verbal Behaviour*, 11, 671–84.

Crook, L.S. and Dean, M.C. (1999). 'Lost in a shopping mall': a breach of professional ethics. *Ethics and Behavior*, 9, 39–50.

Cutler, B.L. and Penrod, S.D. (1995). *Mistaken Identification: The Eyewitness, Psychology and the Law*. New York: Cambridge University Press.

Daley, K. (1987). Encouraging 'habitual' gambling in poker machines. In M.B. Walker (ed.), *Faces of Gambling*, pp. 235–44. Sydney: National Association of Gambling Studies.

Daly, M. and Wilson, M. (1998). *The Truth About Cinderella: Darwinian View of Parenting*. London: Weidenfeld and Nicolson.

Delgardo, J.M.R. (1969). *Physical control of the mind*. New York: Harper and Row.

Della Salla, S. (2005). The anarchic hand. *The Psychologist*, 18, 606–9.

Dement, W. and Kleitman, N. (1957). The relation of eye movements during sleep to dream activity: an objective method for the study of dreaming. *Journal of Experimental Psychology*, 53, 339–46.

Dement, W. and Wolpert, E.A. (1958). The relation of eye movements, body motility, and external stimuli to dream content. Journal *of Experimental Psychology*, 55, 543–53.

Deregowski, J.B. (1972). Pictorial perception and culture. *Scientific American*, 227, 82–8.

Deutsch, M. and associates (eds) (1967). *The Disadvantaged Child*. New York: Basic Books.

Diamond, M. and Sigmundson, K. (1997). Sex reassignment at birth: a long term review and clinical implications. *Archives of Pediatric and Adolescent Medicine*, 151, 298–304.

Dodds, P., Muhamad, R. and Watts, D. (2003). An experimental study of search in global social networks. *Science*, 301, 827–9.

Domjan, M. and Purdy, J.E. (1995). Animal research in psychology: more than meets the eye of the general psychology student. *American Psychologist*, 50, 496–503.

Doms, M. and Avermaet, E. van (1981). The conformity effect: a timeless phenomenon? *Bulletin of the British Psychological Society*, 34, 383–5.

Donaldson, M. (1978). *Children's Minds*. London: Fontana.

Dunbar, R.I.M. (1992). Neocortex size as a constraint on group size in primates. *Journal of Human Evolution*, 22, 469–93.

Dunbar, R.I.M. (1993). Coevolution of neocortical size, group size and language in humans. *Behavioral and Brain Sciences*, 16 (4), 681–735.

Dunn, J. and Deater-Deckard, K. (2001). *Children's Views of Their Changing Families*. York: YPS/Joseph Rowntree Foundation.

Ebbinghaus, H. (1913). *Memory*. New York: Teacher's College Press.

Edwards, J. (1979). *Language and Disadvantage*. London: Arnold.

Elkan, R., Kendrick, D., Hewitt, M., Robinson, J.J.A., Tolley, K., Blair, M., Dewey, M., Williams, D. and Brummell, K. (2003). The effectiveness of domiciliary health visiting: a systematic review of international studies and a selective review of the British literature. *Health Technology Assessment*. 4 (13), 339.

Empson, J. (1989). *Sleep and Dreaming*. London: Faber and Faber.

Eysenck, H.J. (1947). *Dimensions of Personality*. Oxford: Kegan Paul.

Fernald, A. (1985). Four-month-old infants prefer to listen to motherese. *Infant Behavior and Development*, 8, 181–95.

Festinger, L. (1957). *A Theory of Cognitive Dissonance*. Evanston Ill.: Row Peterson.

Festinger, L. and Carlsmith, J.M. (1959). Cognitive consequences of forced compliance. *Journal of Abnormal and Social Psychology*, 58, 203–10.

Fiedler, F.E. (1967). *A Theory of Leadership Effectiveness*. New York: McGraw-Hill.

Findley, M. and Cooper, H. (1981). Introductory psychology textbook citations: a comparison in five research areas. *Personality and Social Psychology Bulletin*, 7, 173–76.

Fischhoff, B, Gonzalez, R., Lerner, J. and Small, D. (2005). Evolving judgements of terror risks: foresight, hindsight and emotion. *Journal of Experimental Psychology: Applied*, 2, 124–39.

Forer, B.R. (1949). The fallacy of personal validation: a classroom demonstration of gullibility. *Journal of Abnormal and Social Psychology*, 44, 118–21.

Fox News (2006). Ky. man freed from jail on dna evidence tries to sue city. Available at http://www.foxnews.com/story/0,2933,191446,00.html (accessed February, 2007).

Fransella, F. and Thomas, L. (eds) (1988). *Experimenting with Personal Construct Theory*. London: Routledge and Kegan Paul.

Freud, S. (1909). Analysis of a phobia of a five-year-old boy. In *The Pelican Freud Library* (1977), Vol. 8, Case Histories 1, pp. 169–306. Harmondsworth: Penguin.

Friedman, M. and Rosenman, R.H. (1959). Association of specific overt behavior pattern with blood and cardiovascular findings. *Journal of American Medical Association*, 169, 1286–96.

Frith, U. (2003). *Autism: Explaining the Enigma*, 2nd edn. Oxford: Basil Blackwell.

Furnham, A. and Varian, C. (1988). Predicting and accepting personality test scores. *Personality and Individual Differences*, 9, 735–48.

Gansberg, M. (1964). Thirty-eight who saw murder didn't call the police. *New York Times*, 27 March.

Gardner, R.A. and Gardner, B.T. (1969). Teaching sign language to a chimpanzee. *Science*, 165, 664–72.

Gatewood, J.B. and Rosenwein, R. (1981). Interactional synchrony: genuine or spurious? A critique of recent research. *Journal of Nonverbal Behavior*, 6, 12–29.

Gergen, M.M. (1988). Building a feminist methodology. *Contemporary Social Psychology*, 13, 47–53.

Gibson, E.J. and Walk, R.D. (1960). The 'visual cliff'. *Scientific American*, 202, 64–71.

Gilovich, T. (1983). Biased evaluations and persistence in gambling. *Journal of Personality and Social Psychology*, 44, 1100–26.

Gladwell, M. (2002). *The Tipping Point: How Little Things Can Make a Big Difference*. London: Abacus.

Glenn, S.M. and Cunningham, C.C. (1983). What do babies listen to most? A developmental study of auditory preferences in nonhandicapped infants and infants with Down's Syndrome. *Developmental Psychology*, 19, 332–7.

Goldberg, E.L. and Comstock, G.W. (1980). Epidemiology of life events: frequency in general populations. *American Journal of Epidemiology*, 111, 736–52.

Goodenough, D.R., Shapiro, A., Holden, M. and Steinschriber, L. (1959). Dreamers and non-dreamers. *Journal of Abnormal and Social Psychology*, 59, 295–302.

Gould, S.J. (1981). *The Mismeasure of Man*. Harmondsworth: Penguin.

Gould, S.J. (1982). A nation of morons. *New Scientist*, 6 May, 349–52.

Gray, J.A. and Wedderburn, A.A.I. (1960). Grouping strategies with simultaneous stimuli. *Quarterly Journal of Experimental Psychology*, 12, 180–4.

Grayson, A. (2006). Autism and developmental psychology. In C.P. Wood, K.S. Littleton and K. Sheehy (eds), *Psychology in Action*, pp. 143–92. Oxford: Blackwell/OU Press.

Griffith, J.D., Cavanaugh, J., Held, J. and Oates, J.A. (1972). Dextroamphetamine: evaluation of psychomimetic properties in man. *Archive of General Psychiatry*, 26, 97–100.

Griffiths, M.D. (1993). Pathological gambling: possible treatment using an audio playback technique. *Journal of Gambling Studies*, 9, 295–7.

Griffiths, M.D. (1994) The role of cognitive bias and skill in fruit-machine gambling. *British Journal of Psychology*, 85, 51–69.

Griffiths, M.D. (1995). *Adolescent Gambling*. London: Routledge.

Gross, R. (1992). *Psychology: The Science of Mind and Behaviour*, 2nd edn. Sevenoaks: Hodder and Stoughton.

Grossman, D. (1995). *On Killing: The Psychological Cost of Learning to Kill in War and Society*. Boston, Mass.: Little Brown.

Guardian (2003). Reading between the letters, *Guardian*, 21 October 2003.

Guthrie, R. (1980). The psychology of Black Americans: an historical perspective. In R. Jones (1980). *Black Psychology*, 2nd edn. London: Harper Collins.

Guthrie, R.V. (1998). *Even the Rat Was White: A Historical View of Psychology* (2nd ed.). Boston: Allyn and Bacon.

Handelsman, M.M. and McLain, J. (1988). The Barnum effect in couples: effects of intimacy, involvement, and sex on acceptance of generalized personality feedback. *Journal of Clinical Psychology*, 44, 430–4.

Haney, C., Banks, W.C. and Zimbardo, P.G. (1973). A study of prisoners and guards in a simulated prison. *Naval Research Review*, 30, 4–17.

Happé, E. (1994). *Autism: An Introduction to Psychological Theory*. London: UCL Press.

Harlow, H.E. (1959). Love in infant monkeys. *Scientific American*, 200, 68–74.

Harlow, H.E. and Harlow, M.K. (1962). Social deprivation in monkeys. *Scientific American*, 207, 136–46.

Harlow L.L., Mulaik S.A. and Steiger J.H. (eds) (1997). *What If There Were No Significance Tests?* Mahwah, N.J.: Lawrence Erlbaum.

Harris, B. (1979). Whatever happened to Little Albert? *American Psychologist*, 34, 151–60.

Haslam, S.A. and McGarty, C. (2001). A hundred years of certitude? Social psychology, the experimental method and the management of scientific uncertainty. *British Journal of Social Psychology*, 40, 1–21.

Haslam, S.A. and Reicher, S. (2003). A tale of two prison experiments. *Psychology Review*, 9, 2–5.

Haslam, S.A. and Reicher, S.D. (2005). The psychology of tyranny. *Scientific American Mind*, 16, 44–51.

Haslam, S.A. and Reicher, S.D. (2006). Stressing the group: social identity and the unfolding dynamics of responses to stress. *Journal of Applied Psychology*, 91, 1037–52.

Haslam, S.A. and Reicher, S.D. (2007). Beyond the banality of evil: three dynamics of an interactionist social psychology of tyranny. *Personality and Social Psychology Bulletin*, 33 (5), 615–22.

Hawthorne, J., Jessop, J., Pryor, J. and Richards, M. (2003). *Supporting Children Through Family Change: A Review of Interventions and Services for Children of Divorcing and Separating Parents*. York: YPS/Joseph Rowntree Foundation.

Hayes, K.J. (1950). Vocalisation and speech in chimpanzees. *American Psychologist*, 5, 275–6.

Hayes, N. (1994). *Foundations of Psychology*. London: Routledge.

Hess, E.H. (1958). 'Imprinting' in animals. *Scientific American*, 198, 81–90.

Hewstone, M., Stroebe, W., Codol, J.P. and Stephenson, G. (1988). *Introduction to Social Psychology: A European Perspective*. Oxford: Blackwell.

Hitchens, C. (2001). *The Trial of Henry Kissinger*. London: Verso Books.

Hodges, I. and Tizard, B. (1989a). IQ and behavioural adjustment of ex-institutional adolescents. *Journal of Child Psychology and Psychiatry*, 30, 53–75.

Hodges, J. and Tizard, B. (1989b). Social and family relationships of ex-institutional adolescents. *Journal of Child Psychology and Psychiatry*, 30, 77–97.

Hofling, K.C., Brotzman, E., Dalrymple, S., Graves, N. and Pierce, C.M. (1966). An experimental study in the nurse–physician relationship. *Journal of Nervous and Mental Disorders*, 143, 171–80.

Hofstadter, R.D. and Dennett, D.C. (1981). *The Mind's I: Fantasies and Reflections on Self and Soul*. Brighton: Harvester Press.

Hofstede, G. (1980). *Culture's consequences*. London: Sage.

Holmes, T.H. and Rahe, R.H. (1967). The social re-adjustment rating scale. *Journal of Psychosomatic Research*, 11, 213–18.

Howitt, D. (1991). *Concerning Psychology*. Milton Keynes: Open University Press.

Hraba, J. and Grant, G. (1970). Black is beautiful: a re-examination of racial preference and identification. *Journal of Personality and Social Psychology*, 16, 398–402.

Hudson, W. (1960). Pictorial depth perception in sub-cultural groups in Africa. *Journal of Social Psychology*, 52, 183–208.

Hyde, T.S. and Jenkins, J.J. (1973). Recall for words as a function of semantic, graphic and syntactic orienting tasks. *Journal of Verbal and Learning Behavior*, 12, 471–80.

Hyman, I.E., Husband, T.H. and Billings, F.J. (1995). False memories of childhood experiences. *Applied Cognitive Psychology*, 9, 181–95.

James, W. (1890). *Principles of Psychology*. New York: Holt.

Janis, I.L. (1983). Stress inoculation in health care: theory and research. In D. Meichenbaum and M.E. Jaremko (eds), *Stress Reduction and Prevention*, pp. 67–99. New York: Plenum.

Janis, I.L. and King, B.T. (1954). The influence of role-playing on opinion change. *Journal of Abnormal and Social Psychology*, 49, 211–18.

Jones, E.E., Kanouse, D.E., Kelley, H.H., Nisbett, R.E., Valins, S. and Weiner, B. (eds) (1972). *Attribution: Perceiving the Causes of Behavior*. Morristown, N.J.: General Learning Press.

Jones, R. (1993). *Black Psychology*, 3rd edn. New York: Cobb and Hen.

Kahneman, D. and Tversky, A. (1973). On the psychology of prediction. *Psychological Review*, 80, 237–51.

Kalat, J.W. (1992). *Biological Psychology* (4th ed.). Belmont, Calif.: Wadsworth.

Kalat, J.W. (1993). *Introduction to Psychology*, 3rd Edition. Pacific Grove, Calif.: Brooks Cole.

Kamin, L. (1977). *The Science and Politics of IQ*. Harmondsworth: Penguin.

Kanner, A.D., Coynes, J.C., Schaefer, C. and Lazarus, R.S. (1981). Comparison of two modes of stress measurement: daily hassles and uplifts versus major life events. *Journal of Behavioural Medicine*, 4, 1–39.

Kelley, H.H. (1967). Attribution theory in social psychology. *Nebraska Symposium on Motivation*, 15, 192–238.

Kellogg, W.N. and Kellogg, L.A. (1933). *The Ape and the Child*. New York: Whittlesey House.

Kelman, H. (1953). Attitude change as a function of response restriction. *Human Relations*, 6, 185-214

Kendon, A. (1970). Movement coordination in social interaction: some examples described. *Acta Psychologica*, 32, 101–25.

Kennedy, A. (1984). *The Psychology of Reading*. London: Methuen.

Kitto, J. (1989). Gender reference terms: separating the women from the girls. *British Journal of Social Psychology*, 28, 185–87.

Kitzinger, C. (2004). The myth of the two biological sexes. *The Psychologist*, 17, 451–4.

Kline, P. (1991) *Intelligence: The Psychometric View*. London: Routledge.

Koff, E. (1983). Through the looking glass of menarche: what the adolescent girl sees. In S. Golub (ed.), *Menarche*, pp. 77–86. Lexington, Mass.: D.C. Heath.

Koluchová, J. (1972). Severe deprivation in twins: a case study. *Journal of Child Psychology and Psychiatry*, 13, 107–14.

Koluchová, J. (1991). Severely deprived twins after 22 years of observation. *Studia Psychologica*, 33, 23–8.

Kossoff, E.H., Vining, E.P.G., Pillas, D.J., Pyzik, P.L., Avellino, A.M., Carson, B.S. and Freeeman, J.M. (2003). Hemispherectomy for intractable unihemispheric epilepsy: etiology vs outcome. *Neurology*, 61, 887–90.

Kozlowski, L.T. and Cutting, J.E. (1977). Recognizing the sex of a walker from a dynamic point-light display. *Perception and Psychophysics*, 21 (6), 575–80.

Kraepelin, E. (1913). *Psychiatry*, 8th edn. Leipzig: Thieme.

Kroll, N.E.A., Parks, I, Parkinson, S.R., Bieber, S.L. and Johnson, A.L. (1970). Short-term memory while shadowing: recall of visually and aurally presented letters. *Journal of Experimental Psychology*, 85, 200–24.

Kutchins, H. and Kirk, S.A. (1997). *Making Us Crazy: DSM – the Psychiatric Bible and the Creation of Mental Disorder*. New York: Free Press.

Labov, W. (1969). The logic of nonstandard English. In P.P. Giglioli (ed.), *Language and Social Context*, pp. 179–215. Harmondsworth, England: Penguin (originally in *Georgetown Monographs on Language and Linguistics*, 22, 1–31).

Lakoff, R. (1975). *Language and Woman's Place*. New York: Harper and Row.

Landfield, A.W. (1971). *Personal Construct Systems in Psychotherapy*. Chicago: Rand McNally.

Lang, P.J. and Lazovik, A.D. (1963). Experimental desensitization of a phobia. *Journal of Abnormal and Social Psychology*, 66, 519–25.

LaPiere, R.T. (1934). Attitudes vs. actions. *Social Forces*, 13, 230–7.

Latané, B. and Darley J.M. (1970). *The Unresponsive Bystander: Why Does He Not Help?* New York: Appleton-Century-Crofts.

Latané, B. and Nida, S. (1981). Ten years of research on group size and helping. *Psychological Bulletin*, 89 (2), 308–24

Lau, R.R. (1982). Origins of health locus of control beliefs. *Journal of Personality and Social Psychology*, 42, 322–34.

Lazarus, R. and Folkman, S. (1984). *Stress, Appraisal and Coping*. New York: Springer.

Le Bon, G. (1895). *The Crowd: A Study of the Popular Mind*. Filiquarian Publishing.

Lenneberg, E.H. (1967). *Biological Foundations of Language*. New York: John Wiley.

Lerner, J.S., Gonzalez, R.M., Small, D.A. and Fischhoff, B. (2003). Emotion and perceived risks of terrorism: a national field experiment. *Psychological Science*, 14, 144–50.

Leslie, A.M. and Frith, U. (1988). Autistic children's understanding of seeing, knowing and believing. *British Journal of Developmental Psychology*, 4, 315–24.

Levine, R.M. (1999). Rethinking bystander non-intervention: social categorisation and the evidence of witnesses at the James Bulger murder trial. *Human Relations*, 52, 1133–55.

Lewin, K., Lippitt, R. and White, R. (1939). Patterns of aggressive behaviour in experimentally created 'social climates'. *Journal of Social Psychology*, 10, 271–99.

Loftus, E. and Ketcham, K. (1994). *The Myth of Repressed Memory*. New York: St. Martin's Press.

Loftus, E. (1997). Creating false memories. *Scientific American*, 277, 3, 70–5. Available at http://faculty.washington.edu/eloftus/Articles/sciam.htm (accessed July 2007).

Loftus, E.F. and Palmer, J.C. (1974). Reconstruction of automobile destruction: an example of the interaction between language and memory. *Journal of Verbal Learning and Verbal Behavior*, 13, 585–9.

Loftus, E.F. and Pickrell, J.E. (1995). The formation of false memories. *Psychiatric Annals*, 25, 720–5.

Lovaas, O.I. (1979). Contrasting illness and behavioural models for the treatment of autistic children: a historical perspective. *Journal of Autism and Developmental Disorders*, 9, 316–22.

Maccoby, E.E. and Jacklin, C.N. (1980). Psychological sex differences. In M. Rutter (ed.), *Developmental Psychiatry*, pp. 92–100. London: Heinemann.

MacDermott, M. (1993). On cruelty, ethics and experimentation. *The Psychologist*, 6, 456–9.

Mackworth, N.H. (1950). Researches on the measurement of human performance. *Medical Research Council Special Report 268*. London: HMSO.

Maguire, E.A., Gadian, D.G., Johnsrode, I.S., Good, C.D., Ashburner, J., Frackowiak, R.S.J. and Frith, C. (2000). Navigation-related structural change in the hippocampi of taxi drivers. *Proceedings of the National Academy of Science, USA*, 97, 4398–403.

Marañon, G. (1924) Contribution a l'etude de l'action emotive de l'adrenaline. *Revue Francaise Endoçrinologie*, 2, 301–25.

Marchetti, C. and Della Salla, S. (1998). Disentangling the alien and anarchic hand. *Cognitive Neuropsychiatry*, 3, 191–208.

Mareschal, D., Johnson, M. and Grayson, A. (2004). Brain and cognitive development. In J.M. Oates and A. Grayson (eds), *Cognitive and Language Development in Children*, pp. 113–61. Oxford: Blackwell/OU Press.

Marshall, G.D. and Zimbardo, P.G. (1979). Affective consequences of inadequately explained physiological arousal. *Journal of Personality and Social Psychology*, 37, 970–88.

Marshall, G.N., Wortman, C.B., Vickers, R.R. Jr., Kusulas, J.W. and Hervig, L.K. (1994). The five-factor model of personality as a framework for personality-health research. *Journal of Personality and Social Psychology*, 67, 278–86.

Matsumoto, D. (1994). *People: Psychology from a Cultural Perspective*. Pacific Grove, Calif.: Brooks/Cole.

McCrae, R.R. and Costa, P.T. (1987). Validation of the five factor model of personality across instruments and observers. *Journal of Personality and Social Psychology*, 52, 81–90.

McCrone, J. (1995). Maps of the mind. *New Scientist*, 7 January, 30–4.

McDermott, M., Opik, L., Smith, S., Taylor, S, and Wills, A. (2002). *The Experiment: Report of the Independent Ethics Panel*. Available at http://www.experimentethics.org.uk.

McDowall, J.J. (1978a). Microanalysis of filmed movement: the reliability of boundary detection by observers. *Environmental Psychology and Nonverbal Behavior*, 3, 77–88.

McDowall, J.J. (1978b). Interactional synchrony: a reappraisal. *Journal of Personality and Social Psychology*, 36, 963–75.

McMasters, C. and Lee, C. (1991). Cognitive dissonance in tobacco smokers. *Addictive Behaviours*, 16, 349–53.

Melzack, R. (1992). Phantom limbs. *Scientific American*, April, 90–6.

Melzack, R. and Wall, P.D. (1985). *The Challenge of Pain*. Harmondsworth: Penguin.

Melzack, R., Wall, P.D. and Ty, T.C. (1982). Acute pain in an emergency clinic: latency of onset and descriptor patterns. *Pain*, 14, 33–43.

Merrin, W. (2005). *Baudrillard and the Media: A Critical Introduction*. Cambridge: Polity.

Miles, R. (1988). *The Women's History of the World*. London: Paladin.

Milgram, S. (1963). Behavioral study of obedience. *Journal of Abnormal and Social Psychology*, 67, 371–8.

Milgram, S. (1967). The small world problem. *Psychology Today*, May, 60–7.

Milgram, S. (1974) *Obedience to Authority*. London: Tavistock.

Miller, D.T., Downs, J.S. and Prentice, D.A. (1998). Minimal conditions for the creation of a unit relationship: the social bond between birthdaymates. *European Journal of Social Psychology*, 28, 475–81.

Miller, G.A. (1956). The magical number seven, plus or minus two: some limits on our capacity for processing information. *Psychological Review*, 63, 81–97.

Miller, G.A. (1966). *Psychology: The Science of Mental Life*. Harmondsworth: Penguin.

Miller, G.A. (1969). Psychology as a means of promoting human welfare. *American Psychologist*, 24, 1063–75.

Moghaddam, F.M., Taylor, D.M. and Wright, S.C. (1993). *Social Psychology in Cross-Cultural Perspective*. New York: W.H. Freeman.

Money, J., and Ehrhardt, A.A. (1972). *Man and Woman, Boy and Girl: Differentiation and Dimorphism of Gender Identity from Conception to Maturity*. Baltimore: Johns Hopkins University Press.

Moscovici, S., Lage, E. and Naffrechoux, M. (1969). Influence of a consistent minority on the response of a majority in a color perception task. *Sociometry*, 32, 365–80.

Murfitt, N. (2002). Jailed! *London Evening Standard*, 2 May, 29–30.

Neisser, U. (1967). *Cognitive Psychology*. New York: Appleton-Century-Croft.

Neisser U. (1979). The control of information pickup in selective looking. In D. Pick (ed.), *Perception and its Development: A Tribute to Eleanor J Gibson*, pp. 201–19. Hillsdale, N.J.: Lawrence ErlbaumAssociates.

Neisser, U. (1981). John Dean's memory: a case study. *Cognition*, 9, 1–22.

Neisser, U. (1982). *Memory Observed*. New York: Freeman.

Neisser U. and Becklen R. (1975). Selective looking: attending to visually specified events. *Cognitive Psychology*, 7, 480–94.

Nisbett, R.E., Caputo, C., Legant, P. and Marecek, J. (1973). Behaviour as seen by the actor and as seen by the observer. *Journal of Personality and Social Psychology*, 27, 154–64.

Nobles, W.W. (1976). Extended self: rethinking the so-called Negro self-concept. *Journal of Black Psychology*, 2, 15–24.

Nobles, W.W. and Goddard, L.L. (1984). *Understanding the Black Family: A Guide for Scholarship and Research*. California: Black Family Institute.

Norman, W.T. (1963). Toward an adequate taxonomy of personality attributes: replicated factor structure in peer nomination personality ratings. *Journal of Abnormal and Social Psycyhology*, 66, 574–83.

Nyborg, H. (1987). Individual differences or different individuals. *Behavioral and Brain Sciences*, 10, 34–5.

O'Connell, A.N. and Russo, N.F. (eds) (2001). *Models of Achievement: Reflections of Eminent Women in Psychology*. New York: Columbia University Press.

Office of National Statistics (2007). http://www.statistics.gov.uk/StatBase/ xsdataset.asp?vlnk=2340&Pos=1&ColRank=1&Rank=192 (accessed July, 2007).

Olds, J. and Milner, P. (1954). Positive reinforcement produced by electrical stimulation of the septal area and other regions of the rat brain. *Journal of Comparative and Physiological Psychology*, 47, 419–27.

Orne, M.T. (1962). On the social psychology of the psychological experiment: with particular reference to demand characteristics and their implications. *American Psychologist*, 17, 776–83.

Orne, M.T. (1966). Hypnosis, motivation and compliance. *American Journal of Psychiatry*, 122, 721–6.

Orne, M.T. and Scheibe, K.E. (1964). The contribution of non-deprivation factors in the production of sensory deprivation effects: the psychology of the 'panic button'. *Journal of Abnormal and Social Psychology*, 68, 3–12.

Pelham, B.W., Mirenberg, M.C. and Jones, J.T. (2002). Why Susie sells seashells by the seashore: implicit egotism and major life decisions. *Journal of Personality and Social Psychology*, 82 (4) 469–87.

Perls, F.S. (1969). *Gestalt Therapy Verbatim*. Moab, Utah: Real People Press.

Perrin, S. and Spencer, C. (1980). The Asch effect: a child of its time? *Bulletin of the British Psychological Society*, 32, 405–6.

Perrin, S. and Spencer, C. (1981). Independence or conformity in the Asch experiment as a reflection of cultural and situational factors. *British Journal of Social Psychology*, 20, 205–9.

Peterson, R.L. and Peterson, M.J. (1959). Short term retention of individual items. *Journal of Experimental Psychology*, 58, 193–8.

Philogene, G. (ed.) (2004). *Racial Identity in Context: The Legacy of Kenneth B. Clark*. Washington: APA.

Piaget, J. (1932). *The Moral Judgement of the Child*. London: Routledge and Kegan Paul.

Piaget, J. (1952). *The Child's Concept of Number*. London: Routledge and Kegan Paul.

Piaget, J. (1976). *The Child's Construction of Reality*. London: Routledge and Kegan Paul. Translated by M. Cook.

Picchioni, M.M. and Murray, R.M. (2007). Schizophrenia. *British Medical Journal*, 335, 91–5.

Pilger, J. (1989). *Heroes*. London: Pan.

Piliavin, M., Rodin, J.A. and Piliavin, J. (1969). Good Samaritanism: an underground phenomenon? *Journal of Personality and Social Psychology*, 13, 289–99.

Pinker, S. (1994). *The Language Instinct: How the Mind Creates Language*. New York: William Morrow.

Plomin, R. and Daniels, D. (1987). Why are children in the same family so different from one another? *Behavioral and Brain Sciences*, 10 (1), 1–16.

Potter, J. and Edwards, D. (1990). Nigel Lawson's tent: discourse analysis, attribution theory and the social psychology of fact. *European Journal of Social Psychology*, 20, 405–24.

Potter, J. and Wetherell, M. (1987). *Discourse and Social Psychology: Beyond Attitudes and Behaviour.* London: Sage.

Potter, J. (1996). Discourse analysis and constructionist approaches: theoretical Background. In J.T.E. Richardson (ed.): *Handbook of Qualitative Research Methods for Psychology and the Social Sciences,* pp. 125–40. Leicester: BPS Books.

Premack, D. and Woodruff, G. (1978). Does the chimpanzee have a theory of mind? *Behavioural and Brain Sciences,* 4, 515–26.

Rachlin, H. (1970). *Introduction to Modern Behaviorism.* San Francisco: W.H. Freeman.

Ragland, D.R. and Brand, R.J. (1988). Type A behavior and mortality from coronary heart disease. *New England Journal of Medicine,* 318, 65–70.

Raine, A., Buchsbaum, M., and LaCasse, L. (1997). Brain abnormalities in murderers indicated by positron emission tomography. *Biological Psychiatry,* 42 (6), 495–508.

Ramachandran, V.S. and Hubbard, E.M. (2001). Psychophysical investigations into the neural basis of synaesthesia. *Proceedings of the Royal Society of London,* 268, 979–83.

Ramachandran, V.S. and Hubbard E.M. (2003). Hearing colors, tasting shapes. *Scientific American,* 288, 42–9.

Ramachandran, V.S. and Rogers-Ramachandran, D. (1996). Synaesthesia in phantom limbs induced with mirrors. *Proceedings of the Royal Society of London,* 263, 377–86.

Rawlins, R. (1979). Forty years of rhesus research. *New Scientist,* 12 April, 108–10.

Rawlinson, G. (1999). Reibadailty. *New Scientist,* 2155, 55.

Rawlinson, G. (1975). How do we recognise words? *New Behaviour,* 2, 336–8.

Reicher, S. and Haslam, S.A. (2006). Rethinking the psychology of tyranny: the BBC prison study. *British Journal of Social Psychology,* 45, 1–40.

Richards, G. (1998). The case of psychology and 'race'. *The Psychologist,* 11, 179–81

Rogers, C. (1951). *Client-Centered Therapy.* New York: Houghton.

Ronson, J. (2005). *The Men Who Stare at Goats.* London: Simon and Schuster.

Rosch, E., Mervis, C.B., Gray, W.D., Johnson, D.M. and Boyes-Graem, P. (1976). Basic objects in natural categories. *Cognitive Psychology,* 8, 382–439.

Rose, S., Kamin, L.J., and Lewontin, R.C. (1984). *Not in our Genes: Biology, Ideology and Human Nature.* Harmondsworth: Penguin.

Rose, R. and Kaprio, J. (1987). Shared experience and similarity of personality: positive data from Finnish and American twins. *Behavioral and Brain Sciences,* 10 (1), 35–6.

Rosenfeld, H.M. (1981). Whither interactional synchrony? In K. Bloom (ed.), *Prospective Issues in Infant research.* Hillsdale, New Jersey: Erlbaum and Associates.

Rosenhan, D.L. (1973). On being sane in insane places. *Science,* 179, 250–8.

Rosenhan, D.L., and Seligman, M.E.P. (1989). *Abnormal Psychology,* 2nd edn. New York: Norton.

Rosenthal, A.M. (1999). *Thirty-Eight Witnesses: The Kitty Genovese Case,* Part 2. Berkeley: University of California Press.

Rosenthal, R. and Fode, K.L. (1963). The effect of experimenter bias on the performance of the albino rat. *Behavioral Science,* 8, 183–9.

Rosenthal, R. and Jacobson, L. (1966). Teachers' expectancies: determinants of pupils' I.Q. gains. *Psychological Reports*, 19, 115–18.

Rotter, J.B. (1966). Generalised expectancies for internal vs external control of reinforcement. *Psychological Monographs*, 80 (1).

Rushton, J. (1990). Race differences, r/K theory and a reply to Flynn. *The Psychologist*, 5, 195–8.

Rymer, R. (1993). *Genie: Escape from a Silent Childhood*. London: Michael Joseph.

Sacks, O. (1986). *The Man Who Mistook his Wife for a Hat*. London: Picador.

Samuel, J. and Bryant, E. (1984). Asking only one question in the conversation experiment. *Journal of Child Psychology and Psychiatry*, 25, 315–18.

Sarafino, E. (1994). *Health Psychology: Biopsychosocial Interactions*, 2nd edn. New York: Wiley.

Scarr, S. (1981). *Race, Social Class and Individual Differences in IQ*. Hillsdale, New Jersey: Lawrence Erlbaum Associates.

Schachter, S. and Singer, J.E. (1962). Cognitive, social, and psychological determinants of emotional state. *Psychological Review*, 69, 379–99.

Schallert, T. (1983). Sensorimotor impairment and recovery of function in brain-damaged rats: reappearance of symptoms during old age. *Behavioral Neuroscience*, 97, 159–64.

Schjelderup-Ebbe, T. (1922). Soziale Verhaltnisse bei Vogeln [Social relationships among birds]. *Zeitschrift fur Psychologie*, 90, 106–7.

Searle, J.R. (1980). Minds, brains, and programs. *The Behavior and Brain Sciences*, 3, 417–57.

Sears, D.O. (1986). College sophomores in the laboratory: influences of a narrow data base on psychology's view of human nature. *Journal of Personality and Social Psychology*, 51, 513–30.

Seligman, M.E.P (1975). *Helplessness: On Depression, Development and Death*. San Francisco: Freeman.

Seligman, M.E.P. and Maier, S.F. (1967). Failure to escape traumatic shock. *Journal of Experimental Psychology*, 74, 1–9.

Sheridan, C. and King, R. (1972). Obedience to authority with an authentic victim. *Proceedings of the 80th Annual Convention, American Psychological Association*, Part 1, 7, 165–6.

Sherif, M. (1956). Experiments in group conflict. *Scientific American*, 195, 54–8.

Shevlin, M. (2003). Research: means and ends. *The Psychologist*, 16 (5), 233.

Shulman, H.G. (1970). Encoding and retention of semantic and phonemic information in short-term memory. *Journal of Verbal Learning and Behavior*, 9, 499–508.

Shulman, H.G. (1972). Semantic confusion errors in short-term memory. *Journal of Verbal Learning and Behavior*, 11, 221–7.

Sifry, D. (2006). *State of the Blogosphere, February 2006 Part 1: On Blogosphere Growth*, posted February 6, 2006. Available at http://www.sifry.com/alerts/archives/000419.html (accessed September 2006).

Simons, D.J. and Chabris, C.F. (1999). Gorillas in our midst: sustained inattentional blindness for dynamic events. *Perception*, 28, 1059–74.

Sizemore, C.C. and Pitillo, E.S. (1977). *I'm Eve*. New York: Doubleday.

Skinner, B.F. (1960). Pigeons in a pelican. *American Psychologist*, 15, 28–37.

Skinner, B.F. (1973). *Beyond Freedom and Dignity*. Harmondsworth: Penguin.

Skinner, B.F. (1974). *About Behaviorism*. Harmondsworth: Penguin.

Slater, M., Antley, A., Davison, A., Swapp, D., Guger, C. et al. (2006).

A Virtual Reprise of the Stanley Milgram Obedience Experiments. *PLoS ONE*. Available at http://www.plosone.org/article/fetchArticle.action?articleURI=info%3Adoi%2F10.1371%2Fjournal.pone.0000039 (accessed 6 February 2007).

Smith, M.L. and Glass, G.V. (1977). Meta-analysis of psychotherapy outcome studies. *American Psychologist*, 32, 752–60.

Smith, P.B., and Bond, M.H. (1993). *Social Psychology Across Cultures*. Hemel Hempstead: Harvester Wheatsheaf.

Snow, C.E. (1979). Conversations with children. In R. Barnes, I. Oates, J Cjapman, V. Lee and R. Czerniewska (eds), *Personality, Development and Learning: A Reader*. Milton Keynes: Open University Press/Hodder and Stoughton.

Snow, R.E. (1969). Unfinished Pygmalion. *Contemporary Psychology*, 14, 197–9.

Sorce, I., Emde, R., Campos, J. and Klinnert, M. (1985). Maternal emotion signalling: its effect on the visual cliff behaviour of 1-year-olds. *Developmental Psychology*, 21, 195–200.

Sperling, G. (1960). The information available in brief visual presentations. *Psychological Monographs*, 74 (11, Whole No. 498).

Sperry, R.W. (1968). Hemisphere deconnection and unity in conscious awareness. *American Psychologist*, 23, 723–33.

Sperry, R.W. (1974). Lateral specialization in the surgically separated hemispheres. In F.O. Schmitt and F.G. Worden (eds), *The Neurosciences: Third Study Programme*, , Ch. I, Vol. 3, pp. 5–19. Cambridge, Mass.: MIT Press.

Spitzer, R.L. (1975). On pseudoscience in science, logic in remission, and psychiatric diagnosis: a critique of Rosenhan's 'On being sane in insane places'. *Journal of Abnormal Psychology*, 84, 442–52.

Stanovich, K.E. (1994). Annotation: does dyslexia exist? *Journal of Child Psychology and Psychiatry*, 35, 579–95.

Stenström, U., Wikby, A., Andersson, P.O. and Ryden, O. (1998). Relationship between locus of control beliefs and metabolic control in insulin-dependent diabetes mellitus. *British Journal of Health Psychology*, 3 (Pt1), 15–25.

Stephenson, G. (1992). *The Psychology of Criminal Justice*. Oxford: Blackwell.

Stetri, A. (1987). Tactile discrimination of shape and intermodal transfer in 2 to 3 month old infants. *British Journal of Developmental Psychology*, 5, 213–20.

Stevenson, J. (1988). Which aspects of reading ability show a 'hump' in their distribution? *Applied Cognitive Psychology*, 2, 77–85.

Strayer, D.L., Drews, F.A. and Johnston, W.A. (2003). Cell phone-induced failures of visual attention during simulated driving. *Journal of Experimental Psychology: Applied*, 9, 23–32.

Suls, J.M. (1972). A two-stage model for the appreciation of jokes and cartoons: an information-processing analysis. In J.H. Goldstein and P.E. McGhee (eds), *The Psychology of Humor*, pp. 81–100. New York: Academic Press.

Tajfel, H. (1970). Experiments in intergroup discrimination. *Scientific American*, 223, 96–102.

Tajfel, H. and Turner, J.C. (1979). An integrative theory of intergroup conflict. In W.G. Autsin and S. Worchel (eds) *The Social Psychology of Intergroup Relations*. Monterey, Calif.: Brooks/Cole.

Taylor, S. (1990). Health psychology: the science and the field. *American Psychologist*, 45, 40–5.

Terrace, H.S. (1979). How Nim Chimpsky changed my mind. *Psychology Today*, November, 65–76.

Thigpen, C.H. and Cleckley, H. (1954). A case of multiple personality. *Journal of Abnormal and Social Psychology*, 49, 135–51.

Tinbergen, N. and Tinbergen, E. (1983). *'Autistic' Children: New Hope for a Cure*. London: Allen and Unwin.

Tinbergen, N. (1952). The curious behavior of the stickleback. *Scientific American*, 187, 22–6.

Tizard, B. (1986). *The Care of the Young: Implications of Recent Research*. London: Thomas Coram Research Unit.

Tizard, B. and Hodges, J. (1978). The effect of institutional rearing on the development of eight-year-old children. *Journal of Child Psychology and Psychiatry*, 19, 99–118.

Travers, J. and Milgram, S. (1969). An experimental study of the small world problem, *Sociometry*, 32, 425–43.

Trotter, R.J. (1985). Muzafer Sherif; a life of conflict and goals: for more than 50 years, his innovative research has helped shape the history of social psychology. *Psychology Today*, 19, 54–8.

Turing, A.M. (1950). Computing machinery and intelligence. *Mind*, 59, 433–60.

Ullman, L.P and Krasner, L. (1965). *Case Studies in Behavior Modification*. London: Holt, Rinehart and Winston.

Underwood, J., Banyard, P. and Davies, M. (in press), Students in digital worlds: lost sin city or reaching Treasure Island? *British Journal of Educational Psychology*.

Valins, S. (1966). Cognitive effects of false heart-rate feedback. *Journal of Personality and Social Psychology*, 4, 400–8.

Vygotsky, L.S. (1962). *Thought and Language*. New York: Wiley.

Wagenaar, W. (1988). *Paradoxes of Gambling Behaviour*. London: Earlbaum.

Watanabe, S., Sakamoto, J. and Wakita, M. (1995). Pigeons' discrimination of paintings by Monet and Picasso. *Journal of the Experimental Analysis of Behavior*, 63, 165–74.

Watson, J.B. (1930). *Behaviorism*, revised edn. New York: W.W. Norton.

Watson, J.B. and Rayner, R. (1920). Conditioned emotional reactions. *Journal of Experimental Psychology*, 3, 1–14.

Watson, P. (1980). *War on the Mind*. Harmondsworth: Penguin.

Weitz, R. (1989). Uncertainty and the lives of persons with AIDS. *Journal of Health and Social Behavior*, 30, 270–81.

Wells, G.L. and Bradfield, A.L. (1998). 'Good, you identified the suspect': feedback to eyewitnesses distorts their reports of the witnessing experience. *Journal of Applied Psychology*, 83, 360–76.

Wessells, M. (2006). Psychologists Aiding Torturers. Available at http://www.tompaine.com/articles/2006/08/16/psychologists_aiding_torturers.php (accessed March 2007).

Williams, J. (1987). *Psychology of Women: Behavior in a Biosocial Context*, 3rd edn. New York: Norton.

Wimmer, H. and Perner, J. (1983). Beliefs about beliefs: representation and constraining function of wrong beliefs in young children's understanding of deception. *Cognition*, 21, 103–28.

Wolpe, J. (1958). *Psychotherapy by Reciprocal Inhibition*. Stanford, Calif.: Stanford University Press.

Wood, D., Bruner, J.S. and Ross, G. (1976). The role of tutoring in problem solving. *Journal of Child Psychology and Psychiatry*, 17, 89–100.

Wood, D., Wood, H. and Middleton, D. (1978). An experimental evaluation of four face-to-face teaching strategies. *International Journal of Behavioral Development*, 1, 131–47.

World Health Organisation (WHO) (2001). Mental health: new understanding, new hope. Available at http://www.who.int/whr/2001/en/ (accessed February, 2007)

World Health Organisation (2004). The importance of caregiver–child interactions for the survival and healthy development of young children. http://www.who.int/child-adolescent-health/publications/CHILD_HEALTH/ISBN_92_4_159134_X.htm (accessed July 2007).

Zimbardo, P. (1973). On the ethics of intervention in human psychological research: with special reference to the Stanford Prison Experiment. *Cognition*, 2, 243–56.

Zimbardo, P. (1989). *Quiet rage: The Stanford Prison Study* [video]. Stanford Calif.: Stanford University.

Zimbardo, P. (2004). A situationist perspective on the psychology of evil: understanding how good people are transformed into perpetrators. In G.A. Miller (ed.), *The Social Psychology of Good and Evil*, pp. 21–50. New York: Guildford Press.

Zimbardo, P. (2006). On rethinking the psychology of tyranny: the BBC prison study. *British Journal of Social Psychology*, 45, 47–53.

INDEX

Note: Items marked with an asterisk are listed separately in the 'Summarized studies' index.

16 PF, 221

A

abnormality, 255, 487–8
    and culture, 196, 200
    long history of, 194
    observed or invented by psychologists, 195, 196–9
    problem of defining, 170, 194, 196–9
    see also *Brain abnormalities in murderers, schizophrenia
addiction, 98
adoption studies, 237
    see also *Social and family relationships of ex-institutional adolescents
Adorno, T.W., 60
adrenalin, 141–2, 143, 144, 483
advertising, 5, 441, 459
    experimental variations in, 191, 428–9, 470
affect, 219, 265
Afrocentric approach, 177–8
    African and Western world views, 178–80
    see also *Extended self
aggression, 155, 169, 484
    in children see *Transmission of aggression
    in monkeys, 116
    and prefrontal cortex, 157
    in 'prison guards' 70, 71, 74, 429
    problem of defining, 446–7
    psychometric analysis, 227, 229
    rats and overpopulation, 126–7
    in sticklebacks, 122
    see also *Transmission of aggression

agreeableness see *Validation of the five-factor model
AIDS
    behaviour resistant to change, 45
    symptoms, 407
    see also *Uncertainty and the lives of persons with AIDS
air traffic controllers, 374, 383
Aitchison, J., 111
Albert B., see *Conditioned emotional reactions
Alexander, G.M. see *Sex differences in response to children's toys in nonhuman primates
alien hands, 139
Allport, G.W., 221
American Association for the Advancement of Science, 16
American Medical Association, 442
American Psychiatric Association, 194, 442
American Psychological Association, 176, 328, 382, 441, 442
    ethical committee of, 16
    see also Miller, G.
American Sign Language (ASL), 109
amnesia, 158, 200, 202
    memory difficulties, 139
amphetamines, 98
    psychosis and schizophrenia see *Dextroamphetamine
anarchic hands, 139
animals
    and language see *Teaching sign language to a chimpanzee
    use of in war, 92
    see also laboratory animals
anthropomorphism, 114, 118, 126, 248
    and study of animal behaviour, 117–18
artefact of experimental procedure, 41, 191, 434, 567–8, 506
    see also demand characteristics, *Effect of experiment

confounding factors, 294, 416, 453–4, 489, 493, 508

congruent validity *see* concurrent validity

Conrad, R., 318

conscientiousness *see* *Validation of the five-factor model

conservation, 277–81

construct validity, 227, 465

constructivism, classical and social, 266, 282, 495

Cool, Nadean, 326, 328

Cooper, H., 427

correlation, 460

Costa, P.T. *see* *Validation of the five-factor model

Craik, F.J.M. *see* *Levels of processing

criminality, lack of distinguishing signs of, 152

criterion validity *see* predictive validity

Crook, L.S., 327

Crosland, Susan, 404

cultural differences, 50, 127, 170, 177–9, 189, 228, 308

    and abnormality, 196, 200

    engineers, 9

    and IQ tests, 231, 233, 447

    in utero, 258, 260, 495

    and psychology *see* psychology

    and test/assessment results, 302, 303

    see also *Extended self, *Logic of non-standard English, *Neonatal behaviour among urban Zambians and Americans, *Pictorial perception and culture

Cunningham, C.C., 293

Cutting, J.E. *see* *Recognizing the sex of a walker

Dance of the neonates *see* *Neonate movement is synchronized with adult speech, 288–92

D

Daniels, D. *see* *Why are children in the same family so different?

Darley, J.M., 6, 18

Darwin, Charles, 87, 177

Dean, M.C., 327

Deater-Deckard, K., 254

debriefing, 16, 72, 78, 327, 432, 471

Delgardo, J.M.R., 98

Della Salla, S., 139

demand characteristics, 49, 213, 279, 418, 467–8, 473, 488, 506

    defined, 421–2

    see also artefact of experimental procedure, experimenter effect, *Asking only one question, *On the social psychology of the psychological experiment

Dement, W. *see* *Relation of eye movements during sleep to dream activity

depth

    perception of, 332–3

    picture perspective, 335–6

Deregowski, J.B. *see* *Pictorial perception and culture

desensitisation therapy *see* systematic desensitization

Deutsch, M., 301

developmental psychology, 243–4, 265–6, 288

    critical period, 250

    and longitudinal studies, 462

    and Piaget, 278

    see also *Analysis of a phobia of a five-year-old boy, *Severe deprivation in twins, *Social and family relationships of ex-institutional adolescents

Diagnostic and Statistical Manual of Mental Disorders (DSM), 194–5

Diamond, M. *see* *Sex reassignment at birth

dichotic listening, 383–7

diffusion of responsibility, 18, 20, 21, 27, 427

discourse analysis, 397, 399

    see also *Nigel Lawsons's tent

Disney, 328

disorders, observed or invented, 195, 196–9

dispositional factors *see* situational v personal/dispositional factors

doctors, long work hours as initiation, 35

Dodds, P. *see* *Experimental study of search in global social networks

dolls

    see *Black is beautiful, *Transmission of aggression

Domjan, M., 418–19

Doms, M., 9

Donaldson, M., 277

dopamine, 98, 152

double-blind design, 437, 510

drapetomania, 177

dreams, 267, 268, 269, 458, 494

    in Shakespeare and Bible, 146

    see also *Relation of eye movements during sleep to dream activity

Dunbar, R.I.M., 127

Dunn, J., 254

dying, fear of, 408

E

Ebbinghaus, H., 307, 309, 311

ecological validity, 16, 30, 56, 61, 215, 311, 383, 506

    defined, 466, 503

    and replicability, 307

    in social psychology, 63

    see also real v realistic conditions

Edwards, D. *see* Nigel Lawson's tent

Edwards, J., 301

egocentrism, 277, 427, 428, 499

elaborated code *see* language deprivation theory

electroencephalogram, 147–18, 203

    see also magneto-encephalography

email, 59, 82–4

emotion

    and physical sensation, 141

    two-factor theory of, 142–5

empirical inquiry, 444

Empson, J., 146

INDEX OF SUMMARIZED STUDIES